Lecture Notes in Computer Science　13203

More information about this series at https://link.springer.com/bookseries/558

Riham AlTawy · Andreas Hülsing (Eds.)

Selected Areas in Cryptography

28th International Conference
Virtual Event, September 29 – October 1, 2021
Revised Selected Papers

 Springer

Editors
Riham AlTawy ⓘD
University of Victoria
Victoria, BC, Canada

Andreas Hülsing ⓘD
Eindhoven University of Technology
Eindhoven, The Netherlands

ISSN 0302-9743   ISSN 1611-3349 (electronic)
Lecture Notes in Computer Science
ISBN 978-3-030-99276-7   ISBN 978-3-030-99277-4 (eBook)
https://doi.org/10.1007/978-3-030-99277-4

This Springer imprint is published by the registered company Springer Nature Switzerland AG
The registered company address is: Gewerbestrasse 11, 6330 Cham, Switzerland

Preface

Selected Areas in Cryptography (SAC) is Canada's annual research conference on cryptography, held since 1994. The 28th edition of SAC was supposed to take place at the University of Victoria in British Columbia, Canada. However, due to the ongoing COVID-19 pandemic, SAC 2021 was held as a virtual event from September 29 to October 1, 2021.

There are four areas covered at each SAC conference. Three of the areas are permanent:

- Design and analysis of symmetric key primitives and cryptosystems, including block and stream ciphers, hash functions, MAC algorithms, cryptographic permutations, and authenticated encryption schemes.
- Efficient implementations of symmetric, public key, and post-quantum cryptography.
- Mathematical and algorithmic aspects of applied cryptology, including post-quantum cryptology.

The fourth area is selected as a special topic for each edition. The special topic for SAC 2021 was

- Privacy enhancing mechanisms and techniques.

We received 60 submissions that were reviewed in a double-blind review process. Regular submissions received three reviews whereas submissions by Program Committee (PC) members were reviewed by five PC members. All in all, 190 reviews were written by our Program Committee, consisting of 38 members, and of course with the help of 28 subreviewers. Eventually, 23 papers were accepted for publication in these proceedings and presentation at the conference.

There were two invited talks at SAC 2021. The Stafford Taveres Lecture was given by Sofía Celi, talking about "How private is secure messaging?". The second invited talk was given by Eyal Ronen on the topic of "Privacy-Preserving Bluetooth Based Contact Tracing—One Size Does Not Fit All". The program of SAC 2021 was completed by a preceding two-day summer school on September 27 and 28, 2021. During the summer school, there was one day of lectures about "Machine-Checked Cryptography with EasyCrypt and Jasmin" held by François Dupressoir, Benjamin Grégoire, and Vincent Laporte. The second day focused on "Communication Privacy" with lectures by Ania M. Piotrowska and Britta Hale. The advantage of an online conference is that almost all lectures as well as the talks were recorded. Therefore, we want to point the interested reader to the YouTube channel of the conference https://www.youtube.com/channel/UCi PgSZ0ho0LQEENlRmhwbBQ.

We would like to thank all our colleagues who helped to make SAC 2021 a success. Especially, we would like to thank the Program Committee members, and their subreviewers, for their hard work during these daring times. We would also like to thank the invited speakers and the summer school lecturers for making the time to give a talk at yet another online conference. Finally, we would like to thank Orr Dunkelman and Michael J. Jacobson, Jr. for their help and advice.

January 2022

Andreas Hülsing
Riham AlTawy

Organization

SAC 2021 was held in cooperation with The International Association for Cryptologic Research (IACR).

Program Chairs

Riham AlTawy	University of Victoria, Canada
Andreas Hülsing	Eindhoven University of Technology, The Netherlands

Program Committee

Riham AlTawy	University of Victoria, Canada
Diego Aranha	Aarhus University, Denmark
Tomer Ashur	Eindhoven University of Technology, The Netherlands, and KU Leuven, Belgium
Paulo Barreto	University of Washington Tacoma, USA
Daniel J. Bernstein	University of Illinois at Chicago, USA, and Ruhr University Bochum, Germany
Jean-François Biasse	University of South Florida, USA
Nina Bindel	University of Waterloo and Institute for Quantum Computing, Canada
Claude Carlet	University of Bergen, Norway, and Université Paris 8, France
Chitchanok Chuengsatiansup	University of Adelaide, Australia
Carlos Cid	Royal Holloway, University of London, UK, and Simula UiB, Norway
Christoph Dobraunig	Lamarr Security Research, Austria
Orr Dunkelman	University of Haifa, Israel
Aleksander Essex	Western University, Canada
Maria Eichlseder	Graz University of Technology, Austria
Britta Hale	Naval Postgraduate School, USA
Andreas Hülsing	Eindhoven University of Technology, The Netherlands
Michael J. Jacobson, Jr.	University of Calgary, Canada
Christian Janson	Technische Universität Darmstadt, Germany
Marcel Keller	CSIRO's Data61, Australia
Péter Kutas	University of Birmingham, UK

Subhamoy Maitra	Indian Statistical Institute Kolkata, India
Christian Majenz	QuSoft and CWI Amsterdam, The Netherlands
Kalikinkar Mandal	University of New Brunswick, Fredericton, Canada
Maria Mendez Real	Université de Nantes, France
Ruben Niederhagen	University of Southern Denmark, Denmark
Abderrahmane Nitaj	University of Caen Normandy, France
Lorenz Panny	Academia Sinica, Taiwan
Christiane Peters	IBM, Belgium
Elizabeth Quaglia	Royal Holloway, University of London, UK
Simona Samardjiska	Radboud University, The Netherlands
Tobias Schneider	NXP Semiconductors, Austria
Nicolas Sendrier	Inria, France
Leonie Simpson	Queensland University of Technology, Australia
Benjamin Smith	Inria and École polytechnique, Institut Polytechnique de Paris, France
Djiby Sow	Cheikh Anta Diop University of Dakar, Senegal
Tyge Tiessen	Technical University of Denmark, Denmark
Yosuke Todo	NTT Corporation, Japan
Yuntao Wang	Japan Advanced Institute of Science and Technology, Japan
Huapeng Wu	University of Windsor, Canada

Additional Reviewers

Kazumaro Aoki	Mounika Pratapa
James Bartusek	Robert Primas
Matthew Dodd	Joost Renes
Jelle Don	Raghvendra Rohit
Shuichi Katsumata	Sumanta Sarkar
Liliya Kraleva	Yu Sasaki
Leah Krehling	Markus Schofnegger
Norman Lahr	Tjerand Silde
Angelique Loe	Patrick Struck
Mohammad Mahzoun	Ha Tran
Liam Medley	Fernando Virdia
Tabitha Ogilvie	Julian Wälde
Richard Petri	Yuval Yarom
Raluca Posteuca	Randy Yee

Invited Talks

How Private is Secure Messaging?

Sofía Celi

Cloudflare, Portugal

Abstract. Secure messaging is on the rise: applications want to implement it, parties want to regulate it, users want to understand it. With a broad arrange of protocols, applications and options, how do users choose the secure messaging option to use? How do they know which security properties they provide? While these initial questions focus on the security part of the secure messaging sphere and its interaction with users, the privacy part is often left out from the discourse. For many, thinking about the privacy notion is integral when talking about secure messaging; while, for others, it is an optional thought. On this talk, we will explore what privacy means in the secure messaging sphere and why we think it is vital to it. We will answer questions such as: what privacy properties are missing from this security idea? Is it only about protecting metadata? what is their impact in the real-world and its policies? Do they translate to a user interface perspective?

Privacy-Preserving Bluetooth Based Contact Tracing—One Size Does Not Fit All

Eyal Ronen

Tel Aviv University, Israel

Abstract. In recent months multiple proposals for contact tracing schemes for combating the spread of COVID-19 have been published. Many of those proposals try to implement this functionality in a decentralized and privacy-preserving manner using Bluetooth Low Energy (BLE). The different schemes provide different trade-offs between privacy, security, and explainability. We claim that different countries, with different needs and cultural norms may require different trade-offs. We present "Hashomer", a contact tracing scheme that has been tailored to needs and cultural norms in Israel. In this talk, we will explain the specific trade-offs we made and the different challenges we faced. Our scheme was adopted by the Israeli Ministry of Health (MoH) and released as part of the national contact tracing application—"Hamagen".

Contents

Privacy and Applications

On Evaluating Anonymity of Onion Routing

Alessandro Melloni$^{(\boxtimes)}$ (iD), Martijn Stam (iD), and Øyvind Ytrehus (iD)

Simula UiB, Bergen, Norway
{alessandro,martijn,oyvindy}@simula.no

Abstract. Anonymous communication networks (ACNs) aim to thwart an adversary, who controls or observes chunks of the communication network, from determining the respective identities of two communicating parties. We focus on low-latency ACNs such as Tor, which target a practical level of anonymity without incurring an unacceptable transmission delay.

While several definitions have been proposed to quantify the level of anonymity provided by high-latency, message-centric ACNs (such as mix-nets and DC-nets), this approach is less relevant to Tor, where user–destination pairs communicate over secure overlay circuits. Moreover, existing evaluation methods of traffic analysis attacks on Tor appear somewhat ad hoc and fragmented. We propose a fair evaluation framework for such attacks against onion routing systems by identifying and discussing the crucial components for evaluation, including how to consider various adversarial goals, how to factor in the adversarial ability to collect information relevant to the attack, and how these components combine to suitable metrics to quantify the adversary's success.

Keywords: Anonymity · Onion routing · Tor · Traffic analysis

1 Introduction

Anonymous communication networks (ACNs) enable users to communicate with each other while hiding as much as possible who said what to whom from an adversary. The focus of anonymity varies depending on what should remain hidden: for instance, who sent to whom versus who sent what. This variation is reflected in a plethora of precise formalizations of anonymity in the context of communication [2,7,27,45], culminating in the recent 'race-car' hierarchy by Kuhn et al. [34, Fig. 3]. Two of the main concepts are unlinkability and unobservability, for instance sender–receiver unlinkability (an adversary cannot tell whether Anna is communicating with Bob or Dad) or sender unobservability (an adversary cannot tell whether Anna is communicating at all).

Of course, not all ACNs will, or even intend to, satisfy all possible notions. In fact, most ACNs belong to one of three main classes: DC nets (after Chaum's dining cryptographers [12]), mix-nets [11], and onion routing [29]. These classes

R. AlTawy and A. Hülsing (Eds.): SAC 2021, LNCS 13203, pp. 3–24, 2022.
https://doi.org/10.1007/978-3-030-99277-4_1

differ in their overhead, both in terms of bandwidth and latency. Typically, the less overhead and hence the more performant the ACN, the less formal guarantees one can hope to obtain [15]. Arguably, onion routing introduces the least inevitable overhead. It involves a user selecting a number of relays and encrypting a message in such a way that each of the relays peels of a layer of encryption until the final message is retrieved at the destination. Onion routing can be defined both in a public-key setting where each message can take its own route [9], or in a symmetric-key setting where a circuit is established on which a secure channel is overlayed [28,47].

Tor [19] is an ACN of the latter type. It aims to improve online anonymity such that even someone monitoring parts of the network cannot easily tell which user is visiting which website, or, more generally, who is connected to whom. As mentioned above, users relay their data over multi-hop circuits, using encryption to hide routing data and thwart easy, content-based correlation of traffic going in and out of any given router. However, to keep overall network latency low, the timing of incoming and outgoing traffic is certainly correlated. Indeed, when Tor was conceived, it was accepted that ingress traffic traces collected at the guard can be linked with the corresponding egress traffic traces collected at the exit node. Thus, an adversary controlling both the guard node and the exit node of a circuit can use traffic analysis to deanonymize such a circuit, thereby linking its user to their destinations.

Yet, in reality the compromise is neither automatic nor complete, and different methods have been proposed to correlate ingress and egress traces [5]. A completely different kind of traffic analysis arises when an adversary fingerprints a list of websites and, with only access to a user's ingress trace, tries to determine which website the user is visiting [43]. In parallel, several defence mechanisms have been suggested to reduce the potency of these attacks (see e.g. [33] for an overview of both attacks and defences).

A natural question is how well these attacks, respectively defences, work: in other words, how to evaluate these attacks and defences. In addition to the two distinct threat models mentioned above, there are various goals that have been considered in the past, for instance determining whether a user is accessing a monitored or unknown website (the 'open' world) versus deciding which of a number of known websites a user is accessing (the 'closed' world). Moreover, different metrics are used to evaluate, depending on the scenario; for the open world's decisional problem one often sees precision and recall, whereas for the closed world's classification problem, accuracy is more common. In some cases, information-theoretic metrics have been used and advocated [4,16,50,52].

What is lacking, though, is a common methodology or perhaps even language how best to evaluate and interpret attacks against and defences for Tor. The attacks themselves can often be regarded considerably less scenario-dependent than their evaluation indicates and for defences there is the legitimate question to what extent their evaluation should depend on current state-of-the-art of attacks. Finally, it is unclear how the attacks and their evaluations relate to the fine-grained formal definitions of anonymity mentioned above.

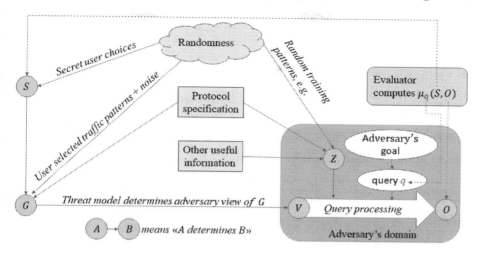

Fig. 1. View of the game and the random variables involved in it: The secret S underlies the game's state G of which an adversary can only observe V. Auxiliary information Z from earlier training is used to extract from V an answer O to the query q.

Our Contribution. We propose a framework for the evaluation of the anonymity offered by low-latency onion routing schemes such as the current Tor design. Our aim is to enable a fair comparison of various traffic analysis methods and related defences, by clarifying the possible threat models and providing a taxonomy of relevant security goals and appropriate metrics.

In Sect. 2, we cast the interplay between Tor and an adversary as a cryptographic game, identifying relevant random variables to express success of an adversary as a population parameter. Figure 1 gives a very high level overview. Even when we cannot hope to ever fully learn the real-life distribution of said variables, for evaluation, one can still set a suitable, hopefully representative distribution and run partially simulated experiments, substituting the true population parameter for a sample statistic on an approximate distribution.

As Tor is used by real people with legitimate privacy concerns, ethical evaluation invariably uses a partially simulated and scaled down version. In a simulation, the evaluator can run multiple experiments, each time knowing the ground truth of who is connected to whom. That sets evaluation apart from an actual adversary trying to learn what is happening during a single snapshot of Tor.

Of course, a real-life adversary will operate against real world Tor and thus the threat models, and possible goals an adversary may have, derive directly from considering the real world. Specifically, an attacker against Tor typically will be able to observe some of the traffic flowing through the network and possibly to manipulate said traffic. Exactly which traffic can be observed depends on the threat model, as we elaborate upon in Sect. 5. For instance, there is a difference between an adversary only observing traffic flowing through the proxy versus an adversary who has corrupted multiple guard and exit nodes.

Table 1. List of random variables in the framework.

Random variable	Description
S	The game's 'secret' mapping of users with destinations
G	The game's full view of the interaction
V	The adversary's limited view of the interaction
Z	Auxiliary information given to or obtained by the adversary
O	The adversary's output, expressing belief about part of the secret

An adversary will use its observations to deduce information about who is connected to whom. There are various ways one can formalize this question in the real world, and some additional ones when considering a simplified simulated setting. We discuss the most common and meaningful scenarios in Sect. 3.

Basic metrics are known in the machine learning community (and beyond) to pose problems; we investigate in Sect. 4, where we also address metrics based on information theory, such as mutual information.

Related Work. Several security definitions have been proposed to quantify the level of anonymity provided by ACNs. While those definitions are suitable to argue about high latency, message-based ACNs (such as mix-nets and DC-nets), as we argue in Sect. 3.1, those definitions are less relevant to low latency, circuit-based onion routing like Tor.

Wagner and Eckhoff [58] provide an overview of possible metrics related to anonymity, including ACNs (see also Sect. 4). Some parallels exist between evaluating ACNs and side-channel attacks (SCA) [54], where a distinguisher wants to recover a subkey given a number of power traces: key recovery is essentially a classification problem and, as for traffic traces, the exact distribution of power traces is typically unknown, yet can be sampled from using real devices.

2   High-Level Framework/Execution Environment

Setup. We apply a perspective of modern cryptology by describing the interaction between an adversary $\mathcal{A}$ and the ACN as a game, where our focus is on identifying the relevant random variables, as summarized in Table 1. For real-life ACNs, the distribution of these random variables might be unknown and difficult to estimate precisely; as we will see, an evaluator typically has far more control over the underlying distributions by using a semi-simulated experimental setting.

Central to our modelling are users who wish to connect to various destinations. We use disjoint sets $\mathcal{U}$ and $\mathcal{D}$ to describe, respectively, users and destinations. In the real-world, users and destinations are typically identified using IP addresses or URLs, possibly even names; abstractly any label suffices.

The choice of the users which destinations to connect to, is modelled by the random variable S, whose sample space is the set of directed bipartite graphs between $\mathcal{U}$ and $\mathcal{D}$. Nodes represent the users and destinations, whereas edges map connections between users and destinations.

The random variable S captures users' behaviour by selecting a single graph from the pool of possible ones, but this abstraction does have some shortcomings when compared to practice. Firstly, our model is static, in the sense that all users simultaneously decide on their destinations. In reality, users come and go and their destinations change over time. Such a dynamic setting seems to have received relatively little attention so far, hence our restriction to static appears standard. Secondly, an evaluator needs to choose a suitable distribution of S that is representative of real usage.

When evaluating, one often considers only simplified distributions for S. For instance, it is common that each user only connects to exactly one destination, so all user nodes have degree one. Additionally, either for all users the destination they connect to is independent and identically distributed (uniformly or based on website popularity metrics) or, in the special case where $|\mathcal{U}| = |\mathcal{D}|$, the graph S might correspond to a permutation, drawn uniformly at random.

For each user $u \in \mathcal{U}$, the destinations they are actually connecting to are denoted by random variable D_u. For some specific users there might be restrictions on the possible destinations, that is the support $\mathcal{D}_u$ of possible destinations is a proper subset of $\mathcal{D}$. Finally, destinations are said to be active if they have non-zero degree.

The state and all the possible observables of the anonymity network are modelled by G. In the case of Tor, G could capture the internal states of routers (identities, cryptographic keys, circuit IDs), traffic traces consisting of vectors of packet sizes and timings, and any other information that may be collected by any party involved (internal or external). Giving an exhaustive, formal definition of G is neither convenient nor necessary, though G should fully determine S.

Adversaries. Most adversaries will only have limited knowledge of G. Their view V of G depends on the specific threat model. For example, a user's ISP will be able to see that user's traffic patterns, but not much more. In contrast, the user's guard node will see that traffic pattern, but additionally know the middle router for that user's circuit. We will discuss threat models in more detail in Sect. 5.

An actual adversary often runs in two stages. During the first 'training' stage, it tries to learn general information about the behaviour of the network. For instance, how traffic traces captured at a proxy depend on the destination, or how traffic traces captured at a proxy differ from the corresponding ones captured at the exit node. This auxiliary information is captured by the random variable Z. Although Z could include an estimation of the distribution of S, it is independent of the random variable S itself. Only in the subsequent second 'challenge' stage the adversary observes V, which it combines with the auxiliary information Z to try and learn something useful about S.

What the adversary tries to learn corresponds to the goal of the adversary, which we capture by a query q that may depend on a target $\mathsf{T} \subseteq \mathcal{U} \times \mathcal{D}$. Given a query q, the target T and the random variable S, there is often a unique answer to this query, which we will denote $S_{|q}$ (with implicit dependency on T). For instance, if q asks which website(s) a user u is connected to, then the target can be encoded as $T = \{u\} \times \mathcal{D}$ and the correct, complete answer $S_{|q}$ is a subset of $\mathcal{D}$. Note that unicity of the answer in the example above is a property of the query, irrespective of either target or instantiation of S.

When discussing possible goals in Sect. 3, we will refer to the users (resp. destinations) component of the target T as $T_{\mathcal{U}}$ (resp. $T_{\mathcal{D}}$), so in the small example above $T_{\mathcal{U}} = \{u\}$ is relevant, whereas $T_{\mathcal{D}} = \mathcal{D}$ is just a formalization artefact (and we may abuse the notation and consider either $T_{\mathcal{U}}$ or $T_{\mathcal{D}}$ to be empty instead).

The adversary processes the information and returns output O_q as response to the query q on target T. If q has unique answers, this output O_q could be the adversary's best guess for $S_{|q}$, or it could be an approximation, a list of possible answers, or a vector of likelihoods for select answers, etc.

Evaluation. When evaluating an attack, we specifically refer to the processing from V into O, possibly in conjunction with how Z is attained and used. On the other hand, when referring to a defence, we are primarily interested in how the random variable G's distribution can be made less susceptible to later attacks.

An evaluation should indicate how well an attack or defence works, which can be done by means of an anonymity metric. In first instance, such a metric is a parameter that summarizes the anonymity, or loss thereof, as indicated by the random variables S and O, or S and V (possibly also including Z). In that sense, a metric can be regarded as a population parameter (or as the difference between two population parameters, cf. the deltas used by Pfitzmann and Hansen [44]).

Although the distribution of G and thus V is typically unknown, one can sample from it, e.g. by connecting to the Internet using the ACN and taking measurements (in an ethically responsible way) or by using a tool like Shadow [31]. Thus, the population parameters can be estimated using sample statistics.

As we will see in Sect. 4, sometimes, metrics are simply expressed as summary statistics (e.g. accuracy), without reference to their potential underlying population parameter. We believe one strength of our framework of making the random variables explicit, is that it helps surface a number of otherwise hidden choices in the evaluation, such as the distribution of S used and how the sampling experiment was set up.

To evaluate an attack, i.e. the processing of V into O_q, one inevitably has to take that output O_q into consideration. As the output is, or is related to, an adversary's best guess for $S_{|q}$, such an output-dependent metric will depend on the adversary's goal. On the other hand, to evaluate a defence, changes in the distribution of V are more relevant, leading to metrics directly on V. Through $S_{|q}$, such input-dependent metrics can still take into account an adversary's goal q, yet without considering how the processing works. Thus, defences can potentially be evaluated independently of the currently best-known attacks.

Traffic traces as contained in V can contain a lot of unstructured data that is computationally expensive to process directly. An adversary may pre-process V

by extracting its most salient features prior to the actual core processing. This core processing itself is often independent of any goal. For instance, for each observed ingress trace and each observed egress trace, it outputs a score how well they match, resulting in a matrix of scores. Subsequent post-processing can take this matrix to return an output specific to a given query q, say by turning the score into a true/false value (based on some threshold) or taking an arg max. Intuitively, such post-processing potentially throws away a lot of information, thus we might also want to consider metrics purely for the core-processing without taking into account any post-processing.

Examples. To illustrate our framework, see Example 1 (and Fig. 2) below.

Example 1 (Website Fingerprinting). Consider the *open world* scenario from Deep Fingerprinting by Sirinam *et al.* [53]. The threat model consists of a local passive adversary sniffing the traffic between a single user and their entry node. Such an adversary wants to verify whether the user is accessing a website from some pre-defined subset $T_\mathcal{D} \subsetneq \mathcal{D}$ or not. In our framework, this translates to:

S The website w accessed by the user, sampled from $\mathcal{D}$ according to a uniform distribution. Using the graph notation, $\mathcal{U} = \{u\}$ and there is a single edge going from u to w.
G The state of the single circuit in the network: identities of the user, nodes, and destination, plus traffic flows from user to destination and vice versa.
V The information in G accessible by the adversary, mainly user's identity and the traffic trace between user and guard node.
goal The query "Is the visited website w an item of $T_\mathcal{D}$?", where $T_\mathcal{D}$ is the target.
Z The training data used by the adversary's distinguisher. It is referred to as *open-world dataset*.
O A binary random variable, answering directly the query q with yes or no.

This process is performed on a single traffic trace at a time, resulting in the binary random variable O. The experiment is repeated in order to collect more data and extrapolate statistical information. *Precision* and *recall* are used to estimate the performance of the distinguisher; moreover, ROC curves are provided to show the trade-off between TPR and FPR.

Example 2, Appendix A, [37] looks at the traffic analysis scenario studied by Nasr *et al.* [38]. There is a key difference between those two examples. In the first one, the adversary attacks a single user at a time, in a way that allows them to scale their approach to multiple users independently of each other. Consequently, the influence on how well the attack performs against a specific user is largely independent of what other users are doing, seemingly contradicting the intuition that the anonymity in onion routing derives from 'hiding among the masses' [19]. In contrast, for the second example all users' traffic traces are pooled together and users may influence each other's anonymity.

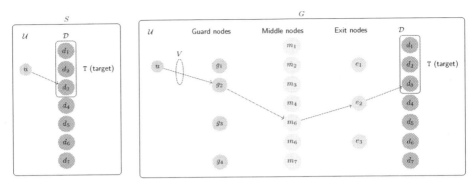

Fig. 2. Bipartite and multipartite graphs representing settings and random variables in Deep Fingerprinting (Example 1). Edges in the secret S are expanded, through protocol specifications, to multiple edges in the multipartite graph G (representing circuits in Tor) and the view of the adversary V.

Relevance. When we say that we focus on evaluation attacks and defences against the anonymity of Tor, our scope is relatively narrow, as we primarily concentrate on fingerprinting and traffic analysis in a scenario where the threat model is fixed (see also Sect. 5). However, an adversary who controls all routers in the Tor network can trivially de-anonymize all circuits, whereas an adversary who controls no routers, proxies, or destinations and cannot observe any traffic, essentially for whom $V = \emptyset$, cannot possibly learn anything useful.

A rational de-anonymization adversary might therefore invest its resources in observing and controlling a chunk of the ACN as large as possible. For a user worried about deanonymisation through ingress–egress traffic analysis, the largest risk arguably lies in the adversary capturing both traffic traces, and less in the adversary's ability to link the traces (if both ends had been acquired within a much larger collection of traces). On the opposite side, deployers of an ACN would probably spend more of their resources in protecting their network from control and widespread observation, rather than incorporating bandwidth-consuming and latency-increasing countermeasures to reduce the damage if an adversary sees both ingress and egress traces [56].

We acknowledge that, rather than minimizing the damage when a threat occurs, it makes sense to minimize the threat happening in the first place and the Tor designer's assumption that all anonymity is lost if both guard and exit node of a circuit are compromised is the correct conservative one. Similarly, guard nodes were introduced in recognition that it is better to sacrifice a few users more severely, than a lot of users a little. Yet that does not take away that figuring out how to compromise in various scenarios, and how to limit those compromises potentially, is an active research area. Whether to deploy a potential defence in practice will be based on its return on investment, essentially a trade-off between the protection offered versus the cost (in comparison with other measures outside the scope of this work).

3   Security Goals and Notions

3.1   Interpreting Privacy Notions

Historical Context. After Chaum [11] initiated the study of ACNs in the early 1980s, it quickly became apparent that a common language was lacking. Pfitzmann and Hansen [44, 45] attempted to consolidate terminology by providing as precise as possible context-free descriptions of various relevant terms, such as unlinkability and unobservability. For specific contexts, they recommend to abstract away certain terms, such as 'sender', 'recipient', and 'message'.

In the context of onion routing, the user establishes a circuit over which bidirectional traffic will flow, making the concepts of sender, receiver, and especially message potentially misleading. Using the existing, default terminology as is might encourage a mental model of a sender sending a single or vector of messages to a receiver. Such a mental model could lead to mismatches in context-specific formalizations, similar to a message-based mental model not quite capturing TLS's record layer security [24]. Thus we speak of users instead of senders and destinations instead of receivers; furthermore, we drop the concept of messages from our framework, arguably the closest analogy would be a circuit.

The privacy notions of unlinkability and unobservability have been formalized for ACNs in a number of works [2, 7, 27]. In particular, Kuhn *et al.* [34] present a thorough formalisation of a wide range of privacy notions, encompassing most previous work. For high latency message-based ACNs, these indistinguishability-based notions are very suitable as they allow expressing (and proving) the security of protocols in a fine-grained manner. However, the notions show some shortcomings when it comes to their applicability to low latency ACNs, such as the inherent dichotomy between success or failure of the attacker in terms of *whether* a formal definition is satisfied or not. This approach is rarely encountered in the literature concerning onion routing in the real world, which commonly rely on measuring *how well* attacks and countermeasures perform. Moreover, they consider asymptotic security as they employ adversaries as probabilistic polynomial time (PPT) algorithms, instead of concrete real-world instantiations.

Our Interpretation. Minding the above, we depart from the indistinguishability -based formalizations and provide an interpretation, specific for onion routing, of observability and linkability (O, L), usually in their negated forms unobservability $(\overline{\mathsf{O}})$ and unlinkability $(\overline{\mathsf{L}})$. Instead of sender and receiver, we maintain our terminology of users (U) and destinations (D). Note that we abstract away any particular onion routing specifications, so our notions are agnostic of, for instance, the use of guard nodes, or the length of the circuits.

Tor's ultimate goal is to avoid any party, different from the user themselves, from learning both user and destination of observed traffic. The corresponding privacy notion is then user–destination unlinkability $((\mathsf{UD})\overline{\mathsf{L}})$. User unobservability $(\mathsf{U}\overline{\mathsf{O}})$ refers to the inability, for the adversary, to observe whether a user is accessing Tor or not. This notion is important, for example, in cases where

Table 2. Privacy notions. A node v of the graph S is active if and only if $\deg(v) > 0$.

Notion	Description
$(UD)\overline{O}$	**1.** No edges can be noticed from either users or destinations; the number of edges can be disclosed. This condition can be expressed as unknown degree value for any of the nodes but known total degree of the graph ($|E_S|$).
$(UD)\overline{L}$	**2.** Degrees of nodes are revealed, but no element e of the edge set E_S is known. In terms of S, no path is completely disclosed, but which users or destinations are active can be revealed.
$U\overline{O}$	**3.** Degree of destinations is known, but not for users'.
$D\overline{O}$	**4.** Which destinations are active is unknown; instead, users' activity may be disclosed.

Tor usage is being censored [20,21,61–63]; the analogous notion ($D\overline{O}$) can be considered for destinations. These two notions could also be combined into user–destination unobservability ($(UD)\overline{O}$), in case neither the user nor the destination can be observed as being connected to the Tor network.

Above, when referring to privacy notions, we only provided intuitive descriptions rather than the formal definition approach mentioned previously. In Table 2 we interpret the privacy notions in terms of the bipartite graph representing S. For example, observing a destination means knowing that the destination is connected to the network, i.e. the corresponding node in the graph has non-zero degree. We will refine further when discussing privacy goals in the next section.

Relationships. Ostensibly, unobservability is a stronger notion than unlinkability (cf. [34,44]). Yet, somewhat counterintuitively when we consider specific threat models against onion routing, it appears that the seemingly stronger looking abstraction (i.e. unobservability) can be the more appropriate. Let us elaborate.

Depending on the threat model (Sect. 5), $(UD)\overline{L}$ may collapse to either $U\overline{O}$ or $D\overline{O}$. For example, assume that the adversary observes the traffic between the user and the guard node, either by corrupting the guard node or by observing traffic in the user's or the guard node's ISP. These observations reveal the user's IP address as well as the traffic patterns from and to the user. Based on this information alone, website fingerprinting may in some cases (with a well fingerprinted server) help the adversary to identify the server and hence the user and destination are linkable. However, if in addition the adversary is able to observe the traffic between the exit node and the destination, it is highly plausible that linking the user and the destination is computationally feasible. Hence, in this scenario, in order to achieve $(UD)\overline{L}$, we need the adversary to be unable to observe the destination of the traffic ($D\overline{O}$). Note that, as it is customary in the literature, such terminology ($\overline{O}$) does not take into account the computational effort needed to infer the desired information (e.g. the end destination) from the available information (e.g. the traffic trace), instead of distinguishing between the concepts of 'unobservability' and 'computational uninferrability'.

3.2   A Taxonomy of Security Goals

Attacks on user–destination anonymity can have different goals, as captured in our framework in terms of queries q on S, where q may furthermore have a specific target T. Distinct goals may require different metrics, which are reflected in the literature, where authors utilise various evaluation metrics to compare their results with others. In order to understand the various metrics, we first need to establish a taxonomy of different goals, which we will do in this section. We divide the goals and the corresponding queries in four distinct categories. From specific to the most general these are distinguishing, decisional, classification, and finally computational. Examples 3–6, Appendix B [37] illustrate these goals.

Distinguishing Goals. Inspired by the classic IND-CPA [6] notion for encryption, distinguishing goals arise in formal cryptologic models of anonymity (see also Sect. 3.1): an adversary is interacting with one of two worlds (say left or right) and needs to figure out which world it is engaged with. A distinguishing goal corresponds to a dichotomous classification problem with a uniform prior and symmetry between the two classification options, with no meaningful distinction between positives and negatives (see Example 3, Appendix B [37]). Assuming the output is a single bit, the typical metric for a distinguishing goal is the distinguishing advantage.

Decisional Goals. Decisional goals are still dichotomous classification problems, but here the prior might be non-uniform and meaning can be associated to positives and negatives. The open world scenario (Example 1) belongs to this category, since $\mathcal{D}$ can be partitioned in monitored/unmonitored destinations and the adversary has to decide whether the observed traffic trace corresponds to a monitored destination or not, without having to pinpoint the exact destination.

In our framework, a query q representing a decisional goal can be regarded as a predicate on S that induces a partition of S's sample space into two subsets: the positive part contains all bipartite graphs satisfying the predicate (e.g., the targeted user connects to a monitored website), whereas for negatives the predicate is false (the user is in the clear). As the concepts of true/false positives/negatives are meaningful, the standard metrics for binary classifiers apply, which we will expand upon in Sect. 4.2.

Decisional goals are often related to the open world scenarios in website fingerprinting, introduced by Panchenko *et al.* [43]. They suggest it as it is closer to a real world scenario (compared to closed world), and it quickly became one of the two main instantiations of website fingerprinting [8,10,26,30,42,49,53,59,60].

Classification Goals. For a more general classification goal, we drop the requirement of only two classes available, thus the query q induces a partition of the sample space of S in more than two subsets. A key difference compared to decisional goals is that, from the adversary's perspective, there is no longer any preference among the possible classes and specifically all misclassifications are treated the same (in sharp contrast to false positives versus false negatives for decisional goals). In that sense, classification goals are closer to distinguishing goals, however for classification goals the prior distribution need not be uniform over the classes.

The closed-world scenario for website fingerprinting is an example of a classification goal; another example arises in traffic analysis attacks when an adversary has to match a single target ingress trace to one of many possible egress traces, or vice versa [55]. Accuracy, corresponding to the probability of classifying correctly, is the most common metric.

Computational Goals. Finally, for computational goals an adversary tries to learn something that perhaps cannot easily be classified and there might not be a single correct answer. For instance, a greedy adversary trying to deanonymize as many users simultaneously as possible. Often there is a notion of proximity or similarity between answers, including not-quite-correct ones, rendering the adversary's job one of best-effort estimation.

A typical example of a computational goal is the matching of ingress traces to egress traces [25,36,38,41,51,55]. Although there is a unique best bipartite graph that correctly identifies all matches without any incorrect ones, an adversary might prefer to only output the matches it is most confident in, or it might even output an inconsistent set of matches in order not to miss any legitimate matches. See also Example 6, Appendix B [37].

Discussion. Some goals that are seemingly identical can be modelled in slightly different ways when evaluating. For instance, when an evaluator is interested how well a website fingerprinting algorithm works on ingress traces, one option is to consider multiple users and target only one (so V is considerable smaller than G), another is to only ever consider a single user (so V contains more of G). When the traces are acquired by live interaction with the ACN (including many unknown users outside $\mathcal{U}$), the two views V might be sufficiently similar to render the single-user simplification representative of the multi-user setting. If, on the other hand, traces are simulated, simplifying away other users may not be warranted.

Goals can also relate to each other in a black-box way, in the sense that an adversary that decides whether an ingress trace and an egress trace are related, might also be used to determine which ingress trace belongs to a given egress trace by selecting one of the matching ingress traces (ideally, there would be exactly one, but this cannot be guaranteed). However, such a black-box approach is likely wasteful if the adversary really creates a score as its core processing and only arrived at a yes/no decision through post-processing. In that case applying a different post-processing instead makes more sense.

We list a number of possible goals in Table 4, Appendix C [37].

4   Metrics

Syverson [56] argues that anonymity metrics should reflect the effort an adversary has to expend in order to reach a goal, and also that to be useful, security metrics should not depend on the values of variables for which we cannot make adequate relevant determinations or predictions. We believe anonymity metrics should be suitable for the security goal at hand, they should allow meaningful comparison between different attacks and countermeasures, and efficient and robust estimation should be feasible. In order to be sufficiently general to accommodate a wide range of goals and attacks, we use the term "metric" in a relaxed manner, without imposing the usual mathematical properties of a metric. What we will assume is that a metric μ does not behave in a non-intuitive way.

Researchers on ACNs like Tor often have limited access to real world data, due to intrinsic difficulties including legal and ethical considerations. Hence, assumptions known to be artificial are regularly employed but seldom explicitly stated. Furthermore, since metrics are used to represent the performance of an attack, they depend on the input data collected by the adversary or by the evaluator for the given attack and not only on the attack itself. The accuracy of a classifier may be influenced by the probability distribution on the input data, by the size of the data set, or by the number of classes. In consequence, metrics used in the literature are often effectively estimates of the adversary's success rate in synthetic settings, while their real world relevance remains less clear [57].

For an attacker, the relevant metrics may be the computational cost and accuracy of an attack, while researchers may be interested in the anonymity level provided by Tor to the average user. Due to these substantial differences, it is of fundamental importance to determine which metrics are pertinent rather than defaulting to some generic ones.

We provide examples illuminating the concepts of this section in Appendix D [37].

4.1   Input-Dependent Metrics

Input-dependent metrics depend on S or $S_{|q}$, G, and V, but not on O. The leakage about the secret random variables S, $S_{|q}$, and G obtained by observing V is naturally expressed in the form of information-theoretic concepts like entropy, conditional entropy, and mutual information [35]. These concepts have already been used to assess anonymity networks [4,16,50,52]. The Shannon entropy

$$\mathrm{H}(S) = -\sum_{s \in S} p_S(s) \log_2 p(s)$$

by itself only expresses the a priori uncertainty about the secret S. In order to evaluate an attack, it is necessary to study the conditional entropy

$$\mathrm{H}(S \mid V) = -\sum_{s \in S, v \in V} p(s, v) \log_2 p(s|v) = \mathbb{E}\left[\mathrm{H}(S \mid V = v)\right]_{v \in V}, \qquad (1)$$

which represents the remaining uncertainty about S after observing the random variable V. Hence, the mutual information $I(S; V) = H(S) - H(S \mid V)$ can be interpreted as the information leakage about S from observing V. Shannon entropy is known to satisfy *monotonicity*, that is, $H(S \mid V) \leq H(S)$, so that information leakage defined as above is always non-negative.

Diaz *et al.* [17] remark that since the RHS of Eq. (1) contains an expectation, there may exist some sample view v that gives more leakage than average, and hence one might be concerned about sample views of this type.

In our model, the view V is a random variable beyond the influence of the adversary, and in a pure Shannon entropic perspective, only the average conditional entropy $H(S \mid V)$ would be important. However, concern about deanonymisation probabilities suggests that more emphasis should be put on this type of sample views (cf. [44, Footnote 34]). Hence, Clauß and Schiffner [13] suggested the use of Rényi entropy and quantiles to measure anonymity. Rényi entropy [1,23,48] is a generalization of Shannon entropy (for convenience, we include a brief summary of relevant concepts in Appendix D [37]), which Clauß and Schiffner argue is more resilient (using different values of α) against the influence of outliers than Shannon entropy. They differentiate between *network* and *application* layers when assessing anonymity, corresponding respectively to G and S in our framework.

In order to compare the performance of attacks in different settings with different sizes of the secret S, some authors [16,58] suggest *normalizing* information metrics by dividing by the secret max entropy $H_0(S) = \log_2 |S|$.

4.2   Output-Dependent Metrics

By definition, the adversary view V contains all of the information the adversary obtains about the secret S, or about the parts $S_{|q}$ of the secret pertinent to a specific query q. However, V is typically complex and the appropriate response to q may not be immediately obvious based on inspection of V. In order to provide an illuminating response O_q that is aligned with the query q, the adversary needs to apply a query-dependent processing of V. An evaluator with access to the secret S (or $S_{|q}$) should be able to compute an *output-dependent* metric function $\mu_q(O_q, S)$ that measures the quality of the (estimated) output O_q relative to S.

It follows by the data processing lemma of information theory [14, Section 2.8] that $I(S; O_q) \leq I(S; V)$ (and similar for Rényi information). Moreover, since V is typically complex and machine learning may be part of the processing, outputs may be unaccompanied by confidence/uncertainty estimates, and thus, the price for the adversary of providing an output O_q in a convenient form is often an information loss. The examples in Appendix D [37] illustrate this.

In the literature, authors have used various output-dependent metrics to quantify the success of attacks. A general consensus on which of these are more insightful for a given type of query still appears lacking. Table 5, Appendix D [37] briefly describes some metrics that have been used in the context of onion routing attacks.

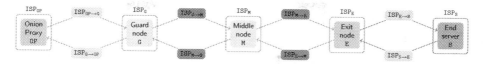

Fig. 3. Example of Tor circuit. As discussed by Sun *et al.* [55], the traffic path may be asymmetric in the forward and backward directions.

Decisional Goals. Queries leading to decisional goals can be considered analogous to binary classifiers, for which the concepts of true/false positive/negative are clear. Two common metrics used for such queries are *Precision* and *Recall*, defined in Table 5, Appendix D [37]. ROC (Receiver operating characteristic) curves [22] provide a more comprehensive description of performance.

Caveat: A binary classifier with non-zero false positive rate which is applied to a random variable with a very low prior probability of being positive suffers from the so called *Base Rate Fallacy*, by which most positive outputs will be incorrect. This scenario has been applied to Tor [32,57], highlighting potential disadvantages of these metrics and calling for more precise description of the setup of experiments and presentation of the results.

Classification Goals. Metrics for classification goals cannot rely on the difference between positive and negative guesses, but only on guesses being either correct or wrong. Thus, they are susceptible to biases in the data sets: for example, if the prior distribution of the data set on three possible classes is {0.9, 0.05, 0.05}, a naïve classifier with constant output 'class 1' has 90% accuracy.

Computational Goals. Computational goals represent the most general case in our framework and are characterised by the concept of "closeness" of the output to the real answer to the query, i.e. guesses by the adversary may be partially correct—in a similar way to fuzzy logic truth values.

5   Adversarial Threat Model

Threat modelling is a central part of the analysis of security and anonymity; we consider the following general adversary characterisations [58] for onion routing:

- *passive* adversaries are only allowed to observe the protocol execution, and as such they can be thought as *honest-but-curious*. *Active* adversaries, on the other hand, can modify, delay, replay, stop the traffic. *Semi-honest* adversaries are a relevant subset of the latter category: they tamper with the traffic in a non-disruptive way only, e.g. by slightly delaying the cells;

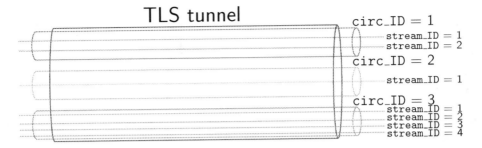

Fig. 4. Multiplexing in onion routing.

- only *internal* adversaries have access to data inside onion nodes, while *external* ones are limited to non-onion nodes. We will refer to adversaries having access to both onion nodes and external parties as *hybrid*;
- *local* adversaries control (observe) only some of the nodes of the network, while *global* ones do not have this limitation. For example, a global internal adversary controls all and only the Tor nodes and global external has access to all and only the Internet infrastructure.

Each of these characteristics is orthogonal to the others, and the terminology reflects these degrees of freedom: passive adversaries tend to *observe* nodes, while active ones *control* them.

According to this characterisation, an active global hybrid adversary is the most powerful. Goldschlag *et al.* [29] explicitly state that onion routing does not aim to protect from global adversaries, regardless of the computational cost of processing all the information or if they are internal or external. On the other hand, local adversaries have a restricted view of the network and they should not be able to link user and destination of the traffic.

While a local adversary is the standard in the literature, other characteristics vary among the different works, with external and passive adversaries being the most common [38,39,41,42,49,53,59]. Some results require the adversary to be not only internal but also semi-honest [36,51,55] or even active [25].

Taking into consideration the Tor protocol specifications [18], it is worth noting that even the same type of adversary may have a more or less granular view of the traffic, depending on their position along the circuit. This is due to the fact that Tor multiplexes traffic on two layers: a single onion circuit can carry several streams (i.e. TCP connections) and nodes multiplex several circuits on the same TLS tunnel (Fig. 4).

In general, internal adversaries have access to more information compared to externals (e.g. single cells, `circ_ID`), but they can be detected and removed from the network [3]. External adversaries observe only TLS-encrypted tunnels but Tor tends, to the proxy, to stream single cells in TLS packets, so they can be inferred by some ISP on the circuit (e.g. ISP_{OP} in Fig. 3).

Assuming for simplicity that the onion proxy creates a single circuit, this is the path from the user to the end destination (cf. Fig. 3):

1. $ISP_{OP \to G}$ and $ISP_{G \to OP}$ observe a single TLS tunnel carrying the user's circuit;
2. ISP_G (and all the others in red in the figure) observe TLS tunnels, possibly carrying multiple circuits;
3. the guard node G and the middle node M observe single cells, but not streams;
4. ISP_E is different, in that they observe also the non-Tor traffic directed to the end destinations. In case of browsing, though, this traffic tends to be encrypted as well [40];
5. exit node E is the only one to have visibility on the `stream_ID` as well, distinguishing different TCP connections originating from OP.

Depending on the settings, this design will prevent many types of adversary from reaching their goal. For example, assume that two users simultaneously create a single circuit each, passing through the same nodes, to different destinations: then, no external adversary can distinguish the streams between the exit node and the end destinations.

6   Application of Our Framework

Our framework allows to clearly describe assumptions underlying attacks and evaluation of anonymity in onion routing; we present a brief list of existing literature expressed in terms of our framework in Table 3.

First, S, G and V are defined taking into consideration the assumptions about the environment. Both the supports of those random variables and their probability distribution are needed to completely characterise the experiment. Furthermore, the definition of V guarantees that also the adversarial model is well specified and understood. The last step of the setup phase is the determination of the query q and optionally a target T. These, on the other hand, influence which type of random variable O_q to employ.

Such process ensures all the game variables are well defined, allowing to establish which type of goal the adversary is trying to achieve. Finally, each case may require different metrics to meaningfully and effectively illustrate the results, while making sure that limitations are apparent and common misunderstanding avoided.

Table 3. Attacks and their instantiation in our framework. Attacks' names have been assigned by the authors of this work for convenience. Adversaries are assumed to be local, for the other features the corresponding initial letter is used. We refer to Table 4, Appendix C [37] for goals.

Ref.	Attack	Adv.	Goal type	Output	Metric
[41]	Wavelet Multi-resolution	E. P	Computational	Pairs (ingress, egress) flows	FP/FN
[51]	Dropmarking	I. S-H	Classification	Pairs (entry, exit) nodes	TPR/TNR/FPR/FNR
[38]	DeepCorr	E. P	Computational	Pairs (ingress, egress) flows	FPR/FNR, ROC curve
[55]	RAPTOR	E. P	Classification	Pairs (ingress, egress) flows	Accuracy
[36]	Cell counting	I. S-H	Classification	Pairs (ingress, egress) flows	Accuracy, detection rate, false positive rate
[25]	Tagging attack	I. A	Decisional	Pairs (ingress, egress) flows	Accuracy
[46]	Fingerprinting with website oracles	E. P	Decisional.Classification	Pairs (trace, website)	Precision, recall
[53]	Deep Fingerprinting	E. P	Decisional, Classification	Pairs (trace, website)	Accuracy
[49]	Fingerprinting with Deep Learning	E. P	Decisional, Classification	Pairs (trace, website)	Accuracy, TPR/FRP.ROC curve
[30]	Correlation with DNS info	E. P	Computational	Intersection of ASes' sets	Precision, recall
[39]	Compressive Traffic Analysis	E. P	Computational	Pairs (flow, noisy flow), pairs (trace, website)	TP/FP, accuracy
[42]	Fingerprinting at Internet scale	E. P	Decisional, Classification	Pairs (trace, website)	Accuracy, precision
[59]	k-NN Website Fingerprinting	E. P	Decisional, Classification	Pairs (trace, website)	TPR/FPR, accuracy
[10]	Circuit clogging	I. S-H	Classification	Pairs (user, onion nodes)	TPR/FRP, ROC curve
[60]	SVM Fingerprinting	E. P	Decisional, Classification	Pairs (trace, website)	Accuracy, TP/FP
[26]	Induced throttling	I. S-H	Classification	Pairs (user, onion nodes)	Percentile, degrees of anonymity, client probability
[8]	DLSVM	E. P	Decisional	Pairs (trace, website)	TPR/FPR, success rate
[43]	Website fingerprinting	E. P	Decisional, Classification	Pairs (trace, website)	Accuracy, TPR/FPR

7   Conclusion

We highlighted several of the challenges when evaluating onion routing and described a framework that helps to benchmark different attacks and counter-measures. Although we did not explicitly mention all features of Tor, we expect that for instance so-called leaky pipes and hidden services can be easily integrated into our framework.

We leave open the dynamic situation, where users come and go, and an adversary might actively try to influence the (re)establishment of circuits. Formally making the various random variables time-dependent is easy enough, simply by writing $S(t)$ instead of S. However, one main challenge we see are determining meaningful, possibly adversarially affected, evolutions of the secret $S(t)$. A fixed uniform distribution as often used for a static S somewhat defeats the purpose of the dynamic setting, but could still serve a situation where an adversary can trigger (as in Tor) circuit teardowns that are subsequently re-established, making the overall view of the system G depend on the adversary.

References

1. Arimoto, S.: Information measures and capacity of order α for discrete memory-less channels. In: Topics in Information Theory. Colloquia Mathematica Societatis János Bolyai, vol. 16, pp. 41–52 (1977)
2. Backes, M., Kate, A., Manoharan, P., Meiser, S., Mohammadi, E.: AnoA: a framework for analyzing anonymous communication protocols. In: Cortier, V., Datta, A. (eds.) CSF 2013 Computer Security Foundations Symposium, pp. 163–178. IEEE Computer Society Press (2013). https://doi.org/10.1109/CSF.2013.18
3. Bagueros, I.: Tor security advisory: exit relays running sslstrip in May and June 2020, August 2020. https://blog.torproject.org/bad-exit-relays-may-june-2020
4. Barton, A., Wright, M., Ming, J., Imani, M.: Towards predicting efficient and anonymous Tor circuits. In: Enck, W., Felt, A.P. (eds.) USENIX Security 2018, pp. 429–444. USENIX Association, August 2018
5. Bauer, K.S., McCoy, D., Grunwald, D., Kohno, T., Sicker, D.C.: Low-resource routing attacks against Tor. In: Ning, P., Yu, T. (eds.) WPES 2007, pp. 11–20. ACM, New York, October 2007. https://doi.org/10.1145/1314333.1314336
6. Bellare, M., Desai, A., Jokipii, E., Rogaway, P.: A concrete security treatment of symmetric encryption. In: 38th FOCS, pp. 394–403. IEEE Computer Society Press, October 1997. https://doi.org/10.1109/SFCS.1997.646128
7. Bohli, J.-M., Pashalidis, A.: Relations among privacy notions. In: Dingledine, R., Golle, P. (eds.) FC 2009. LNCS, vol. 5628, pp. 362–380. Springer, Heidelberg (2009). https://doi.org/10.1007/978-3-642-03549-4_22
8. Cai, X., Zhang, X.C., Joshi, B., Johnson, R.: Touching from a distance: website fingerprinting attacks and defenses. In: Yu, T., Danezis, G., Gligor, V.D. (eds.) ACM CCS 2012, pp. 605–616. ACM Press, October 2012. https://doi.org/10.1145/2382196.2382260
9. Camenisch, J., Lysyanskaya, A.: A formal treatment of onion routing. In: Shoup, V. (ed.) CRYPTO 2005. LNCS, vol. 3621, pp. 169–187. Springer, Heidelberg (2005). https://doi.org/10.1007/11535218_11
10. Chan-Tin, E., Shin, J., Yu, J.: Revisiting circuit clogging attacks on Tor. In: ARES 2013, pp. 131–140. IEEE Computer Society, September 2013. https://doi.org/10.1109/ARES.2013.17
11. Chaum, D.: Untraceable electronic mail, return addresses, and digital pseudonyms. Commun. Assoc. Comput. Mach. **24**(2), 84–90 (1981). https://doi.org/10.1145/358549.358563
12. Chaum, D.: The dining cryptographers problem: *Unconditional sender and recipient untraceability*. J. Cryptol. **1**(1), 65–75 (1988). https://doi.org/10.1007/BF00206326
13. Clauß, S., Schiffner, S.: Structuring anonymity metrics. In: Juels, A., Winslett, M., Goto, A. (eds.) WDIM 2006, pp. 55–62. ACM, November 2006. https://doi.org/10.1145/1179529.1179539
14. Cover, T.M., Thomas, J.A.: Elements of Information Theory. Wiley, USA (2006). https://doi.org/10.1002/047174882X

15. Das, D., Meiser, S., Mohammadi, E., Kate, A.: Anonymity trilemma: strong anonymity, low bandwidth overhead, low latency - choose two. In: 2018 IEEE Symposium on Security and Privacy, pp. 108–126. IEEE Computer Society Press, May 2018. https://doi.org/10.1109/SP.2018.00011

16. Díaz, C., Seys, S., Claessens, J., Preneel, B.: Towards measuring anonymity. In: Dingledine, R., Syverson, P. (eds.) PET 2002. LNCS, vol. 2482, pp. 54–68. Springer, Heidelberg (2003). https://doi.org/10.1007/3-540-36467-6_5

17. Díaz, C., Troncoso, C., Danezis, G.: Does additional information always reduce anonymity? In: Ning, P., Yu, T. (eds.) WPES 2007, pp. 72–75. ACM, New York, October 2007. https://doi.org/10.1145/1314333.1314347

18. Dingledine, R., Mathewson, N.: Tor protocol specification, August 2021. Commit 6d1e05d, https://raw.githubusercontent.com/torproject/torspec/c17c36c57635a9ebf88b2b41dc41cbddcf56f7ef/tor-spec.txt

19. Dingledine, R., Mathewson, N., Syverson, P.F.: Tor: The second-generation onion router. In: Blaze, M. (ed.) USENIX Security 2004, pp. 303–320. USENIX Association, August 2004

20. Dyer, K.P., Coull, S.E., Ristenpart, T., Shrimpton, T.: Protocol misidentification made easy with format-transforming encryption. In: Sadeghi, A.R., Gligor, V.D., Yung, M. (eds.) ACM CCS 2013, pp. 61–72. ACM Press, November 2013. https://doi.org/10.1145/2508859.2516657

21. Ensafi, R., Winter, P., Mueen, A., Crandall, J.R.: Analyzing the great firewall of China over space and time. PoPETs $2015(1)$, 61–76 (2015). https://doi.org/10.1515/popets-2015-0005

22. Fawcett, T.: An introduction to ROC analysis. Pattern Recogn. Lett. $27(8)$, 861–874 (2006). https://doi.org/10.1016/j.patrec.2005.10.010

23. Fehr, S., Berens, S.: On the conditional Rényi entropy. IEEE Trans. Inf. Theory $60(11)$, 6801–6810 (2014). https://doi.org/10.1109/TIT.2014.2357799

24. Fischlin, M., Günther, F., Marson, G.A., Paterson, K.G.: Data is a stream: security of stream-based channels. In: Gennaro, R., Robshaw, M. (eds.) CRYPTO 2015. LNCS, vol. 9216, pp. 545–564. Springer, Heidelberg (2015). https://doi.org/10.1007/978-3-662-48000-7_27

25. Fu, X., Ling, Z.: One cell is enough to break Tor's anonymity (2009)

26. Geddes, J., Jansen, R., Hopper, N.: How low can you go: balancing performance with anonymity in Tor. In: De Cristofaro, E., Wright, M. (eds.) PETS 2013. LNCS, vol. 7981, pp. 164–184. Springer, Heidelberg (2013). https://doi.org/10.1007/978-3-642-39077-7_9

27. Gelernter, N., Herzberg, A.: On the limits of provable anonymity. Cryptology ePrint Archive, Report 2013/531 (2013). https://eprint.iacr.org/2013/531

28. Goldschlag, D.M., Reed, M.G., Syverson, P.F.: Hiding routing information. In: Anderson, R. (ed.) IH 1996. LNCS, vol. 1174, pp. 137–150. Springer, Heidelberg (1996). https://doi.org/10.1007/3-540-61996-8_37

29. Goldschlag, D.M., Reed, M.G., Syverson, P.F.: Onion routing. Commun. Assoc. Comput. Mach. $42(2)$, 39–41 (1999). https://doi.org/10.1145/293411.293443

30. Greschbach, B., Pulls, T., Roberts, L.M., Winter, P., Feamster, N.: The effect of DNS on Tor's anonymity. In: NDSS 2017. The Internet Society, February/March 2017

31. Jansen, R., Hopper, N.: Shadow: running Tor in a box for accurate and efficient experimentation. In: NDSS 2012. The Internet Society, February 2012

32. Juárez, M., Afroz, S., Acar, G., Díaz, C., Greenstadt, R.: A critical evaluation of website fingerprinting attacks. In: Ahn, G.J., Yung, M., Li, N. (eds.) ACM CCS

2014, pp. 263–274. ACM Press, November 2014. https://doi.org/10.1145/2660267. 2660368

33. Karunanayake, I., Ahmed, N., Malaney, R., Islam, R., Jha, S.: Anonymity with Tor: a survey on Tor attacks (2020). https://arxiv.org/abs/2009.13018

34. Kuhn, C., Beck, M., Schiffner, S., Jorswieck, E.A., Strufe, T.: On privacy notions in anonymous communication. PoPETs **2019**(2), 105–125 (2019). https://doi.org/ 10.2478/popets-2019-0022

35. Li, S., Guo, H., Hopper, N.: Measuring information leakage in website fingerprinting attacks and defenses. In: Lie, D., Mannan, M., Backes, M., Wang, X. (eds.) ACM CCS 2018, pp. 1977–1992. ACM Press, October 2018. https://doi.org/10.1145/ 3243734.3243832

36. Ling, Z., Luo, J., Yu, W., Fu, X., Xuan, D., Jia, W.: A new cell-counting-based attack against Tor. IEEE/ACM Trans. Networking **20**(4), 1245–1261 (2012). https://doi.org/10.1109/TNET.2011.2178036

37. Melloni, A., Stam, M., Ytrehus, Ø.: On evaluating anonymity of onion routing (2021), full version. https://ece.engr.uvic.ca/~raltawy/SAC2021/17.pdf

38. Nasr, M., Bahramali, A., Houmansadr, A.: DeepCorr: strong flow correlation attacks on Tor using deep learning. In: Lie, D., Mannan, M., Backes, M., Wang, X. (eds.) ACM CCS 2018, pp. 1962–1976. ACM Press, October 2018. https://doi. org/10.1145/3243734.3243824

39. Nasr, M., Houmansadr, A., Mazumdar, A.: Compressive traffic analysis: a new paradigm for scalable traffic analysis. In: Thuraisingham, B.M., Evans, D., Malkin, T., Xu, D. (eds.) ACM CCS 2017, pp. 2053–2069. ACM Press, October/November 2017. https://doi.org/10.1145/3133956.3134074

40. Naylor, D., et al.: The Cost of the "S" in HTTPS. In: Seneviratne, A., Diot, C., Kurose, J., Chaintreau, A., Rizzo, L. (eds.) CoNEXT 2014, CoNEXT 2014, pp. 133–140. ACM, December 2014. https://doi.org/10.1145/2674005.2674991

41. Palmieri, F.: A distributed flow correlation attack to anonymizing overlay networks based on wavelet multi-resolution analysis. IEEE Trans. Dependable Secur. Comput. (To appear). https://doi.org/10.1109/TDSC.2019.2947666

42. Panchenko, A., et al.: Website fingerprinting at internet scale. In: NDSS 2016. The Internet Society, February 2016

43. Panchenko, A., Niessen, L., Zinnen, A., Engel, T.: Website fingerprinting in onion routing based anonymization networks. In: Chen, Y., Vaidya, J. (eds.) WPES 2011, pp. 103–114. ACM, October 2011. https://doi.org/10.1145/2046556.2046570

44. Pfitzmann, A., Hansen, M.: A terminology for talking about privacy by data minimization: Anonymity, unlinkability, undetectability, unobservability, pseudonymity, and identity management (Aug 2010), version v0.34. https://dud. inf.tu-dresden.de/literatur/Anon_Terminology_v0.34.pdf

45. Pfitzmann, A., Köhntopp, M.: Anonymity, unobservability, and pseudonymity — a proposal for terminology. In: Federrath, H. (ed.) Designing Privacy Enhancing Technologies. LNCS, vol. 2009, pp. 1–9. Springer, Heidelberg (2001). https://doi. org/10.1007/3-540-44702-4_1

46. Pulls, T., Dahlberg, R.: Website fingerprinting with website oracles. PoPETs **2020**(1), 235–255 (2020). https://doi.org/10.2478/popets-2020-0013

47. Reed, M.G., Syverson, P.F., Goldschlag, D.M.: Proxies for anonymous routing. In: ACSAC 1996, pp. 95–104. IEEE Computer Society (1996). https://doi.org/10. 1109/CSAC.1996.569678

48. Rényi, A.: On measures of entropy and information. In: Neyman, J. (ed.) Proceedings of the Fourth Berkeley Symposium on Mathematical Statistics and Prob-

ability, Volume 1. vol. 4.1, pp. 547–561. University of California Press, January 1961

49. Rimmer, V., Preuveneers, D., Juárez, M., van Goethem, T., Joosen, W.: Automated website fingerprinting through deep learning. In: NDSS 2018. The Internet Society, February 2018

50. Rochet, F., Pereira, O.: Waterfilling: balancing the Tor network with maximum diversity. PoPETs **2017**(2), 4–22 (2017). https://doi.org/10.1515/popets-2017-0013

51. Rochet, F., Pereira, O.: Dropping on the edge: flexibility and traffic confirmation in onion routing protocols. PoPETs **2018**(2), 27–46 (2018). https://doi.org/10.1515/popets-2018-0011

52. Serjantov, A., Danezis, G.: Towards an information theoretic metric for anonymity. In: Dingledine, R., Syverson, P. (eds.) PET 2002. LNCS, vol. 2482, pp. 41–53. Springer, Heidelberg (2003). https://doi.org/10.1007/3-540-36467-6_4

53. Sirinam, P., Imani, M., Juárez, M., Wright, M.: Deep fingerprinting: undermining website fingerprinting defenses with deep learning. In: Lie, D., Mannan, M., Backes, M., Wang, X. (eds.) ACM CCS 2018, pp. 1928–1943. ACM Press, October 2018. https://doi.org/10.1145/3243734.3243768

54. Standaert, F.-X., Malkin, T.G., Yung, M.: A unified framework for the analysis of side-channel key recovery attacks. In: Joux, A. (ed.) EUROCRYPT 2009. LNCS, vol. 5479, pp. 443–461. Springer, Heidelberg (2009). https://doi.org/10.1007/978-3-642-01001-9_26

55. Sun, Y., Edmundson, A., Vanbever, L., Li, O., Rexford, J., Chiang, M., Mittal, P.: RAPTOR: routing attacks on privacy in Tor. In: Jung, J., Holz, T. (eds.) USENIX Security 2015, pp. 271–286. USENIX Association, August 2015

56. Syverson, P.F.: Why I'm not an entropist. In: Christianson, B., Malcolm, J.A., Matyas, V., Roe, M. (eds.) SPW 2009. LNCS, vol. 7028, pp. 231–239. Springer, Heidelberg (2009)

57. The23rd Raccoon: How I Learned to Stop Ph34ring NSA and Love the Base Rate Fallacy (2008). https://archives.seul.org/or/dev/Sep-2008/msg00016.html

58. Wagner, I., Eckhoff, D.: Technical privacy metrics: a systematic survey. ACM Comput. Surv. **51**(3), 57:1–57:38 (2018). https://doi.org/10.1145/3168389

59. Wang, T., Cai, X., Nithyanand, R., Johnson, R., Goldberg, I.: Effective attacks and provable defenses for website fingerprinting. In: Fu, K., Jung, J. (eds.) USENIX Security 2014, pp. 143–157. USENIX Association, August 2014

60. Wang, T., Goldberg, I.: Improved website fingerprinting on Tor. In: Sadeghi, A., Foresti, S. (eds.) WPES 2013, pp. 201–212. ACM, November 2013. https://doi.org/10.1145/2517840.2517851

61. Winter, P.: Towards a censorship analyser for Tor. In: Crandall, J.R., Wright, J. (eds.) FOCI 2013. USENIX Association, Washington, D.C. (2013)

62. Winter, P., Lindskog, S.: How the great firewall of China is blocking Tor. In: Dingledine, R., Wright, J. (eds.) FOCI 2012. USENIX Association, Bellevue, WA (2012)

63. Winter, P., Pulls, T., Fuss, J.: ScrambleSuit: a polymorphic network protocol to circumvent censorship. In: Sadeghi, A., Foresti, S. (eds.) WPES 2013. ACM, November 2013. https://doi.org/10.1145/2517840.2517856

Revisiting Driver Anonymity in ORide

Deepak Kumaraswamy[1]([⊠]) [ID], Shyam Murthy[2] [ID], and Srinivas Vivek[2] [ID]

[1] National Institute of Technology Karnataka, Mangalore, India
deepakkumaraswamy99@gmail.com
[2] International Institute of Information Technology Bangalore, Bangalore, India
{shyam.sm,srinivas.vivek}@iiitb.ac.in

Abstract. Ride Hailing Services (RHS) have become a popular means of transportation, and with its popularity comes the concerns of privacy of riders and drivers. ORide is a privacy-preserving RHS proposed at the USENIX Security Symposium 2017 and uses Somewhat Homomorphic Encryption (SHE). In their protocol, a rider and all drivers in a zone send their encrypted coordinates to the RHS Service Provider (SP) who computes the squared Euclidean distances between them and forwards them to the rider. The rider decrypts these and selects the optimal driver with least Euclidean distance.

In this work, we demonstrate a location-harvesting attack where an honest-but-curious rider, making only a single ride request, can determine the exact coordinates of about half the number of responding drivers even when only the distance between the rider and drivers are given. The significance of our attack lies in inferring locations of other drivers in the zone, which are not (supposed to be) revealed to the rider as per the protocol.

We validate our attack by running experiments on zones of varying sizes in arbitrarily selected big cities. Our attack is based on enumerating lattice points on a circle of sufficiently small radius and eliminating solutions based on conditions imposed by the application scenario. Finally, we propose a modification to ORide aimed at thwarting our attack and show that this modification provides sufficient driver anonymity while preserving ride matching accuracy.

Keywords: Ride hailing services · Privacy and censorship · Applied cryptography · Lattice points

1 Introduction

Ride Hailing Services such as Uber, Lyft are becoming popular world-wide year over year. According to Pew Research [23], the number of Americans who have used RHS has more than doubled since 2015. In order to provide the service, RHS Service Providers (SP) collect upfront information about individuals desiring to use their services, which include riders and drivers who are part of the network. In addition, details of rides offered and accepted are also collected as

© The Author(s), under exclusive license to Springer Nature Switzerland AG 2022
R. AlTawy and A. Hülsing (Eds.): SAC 2021, LNCS 13203, pp. 25–46, 2022.
https://doi.org/10.1007/978-3-030-99277-4_2

part of their billing and statistics gathering. This raises a number of privacy concerns among the individual users. Though the SP would, in general, keep the information secure given the need to keep its reputation high, there is nothing to prevent breach of privacy if either the provider turns malicious or if someone with access to information internal to the provider wants to mine the information for personal gain [20].

A ride hailing service consists of three parties, namely, the SP, a rider who has subscribed for services of the SP and a set of drivers involved in ride selection. The SP is modeled as an honest-but-curious adversary. We consider the threat model where the rider attempts to mount a location-harvesting attack on participating drivers. While there are a number of solutions proposed in the last few years that preserve privacy of riders and drivers with respect to the SP, there are only a few works that look at privacy issues of drivers with respect to riders. The work *Geo-locating Drivers* [38] does an analysis of features and web APIs of non-privacy preserving RHS apps which can be used to extract privacy sensitive driver data. *PrivateRide* by Pham *et al.* [25] describes how riders or other malicious outsiders posing as riders can harvest personal information of drivers for purposes of stalking, blackmailing or other malicious activities. Apart from user-profiling, there are several instances where leakage of information regarding driver locations can lead to serious threats (refer Sect. 2.5).

One of the early privacy-preserving ride hailing services is *ORide* [24]. While the primary focus of this proposal was to provide an oblivious ride-matching solution to riders while preserving the privacy of riders and drivers from the SP, it also considers location-harvesting attacks against drivers by a malicious set of riders who create and cancel fake ride requests simultaneously from multiple locations. ORide ensures the anonymity of the drivers and riders with respect to SP primarily through the use of a Somewhat Homomorphic Encryption (SHE) scheme. There are more recent works that also propose privacy-preserving RHS, and an overview of the works related to RHS is given in Sect. 4.

In ORide, the SP collects SHE encrypted coordinates of the drivers in the zone of the rider, homomorphically computes the Euclidean distances between the rider and drivers, and then sends these encrypted values to the rider. The rider then decrypts the encrypted distances, chooses the nearest driver and proceeds with ride establishment (the ORide protocol is recalled in Sect. 2.1). This clearly leaks the distances of even those drivers who were *not* selected to offer the ride. But given that there are many possibilities for the coordinates of the driver, even if only their distance is known, one would expect that in practice the exact driver location is anonymous. However, we show that while the protocol hides personal information of the drivers it offers only limited anonymity for the drivers' locations w.r.t. a rider who requests a ride.

1.1   Our Contribution

In this work, we show a location-harvesting attack on the drivers in the ORide protocol. Along with the privacy for riders and drivers with respect to the SP, ORide also claims that its design offers location privacy for drivers with respect to riders by preventing location-harvesting attacks. This is done using deposit tokens and permutation of driver indices for each ride request, which prevents a malicious rider from making fake ride requests and triangulating locations of all drivers in the zone [24, §8]. We show in Sect. 2.3 that even an honest-but-curious rider, with only one ride request and response, can recover the exact coordinates of about half the number of drivers who respond to her ride request. Such an attack is not easy for the SP to detect unlike attacks that involve simultaneous ride requests and cancellations. We remark here that except driver location information, no personal driver information is revealed in our attack. Nonetheless, in Sect. 2.5 we discuss practical scenarios where revealing only the drivers locations (without their identities) can be harmful.

Our attack is motivated by the classical *Gauss' circle problem* [29, Ch. 9]. ORide uses a map-projection system such as UTM [33] to work with planar integer coordinates. Recovering the integer coordinates (X_d, Y_d) of the driver by the rider reduces to solving $(X_r - X_d)^2 + (Y_r - Y_d)^2 = N$, where X_r, Y_r, N are non-negative integers that are known to the rider. Relabelling this equation as $x^2 + y^2 = N$ results in a variant of the Gauss' circle problem. Since N is sufficiently small, it is feasible to enumerate all the lattice points (i.e., points with integer coordinates) on the circle of radius $\sqrt{N}$. In our case, since N always corresponds to the case where a solution is known to exist, we experimentally observe that the number of solutions to be about 20 on average (over our choice of zones in Table 1). Then we use the following ideas to further eliminate the potential solutions: (i) the driver coordinates must be in the same zone as that of the rider, (ii) the driver is typically expected to be at a motorable location such as road though the rider can book the ride from anywhere. This allows us to eliminate most of the possibilities (see Algorithm 1 in Sect. 2) and reduce the number of solutions from 20 to about 2 on average. In Sect. 2.4, we validate our attack by running experiments over zones of different sizes for four arbitrarily chosen big cities, and show that a rider can determine the *exact* locations of 45% of the responding drivers (see Table 1). Our attacks take an average only 2 s per driver on a commodity laptop. We stress that we are not only using the geographical information to eliminate locations, but also the fact that all coordinates are encoded as integers and hence there are only a handful of locations to enumerate on the circle in the first place. Our attack exploits an inherent property of SHE schemes – namely the requirement of integer-like encoded inputs for *exact* arithmetic [5]. We also believe that the abstraction of our attack as enumerating lattice points on a circle (and also our extension to other distance metrics in Appendix A) is generic and will motivate similar exploits in other privacy preserving solutions that use SHE.

In Sect. 3, we propose a modification to the ORide protocol which serves as a solution to overcome our attack. Here the driver obfuscates her location by choosing random coordinates within a certain distance R from her original location. Now the rider receives Euclidean distances that are homomorphically computed between her and the driver's anonymized location. Accordingly we modify the rider's attack from Sect. 2 to account for the fact that these anonymized coordinates (which are represented by different lattice solutions) may not lie on road.

However the anonymized coordinates will definitely have a road within proximity R, since the driver was originally on road. Through experiments we analyze this new attack on the proposed modification and evaluate its effect on driver anonymity and accuracy (refer Table 2). The optimal driver chosen in this case (based on least Euclidean distance between the rider and anonymized drivers' locations) is sufficiently close to the time-wise closest driver (who takes the least time to arrive at rider's location). Our solution is therefore viable in practice and is successful in preserving driver anonymity.

In Appendix A, we investigate possible alternate modifications to ORide in an attempt to mitigate our attack. However we show that these non-trivial techniques are eventually vulnerable to the same attack.

In Sect. 4, we discuss related works on privacy-preserving RHS and also briefly discuss the applicability of our attacks to these works. We also discuss other techniques that are available in the literature for location obfuscation.

2   Analysis of ORide Protocol

In this section we briefly recall the ORide protocol of [24], followed by a security analysis of the protocol at the rider's end. We then describe our attack that would allow a rider to predict a driver's location with good accuracy, and present the results of practical experiments.

2.1   ORide: A Privacy-Preserving Ride Hailing Service

As mentioned in Sect. 1, ORide is a privacy-preserving ride hailing service that uses an SHE scheme to match riders with drivers. In the process, identities and locations of drivers and riders are not revealed to the SP. The protocol provides accountability for SP and law-enforcement agencies in case of a malicious driver or rider. It also supports convenience features like automatic payment and reputation-rating of drivers/riders. In short, it is a complete and practical solution along with novel methods that help keep the identity of drivers and riders oblivious to the SP, together with accountability and convenience. The experiments done in their paper use real datasets consisting of taxi rides in New York city [26]. Their instantiation provides 112-bit security, based on the FV SHE scheme [7] which relies on the hardness of the Ring Learning With Errors (RLWE) problem.

We give below a high-level overview of the ORide protocol relevant to our attack. (For more details, the reader is referred to the original paper). The registered drivers periodically advertise their geographical zones to the SP. These zones are predefined by the SP and available to drivers and riders. The size of a zone is chosen in such a way that there are sufficiently many riders and drivers to ensure anonymity while maintaining the efficiency of ride-matching. When a rider wishes to hail a ride, she generates an ephemeral FV public/private key-pair (p_k, s_k). She encrypts her planar coordinates using this key and sends it to the SP along with p_k and her zone $\mathcal{Z}$. SP broadcasts the public key p_k received from the rider to each driver in $\mathcal{Z}$. The ith driver D_i encrypts her planar coordinates using p_k and sends it to SP. SP homomorphically computes the squared values of the Euclidean distances between each driver and the rider in parallel, and sends the encrypted result to the rider. The rider decrypts the ciphertext sent by SP to obtain the squared Euclidean distance to each driver D_i. She then selects the driver with smallest squared Euclidean distance and then notifies the SP of the selected driver. This selected driver is in turn notified by the SP. As part of the ride establishment protocol a secure channel is then established between the rider and the driver. They then proceed to service the ride request as per the protocol. Further steps, although important, are not relevant to our work and, hence, we do not mention them here.

2.2   ORide: Threat Model

The threat model considered in ORide is that of an honest-but-curious SP, whereas the drivers and riders are active adversaries who do not collude with the SP. We consider the same adversarial model in this paper as well. All the plaintext information is encoded as integer polynomials before encrypting with the FV SHE scheme. In ORide, the apps on the drivers and riders use a map-projection system such as UTM [33] to convert pairs of floating-point latitudes and longitudes to planar integer coordinates. Drivers use third-party services like Google Maps or TomTom for navigation.

2.3   Attack: Predicting Driver Locations

We now analyze the ORide protocol from the rider's end. For ease of explana-tion, the rest of our paper shall refer to the squared Euclidean distance between two points as simply the Euclidean distance. In the ORide protocol, before a rider finally chooses the closest driver, she is given a list of Euclidean distances corresponding to drivers in her zone. In this case, the rider only gets to know the Euclidean distance to each driver, and not the driver's exact coordinates. Math-ematically, this would mean that there are infinite possibilities for the driver's location on the circumference of a circle defined from the rider's perspective.

On the contrary, we show that the driver's Euclidean distance allows the rider to identify the actual location of a driver with good probability. We show that by identifying road networks on a live map (using Google Maps API [9]), along with the fact that ORide uses integer coordinates, the number of possible driver locations from the rider's perspective can be reduced significantly, to around 2 locations on average.

Remark. While we make use of the fact that ORide uses integers coordinates, our attack would also work for fixed- point encoding of the coordinates. This is because the current (exact) techniques for fixed-point encodings for RLWE-based SHE schemes essentially use the scaled-integer representation [5].

Before we proceed with our analysis, we make the assumption that when the rider requests a ride and when each driver in the zone sends her encrypted

---

Algorithm 1: Location-harvesting Attack on ORide

Input : The rider's zone $\mathcal{Z}$, number of drivers n inside $\mathcal{Z}$, rider's coordinates (X_r, Y_r), Euclidean distances d_i between the rider and driver D_i $(\forall i = 1, \cdots, n)$

Output: For each driver D_i, $\mathcal{S}'_i$ denotes the prediction set made for the location of D_i by the rider

Procedure Predict_Driver($\mathcal{Z}, n, (X_r, Y_r), \{d_i\}_{i=1}^n$) :

    $avg = 0;\ exact = 0$
    for each driver D_i **do**
        Receive: d_i from SP
        $\mathcal{S}_i = \phi$ /* Store unique lattice points */
        for $x = 0$ **to** $\lfloor \sqrt{d_i} \rfloor$ **do**
            $y = \sqrt{d_i - x^2}$
            if y *is an integer* **then**
                $T = \{\ (x, y), (-x, y), (-x, -y), (x, -y),$
                                          $(y, x), (-y, x), (-y, -x), (y, -x)\ \}$
                for $(x', y') \in T$ **do**
                    /* Compute predicted location for D_i */
                    $X_d = X_r + x';\ Y_d = Y_r + y'$
                    if (X_d, Y_d) is inside $\mathcal{Z}$ **then**
                        $\mathcal{S}_i := \mathcal{S}_i \cup \{\ (x, y)\ \}$
                    end
                end
            end
        end
        $\mathcal{S}'_i = \phi$ /* Filtered lattice points on road */
        for $(X_d, Y_d) \in \mathcal{S}_i$ **do**
            /* Use Google Maps API to check if the coordinates lie on road */
            $(x, y)_{road} = \mathsf{RoadAPI}(\ (X_d, Y_d)\ )$
            if distance between (X_d, Y_d) and $(x, y)_{road} <= 3$ metres **then**
                $\mathcal{S}'_i := \mathcal{S}'_i \cup \{\ (X_d, Y_d)\ \}$
            end
        end
        /* $\|\mathcal{S}'_i\|$ is the number of locations that the rider has predicted for D_i */
        $avg := avg + \|\mathcal{S}'_i\|$
        if $\|\mathcal{S}'_i\|\ == 1$ **then**
            $exact + = 1$ /* Exact driver loc predictions */
        end
    end
    $avg := avg\ /\ n;\ exact := exact\ /n \times 100$
    Output: $exact,\ avg,\ \mathcal{S}'_i$

---

coordinates to SP, the drivers are on road (since we use Google Maps API in our experiments, these include city roads, parking lot roads and many other categories, as specified by the definition of a *road segment* by Google Maps [9]). This assumption is reasonable since a vast majority of the active drivers at any point in time constantly move around the city looking for potential rides or about to finish serving another ride.

When we say that a driver's coordinates lie on road, we mean that the coordinates lie within the borders of the road. The current standards for lane width in the United States recommends that each lane is 3 m wide on average [19]. Since many roads within a city consist of 2 lanes, we assume that a pair of coordinates lie on road if the location is within 3 m from the centre of a road (neighborhoods in many cities around the world consist mostly of 2 lane roads, so our experiments give a fairly accurate idea of location recovery probabilities). We stress that the drivers can be anywhere in the zone on any road and our experiments indeed follow this distribution.

Rider's Attack. A rider performs the following attack to obtain a set of possible locations for a driver. At the time of ride request, let the rider coordinates be (X_r, Y_r) and the driver coordinates be (X_d, Y_d), which the rider does not know. Let the rider's zone be denoted by $\mathcal{Z}$. SP receives the encrypted values of X_r, X_d, Y_r, Y_d, then homomorphically computes the Euclidean distance in encrypted form, and the rider decrypts this to obtain $N = (X_r - X_d)^2 + (Y_r - Y_d)^2$. If N is not too large (refer to Sect. 2.4 for a concrete discussion on bounds for N), the rider can efficiently find all integer solutions to the equation $x^2 + y^2 = N$. The rider could use an $O(\sqrt{N})$ algorithm to accomplish this: keep a solution-set, and for every integer $x' \in [0, \lfloor \sqrt{N} \rfloor]$, compute $y' = (N - x'^2)^{1/2}$. If y' is an integer, add the coordinates (x', y'), $(x', -y')$, $(-x', y')$, $(-x', -y')$, (y', x'), $(y', -x')$, $(-y', x')$ and $(-y', -x')$ into this set.

Now, rider maintains a set $\mathcal{S}$ containing the possible driver locations. For each integral solution x_i, y_i satisfying $x_i^2 + y_i^2 = N$, the rider identifies potential driver coordinates as $(X'_{d,i} = X_r + x_i, Y'_{d,i} = Y_r + y_i)$ and adds $(X'_{d,i}, Y'_{d,i})$ to $\mathcal{S}$ if $(X'_{d,i}, Y'_{d,i})$ is inside $\mathcal{Z}$.

Once the rider obtains these possible driver coordinates in $\mathcal{S}$, she checks whether each solution lies on road. (Google Maps Road API [9] can be used to achieve this). The rider now obtains a filtered set of coordinates $\mathcal{S}' \subseteq \mathcal{S}$ that are inside $\mathcal{Z}$, and also lie on a road. Note that since the actual coordinates of the driver also satisfy these conditions, it is *always* present in this set. The cardinality of $\mathcal{S}'$ would denote the number of predicted locations for a driver. If this cardinality is exactly one, then the rider has successfully predicted the driver's exact location. Our attack is summarized in Algorithm 1. The algorithm takes as input the Euclidean distances of drivers in the zone and, for each driver, outputs the set of filtered coordinates $\mathcal{S}'$. It outputs the number of predicted locations *avg*, averaged over all drivers. Finally, it outputs *exact* which denotes the number of drivers for whom exactly one location is predicted.

We present an illustrative example in Fig. 1. Consider a large zone in Dallas, USA, with a cartesian grid embedded over the road view of the map. Consider a driver and a rider pair inside this zone. The rider is said to be located at the origin, and let the driver be at coordinates $(4, 3)$ (which agrees with our assumption that drivers lie on road). The rider is given the Euclidean distance 25 to this driver. She then obtains all lattice points lying on this circle: $\mathcal{S} = \{(\pm 3, \pm 4), (\pm 4, \pm 3), (\pm 5, 0), (0, \pm 5)\}$. Out of these, the rider filters out coordinates that lie on road (shown as green dots in Fig. 1) to obtain $\mathcal{S}' = \{(-4, 3), (4, 3), (5, 0), (0, -5)\}$. Note that the driver's actual coordinates belong to $\mathcal{S}'$. Note also that if the rider's location, her zone and the Euclidean distance to this driver was given as input to Algorithm 1, we would receive as outputs $\mathcal{S}' = \{(-4, 3), (4, 3), (5, 0), (0, -5)\}, avg = 4, exact = 0$.

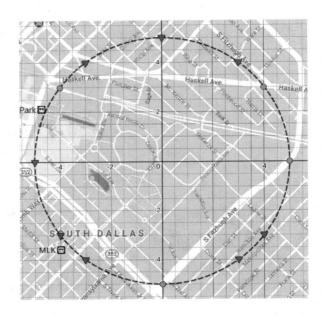

Fig. 1. Illustrative example of location prediction of a single driver by a rider. (Color figure online)

Remark. In the scenario of ORide, the rider's zone usually consists of multiple drivers. Note that in Algorithm 1, when calculating the possible coordinates $\mathcal{S}'_i$ for the ith driver D_i, the analysis that a rider performs for one driver is *independent* of the analysis for other drivers. Therefore, the averaged results for multiple drivers in one execution of the attack (if the driver locations are randomly and independently sampled subject to above conditions) is equivalent to the averaged results over multiple executions of the attack in the case of only a single driver present inside the zone.

Our implementation of the attack will therefore consider one driver inside the zone, and average the results over multiple experiments, considering randomly chosen rider and driver locations each time.

2.4   Implementation of Our Attack

Using Google Maps API for Python [10], we performed experiments to validate our attack across four arbitrarily chosen cities: New York city, Dallas, Los

Angeles and London[1]. We ran our experiments over zones of sizes $A = \{\, 1\,\text{km}^2,$ $4\,\text{km}^2,\ 9\,\text{km}^2,\ 25\,\text{km}^2,\ 100\,\text{km}^2,\ 400\,\text{km}^2,\ 900\,\text{km}^2\,\}$ (with the exception of New York city due to its geography having multiple smaller discontiguous areas). For each city, and for each zone size $a \in A$, we performed 30 experiments. In each experiment, a random square zone $\mathcal{Z}_a$ of area equal to a, was chosen. We chose a random latitude-longitude pair inside $\mathcal{Z}_a$ for the rider in this zone. For a driver, we similarly chose a random latitude-longitude pair inside $\mathcal{Z}_a$ that was on road (Google Maps Road API was used to accomplish this).

These coordinates were converted to UTM coordinates using the *utm* library for Python [3]. The Euclidean distance between these UTM coordinates was made available to the rider. Finally, we obtained the driver's filtered set of probable locations as described in Algorithm 1. After obtaining the predicted driver coordinates, we averaged the number of such predicted locations over multiple experiments. We also counted the percentage of experiments in which the rider predicted exactly one location. With these considerations, our results for varying grid sizes and cities are shown in Table 1.

Table 1. The rider's prediction based on Algorithm 1, averaged over 30 experiments.

Zone Size (km^2)	Number of possible driver locations (Output *avg* of Algorithm 1)				Exact driver locations prediction (Output *exact* of Algorithm 1)			
	New York	Dallas	Los Angeles	London	New York	Dallas	Los Angeles	London
1	2.6	1.8	2.5	1.6	32%	52%	32%	60%
2	2.4	1.6	2.1	1.6	48%	52%	36%	68%
4	2.0	2.0	1.8	1.7	44%	44%	52%	56%
9	2.7	1.9	2.1	2.3	38%	56%	48%	40%
25	2.6	2.2	2.4	2.1	36%	44%	36%	48%
100	2.7	2.1	2.2	1.8	32%	44%	44%	56%
400	2.3	2.1	2.5	1.8	36%	48%	28%	56%
900	–	2.8	3.1	2.4	–	40%	24%	40%

Timings. Our experiments were performed on an Intel Core i5-8250U CPU @ 1.60 GHz with 8 GB RAM running Ubuntu 18.04.4 LTS. On an average, one experiment (as described above) took 2 s for each driver, showing that our attack is indeed efficient, thus allowing a rider to practically obtain any driver's coordinates with good confidence.

Interpretation of Values in Table 1. Our experiments showed that the average number of solutions to $x^2 + y^2 = N$ over all the aforementioned zone sizes was 20. When we filter these solutions based on whether they lie inside a zone and on road, the average possible driver coordinates were 2 in number (as

---

[1] The code for our attack presented in Sect. 2 can be accessed at https://github.com/deepakkavoor/rhs-attack.

indicated by the value *avg* in Table 1), which is a significant reduction. Although it may seem that Euclidean distance gives fair anonymity to driver coordinates, our attack shows that in practice, this is not the case, and a rider can indeed find the driver's location with good probability. We also note from the average value of *exact* in Table 1 that the rider can predict the driver's exact location around 45% of the times.

Note that in each city, as zones get bigger, the number of lattice solutions and filtered coordinates tend to increase leading to higher *avg*. More lattice solutions imply that the event when a rider predicts exactly one location for a driver is rare, thus decreasing the value of *exact*. This trend can be verified from Table 1.

Anonymity Sets. In ORide, when the rider makes a request, she sends her zone identity to SP, and the SP now knows which zone the rider is in. This zone could contain the rider's home/work address. As pointed out in the ORide paper [24], SP might be able to guess the identities of the riders if this pick-up zone had a limited number of ride activities, and a limited number of riders (as an extreme example, a zone where only one rider lives). Therefore, ORide defines zones in such a way that each zone has at least a large minimum number of ride requests per day. This large minimum is referred to by them as the *anonymity-set* size. The choice of size of these zones is left to the SP, based on balancing the communication bandwidth requirements and sizes of anonymity sets in those zones. (A very high anonymity set would mean that the demand for rides in that zone is high, leading to longer ride matching times and higher bandwidth usage).

We justify our choice of choosing zones of sizes $a \in A$ for our experiments:

- In a densely populated city like New York City (population density[2] 11,084 persons/km^2), where more people tend to use ride hailing services, a smaller zone size would suffice to achieve the required anonymity-set size. In a sparse city like Dallas (population density 1,590 persons/km^2), where fewer ride-hailing activities occur, these zones would have to be bigger in size to achieve the same anonymity for riders. Taking into consideration the different possible zone sizes in both densely populated and sparse cities, the experiments validate our attack in zones of areas ranging from $1\,km^2$ to $900\,km^2$.
- We analyzed the NYC Uber-Dataset [21] for May 2019, and deduced that the demand for taxi rides was very high in Manhattan compared to the other boroughs of NYC. We chose May since this month had one of the highest ride requests for Uber in 2019. Based on this, we followed the zone demarcation that was proposed by ORide: each Census Tract (CT) [22] in Manhattan is considered as one zone. The boroughs of Queens and Bronx are merged into one zone, and the boroughs of Brooklyn and Staten Island are merged into one zone. The size of each CT in Manhattan varies between $1\,km^2$ and $4\,km^2$ that correspond to zone size of higher activity. Since the boroughs other than Manhattan have lesser activity, these zones are expected to have a larger area. Indeed, the combined area of Queens and Bronx is around $390\,km^2$, and the

---

[2] https://worldpopulationreview.com/us-cities.

combined area of Brooklyn and Staten Island is around $330\,\text{km}^2$. Since this is the primary zone demarcation proposed by the authors of ORide, we found it reasonable to include these ranges of areas for our experiments in Table 1.

We next discuss few details involved in the implementation of our attack.

- Although zones can be of any geographical shape, we chose square zones for ease of choosing random coordinates inside its boundary, and to simplify checking whether a given coordinate lies inside the zone.
- Latitude-longitude coordinates were converted into UTM formats using the *utm* library for Python. On an average, this conversion results in a difference of $0.5\,\text{m}$ between the original coordinate and the planar coordinate's representation. For all practical purposes, this difference is very small, and the two coordinates can be considered to represent the same location.
- As discussed earlier, based on the NYC Uber-Dataset and ORide's proposed demarcation, even large sparse zones that have a sufficiently big anonymity-set would rarely exceed $30 \times 30 = 900\,\text{km}^2$. Note that the Euclidean distance between two UTM coordinates is equal to the distance (in metres) between latitude-longitude representation of those points. Hence, the maximum value of N for a $d \times d$ grid would be $2d^2$. For a $30\,\text{km} \times 30\,\text{km}$ grid, d would be $30{,}000$. Since there exists an $O(\sqrt{N}) = O(d)$ algorithm to compute solutions to $x^2 + y^2 = N$, it is indeed feasible for the rider to perform this analysis on modern computers in very less time, even for different zone structures chosen by SP.

Remark. We give a brief insight into the number of drivers inside a zone, which averages to 400. The zone demarcation proposed for New York by the authors of ORide was discussed briefly above. According to ride information for May 2019 in the NYC Uber-Dataset, a zone in Manhattan had at most 6,000 ride requests per day. (We chose the month of May since it experienced the most ride-requests in the year 2019). We make the same assumption that the authors of ORide did: the drop-off zone for a driver is her waiting zone for new ride requests. Moreover, as in ORide, we assume that the waiting time between a driver's drop-off event and her next pick-up event is at most 30 min. This would mean that during a ride-request event, the available drivers to answer this request are the ones who had a drop-off event inside that zone in the last 30 min since the ride-request. We considered the top 20 high-ride zones, and for each zone, grouped the ride requests for a day based on 30 min intervals. Each 30 min interval consisted of at most 400 drop-off events inside each zone. This would imply that when a ride request occurs at any time of the day, at most 400 drivers would be waiting in that zone to service this request. We stress that there are at most 400 drivers in all zone demarcations considered above, and as the zone size increases the density of drivers (the number of drivers available for ride request in $1\,\text{km}^2$) in that zone decreases.

2.5   Impact and Consequences of Our Attack

We have experimentally shown that our location-harvesting attack can identify the exact locations of a driver in about 45% of the cases. Equivalently, this means that in a zone of around 400 available drivers, a ride request leaks the locations of around 180 drivers to the rider, which is a significant number. Although our attack doesn't reveal additional driver data such as user profiles, this leak of location information could still cause potential threats to drivers and ultimately affect the SP's reputation. For instance, according to [12], it is claimed that non-SP taxi drivers try to identify locations of Uber vehicles and attack them. There are also reports of people using ride-hailing apps to locate and rob drivers registered to the SP [30]. Zhao et al. [38] investigate several approaches through which information regarding drivers' locations can lead to statistical attacks and exploits. A potential competitor to ORide can use our attack and make queries to ORide as an honest-but-curious rider over a period of time. It can then get to know the distribution/density of different drivers in the city without raising suspicions. This distribution could indicate regions where there is high demand for ride hailing services. The competitor could focus on deploying their drivers and taxis in that region.

In general, ensuring privacy of the locations of drivers in the zone should be an important aspect of any privacy-preserving RHS. The authors of ORide claim that an adversary cannot obtain a snapshot of drivers' locations (say, a malicious rider who makes multiple fake ride requests with the goal of harvesting drivers' locations) [24, §8], thus preserving their anonymity. In contrast, our work refutes this claim made in ORide using just a single ride request by an honest-but-curious rider. We think that this flaw in ORide is not merely an implementation error. The requirement of integer-encoded inputs is inherent to current SHE schemes, and this helps us obtain small number of lattice points on the circle.

Remark.   One of our motivations behind considering privacy of driver locations is to prevent physical attacks on the drivers in a zone. It can be argued that even if locations of these drivers are not revealed, a malicious rider can request a ride in an honest manner, and attack the chosen driver when she arrives at the pick-up location. While this is true, and in fact, at the end of any ride hailing service (whether it preserves privacy or not), the selected driver *must* arrive at the rider's pick-up location and so, this attack scenario is nearly impossible to thwart. However, in almost all apps (including ORide), the identity information of the rider (name, phone number etc.) is revealed to the driver selected for the ride (and vice-versa) which act as a deterrent for such attacks. The possibility of fake accounts can be eliminated by enforcing identity verification at the time of registration. This does not violate rider privacy since ORide assigns anonymous tokens to all entities during the ride request process. Using our attack from Sect. 2.3, a rider can get to know even the locations of *non-selected* drivers in the zone, namely the other drivers who have no information about the identity of the rider. Finally, we remark that if the driver has moved from her last revealed location or does not have a logo/sticker on her car (advertising that she belongs to a particular RHS) then it would be hard for the rider to carry out physical attacks.

3 Mitigation of Our Attack

We propose a solution where the driver can thwart our attack by anonymizing her location. Each driver could choose a random coordinate within a circle of fixed radius around herself, encrypt and send these random coordinates to the SP instead of her original coordinates. We show that this modification to ORide provides sufficient anonymity while preserving ride matching accuracy, and is therefore a reasonable solution to mitigate our attack. The idea of adding noise to geographical data to preserve privacy has been addressed in several works in the literature. In Sect. 4, we discuss some of these techniques and their relevance to our setting. We analyze the effect of this technique on driver anonymity and provide concrete values for ride matching accuracy through experiments using Google Maps API.

Remark. In Appendix A, we discuss other ideas that may intuitively seem to thwart our attack. However, we show that those modifications are vulnerable to our attack from Sect. 2 and hence do not preserve driver anonymity.

3.1 Anonymizing Driver Locations

By anonymizing her location, each driver may try to preserve the privacy of her location with respect to a rider. Let each driver D_i (at coordinates L_i) choose a circle of radius R centered at her location (where R is publicly known), and pick a random UTM coordinates L_i' inside this circle. The driver encrypts L_i' (instead of L_i as suggested by ORide) and sends it to SP. We refer to L_i' as the anonymized driver coordinates.

As per the original attack in Sect. 2, the rider obtains a Euclidean distance N_i and enumerates all lattice points that correspond to this distance. Due to the changes described above, these lattice points need not correspond to possible driver coordinates. They instead represent possible *anonymized* driver coordinates. The rider would have next proceeded to filter each lattice point based on whether it is on road or not. But a lattice point which represents an anonymized driver location may not lie a point on road, although the original driver did. Filtering in this way would lead to erroneous conclusions by the rider, and she may throw out a lattice point that actually corresponds to the driver location.

Observe that within distance R of anonymized driver coordinates, there will always lie a road (since the original driver was on road). We modify the rider's attack accordingly to cope with this fix. Suppose there was a lattice point discovered by the rider. Within a circle of radius R centered at this point, if there were no roads at all (for instance a lattice point that was in the middle of a park) the rider can then conclude that this point is not the driver's anonymized coordinates. So, the best option that a rider has (to improve her attack against this obfuscation technique) is to filter each lattice point based on whether there is a road within distance R of that point. As we see in Sect. 3.2, the possibility that a lattice point is filtered out in a dense city is low if we choose an appropriate value of R. This prevents a rider from eliminating many lattice points thus improving driver anonymity. Moreover, this technique preserves accuracy when compared to ORide as we show next.

3.2   Anonymity of Drivers with Respect to Rider

The value of R is public and should be decided by the SP, who can in fact implement the end-user application in such a way that the driver's device locally computes R based on the current location of the driver. If the driver's local device senses that she is in a densely populated city (and thus there are many roads within close proximity of an arbitrary point in that region of the city), a smaller R can be chosen. On the other hand, if the device understands that the driver is in a location where there are very few roads within distance R from an arbitrary point in that region, a larger R is chosen (for instance, in a sparsely populated city with low road density). This choice of R based on the concentration of roads around the driver is motivated by the modification to rider's attack discussed at the end of Sect. 3.1 (the rider's attack now tries to filter lattice points based on the availability of roads within distance R from each lattice point solution). We consider the number of (anonymized) driver locations predicted by a rider as a measure of anonymity for that driver. This depends on the number of lattice solutions for the Euclidean distance between (anonymized) driver location and rider. Along with this, it also depends on the number of solutions that the rider can further filter based on availability of roads within distance R from each solution. We expect anonymity to increase with R due to higher probability of finding a road within distance R of any location.

Similar to the setup in Sect. 2.4, in the following discussion we average results over 25 experiments where each experiment chooses a random zone of size $4\,\mathrm{km}^2$ in the mentioned city (along with random coordinates for a rider and driver) and runs the modified rider's attack for filtering coordinates. For a small value of R such as $10\,\mathrm{m}$, any coordinate within distance R of some point is practically the same location. We experimentally observed that the average anonymity for a driver in Los Angeles was around 3, which is close to what we observe in the original attack (see Table 1). Hence small values of R should not be chosen since they offer low anonymity. In a densely populated city such as Los Angeles, most locations within the city are expected to have roads within reasonable distance. For $R = 50\,\mathrm{m}$ we observed that the area surrounding *most* lattice points in Los Angeles had at least one road within $50\,\mathrm{m}$. From a rider's perspective, this would mean that most lattice solutions obtained by her are possible choices for the anonymized driver coordinates. Experiments showed that the average number of filtered lattice points when $R = 50$ m was 14 (meaning the rider has 14 possible *anonymized* locations of a driver). This provides sufficient anonymity to a driver in practice, since the probability of correctly predicting a driver's anonymized coordinate is only 1/14. This is certainly an improvement compared to 1/1.8 for ORide (Table 1). Considering Dallas, a city with relatively sparse road density, we observed that a significant number of locations did not have roads within 50 m, and this allowed the rider to filter out many possible lattice solutions. Our experiments suggest that choosing $R = 150$ m prevents the rider from doing so and offers sufficient anonymity, which averaged around 16.

Remark. As seen above, the rider ends up with around 15 equally probable solutions for the driver's obfuscated location. This means that even if the rider applies clustering algorithms over multiple queries to eliminate noise and tries to find the actual driver's location, there will still be many equally probable locations for the driver (>10) thus providing high anonymity.

3.3   Accuracy of Ride-Matching

When a driver chooses random coordinates within distance R instead of her own location, the Euclidean distance is now computed between the rider's location and the *anonymized* driver location.

Among all drivers in the zone, suppose an optimal driver is chosen according to some metric M. For example, if M represents Euclidean distance, the optimal driver is the one with least Euclidean distance from her location to the rider in the case of ORide, and the one with least Euclidean distance from her anonymized location to the rider in the case of our modified solution. Let t_M be the time taken for this optimal driver to reach rider. Let t_T be the minimum time taken among all drivers in the zone to reach rider (corresponding to the time-wise closest driver). We evaluate the accuracy of metric M as the percentage of experiments in which $|t_M - t_T|$ is less than or equal to 1 min (in practice it is okay for the rider to wait another extra minute compared to the time-wise closest driver). Google Maps API was used to determine the time taken for a driver to reach the rider.

We chose zones of varying sizes in Los Angeles and Dallas. In each experiment a random rider and 400 drivers were chosen in each zone. We compared the accuracy of Euclidean metric for $R = 50$ m and $R = 150$ m in both scenarios – when used in the context of ORide (computed between the rider and driver's actual location) and when used in the fix to our attack (computed between the rider and driver's anonymized location). As discussed previously, we chose $R = 50$ m for Los Angeles and $R = 150$ m for Dallas, respectively, to ensure sufficient anonymity. Moreover, the sizes of zones are chosen to be smaller in Los Angeles (refer Sect. 2.4) and larger in Dallas. The inferred accuracies were averaged over 25 experiments (refer Table 2). We see that our solution indeed provides sufficient driver anonymity with respect to rider while preserving accuracy of ride matching compared to ORide.

Choosing large R to achieve greater anonymity in a small zone (where driver density is high) leads to loss of accuracy. This seems intuitively correct, since having a large anonymity radius in a small zone with high driver density greatly changes the ordering of drivers based on Euclidean distances. To concretely verify this, we used a similar setup described above and observed that with $R = 150$ m and a 4 km^2 zone size in Los Angeles the accuracy of ORide was around 84%

whereas that of the modified solution was only 70%. So, R should increase with zone size both to preserve accuracy and driver anonymity (prevent filtering of lattice solutions based on availability of roads).

Table 2. Comparison of accuracy of selecting best driver in ORide vs. our solution (with anonymized driver locations), averaged over 25 experiments.

City	Zone Size (km^2)	Radius R (m)	ORide	Our solution
Los Angeles	4	50	84%	80%
	25	50	92%	90%
Dallas	100	150	83%	83%

4   Related Works

Among providers of RHS namely Lyft, DiDi, OLA, taxify and others, Uber is one of the popular ride service providers. An in-depth analysis of the practices followed by Uber and the impact of price-surging on passengers and drivers are done by Chen et al. [4]. *The Guardian* [11] reports how anonymized details of New York city taxi drivers can be used to easily convert the data to its original format to obtain personal information. Different threat models are widely considered in the literature, namely, a malicious driver targeting riders, and an honest-but-curious SP harvesting information about riders and drivers with the intention of selling it to other entities for advertising purposes, or with potentially malicious intentions to target high profile individuals. Privacy of the driver is given much less attention; so much so that in a few papers the actual driver locations are revealed to the SP as well as the rider [14] and [2]. As motivated in Sect. 1 there can be instances where a malicious rider can target drivers of a specific SP. For example, a competitor SP can masquerade as rider to collect driver profile information or statistics to target the drivers belonging to the specific SP. *Geolocating Drivers* by Zhao et al. [38] does a study of leakage of sensitive data, in particular, it evaluates the threat to driver information. They show it is possible to harvest driver data by a malicious outsider SP by analyzing APIs in non-privacy preserving apps provided to drivers by Uber, Lyft and other popularly deployed SPs.

PrivateRide by Pham et al. [25] is one of the first papers to address privacy in RHS. The location of the riders are kept hidden by means of a cloaked region, and location privacy is preserved by using cryptographically secure constructs. Details of rider and selected driver are mutually exchanged only after the ride request is fulfilled and when they both are in close proximity, to prevent a malicious outsider trying to harvest driver information. A recent work by Khazbak et al. [14] improves upon the solution of *PrivateRide* by providing obfuscation techniques (spatial and temporal cloaking), of rider locations, to achieve better results in terms of selecting the closest driver, at the cost of slightly more computational overhead. However, the drivers' locations are revealed to the rider.

ORide [24] is a follow-up work by the same authors of *PrivateRide* that provides more robust privacy and accountability guarantees, and has been described earlier in this paper. All the following works try to improve upon ORide by proposing different models of privacy-preserving closest driver selection by the SP. We note here that our attack is relevant in cases where the rider gets to make a choice, and is not applicable in situations where the SP selects a single suitable driver and provides the same to the rider. *pRide* by Luo *et al.* [15] proposes a privacy-preserving ride-matching service involving two non-colluding servers with one being the SP and the other a third-party Crypto Provider (CP). The solution makes use of Road Network Embedding (RNE) [27] technique to transform a road network into a higher dimensional space so that the distance computation between any two nodes in the network can be performed efficiently. They propose two solutions, one using the Paillier cryptosystem and another using BGN cryptosystem. The homomorphically encrypted driver and rider locations received by the SP are sent to the CP along with a random noise where it is decrypted and garbled. The SP then uses a garbled circuit to find the closest driver to the rider and completes the ride request. They show high accuracy in matching the closest driver while preserving the privacy of driver and rider locations. The disadvantage of this scheme is their use of a second Crypto Server that does not collude with the SP, which may be inconvenient to realize in practice, and also the high communication cost between the two servers. *lpRide* by Yu *et al.* [37] improves upon *pRide* to perform all the homomorphic distance computation algorithms on a single SP server thus eliminating high communication cost when two servers are involved. They use modified Paillier cryptosystem [18] for encrypting RNE transformed locations of rider and driver. However, [31] proposed an attack on the modified Paillier scheme used in lpRide, allowing the service provider to recover locations of all riders and drivers in the region. Wang *et al.* propose *TRACE* [32] that uses bilinear pairing for encrypting driver and rider locations. *PSRide* by Yu *et al.* [35] uses Paillier cryptosystem and Yao's garbled circuit with two servers on the same lines as *pRide* and hence suffers from some of the disadvantages mentioned above. *EPRide* by Yu *et al.* [36] efficiently finds the exact shortest road distance using a road network hypercube embedding. They experimentally show significant improvements in accuracy and efficiency compared to *ORide* and *pRide*. Xie *et al.* [34] compute shortest distances using road network embeddings along with property-preserving hash functions. In doing so, they remove the need for a trusted third-party server.

Maouche *et al.* [16] propose a user re-identification attack on four different mobility datasets obfuscated using three different Location Preserving Privacy Mechanisms (LLPM), with one of the datasets in the RHS setting. Their attack makes use of previously learned user profiles and tries to re- associate the same to obfuscated data. A number of LLPMs are available in the literature that anonymize private data. Differential privacy and k-anonymity are two popular techniques. Differential privacy, introduced by the seminal work of Dwork *et al.* [6] can be applied wherever aggregate information from several similar entities are available. Geo-indistinguishability by Andrés *et al.* [1] adds exponentially decaying noise from a Laplace distribution around the point of interest thereby obfuscating the point of interest. The notion of k-anonymity by Sweeney [28] obfuscates an entity by introducing $k - 1$ dummy uniformly distributed entities which are indistinguishable by the adversary. In our case, the driver applies noise to her coordinates before encrypting and sending to SP. SP homomorphically computes the Euclidean distance between the rider and each driver. Using this (noisy) Euclidean distance, the rider solves the Gauss circle problem and filters out solutions depending on whether they have a road in their vicinity. Finally, the rider ends up with not one, but many possible choices for the anonymized driver location. This is a combination of both differential privacy (where the driver applies noise to her location) and k-anonymity (the rider has many equally possible choices for the driver's obfuscated location). Empirically, we see that our method of adding uniformly random noise is sufficient to provide high anonymity to the driver. Also, our method of filtering out non-plausible driver locations is based on the region's topography. We leave the analysis of using other obfuscation techniques to thwart our attack for future work.

5   Conclusion

In this paper we present an attack on a privacy-preserving RHS, ORide [24]. We show that an honest-but-curious rider can determine the coordinates of nearly half the number of drivers in a zone even when only the Euclidean distance between the rider and a driver is available to the rider. Our attack involves enumeration of lattice points on a circle of appropriate radius and subsequent elimination of lattice points based on geographic conditions. Finally we propose a modification to the ORide protocol as a strategy to mitigate our attack. Here a driver anonymizes her location by choosing a random coordinate within a circle of certain radius around herself. We show through concrete experiments that this technique preserves driver anonymity and accuracy of ride matching.

   Although protocols may seem secure in theory, there may arise several complications and vulnerabilities when they are deployed practically, as demonstrated by our attack in Sect. 2. In the future it will be interesting to experimentally investigate the notion of driver privacy with respect to both the SP and rider in more recent works following ORide (*lpRide*, [37], *pRide* [15]).

Acknowledgement. The authors would like to thank Sonata Software Limited, Bengaluru, India for funding this work. We also thank the anonymous reviewers of ACM CCS2020, USENIX Security 2021 and SAC 2021 for their valuable comments and suggestions.

A   Appendix: Further Attacks

We look at potential ways in which our attack can be thwarted and analyze their efficacy. In the first scenario, in order to obfuscate driver locations, the

SP homomorphically adds noise to driver distances before sending them to the rider. For this case, we show that a rider can still break anonymity by recovering the original distances between the rider and the drivers. In the second scenario, the SP uses p-norm metric instead of the Euclidean distance and we show that our attack also extends to this case. Note that increasing zone sizes is not a countermeasure to our attack. As discussed in Sect. 2.4, zone sizes should be small enough (less than $1000\,\mathrm{km}^2$ in practice) to ensure efficient ride-matching times and lower bandwidth costs.

A.1   Homomorphic Noise Addition by SP

In order to thwart our attack, the SP could try to obfuscate driver locations by transforming the (encrypted squared) Euclidean distances using a random monotonic polynomial F with integer coefficients and of a small degree, as suggested by Kesarwani et al. [13]. Integer coefficients are needed for ease of representation in homomorphic computations, monotonicity is needed to maintain the sorting order of the distance inputs (so that the rider obtains the correct order upon decryption), and low polynomial degree is required for efficient homomorphic evaluation. Let N_i be the Euclidean distance between the rider and a driver D_i in her zone. The rider would get to know from the SP, for each driver D_i in her zone, the values $F(N_i)$ for some random monotonic integer polynomial F of low degree. Note that F is unknown to the rider, but the degree d, range of coefficients of the polynomial $[1, 2^\alpha - 1]$ and range of N_i ($[0, 2^\beta - 1]$) are publicly known. We claim that the rider can obtain the actual distance N_i.

[17] provides a method of recovering a monotonic integer polynomial of low degree and bounded input range when only sufficiently many outputs evaluated at integer points are provided. We used the publicly available SageMath [8] code from the authors of [17] with parameters similar to that described in [13], namely $d = 9$, $\alpha = 32$ and $\beta = 28$. Next one obtains outputs $F(N_i)$ by evaluating this polynomial on the distances N_i. These two steps are the same as what the SP would do (homomorphically) once it receives inputs from the rider and all drivers in a particular zone. The $F(N_i)$ values, d, α and β are the only values given to the SageMath code in the experiments to recover (squared) Euclidean distances to drivers for various zone sizes. We correlated back the results of the recovery with the input distances and verified that in all cases the recovered distances matched correctly, which means that the rider can proceed with the attack mentioned in Sect. 2 after recovering N_i values.

A.2 p-norm Metric by SP

In order to mitigate our attack in Sect. 2, the SP may try to homomorphically compute the p-norm (instead of Euclidean distance) of ciphertexts and send it to rider. Let $(x_R, y_R), (x_{D_i}, y_{D_i})$ denote coordinates of a rider and driver D_i, respectively. The rider would thus obtain $N_i = |x_R - x_{D_i}|^p + |y_R - y_{D_i}|^p$ for each driver D_i in her zone (the value of p should not be too large to allow efficient homomorphic computations by SP).

Note that if p is odd, $(x_R - x_{D_i})^p + (y_R - y_{D_i})^p$ could represent a negative value. Since ORide uses *ciphertext packing* and non-Boolean circuit representation with the underlying SHE library [24], it is very inefficient to compute the absolute value homomorphically. Hence, the SP would have to use only even values for p. Let $p = 2q$. In the rider's attack, she has to now enumerate all lattice points satisfying the equation $x^p + y^p = N_i$. Observe that if (x, y) is a solution to this equation, then the lattice point (x^q, y^q) is a solution to $x^2 + y^2 = N_i$. This implies that the solution set comprising of lattice points satisfying $x^p + y^p = N_i$ is smaller than the solution set of lattice points satisfying $x^2 + y^2 = N_i$. Based on our experiments on various zones and cities, we have estimated the number of lattice points satisfying $x^2 + y^2 = N_i$ to be around 20 (refer to Sect. 2.4). This means that on average, the lattice points satisfying $x^p + y^p = N_i$ cannot be greater than 20 in number. The rider (similar to the rest of the attack) can then check whether each lattice point lies in the zone and on road, to reduce the number of possible predicted driver locations. In this way, our attack also applies when the SP uses p-norm instead of Euclidean distance.

References

1. Andrés, M., Bordenabe, N., Chatzikokolakis, K., Palamidessi, C.: Geo-indistinguishability: differential privacy for location-based systems. In: Proceedings of the ACM Conference on Computer and Communications Security (2013)
2. Baza, M., Lasla, N., Mahmoud, M., Srivastava, G., Abdallah, M.: B-ride: ride sharing with privacy-preservation, trust and fair payment atop public blockchain. IEEE Trans. Network Sci. Eng. **8**, 1214–1229 (2019)
3. Bieniek, T.: Utm 0.5.0 (2019). https://pypi.org/project/utm/. Accessed 3 Apr 2020
4. Chen, L., Mislove, A., Wilson, C.: Peeking Beneath the Hood of Uber. In: Cho, K., Fukuda, K., Pai, V.S., Spring, N. (eds.) Proceedings of the 2015 ACM Internet Measurement Conference, IMC 2015, Tokyo, Japan, 28–30 October, 2015, pp. 495–508. ACM (2015)
5. Costache, A., Smart, N.P., Vivek, S., Waller, A.: Fixed-point arithmetic in SHE schemes. In: Avanzi, R., Heys, H. (eds.) SAC 2016. LNCS, vol. 10532, pp. 401–422. Springer, Cham (2017). https://doi.org/10.1007/978-3-319-69453-5_22
6. Dwork, C., McSherry, F., Nissim, K., Smith, A.: Calibrating noise to sensitivity in private data analysis. In: Halevi, S., Rabin, T. (eds.) TCC 2006. LNCS, vol. 3876, pp. 265–284. Springer, Heidelberg (2006). https://doi.org/10.1007/11681878_14
7. Fan, J., Vercauteren, F.: Somewhat practical fully homomorphic encryption. Cryptology ePrint Archive (2012). http://eprint.iacr.org/2012/144
8. GitHub: SAGE code for polynomial recovery (2019). https://github.com/shyamsmurthy/knn_polynomial_recovery. Accessed 12 June 2020
9. Google: Google Maps Platform (2019). https://developers.google.com/maps/documentation/roads/intro/. Accessed 3 Apr 2020
10. Google: Google Maps Platform, client libraries for google maps web services (2019). https://developers.google.com/maps/web-services/client-library. Accessed 3 Apr 2020
11. Guardian, T.: New York Taxi Details can be Extracted from Anonymised Data, Researchers Say (2014). https://www.theguardian.com/technology/2014/jun/27/new-york-taxi-details-anonymised-data-researchers-warn. Accessed 20 Mar 2020

12. Hurriyet Daily News: Istanbul taxi drivers hunt down, beat up Uber drivers as tensions rise (2018). https://www.hurriyetdailynews.com/istanbul-taxi-drivers-hunt-down-beat-up-uber-drivers-as-tensions-rise-128443. Accessed 11 June 2020
13. Kesarwani, M., et al.: Efficient secure k-nearest neighbours over encrypted data. In: Proceedings of the 21th International Conference on Extending Database Technology, EDBT 2018, Vienna, Austria, 26–29 March, 2018, pp. 564–575 (2018)
14. Khazbak, Y., Fan, J., Zhu, S., Cao, G.: Preserving location privacy in ride-hailing service. In: 2018 IEEE Conference on Communications and Network Security, CNS 2018, Beijing, China, 30 May–1 June 2018, pp. 1–9. IEEE (2018)
15. Luo, Y., Jia, X., Fu, S., Xu, M.: pRide: privacy-preserving ride matching over road networks for online ride-hailing service. IEEE Trans. Inf. Forensics Secur. **14**(7), 1791–1802 (2019)
16. Maouche, M., Mokhtar, S., Bouchenak, S.: AP-attack: a novel user re-identification attack on mobility datasets. In: MobiQuitous 2017–14th EAI International Conference on Mobile and Ubiquitous Systems: Computing, Networking and Services, pp. 48–57, November 2017
17. Murthy, S., Vivek, S.: Cryptanalysis of a protocol for efficient sorting on SHE encrypted data. In: Albrecht, M. (ed.) IMACC 2019. LNCS, vol. 11929, pp. 278–294. Springer, Cham (2019). https://doi.org/10.1007/978-3-030-35199-1_14
18. Nabeel, M., Appel, S., Bertino, E., Buchmann, A.: Privacy preserving context aware publish subscribe systems. In: Lopez, J., Huang, X., Sandhu, R. (eds.) NSS 2013. LNCS, vol. 7873, pp. 465–478. Springer, Heidelberg (2013). https://doi.org/10.1007/978-3-642-38631-2_34
19. NACTO: Urban Street Design Guide (2019). https://nacto.org/publication/urban-street-design-guide/street-design-elements/lane-width/. Accessed 12 Mar 2020
20. NortonLifeLock: Uber Announces New Data Breach Affecting 57 million Riders and Drivers (2020). https://us.norton.com/internetsecurity-emerging-threats-uber-breach-57-million.html. Accessed 10 Apr 2020
21. NYC Taxi and Limousine Commission: TLC Trip Record Data. https://www1.nyc.gov/site/tlc/about/tlc-trip-record-data.page. Accessed 14 Apr 2020
22. NYU Spatial Data Repository: 2010 New York City Census Tract Boundaries. https://geo.nyu.edu/catalog/nyu-2451-34513. Accessed 14 Apr 2020
23. Pew Research Center: More Americans Are Using Ride-Hailing Apps (2019). https://www.pewresearch.org/fact-tank/2019/01/04/more-americans-are-using-ride-hailing-apps/. Accessed 18 Feb 2020
24. Pham, A., Dacosta, I., Endignoux, G., Troncoso-Pastoriza, J.R., Huguenin, K., Hubaux, J.: ORide: a privacy-preserving yet accountable ride-hailing service. In: Kirda, E., Ristenpart, T. (eds.) 26th USENIX Security Symposium, USENIX Security 2017, Vancouver, BC, Canada, 16–18 August, 2017, pp. 1235–1252. USENIX Association (2017)
25. Pham, A., et al.: PrivateRide: a privacy-enhanced ride-hailing service. PoPETs **2017**(2), 38–56 (2017). https://doi.org/10.1515/popets-2017-0015
26. Schneider, T.: NYC Taxi Data (2019). https://github.com/toddwschneider/nyc-taxi-data. Accessed 14 April 2020
27. Shahabi, C., Kolahdouzan, M.R., Sharifzadeh, M.: A road network embedding technique for k-nearest neighbor search in moving object databases. In: Voisard, A., Chen, S. (eds.) ACM-GIS 2002, Proceedings of the Tenth ACM International Symposium on Advances in Geographic Information Systems, McLean, VA (near Washington, DC), USA, USA, 8–9 November, 2002, pp. 94–10. ACM (2002)
28. Sweeney, L.: k-anonymity: a model for protecting privacy. Int. J. Uncertainty Fuzziness Knowl.Based Syst. **10**, 557–570 (2012)

29. Takloo-Bighash, R.: A Pythagorean Introduction to Number Theory: Right Triangles, Sums of Squares, and Arithmetic. Undergraduate Texts in Mathematics, Springer International Publishing (2018). https://books.google.co.in/books?id=_td7DwAAQBAJ

30. thejournal.ie: West Dublin gang using hailing apps to target older taxi drivers (2019). https://www.thejournal.ie/west-dublin-taxi-robbery-4420178-Jan2019/. Accessed 11 June 2020

31. Vivek, S.: Attacks on a privacy-preserving publish-subscribe system and a ride-hailing service. CoRR (2021). https://arxiv.org/abs/2105.04351

32. Wang, F., Zhu, H., Liu, X., Lu, R., Li, F., Li, H., Zhang, S.: Efficient and privacy-preserving dynamic spatial query scheme for ride-hailing services. IEEE Trans. Veh. Technol. **67**(11), 11084–11097 (2018)

33. Wikipedia contributors: Universal Transverse Mercator coordinate system (2020). https://en.wikipedia.org/wiki/Universal_Transverse_Mercator_coordinate_system. Accessed 27 Apr 2020

34. Xie, H., Guo, Y., Jia, X.: A privacy-preserving online ride-hailing system without involving a third trusted server. IEEE Trans. Inf. Forensics Secur. **16**, 3068–3081 (2021)

35. Yu, H., Jia, X., Zhang, H., Yu, X., Shu, J.: Psride: privacy-preserving shared ride matching for online ride hailing systems. IEEE Trans. Dependable Secure Comput., 1 (2019)

36. Yu, H., Jia, X., Zhang, H., Shu, J.: Efficient and privacy-preserving ride matching using exact road distance in online ride hailing services. IEEE Trans. Serv. Comput., 1 (2020)

37. Yu, H., Shu, J., Jia, X., Zhang, H., Yu, X.: lpride: lightweight and privacy-preserving ride matching over road networks in online ride hailing systems. IEEE Trans. Vehicular Technol. **68**(11), 10418–10428 (2019)

38. Zhao, Q., Zuo, C., Pellegrino, G., Lin, Z.: Geo-locating drivers: a study of sensitive data leakage in ride-hailing services. In: 26th Annual Network and Distributed System Security Symposium, NDSS 2019, San Diego, California, USA, 24–27 February, 2019. The Internet Society (2019). https://www.ndss-symposium.org/ndss-paper/geo-locating-drivers-a-study-of-sensitive-data-leakage-in-ride-hailing-services/

The Boneh-Katz Transformation, Revisited: Pseudorandom/Obliviously-Samplable PKE from Lattices and Codes and Its Application

Keita Xagawa[✉]

NTT Social Informatics Laboratories, Tokyo, Japan
keita.xagawa.zv@hco.ntt.co.jp

Abstract. The Boneh-Katz transformation (CT-RSA 2005) converts a selectively-secure identity/tag-based encryption scheme into a public-key encryption scheme secure against chosen-ciphertext attacks. We show that if the underlying primitives are pseudorandom, then the public-key encryption scheme obtained by the Boneh-Katz transformation is also pseudorandom. A similar result holds for oblivious sampleability (Canetti and Fischlin (CRYPTO 2001)). As applications, we can construct

- pseudorandom and obliviously-samplable public-key encryption schemes from lattices and codes,
- universally-composable non-interactive bit-commitment from lattices,
- public-key steganography which is steganographically secure against adaptive chosen-covertext attacks and steganographic key-exchange from lattices and codes,
- anonymous authenticated key exchange from lattices and codes,
- public-key encryption secure against simulation-based, selective-opening chosen-ciphertext attacks from lattices and codes.

Keywords: Public-key encryption · Tag-based encryption · Post-quantum cryptography · The Boneh-Katz transformation · Selective-opening security · Anonymity

1 Introduction

Public-key encryption (PKE) is the most basic primitive in asymmetric-key cryptography since it allows us to transmit data over the public channel securely if the receiver's encryption key is available. There are several security notions and properties of PKE and the researchers exploited those to construct interesting primitives and protocols. One of the most basic security notions is indistinguishability (IND-security) which means that any efficient adversary cannot distinguish a ciphertext of a plaintext with another ciphertext of another plaintext [27].

© The Author(s), under exclusive license to Springer Nature Switzerland AG 2022
R. AlTawy and A. Hülsing (Eds.): SAC 2021, LNCS 13203, pp. 47–67, 2022.
https://doi.org/10.1007/978-3-030-99277-4_3

Anonymity and Pseudorandomness: Although indistinguishability under chosen-plaintext/ciphertext attacks (IND-CPA/CCA security) ensures the confidentiality of contents [27,41,43], it does not imply anonymity and privacy of the receiver. Bellare, Boldyreva, Desai, and Pointcheval [4] defined indistinguishability of keys under chosen-plaintext/ciphertext attacks (IK-CPA/CCA security) to capture anonymity; in the security game, the adversary is, given two encryption keys, asked to determine which encryption key is used to encrypt a plaintext. This security notion has several applications: anonymous communication, anonymous authentication [13], auction [46], and so on.

We also note that pseudorandom PKE is related to anonymity. We say a PKE scheme is pseudorandom (PR-secure) if its ciphertext is indistinguishable from a random string from a set specified by the security parameter, encryption key, and the length of the message. We also say a PKE scheme is strongly pseudorandom (SPR-secure) if the set is independent of an encryption key. It is easy to see that strongly-pseudorandom PKE scheme is anonymous. Pseudorandom PKE also has applications for public-key steganography and steganographic key exchange [48], and backdoored pseudorandom generators (PRG) [19]. We also note that we have subliminal communication based on pseudorandom key-exchange [29], which can be constructed from PR-CPA-secure PKE if its encryption key is pseudorandom.

The constructions of SPR-CCA-secure PKE schemes from elliptic curves [40] and the DDH group [28] are known. To the authors' best knowledge, we have no *explicit* construction of post-quantum (S)PR-CCA-secure ones *in the standard model* except one from puncturable pseudorandom function (PRF) and indistinguishablity obfuscation (iO) [36,45].

Oblivious Sampleability: Canetti and Fischlin [14] introduced *oblivious sampleability (OS-security)*, which is an enhancement of PR-security; oblivious sampleability requires (1) a ciphertext is indistinguishable from a random string generated by a sampling algorithm on input the encryption key and (2) an explanation algorithm to explain how one samples the random string, e.g., if a ciphertext consists of group elements, then the randomness used to make the group elements are required. Combining OS-CCA-secure PKE with trapdoor commitments, they obtain UC-secure non-interactive bit commitment against adaptive corruption without erasure [14]. We do not know whether every IND-CCA-secure PKE scheme is OS-CCA-secure or not[1].

This security notion is strongly related to efficiently-samplable and explainable (ESE) ciphertext space. See [23,36] for its application to simulation-based, sender selective-opening security against chosen-ciphertext attacks (SIM-SSO-CCA security) of PKE.

Although there are several OS-CCA-secure PKE/KEM schemes from number-theoretic assumptions (see [14,23,36]), we have no *explicit* construc-

---

[1] Ishai et al. [30] refuted the hypothesis that every efficiently-samplable distribution has an invertible-sampling algorithm assuming the strong version of extractable OWF and NIWI proofs for all NP (or assuming non-interactively extractable OWF and NIZK proofs for all NP). Although this is not applicable to PKE, this is supporting evidence.

tion of post-quantum OS-CCA-secure ones *in the standard model* except one from puncturable pseudo-random function PRF and iO [36,45].

1.1 Our Contribution

The Boneh-Katz Transformation, Revisited: We revisit the Boneh-Katz (BK) transformation [9,10], which obtains IND-CCA-secure PKE from selectively-secure identity-based encryption (IBE) (or tag-based encryption (TBE)), weakly-secure commitment, and secure message authentication code (MAC). We show that the BK transformation *preserves* pseudorandomness and oblivious sampleability: If the underlying primitives are pseudorandom and obliviously-samplable, then the PKE scheme obtained by the transformation is also pseudorandom and obliviously-samplable, respectively.
SPR-CCA/SOS-CCA-*secure PKEs:* Using the above theorem, we obtain SPR-CCA-secure and SOS-CCA-secure PKEs from lattices and codes with various parameter settings upon existing IBE/TBE schemes [1,6,16,21,22,32,39,51]. As a byproduct, we show the Kiltz-Masny-Pietrzak TBE scheme [32] and the Yu-Zhang TBE scheme [51] based on the LPN problems are indeed pseudorandom and obliviously-samplable without changing the assumptions.

Applications: Employing them, we then obtain

- non-interactive bit commitment that is adaptively UC-secure in the non-erasure model under a re-usable common reference string from lattices through [14],
- public-key steganography which is steganographically secure against adaptive chosen-covertext attacks and steganographic key-exchange from lattice and codes through [7,28]
- anonymous authenticated key exchange from lattices and codes through [25], and
- public-key encryption secure against simulation-based, selective-opening chosen-ciphertext attacks from lattices and codes through [36].

Note on the Canetti-Halevi-Katz (CHK) Transformation: The Canetti-Halevi-Katz (CHK) transformation [9] allows us to obtain IND-CCA-secure PKE from selectively-secure identity-based encryption (IBE) (or tag-based encryption (TBE)) and one-time signature. Moreover, the CHK transformation preserves anonymity: See Paterson and Srinivasan [42] and Yoshida, Morozov, and Tanaka [50].

Unfortunately, a PKE scheme obtained by the CHK transformation cannot be obliviously-samplable even if the underlying IBE/TBE is obliviously-samplable, since we can verify the one-time signature in the ciphertext of PKE. The random string should contain the verification key of one-time signature and signature on the ciphertext of IBE/TBE. Roughly speaking, we cannot explain the randomness of the key generation of one-time signature, because once this randomness is leaked, then we can forge any message under the verification key and may be able to mount chosen-ciphertext attacks.[2]

1.2 Related Works

Anonymous PKE: Bellare et al. [4] put forth the notion of anonymity of PKE and introduced indistinguishability of keys (IK-security). (See also Camenisch and Lysyanskaya [13] and Sako [46].) Paterson and Srinivasan [42] defined Trusted Authority's anonymity (TA anonymity) of IBE. They showed that if the underlying IBE scheme satisfies TA anonymity, then the PKE scheme obtained by the CHK transformation is also key-private. As we explained, this is not pseudorandom. They refer to the BK transformation but omit the detail. This work can be considered as the follow-up of the case of the BK transformation. We note that the anonymity of PKE is insufficient for UC-secure commitment and SIM-SSO-CCA-secure PKE.

Yoshida et al. [50] proposed two anonymous code-based PKE schemes in the standard model through the CHK-like transformation, which are not pseudorandom.

Obliviously-Samplable PKE/KEM: Canetti and Fischlin [14] introduced the notion of *oblivious sampleability (OS-security)* and its application to UC-secure commitment. They showed that the Cramer-Shoup PKE [17] over the subgroup $\mathbb{G} \subseteq \mathbb{Z}_p^*$ of prime order $q \mid p-1$ satisfies their requirements because we can *explain* how to generate a random element in $\mathbb{G}$. As far as we know, there is no explicit construction of post-quantum PKE scheme satisfying OS-CCA security in the standard model except one from puncturable PRF and iO [36,45]. Thus, this paper first gives a post-quantum OS-CCA-secure PKE scheme without iO.

Concurrent Work: Leveraging key-dependent-message (KDM) security of DEM, Kitagawa, Matsuda, and Tanaka [34][3] proposed a SPR-CCA-secure KEM scheme from SPR-CPA-secure KEM, one-time key-dependent-message secure DEM with pseudorandom ciphertext property, and target-collision-resistance hash function [34, Sect. 6.4]. Concurrently, they also construct SIM-SSO-CCA-secure PKE scheme from it through the framework by Liu and Paterson [36] as ours, whose underlying KEM, DEM, and hash function can be constructed by either the CDH assumption, the LWE assumption, or the low-noise LPN assumption.

---

[2] If the underlying IBE/TBE is malleable, we modify the ciphertext of the IBE/TBE, sign it with the signing key of the one-time signature, and obtain a new valid ciphertext related to the challenge ciphertext.

[3] [34] is Jun. 2021 version of [33] on Cryptology ePrint Archive.

1.3   Organization

We review notations and cryptographic schemes in Sect. 2. We review the Boneh-Katz transformation and prove its pseudorandomness and oblivious sampleability in Sect. 3. We discuss how to instantiate applications through PR-CCA-secure/OS-CCA-secure PKE in Sect. 4. In the full version, we review the LPN-related assumptions, review the Kiltz-Masny-Pietrzak TBE scheme and the Yu-Zhang TBE scheme and prove their PR-CCA-security.

2   Definitions

Notations: A security parameter is denoted by κ. We use the standard O-notations. DPT and PPT stand for deterministic polynomial time and probabilistic polynomial time. A function $f(\kappa)$ is said to be *negligible* if $f(\kappa) = \kappa^{-\omega(1)}$. We denote a set of negligible functions by $\mathsf{negl}(\kappa)$. For a distribution χ, we often write "$x \leftarrow \chi$," which indicates that we take a sample x according to χ. For a finite set S, $U(S)$ denotes the uniform distribution over S. We often write "$x \leftarrow S$" instead of "$x \leftarrow U(S)$." For a set S and a deterministic algorithm A, $\mathsf{A}(S)$ denotes the set $\{\mathsf{A}(x) \mid x \in S\}$. If inp is a string, then "out $\leftarrow \mathsf{A}(\mathsf{inp})$" denotes the output of algorithm A when run on input inp. If A is deterministic, then out is a fixed value and we write "out $:= \mathsf{A}(\mathsf{inp})$." We also use the notation "out $:= \mathsf{A}(\mathsf{inp}; r)$" to make the randomness r explicit.

For a statement P (e.g., $r \in [0, 1]$), we define $\mathsf{boole}(P) = 1$ if P is satisfied and 0 otherwise.

Efficiently-Samplable and Explainable Domain: A domain $\mathcal{D}$ is said to be *efficiently samplable and explainable (ESE)* [23] if there are two PPT algorithms defined as follows:

- $\mathsf{Sample}(\mathcal{D}; \rho)$: On input domain $\mathcal{D}$ and random coins $\rho \leftarrow \mathcal{R}$, this algorithm outputs an element x according to the uniform distribution over $\mathcal{D}$.
- $\mathsf{Sample}^{-1}(\mathcal{D}, x)$: On input domain $\mathcal{D}$ and any $x \in \mathcal{D}$, this algorithm outputs ρ that is uniformly distributed over the set $\{\rho \in \mathcal{R} \mid \mathsf{Sample}(\mathcal{D}; \rho) = x\}$.

For example, $\mathcal{D} = \{0, 1\}^\kappa$ is ESE with $\rho = \mathsf{Sample}(\mathcal{D}; \rho) = \mathsf{Sample}^{-1}(\mathcal{D}, \rho)$. Damgård and Nielsen [18] showed that any dense subset of an efficiently samplable domain is ESE if the dense subset allows an efficient membership test.

2.1   Public-Key Encryption (PKE)

The model for PKE schemes is summarized as follows:

Definition 2.1. *A PKE scheme* PKE *consists of the following triple of PPT algorithms* $(\mathsf{Gen}_{\mathsf{PKE}}, \mathsf{Enc}_{\mathsf{PKE}}, \mathsf{Dec}_{\mathsf{PKE}})$.

- $\mathsf{Gen}_{\mathsf{PKE}}(1^\kappa) \rightarrow (ek, dk)$: *a key-generation algorithm that on input* 1^κ, *where* κ *is the security parameter, outputs a pair of keys* (ek, dk). *ek and dk are called the encryption key and decryption key, respectively.*

52   K. Xagawa

- $\mathsf{Enc_{PKE}}(ek, m) \rightarrow c$: *an encryption algorithm that takes as input encryption key ek and message $m \in \mathcal{M}$ and outputs ciphertext $c \in \mathcal{C}$.*
- $\mathsf{Dec_{PKE}}(dk, c) \rightarrow m/\bot$: *a decryption algorithm that takes as input decryption key dk and ciphertext c and outputs message $m \in \mathcal{M}$ or a rejection symbol $\bot \notin \mathcal{M}$.*

Definition 2.2 (Correctness). *We say* $\mathsf{PKE} = (\mathsf{Gen_{PKE}}, \mathsf{Enc_{PKE}}, \mathsf{Dec_{PKE}})$ *has perfect correctness if for any* (ek, dk) *generated by* $\mathsf{Gen_{PKE}}$ *and for any* $m \in \mathcal{M}$, *we have*
$$\Pr[c \leftarrow \mathsf{Enc_{PKE}}(ek, m) : \mathsf{Dec_{PKE}}(dk, c) = m] = 1.$$

Security Notions: We review indistinguishability under chosen-ciphertext attacks (IND-CCA) [5,43], pseudorandom under chosen-ciphertext attacks (PR-CCA) (as known as IND\$-CCA) [28,48], oblivious sampleability under chosen-ciphertext attacks (OS-CCA) [14] and their strong versions (SPR-CCA and SOS-CCA) for PKE.

In order to define oblivious sampleability, we introduce two additional algorithms, $\mathsf{Rnd_{PKE}}$ and $\mathsf{Expl_{PKE}}$: $\mathsf{Rnd_{PKE}}$ takes an encryption key ek, a length of message 0^ℓ, and randomness $\rho \in \mathcal{R}_{\mathsf{Rnd_{PKE}}, ek, \ell}$ and outputs $c \in \mathcal{C}$; $\mathsf{Expl_{PKE}}$ takes ek and $c \in \mathcal{C}$ and outputs a randomness ρ. Roughly speaking, we say a PKE scheme is obliviously samplable if there exist $\mathsf{Rnd_{PKE}}$ and $\mathsf{Expl_{PKE}}$ that a dummy ciphertext c generated by $\mathsf{Rnd_{PKE}}$ with randomness ρ and a real ciphertext c^* of m^* and corresponding fake randomness ρ^* generated by $\mathsf{Expl_{PKE}}$ are indistinguishable.

Definition 2.3 (Security notions for PKE). *Let* $\mathcal{D}_\mathcal{M}$ *be a distribution over the message space* $\mathcal{M}$. *For any adversary* $\mathcal{A}$, *we define its* IND-CCA, PR-CCA, *and* OS-CCA *advantages against a PKE scheme* $\mathsf{PKE} = (\mathsf{Gen_{PKE}}, \mathsf{Enc_{PKE}}, \mathsf{Dec_{PKE}})$ *and two additional PPT algorithms* $\mathsf{Rnd_{PKE}}$ *and* $\mathsf{Expl_{PKE}}$ *as follows:*

$$\mathsf{Adv}^{\mathrm{ind\text{-}cca}}_{\mathsf{PKE},\mathcal{A}}(\kappa) := \left| \Pr[\mathsf{Expt}^{\mathrm{ind\text{-}cca},0}_{\mathsf{PKE},\mathcal{A}}(\kappa) = 1] - \Pr[\mathsf{Expt}^{\mathrm{ind\text{-}cca},1}_{\mathsf{PKE},\mathcal{A}}(\kappa) = 1] \right|,$$
$$\mathsf{Adv}^{\mathrm{pr\text{-}cca}}_{\mathsf{PKE},\mathcal{A}}(\kappa) := \left| \Pr[\mathsf{Expt}^{\mathrm{pr\text{-}cca},0}_{\mathsf{PKE},\mathcal{A}}(\kappa) = 1] - \Pr[\mathsf{Expt}^{\mathrm{pr\text{-}cca},1}_{\mathsf{PKE},\mathcal{A}}(\kappa) = 1] \right|,$$
$$\mathsf{Adv}^{\mathrm{os\text{-}cca}}_{\mathsf{PKE},\mathcal{A}}(\kappa) := \left| \Pr[\mathsf{Expt}^{\mathrm{os\text{-}cca},0}_{\mathsf{PKE},\mathcal{A}}(\kappa) = 1] - \Pr[\mathsf{Expt}^{\mathrm{os\text{-}cca},1}_{\mathsf{PKE},\mathcal{A}}(\kappa) = 1] \right|,$$

where $\mathsf{Expt}^{\mathrm{ind\text{-}cca},b}_{\mathsf{PKE},\mathcal{A}}(\kappa)$, $\mathsf{Expt}^{\mathrm{pr\text{-}cca},b}_{\mathsf{PKE},\mathcal{A}}(\kappa)$, *and* $\mathsf{Expt}^{\mathrm{os\text{-}cca},b}_{\mathsf{PKE},\mathcal{A}}(\kappa)$ *are experiments described in Fig. 1. We say that* PKE *is* IND-CCA-*secure,* PR-CCA-*secure, and* OS-CCA-*secure if* $\mathsf{Adv}^{\mathrm{ind\text{-}cca}}_{\mathsf{PKE},\mathcal{A}}(\kappa)$, $\mathsf{Adv}^{\mathrm{pr\text{-}cca}}_{\mathsf{PKE},\mathcal{A}}(\kappa)$, *and* $\mathsf{Adv}^{\mathrm{os\text{-}cca}}_{\mathsf{PKE},\mathcal{A}}(\kappa)$ *is negligible for any PPT adversary* $\mathcal{A}$, *respectively.*

We also say that PKE *is* SPR-CCA-*secure if it is* PR-CCA-*secure and its ciphertext space* $\mathcal{C}$ *depends on only* κ *and is independent from* ek. *We also say that* PKE *is* SOS-CCA-*secure if it is* OS-CCA-*secure and its additional algorithms take* 1^κ *instead of* ek *as a part of input.*

Remark 2.1. We note that if a PKE scheme is PR-CCA-secure and its ciphertext space $\mathcal{C}$ is ESE, then the PKE scheme is OS-CCA-secure.

$\text{Expt}_{\text{PKE},\mathcal{A}}^{\text{ind-cca},b}(\kappa)$	$\text{Expt}_{\text{PKE},\mathcal{A}}^{\text{pr-cca},b}(\kappa)$	$\text{Expt}_{\text{PKE},\mathcal{A}}^{\text{os-cca},b}(\kappa)$
$(ek, dk) \leftarrow \text{Gen}_{\text{PKE}}(1^\kappa)$	$(ek, dk) \leftarrow \text{Gen}_{\text{PKE}}(1^\kappa)$	$(ek, dk) \leftarrow \text{Gen}_{\text{PKE}}(1^\kappa)$
$(m_0, m_1, st) \leftarrow \mathcal{A}_1^{\text{DEC}_\perp(\cdot)}(ek)$	$(m, st) \leftarrow \mathcal{A}_1^{\text{DEC}_\perp(\cdot)}(ek)$	$(m, st) \leftarrow \mathcal{A}_1^{\text{DEC}_\perp(\cdot)}(ek)$
$c^* \leftarrow \text{Enc}_{\text{PKE}}(ek, m_b)$	$c_0^* \leftarrow \text{Enc}_{\text{PKE}}(ek, m)$	$c_0^* \leftarrow \text{Enc}_{\text{PKE}}(ek, m)$
$b' \leftarrow \mathcal{A}_2^{\text{DEC}_{c^*}(\cdot)}(c^*, st)$	$c_1^* \leftarrow \mathcal{C}_{ek}$	$\rho_0^* \leftarrow \text{Expl}_{\text{PKE}}(ek, c_0^*)$
return b'	$b' \leftarrow \mathcal{A}_2^{\text{DEC}_{c_b^*}(\cdot)}(c_b^*, st)$	$\rho_1^* \leftarrow \mathcal{R}_{\text{Rnd}_{\text{PKE}}, ek, \|m\|}$
	return b'	$c_1^* \leftarrow \text{Rnd}_{\text{PKE}}(ek, 0^{\|m\|}; \rho_1^*)$
$\underline{\text{DEC}_a(c)}$		$b' \leftarrow \mathcal{A}_2^{\text{DEC}_{c_b^*}(\cdot)}(c_b^*, \rho_b^*, st)$
if $c = a$, return $\perp$		**return** b'
$m \leftarrow \text{Dec}_{\text{PKE}}(dk, c)$		
return m		

Fig. 1. Games for PKE schemes

2.2 Tag-Based Encryption (TBE)

MacKenzie, Reiter, and Yang [37] introduced a notion of *tag-based encryption* (TBE). They show that applying the CHK transformation to TBE results in IND-CCA-secure PKE independently.

The model for TBE schemes is summarized as follows:

Definition 2.4. *A TBE scheme* TBE *consists of the following triple of PPT algorithms* $(\text{Gen}_{\text{TBE}}, \text{Enc}_{\text{TBE}}, \text{Dec}_{\text{TBE}})$.

- $\text{Gen}_{\text{TBE}}(1^\kappa) \to (ek, dk)$: *a key-generation algorithm that on input* 1^κ, *where* κ *is the security parameter, outputs a pair of keys* (ek, dk). ek *and* dk *are called the encryption key and decryption key, respectively.*
- $\text{Enc}_{\text{TBE}}(ek, \tau, m) \to c$: *an encryption algorithm that takes as input encryption key* ek, *tag* $\tau \in \mathcal{T}$, *and message* $m \in \mathcal{M}$ *and outputs ciphertext* $c \in \mathcal{C}$.
- $\text{Dec}_{\text{TBE}}(dk, \tau, c) \to m/\perp$: *a decryption algorithm that takes as input decryption key* dk, *tag* τ, *and ciphertext* c *and outputs message* $m \in \mathcal{M}$ *or a rejection symbol* $\perp \notin \mathcal{M}$.

Definition 2.5 (Correctness). *We say* TBE $= (\text{Gen}_{\text{TBE}}, \text{Enc}_{\text{TBE}}, \text{Dec}_{\text{TBE}})$ *has perfect correctness if for any* (ek, dk) *generated by* Gen_{TBE}, *for any tag* $\tau \in \mathcal{T}$ *and for any* $m \in \mathcal{M}$, *we have*

$$\Pr[c \leftarrow \text{Enc}_{\text{TBE}}(ek, \tau, m) : \text{Dec}_{\text{TBE}}(dk, \tau, c) = m] = 1.$$

Security Notions: We review indistinguishability under selective-tag and weak chosen-ciphertext attacks IND-ST-wCCA [31]. In addition, we define PR-ST-wCCA and OS-ST-wCCA by using Rnd_{TBE} and Expl_{TBE}.

In order to define oblivious sampleability, we introduce two additional algorithms, Rnd_{TBE} and Expl_{TBE}: Rnd_{TBE} takes an encryption key ek, a length of message 0^ℓ, and randomness $\rho \in \mathcal{R}_{\text{Rnd}_{\text{TBE}}, ek, \ell}$ and outputs $c \in \mathcal{C}$; Expl_{PKE} takes ek and $c \in \mathcal{C}$ and outputs a randomness ρ.

$\mathsf{Expt}_{\mathsf{TBE},\mathcal{A}}^{\mathrm{ind\text{-}st\text{-}wcca},b}(\kappa)$	$\mathsf{Expt}_{\mathsf{TBE},\mathcal{A}}^{\mathrm{pr\text{-}st\text{-}wcca},b}(\kappa)$	$\mathsf{Expt}_{\mathsf{TBE},\mathcal{A}}^{\mathrm{os\text{-}st\text{-}wcca},b}(\kappa)$
$(\tau^*, st) \leftarrow \mathcal{A}_0(1^\kappa)$	$(\tau^*, st) \leftarrow \mathcal{A}_0(1^\kappa)$	$(\tau^*, st) \leftarrow \mathcal{A}_0(1^\kappa)$
$(ek, dk) \leftarrow \mathsf{Gen}_{\mathsf{TBE}}(1^\kappa)$	$(ek, dk) \leftarrow \mathsf{Gen}_{\mathsf{TBE}}(1^\kappa)$	$(ek, dk) \leftarrow \mathsf{Gen}_{\mathsf{TBE}}(1^\kappa)$
$(m_0, m_1, st) \leftarrow \mathcal{A}_1^{\mathrm{Dec}_{\tau^*}(\cdot)}(ek, st)$	$(m, st) \leftarrow \mathcal{A}_1^{\mathrm{Dec}_{\tau^*}(\cdot)}(ek, st)$	$(m, st) \leftarrow \mathcal{A}_1^{\mathrm{Dec}_{\tau^*}(\cdot)}(ek, st)$
$c^* \leftarrow \mathsf{Enc}_{\mathsf{TBE}}(ek, \tau^*, m_b)$	$c_0^* \leftarrow \mathsf{Enc}_{\mathsf{TBE}}(ek, \tau^*, m)$	$c_0^* \leftarrow \mathsf{Enc}_{\mathsf{TBE}}(ek, \tau^*, m)$
$b' \leftarrow \mathcal{A}_2^{\mathrm{Dec}_{\tau^*}(\cdot)}(c^*, st)$	$c_1^* \leftarrow \mathcal{C}$	$\rho_0^* \leftarrow \mathsf{Expl}_{\mathsf{TBE}}(ek, c_0^*)$
return b'	$b' \leftarrow \mathcal{A}_2^{\mathrm{Dec}_{\tau^*}(\cdot)}(c_b^*, st)$	$\rho_1^* \leftarrow \mathcal{R}_{\mathsf{Rnd}_{\mathsf{TBE}}.ek,|m|}$
	return b'	$c_1^* \leftarrow \mathsf{Rnd}_{\mathsf{TBE}}(ek, 0^{|m|}; \rho_1^*)$
		$b' \leftarrow \mathcal{A}_2^{\mathrm{Dec}_{\tau^*}(\cdot)}(c_b^*, \rho_b^*, st)$
$\underline{\mathrm{Dec}_{\tau^*}(\tau, c)}$		**return** b'
if $\tau = \tau^*$, **return** $\bot$		
$m \leftarrow \mathsf{Dec}_{\mathsf{TBE}}(dk, \tau, c)$		
return m		

Fig. 2. Games for TBE schemes

Definition 2.6 (Security notion for TBE). *For any adversary $\mathcal{A}$, we define its* IND-ST-wCCA *and* OS-ST-wCCA *advantages against a TBE scheme* TBE $= (\mathsf{Gen}_{\mathsf{TBE}}, \mathsf{Enc}_{\mathsf{TBE}}, \mathsf{Dec}_{\mathsf{TBE}})$ *with additional PPT algorithms* $\mathsf{Rnd}_{\mathsf{TBE}}$ *and* $\mathsf{Expl}_{\mathsf{TBE}}$ *as follows:*

$$\mathsf{Adv}_{\mathsf{TBE},\mathcal{A}}^{\mathrm{ind\text{-}st\text{-}wcca}}(\kappa) := \left| \Pr[\mathsf{Expt}_{\mathsf{TBE},\mathcal{A}}^{\mathrm{ind\text{-}st\text{-}wcca},0}(\kappa) = 1] - \Pr[\mathsf{Expt}_{\mathsf{TBE},\mathcal{A}}^{\mathrm{ind\text{-}st\text{-}wcca},1}(\kappa) = 1] \right|,$$

$$\mathsf{Adv}_{\mathsf{TBE},\mathcal{A}}^{\mathrm{pr\text{-}st\text{-}wcca}}(\kappa) := \left| \Pr[\mathsf{Expt}_{\mathsf{TBE},\mathcal{A}}^{\mathrm{pr\text{-}st\text{-}wcca},0}(\kappa) = 1] - \Pr[\mathsf{Expt}_{\mathsf{TBE},\mathcal{A}}^{\mathrm{pr\text{-}st\text{-}wcca},1}(\kappa) = 1] \right|,$$

$$\mathsf{Adv}_{\mathsf{TBE},\mathcal{A}}^{\mathrm{os\text{-}st\text{-}wcca}}(\kappa) := \left| \Pr[\mathsf{Expt}_{\mathsf{TBE},\mathcal{A}}^{\mathrm{os\text{-}st\text{-}wcca},0}(\kappa) = 1] - \Pr[\mathsf{Expt}_{\mathsf{TBE},\mathcal{A}}^{\mathrm{os\text{-}st\text{-}wcca},1}(\kappa) = 1] \right|,$$

where $\mathsf{Expt}_{\mathsf{TBE},\mathcal{A}}^{\mathrm{ind\text{-}st\text{-}wcca},b}(\kappa)$, $\mathsf{Expt}_{\mathsf{TBE},\mathcal{A}}^{\mathrm{pr\text{-}st\text{-}wcca},b}(\kappa)$, *and* $\mathsf{Expt}_{\mathsf{TBE},\mathcal{A}}^{\mathrm{os\text{-}st\text{-}wcca},b}(\kappa)$ *are experiments described in Fig. 2. We say that* TBE *is* IND-ST-wCCA-*secure,* PR-ST-wCCA-*secure, and* OS-ST-wCCA-*secure if* $\mathsf{Adv}_{\mathsf{TBE},\mathcal{A}}^{\mathrm{ind\text{-}st\text{-}wcca}}(\kappa)$, $\mathsf{Adv}_{\mathsf{TBE},\mathcal{A}}^{\mathrm{pr\text{-}st\text{-}wcca}}(\kappa)$, *and* $\mathsf{Adv}_{\mathsf{TBE},\mathcal{A}}^{\mathrm{os\text{-}st\text{-}wcca}}(\kappa)$ *are negligible for any PPT adversary $\mathcal{A}$, respectively.*

We also say that TBE *is* SPR-ST-wCCA-*secure if it is* PR-ST-wCCA-*secure and its ciphertext space $\mathcal{C}$ depends on only κ and is independent from ek. We also say that* TBE *is* SOS-ST-wCCA-*secure if it is* OS-ST-wCCA-*secure and its additional algorithms take 1^κ instead of ek.*

Remark 2.2. Again, we note that if a TBE scheme is PR-ST-wCCA-secure and its ciphertext space $\mathcal{C}$ is ESE, then the TBE scheme is OS-ST-wCCA-secure.

2.3   Weak Commitment also Known as Encapsulation

Boneh et al. introduced the concept of encapsulation [9], which is a weak variant of commitment [8] and we here call it *weak commitment*. Weak commitment is summarized as follows:

Definition 2.7. *A* weak commitment scheme wCom *consists of the following triple of PPT algorithms* (Init, S, R):

- Init$(1^\kappa) \rightarrow pp$: *an initialization algorithm that takes on input* 1^κ, *where* κ *is the security parameter, and outputs a string pp.*
- S$(1^\kappa, pp) \rightarrow (r, com, dec)$: *a sender algorithm that takes as input* 1^κ *and pp and outputs* (r, com, dec) *with* $r \in \{0,1\}^\kappa$, *where we refer to com as the commitment string and dec as the decommitment string.*
- R$(pp, com, dec) \rightarrow r/\bot$: *a receiver algorithm that takes as input* (pp, com, dec) *and outputs* $r \in \{0,1\}^\kappa$ *or a rejection symbol* $\bot \notin \{0,1\}^\kappa$.

Definition 2.8 (Correctness). *We say* wCom $=$ (Init, S, R) *has* perfect correctness *if for any pp generated by* Init, *we have*

$$\Pr[(r, com, dec) \leftarrow S(1^\kappa, pp) : R(pp, com, dec) = r] = 1.$$

We review the definitions of hiding property and binding property [9]. We here only require binding *for honestly generated commitments*. In addition, we define oblivious sampleability of weak commitment by using $\mathsf{Rnd}_{\mathsf{wCom}}$ and $\mathsf{Expl}_{\mathsf{wCom}}$. We also define non-invertibility, which states it is hard to generate meaningful decommitment for obliviously-sampled *com* and ρ.

Definition 2.9. *For any adversary* $\mathcal{A}$, *we define its four advantages against an encapsulation scheme* wCom $=$ (Init, S, R) *and two PPT algorithms* $(\mathsf{Rnd}_{\mathsf{wCom}}, \mathsf{Expl}_{\mathsf{wCom}})$ *as follows:*

$$\mathsf{Adv}^{\mathrm{hiding}}_{\mathsf{wCom},\mathcal{A}}(\kappa) := \left| \Pr[\mathsf{Expt}^{\mathrm{hiding},0}_{\mathsf{wCom},\mathcal{A}}(\kappa) = 1] = \Pr[\mathsf{Expt}^{\mathrm{hiding},1}_{\mathsf{wCom},\mathcal{A}}(\kappa) = 1] \right|,$$

$$\mathsf{Adv}^{\mathrm{binding}}_{\mathsf{wCom},\mathcal{A}}(\kappa) := \Pr[\mathsf{Expt}^{\mathrm{binding}}_{\mathsf{wCom},\mathcal{A}}(\kappa) = 1],$$

$$\mathsf{Adv}^{\mathrm{os}}_{\mathsf{wCom},\mathcal{A}}(\kappa) := \left| \Pr[\mathsf{Expt}^{\mathrm{os},0}_{\mathsf{wCom},\mathcal{A}}(\kappa) = 1] - \Pr[\mathsf{Expt}^{\mathrm{os},1}_{\mathsf{wCom},\mathcal{A}}(\kappa) = 1] \right|,$$

$$\mathsf{Adv}^{\mathrm{non\text{-}inv}}_{\mathsf{wCom},\mathcal{A}}(\kappa) := \Pr[\mathsf{Expt}^{\mathrm{non\text{-}inv}}_{\mathsf{wCom},\mathcal{A}}(\kappa) = 1],$$

where $\mathsf{Expt}^{\mathrm{hiding},b}_{\mathsf{wCom},\mathcal{A}}(\kappa)$, $\mathsf{Expt}^{\mathrm{binding}}_{\mathsf{wCom},\mathcal{A}}(\kappa)$, $\mathsf{Expt}^{\mathrm{os},b}_{\mathsf{wCom},\mathcal{A}}(\kappa)$, *and* $\mathsf{Expt}^{\mathrm{non\text{-}inv}}_{\mathsf{wCom},\mathcal{A}}(\kappa)$ *are experiments described in Fig. 3.*

We say that wCom *is* secure *if* $\mathsf{Adv}^{\mathrm{hiding}}_{\mathsf{wCom},\mathcal{A}}(\kappa)$ *and* $\mathsf{Adv}^{\mathrm{binding}}_{\mathsf{wCom},\mathcal{A}}(\kappa)$ *are negligible for any PPT adversary* $\mathcal{A}$. *We also say that* wCom *is* OS-secure *if* $\mathsf{Adv}^{\mathrm{os}}_{\mathsf{wCom},\mathcal{A}}(\kappa)$ *is negligible for any PPT adversary* $\mathcal{A}$. *We also say that* wCom *is* non-invertible *if* $\mathsf{Adv}^{\mathrm{non\text{-}inv}}_{\mathsf{wCom},\mathcal{A}}(\kappa)$ *is negligible for any PPT adversary* $\mathcal{A}$.

Concrete Construction: Let $\mathcal{H}_{\mathrm{uow}} = \{H_s \colon \{0,1\}^{k_1} \rightarrow \{0,1\}^k\}$ be a family of universal one-way hash function (UOWHF) and let $\mathcal{H} = \{h \colon \{0,1\}^{k_1} \rightarrow \{0,1\}^k\}$ be a family of pairwise-independent hash function. Let $k_1 = 2k + \delta$. Boneh and Katz [10] gave a concrete construction of weak commitments from them as follows:

- Init(1^κ): choose H_s and h and output $pp = (h, s)$.

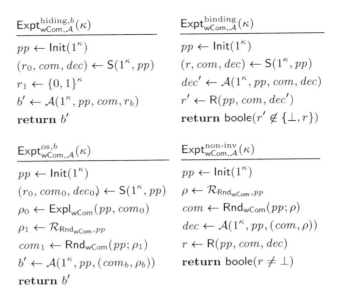

$$\underline{\mathsf{Expt}^{\mathrm{hiding},b}_{\mathsf{wCom},\mathcal{A}}(\kappa)}$$

$pp \leftarrow \mathsf{Init}(1^\kappa)$
$(r_0, com, dec) \leftarrow \mathsf{S}(1^\kappa, pp)$
$r_1 \leftarrow \{0,1\}^\kappa$
$b' \leftarrow \mathcal{A}(1^\kappa, pp, com, r_b)$
return b'

$$\underline{\mathsf{Expt}^{\mathrm{binding}}_{\mathsf{wCom},\mathcal{A}}(\kappa)}$$

$pp \leftarrow \mathsf{Init}(1^\kappa)$
$(r, com, dec) \leftarrow \mathsf{S}(1^\kappa, pp)$
$dec' \leftarrow \mathcal{A}(1^\kappa, pp, com, dec)$
$r' \leftarrow \mathsf{R}(pp, com, dec')$
return $\mathsf{boole}(r' \notin \{\bot, r\})$

$$\underline{\mathsf{Expt}^{\mathrm{os},b}_{\mathsf{wCom},\mathcal{A}}(\kappa)}$$

$pp \leftarrow \mathsf{Init}(1^\kappa)$
$(r_0, com_0, dec_0) \leftarrow \mathsf{S}(1^\kappa, pp)$
$\rho_0 \leftarrow \mathsf{Expl}_{\mathsf{wCom}}(pp, com_0)$
$\rho_1 \leftarrow \mathcal{R}_{\mathsf{Rnd}_{\mathsf{wCom}}, pp}$
$com_1 \leftarrow \mathsf{Rnd}_{\mathsf{wCom}}(pp; \rho_1)$
$b' \leftarrow \mathcal{A}(1^\kappa, pp, (com_b, \rho_b))$
return b'

$$\underline{\mathsf{Expt}^{\mathrm{non\text{-}inv}}_{\mathsf{wCom},\mathcal{A}}(\kappa)}$$

$pp \leftarrow \mathsf{Init}(1^\kappa)$
$\rho \leftarrow \mathcal{R}_{\mathsf{Rnd}_{\mathsf{wCom}}, pp}$
$com \leftarrow \mathsf{Rnd}_{\mathsf{wCom}}(pp; \rho)$
$dec \leftarrow \mathcal{A}(1^\kappa, pp, (com, \rho))$
$r \leftarrow \mathsf{R}(pp, com, dec)$
return $\mathsf{boole}(r \neq \bot)$

Fig. 3. Games for weak commitment schemes

- $\mathsf{S}(pp)$: take $x \leftarrow \{0,1\}^{k_1}$ and output $(r, com, dec) = (h(x), H_s(x), x)$.
- $\mathsf{R}(pp, com, dec)$: output $h(dec)$ if $H_s(dec) = com$ and $\bot$ otherwise.

We require the following properties:

- H_s is universal one-way for the binding property. (See [9, Theorem 4].)
- $2 \cdot 2^{\frac{2k-k_1}{3}} = 2^{-\delta/3+1}$ is negligible in the security parameter for the hiding property. (See [9, Theorem 4].)
- $H_s(U(\{0,1\}^{k_1}))$ is pseudorandom for the OS property. See Lemma 2.1 below.
- $H_s(U(\{0,1\}^{k_1}))$ is pseudorandom and one-way for the non-invertible property. See Lemma 2.2 below.

We have several instantiating way of H_s.

- The easiest way is employing the standard hash functions, say, $H_s(x) = \mathsf{SHA3\text{-}256}(s, x)$. This keyed function is collision-resistant; and it is reasonable to assume that $(s, H_s(u))$ with $u \leftarrow \{0,1\}^{k_1}$ is close to uniform.
- (From lattices:) for example, Ajtai's hash function from lattices is collision-resistant if SIS is hard [2,26]. This hash function is strongly universal (see e.g., Regev [44, Sect. 5]) and, thus, pseudorandom.
- (From codes:) for example, we can use the Expand-then-Shrink hash function as known as FSB [3,12,52]. Let $k_1 = k_1' \cdot w$ and $m = k_1' \cdot 2^w$ for some w. Let e_i is the i-th unit vector of dimension 2^w. The hash function is defined as $h_M(x) = M \cdot \mathsf{Expand}(x)$, where $M \leftarrow \mathbb{Z}_2^{k \times m}$ and $\mathsf{Expand}(x) =$

$e_{\mathsf{int}(x_1)} \| \cdots \| e_{\mathsf{int}(x_{k'_1})} \in \mathbb{Z}_2^m$ with $x = x_1 \| \cdots \| x_{k'_1}$ for each $x_i \in \mathbb{Z}_2^w$. Brakerski et al. [12] and Yu et al. [52] showed that their hash functions are collision-resistant assuming the extremely low-noise LPN. We can show its pseudorandomness by assuming the hash function is one-way by applying the result of Mol and Micciancio [38], which states pseudorandomness of $(g, \sum_i x_i \cdot g_i)$ with $g \leftarrow \mathbb{G}^m$ and $x \leftarrow \mathcal{X}$, where $\mathcal{X}$ is an arbitrary distribution over $\{0,1\}^m$, if $(g, f_g(x))$ is one-way.

Lemma 2.1. *Suppose that $(H_s, H_s(x))$ is computationally indistinguishable from (H_s, u), where $H_s \leftarrow \mathcal{H}_{\mathsf{uow}}, x \leftarrow \{0,1\}^{k_1}$, and $u \leftarrow \{0,1\}^k$. Then, the scheme is obliviously sampleable with $\mathcal{R}_{\mathsf{Rnd}_{\mathsf{wCom}}, pp} = \{0,1\}^k$, $\mathsf{Rnd}_{\mathsf{wCom}}(pp, \cdot)$ and $\mathsf{Expl}_{\mathsf{wCom}}(pp, \cdot)$ are the identity function over $\{0,1\}^k$.*

Proof. We consider the following three games:

- Game 0: $H_s \leftarrow \mathcal{H}_{\mathsf{uow}}, h \leftarrow \mathcal{H}, x \leftarrow \{0,1\}^{k_1}, com_0 \leftarrow H_s(x)$, and $\rho_0 \leftarrow \mathsf{Expl}_{\mathsf{wCom}}(pp, com_0) = com_0$. Output $b' \leftarrow \mathcal{A}(1^\kappa, (H_s, h), (com_0, \rho_0))$.
- Hybrid: $H_s \leftarrow \mathcal{H}_{\mathsf{uow}}, h \leftarrow \mathcal{H}, x \leftarrow \{0,1\}^{k_1}, com \leftarrow \{0,1\}^k$, and $\rho \leftarrow \mathsf{Expl}_{\mathsf{wCom}}(pp, com) = com$. Output $b' \leftarrow \mathcal{A}(1^\kappa, (H_s, h), (com, \rho))$.
- Game 1: $H_s \leftarrow \mathcal{H}_{\mathsf{uow}}, h \leftarrow \mathcal{H}, x \leftarrow \{0,1\}^{k_1}, \rho_1 \leftarrow \{0,1\}^k$, and $com_1 \leftarrow \mathsf{Rnd}_{\mathsf{wCom}}(pp, \rho_1) = \rho_1$. Output $b' \leftarrow \mathcal{A}(1^\kappa, (H_s, h), (com_1, \rho_1))$.

We suppose that $(H_s, H_s(x))$ is computationally indistinguishable from (H_s, u), where $H_s \leftarrow \mathcal{H}_{\mathsf{uow}}, x \leftarrow \{0,1\}^{k_1}$, and $u \leftarrow \{0,1\}^k$. Thus, it is easy to see that Game 0 and Hybrid are computationally indistinguishable. It is obvious that Hybrid and Game 1 are equivalent. Hence, the lemma follows. □

Lemma 2.2. *Suppose that $(H_s, H_s(x))$ is computationally indistinguishable from (H_s, u), where $H_s \leftarrow \mathcal{H}_{\mathsf{uow}}, x \leftarrow \{0,1\}^{k_1}$, and $u \leftarrow \{0,1\}^k$. Moreover, suppose that H_s is one-way. Then, the scheme is non-invertible.*

Proof. We consider the following two games:

- Game 0: $H_s \leftarrow \mathcal{H}_{\mathsf{uow}}, h \leftarrow \mathcal{H}, \rho \leftarrow \{0,1\}^k$, and $com \leftarrow \mathsf{Rnd}_{\mathsf{wCom}}(pp, \rho) = \rho$. $dec \leftarrow \mathcal{A}(1^\kappa, (H_s, h), (com, \rho))$. Output 1 if $H_s(dec) = com$ and 0 otherwise.
- Game 1: $H_s \leftarrow \mathcal{H}_{\mathsf{uow}}, h \leftarrow \mathcal{H}, x \leftarrow \{0,1\}^{k_1}, com \leftarrow H_s(x)$, and $\rho \leftarrow \mathsf{Expl}_{\mathsf{wCom}}(pp, com) = com$. $dec \leftarrow \mathcal{A}(1^\kappa, (H_s, h), (com, \rho))$. Output 1 if $H_s(dec) = com$ and 0 otherwise.

Game 0 is $\mathsf{Expt}_{\mathsf{wCom}, \mathcal{A}}^{\mathsf{non\text{-}inv}}(\kappa)$. In the hypothesis, we suppose that $(H_s, H_s(x))$ is computationally indistinguishable from (H_s, u), where $H_s \leftarrow \mathcal{H}_{\mathsf{uow}}, x \leftarrow \{0,1\}^{k_1}$, and $u \leftarrow \{0,1\}^k$. Thus, it is easy to see that Game 0 and Game 1 are computationally indistinguishable. Moreover, it is easy to verify that there exists an adversary $\mathcal{A}_{\mathsf{ow}}$ breaking one-wayness of H_s whose advantage is equivalent to $\Pr[\mathcal{A}$ wins Game 1]. Now, the lemma follows. □

$$\underline{\mathsf{Expt}_{\mathsf{MAC},\mathcal{A}}^{\mathrm{seuf\text{-}ot\text{-}cma}}(\kappa)} \qquad\qquad \underline{\mathsf{Expt}_{\mathsf{MAC},\mathcal{A}}^{\mathrm{os},b}(\kappa)}$$

$r \leftarrow \{0,1\}^{\kappa}, (\mu,\sigma) \leftarrow (\bot,\bot)$	$r \leftarrow \{0,1\}^{\kappa}$
$(\mu^*,\sigma^*) \leftarrow \mathcal{A}^{\mathrm{TAG}(\cdot)}(1^{\kappa})$	$(\mu^*, st) \leftarrow \mathcal{A}_0(1^{\kappa})$
$d \leftarrow \mathsf{V}(r,\mu^*,\sigma^*)$	$\sigma_0 \leftarrow \mathsf{T}(r,\mu^*)$
$p \leftarrow \mathrm{boole}((\mu,\sigma) \neq (\mu^*,\sigma^*))$	$\rho_0 \leftarrow \mathsf{Expl}_{\mathsf{MAC}}(\sigma_0)$
return $p \wedge d$	$\rho_1 \leftarrow \mathcal{R}_{\mathsf{Rnd}_{\mathsf{MAC}}}$
	$\sigma_1 \leftarrow \mathsf{Rnd}_{\mathsf{MAC}}(1^{\kappa}; \rho_1)$
$\underline{\mathrm{TAG}(\mu)}$	$b' \leftarrow \mathcal{A}_1(1^{\kappa}, (\sigma_b, \rho_b), st)$
if $\sigma \neq \bot$ **then return** $\bot$	**return** b'
else $\sigma \leftarrow \mathsf{T}(r,\mu)$	
return σ	

Fig. 4. Games for MAC schemes

2.4   Message Authentication Code (MAC)

The model for MAC is summarized as follows:

Definition 2.10. *A* MAC *scheme* MAC *consists of the following pair of polynomial-time algorithms* (T,V):

- $\mathsf{T}(r,\mu) \to \sigma$: *a tagging algorithm that takes on input* $r \in \{0,1\}^{\kappa}$ *and a message* $\mu \in \{0,1\}^*$, *where* κ *is the security parameter, and outputs a tag* σ.
- $\mathsf{V}(r,\mu,\sigma) \to \top/\bot$: *a verification algorithm that takes as input* r, μ, *and a tag* σ, *and outputs* $\top$ *as "acceptance" or* $\bot$ *as "rejection."*

Definition 2.11 (Correctness). *We say* MAC $= (\mathsf{T},\mathsf{V})$ *has* perfect correctness *if for any* $r \in \{0,1\}^{\kappa}$ *and* $\mu \in \{0,1\}^*$, *we have*

$$\Pr[\sigma \leftarrow \mathsf{T}(r,\mu) : \mathsf{V}(r,\mu,\sigma) = \top] = 1.$$

We define strong existential-unforgeability against one-time chosen-message attack. In addition, we define oblivious sampleability by using $\mathsf{Rnd}_{\mathsf{MAC}}$ and $\mathsf{Expl}_{\mathsf{MAC}}$.

Definition 2.12. *For any adversary* $\mathcal{A}$, *we define its advantages against a MAC scheme* MAC $= (\mathsf{T},\mathsf{V})$ *and two PPT algorithms* $(\mathsf{Rnd}_{\mathsf{MAC}}, \mathsf{Expl}_{\mathsf{MAC}})$ *as follows:*

$$\mathsf{Adv}_{\mathsf{MAC},\mathcal{A}}^{\mathrm{seuf\text{-}ot\text{-}cma}}(\kappa) := \Pr[\mathsf{Expt}_{\mathsf{MAC},\mathcal{A}}^{\mathrm{seuf\text{-}ot\text{-}cma}}(\kappa) = 1],$$

$$\mathsf{Adv}_{\mathsf{MAC},\mathcal{A}}^{\mathrm{os}}(\kappa) := \left| \Pr[\mathsf{Expt}_{\mathsf{MAC},\mathcal{A}}^{\mathrm{os},0}(\kappa) = 1] - \Pr[\mathsf{Expt}_{\mathsf{MAC},\mathcal{A}}^{\mathrm{os},1}(\kappa) = 1] \right|,$$

where $\mathsf{Expt}_{\mathsf{MAC},\mathcal{A}}^{\mathrm{seuf\text{-}ot\text{-}cma}}(\kappa)$ *and* $\mathsf{Expt}_{\mathsf{MAC},\mathcal{A}}^{\mathrm{os},b}(\kappa)$, *are the experiments described in Fig. 4.*

We say that MAC *is* sEUF-OT-CMA-*secure and* OS-*secure if* $\mathsf{Adv}_{\mathsf{MAC},\mathcal{A}}^{\mathrm{seuf\text{-}ot\text{-}cma}}(\kappa)$ *and* $\mathsf{Adv}_{\mathsf{MAC},\mathcal{A}}^{\mathrm{os}}(\kappa)$ *is negligible for any PPT adversary* $\mathcal{A}$, *respectively.*

Concrete Construction: It is known that the standard universal hash function provides a one-time secure MAC as follows: Let us identify $\{0,1\}^k$ with $GF(2^k)$. For $a, b \in \{0,1\}^k$, we define $H_{a,b} : \{0,1\}^k \to \{0,1\}^k : \mu \mapsto a\mu + b \in \{0,1\}^k$. Thus, we have an sEUF-OT-CMA-secure MAC scheme unconditionally. Combining with collision-resistant hash function $h : \{0,1\}^* \to \{0,1\}^k$, we can extend the domain of the MAC as we want. Moreover, this extended MAC is OS-secure since the distribution of $\sigma = H_{a,b}(h(\mu))$ is uniform over $\{0,1\}^k$ if $a, b \leftarrow \{0,1\}^k$.

3 The Boneh-Katz Transformation, Revisited

Let us review the Boneh-Katz transformation [9, Sect. 5] for IBE, but we here adapt it for TBE.

Let TBE = $(Gen_{TBE}, Enc_{TBE}, Dec_{TBE})$ be a TBE scheme whose plaintext space is $\mathcal{M}_{TBE} = \mathcal{M} \times \mathcal{D}$ and tag space is $\mathcal{T}$. Let wCom = $(Init, S, R)$ be a weak commitment scheme whose commitment space is $\mathcal{T}$ and decommitment space is $\mathcal{D}$. Let MAC = (T, V) be a MAC scheme. PKE = $(Gen_{PKE}, Enc_{PKE}, Dec_{PKE})$ = BK[TBE, wCom, MAC] is defined as follows:

- $Gen_{PKE}(1^\kappa)$: Generate $(ek_{TBE}, dk_{TBE}) \leftarrow Gen_{TBE}(1^\kappa)$ and $pp \leftarrow Init(1^\kappa)$. Set $ek := (ek_{TBE}, pp)$ and $dk := dk_{TBE}$. Return (ek, dk).
- $Enc_{PKE}(ek, m)$: Compute $(r, com, dec) \leftarrow S(1^\kappa, pp)$. Compute $c \leftarrow Enc_{TBE}(ek_{TBE}, com, (m, dec))$ and $\sigma \leftarrow T(r, c)$. Set $ct := (com, c, \sigma)$. Return **return** ct.
- $Dec_{PKE}(dk, ct)$: Parse $ct = (com, c, \sigma)$. Compute $(m, dec) \leftarrow Dec_{TBE}(dk_{TBE}, com, c)$. If $(m, dec) = \perp$, then return $\perp$. Compute $r \leftarrow R(pp, com, dec)$. If $r = \perp$, then return $\perp$. If $V(r, c, \sigma) = \perp$, then return $\perp$. Otherwise return m.

Table 1. Summary of Games for the Proof of Theorem 3.1: Expl implies ρ_X^* is generated by $Expl_X$. Rand implies ρ_X^* is chosen from $\mathcal{R}_{Rand_X}$ and a part of ct is generated by $Rand_X$.

Game	,*	c^*	σ^*	ρ_{wCom}^*	ρ_{TBE}^*	ρ_{MAC}^*	DEC	When ,* is generated
Game$_0$	Real	Real	$T(r^*, c^*)$	Expl	Expl	Expl	Original	Original
Game$_1$	Real	Real	$T(r^*, c^*)$	Expl	Expl	Expl	Original	At the beginning
Game$_2$	Real	Real	$T(r^*, c^*)$	Expl	Expl	Expl	Reject if ,=,*	At the beginning
Game$_3$	Real	Rand	$T(r^*, c^*)$	Expl	Rand	Expl	Reject if ,=,*	At the beginning
Game$_4$	Real	Rand	$T(r^+, c^*)$	Expl	Rand	Expl	Reject if ,=,*	At the beginning
Game$_5$	Real	Rand	Rand	Expl	Rand	Rand	Reject if ,=,*	At the beginning
Game$_6$	Rand	Rand	Rand	Rand	Rand	Rand	Reject if ,=,*	At the beginning
Game$_7$	Rand	Rand	Rand	Rand	Rand	Rand	Original	Original

Adjusting the security proof in [9], we can show that PKE is IND-CCA secure if TBE is IND-sID-CPA secure, wCom is secure, and MAC is sEUF-OT-CMA secure, as noted (but not proven) in Kiltz [31, Sect. 4].

We here show that PKE is OS-CCA-secure if the underlying primitives are OS-CCA-secure. The proof is easily adapted into the PR-CCA case.

Theorem 3.1. *If* TBE *is* OS-ST-wCCA-*secure,* wCom *is secure and OS-secure, and* MAC *is* sEUF-OT-CMA-*secure and OS-secure, then,* PKE *is* OS-CCA-*secure.*

We use the game-hopping proof. We will define eight games $\mathsf{Game}_0, \ldots, \mathsf{Game}_7$. See Table 1 for the summary of games. Let S_i denote the event that the adversary outputs $b' = 1$ in the i-th game Game_i for $i = 0, 1, \ldots, 7$. Let Q denote the number of decryption queries the adversary makes. The proofs of Lemmas 3.1–3.7 (the bound between Game_0 and Game_4) are straightforward adaption of those in Boneh and Katz [10]. Due to space limitations, we omit the proofs for lemmas. See the full version [49] of this paper for the proofs.

Game_0: This is the original game for $b = 0$. The challenge is

$$ct_0^* = (com^*, c^*, \sigma^*) = \left(com^*, \mathsf{Enc}_{\mathsf{TBE}}(ek_{\mathsf{TBE}}, com^*, (m^*, dec^*)), \mathsf{T}(r^*, c^*) \right),$$

$$\rho_0^* = (\rho_{\mathsf{wCom}}^*, \rho_{\mathsf{TBE}}^*, \rho_{\mathsf{MAC}}^*) = \left(\mathsf{Expl}_{\mathsf{wCom}}(pp, com^*), \mathsf{Expl}_{\mathsf{TBE}}(ek_{\mathsf{TBE}}, c^*), \mathsf{Expl}_{\mathsf{MAC}}(1^\kappa, \sigma^*) \right),$$

where $(r^*, com^*, dec^*) \leftarrow \mathsf{S}(1^\kappa, pp)$. We have $\Pr[S_0] = \Pr[\mathsf{Expt}_{\mathsf{PKE},\mathcal{A}}^{\text{os-cca},0} = 1]$. Game_1: We modify the game as follows: In this game, the challenger generates $pp \leftarrow \mathsf{Init}(1^\kappa)$, $(r^*, com^*, dec^*) \leftarrow \mathsf{S}(pp)$, and $(ek_{\mathsf{TBE}}, dk_{\mathsf{TBE}}) \leftarrow \mathsf{Gen}_{\mathsf{TBE}}(1^\kappa)$. It then runs the adversary on input $ek = (ek_{\mathsf{TBE}}, pp)$.

Since, this change is just conceptual, the two games are equivalent.

Lemma 3.1. *We have* $\Pr[S_0] = \Pr[S_1]$.

Game_2: We modify Game_1 as follows: The decryption oracle always rejects a query $ct = (com, c, \sigma)$ if $com = com^*$.

We define Valid as the event that $\mathcal{A}$ submits a query $ct = (com^*, c, \sigma) \neq ct^*$ which is valid, that is, the decryption result is not $\perp$. Since Game_1 and Game_2 are equivalent until Valid occurs, we have the following lemma.

Lemma 3.2. *We have* $|\Pr[S_1] - \Pr[S_2]| \leq \Pr[\mathsf{Valid}_1] = \Pr[\mathsf{Valid}_2]$.

Let us decompose Valid into two events:

- We define NoBind as the event that $\mathcal{A}$ queries a ciphertext $ct = (com^*, c, \sigma)$ such that $(m', dec') \leftarrow \mathsf{Dec}_{\mathsf{TBE}}(dk_{\mathsf{TBE}}, com^*, c)$, $r \leftarrow \mathsf{R}(pp, com^*, dec')$, and $r \notin \{r^*, \perp\}$.
- We also define Forge as the event that $\mathcal{A}$ queries $ct = (com^*, c, \sigma)$ such that $(c, \sigma) \neq (c^*, \sigma^*)$ and $\mathsf{V}(r^*, c, \sigma) = \top$.

Clearly, we have the following lemma:

Lemma 3.3. *We have* $\Pr[\mathsf{Valid}_2] \leq \Pr[\mathsf{NoBind}_2] + \Pr[\mathsf{Forge}_2]$.

We show that the adversary making NoBind_2 true breaks the binding property of wCom.

Lemma 3.4. *There exists a PPT adversary* $\mathcal{A}_{\mathsf{wCom}}$ *satisfying* $\Pr[\mathsf{NoBind}_2] \leq$ $\mathsf{Adv}^{\mathrm{binding}}_{\mathsf{wCom},\mathcal{A}_{\mathsf{wCom}}}(\kappa).$

Game$_3$: We modify Game$_2$ as follows: In this game, the challenge ciphertext is

$$ct^* = (com^*, c^*, \sigma^*) = \Big(com^*, \mathsf{Rnd}_{\mathsf{TBE}}(ek_{\mathsf{TBE}}, 0^{|m|+|dec^*|}; \rho^*_{\mathsf{TBE}}), \mathsf{T}(r^*, c^*)\Big),$$

$$\rho^* = (\rho^*_{\mathsf{wCom}}, \rho^*_{\mathsf{TBE}}, \rho^*_{\mathsf{MAC}}) = \Big(\mathsf{Expl}_{\mathsf{wCom}}(com^*), \rho^*_{\mathsf{TBE}}, \mathsf{Expl}_{\mathsf{MAC}}(\sigma^*)\Big).$$

We have the following lemmas.

Lemma 3.5. *There exists a PPT adversary* $\mathcal{A}_{\mathsf{TBE}}$ *satisfying* $|\Pr[S_2] - \Pr[S_3]| \leq$ $\mathsf{Adv}^{\mathrm{os\text{-}st\text{-}wcca}}_{\mathsf{TBE},\mathcal{A}_{\mathsf{TBE}}}(\kappa).$

Lemma 3.6. *There   exists   a   PPT   adversary* $\mathcal{A}'_{\mathsf{TBE}}$ *satisfying* $|\Pr[\mathsf{Forge}_2] - \Pr[\mathsf{Forge}_3]| \leq \mathsf{Adv}^{\mathrm{os\text{-}st\text{-}wcca}}_{\mathsf{TBE},\mathcal{A}'_{\mathsf{TBE}}}(\kappa).$

Game$_4$: We modify Game$_3$ as follows: In this game, the challenge ciphertext is

$$ct^* = (com^*, c^*, \sigma^*) = \Big(com^*, \mathsf{Rnd}_{\mathsf{TBE}}(ek_{\mathsf{TBE}}, 0^{|m|+|dec^*|}; \rho^*_{\mathsf{TBE}}), \mathsf{T}(r^+, c^*)\Big),$$

$$\rho^* = (\rho^*_{\mathsf{wCom}}, \rho^*_{\mathsf{TBE}}, \rho^*_{\mathsf{MAC}}) = \Big(\mathsf{Expl}_{\mathsf{wCom}}(com^*), \rho^*_{\mathsf{TBE}}, \mathsf{Expl}_{\mathsf{MAC}}(\sigma^*)\Big),$$

where $r^+ \leftarrow \{0,1\}^\kappa$.

We define Forge_4 as the event that $\mathcal{A}$ queries $ct = (com^*, c, \sigma)$ such that $(c,\sigma) \neq (c^*, \sigma^*)$ and $\mathsf{V}(r^+, c, \sigma) = \top$ (instead of $\mathsf{V}(r^*, c, \sigma) = \top$). We have the following lemmas.

Lemma 3.7. *There exists a PPT adversary* $\mathcal{A}'_{\mathsf{wCom}}$ *satisfying* $|\Pr[S_3] - \Pr[S_4]| \leq$ $\mathsf{Adv}^{\mathrm{hiding}}_{\mathsf{wCom},\mathcal{A}'_{\mathsf{wCom}}}(\kappa).$

Lemma 3.8. *There   exists   a   PPT   adversary* $\mathcal{A}''_{\mathsf{wCom}}$ *satisfying* $|\Pr[\mathsf{Forge}_3] - \Pr[\mathsf{Forge}_4]| \leq \mathsf{Adv}^{\mathrm{hiding}}_{\mathsf{wCom},\mathcal{A}''_{\mathsf{wCom}}}(\kappa).$

Lemma 3.9. *There exists a PPT adversary* $\mathcal{A}_{\mathsf{MAC}}$ *satisfying* $\Pr[\mathsf{Forge}_4] \leq Q \cdot$ $\mathsf{Adv}^{\mathrm{seuf\text{-}ot\text{-}cma}}_{\mathsf{MAC},\mathcal{A}_{\mathsf{MAC}}}(\kappa).$

Game$_5$: We modify Game$_4$ as follows: In this game, the challenge ciphertext is

$$ct^* = (com^*, c^*, \sigma^*) = \Big(com^*, \mathsf{Rnd}_{\mathsf{TBE}}(ek_{\mathsf{TBE}}, 0^{|m|+|dec^*|}; \rho^*_{\mathsf{TBE}}), \mathsf{Rnd}_{\mathsf{MAC}}(1^\kappa; \rho^*_{\mathsf{MAC}})\Big),$$

$$\rho^* = (\rho^*_{\mathsf{wCom}}, \rho^*_{\mathsf{TBE}}, \rho^*_{\mathsf{MAC}}) = \Big(\mathsf{Expl}_{\mathsf{wCom}}(com^*), \rho^*_{\mathsf{TBE}}, \rho^*_{\mathsf{MAC}}\Big)$$

We have the following lemma.

Lemma 3.10. *There exists a PPT adversary* $\mathcal{A}'_{\mathsf{MAC}}$ *satisfying* $|\Pr[S_4] - \Pr[S_5]| \leq$ $\mathsf{Adv}^{\mathrm{os}}_{\mathsf{MAC},\mathcal{A}'_{\mathsf{MAC}}}(\kappa).$

Game$_6$: We modify Game$_5$ as follows: In this game, the challenge ciphertext is

$$ct^* = (com^*, c^*, \sigma^*) = \Big(\mathsf{Rnd}_{\mathsf{wCom}}(pp; \rho^*_{\mathsf{wCom}}), \mathsf{Rnd}_{\mathsf{TBE}}(ek_{\mathsf{TBE}}, 0^{|m|+|dec^*|}; \rho^*_{\mathsf{TBE}}), \mathsf{Rnd}_{\mathsf{MAC}}(1^\kappa; \rho^*_{\mathsf{MAC}}) \Big),$$

$$\rho^* = (\rho^*_{\mathsf{wCom}}, \rho^*_{\mathsf{TBE}}, \rho^*_{\mathsf{MAC}}).$$

We have the following lemma.

Lemma 3.11. *There exists a PPT adversary $\mathcal{A}'''_{\mathsf{wCom}}$ satisfying* $|\Pr[S_5] - \Pr[S_6]| \le \mathsf{Adv}^{\mathsf{os}}_{\mathsf{wCom}, \mathcal{A}'''_{\mathsf{wCom}}}(\kappa)$.

Game$_7$: We modify Game$_6$ as follows: In this game, the challenger generates $(ek_{\mathsf{TBE}}, dk_{\mathsf{TBE}}) \leftarrow \mathsf{Gen}_{\mathsf{TBE}}(1^\kappa)$, $pp \leftarrow \mathsf{Init}(1^\kappa)$ and runs the adversary with $ek = (ek_{\mathsf{TBE}}, pp)$. It generates $com^* \leftarrow \mathsf{Rnd}_{\mathsf{wCom}}(pp)$ when it generates the challenge ciphertext as in Game$_0$. The decryption oracle decrypts a query $ct = (com^*, c, \sigma)$ if $(c, \sigma) \ne (c^*, \sigma^*)$ as in Game$_0$.

By the definition, we have $\Pr[S_7] = \Pr[\mathsf{Expt}^{\mathsf{os\text{-}cca},1}_{\mathsf{PKE}, \mathcal{A}}(\kappa) = 1]$.

We again recall the event Valid that the adversary queries a valid ciphertext $ct = (com^*, c, \sigma)$ with $(c, \sigma) \ne (c^*, \sigma^*)$. Since Game$_6$ and Game$_7$ are equivalent until Valid occurs, we have the following lemma:

Lemma 3.12. *We have* $|\Pr[S_6] - \Pr[S_7]| \le \Pr[\mathsf{Valid}_6] = \Pr[\mathsf{Valid}_7]$.

Let us consider what is a valid ciphertext. If (com^*, c, σ) is valid, we have $(m, dec) \leftarrow \mathsf{Dec}_{\mathsf{TBE}}(dk_{\mathsf{TBE}}, com^*, c)$ with $(m, dec) \ne \bot$, $r \leftarrow \mathsf{R}(pp, com^*, dec)$ with $r \ne \bot$, and $\mathsf{V}(r, c, \sigma) = \top$ in decryption.

We define an event Inv as the event that we have $r \ne \bot$ in decryption. Notice that if Valid occurs, then Inv should occur internally. Thus, we have $\Pr[\mathsf{Valid}_7] \le \Pr[\mathsf{Inv}_7]$. We also have the following lemma.

Lemma 3.13. *There exists a PPT adversary $\mathcal{A}''''_{\mathsf{wCom}}$ satisfying* $\Pr[\mathsf{Valid}_7] \le \Pr[\mathsf{Inv}_7] \le \mathsf{Adv}^{\mathsf{non\text{-}inv}}_{\mathsf{wCom}, \mathcal{A}''''_{\mathsf{wCom}}}(\kappa)$.

Summary: Summing up the bounds in the previous lemmas, we obtain Theorem 3.1:

4 Instantiations and Applications

Instantiations: We have several lattice/code-based IBE/TBE schemes allowing us to construct OS-CCA/PR-CCA-secure PKE schemes by combining them with an appropriate commitment scheme and MAC scheme from symmetric-key primitives.

From Lattices: The CHKP IBE scheme [16], the ABB IBE scheme [1], the MP TBE scheme [39], and the BBDQ TBE scheme [6] from lattices are PR-ST-wCCA-secure under the LWE assumptions with suitable parameter settings. Moreover, their ciphertext spaces are of the form $\mathbb{Z}_q^k$ for positive integers q and k and, thus, the ciphertext spaces are ESE.

From Codes: The DMQN09 TBE scheme [22] and the DMQN12 TBE scheme [21] are also PR-ST-wCCA-secure under the assumption that their keys are pseudorandom and the LPN assumptions. Their ciphertext spaces are of the form $\mathbb{F}_2^k$ for positive integer k and, thus, the ciphertext spaces are ESE.

The KMP TBE scheme [32] and the YZ TBE scheme [51] are IND-ST-wCCA-secure under the assumption that the low-noise LPN problem is hard and the assumption that the constant-noise LPN problem is sub-exponentially hard, respectively. Fortunately, we can show that they are PR-ST-wCCA-secure under the same assumptions.

Fully-Equipped, UC-secure Bit Commitment: Canetti and Fischlin [14] constructed a UC-secure non-interactive bit commitment for adaptive corruption without erasures in the re-usable CRS model from trapdoor commitment (as known as chameleon hash function [35]) and OS-CCA-secure PKE.

We have a trapdoor commitment scheme from lattices [16]. Combining it with OS-CCA-secure PKE scheme from lattice, we obtain fully-equipped, UC-secure bit commitment under the LWE assumption.

Unfortunately, we do not know any non-interactive trapdoor commitment scheme from codes/LPN and this is a long-standing open problem. The construction of fully-equipped UC-secure commitment from codes/LPN is still an open problem, although we have *interactive* UC-secure commitment from LPN, for example, one obtained by combining UC-secure commitment in the OT-hybrid model [15] and 2-round OT from LPN [20].

Public-Key Steganography: Hopper [28] gave a construction of public-key steganography secure against adaptive chosen-covertext attacks (SS-CCA-security) for a single channel from SPR-CCA-secure PKE. Berndt and Liśkiewicz [7] improved the existing constructions to achieve SS-CCA-secure public-key steganography for every memoryless channel from SPR-CCA-secure PKE, PRPs, and CRHFs.

Since we have SPR-CCA-secure PKE from lattices and codes, we obtain SS-CCA-secure public-key steganography from lattices and codes through [7,28].

Anonymous AKE: KEM-based AKEs [11,24,25,47] can achieve anonymity. Such AKEs employ IND-CCA-secure KEM and IND-CPA-secure KEM. Roughly speaking, the first message from Alice is $pk_{\mathrm{tmp}}, ct_{A \to B} = \mathsf{Enc}_{\mathsf{cca}}(pk_B)$ and the second message from Bob is $ct_{\mathrm{tmp}} = \mathsf{Enc}_{\mathsf{cpa}}(pk_{\mathrm{tmp}}), ct_{B \to A} = \mathsf{Enc}_{\mathsf{cca}}(pk_A)$. Thus, if the ciphertexts of IND-CCA-secure KEM are pseudorandom, then the AKE is anonymous from the outsider's view.

SIM-SSO-CCA PKE: Following and repairing Fehr, Hofheinz, Kiltz, and Wee [23], Liu and Paterson [36] constructed a SIM-SSO-CCA secure PKE scheme using a special KEM scheme, which they call "tailored" KEM; roughly speaking, they required the following properties: 1) *ESE domains:* the key space and ciphertext space are efficiently samplable and explainable (ESE), 2) *tailored decapsulation:* the valid ciphertexts should be a small subset of ciphertext space, and 3) *tailored security:* it should satisfy tailored, constrained CCA security, which is weaker than IND-CCA security.

It is easy to convert OS-CCA-secure PKE scheme into OS-CCA-secure KEM scheme if the message space is ESE; choosing a key $K \leftarrow \mathcal{M}$ and encrypting it as $C = \mathsf{Enc}_{\mathsf{PKE}}(ek, K; \rho)$. We note that the OS-CCA-secure PKE scheme obtained by the BK transformation satisfies the tailored decapsulation since its ciphertext contains a MAC tag. Thus, following [36], OS-CCA-secure PKE (with an ESE key space) implies SIM-SSO-CCA secure PKE. Instantiating OS-CCA-secure from lattices and codes, we obtain SIM-SSO-CCA-secure PKEs in the standard model from lattice and codes, respectively.

References

1. Agrawal, S., Boneh, D., Boyen, X.: Efficient lattice (H)IBE in the standard model. In: Gilbert, H. (ed.) EUROCRYPT 2010. LNCS, vol. 6110, pp. 553–572. Springer, Heidelberg (2010). https://doi.org/10.1007/978-3-642-13190-5_28

2. Ajtai, M.: Generating hard instances of lattice problems (extended abstract). In: 28th ACM STOC, pp. 99–108, May 1996

3. Augot, D., Finiasz, M., Sendrier, N.: A family of fast syndrome based cryptographic hash functions. In: Dawson, E., Vaudenay, S. (eds.) Mycrypt 2005. LNCS, vol. 3715, pp. 64–83. Springer, Heidelberg (2005). https://doi.org/10.1007/11554868_6

4. Bellare, M., Boldyreva, A., Desai, A., Pointcheval, D.: Key-privacy in public-key encryption. In: Boyd, C. (ed.) ASIACRYPT 2001. LNCS, vol. 2248, pp. 566–582. Springer, Heidelberg (2001). https://doi.org/10.1007/3-540-45682-1_33

5. Bellare, M., Desai, A., Pointcheval, D., Rogaway, P.: Relations among notions of security for public-key encryption schemes. In: Krawczyk, H. (ed.) CRYPTO 1998. LNCS, vol. 1462, pp. 26–45. Springer, Heidelberg (1998). https://doi.org/10.1007/BFb0055718

6. Benhamouda, F., Blazy, O., Ducas, L., Quach, W.: Hash proof systems over lattices revisited. In: Abdalla, M., Dahab, R. (eds.) PKC 2018. LNCS, vol. 10770, pp. 644–674. Springer, Cham (2018). https://doi.org/10.1007/978-3-319-76581-5_22

7. Berndt, S., Liśkiewicz, M.: On the gold standard for security of universal steganography. In: Nielsen, J.B., Rijmen, V. (eds.) EUROCRYPT 2018. LNCS, vol. 10820, pp. 29–60. Springer, Cham (2018). https://doi.org/10.1007/978-3-319-78381-9_2

8. Blum, M.: Coin flipping by telephone. In: CRYPTO 1981, vol. ECE Report 82-04, pp. 11–15 (1981)

9. Boneh, D., Canetti, R., Halevi, S., Katz, J.: Chosen-ciphertext security from identity-based encryption. SIAM J. Comput. **36**(5), 1301–1328 (2007)

10. Boneh, D., Katz, J.: Improved efficiency for CCA-secure cryptosystems built using identity-based encryption. In: Menezes, A. (ed.) CT-RSA 2005. LNCS, vol. 3376, pp. 87–103. Springer, Heidelberg (2005). https://doi.org/10.1007/978-3-540-30574-3_8

11. Boyd, C., Cliff, Y., González Nieto, J.M., Paterson, K.G.: One-round key exchange in the standard model. Int. J. Appl. Cryptogr. **1**(3), 181–199 (2009)

12. Brakerski, Z., Lyubashevsky, V., Vaikuntanathan, V., Wichs, D.: Worst-case hardness for LPN and cryptographic hashing via code smoothing. In: Ishai, Y., Rijmen,

V. (eds.) EUROCRYPT 2019. LNCS, vol. 11478, pp. 619–635. Springer, Cham (2019). https://doi.org/10.1007/978-3-030-17659-4_21

13. Camenisch, J., Lysyanskaya, A.: An efficient system for non-transferable anonymous credentials with optional anonymity revocation. In: Pfitzmann, B. (ed.) EUROCRYPT 2001. LNCS, vol. 2045, pp. 93–118. Springer, Heidelberg (2001). https://doi.org/10.1007/3-540-44987-6_7

14. Canetti, R., Fischlin, M.: Universally composable commitments. In: Kilian, J. (ed.) CRYPTO 2001. LNCS, vol. 2139, pp. 19–40. Springer, Heidelberg (2001). https://doi.org/10.1007/3-540-44647-8_2

15. Cascudo, I., Damgård, I., David, B., Döttling, N., Nielsen, J.B.: Rate-1, linear time and additively homomorphic UC commitments. In: Robshaw, M., Katz, J. (eds.) CRYPTO 2016. LNCS, vol. 9816, pp. 179–207. Springer, Heidelberg (2016). https://doi.org/10.1007/978-3-662-53015-3_7

16. Cash, D., Hofheinz, D., Kiltz, E., Peikert, C.: Bonsai trees, or how to delegate a lattice basis. J. Cryptol. 25(4), 601–639 (2012)

17. Cramer, R., Shoup, V.: A practical public key cryptosystem provably secure against adaptive chosen ciphertext attack. In: Krawczyk, H. (ed.) CRYPTO 1998. LNCS, vol. 1462, pp. 13–25. Springer, Heidelberg (1998). https://doi.org/10.1007/BFb0055717

18. Damgård, I., Nielsen, J.B.: Improved non-committing encryption schemes based on a general complexity assumption. In: Bellare, M. (ed.) CRYPTO 2000. LNCS, vol. 1880, pp. 432–450. Springer, Heidelberg (2000). https://doi.org/10.1007/3-540-44598-6_27

19. Dodis, Y., Ganesh, C., Golovnev, A., Juels, A., Ristenpart, T.: A formal treatment of backdoored pseudorandom generators. In: Oswald, E., Fischlin, M. (eds.) EUROCRYPT 2015. LNCS, vol. 9056, pp. 101–126. Springer, Heidelberg (2015). https://doi.org/10.1007/978-3-662-46800-5_5

20. Döttling, N., Garg, S., Hajiabadi, M., Masny, D., Wichs, D.: Two-round oblivious transfer from CDH or LPN. In: Canteaut, A., Ishai, Y. (eds.) EUROCRYPT 2020. LNCS, vol. 12106, pp. 768–797. Springer, Cham (2020). https://doi.org/10.1007/978-3-030-45724-2_26

21. Döttling, N., Müller-Quade, J., Nascimento, A.C.A.: IND-CCA secure cryptography based on a variant of the LPN problem. In: Wang, X., Sako, K. (eds.) ASIACRYPT 2012. LNCS, vol. 7658, pp. 485–503. Springer, Heidelberg (2012). https://doi.org/10.1007/978-3-642-34961-4_30

22. Dowsley, R., Müller-Quade, J., Nascimento, A.C.A.: A CCA2 secure public key encryption scheme based on the McEliece assumptions in the standard model. In: Fischlin, M. (ed.) CT-RSA 2009. LNCS, vol. 5473, pp. 240–251. Springer, Heidelberg (2009). https://doi.org/10.1007/978-3-642-00862-7_16

23. Fehr, S., Hofheinz, D., Kiltz, E., Wee, H.: Encryption schemes secure against chosen-ciphertext selective opening attacks. In: Gilbert, H. (ed.) EUROCRYPT 2010. LNCS, vol. 6110, pp. 381–402. Springer, Heidelberg (2010). https://doi.org/10.1007/978-3-642-13190-5_20

24. Fujioka, A., Suzuki, K., Xagawa, K., Yoneyama, K.: Practical and post-quantum authenticated key exchange from one-way secure key encapsulation mechanism. In: ASIACCS 2013, pp. 83–94. ACM Press, May 2013

25. Fujioka, A., Suzuki, K., Xagawa, K., Yoneyama, K.: Strongly secure authenticated key exchange from factoring, codes, and lattices. Des. Codes Crypt. 76(3), 469–504 (2014). https://doi.org/10.1007/s10623-014-9972-2

26. Goldreich, O., Goldwasser, S., Halevi, S.: Collision-free hashing from lattice problems. Cryptology ePrint Archive, Report 1996/009 (1996). https://eprint.iacr.org/1996/009

27. Goldwasser, S., Micali, S.: Probabilistic encryption. J. Comput. Syst. Sci. **28**(2), 270–299 (1984)

28. Hopper, N.: On steganographic chosen covertext security. In: Caires, L., Italiano, G.F., Monteiro, L., Palamidessi, C., Yung, M. (eds.) ICALP 2005. LNCS, vol. 3580, pp. 311–323. Springer, Heidelberg (2005). https://doi.org/10.1007/11523468_26

29. Horel, T., Park, S., Richelson, S., Vaikuntanathan, V.: How to subvert backdoored encryption: security against adversaries that decrypt all ciphertexts. In: ITCS 2019. LIPIcs, vol. 124, pp. 42:1–42:20, January 2019

30. Ishai, Y., Kumarasubramanian, A., Orlandi, C., Sahai, A.: On invertible sampling and adaptive security. In: Abe, M. (ed.) ASIACRYPT 2010. LNCS, vol. 6477, pp. 466–482. Springer, Heidelberg (2010). https://doi.org/10.1007/978-3-642-17373-8_27

31. Kiltz, E.: Chosen-ciphertext security from tag-based encryption. In: Halevi, S., Rabin, T. (eds.) TCC 2006. LNCS, vol. 3876, pp. 581–600. Springer, Heidelberg (2006). https://doi.org/10.1007/11681878_30

32. Kiltz, E., Masny, D., Pietrzak, K.: Simple chosen-ciphertext security from low-noise LPN. In: Krawczyk, H. (ed.) PKC 2014. LNCS, vol. 8383, pp. 1–18. Springer, Heidelberg (2014). https://doi.org/10.1007/978-3-642-54631-0_1

33. Kitagawa, F., Matsuda, T., Tanaka, K.: CCA security and trapdoor functions via key-dependent-message security. In: Boldyreva, A., Micciancio, D. (eds.) CRYPTO 2019. LNCS, vol. 11694, pp. 33–64. Springer, Cham (2019). https://doi.org/10.1007/978-3-030-26954-8_2

34. Kitagawa, F., Matsuda, T., Tanaka, K.: CCA security and trapdoor functions via key-dependent-message security. Cryptology ePrint Archive, Report 2019/291 (2019). June 2021 version

35. Krawczyk, H., Rabin, T.: Chameleon signatures. In: NDSS 2000, February 2000

36. Liu, S., Paterson, K.G.: Simulation-based selective opening CCA security for pke from key encapsulation mechanisms. In: Katz, J. (ed.) PKC 2015. LNCS, vol. 9020, pp. 3–26. Springer, Heidelberg (2015). https://doi.org/10.1007/978-3-662-46447-2_1

37. MacKenzie, P., Reiter, M.K., Yang, K.: Alternatives to non-malleability: definitions, constructions, and applications. In: Naor, M. (ed.) TCC 2004. LNCS, vol. 2951, pp. 171–190. Springer, Heidelberg (2004). https://doi.org/10.1007/978-3-540-24638-1_10

38. Micciancio, D., Mol, P.: Pseudorandom knapsacks and the sample complexity of LWE search-to-decision reductions. In: Rogaway, P. (ed.) CRYPTO 2011. LNCS, vol. 6841, pp. 465–484. Springer, Heidelberg (2011). https://doi.org/10.1007/978-3-642-22792-9_26

39. Micciancio, D., Peikert, C.: Trapdoors for lattices: simpler, tighter, faster, smaller. In: Pointcheval, D., Johansson, T. (eds.) EUROCRYPT 2012. LNCS, vol. 7237, pp. 700–718. Springer, Heidelberg (2012). https://doi.org/10.1007/978-3-642-29011-4_41

40. Möller, B.: A public-key encryption scheme with pseudo-random ciphertexts. In: Samarati, P., Ryan, P., Gollmann, D., Molva, R. (eds.) ESORICS 2004. LNCS, vol. 3193, pp. 335–351. Springer, Heidelberg (2004). https://doi.org/10.1007/978-3-540-30108-0_21

41. Naor, M., Yung, M.: Universal one-way hash functions and their cryptographic applications. In: STOC 1989, pp. 33–43, May 1989

42. Paterson, K.G., Srinivasan, S.: Security and anonymity of identity-based encryption with multiple trusted authorities. In: Galbraith, S.D., Paterson, K.G. (eds.) Pairing 2008. LNCS, vol. 5209, pp. 354–375. Springer, Heidelberg (2008). https://doi.org/10.1007/978-3-540-85538-5_23

43. Rackoff, C., Simon, D.R.: Non-interactive zero-knowledge proof of knowledge and chosen ciphertext attack. In: Feigenbaum, J. (ed.) CRYPTO 1991. LNCS, vol. 576, pp. 433–444. Springer, Heidelberg (1992). https://doi.org/10.1007/3-540-46766-1_35

44. Regev, O.: On lattices, learning with errors, random linear codes, and cryptography. J. ACM **56**(6), 34:1–34:40 (2009)

45. Sahai, A., Waters, B.: How to use indistinguishability obfuscation: deniable encryption, and more. In: STOC 2014, pp. 475–484, May/June 2014

46. Sako, K.: An auction protocol which hides bids of losers. In: Imai, H., Zheng, Y. (eds.) PKC 2000. LNCS, vol. 1751, pp. 422–432. Springer, Heidelberg (2000). https://doi.org/10.1007/978-3-540-46588-1_28

47. Schwabe, P., Stebila, D., Wiggers, T.: Post-quantum TLS without handshake signatures. In: ACM CCS 2020, pp. 1461–1480 (2020)

48. von Ahn, L., Hopper, N.J.: Public-key steganography. In: Cachin, C., Camenisch, J.L. (eds.) EUROCRYPT 2004. LNCS, vol. 3027, pp. 323–341. Springer, Heidelberg (2004). https://doi.org/10.1007/978-3-540-24676-3_20

49. Xagawa, K.: The Boneh-Katz transformation, revisited: pseudorandom/obliviously-samplable PKE from lattices and codes and its application. Cryptology ePrint Archive, Report 2021/740 (2021). https://eprint.iacr.org/2021/740

50. Yoshida, Y., Morozov, K., Tanaka, K.: CCA2 key-privacy for code-based encryption in the standard model. In: Lange, T., Takagi, T. (eds.) PQCrypto 2017. LNCS, vol. 10346, pp. 35–50. Springer, Cham (2017). https://doi.org/10.1007/978-3-319-59879-6_3

51. Yu, Yu., Zhang, J.: Cryptography with auxiliary input and trapdoor from constant-noise LPN. In: Robshaw, M., Katz, J. (eds.) CRYPTO 2016. LNCS, vol. 9814, pp. 214–243. Springer, Heidelberg (2016). https://doi.org/10.1007/978-3-662-53018-4_9

52. Yu, Yu., Zhang, J., Weng, J., Guo, C., Li, X.: Collision resistant hashing from sub-exponential learning parity with noise. In: Galbraith, S.D., Moriai, S. (eds.) ASIACRYPT 2019. LNCS, vol. 11922, pp. 3–24. Springer, Cham (2019). https://doi.org/10.1007/978-3-030-34621-8_1

ZKAttest: Ring and Group Signatures for Existing ECDSA Keys

Armando Faz-Hernández[1], Watson Ladd[1(✉)], and Deepak Maram[2]

[1] Cloudflare, Inc., San Francisco, USA
armfazh@cloudflare.com, watsonbladd@gmail.com
[2] Cornell Tech, New York, USA
sm2686@cornell.edu

Abstract. Cryptographic keys are increasingly stored in dedicated hardware or behind software interfaces. Doing so limits access, such as permitting only signing via ECDSA. This makes using them in existing ring and group signature schemes impossible as these schemes assume the ability to access the private key for other operations. We present a Σ-protocol that uses a committed public key to verify an ECDSA or Schnorr signature on a message, without revealing the public key. We then discuss how this protocol may be used to derive ring signatures in combination with Groth–Kohlweiss membership proofs and other applications. This scheme has been implemented and source code is freely available.

Keywords: Ring signature · Zero-knowledge proof · Σ-protocol

1 Introduction

A *ring signature* scheme allows a signer to sign a message without revealing their identity, thereby providing anonymity behind a ring. A verifier can check the validity of the signature, but cannot know who among the ring members generated the signature. This notion was introduced by Rivest *et al.* [28]. For example, a whistleblower belonging to an organization could reveal sensitive documents using a ring of all members within the organization, demonstrating the authenticity of their claim to be a member while still remaining anonymous.

Existing schemes typically presuppose that every member of the ring has ready access to a suitable key. But establishing such keys across a large group of members purely for the purpose of whistleblowing may attract unwanted attention. Furthermore it is unlikely that organizations would cooperate in issuing keys for use with ring signatures. This problem can be avoided if a ring signature could use *already existing keys*, such as those stored in a hardware security module. A ring signature scheme would then be usable without requiring changes to the hardware or the distribution of new keys across an organization.

For example, WebAuthn [21], a popular standard for hardware authenticators, provides support only for signing messages through a standardized algorithm such as ECDSA [23]. These signatures, and the certificate chain that shows

R. AlTawy and A. Hülsing (Eds.): SAC 2021, LNCS 13203, pp. 68–83, 2022.
https://doi.org/10.1007/978-3-030-99277-4_4

the authenticity of the public key, reveal which authenticator was used when carrying out attestation, creating a trade-off between confidence in authentication and privacy. Changing the install base of such modules to enhance privacy, for example by supporting an existing ring signature scheme, will take years. Therefore a privacy enhancing form of WebAuthn attestation that works with existing keys is highly desirable: this is the core motivation for ZKAttest.

The core primitive in ZKAttest is *proof of valid ECDSA signature under a committed public key*. A verifier can check signature validity by verifying this proof but learns nothing about the public key, thanks to the hiding commitment. Zero–knowledge proofs then enable us to show additional properties of the public key. For instance we can show that C is a commitment to a value on a public list of keys, thereby producing a ring signature.

Outline. Section 2 contains definitions and recalls facts about Σ-protocols, Pedersen commitments, ring signatures and other things we use. Section 3 lists parameters of the groups used. Section 4 discusses proofs of point addition that we then use in Sect. 5 to prove knowledge of scalar multiplications. We then apply these scalar multiplication proofs to proof of signature under a committed key in Sect. 6, and use that proof to derive ring and group signatures in Sect. 7. We discuss an implementation and application to WebAuthn privacy in Sect. 8.

2   Preliminaries

We will write G for the group of points on an elliptic curve and $g, h, g_1, g_2, \ldots$ be generators of the group. In our construction, we will use two different sets of elliptic curves, and pick one from each. One set, denoted G_{NIST} are standardized elliptic curves, and the other G_{Tom} is a set of elliptic curves such that the group order equals the size of the base field of G_{NIST}.

We write $com(x; r) = xg + rh$ to denote the computation of a Pedersen commitment to x with randomness r. Pedersen commitments are unconditionally hiding, computationally binding, and additively homomorphic [26].

We recall some basic Σ-protocols and their definition and properties [12,16]. A protocol is a Σ-protocol if it is a three round protocol satisfying Special Honest-Verifier Zero-Knowledge (SHVZK) and Special soundness. SHVZK implies that we are able to sample from the distribution of transcripts without any knowledge of the witness. Special soundness means given several transcripts with identical commitment phases and different challenges a witness can be extracted.

Σ-protocols compose in parallel. In this paper we apply this result to prove multiple properties of a common set of commitments, without being forced to spell out each proof. Given commitments $C_1 = xg + r_1h$, $C_2 = yg + r_2h$, and a commitment C_3 to the sum, product, difference, or quotient of x and y, there is a Σ-protocol that proves that C_3 is in fact a commitment to the sum, product, difference, or quotient of x and y. Σ-protocols can be combined to prove that two statements are simultaneously true, or that one of two statements is true [14].

From a Σ-protocol we can apply the Fiat-Shamir transform to achieve a *non-interactive zero-knowledge proof* (NIZK) [6,9]. The security definitions of a NIZK in the random oracle model (ROM) involve the existence of a simulator, that can interact with a verifier and produce true seeming proofs by programming the oracle, and an extractor, that interacts with a prover and obtains witnesses.

We recall ring signatures following definitions given by Bender, Katz, and Morselli [8]. Intuitively ring signatures permit signers to hide among a group of their choice, generating only a proof that one among the ring singed without revealing who. Ideally even if all members of the ring have their private keys exposed, the signer will not be discovered. Thus in addition to unforgeability we have a requirement of anonymity.

Definition 2.1. *A ring signature scheme is a triple of algorithms* (**Gen**, **Sign**, **Verify**) *such that* **Gen**(1^k) *outputs keys* (sk, pk), **Sign**(m, sk_i, R) *produces a signature* σ *on the message* m *with respect to the ring* $R = \{pk_1, \ldots, pk_n\}$, *and* **Verify**$(\sigma, m, R)$ *accepts or rejects the signature.*

Definition 2.2. *A ring signature scheme is* complete *if* **Verify** *accepts when run on signatures generated by* **Sign**.

Definition 2.3. *A ring signature scheme is* anonymous against full key exposure *if the adversarial advantage in the following game is negligible:*

1. *A set S of public keys pk_i is generated with* **Gen**.
2. *The adversary is given access to an oracle* **Corrupt** *that on input i returns the randomness used to generate pk_i.*
3. *The adversary is given access to an oracle* **OSign** *to sign messages of their choice with rings of their choice.*
4. *The adversary outputs a message m, a ring R and a pair of indices i_0 and i_1 such that pk_{i_0} and pk_{i_1} are both in the ring. The game picks a random bit b and sends back* **Sign**(m, sk_{i_b}, R). *The adversary then attempts to guess who signed. There are no restrictions on picking corrupted indices in this step.*

Definition 2.4. *A ring signature scheme is* unforgeable against insider corruption *if the adversarial advantage in the following game is negligible:*

1. *A set S of public keys PK_s is generated by* **Gen** *and given to the adversary.*
2. *The adversary is given a signing oracle* **OSign**$(s, M, R) = $ **Sign**(m, sk_s, R) *for $PK_s \in S$, where $PK_s \in R$.*
3. *The adversary is also given an oracle* **Corrupt** *such that* **Corrupt**(i) *returns sk_i.*
4. *The adversary outputs (R^*, M^*, σ^*). The adversary wins if* **Verify**(σ^*, M^*, R^*) *accepts, R^* does not contain corrupted users and is a subset of S and the adversary did not ask the signature oracle to sign M^* with the ring R^*.*

3 Tom Curves

Digital signatures are generated using standardized elliptic curves defined over prime fields [25, 30]. These curves are defined by $E/\mathbb{F}_p\colon y^2 = x^3 - 3x + b$, which in turn leads to a prime order group $G_{\text{NIST}} = E(\mathbb{F}_p)$.

In order to prove relations among commitments to values in $\mathbb{F}_p$, (for example, commitments of the coordinates of a point), it is convenient to operate in a group that has order p. If we had to use a group that did not have this order, then to prove knowledge of openings of C_1, C_2, C_3 to $x, y, xy \bmod p$, we would need to have a group of size at least p^2 so that we could prove knowledge of C_4 opening to xy over the integers then prove that there was a number r of size at most p such that $t = xy - rp$. This would require an additional range proof and many auxiliary commitments. Furthermore we cannot make use of homomorphisms to carry out addition of commitments.

Instead, we follow the method of Bröker [11] to generate elliptic curves with the desired order, and we call these curves the *Tom curves*. Hence, for a prime q, a Tom curve $E'/\mathbb{F}_q\colon y^2 = x^3 + a_4 x + a_6$ results in a group $G_{\text{Tom}} = E'(\mathbb{F}_q)$ of prime order equal to p. Correspondingly, we use Com_{Tom} and Com_{NIST} to distinguish between the two commitment functions.

To generate these curves we used complex multiplication. The starting point is searching through (negative) discriminants d for one that allows an integral solution to the problem $x^2 - dy^2 = 4p$. Given such a solution, $q = p + 1 - x$ or $p + 1 + x$ are possible base fields if they are prime. Once the base field is found, creating the curve requires computing the Hilbert class polynomial of d and taking a root modulo q. It is possible that the curve found is the twist of the one that is sought, and this can be determined by point-counting.

In the smaller cases, curve generation took few seconds on a commodity laptop, and up to two minutes for the largest instance. The main complexity is computation of the Hilbert class polynomial, which is built into PARI/GP [32]. For a one-time computation our script runs efficiently enough, taking a few minutes wall clock time.

Generating curves whose order is a small multiple of p to have a faster arithmetic (such as in Edwards curves) is also possible. However, it requires a slightly more complicated search for elements of small norm, and one must apply the Decaf group interface to deal with cofactors. To simplify the presentation we focus on prime order Tom curves.

Table 1 shows Tom curves associated to commonly used curves from the FIPS 186-2 [25] and SEC 2 [31] standards.

4 Proof of Point Addition

Let a, b, t be points on G_{NIST} with coordinates $a_x, a_y, b_x, b_y, t_x, t_y$ and $C_1, \ldots, C_6$ be the corresponding commitments computed on the Tom curve (i.e., $C_1 = \text{Com}_{\text{Tom}}(a_x)$, and so on). Now suppose we wish to prove the relation $a + b = t$. There are several special cases.

Table 1. Tom curves and their associated parameters.

Standard curve $E(\mathbb{F}_p)$	Tom curve $E'(\mathbb{F}_q)$
P-256	**T-256** $d = -4155$ $q = \mathtt{ffffffff0000000100000000000000017e72b42b30e73177931}$ $\mathtt{35661b1c4b117}$ $a_4 = \mathtt{776679e96d94aff61a5fb6d256dece8a9162868d9a3fcbcead}$ $\mathtt{27946509c31405}$ $a_6 = \mathtt{c0450ed15e63704c6dfdd9be22fd6bbdfe5f4ccbc43c4d88a2}$ $\mathtt{ec905a2af4fef7}$
P-384	**T-384** $d = -619$ $q = \mathtt{ffffffffffffffffffffffffffffffffffffffffffffffffeaf5}$ $\mathtt{f689f8669fb41b08d5f5edffd26599c434bbd978917c5}$ $a_4 = \mathtt{821dfdc940e7f074ac481f8b2870c48962cce56abd72dfc428}$ $\mathtt{13a944cea15df78dc0a2d97fbf031ed26c9076826940ba}$ $a_6 = \mathtt{9b5b584b655fdcb087d37f8c4fee893c0499223db5e004c674}$ $\mathtt{ea0dee48a4ec0c9e9f684099f2a51c62a2cce400cb1e4b}$
P-521	**T-521** $d = -28243$ $q = \mathtt{20000000000000000000000000000000000000000000000000000}$ $\mathtt{000000000000002c54be78524c33584f734a266748b2063accf5028}$ $\mathtt{e6778dc5056476d0690853249}$ $a_4 = \mathtt{ef6432c21701cc48c63fb9263e14ba76d4a94ba14d173b134e}$ $\mathtt{3032b0e2e543180eb6725125992a7d00162a5f57d21918b0766364e}$ $\mathtt{eb53c53bb12f405dac1d527e2}$ $a_6 = \mathtt{3cbc65d1e0245d79703b18e9aaea1ac6d67f87a2cd4bd84b9e}$ $\mathtt{6df6a45a979c481825ca5a857270fc890352f9fac7fd6020deaabb2}$ $\mathtt{8d099718f0f77a4eec222871d}$

We start with the general case of $a_x \neq b_x$ in which the following affine addition formula [29, Chapter III, Section 2] holds:

$$t_x = \left(\frac{b_y - a_y}{b_x - a_x}\right)^2 - a_x - b_x, \quad \text{and } t_y = \left(\frac{b_y - a_y}{b_x - a_x}\right)(b_x - t_x) - a_y.$$

To prove $a + b = t$, the prover computes auxiliary commitments

$$C_7 = \mathrm{Com_{Tom}}(b_x - a_x) \qquad C_8 = \mathrm{Com_{Tom}}\left((b_x - a_x)^{-1}\right)$$
$$C_9 = \mathrm{Com_{Tom}}(b_y - a_y)$$

$$C_{10} = \mathrm{Com_{Tom}}\left(\frac{b_y - a_y}{b_x - a_x}\right) \qquad C_{11} = \mathrm{Com_{Tom}}\left(\left(\frac{b_y - a_y}{b_x - a_x}\right)^2\right)$$

$$C_{12} = \mathrm{Com_{Tom}}(b_x - t_x) \qquad C_{13} = \mathrm{Com_{Tom}}\left(\left(\frac{b_y - a_y}{b_x - a_x}\right)(b_x - t_x)\right)$$

and then proves in parallel that each of these auxiliary commitments opens to the proper value as a sum or product of previous one, and then finally that

$$C_5 = C_{11} - C_1 - C_3, \quad \text{and} \quad C_6 = C_{13}C_{12} - C_2.$$

Each of these auxiliary proofs can be done through either proving a correct multiplication or addition, via known techniques [14]. Note that a proof of proper inversion can be achieved through a proof of multiplication as proving $C_8 = C_7^{-1}$ is equivalent to proving $C_8 C_7 = \mathrm{Com_{Tom}}(1)$.

For our application, the points we must add are unlikely to be in exceptional cases. And if ever they are, the prover can simply try the entire protocol again, as the probability of an exceptional case $a = -b$ or $a = b$ is just $2/|G|$. This proof does not demonstrate that the points are on the curve, but if a and b are then t is guaranteed to be.

To handle the special cases in our addition law we extend our proof to show that $a_x - b_x$ is not zero via showing it has an inverse. Then the two remaining cases possibilities are that $a_y = b_y$ in which case we have a point doubling, or the result is the point at infinity, which cannot be represented in affine coordinates. Since the result is represented in affine coordinates, it cannot be the point at infinity.

Therefore it suffices to prove the following statement, using the OR and AND compositions of Σ-protocols: $(a_x - b_x \neq 0 \wedge t = a + b) \vee (a_x = b_x \wedge a_y = b_y \wedge t = 2a)$. This demonstrates that $t = a + b$ provided the output can be written in affine coordinates.

The cost of this proof is dominated by the number of field multiplications and field inversions; each of them amounts to a proof of multiplication. Therefore, in the proof-space, the affine formulas are the most efficient formulas to use. A more complicated complete formulas such as the ones from Renes et al. [27] would require significantly more operations. A cheaper unified formula that applies to both addition and multiplication in affine coordinates is unknown to the authors.

5 Proof of Scalar Multiplication

To make the notation nicer, group elements and commitments of G_{NIST} will be unprimed while those on G_{Tom} primed. For example g, h refer to points on G_{NIST} while g', h' to points on G_{Tom}.

In this protocol, the prover starts with commitments $C_1 = \text{Com}_{\text{NIST}}(\lambda)$, $C_2' = \text{Com}_{\text{Tom}}(x)$ and $C_3' = \text{Com}_{\text{Tom}}(y)$. Their goal is to prove knowledge of opening of these commitments C_1, C_2', C_3' to values x, y and λ such that $(x, y) = \lambda g$ where g is a point of G_{NIST}.

This proof is a corrected form of one that appears in Agrawal *et al.* [1]. We discuss the correction towards the end of this section. We now describe a round of the Σ-protocol. For 128-bit security, we do 128 parallel instances of the below protocol.

1. The prover picks $\alpha, \beta_1, \beta_2, \beta_3$ at random and computes $(\gamma_1, \gamma_2) = \alpha g$, $a_1 = \alpha g + \beta_1 h$, $a_2' = \gamma_1 g' + \beta_2 h'$, and $a_3' = \gamma_2 g' + \beta_3 h'$.
2. The prover lets C_4', C_5' be commitments to the x and y coordinates of $(\alpha - \lambda)g$. It sends $a_1, a_2', a_3', C_4', C_5'$ to the verifier. It also sends the commitments for a point addition proof showing that (a_2', a_3') and (C_2', C_3') sum to the point (C_4', C_5').
3. The verifier responds with a challenge string $c = (c_0, c_1)$ where c_0 is a single bit, and c_1 a challenge for the point addition protocol.
4. If $c_0 = 0$ the prover computes $z_1 = \alpha, z_2 = \beta_1, z_3 = \beta_2, z_4 = \beta_3$ and responds with (z_1, z_2, z_3, z_4).
5. If $c_0 = 1$ the prover computes $z_1 = \alpha - \lambda$, $z_2 = \beta_1 - r$. The prover uses the point addition protocol (Sect. 4) to prove knowledge of an opening of a_2', a_3', C_2', C_3' and C_4', C_5' to $\gamma_1, \gamma_2, x, y, u, v$ respectively such that $(u, v) = (\gamma_1, \gamma_2) - (x, y)$ using challenge c_1. Call the response π. The prover sends (π, z_1, z_2) to the verifier as well as the opening of C_4' and C_5'.
6. If $c_0 = 0$, the verifier simply verifies that the commitments a_1, a_2', a_3' are opened correctly by $(\alpha, \beta_1, \beta_2, \beta_3)$. If $c_0 = 1$, then the verifier validates π using c_1 and checks that $z_1 g + z_2 h + C_1 = a_1$, as well as verifying the opening of C_4' and C_5' to $z_1 g$.

We added the verification step $z_1 g + z_2 h + C_1 = a_1$ to the verification algorithm in [1]. Without this the verification ignored C_1 entirely, and therefore did not demonstrate knowledge of an opening of C_1.

Theorem 5.1. *The above protocol is a Σ-protocol.*

Proof. It is easy to see that the protocol is three rounds and that the challenge is a random string of bits. What is not clear is the Special Honest-Verifier Zero-Knowledge and Soundness properties. We prove each one at a time.

Special Honest-Verifier Zero-Knowledge: Our goal is to construct a simulator such that the output of the simulator is statistically indistinguishable from the transcript of the protocol with a prover. On the input of challenge c, the simulator does the following: If $c_0 = 0$, pick $(\alpha, \beta_1, \beta_2, \beta_3)$ at random and compute $a_1, a_2', a_3', C_4', C_5'$ using the same process as above, then reveal the openings. If $c_0 = 1$, pick z_1, z_2 at random and compute $a_1 = z_1 g_1 + z_2 h + C_1$, and let C_4', C_5' be commitments to the x and y coordinates of $z_1 g$. Then invoke the simulator for the point addition proof, and send over the last move. Since Pedersen commitments are unconditionally hiding and not binding if the discrete logarithm is known, the statement being proved by the point addition proof is true, so the transcript can be simulated.

Soundness: We demonstrate that the witnesses (λ, x, y) may be extracted given three accepting transcripts for the same commitment: one with $c_0 = 0$ and two with $c_0 = 1$ and differing c_1.

Note that $\lambda = z_1 - \widehat{z_1}$ where z_1 is from the transcript with $c_0 = 0$ and $\widehat{z_1}$ is from one of the others. Further the prover must have a'_2, a'_3 on the curve as they open them when $c_0 = 0$, and C_4, C_5 on the curve as they open them when $c_0 = 1$. Therefore C'_2 and C'_3 are on the curve as they satisfy the addition proof. We have openings of the commitments involved in π by the extractability of π, and know that a'_2 and a'_3 are commitments to the x and y coordinates of $\alpha g + \beta_1 h$ for some α. Furthermore we know that $z_1 g + z_2 h + C_1 = a_1 = \alpha g + \beta_1 h$, and that C'_2, C'_3 are commitments to the x and y coordinates of a point t such that $z_1 g + t = \alpha g$ as the openings are extractable from π. Therefore $t = (x, y)$ can be extracted as $t = (\alpha - z_1)g$ and $C_1 = (\alpha - z_1)g + (z_2 - \beta_1)h$, which is exactly what is needed to show: C_1 is a commitment to the discrete logarithm of t.   □

6   Proof of Knowledge of ECDSA Signature

We have a proof of scalar multiplication, but it does not immediately apply to verification of signatures under committed public keys. To apply these techniques to ECDSA we slightly recast the verification equation to make it more amenable to our techniques. Ordinarily ECDSA verification of a signature (r, s) on a message m takes the form of evaluating $R = u_1 g + u_2 q$ for the public key q, and then verifying that the truncation of the x coordinate of R equals r. In this equation $u_1 = ts^{-1} \bmod n$ and $u_2 = rs^{-1} \bmod n$ where t is a function of $H(m)$.

An alternative signature scheme instead transmits $(R, z = s/r)$ as the signature, and then verifies the equation $zR - tr^{-1}g = q$ (obtained by multiplying z on both sides of the previous equation). This equation is much more amenable to a zero-knowledge proof. R is independent of the public key, as it is kg for some random k, and t is a function of the message alone. Therefore R is independent of the key. Note that this scheme is as secure as ECDSA since the verification equations are equivalent.

It is in this form we apply the scalar multiplication proof to get our protocol. Let Q be the committed public key. The prover transmits R, and a commitment to the scalar z. The prover uses the scalar multiplication proof to demonstrate correctness of a commitment to zR, and then use the point addition proof to demonstrate that the committed Q satisfies $zR - tr^{-1}g = Q$. As $tr^{-1}g$ is a public value, the prover can simply display the opening of its commitments to $tr^{-1}g$ to verify its correctness.

More formally we let $C_{qx}, C_{qy} = \mathrm{Com_{Tom}}(Q_x), \mathrm{Com_{Tom}}(Q_y)$ and $C_z = zR + rh$ for a random r. Now, as R is an adversarially chosen point, we would have a problem if $R = kh$ for some k known to the adversary. To solve this we must adjust h by generating it via hashing to the NIST curve based on R (refer to Faz-Hernández et al. [18] for standard methods for hashing to curves). Then the prover generates an auxiliary commitment $C_{sx}, C_{sy} = \mathrm{Com}_{\mathrm{Tom}}(tr^{-1}g)$. The prover then generates C_2, C_3 commitments to the x and y coordinates of zR.

Lastly the prover proves knowledge of openings of C_{sx}, C_{sy}, C_{qx}, C_{qy}, C_2, C_3, C_z such that C_{sx}, C_{sy} open to $tr^{-1}g$; C_2, C_3 open to the x and y coordinates of zR; and $zR - tr^{-1}g = Q$.

We can handle some variations of Schnorr signatures similarly, although not EdDSA [10]. Given a message m and public key $Q = xg$, the signature is (R, s) where $R = kg$, $e = H(R, m)$ and $s = k - xe$. The verification equation is then $sg + eQ = R$. We can recast this as $Q = e^{-1}R - e^{-1}sg$. Here the prover sends R, and a commitment to $e^{-1}s$, then proves that the committed public key is the sum of $e^{-1}R$, known to both, and $e^{-1}sg$, computable through a scalar multiplication proof. Since EdDSA incorporates the public key of the signer into what is hashed, it is difficult to preserve signer privacy while permitting verification. SNARK based approaches would be able to handle this type of signature [19].

7 Applications

Having demonstrated that a message is signed with a committed key, we can then prove additional properties of the key. Depending on the properties chosen we obtain group signatures, ring signatures, and proof of non-revocation.

7.1 Ring Signatures

Given a list of public keys $k_1, k_2, \ldots, k_n$ in the ring, a signer takes the private key corresponding to their key k_i, commits to k_i, signs the message m, creates a proof of signature under committed key (Sect. 6), and then proves that the commitment is to one of the keys in the list via Groth–Kohlweiss proofs [20]. More formally:

- **Gen** generates an ECDSA keypair.
- **Sign** carries out an ECDSA signature, commits to the key, and proves the signature verifies and the key is on the list.
- **Verify** verifies the proof.

We now formally demonstrate correctness of this application. We start with unforgeability. In Sect. 2 we recalled a game based definition of the strongest variants unforgeability and anonymity. We now show that our construction achieves both of these, à la Chase and Lysyanskaya [15]. To avoid an unfortunate collision in notation we will call the ring Γ.

Theorem 7.1. *Our ring signature scheme achieves anonymity against full key exposure.*

Proof. Consider the adversary in Step 4 of Definition 2.3. They have received R and a NIZK for the statement "There is a modified ECDSA signature (R, z) that verifies under a public key Q that is on the list of public keys". But both sk_{i_0} and sk_{i_1} would produce witnesses for this statement. Now consider the adversary interacting with a game that switches which witness is used. By witness indistinguishability, the adversary would produce the same result. Therefore the adversarial advantage must be negligible.

Theorem 7.2. *Our ring signature scheme achieves unforgeability against insider corruption assuming that ECDSA is unforgeable.*

Proof. Let **Sim** and **Ext** be the simulator and extractor for our NIZK. We take the adversary in the unforgeability game and provide it with **OSign** that works as follows: Given a private key sk_i, ring Γ, and associated public key pk_i it computes random commitments C for use in our scheme. It generates a proof that R is the R for a signature of a message under a public key in the ring using the simulator, with no witness. This produces a valid signature σ for the ring signature scheme that it returns thanks to the simulator. Corruptions we handle by handing back the private key that is requested.

The adversary has no way to know the difference between this game and the original one by the NIZK properties of the Fiat-Shamir transform.

At the final step of the game the adversary returns a signature for a ring it has not queried, that does not contain any corrupted key. Assume this proof is valid. This is the proof we apply **Ext** to, obtaining an ECDSA signature and a public key pk_i such that the signature is valid and pk_i is in the ring. Now at no point was the adversary given a value that reveals information theoretically any private key or ECDSA signature of a value in the ring. Therefore this extracted signature violates the unforgeability of ECDSA.

We do want to note a subtlety: our signature scheme proves knowledge of a signature on a message. Therefore an adversary who obtains an ECDSA signature of a message under a users key can create their own ring signature showing that someone in a ring containing the user signed the message. This sort of multiprotocol attack is not present in the security definition of ring signatures.

7.2   Group Signatures

Once again Chase and Lysynaskaya anticipate us, as do Bellare *et al.* [5,15]. Both papers combine a public-key encryption scheme, a signature scheme, and a zero-knowledge proof system into a group signature scheme. A signer signs with their private key and encrypts the public key to the group manager, and the signature is a zero-knowledge proof that the private key was used to sign the message and that the public key is encrypted to the group manager and is in an accumulator.

Our zero-knowledge proof can be used to show a committed public key was used to sign, and if encryption to the group manager is done via ElGamal encryption [17] the same proof techniques can show the committed public key is correctly encrypted. We can also hash public keys via a Pedersen hash: after chopping the bit expansion of the x-coordinate of the key up into small pieces x_0, x_1, x_2 we can take $x_0 g_1 + x_2 g_2 + x_3 g_3 + t g_4$ as the hash using our proof of scalar multiplication, where t is a parameter used by the prover to make the output have a prime x-coordinate. This enables our scheme to be used together with an RSA accumulator, using proofs for membership of Benarroch *et al.* [7].

7.3 Non-revocation

Another application which we shall not treat formally is demonstrating non-membership on a list. In applications such as WebAuthn, attestations are signatures under a key built into the device. Revealing the key reveals the issuing device, harming user privacy. At the same time revocation is necessary to ensure that compromised devices are distrusted. By using a Bayer–Groth proof of non-membership [4], we obtain a proof of signature guaranteeing the use of an unrevoked key; moreover, this proof does not reveal which key was used.

We also discuss a non-application. It is tempting to apply our technique to the case of anonymous credentials [13], where the issuer would sign a message with ECDSA, and a zero-knowledge proof of the credential is then used to anonymize the credential itself. However our scheme hides the identity of the key, not the signature itself, and therefore repeat proofs with the same signature are linkable. Our scheme reveals the commitment to randomness used in the signature, but this alone cannot reveal the key as it is independent of the key.

8 Implementation

ZKAttest originated as an effort to improve the privacy of WebAuthn attestation, to enable it to be used as an alternative to CAPTCHAs [2]. WebAuthn attestation takes the form of signing an attestation message with a device attestation key that chains up to a manufacturer's key via the PKI. However, each attestation does reveal a hard-coded certificate associated with the device class. If the certificate were unique, it could be used to track a user's attestation across multiple challenges and make inferences about that user's browsing patterns. The FIDO standard [3, Section 4.1.2.1.1] that specifies certificates should be batched and shared across at least 100,000 devices, so there is a moderately sized list of all valid attestation keys. By using our ring signature to sign the attestation message instead of presenting the ECDSA signature and chain, the user's privacy is further protected as all that is learned is that they have a WebAuthn device that is trusted, rather than which one they have. Currently we have deployed a proof of concept implementation that dynamically adds the attestation key to a much smaller list of randomly generated keys, and then verifies the ring signature server side.

Because our demonstration runs in the browser we wrote our implementation in TypeScript, and implemented our proof for ECDSA with the P-256 curve. No other language would allow us to run in the browser without a complex transpilation step. Internally, we use JavaScript's native big integer library [24] and built on top of it elliptic curve arithmetic for the NIST and Tom curves. The source code is available at https://github.com/cloudflare/zkp-ecdsa.

Note that JavaScript's runtime does not guarantee that operations on big integers run in constant-time; moreover, some operations can be performed much faster when targeting a specific computer architecture. These impact performance negatively, but we still get adequate performance for occasional interactive use by users. Our implementation is capable of proving membership on a list within ten seconds, and can prove membership on lists of up to several thousand with no appreciable slowdown. Verification time is half a second, albeit with an acceptable soundness loss through verifying only some parallel compositions.

We trade soundness for performance by checking a randomly chosen subset of the cases for the scalar multiplication proof. This ensures sufficient security for our application while accelerating verification time. Each case has the same $1/2$ failure probability, so after checking 20 cases the probability of forgery is now 2^{-20}. As the relations to be checked are not known to the prover ahead of time, they must interact with the verifier to attempt cheating. In our application, requiring a million interactions for a single successful forgery is acceptable, because we have other means for rate limiting malicious actors and can afford a small false positive rate. As we continue to optimize our implementation, we can reduce this rate even more. The cost of these checks is linear in the number performed.

Several high-level optimizations were required to achieve this level of performance. The major one is batching verification equations. In our protocol we have a set of commitments, some from the theorems that are to be proven and some from the proofs, $C_1, \ldots C_n$, that are then hashed to form a challenge e; and then a set of revealed scalars s_{ij} such that $\sum s_{ij} C_i = 0$ for all j. Verifying each of these equations separately is expensive. Our implementation instead selects a random vector of scalars r_i, and verifies that $\sum s_{ij} C_i r_i = 0$. If any of the $\sum s_{ij} C_i$ are not the identity, the probability that r_i lies in the kernel of the resulting linear operator is at most $1/|G|$. This technique was also used by Bernstein *et al.* [10] to accelerate verification of multiple signatures.

Some limitations of JavaScript prevent from performing well-known low-level optimizations. For instance, JavaScript's multiprecision arithmetic operators [24] are limited in expressiveness so every field operation involves a full division by the modulus. Montgomery arithmetic is hard to express. Inversion has to be accomplished through either Fermat's little theorem or extended Euclidean algorithm: there is no way to approximate the quotient efficiently for use in asymptotically faster gcd algorithms to make up for the slow division. Each step of the extended Euclidean algorithm is an expensive division even though the quotients are usually small. We have not investigated the use of binary algorithms to accelerate the Euclidean algorithm to potentially accelerate it.

Access to machine word operations is central for obtaining better performance for field operations. An alternative is moving computations to either WebAssembly or AssemblyScript, but we did not explore that path due to time constraints.

9   Related Work

There is a rich literature on anonymous credentials, ring signatures, and group signatures, only some of which we have consulted. Agrawal *et al.* [1] presented a proof of exponentiation relation, that our scalar multiplication proof is related to. Their proof had a verification equation that did not include C_1. Therefore an attacker could generate any C_1 value and the verifier would accept it, contradicting the security claim of that paper. We have verified the correction we present with the authors of that paper. Agrawal *et al.* consider the challenges of proving statements with both algebraic relations and "arithmetic" ones, while our techniques avoid "arithmetic" relations. In addition Agrawal *et al.* say that the complex multiplication method is quite inefficient and makes protocols impractical, choosing to use a fixed, much larger group instead. The opposite is true: a short one time calculation reduces the number of commitments and the size of the group.

The general approach of constructing ring signatures via proofs on signatures is found in Chase and Lysyanskaya [15], although they approach the question with an eye toward delegatable anonymous credentials, and do not provide a proof of the intuitive claim that their ring signature scheme is secure. Our work can be seen as instantiating their scheme for an ECDSA signature, but in settings where the message is public.

SNARKs provide a general method to create a succinct argument of knowledge for any circuit [19]. One could apply such a technique to the ECDSA verification circuit and thus obtain a proof of signature generically, just as we have applied the composition of Σ-protocols to obtain one by hand. SNARKs are deployed in Zcash [22] where proofs of signatures are used and efficient verification is a requirement. However SNARK design and compilation is tricky, with very few tools targeting JavaScript and SNARKs depend on unfalsifiable assumptions even in the CRS model, and the common reference strings are large. In the future these barriers are likely to improve with further research.

Groth and Kohlweiss considered applying their one-out-of-many scheme to produce ring signatures that use a preexisting PKI [20]. A user would reveal that they know how to open their public key to zero, and use this for a ring signature scheme. Our work can be seen as a natural extension to use preexisting infrastructure such as smart cards or other forms of hardware with a limited interface for the use of private keys.

10   Conclusion

We have presented a practical scheme with minimal assumptions for proving knowledge of an ECDSA signature under a committed key. Our approach does not use expensive pairing computations, is practical and efficient, and widely applicable. Unlike SNARK based approaches we do not have a large common reference string and our security does not need knowledge assumptions [19]. By decoupling the proof of the signature from proving information about the key it enables a great array of applications, such as improving the privacy of remote attestation and demonstrating that keys have not been revoked. Our proof-of-concept implementation demonstrates that our techniques are practical even in a limited computing environment, such as a web browser. We believe ZKAttest has numerous additional applications.

Acknowledgements. We would like to thank SAC reviewers for providing feedback that helped us to improve the article. We also want to thank Alex Davidson for thoughtful discussions during the early stages of this work.

References

1. Agrawal, S., Ganesh, C., Mohassel, P.: Non-interactive zero-knowledge proofs for composite statements. In: Shacham, H., Boldyreva, A. (eds.) CRYPTO 2018. LNCS, vol. 10993, pp. 643–673. Springer, Cham (2018). https://doi.org/10.1007/978-3-319-96878-0_22
2. von Ahn, L., Blum, M., Hopper, N.J., Langford, J.: CAPTCHA: using hard AI problems for security. In: Biham, E. (ed.) EUROCRYPT 2003. LNCS, vol. 2656, pp. 294–311. Springer, Heidelberg (2003). https://doi.org/10.1007/3-540-39200-9_18
3. Balfanz, D., ˙et al.: FIDO UAF protocol specification v1.0. FIDO alliance standard, FIDO (December 2014). https://fidoalliance.org/specs/fido-uaf-v1.0-ps-20141208/fido-uaf-protocol-v1.0-ps-20141208.html
4. Bayer, S., Groth, J.: Zero-knowledge argument for polynomial evaluation with application to blacklists. In: Johansson, T., Nguyen, P.Q. (eds.) EUROCRYPT 2013. LNCS, vol. 7881, pp. 646–663. Springer, Heidelberg (2013). https://doi.org/10.1007/978-3-642-38348-9_38
5. Bellare, M., Micciancio, D., Warinschi, B.: Foundations of group signatures: formal definitions, simplified requirements, and a construction based on general assumptions. In: Biham, E. (ed.) EUROCRYPT 2003. LNCS, vol. 2656, pp. 614–629. Springer, Heidelberg (2003). https://doi.org/10.1007/3-540-39200-9_38
6. Bellare, M., Rogaway, P.: Random oracles are practical: a paradigm for designing efficient protocols. In: Denning, D.E., Pyle, R., Ganesan, R., Sandhu, R.S., Ashby, V. (eds.) CCS 1993, Proceedings of the 1st ACM Conference on Computer and Communications Security, Fairfax, Virginia, USA, 3–5 November 1993, pp. 62–73. ACM (1993). https://doi.org/10.1145/168588.168596
7. Benarroch, D., Campanelli, M., Fiore, D., Kolonelos, D.: Zero-knowledge proofs for set membership: Efficient, succinct, modular. Cryptology ePrint Archive, Report 2019/1255 (October 2019). https://eprint.iacr.org/2019/1255
8. Bender, A., Katz, J., Morselli, R.: Ring signatures: stronger definitions, and constructions without random oracles. J. Cryptol. **22**(1), 114–138 (2007). https://doi.org/10.1007/s00145-007-9011-9
9. Bernhard, D., Pereira, O., Warinschi, B.: How not to prove yourself: pitfalls of the fiat-shamir heuristic and applications to helios. In: Wang, X., Sako, K. (eds.) ASIACRYPT 2012. LNCS, vol. 7658, pp. 626–643. Springer, Heidelberg (2012). https://doi.org/10.1007/978-3-642-34961-4_38
10. Bernstein, D.J., Duif, N., Lange, T., Schwabe, P., Yang, B.Y.: High-speed high-security signatures. J. Cryptogr. Eng. **2**(2), 77–89 (2012). https://doi.org/10.1007/s13389-012-0027-1

11. Bröker, R.: Constructing Elliptic Curves of Prescribed Order. Ph.D. thesis, Leiden (2006)
12. Camenisch, J.: Group signature schemes and payment systems based on the discrete logarithm problem. Ph.D. thesis, ETH Zurich (1998)
13. Camenisch, J., Lysyanskaya, A.: An efficient system for non-transferable anonymous credentials with optional anonymity revocation. In: Pfitzmann, B. (ed.) EUROCRYPT 2001. LNCS, vol. 2045, pp. 93–118. Springer, Heidelberg (2001). https://doi.org/10.1007/3-540-44987-6_7
14. Camenisch, J., Michels, M.: Proving in zero-knowledge that a number is the product of two safe primes. In: Stern, J. (ed.) EUROCRYPT 1999. LNCS, vol. 1592, pp. 107–122. Springer, Heidelberg (1999). https://doi.org/10.1007/3-540-48910-X_8
15. Chase, M., Lysyanskaya, A.: On signatures of knowledge. In: Dwork, C. (ed.) CRYPTO 2006. LNCS, vol. 4117, pp. 78–96. Springer, Heidelberg (2006). https://doi.org/10.1007/11818175_5
16. Damgård, I.: On Σ-protocols (2010). https://www.cs.au.dk/~ivan/Sigma.pdf
17. ElGamal, T.: A public key cryptosystem and a signature scheme based on discrete logarithms. In: Blakley, G.R., Chaum, D. (eds.) CRYPTO 1984. LNCS, vol. 196, pp. 10–18. Springer, Heidelberg (1985). https://doi.org/10.1007/3-540-39568-7_2
18. Faz-Hernández, A., Scott, S., Sullivan, N., Wahby, R.S., Wood, C.A.: Hashing to elliptic curves. internet-draft, internet engineering task force (April 2021). https://datatracker.ietf.org/doc/draft-irtf-cfrg-hash-to-curve/, (work in progress)
19. Groth, J.: On the size of pairing-based non-interactive arguments. In: Fischlin, M., Coron, J.-S. (eds.) EUROCRYPT 2016. LNCS, vol. 9666, pp. 305–326. Springer, Heidelberg (2016). https://doi.org/10.1007/978-3-662-49896-5_11
20. Groth, J., Kohlweiss, M.: One-out-of-many proofs: or how to leak a secret and spend a coin. In: Oswald, E., Fischlin, M. (eds.) EUROCRYPT 2015. LNCS, vol. 9057, pp. 253–280. Springer, Heidelberg (2015). https://doi.org/10.1007/978-3-662-46803-6_9
21. Hodges, J., Jones, J., Jones, M.B., Kumar, A., Lundberg, E.: Web Authentication: An API for accessing Public Key Credentials - Level 2. W3C recommendation, W3C (April 2021). https://www.w3.org/TR/webauthn-2
22. Hopwood, D., Bowe, S., Hornby, T., Wilcox, N.: Zcash protocol specification (August 2021). https://zips.z.cash/protocol/protocol.pdf
23. Johnson, D., Menezes, A., Vanstone, S.: The elliptic curve digital signature algorithm (ECDSA). Int. J. Inf. Secur. 1(1), 36–63 (2001). https://doi.org/10.1007/s102070100002
24. MDN contributors: Bigint (2021). https://developer.mozilla.org/en-US/docs/Web/JavaScript/Reference/Global_Objects/BigInt
25. National Institute of Standards and Technology: FIPS 186-2: Digital Signature Standard (DSS). Federal Information Processing Standards Publication (January 2000). https://csrc.nist.gov/CSRC/media/Publications/fips/186/2/archive/2000-01-27/documents/fips186-2.pdf
26. Pedersen, T.P.: Non-interactive and information-theoretic secure verifiable secret sharing. In: Feigenbaum, J. (ed.) CRYPTO 1991. LNCS, vol. 576, pp. 129–140. Springer, Heidelberg (1992). https://doi.org/10.1007/3-540-46766-1_9
27. Renes, J., Costello, C., Batina, L.: Complete addition formulas for prime order elliptic curves. In: Fischlin, M., Coron, J.-S. (eds.) EUROCRYPT 2016. LNCS, vol. 9665, pp. 403–428. Springer, Heidelberg (2016). https://doi.org/10.1007/978-3-662-49890-3_16

28. Rivest, R.L., Shamir, A., Tauman, Y.: How to leak a secret. In: Boyd, C. (ed.) ASIACRYPT 2001. LNCS, vol. 2248, pp. 552–565. Springer, Heidelberg (2001). https://doi.org/10.1007/3-540-45682-1_32
29. Silverman, J.H.: The Geometry of Elliptic Curves. In: The Arithmetic of Elliptic Curves. GTM, vol. 106, pp. 41–114. Springer, New York (2009). https://doi.org/10.1007/978-0-387-09494-6_3
30. Solinas, J.A.: Generalized Mersenne Numbers. Technical report, Centre for Applied Cryptographic Research, University of Waterloo (June 1999). https://cacr.uwaterloo.ca/techreports/1999/corr99-39.pdf
31. Standards for Efficient Cryptography Group: SEC 2: Recommended Elliptic Curve Domain Parameters. Standards for Efficient Cryptography (SEC) (September 2000). https://www.secg.org/sec2-v1.pdf
32. The PARI Group, Univ. Bordeaux: PARI/GP version 2.13.0 (2019). http://pari.math.u-bordeaux.fr/

Implementation, PUFs and MPC

A Low-Randomness Second-Order Masked AES

Tim Beyne, Siemen Dhooghe[(✉)], Adrián Ranea, and Danilo Šijačić

imec-COSIC, ESAT, KU Leuven, Leuven, Belgium
{tim.beyne,siemen.dhooghe,adrian.ranea,danilo.sijacic}@esat.kuleuven.be

Abstract. We propose a second-order masking of the AES in hardware that requires an order of magnitude less random bits per encryption compared to previous work. The design and its security analysis are based on recent results by Beyne *et al.* from Asiacrypt 2020. Applying these results to the AES required overcoming significant engineering challenges by introducing new design techniques. Since the security analysis is based on linear cryptanalysis, the masked cipher needs to have sufficient diffusion and the S-box sharing must be highly nonlinear. Hence, in order to apply the changing of the guards technique, a detailed study of its effect on the diffusion of the linear layer becomes important. The security analysis is automated using an SMT solver. Furthermore, we propose a sharpening of the glitch-extended probing model that results in improvements to our concrete security bounds. Finally, it is shown how to amortize randomness costs over multiple evaluations of the masked cipher.

Keywords: Hardware · Linear cryptanalysis · Masking · Probing security · Side-channel analysis · Threshold implementations

1 Introduction

The Advanced Encryption Standard (AES) [10] has been an important building block for many cryptographic applications. For over twenty years, the cipher has largely withstood cryptanalytic attacks. However, just like any other symmetric primitive, naive implementations of the AES are vulnerable to side-channel attacks such as Differential Power Analysis (DPA) due to Kocher *et al.* [16]. To counter these attacks, several adversarial models and side-channel countermeasures have been developed during the past two decades. Masking methods are a common theme among different countermeasures. These methods split all key-dependent variables in the circuit into $d + 1$ or more random shares and provide security against d^{th}-order DPA attacks.

Over the years, several first- and even higher-order secure maskings of the AES have appeared in the literature. In particular, several second-order maskings have been proposed: a higher-order threshold implementation [11], a private circuits variant [14], and a multiplicative masking [12]. Despite these advances, all of these works still require significant randomness resources for each evaluation of the round function, namely more than ten-thousand random bits. There are several important downsides to strong randomness requirements. The security requirements for embedded random number generators used by masking schemes are currently not well understood. As mentioned in NIST's threshold cryptography project roadmap [6], random number generators can be single points of failure. As a result, considerable efforts were made to reduce the randomness costs of maskings. This research culminated in the development of first-order maskings of the AES that did not require fresh randomness [23,25]. So far, it is not known how to similarly reduce the randomness requirements for higher-order secure maskings of the AES.

Threshold Implementations, proposed by Nikova et al. [20], are key to the design of first-order low-randomness maskings. Until recently, this method has had limited success in the higher-order setting as it was only secure against univariate attacks [21]. At Asiacrypt 2020, Beyne et al. [2] demonstrated how to design multivariate secure threshold implementations without significantly increasing the randomness costs. Their approach uses linear cryptanalysis to show that the information obtained by second-order probing adversaries cannot be reliably exploited with a finite but large number of queries to the masked cipher.

Although the work of Beyne et al. represents an important step towards secure higher-order threshold implementations, it is still quite theoretical and its application was limited to a 7-share masking of the block cipher LED. In addition, it imposes strong requirements such as uniformity and higher-order non-completeness on each shared function. However, there is currently no known uniform sharing of the AES S-box. In the first-order case, the "changing of the guards" method of Daemen [7] can be used to achieve uniformity without fresh randomness. However, as noted by Beyne et al., a direct application of the changing of the guards method would "alter the diffusion of the shared cipher and consequently demand a more detailed security analysis" [2, §8.2]. Finally, for more complicated maskings, the security analysis becomes cumbersome without the use of automated tools.

Contribution. This paper applies the techniques from [2] to design a second-order masking of the AES in hardware. This requires overcoming the difficulties outlined above. The design is based on four shares and requires an order of magnitude fewer random bits per encryption operation than previous work, namely we require only 1800 random bits per encryption including the sharing of the plaintext and key. This randomness cost can be compared with second-order designs such as the one by Groß et al. [14] requiring a total of 11312 bits or the work by De Meyer et al. [12] requiring 11112 bits.

After reviewing the necessary preliminary material in Sect. 2, the proposed design is described in Sect. 3. Several novel design concepts are introduced along the way. It is shown how the second-order non-completeness requirement can be relaxed by means of additional randomness. However, by using the techniques from [2], we are able to show that this randomness can be reused across all S-boxes. In order to maintain strong diffusion even when the changing of the guards method is used to ensure the uniformity of the S-box layer, the "guards in formation" technique is introduced. This technique relies on a detailed analysis of the interaction between the changing of the guards structure and the linear layer of the cipher.

The design choices made in Sect. 3 pay off in the security analysis, which is presented in Sect. 4. As a result, a concrete upper bound on the advantage of bounded-query second-order probing adversaries is obtained. In addition, Sect. 4 shows how Satisfiability Modulo Theories (SMT) solvers can be used to automate a large portion of the security analysis by identifying optimal linear trails in the masked cipher.

Section 5 investigates the glitch-extended probing model of Faust *et al.* [13] and proposes a sharpened variant. This sharpening results in significant improvements to the security bound of our second-order masking of the AES. We adapt the bounded-query probing model appropriately and apply the necessary changes to the theoretical results from [2]. Our proposals are based on realistic simulations of the behavior of glitches in the masked AES S-box.

Finally, Sect. 6 proposes a technique to amortize randomness over multiple masked AES calls by extracting randomness during its execution. Moreover, it is shown that this extraction process can be used several thousands of times without a significant security loss. A concrete upper bound on the advantage of bounded-query probing adversaries is derived. This technique allows us to reduce the total number of random bits required to 840 bits per masked encryption call.

2 Preliminaries

This section introduces the bounded-query probing model and the key results from [2] related to the security analysis of higher-order threshold implementations. For convenience, all random variables in this paper are denoted in boldface.

2.1 The Bounded-Query Probing Model

This section introduces the bounded-query probing model of Beyne *et al.* [2] and the main theorem that can be used to prove the security of higher-order masked implementations in this model.

Threshold Probing. A dth-order (or d-threshold) probing adversary $\mathcal{A}$, as first proposed by Ishai *et al.* [15], can view up to d gates or wires in a circuit. This circuit encodes an operation, such as a cipher call, and consists of gates, such as AND or XOR gates, and wires. The adversary $\mathcal{A}$ is computationally unbounded, and must specify the location of the probes before querying the circuit. However, the adversary can change the location of the probes over multiple circuit queries. The adversary's interaction with the circuit is mediated through encoder and decoder algorithms, neither of which can be probed.

In the bounded query model, the security of a circuit C with input k against a dth-order probing adversary is quantified by means of the left-or-right security game. The challenger picks a random bit b and provides an oracle $\mathcal{O}^b$, to which adversary $\mathcal{A}$ is given query access. The adversary queries the oracle by choosing up to d wires to probe – we denote this set of probe positions by $\mathcal{P}$ – and sends it to the oracle along with chosen inputs k_0 and k_1. The oracle responds with the probed wire values of $C(k_b)$. After a total of q queries, the adversary responds to the challenger with a guess for b. For $b \in \{0, 1\}$, denote the result of the adversary after interacting with the oracle $\mathcal{O}^b$ using q queries by $\mathcal{A}^{\mathcal{O}^b}$. The left-or-right advantage of the adversary $\mathcal{A}$ is then as defined as

$$\mathrm{Adv\text{-}thr}(\mathcal{A}) = |\Pr[\mathcal{A}^{\mathcal{O}^0} = 1] - \Pr[\mathcal{A}^{\mathcal{O}^1} = 1]|.$$

The above model is extended to capture the effect of glitches on hardware. Whereas a probe normally results in the value of a single wire, a glitch-extended probe allows observing all value used in the calculation of the probed wire up to the previous register layer. More information can be found in the work by Faust et al. [13].

Security Analysis. The main theoretical result of [2] is that the bounded-query probing security of a masked cipher can be related to its linear cryptanalysis. The first step towards this result is provided by Theorem 1 below, which relates the security of the masked cipher to the Fourier transform of the probability distribution of wire values obtained by probing. The link with linear cryptanalysis will be developed in detail in Sect. 2.4.

The Fourier transform of a function $V \to \mathbb{C}$, where V is a subspace of $\mathbb{F}_2^n$, can be defined as in Definition 1 below. For the purposes of this section, only probability mass functions on $\mathbb{F}_2^n$ need be considered. Despite this, Definition 1 considers more general functions on an arbitrary subspace $V \subseteq \mathbb{F}_2^n$. Since any vector space over $\mathbb{F}_2$ is isomorphic to $\mathbb{F}_2^n$ for some n, this generalization is mostly a matter of notation. Nevertheless, this extended notation will be convenient in Sect. 2.4.

Definition 1 ([2], **Sect. 2.1**). *Let $V \subseteq \mathbb{F}_2^n$ be a vector space and $f : V \to \mathbb{C}$ a complex-valued function on V. The Fourier transformation of f is a function $\widehat{f} : \mathbb{F}_2^n / V^\perp \to \mathbb{C}$ defined by*

$$\widehat{f}(u) = \sum_{x \in V} (-1)^{u^\top x} f(x),$$

where we write u for $u + V^\perp$. Equivalently, $\widehat{f}$ is the representation of f in the basis of functions $x \mapsto (-1)^{u^\top x}$ for $u \in \mathbb{F}_2^n / V^\perp$.

Recall that the orthogonal complement $V^\perp$ of a subspace V of $\mathbb{F}_2^n$ is the vector space $V^\perp = \{x \in \mathbb{F}_2^n \mid \forall v \in V : v^\top x = 0\}$. The quotient space $\mathbb{F}_2^n / V^\perp$ is by definition the vector space of cosets of $V^\perp$. For convenience, an element $x + V^\perp \in \mathbb{F}_2^n / V^\perp$ will simply be denoted by x. For $x \in \mathbb{F}_2^n / V^\perp$ and $v \in V$, the expression $x^\top v$ is well-defined. Consequently, the above definition is proper.

The main theorem on the advantage of an adversary in the bounded-query probing model can now be stated. It relies on the observation that, for a bounded-query probing secure circuit, all probed wire values either closely resemble uniform randomness or reveal nothing about the secret input.

Theorem 1 ([2], Sect. 4). *Let $\mathcal{A}$ be a t-threshold-probing adversary for a circuit C. Assume that for every query made by $\mathcal{A}$ on the oracle $\mathcal{O}^b$, there exists a partitioning (depending only on the probe positions) of the resulting wire values into two random variables $\mathbf{x}$ ('good') and $\mathbf{y}$ ('bad') such that*

1. *The conditional probability distribution $p_{\mathbf{y}|\mathbf{x}}$ satisfies $\mathbb{E}_{\mathbf{x}}\|\widehat{p}_{\mathbf{y}|\mathbf{x}} - \delta_0\|_2^2 \leq \varepsilon$ with δ_0 the Kronecker delta function,*
2. *Any t-threshold-probing adversary for the same circuit C and making the same oracle queries as $\mathcal{A}$, but which only receives the 'good' wire values (i.e. corresponding to $\mathbf{x}$) for each query, has advantage zero.*

The advantage of $\mathcal{A}$ can be upper bounded as

$$\mathrm{Adv}_{t\text{-thr}}(\mathcal{A}) \leq \sqrt{2\,q\,\varepsilon}\,,$$

where q is the number of queries to the oracle $\mathcal{O}^b$.

The advantage of a probing adversary against the circuit can be upper bounded in terms of $\|\widehat{p}_{\mathbf{z}} - \delta_0\|_2$ where $p_{\mathbf{z}}$ is the probability distribution of any measured set of 'bad' wire values, possibly conditioned on several 'good' wire values. The conditioning on 'good' values simply corresponds to fixing some variables in the circuit to constants. Section 2.4 provides the essential link between $\widehat{p}_{\mathbf{z}}$ and the linear cryptanalysis of the shared circuit that will enable us to upper bound the quantity $\|\widehat{p}_{\mathbf{z}} - \delta_0\|_2$ for concrete masked ciphers.

2.2   Boolean Masking and Threshold Implementations

Boolean masking is a technique based on splitting each secret variable $x \in \mathbb{F}_2$ in the circuit into shares $\bar{x} = (x^1, x^2, \ldots, x^{s_x})$ such that $x = \sum_{i=1}^{s_x} x^i$ over $\mathbb{F}_2$. A random Boolean masking of a fixed secret is uniform if all sharings of that secret are equally likely.

There are several approaches to masking a circuit. In this work, we make use of threshold implementations, proposed by Nikova *et al.* [20]. This approach has been extended to capture higher-order univariate attacks by Bilgin *et al.* [4]. In the following, the main properties of threshold implementations are reviewed.

Let $\bar{F}$ be a layer in the threshold implementation corresponding to a part of the circuit $F : \mathbb{F}_2^n \rightarrow \mathbb{F}_2^m$. The function $\bar{F} : \mathbb{F}_2^{ns_x} \rightarrow \mathbb{F}_2^{ms_y}$, where we assume s_x shares per input bit and s_y shares per output bit, will be called a *sharing* of F. The ith share of the function $\bar{F}$ is denoted by $F^i : \mathbb{F}_2^{ns_x} \rightarrow \mathbb{F}_2^m$, for $i \in \{1, .., s_y\}$. Sharings can have a number of properties that are relevant in the security argument for a threshold implementation; these properties are summarized in Definition 2.

Definition 2 (Properties of sharings [4,20]). *Let $F : \mathbb{F}_2^n \rightarrow \mathbb{F}_2^m$ be a function and $\bar{F} : \mathbb{F}_2^{ns_x} \rightarrow \mathbb{F}_2^{ms_y}$ be a sharing of F. The sharing $\bar{F}$ is said to be*

1. *correct if $\sum_{i=1}^{s_y} F^i(x^1, \ldots, x^{s_x}) = F(x)$ for all $x \in \mathbb{F}_2^n$ and for all shares $x^1, \ldots, x^{s_x} \in \mathbb{F}_2^n$ such that $\sum_{i=1}^{s_x} x^i = x$,*

2. d^{th}-order non-complete *if any function in d or fewer shares F^i depends on at most $s_x - 1$ input shares,*
3. uniform *if $\bar{F}$ maps a uniform random sharing of any $x \in \mathbb{F}_2^n$ to a uniform random sharing of $F(x) \in \mathbb{F}_2^m$.*

2.3   Changing of the Guards

The changing of the guards method proposed by Daemen [7] is a technique that transforms a non-complete sharing into a uniform and non-complete sharing. The technique works by embedding the sharing into a Feistel-like structure. In this paper, we slightly generalize the method by considering a (higher-order) probing secure sharing. Such a sharing potentially requires multiple register stages and extra randomness to guarantee its security. However, the changing of the guards method still ensures the uniformity of the output. An example of the method with four shares is shown in Fig. 1.

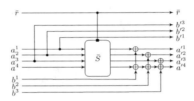

Fig. 1. Changing of the guards method with four shares where the shared S-box $\bar{S}$ uses the randomness $\bar{r}$.

2.4   Cryptanalysis of Higher-Order Threshold Implementations

As discussed in Sect. 2.1, Theorem 1 allows proving the security of higher-order threshold implementations given an upper bound on the Fourier coefficients of probability distributions of wire values obtained by probing. This section shows how such an upper bound can be obtained using linear cryptanalysis.

For any linear masking scheme, there exists a vector space $\mathbb{V} \subset \mathbb{F}_2^\ell$ of valid sharings of zero. More specifically, an $\mathbb{F}_2$-linear secret sharing scheme is an algorithm that maps a secret $x \in \mathbb{F}_2^n$ to a random element of a corresponding coset of the vector space $\mathbb{V}$. Let $\rho : \mathbb{F}_2^n \to \mathbb{F}_2^\ell$ be a map that sends secrets to their corresponding coset representative. For convenience, we denote $\mathbb{V}_a = a + \mathbb{V}$.

Let $\bar{G}$ be a correct sharing of a function $G : \mathbb{F}_2^n \to \mathbb{F}_2^n$ in the sense of Definition 2. Fix any $x \in \mathbb{F}_2^n$ and let $a = \rho(x)$ and $b = \rho(G(x))$. The correctness property implies that $\bar{G}(\mathbb{V}_a) \subseteq \mathbb{V}_b$. It follows that the restriction $F : \mathbb{V}_a \to \mathbb{V}_b$ of $\bar{G}$ defined by $F(x) = \bar{G}(x)$ is a well defined function.

Linear cryptanalysis is closely related to the propagation of the Fourier transformation of a probability distribution under a function $F : \mathbb{V}_a \to \mathbb{V}_b$. This leads to the notion of correlation matrices due to Daemen *et al.* [8]. The action of F on probability distributions can be described by a linear operator. The coordinate representation of this operator with respect to the standard basis $\{\delta_x\}_{x \in V}$ may be called the *transition matrix* of F. Following [1], the correlation matrix of F is then the same operator expressed with respect to the Fourier basis. The correlation matrix of a sharing can be defined as follows. Note that it only depends on the spaces $\mathbb{V}_a$ and $\mathbb{V}_b$, not on the specific choice of the representatives a and b.

Definition 3 (Correlation matrix). *For a subspace $\mathbb{V} \subseteq \mathbb{F}_2^\ell$, let $F : \mathbb{V}_a \to \mathbb{V}_b$ be a function. The correlation matrix C^F of F is a real $|\mathbb{V}_b| \times |\mathbb{V}_a|$ matrix with coordinates indexed by elements $u, v \in \mathbb{F}_2^n / \mathbb{V}^\perp$ and equal to*

$$C_{v,u}^F = \frac{1}{|\mathbb{V}|} \sum_{x \in \mathbb{V}_a} (-1)^{u^\top x + v^\top F(x)}.$$

The relation between Definition 3 and linear cryptanalysis is as follows: the coordinate $C_{v,u}^F$ is equal to the correlation of a linear approximation over F with input mask u and output mask v. That is, $C_{v,u}^F = 2 \Pr[v^\top F(\mathbf{x}) = u^\top \mathbf{x}] - 1$ for $\mathbf{x}$ uniform random on $\mathbb{V}_a$. An important difference with ordinary linear cryptanalysis is that, for shared functions, the masks u and v correspond to equivalence classes. This formalizes the intuitive observation that masks which differ by a vector orthogonal to the space $\mathbb{V}$ lead to identical correlations.

From this point on, we restrict to second-order probing adversaries. The description of the link with linear cryptanalysis presented in [2], is completed by Theorem 2 below. It shows that the coordinates of $\widehat{p}_\mathbf{z}$ are entries of the correlation matrix of the state-transformation between the specified probe locations. In Theorem 2, the restriction of $x \in \mathbb{V}_a$ to an index set $I = \{i_1, \ldots, i_m\}$ is denoted by $x_I = (x_{i_1}, \ldots, x_{i_m}) \in \mathbb{F}_2^{|I|}$. This definition depends on the specific choice of the representative a, but the result of Theorem 2 does not.

Theorem 2 ([2], Sect. 5.2). *Let $F : \mathbb{V}_a \to \mathbb{V}_b$ be a function with $\mathbb{V} \subset \mathbb{F}_2^\ell$ and $I, J \subset \{1, \ldots, \ell\}$. For $\mathbf{x}$ uniform random on $\mathbb{V}_a$ and $\mathbf{y} = F(\mathbf{x})$, let $\mathbf{z} = (\mathbf{x}_I, \mathbf{y}_J)$. The Fourier transformation of the probability mass function of $\mathbf{z}$ then satisfies*

$$|\widehat{p}_\mathbf{z}(u, v)| = |C_{\widetilde{v}, \widetilde{u}}^F|,$$

where $\widetilde{u}, \widetilde{v} \in \mathbb{F}_2^\ell / \mathbb{V}^\perp$ are such that $\widetilde{u}_I = u$, $\widetilde{u}_{[\ell] \setminus I} = 0$, $\widetilde{v}_J = v$ and $\widetilde{v}_{[\ell] \setminus J} = 0$.

Theorem 2 relates the linear approximations of F to $\widehat{p}_\mathbf{z}(u)$ and hence provides a method to upper bound $\|\widehat{p}_\mathbf{z} - \delta_0\|_2$ based on linear cryptanalysis. Upper bounding the absolute correlations $|C_{\widetilde{v}, \widetilde{u}}^F|$ is nontrivial in general. However, the piling-up principle [17,24] can be used to obtain heuristic estimates.

Importantly, Theorem 2 relates to linear cryptanalysis with respect to $\mathbb{V}$ rather than $\mathbb{F}_2^\ell$. The differences are mostly minor, but there is a subtle difference in relation to the important notion of 'activity'. In standard linear cryptanalysis, an S-box is said to be active if its output mask is nonzero. The same definition applies for linear cryptanalysis with respect to $\mathbb{V}$, but one must take into account that the mask is now an element of the quotient space $\mathbb{F}_2^\ell / \mathbb{V}^\perp$. In particular, if the mask corresponding to the shares of a particular bit can be represented by an all-one vector $(1, 1, \ldots, 1)^\top$, it may be equivalently represented by the zero vector. It is still true that a valid linear approximation for a permutation must have either both input masks equivalent to zero or neither equivalent to zero. More generally, this condition is ensured by any uniform sharing.

3   A Low-Randomness Second-Order Secure AES

In this section, our second-order masking of the AES is introduced.

3.1   Masking Details

Masking State and Key. For the sharing of the AES state and key, we use classical Boolean masking. The 128-bit state is shared using four shares per bit, requiring a total of $128 \times 3 = 384$ random bits. The 128-bit key is also shared using four shares, and this also costs 384 random bits. Finally, we extend the state by an additional column where each cell contains three shares of randomness. This requires an additional $32 \times 3 = 96$ random bits and is necessary for the "guards in formation" technique that will be described in Theorem 3.3. It will be used over the rows of the state for the S-box layer. An overview of the shared AES round function is shown in Fig. 2. The following sections discuss further aspects of this sharing.

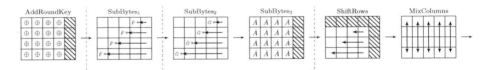

Fig. 2. One round of the masked AES. The locations of the registers are indicated by dashed lines. The nonlinear operations require an additional register stage, which is not shown on the figure. Hatched cells remain unchanged through the operation.

Sharing the Affine Transformations. The masking of the linear transformations ShiftRows and MixColumns is simply done share-wise. Constants are added to the first share of the relevant variable.

Sharing the S-Box. The AES S-box consists of an inversion S over $\mathbb{F}_{2^8}$ and an affine layer A. Similar to the other linear layers of the AES, the affine layer is masked using a share-wise approach. Following the work by Wegener *et al.* [25], the inversion $(x \mapsto x^{254})$ is decomposed into two cubic functions. Specifically, we consider

$$x^{254} = \left(x^{26}\right)^{49} = G(F(x)).$$

The sharings $\bar{F}$ and $\bar{G}$ of F and G respectively are chosen such that they are first-order non-complete and second-order probing secure. That is, none of the output shares depends on all of the input shares and placing two probes in the sharing does not reveal any secret values. While the need for second-order probing security is clear, non-completeness is required such that, even when randomness is re-used, a security analysis over multiple rounds remains possible. More details are given in Sect. 4.2.

Non-complete sharings of F and G can be achieved by using four input shares. More specifically, we use the direct four-sharing of F and G as defined in the thesis of Bilgin [3, pg. 36]. To achieve second-order probing security, the sharings $\bar{F}$ and $\bar{G}$ are split into two stages separated by a register such that $\bar{F} = \bar{F}_2 \circ \bar{F}_1$ and $\bar{G} = \bar{G}_2 \circ \bar{G}_1$ with $\bar{F}_1, \bar{F}_2, \bar{G}_1$ and $\bar{G}_2$ second-order non-complete. In particular, $\bar{F}_2$ and $\bar{G}_2$ merely implement a linear compression of shares into four output shares. To ensure the second-order probing security of $\bar{F}$ and $\bar{G}$, randomness is added at the end of the stages $\bar{F}_1$ and $\bar{G}_1$.

Finally, the sharing is made uniform using the changing of the guards approach of Daemen [7] which was recalled in Sect. 2.3.

Key Schedule. The key schedule is masked similar to the state. Meaning that linear layers are masked share-wise and the masked S-box follows the method above.

Using the linear cryptanalysis tool introduced in Sect. 4, we find that using the above masked AES S-box with changing of the guards over the four S-boxes does not result in a secure masking of the key-schedule. In fact, one can easily find trails with nonzero correlation over few rounds with a small number of active S-boxes. One such trail is shown in Appendix A. Hence, we instantiate the additional cell due to the changing of the guards technique with fresh randomness in every evaluation. This costs 24 random bits for every $\bar{F}$ or $\bar{G}$ layer for a total randomness cost of $20 \times 24 = 480$ bits plus an additional 384 random bits for the initial sharing of the master key. The 456 random bits to ensure the local second-order probing security of the masked S-box can be re-used from the masked S-boxes in the state.

3.2   Optimizing the S-Box Sharing

As explained in Sect. 3.1, the S-box sharing is realized using a particular technique to ensure second-order non-completeness over each register stage and first-order non-completeness over both stages. This section shows how to minimize the randomness costs by reducing the number of output shares in the second-order non-complete expansion layers $\bar{F}_1$ and $\bar{G}_1$.

We start with a straightforward method to choose $\bar{F}_1$ and $\bar{G}_1$. Denote the output bits of $\bar{F}$ (similarly $\bar{G}$) by $y_i^1, y_i^2, y_i^3, y_i^4$ for $i \in \{1, ..., 8\}$. Each output bit is a function of at most three shares of each input bit due to $\bar{F}$ being non-complete. One can again find a second-order non-complete sharing for each of these three-shared functions. This would indeed result in a decomposition of $\bar{F}$

that is second-order non-complete in each stage, while maintaining the first-order non-completeness of $\bar{F}$.

The above method has the downside that it results in functions $\bar{F}_1$ with a large number of shares. This can be optimized further. Instead of using a second-order non-complete sharing of each F^i (or G^i), we can re-share some functions using a first-order non-complete covering scheme. The optimized covering scheme is shown in Table 1. The third column shows which input shares can be combined in $\bar{F}_1$ (or $\bar{G}_1$). For example, F^1 is re-shared such that each output bit can use only either the first and second share of an input bit or the first and third. This covering scheme is verified to be second-order non-complete. For example, it is clear that one probe can never learn the second and third share of an input bit.

Table 1. This table depicts the share dependencies of an input bit for $\bar{F}$, $\bar{G}$ or $\bar{F}_1$, $\bar{G}_1$. It also shows which random bits are added to the output of $\bar{F}_1$ or $\bar{G}_1$.

Output share	$\bar{F}$ or $\bar{G}$	$\bar{F}_1$ or $\bar{G}_1$	Used random bits
1	$\{x^1, x^2, x^3\}$	$\{x^1, x^2\}, \{x^1, x^3\}$	$r_1, ..., r_{96}$
2	$\{x^2, x^3, x^4\}$	$\{x^2\}, \{x^3\}, \{x^4\}$	$r_{97}, ..., r_{456}$
3	$\{x^1, x^3, x^4\}$	$\{x^1, x^3\}, \{x^1, x^4\}$	$r_1 + r_{97}, ..., r_{96} + r_{192}$
4	$\{x^1, x^2, x^4\}$	$\{x^1, x^2\}, \{x^1, x^4\}$	$r_1 + r_{193}, ..., r_{96} + r_{288}$

While Table 1 shows a second-order non-complete covering scheme for $\bar{F}_1$ and $\bar{G}_1$, we still need to share $\bar{F}$ or $\bar{G}$ following those requirements. For this, we use the covering schemes from the work by Bozilov [5]. This work provides a covering such that each function F^1, F^3, and F^4 is re-shared to have 12 output shares and F^2 can be re-shared to have 45 output shares. Thus, we have a total of $45 \cdot 8 + 24 \cdot 12 = 648$ output shares for $\bar{F}_1$ (similarly $\bar{G}_1$).

In order to ensure the second-order probing security of the sharings of $\bar{F}$ and $\bar{G}$, a total of 648 random bits are added to the second-order non-complete sharing before re-compression. We can reduce this number by observing that the security condition boils down to requiring that all values seen by the probing adversary need to be masked with a unique random bit. In Table 1, we show a reduction of this randomness to 456 bits. By probing, an adversary can see all random bits related to an output share listed in the table. One can see that, even if two output shares are probed, all observed bits in the expansion are masked with a unique random bit. For example, probing output shares 2 and 3, the adversary observes $r_{97}, ..., r_{456}$ and $r_1 + r_{97}, ..., r_{96} + r_{193}$. The observations are then still masked by the unique random bits $r_{97}, ..., r_{456}$ and $r_1, ..., r_{96}$.

3.3   Guards in Formation

This section discusses the application of the changing of the guards technique to the S-box layer. Recall from Fig. 1 that three out of four shares of one input (b^1, b^2, b^3) are used to re-mask the other branch (a'^1, a'^2, a'^3, a'^4) in the Feistel structure. However, when used in a straightforward way, this operation is not second-order non-complete as three shares are used to mask the fourth share of the other branch. In order to make the re-masking operation second-order probing secure, it can be spread across the two stages of the sharing $\bar{F}$ (or $\bar{G}$).

It is also important to consider how the changing of the guards structure links the different cells of the state. As the cryptanalytic properties of our masking affect its security, the diffusion resulting from the linear layer plays an important role. However, from the perspective of linear-cryptanalysis, placing a changing of the guards structure over the S-box layer reduces diffusion. To improve diffusion while keeping the cost minimal, we look for inspiration in the Rijndael-160 cipher [9].

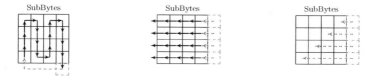

Fig. 3. Three examples of diffusion patterns using the changing of the guards technique. Additional cells are outlined by dashed gray lines. The third example chains all cells in a row.

A traditional application of the changing of the guards method would result in one additional state cell. This extra cell is instantiated with a random sharing of zero at the start of execution. One has several options on how to lay out the changing of the guards structure in this case, one example is shown in the leftmost illustration in Fig. 3. Since the changing of the guards method now mixes shares from different cells, it affects the diffusion of the shared cipher. Using the security analysis tool that will be introduced in Sect. 4, one finds that the example in Fig. 3 results in linear trails with few active S-boxes. Consequently, the security bound obtained using Theorem 1 would not be satisfactory.

Instead, we shorten the chain of cells linked by the changing of the guards structure by increasing the number of additional cells. Specifically, the changing of the guards method is applied to the S-boxes in each of the rows of the state independently. This is illustrated in the middle illustration of Fig. 3. Furthermore, the diffusion properties over the enlarged state are improved by also applying a `MixColumns` operation over the four extra cells. Finally, to complete the analogy with Rijndael-160, a 'shift' is introduced in the changing of the guards structure. The shifting offset depends on the row number as depicted in the rightmost part of Fig. 3. The final result is shown in Fig. 2.

4   Security Analysis

This section determines an upper bound on the advantage of second-order probing adversaries for the masked AES construction from Sect. 3.

4.1   Single Round

In this section, we argue that one round of the masked AES is second-order probing secure. Recall that, without loss of generality, it may be assumed that all probes are placed right before a register stage. Probes placed in linear layers only return one share per input bit. Probing two linear layers is trivially secure, and probing a linear layer and an S-box can be reduced to the following cases where two S-boxes are probed. Hence, only two cases must be considered: both probes placed within the same shared S-box (either $\bar{F}$ or $\bar{G}$), or probes positioned in two different shared S-boxes.

For the first case, consider that the adversary places both probes in $\bar{F}$ (the argument is the same for $\bar{G}$). If both probes are placed in $\bar{F}_1$, the adversary does not receive all shares of any secret bit since $\bar{F}_1$ is a second-order non-complete sharing. Thus, consider the case where the adversary probes the compression layer $\bar{F}_2$. As shown in Table 1, each bit at the input of the expansion layer is masked with a unique random bit. Thus, whatever the choice of the second probe position, the adversary cannot infer any information about an input secret of $\bar{F}$. As a result, the sharings $\bar{F}$ and $\bar{G}$ are second-order probing secure.

Consider the second case, *i.e.* the two probes are placed in different S-boxes. If both probes are placed in the $\bar{F}$-part of the S-box sharings (similarly $\bar{G}$) then, due to first-order non-completeness, the adversary does not learn any secret bits. Hence, we consider the case where one probe is placed in $\bar{F}$ and one is placed in $\bar{G}$. Consider that $\bar{b}$ denotes the additional branch used for the changing of the guards technique. This branch $\bar{b}$ is a uniform random sharing of zero and is used to re-mask the output of $\bar{F}$. From the probe in $\bar{F}$, the adversary learns at most one output share of $\bar{F}$. We argue that the probe in $\bar{G}$ cannot reveal all of the other output shares. The argument is based on the consistent use of the same covering scheme for both sharings:

- Due to the second-order non-completeness of the expansion layer $\bar{G}_1$ of $\bar{G}$, probing $\bar{G}_1$ does not reveal any of the other three output shares of $\bar{F}$.
- When probing the compression layer $\bar{G}_2$ of $\bar{G}$, the resulting values are masked by the randomness $\bar{r}$. The adversary can only see the same bits of $\bar{r}$ as obtained from the probe in $\bar{F}$ when the indices of the probed output shares of $\bar{F}$ and $\bar{G}$ are the same. The covering scheme used for non-completeness (second column of Table 1) guarantees that the adversary does not obtain all of the output shares of $\bar{F}$.

The above security argument also holds for the key schedule, as it uses the same masked S-box. In particular, the four S-boxes in one round of the key schedule can be considered to be parallel to the 16 S-boxes in the round function.

4.2   Multiple Rounds

Following Theorems 1 and 2, we argue the second-order probing security of multiple rounds of the masked AES by bounding the correlation of all linear trails resulting from two probes placed in different rounds. Specifically, by Theorem 2, bounding the correlation of linear approximations in the masked cipher results in an upper bound on $\|\widehat{p}_{\mathbf{z}} - \delta_0\|_2$ where $p_{\mathbf{z}}$ is the probability distribution of the probed values. In turn, by Theorem 1, this provides a bound on the advantage of second-order probing adversaries.

All of the randomness which is re-used across S-boxes, can be labeled as 'good' in the terminology of Theorem 1. This is safe, since an adversary only probing these values cannot obtain any secret information. Consequently, in the linear cryptanalysis of the masked cipher, these random bits must be considered to be constant. Since F and G are shared in a non-complete way even without the use of randomness, we can assume that any probe placed by the adversary results in a set of non-complete input shares. This is important, since it implies only linear approximations with nonzero input and output masks must be considered.

To ensure the security of the masking, all linear approximations over the sharings $\bar{G}$ and $\bar{F}$ should have a low absolute correlation. Verifying this property is slow since the masked S-box has 32 input bits. Using optimized verification software, it takes 1500 core hours on an Intel(R) Xeon(R) Gold 6230 CPU with a clock frequency of 2.10 GHz to compute the linear approximation table of a sharing for one input secret (one restriction). The search revealed sharings of the F and G with the following properties.

Claim 1. *Let $\bar{F} : \mathbb{V}_a \to \mathbb{V}_b$ be any restriction of the sharing of F obtained in Section 3.1. Denote its absolute correlation matrix by $|C^{\bar{F}}|$. For any $u, v \in \mathbb{F}_2^\ell / \mathbb{V}^\perp$ not both equal to zero, it holds that $\left|C_{u,v}^{\bar{F}}\right| \leq 2^{-3}$ and, moreover, $\left|C_{0,v}^{\bar{F}}\right| \leq 2^{-3.8}$.*

Claim 2. *Let $\bar{G} : \mathbb{V}_a \to \mathbb{V}_b$ be any restriction of the sharing of G obtained in Section 3.1. Denote its absolute correlation matrix by $|C^{\bar{G}}|$. For any $u, v \in \mathbb{F}_2^\ell / \mathbb{V}^\perp$ not both equal to zero, it holds that $\left|C_{u,v}^{\bar{G}}\right| \leq 2^{-2.6}$ and, moreover, $\left|C_{0,v}^{\bar{G}}\right| \leq 2^{-4}$.*

The above two claims can be verified from the linear approximation table of the sharings. However, the above two results are claims since they were only verified for a couple of secrets.

To upper bound the maximum absolute correlation of linear trails between the observed values (corresponding to nonzero masks), we use a slight refinement of the standard a wide-trail type argument. That is, we search for the best trail activity patterns over the masked AES, but we take into account both cases in Claims 1 and 2. All of this is done using automated tools. Specifically, we encode this search problem as a sequence of Satisfiability Modulo Theories (SMT) problems in the bit-vector theory. These problems are then solved with the off-the-shelf SMT solver Boolector [19]. A similar approach was originally used by Mouha *et al.* [18] to search for activity patterns of the unmasked AES using Mixed Integer Linear Programming. Whereas the approach of Mouha *et al.* is to search for activity patterns with a minimal number of active S-boxes, our approach is to look for activity patterns with maximal absolute correlation. To create and solve these SMT problems we used a development version of ArxPy[1].

---

[1] https://github.com/ranea/ArxPy

To model the correlation of the shared S-boxes, we consider the worst case scenarios from Claims 1 and 2, that is, replacing the inequalities for both cases by equalities. Thus, the correlation of the activity patterns found by our SMT-based method provides an upper bound on the correlation of all linear trails compatible with a specified activity pattern for the input and output masks. An optimal trail is shown in Appendix C. It spans three rounds and has absolute linear correlation at most $2^{-55.20}$. Therefore, the absolute correlation of all relevant linear trails is bounded by $2^{-55.20}$. It follows that the squared 2-norm of the nontrivial Fourier coefficients of the observed bits $\mathbf{z}$ can be upper bounded by

$$\varepsilon := \|\widehat{p_{\mathbf{z}}} - \delta_0\|_2^2 \le |\mathrm{supp}\,\widehat{p_{\mathbf{z}}}|\, \|\widehat{p_{\mathbf{z}}} - \delta_0\|_\infty^2 \le 2^{48}\, 2^{-110.40} = 2^{-62.40},$$

where we have used the inequality $|\mathrm{supp}\,\widehat{p_{\mathbf{z}}}| \le 2^{48}$. The latter follows from the fact that the observed value $\mathbf{z}$ consists of at most 48 bits in the glitch-extended probing model: if an output coordinate of $\bar{F}$ or $\bar{G}$ is read, at most 24 shares are learned; if an output of the shared linear layer is probed, at most seven shares are observed.

We also built an SMT model for the key schedule. The best trail was found to span eight rounds and activates 21 masked S-boxes. The absolute correlation of the trail is upper bounded by $2^{-63.60}$. Thus, the squared 2-norm of the nontrivial Fourier coefficients of observed bits in the key schedule can be bounded by $\varepsilon \le 2^{-79.20}$. As the trails through the state transformation have a larger absolute correlation, the upper bound on the maximum advantage of a second-order probing adversary is determined by the bound $\varepsilon \le 2^{-62.40}$.

4.3   Security Claim

Due to the analysis in Sects. 4.1 and 4.2, Theorem 1 can be applied with the upper bound $\varepsilon \le 2^{-62.40}$. It follows that the following security claim can be made.

Security Claim 1. *For the masked AES described in Sect. 3, the following bound on the advantage of the adversary (assuming piling-up) in the probing model is claimed:*

$$\mathrm{Adv}_{\text{2-thr}}(\mathcal{A}) \le \sqrt{\frac{q}{2^{61.4}}}\,.$$

Although the above bound is expressed in terms of the number of probing queries, it can be interpreted in terms of the number of traces taken by an adversary subject to a few assumptions. If the attacker mounts a second-order DPA attack using at most two time samples in a power trace, then the number of queries corresponds to the number of traces. If an adversary does not gather more than 2^{27} (100 million) traces, the above bound shows that the advantage of any attack is at most $2^{-17.2}$. We note that most of the side-channel literature verifies implementations using 100 million traces [11,12]. The next section shows that this bound can be significantly improved by taking a closer look at the glitch model, leading to a much lower advantage in practice.

5   Sharpening the Glitch Model

In Sect. 4, an upper bound on the advantage of a second-order probing adversary for the masked AES of Sect. 3 was obtained. However, we observe that this bound is significantly negatively impacted by the large support of the Fourier transformation of the observed values. Indeed, this leads to an increase in advantage by a factor 2^{24} due to the possibility that a glitch-extended probe may observe 24 bits. In this section, we propose a modified glitch model (supported by simulations) that leads to an improved bound.

We adapt the glitch-extended probing model from Sect. 2.1. Instead of an adversary which observes the values of all wires that depend on the probed wire (up to the preceding register stage), the new model proposes that the adversary chooses an arbitrary Boolean function of those values. For example, suppose that the adversary places a glitch-extended probe on a masked function $g(x_1, \ldots, x_n)$. Instead of receiving all of the input values $x_1, \ldots, x_n$, the adversary can choose a function $f : \mathbb{F}_2^n \to \mathbb{F}_2$ and receives the value $f(x_1, \ldots, x_n)$ instead. The function f will be referred to as the *glitch function*.

The idea is that, intuitively, the glitch function cannot be completely arbitrary: most Boolean functions in many variables are not easily realized with a small, structured circuit. We formalize this intuition by postulating that the 1-norm of the Walsh-Hadamard transform of the glitch function can not be too large. To exploit this assumption, the following refinement of Theorem 2 is proposed.

Theorem 3. *Let $F : \mathbb{V}_a \to \mathbb{V}_b$ be a permutation with $\mathbb{V} \subset \mathbb{F}_2^\ell$ and $I, J \subset \{1, \ldots, \ell\}$. For $\mathbf{x}$ uniform random on $\mathbb{V}_a$ and $\mathbf{y} = F(\mathbf{x})$, let $\mathbf{z} = (g_1(\mathbf{x}_I), g_2(\mathbf{y}_J))$, $f_1 = 2^{-|I|}(-1)^{g_1}$, and $f_2 = 2^{-|J|}(-1)^{g_2}$. The Fourier transformation of the probability mass function of $\mathbf{z}$ then satisfies*

$$\|\widehat{p_{\mathbf{z}}} - \delta_0\|_2 \leq \|\widehat{f_1}\|_1 \|\widehat{f_2}\|_1 \max_{w, w' \in \mathbb{F}_2^\ell / \mathbb{V}^\perp} |C_{w, w'}^F|,$$

where $w, w' \in \mathbb{F}_2^\ell / \mathbb{V}^\perp$ are such that $w'_{[\ell] \setminus I} = 0$ and $w_{[\ell] \setminus J} = 0$.

Proof. Let $\mathbf{z}' = (\mathbf{x}_I, \mathbf{y}_J)$. By Theorem 2, it holds that $\widehat{p_{\mathbf{z}'}}(u, v) = C_{\tilde{v}, \tilde{u}}^F$ where $\tilde{u}, \tilde{v} \in \mathbb{F}_2^\ell / \mathbb{V}^\perp$ are such that $\tilde{u}_I = u$, $\tilde{u}_{[\ell] \setminus I} = 0$, $\tilde{v}_J = v$, and $\tilde{v}_{[\ell] \setminus J} = 0$. In addition, it holds that

$$\widehat{p_{\mathbf{z}}}(1, 1) = \left[(C^{f_1} \otimes C^{f_2}) \widehat{p_{\mathbf{z}'}}\right]_{1, 1} = \sum_{u \in \mathbb{F}_2^{|I|}, v \in \mathbb{F}_2^{|J|}} \widehat{f_1}(u) \widehat{f_2}(v) C_{\tilde{v}, \tilde{u}}^F.$$

Since $\widehat{p_{\mathbf{z}}}(0, 0) = 1$, $\widehat{p_{\mathbf{z}}}(0, 1) = 0$, and $\widehat{p_{\mathbf{z}}}(1, 0) = 0$, it holds that $\|\widehat{p_{\mathbf{z}}} - \delta_0\|_2 = |\widehat{p_{\mathbf{z}}}(1, 1)|$. The absolute value of $\widehat{p_{\mathbf{z}}}(1, 1)$ can be upper-bounded using the triangle inequality:

$$|\widehat{p_{\mathbf{z}}}(1, 1)| \leq \sum_{u \in \mathbb{F}_2^{|I|}, v \in \mathbb{F}_2^{|J|}} |\widehat{f_1}(u)| |\widehat{f_2}(v)| |C_{\tilde{v}, \tilde{u}}^F| \leq \|\widehat{f_1}\|_1 \|\widehat{f_2}\|_1 \max_{w, w' \in \mathbb{F}_2^\ell / \mathbb{V}^\perp} |C_{w, w'}^F|.$$

The above theorem shows that we can improve the bound on a probing adversary if we know the 1-norm of the Walsh-Hadamard transformation of the glitch functions. In order to upper bound this 1-norm, one can simulate the effect of glitches on the circuit.

Our simulation setup is based on the work of Šijačić *et al.* [22]. We obtain gate-level netlists using Synopsys DesignCompiler with a 45 nm standard-cell library from NanGate. Composite Current Source (CCS) models provide detailed timing information with 1 ps precision. CCS timing also captures different gate propagation delays for every pin and signal edge (rising or falling). Thus, we include the effects of data-dependent glitches in the simulations. The distribution of data-dependent glitches is also affected by the routing wires delays and random fluctuations of the operating environment (*e.g.* noise, temperature, and operating voltage). To account for these influences, we annotate delays of all ports and wires using random values drawn from a normal distribution with mean 100 ps and variance $30\,(\text{ps})^2$. We use MentorGraphics QuestaSim for logic simulation. Lastly, we develop custom parsers to obtain continuous identity function traces from logic simulation outputs.

We simulate the masked AES S-box from Sect. 3 and compute its Walsh-spectrum for different probe positions. However, since the masked AES S-box has 32 input bits, the memory requirements for performing many experiments are large. To provide an additional example, we also simulate a 9-bit XOR. The spectrum and 1-norms for different input delays, initial states, and different probe positions and time samples for the masked AES S-box and 9-bit XOR is given in Appendix B.

Using the observed 1-norm and the above theorem, we can improve the security bound for the masked AES from Sect. 3. From Fig. 6 in Appendix B, we observe that the 1-norm of the Walsh-Hadamard transform of the glitch functions for the masked AES S-box is between 600 and $1635 \approx 2^{10.68}$. By applying Theorem 3, the squared 2-norm of the nontrivial Fourier coefficients of the observed bits $\mathbf{z}$ can be upper bounded by

$$\|\widehat{p_{\mathbf{z}}} - \delta_0\|_2^2 \leq 2^{21.36}\, 2^{-110.40} = 2^{-89.04},$$

This gives the following refined security claim.

Security Claim 2. *For the masked AES described in Sect. 3, the following bound on the advantage of the adversary (assuming piling-up) in the probing model with refined glitches is claimed:*

$$\mathrm{Adv}_{2\text{-thr}}(\mathcal{A}) \leq \sqrt{\frac{q}{2^{88.04}}}\,.$$

6   Amortizing Randomness Over Multiple Queries

This section introduces a method to safely extract randomness from the state of the masked AES from Sect. 3 for usage in the next call. This further reduces the requirements on the (true) random number generator used in the implementation.

The technique works by extracting the randomness from the masked state in certain rounds. Here extraction means taking three out of four shares of each bit of the state for subsequent use. Directly using the extracting state bits as randomness in the next masked cipher call would be insecure in the probing model. Instead, we extract randomness from multiple rounds and add it together. A total of twice the shared state size, 960 random bits, is extracted per masked cipher call.

Suppose that the randomness is refreshed after every l calls to the masked cipher, *i.e.* after l blocks have been encrypted. To assess the security of such a construction, one can rely on a variant of the bounded query probing model from Sect. 2.1. Since the regular circuit oracle only generates new randomness every l calls, it is more convenient to consider an oracle for which each query corresponds to l invocations of the masked cipher. Equivalently, the adversary is given oracle access to a circuit that consists of l blocks which are only connected by the circuitry required to reuse randomness. The adversary is allowed to reposition the probes after each invocation of the masked circuit, so up to $2l$ probes per query are provided. However, only two probes per block are allowed. An adversary with this access structure may be called an l-block 2-threshold adversary.

It is straightforward to adapt Theorem 1 to l-block 2-threshold adversaries. The only difference is in the admissible probe positions. However, when applying this result to determine the security bound, care must be taken in the labeling (as 'good' or 'bad') of probed values. In the $l = 1$ case, probed values resulting from two probes placed within the same S-box were marked as 'good'. This helps to avoid corner cases that do not threaten the probing security, but that prevent the direct replacement of these values with uniform randomness in the proof of Theorem 1. For $l \geq 2$, the presence of probes in other blocks makes this labeling incorrect and an additional reduction is required before applying the theorem. In this initial step, the set of values obtained by placing both probes of a block in the same S-box is modified (expanded) to a set of values with a uniform random *marginal* distribution. By simply returning all but one of the input shares of the S-box, this is achieved without any loss in security. The modified values can then be labeled as 'bad'.

To complete the argument, an upper bound on $\|\widehat{p}_{\mathbf{z}} - \delta_0\|_2^2$ must be determined. Here, $\mathbf{z}$ consists of the (modified) probed values conditioned on any values labeled as 'good'. This requires an analysis of linear trails, including trails that run across multiple blocks through the randomness extraction mechanism.

Suppose that $\varepsilon = 2^b \times c^2$, where b is the maximum number of bits seen by any pair of probes (possibly in different blocks) and c^2 an upper bound on the squared correlation of any linear approximation between such a pair of probes. Grouping masks by the number of active probes, and applying the piling-up principle, one obtains the upper bound

$$\|\widehat{p}_{\mathbf{z}} - \delta_0\|_2^2 \le \sum_{n=2}^{2l} \binom{2l}{n} \varepsilon^{n-1} = \varepsilon^{-1}\left[(1+\varepsilon)^{2l} - (1 + 2l\,\varepsilon)\right] \le l(2l-1)\varepsilon.$$

The actual number of probes could be lower than $2l$ due to the initial reduction that essentially combines two probes placed in one S-box into a single probe. It follows that a second-order probing adversary making a total of q queries has advantage bounded by

$$\mathrm{Adv}_{l\text{-blk},2\text{-thr}}(\mathcal{A}) \le \sqrt{2l-1} \times \sqrt{2q\,\varepsilon}.$$

That is, a factor of at most $\sqrt{2l-1}$ is lost when randomness is reused over l masked cipher calls. This loss is due to the adversary's capability of placing two probes in each query in arbitrary positions. However, the information gathered in each query does not directly relate to a secret. Instead, many queries are needed to distinguish this information from uniform random. Thus, it is unclear whether these attacks relate to second-order DPA attacks. Hence when factoring in noise, we expect that the above bound can be significantly improved. We pose this improvement as an open problem.

Using SMT-based search tools, we find the best linear trail with two probes in one AES circuit and an arbitrary non-zero mask on the extracted randomness. Optimal trails are shown in Appendix D. The best trail with a non-zero mask on the extracted randomness has absolute correlation at most $2^{-61.0}$. Thus, the dominant trails are still those given in Sect. 4.2 and we again have the bound $\varepsilon \le 2^{-62.40}$.

Security Claim 3. *For the masked AES with randomness reuse, the following bound on the advantage of the adversary (assuming piling-up) in the probing model is claimed:*

$$\mathrm{Adv}_{l\text{-blk},2\text{-thr}}(\mathcal{A}) \le \sqrt{2l-1} \times \sqrt{\frac{q}{2^{61.4}}}.$$

By making use of the sharpened glitch model from Sect. 5, the above bound can again be improved significantly.

This technique generates a total of 960 random bits per masked cipher call. In total, the masked AES from Sect. 3 requires 1800 random bits, 936 bits for the state and 864 bits for the key. By choosing $l > 936$, the effective number of random bits for the state is less than one per call. This increases the maximum advantage of a second-order probing adversaries by a factor less than 2^6.

7 Conclusion

A second-order masked AES using less than 2000 bits of randomness was developed. Furthermore, it was shown how the randomness cost can be amortized over several cipher calls. This resulted in a total cost of less than 1000 random bits per encrypted block. These low randomness costs are the result of careful design choices guided by a detailed security analysis in the bounded-query probing model. In particular, the sharing of the nonlinear layer is based on a variant of the changing of the guards method, which we call "guards in formation" and improves the diffusive properties of the masked cipher. An automated tool based on SMT solvers was used to bound the absolute correlation of linear trails through the masked cipher. This resulted in concrete upper bounds on the advantage of probing adversaries.

The main open problem of this work is the efficiency of the masking. We note that our S-box masking extends the one from Wegener *et al.* [25], who reported that the S-box costs over 20k GE when unrolled. Synthesis of our unrolled S-box shows that it requires over 40k GE. Hence, the presented AES masking will not competitive with the current state-of-the-art in terms of area-requirements. However, we expect that future work will improve the efficiency of the implementation.

Acknowledgment. We thank Vincent Rijmen, Svetla Nikova, Lauren De Meyer, and Victor Arribas for interesting discussions. We also thank Dušan Božilov for his help on coverings. Tim Beyne, Siemen Dhooghe, and Adrián Ranea are supported by a PhD Fellowship from the Research Foundation – Flanders (FWO).

A   Trails in the Second-Order Masked Key Schedule

This appendix provides the activity-pattern of a trail with non-zero correlation over two rounds of the second-order masked key schedule of the AES. This is the key-schedule described in Sect. 3.1, but *without using fresh randomness* for the changing of the guards technique. The trail is depicted in Fig. 4. Recall that the AES S-box is split in two cubic maps and that the additional cell used for the changing of the guards technique is passed on to the next nonlinear operation.

B   Walsh Spectra of the AES and XOR

In this appendix we simulate the masked AES S-box from Sect. 3 and compute its Walsh-spectrum for different probe positions. The spectrum for a single input delay and initial state but different probe positions and time samples for the masked AES S-box is given in Fig. 5a. The spectrum for different input delays, initial states, probe positions, and time samples for the 9-bit XOR is given in Fig. 5b. The distributions of the 1-norms are illustrated in Figure 6 using a box plot.

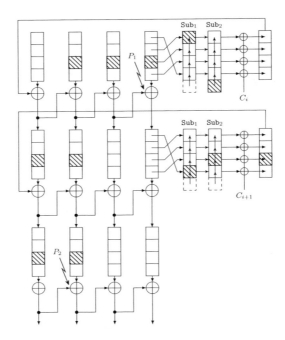

Fig. 4. Activity pattern of a trail with non-zero correlation through two rounds of the second-order masked key schedule of AES caused by two probes. Hatched cells correspond to active cells. The lightning signs denote the two probes.

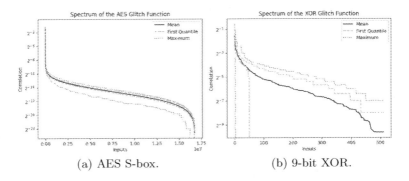

(a) AES S-box.   (b) 9-bit XOR.

Fig. 5. Sorted absolute Walsh-spectrum of glitch functions for the AES S-box and the 9-bit XOR for different probe positions, times, inputs delays, and initial states.

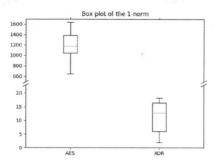

Fig. 6. Box plot of the 1-norm of the Walsh-Hadamard transform of the glitch functions for the masked AES and the XOR, for different probe positions, times, input delays and initial states.

C   Trails in the Second-Order Masked State

In this appendix we give trails through the state of the second-order masked AES. We give the best trail with absolute linear correlation at most $2^{-55.20}$ in Fig. 7.

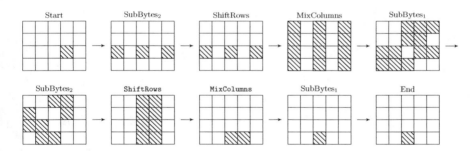

Fig. 7. An optimal trail (for two probes) with non-zero correlation through the second-order masked AES. The hatched cells denote active cells of the output of the operation.

D   Trails in the Generation of Randomness

In this appendix we give trails of the second-order masked AES where randomness is generated following the method described in Sect. 6. We give the best trail with absolute linear correlation at most $2^{-61.0}$ in Fig. 8. The hatched cells in these figures denote the active cells in the output masks for the indicated transformations.

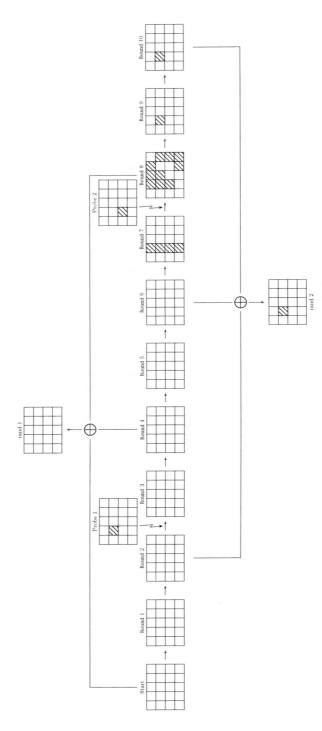

Fig. 8. A trail achieving the highest correlation on the extracted randomness. The trail essentially follows the one given in Fig. 7.

References

1. Beyne, T.: Block cipher invariants as eigenvectors of correlation matrices. In: Peyrin, T., Galbraith, S. (eds.) ASIACRYPT 2018. LNCS, vol. 11272, pp. 3–31. Springer, Cham (2018). https://doi.org/10.1007/978-3-030-03326-2_1

2. Beyne, T., Dhooghe, S., Zhang, Z.: Cryptanalysis of masked ciphers: a not so random idea. In: Moriai, S., Wang, H. (eds.) ASIACRYPT 2020. LNCS, vol. 12491, pp. 817–850. Springer, Cham (2020). https://doi.org/10.1007/978-3-030-64837-4_27

3. Bilgin, B.: Threshold implementations : as countermeasure against higher-order differential power analysis. Ph.D. thesis, University of Twente, Enschede, Netherlands (2015). http://purl.utwente.nl/publications/95796

4. Bilgin, B., Gierlichs, B., Nikova, S., Nikov, V., Rijmen, V.: Higher-order threshold implementations. In: Sarkar, P., Iwata, T. (eds.) ASIACRYPT 2014. LNCS, vol. 8874, pp. 326–343. Springer, Heidelberg (2014). https://doi.org/10.1007/978-3-662-45608-8_18

5. Bozilov, D.: On optimality of d + 1 TI shared functions of 8 bits or less. IACR Cryptol. ePrint Arch. 2020, 570 (2020). https://eprint.iacr.org/2020/570

6. Brandão, L.T.A.N., Davidson, M., Vassilev, A.: NIST roadmap toward criteria for threshold schemes for cryptographic primitives. National Institute of Standards and Technology (NIST), U.S. Department of Commerce (2020). https://csrc.nist.gov/publications/detail/nistir/8214a/final

7. Daemen, J.: Changing of the guards: a simple and efficient method for achieving uniformity in threshold sharing. In: Fischer, W., Homma, N. (eds.) CHES 2017. LNCS, vol. 10529, pp. 137–153. Springer, Cham (2017). https://doi.org/10.1007/978-3-319-66787-4_7

8. Daemen, J., Govaerts, R., Vandewalle, J.: Correlation matrices. In: Preneel, B. (ed.) FSE 1994. LNCS, vol. 1008, pp. 275–285. Springer, Heidelberg (1995). https://doi.org/10.1007/3-540-60590-8_21

9. Daemen, J., Rijmen, V.: The block cipher rijndael. In: Quisquater, J.-J., Schneier, B. (eds.) CARDIS 1998. LNCS, vol. 1820, pp. 277–284. Springer, Heidelberg (2000). https://doi.org/10.1007/10721064_26

10. Daemen, J., Rijmen, V.: Advanced Encryption Standard (AES). National Institute of Standards and Technology (NIST), FIPS PUB 197, U.S. Department of Commerce (2001)

11. De Cnudde, T., Reparaz, O., Bilgin, B., Nikova, S., Nikov, V., Rijmen, V.: Masking AES with $d+1$ shares in hardware. In: Gierlichs, B., Poschmann, A.Y. (eds.) CHES 2016. LNCS, vol. 9813, pp. 194–212. Springer, Heidelberg (2016). https://doi.org/10.1007/978-3-662-53140-2_10

12. De Meyer, L., Reparaz, O., Bilgin, B.: Multiplicative masking for AES in hardware. IACR TCHES **2018**(3), 431–468 (2018). https://doi.org/10.13154/tches.v2018.i3.431-468, https://tches.iacr.org/index.php/TCHES/article/view/7282

13. Faust, S., Grosso, V., Pozo, S.M.D., Paglialonga, C., Standaert, F.: Composable masking schemes in the presence of physical defaults & the robust probing model. IACR Trans. Cryptogr. Hardw. Embed. Syst. **2018**(3), 89–120 (2018)

14. Gross, H., Mangard, S., Korak, T.: An efficient side-channel protected AES implementation with arbitrary protection order. In: Handschuh, H. (ed.) CT-RSA 2017. LNCS, vol. 10159, pp. 95–112. Springer, Cham (2017). https://doi.org/10.1007/978-3-319-52153-4_6

15. Ishai, Y., Sahai, A., Wagner, D.: Private circuits: securing hardware against probing attacks. In: Boneh, D. (ed.) CRYPTO 2003. LNCS, vol. 2729, pp. 463–481. Springer, Heidelberg (2003). https://doi.org/10.1007/978-3-540-45146-4_27

16. Kocher, P., Jaffe, J., Jun, B.: Differential power analysis. In: Wiener, M. (ed.) CRYPTO 1999. LNCS, vol. 1666, pp. 388–397. Springer, Heidelberg (1999). https://doi.org/10.1007/3-540-48405-1_25

17. Matsui, M.: Linear cryptanalysis method for DES cipher. In: Helleseth, T. (ed.) EUROCRYPT 1993. LNCS, vol. 765, pp. 386–397. Springer, Heidelberg (1994). https://doi.org/10.1007/3-540-48285-7_33

18. Mouha, N., Wang, Q., Gu, D., Preneel, B.: Differential and linear cryptanalysis using mixed-integer linear programming. In: Wu, C.-K., Yung, M., Lin, D. (eds.) Inscrypt 2011. LNCS, vol. 7537, pp. 57–76. Springer, Heidelberg (2012). https://doi.org/10.1007/978-3-642-34704-7_5

19. Niemetz, A., Preiner, M., Biere, A.: Boolector 2.0 system description. J. Satisfiabil. Boolean Model. Comput. **9**, 53–58 (2015)

20. Nikova, S., Rechberger, C., Rijmen, V.: Threshold implementations against side-channel attacks and glitches. In: Ning, P., Qing, S., Li, N. (eds.) ICICS 2006. LNCS, vol. 4307, pp. 529–545. Springer, Heidelberg (2006). https://doi.org/10.1007/11935308_38

21. Reparaz, O.: A note on the security of higher-order threshold implementations. Cryptology ePrint Archive, Report 2015/001 (2015). http://eprint.iacr.org/2015/001

22. Šijačić, D., Balasch, J., Yang, B., Ghosh, S., Verbauwhede, I.: Towards efficient and automated side-channel evaluations at design time. J. Cryptogr. Eng. **10**(4), 305–319 (2020). https://doi.org/10.1007/s13389-020-00233-8

23. Sugawara, T.: 3-share threshold implementation of AES s-box without fresh randomness. IACR Trans. Cryptogr. Hardw. Embed. Syst. **2019**(1), 123–145 (2019)

24. Tardy-Corfdir, A., Gilbert, H.: A known plaintext attack of FEAL-4 and FEAL-6. In: Feigenbaum, J. (ed.) CRYPTO 1991. LNCS, vol. 576, pp. 172–182. Springer, Heidelberg (1992). https://doi.org/10.1007/3-540-46766-1_12

25. Wegener, F., Moradi, A.: A first-order SCA resistant AES without fresh randomness. In: Fan, J., Gierlichs, B. (eds.) COSADE 2018. LNCS, vol. 10815, pp. 245–262. Springer, Cham (2018). https://doi.org/10.1007/978-3-319-89641-0_14

How Do the Arbiter PUFs Sample the Boolean Function Class?

Animesh Roy[1], Dibyendu Roy[2(✉)], and Subhamoy Maitra[1]

[1] Indian Statistical Institute, Kolkata, India
animesh.roy03@gmail.com, subho@isical.ac.in
[2] Indian Institute of Information Technology Vadodara (Gandhinagar Campus),
Gandhinagar, India
dibyendu.roy@iiitvadodara.ac.in

Abstract. Arbiter based Physical Unclonable Function (sometimes called Physically Unclonable Function, or in short PUF) is a hardware based pseudorandom bit generator. The pseudorandomness in the output bits depends on device specific parameters. For example, based on the delay parameters, an n-length Arbiter PUF can be considered as an n-variable Boolean function. We note that the random variation of the delay parameters cannot exhaust all the Boolean functions and the class is significantly smaller as well as restricted. While this is expected (as the autocorrelation property in certain cases is quite biased), we present a more disciplined and first theoretical combinatorial study in this domain. Our work shows how one can explore the functions achieved through an Arbiter based PUF construction with random delay parameters. Our technique mostly shows limitation of such functions from the angle of cryptographic evaluation as the subclass of the Boolean function can be identified with much better efficiency (much less complexity) than random. On the other hand, we note that under certain constraints on the weights of inputs, such a simple model of Arbiter PUFs provide good cryptographic parameters in terms of differential analysis. In this regard, we theoretically solve the problem of autocorrelation properties in a restricted space of input variables with a fixed weight. Experimental evidences complement our theoretical findings.

Keywords: Bias · Boolean function · Non-uniformity · Physically Unclonable Function (PUF) · Pseudorandomness · Restricted domain

1 Introduction

Arbiter based Physically Unclonable Functions (PUFs) were first introduced in [8]. This is a hardware based pseudorandom bit generator which is used to generate cryptographic keys and related applications in device authentications [5,9,10]. PUFs are used to generate keys during the execution of the algorithms without storing them in an insecure memory. To meet the security needs, these constructions must be one-way and should not be cloned in different

© The Author(s), under exclusive license to Springer Nature Switzerland AG 2022
R. AlTawy and A. Hülsing (Eds.): SAC 2021, LNCS 13203, pp. 111–130, 2022.
https://doi.org/10.1007/978-3-030-99277-4_6

devices. The design of PUFs basically depends on multiple device parameters. Due to this, such devices supposedly generate uncorrelated output bit-stream. An n-length Arbiter PUF takes an n-bit long challenge and based on the manufacturing variations, it generates one pseudorandom output bit. Thus an n-length Arbiter based PUF can be treated as a Boolean function from $\{0,1\}^n$ to $\{0,1\}$, as described in [12]. Due to the pseudorandom nature of the output bits, one can exploit them for security related tools and thus PUF has certain practical applications, e.g., smart cards [1]. An Arbiter based PUF supports a large amount of Challenge-Response Pairs (CRPs) and therefore an adversary should not be able to predict the CRPs.

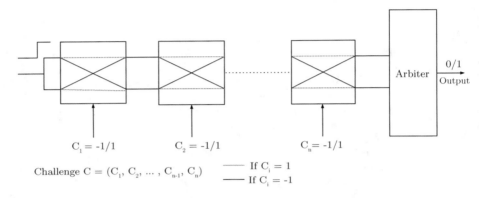

Fig. 1. Basic structure of an Arbiter based PUF.

An ideal PUF should exhibit some important cryptographic features, like uniformity, uniqueness, reliability as PUF is used to generate keys for cryptographic purpose. Uniformity describes the distribution of the output bits of a PUF. If a PUF produces an equal number of 0's and 1's in the output then that PUF is said to be uniform or balanced. The uniqueness property says that if we provide the same input to different PUFs, then the output of one PUF should not be predicted from the other. That means each PUF should be unique in nature. It will have good reliability if the same device produces the same output for the same input in different instances. In real life, achieving all these cryptographic properties together is difficult as the device specific and environmental parameters may inject noise in the output bits. Thus the reducing noise in the output bits becomes an important task in practice. In [7], Gassend has shown that error correcting codes can be used to tackle the noisy situations.

As we have already described, an Arbiter based PUF can act as an n-variable Boolean function. In most of the cryptographic applications, the input bits of a Boolean function are usually considered independent and taken uniformly from the domain. In such a scenario, the question is on pseudo-randomness measures of the output bits. If this is violated, then the PUF model should not be accepted for cryptographic applications. There are several attacks in this direction [1,2,18–22] and the recent trend shows significant works in this direction using Machine Learning tools [11,16,20,22]. Several counter-measures are also proposed to resist such attacks and thus new designs are introduced [6,10,11]. On an orthogonal context, we are more interested in combinatorial and statistical aspects in evaluating the Boolean functions generated out of varying delays in Arbiter PUFs. In this direction, we refer to [24], where several non-randomness results had been demonstrated theoretically.

From [24], it can be referred that if one generates output bits corresponding to two challenge inputs $C = (C_1, C_2, \ldots, C_n)$ and $\tilde{C} = (\tilde{C}_1, \tilde{C}_2, \ldots, \tilde{C}_n)$, where C and $\tilde{C}$ belong to $\{-1, 1\}^n$ and differ only at the most significant bit (MSB) position (i.e., $C_1 + \tilde{C}_1 = 0$), then the output bits will match with high probability. The position of the differed challenge bit plays an important role in producing the bias. One can look into Fig. 1 to understand the position of the challenge bits. This bias reduces with the location of the bit difference at the inputs. The least bias occurs for the middle-most bit. Naturally, this lack of randomness provides a direction that the PUF devices can only produce a restricted class of Boolean functions, not all. Consequently, the immediate scientific question is to explore the set of Boolean functions such Arbiter PUFs are generating. In this regard, here we present relevant combinatorial results to show certain necessary conditions regarding the existence or non-existence of Boolean functions generated out of the Arbiter PUFs. Then we try to find out for what kinds of combinatorial properties the functions from Arbiter PUFs resemble a randomly chosen Boolean function better. We note that if one considers a certain autocorrelation measure after restricting the input bit pattern to a fixed weight, then such bias disappears. Thus, if one can restrict the attack model with such a constraint, then the use of Arbiter PUFs in certain applications (such as lightweight environment) might be recommended.

As a passing remark, we should also mention the thin connectivity with certain stream ciphers like FLIP [13], which are used as integral components in Fully Homomorphic Encryption (FHE) [3]. In this direction, several properties of Boolean functions over restricted domain (definition of the restricted domain is described in Sect. 1.2 in more detail) were studied in [4,14,15,17]. Our results show that while there is significant bias in the Arbiter PUFs in certain autocorrelation measures [24], this is absent if challenge inputs are chosen from a restricted domain.

Before proceeding further, let us now present the outline of the paper.

1.1 Contribution and Organization

In Sect. 1.2, we discuss the basic definitions and notations, introducing the existing results and the problems we consider. The contributions of this paper are the followings, in one case it shows the limitation of Arbiter PUFs, and in another case it demonstrates still how they can be useful in restricted domain.

– In Sect. 2, we study the limitation of Arbiter PUFs in representing the class of Boolean functions. We provide examples of functions that can or cannot be generated through different delay parameters. An upper bound on the number of such functions are also provided, which shows that the proportions of different functions will be vanishing compared to the total class of Boolean functions as the number of input variables increases. We show that the ratio of distinct Boolean functions arising out of n-length Arbiter PUFs and the total number of n-variable Boolean functions is less than $\frac{1}{2^{5 \cdot 2^{n-4}}}$ for $n \geq 4$. The analysis also identifies the nature of the functions arriving out of the Arbiter PUFs with better efficiency.

– Then, in Sect. 3, we show that the nature of autocorrelation distributions of Arbiter PUFs and Boolean functions do not differ much if the inputs are chosen from a restricted domain. In particular, we consider when the weight of the inputs are fixed and the inputs must always differ at an already selected bit. We provide a theoretical proof in this regard. This shows that in certain restricted applications, such simple Arbiter PUFs can still be useful.

Section 4 concludes the paper.

1.2 Preliminaries

In this section we talk about some basic terminologies and definitions.

Arbiter PUF. It is a hardware based pseudorandom bit generator model, where the basic idea is to initiate a digital race condition on two paths on the chip and decide which of the two paths won the race. In Arbiter PUF construction, there are n-many Arbiter switches present, one after the other, as shown in Fig. 1. Each switch has two multiplexers symmetrically placed. Each input bit is fed to each Arbiter switch. A common pulse is also transmitted through the switches and received at the end by an Arbiter. Based on the input bits, the pulse selects the path inside the Arbiter switches. If an input bit is 1, the path of the pulse remains unchanged. Else it gets swapped. Due to process variations, the pulse will traverse through one path, faster than the other. At the end, the Arbiter finally produces the response 0 or 1 based on the top or bottom path is reached first. For each device, these paths for a given challenge act differently due to delay parameters and hence the output will differ for different devices. This is an informal description of the device. For our purpose, we need to follow the mathematical definition more formally. This is as follows.

An n-length (or n-variable) Arbiter based PUF takes an input of length n from $\{-1, 1\}^n$ and generates either 0 or 1. Note that, by abuse of notation, we interchangeably consider the mapping $a \to (-1)^a$, for $a \in \{0, 1\}$ sometime in Boolean treatment here. For our analysis we consider the domain of n-length PUF as $\{-1, 1\}^n$ instead of $\{0, 1\}^n$ whereas in general the domain of n-variable Boolean function is considered as $\{0, 1\}^n$. The input to the Arbiter PUF is known as challenge and the output is known as response. In [11] it has been shown that an n-length Arbiter PUF can be modelled mathematically in the following form.

$$\Delta(C) = \alpha_1 P_0 + (\alpha_2 + \beta_1)P_1 + \cdots + (\alpha_n + \beta_{n-1})P_{n-1} + P_n\beta_n. \tag{1}$$

Here C is the challenge to the PUF, $C = (C_1, \ldots, C_n) \in \{-1, 1\}^n$, α_i and β_i depend on the delay parameters p_i, q_i, r_i, s_i. Usually in a mathematical model of PUF, we assume that these delay parameters follows normal distribution with mean μ and standard deviation σ, i.e., the distribution follows $\mathcal{N}(\mu, \sigma)$. The formula through which these α_i, β_i are connected with p_i, q_i, r_i, s_i are $\alpha_i = \frac{p_i - q_i}{2} + \frac{r_i - s_i}{2}$, and $\beta_i = \frac{p_i - q_i}{2} - \frac{r_i - s_i}{2}$. It can be easily verified that if $p_i, q_i, r_i, s_i \sim \mathcal{N}(\mu, \sigma)$ then $\alpha_i, \beta_i \sim \dot{\mathcal{N}}(0, \sqrt{2}\sigma)$. The term $P_k = \prod_{i=k+1}^{n} C_i$, for $k = 0, \ldots, n-1$ and $P_n = 1$. For a challenge $C \in \{-1, 1\}^n$, the value of $\Delta(C)$ can either be positive or negative. If the sign of $\Delta(C)$ is positive, the output from the PUF will be 1 and if the sign of $\Delta(C)$ is negative then the output from the PUF will be 0. We will be using the notation $\mathcal{B}_n^{\mathsf{PUF}}$ to denote the set of n-variable Boolean functions exhaustively generated through n-step Arbiter PUFs, whereas the set of all Boolean functions involving n-variables are usually denoted by $\mathcal{B}_n$. One can note that implementation of an n-variable Boolean function requires exponential number of gates. In practical life, we always prefer to have those circuits which can be implemented using a polynomial number of gates. Arbiter based PUFs are those class circuits that can be implemented using $\mathcal{O}(n)$ units. Thus the Boolean functions constructed using PUF are of great interest. In this paper, we are first time finding such class of Boolean functions and also showing that in a special case it exhibits good property.

Restricted Domain. Let f be a function from $\{-1, 1\}^n$ to $\{0, 1\}$. Further, let the function be defined over a restricted domain when it takes input from a subset of $\{-1, 1\}^n$. We know that the weight of $\mathbf{x} \in \{0, 1\}^n$ (i.e., $wt(\mathbf{x})$) is considered as the number of 1's present in $\mathbf{x}$. In the similar convention along with the transformation $a \rightarrow (-1)^a$ here we define $wt(\mathbf{x})$ for $\mathbf{x} \in \{-1, 1\}^n$. The weight of $\mathbf{x} \in \{-1, 1\}^n$ is the total number of -1's present in $\mathbf{x}$. This is the total number of 1's if we consider the string of 0's and 1's. The set $E_{n,k}$ denotes the set of all n-length points whose weight is k, i.e., $E_{n,k} = \{\mathbf{x} : \mathbf{x} \in \{-1, 1\}^n \text{ and } wt(\mathbf{x}) = k\}$. Here $|E_{n,k}| = \binom{n}{k}$. It can be noticed that $E_{n,k}$ is a restricted domain, where the restriction is that the all the points in $E_{n,k}$ will be of length n and weight k.

Autocorrelation of an n-variable Boolean function $f : \{0, 1\}^n \rightarrow \{0, 1\}$ is defined by

$$\mathcal{A}_f(\mathbf{a}) = \sum_{\mathbf{x} \in \{0,1\}^n} (-1)^{f(\mathbf{x}) \oplus f(\mathbf{x} \oplus \mathbf{a})}, \mathbf{a} \in \{0, 1\}^n.$$

It can be noticed this definition of autocorrelation can not be used directly to compute autocorrelation of f in $E_{n,k}$. As if we take any $\mathbf{x} \in E_{n,k}$ and take any $\mathbf{a} \in \{0, 1\}^n$ then $\mathbf{x} \oplus \mathbf{a}$ may not belong to $E_{n,k}$. For an $\mathbf{x} \in E_{n,k}$, we need to select an $\mathbf{a}$ selectively such that $\mathbf{x} \oplus \mathbf{a}$ should also belong to $E_{n,k}$. As we have already pointed out (see the discussion in Sect. 1.3 below), significant bias could be identified in $\mathcal{A}_f(\mathbf{a})$ when $wt(\mathbf{a}) = 1$. In a similar line, we consider a special case, where a specific input bit will be selected, where the differential will exist. However, the weight of the two inputs should be of the same weight.

Let f be an n-variable Boolean function. Let S_1 and S_2 be two sets defined as $S_1 = \{\mathbf{x} \in E_{n,k} \mid \text{u-th bit of } \mathbf{x} \text{ is } -1\}$, $S_2 = \{\mathbf{x} \in E_{n,k} \mid \text{u-th bit of } \mathbf{x} \text{ is } 1\}$. Note that $E_{n,k} = S_1 \cup S_2$ and $S_1 \cap S_2 = \phi$. The restricted autocorrelation of f over $E_{n,k}$ is defined as

$$\mathcal{A}_f^{E_{n,k}} = \sum_{\mathbf{x}_1 \in S_1, \mathbf{x}_2 \in S_2} (-1)^{f(\mathbf{x}_1) \oplus f(\mathbf{x}_2)}.$$

It is evident that $|S_1| = \binom{n-1}{k-1}$ and $|S_2| = \binom{n-1}{k}$. We are not concerned about the bit position u as it will be proved that this expression actually does not depend on u for an n-length Arbiter PUF.

The purpose of defining restricted autocorrelation is to study the autocorrelation spectrum of PUF in a restricted domain, where the simple construction of Arbiter PUF does not provide any bias.

1.3 Motivation of Our Work

Theoretical estimation of autocorrelation of an n-variable PUF over a complete domain $\{-1, 1\}^n$ is discussed in [24]. In the same paper, it has also been shown that the outputs corresponding to inputs are heavily biased when two inputs differ at the first position. It means that the autocorrelation value of $f \in \mathcal{B}_n^{\mathsf{PUF}}$ is not good for certain $\mathbf{a} \in \{0, 1\}^n$. To verify the theoretical analysis presented in [24] we have performed a simulation. We have taken random values of delay parameters from a normal distribution and generated 1024 many random 12-length PUFs. For each of these 12-length PUFs we have considered two inputs $C, \tilde{C} \in \{-1, 1\}^{12}$ where $C, \tilde{C}$ differ only in one location i i.e., if $C = (C_1, \ldots, C_i, \ldots, C_{12})$ and $\tilde{C} = (C_1, \ldots, -C_i, \ldots, C_{12})$. For each of these two inputs we compute the output bits from the PUF. Let z_C and $z_{\tilde{C}}$ be the output bits corresponding to C and $\tilde{C}$ respectively. Finally, we compute $Pr[z_C = z_{\tilde{C}}]$. The observed experimental result is presented in Fig. 2 and Table 1 are completely in the same direction of the theoretical results presented in [24]. From Lemma 1 of [24] it is also evident that the bias ϵ (i.e., $Pr[z_C = z_{\tilde{C}}] = \frac{1}{2} \pm \epsilon$) increases with the increase in the length of the PUF.

To understand the autocorrelation values we consider a 12-variable PUF and two inputs C and $\tilde{C}$ where C and $\tilde{C}$ differ at only one location. From the result of [24] we know that the output z_C and $z_{\tilde{C}}$ are highly biased for certain bit difference locations. The experimental $Pr[z_C = z_{\tilde{C}}]$ for different single bit difference locations is provided in Table 1. From Table 1 and Fig. 2 it can be observed that the bias is highest when the bit difference location is either first or last and bias is least when the bit difference location is in the middle. Thus for certain values of $\mathbf{a} \in \{0, 1\}^n$ the expected autocorrelation value of $f \in \mathcal{B}_n^{\mathsf{PUF}}$ significantly differs from 0.5.

Table 1. Experimental Bias of PUFs ($n = 12$) in complete domain (over 1024 randomly chosen Arbiter PUFs) for single bit difference, matching with the theoretical values from [24]

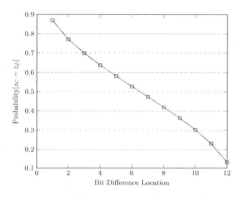

Fig. 2. Representation of Table 1

Bit Difference Location	$\Pr[z_C = z_{\tilde{C}}]$
1	0.8691
2	0.7699
3	0.6982
4	0.6368
5	0.5804
6	0.5266
7	0.4734
8	0.4196
9	0.3632
10	0.3017
11	0.2300
12	0.1309

To get a clearer idea about the autocorrelation distribution of PUF we perform statistical analysis. We consider all 4-variable Boolean functions and PUFs and measure the average number of Boolean functions and PUFs corresponding to different possible autocorrelation values $\{-16, -8, -4, 0, 4, 8, 12, 16\}$. From Fig. 3 it can be observed that the distribution of PUF differs significantly from the distribution of Boolean function.

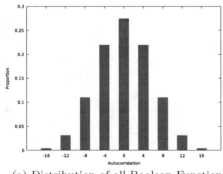

(a) Distribution of all Boolean Functions

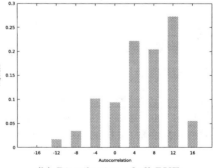

(b) Distribution of all PUFs

Fig. 3. Comparison of autocorrelation distribution in complete domain

Now we provide a clear answer why the autocorrelation distribution is highly biased for PUF for single bit difference. The basic reason is that the Arbiter PUFs cannot exhaustively generate all possible Boolean functions. This observation motivates us to investigate the following.

- How to estimate the set $\mathcal{B}_n^{\mathsf{PUF}}$?
- Can we obtain a restricted definition of autocorrelation so that the Arbiter PUFs do not expose a significant bias?

2   Relation Between $\mathcal{B}_n^{\mathsf{PUF}}$ and $\mathcal{B}_n$

In this section, we explore the class of Boolean functions generated from n-variable PUFs i.e., $\mathcal{B}_n^{\mathsf{PUF}}$. To compute the number of distinct Boolean functions which can be constructed using PUFs we start with $n = 1$. The total number of Boolean functions involving 1-variable is $|\mathcal{B}_1| = 2^{2^1} = 4$. We all know that a PUF can be seen as a Boolean function. Thus, the obvious question is if we consider 1-length PUF, can that generate all possible Boolean functions given different delay parameters. To answer this question we state the following proposition.

Proposition 1. *All possible Boolean functions involving 1-variable can be generated by using 1-length PUFs i.e., $\mathcal{B}_1^{\mathsf{PUF}} = \mathcal{B}_1$.*

Proof. This proposition can be proven by exhaustively enumerating $\mathcal{B}_1^{\mathsf{PUF}}$. We have considered 1-length PUFs for different random delay parameters and observed that all the possible truth tables are generated in our experiment. Thus $|\mathcal{B}_1^{\mathsf{PUF}}| = |\mathcal{B}_1| = 4$.   □

Now we move towards the case for $n = 2$. The total number of Boolean functions in this case is $|\mathcal{B}_2| = 2^{2^2} = 16$. Interestingly, from our experiments, we have observed that 14 many Boolean functions can be constructed from 2-length Arbiter PUFs, i.e., $|\mathcal{B}_2^{\mathsf{PUF}}| = 14$. Truth tables of two specific Boolean functions can never be constructed using 2-length Arbiter PUFs. In this regard, we will state the following result.

Proposition 2. *The following two Boolean functions f_1 and f_2 do not belong to $\mathcal{B}_2^{\mathsf{PUF}}$.*

C_2	C_1	f_1	f_2
1	1	1	0
1	−1	0	1
−1	1	1	0
−1	−1	0	1

Proof. The mathematical model of 2-length PUF is $\Delta(C) = \alpha_1 P_0 + (\alpha_2 + \beta_1) P_1 + \beta_2$, where $P_0 = C_1 C_2$ and $P_1 = C_2$. Here α_i, β_i are the delay parameters. We consider the truth table of f_1 first. It can be observed that if the sign($\Delta(C)$) and sign(C_1) are the same then only the truth table f_1 can be generated from 2-length PUF. Thus, to generate the same truth values from a 2-length PUF, we need to have the following scenarios.

C_2	C_1	$\Delta(C)$
1	1	$\alpha_1 + (\alpha_2 + \beta_1) + \beta_2 > 0$
1	-1	$-\alpha_1 + (\alpha_2 + \beta_1) + \beta_2 < 0$
-1	1	$-\alpha_1 - (\alpha_2 + \beta_1) + \beta_2 > 0$
-1	-1	$\alpha_1 - (\alpha_2 + \beta_1) + \beta_2 < 0$

If the above conditions hold for at least one pair of $\alpha_1, \alpha_2, \beta_1, \beta_2$ then only the truth values of f_1 can be generated. If we add two > 0 inequalities then we will have $\beta_2 > 0$ and if we add two < 0 inequalities then we will have $\beta_2 < 0$. This generates a contradiction. Hence the truth table of f_1 can not be generated from the 2-length Arbiter PUF structure. Similarly, it can be shown that it is not possible to generate the truth table of f_2 using a 2-length PUF. Thus $f_1, f_2 \notin \mathcal{B}_2^{\mathsf{PUF}}$.   □

Using the transformation $a \rightarrow (-1)^a$ for $a \in \{0, 1\}$, the Algebraic Normal Form (ANF) of f_1, f_2 are $f_1(x_1, x_2) = 1 \oplus x_1$ and $f_2(x_1, x_2) = x_1$ respectively. Here x_1 corresponds to C_1.

Proposition 2 justifies that $|\mathcal{B}_2^{\mathsf{PUF}}| = 14$ as we noted from exhaustive experiment and directs us towards the following result.

Lemma 1. *For any n-variable Boolean function $f \notin \mathcal{B}_n^{\mathsf{PUF}}$ if and only if $(1 \oplus f) \notin \mathcal{B}_n^{\mathsf{PUF}}$.*

Proof. To prove this, we assume that there exists an n-variable Boolean function $f \in \mathcal{B}_n^{\mathsf{PUF}}$ but $1 \oplus f \notin \mathcal{B}_n^{\mathsf{PUF}}$. Let the n-length PUF be $\Delta(C) = \alpha_1 P_0 + (\alpha_2 + \beta_1)P_0 + (\alpha_3 + \beta_2)P_2 + \cdots + (\alpha_n + \beta_{n-1})P_{n-1} + \beta_n$. Here, α_i, β_i are the delay parameters. We know that depending on the sign of $\Delta(C)$, the truth table of $1 \oplus f$ is generated. Now if we consider a PUF with the delay parameters $\alpha_i' = -\alpha_i$ and $\beta_i' = -\beta_i$ and construct the PUF $\Delta(C)' = \alpha_1' P_0 + (\alpha_2' + \beta_1')P_0 + (\alpha_3' + \beta_2')P_2 + \cdots + (\alpha_n' + \beta_{n-1}')P_{n-1} + \beta_n'$, then $\operatorname{sign}(\Delta(C))$ and $\operatorname{sign}(\Delta(C)')$ will be opposite for the same challenge values. Thus the truth table generated from $\Delta(C)'$ will be the truth table of $1 \oplus (1 \oplus f) = f$. Which contradicts our assumption. Hence if a Boolean function $f \notin \mathcal{B}_n^{\mathsf{PUF}}$ then $(1 \oplus f) \notin \mathcal{B}_n^{\mathsf{PUF}}$. Similarly if $(1 \oplus f) \notin \mathcal{B}_n^{\mathsf{PUF}}$ then $f \notin \mathcal{B}_n^{\mathsf{PUF}}$.   □

We know that any $(n+1)$-variable Boolean function f can be expressed as $f(x_1, \ldots, x_{n+1}) = (1 \oplus x_{n+1})f_1(x_1, \ldots, x_n) \oplus x_{n+1}f_2(x_1, \ldots, x_n)$, where f_1, f_2 are two Boolean functions involving n variables. This is basically equivalent to $f(x_1, \ldots, x_{n+1}) = f_1(x_1, \ldots, x_n) \parallel f_2(x_1, \ldots, x_n)$, in terms of concatenating the truth tables. That is, the truth table of f can be divided into two halves. In upper half if we consider $x_{n+1} = 0$, then it will contain the truth values of f_1 and in lower half if we consider $x_{n+1} = 1$ then it will contain the truth values of f_2.

Every 3-variable Boolean function f can be written as $f = f_1 \parallel f_2$, where f_1 and f_2 are two Boolean functions involving 2 variables. As the constructions of PUFs depend on parameters from normal distributions, the natural question is that if we consider a 3-variable PUF then can it be of the form $F = f \parallel f_1$ or $F = f_1 \parallel f$, where $f_1 = (1\ 0\ 1\ 0) \notin \mathcal{B}_2^{\mathsf{PUF}}$ (see Proposition 2) and $f \in \mathcal{B}_2$. The mathematical model of 3-variable PUF is $\Delta(C) = \alpha_1 P_0 + (\alpha_2 + \beta_1)P_1 + (\alpha_3 + \beta_2)P_2 + \beta_3$, where $P_0 = C_1 C_2 C_3$, $P_1 = C_2 C_3$ and $P_2 = C_3$. We prepare a truth table of a 3-variable PUF $F = f_1 \parallel f$ where $f_1 = (1\ 0\ 1\ 0) \notin \mathcal{B}_2^{\mathsf{PUF}}$ and $f \in \mathcal{B}_2$. We now break the truth table into two parts. In the upper part $C_3 = 1$ and in the lower part $C_3 = -1$. Without loss of generality we consider $f = (0\ 0\ 0\ 0)$. The final truth table of F will be of the following form.

C_3	C_2	C_1	$\Delta(C)$	$F = f_1 \parallel f$
1	1	1	$\alpha_1 + (\alpha_2 + \beta_1) + (\alpha_3 + \beta_2) + \beta_3 > 0$	1
1	1	-1	$-\alpha_1 + (\alpha_2 + \beta_1) + (\alpha_3 + \beta_2) + \beta_3 < 0$	0
1	-1	1	$-\alpha_1 - (\alpha_2 + \beta_1) + (\alpha_3 + \beta_2) + \beta_3 > 0$	1
1	-1	-1	$\alpha_1 - (\alpha_2 + \beta_1) + (\alpha_3 + \beta_2) + \beta_3 < 0$	0
-1	1	1	$-\alpha_1 - (\alpha_2 + \beta_1) - (\alpha_3 + \beta_2) + \beta_3 < 0$	0
-1	1	-1	$\alpha_1 - (\alpha_2 + \beta_1) - (\alpha_3 + \beta_2) + \beta_3 < 0$	0
-1	-1	1	$\alpha_1 + (\alpha_2 + \beta_1) - (\alpha_3 + \beta_2) + \beta_3 < 0$	0
-1	-1	-1	$-\alpha_1 + (\alpha_2 + \beta_1) - (\alpha_3 + \beta_2) + \beta_3 < 0$	0

We consider the following pairs of equations from the upper part of the above truth table.

$$\begin{cases} -\alpha_1 + (\alpha_2 + \beta_1) + (\alpha_3 + \beta_2) + \beta_3 < 0 \\ \alpha_1 - (\alpha_2 + \beta_1) + (\alpha_3 + \beta_2) + \beta_3 < 0 \end{cases} \tag{2}$$

$$\begin{cases} \alpha_1 + (\alpha_2 + \beta_1) + (\alpha_3 + \beta_2) + \beta_3 > 0 \\ -\alpha_1 - (\alpha_2 + \beta_1) + (\alpha_3 + \beta_2) + \beta_3 > 0 \end{cases} \tag{3}$$

From Eq. (2) we get $(\alpha_3 + \beta_2) + \beta_3 < 0$ and from Eq. (3) we get $(\alpha_3 + \beta_2) + \beta_3 > 0$, which is a contradiction. Thus for any $f \in \mathcal{B}_3^{\mathsf{PUF}}$ it can not be of the form $f_1 \parallel f_2$ or $f_2 \parallel f_1$ where $f_1 = (1\ 0\ 1\ 0) \notin \mathcal{B}_2^{\mathsf{PUF}}$. Similarly we can prove that for any $f \in \mathcal{B}_3^{\mathsf{PUF}}$ it can not be of the form $(1 \oplus f_1) \parallel f_2$ or $f_2 \parallel (1 \oplus f_1)$ where $f_1 = \notin \mathcal{B}_2^{\mathsf{PUF}}$. In this regard, we present the following important result.

Theorem 1. *If $f_1 \notin \mathcal{B}_n^{\mathsf{PUF}}$, then there does not exist any $F \in \mathcal{B}_{n+1}^{\mathsf{PUF}}$ of the form $f_1 \parallel f$ or $f \parallel f_1$.*

Proof. Assume that there exists an $F \in \mathcal{B}_{n+1}^{\mathsf{PUF}}$ such that $F = f_1 \parallel f$ and $f_1 \notin \mathcal{B}_n^{\mathsf{PUF}}$. Let the challenge input to the $(n+1)$-variable PUF be $C = (C_1, \ldots, C_{n+1})$. The mathematical model of the $(n + 1)$-variable PUF corresponding to F is

$$\Delta(C) = \alpha_1 P_0 + (\alpha_2 + \beta_1)P_1 + \cdots + (\alpha_{n+1} + \beta_n)P_n + \beta_{n+1}, \tag{4}$$

where $P_k = \prod_{i=k+1}^{n+1} C_i$. As $F \in \mathcal{B}_{n+1}^{\mathsf{PUF}}$, the inequalities constructed from $\Delta(C)$ in Eq. (4) and the truth table corresponding to F will provide a solution for α_i and

β_i. Let us look at the truth table of F into two equal parts. In the upper half $C_{n+1} = 1$ and lower half $C_{n+1} = -1$. It can be noticed that the upper half of the truth table of F should be exactly the same as the truth table of f_1 and the lower half should be exactly the same as the truth table of f. Using the values of α_i and β_i we prepare the following model of n-variable PUF

$$\Delta(C)' = \alpha_1' P_0 + (\alpha_2' + \beta_1') P_1 + \cdots + (\alpha_n' + \beta_{n-1}') P_n + \beta_n', \tag{5}$$

with $\alpha_i' = \alpha_i$ for $i = 1, \ldots, n$; $\beta_i' = \beta_i$ for $i = 1, \ldots n-1$ and $\beta_n' = (\alpha_{n+1} + \beta_n) + \beta_{n+1}$. The existence of α_i, β_i guarantees that the PUF described in Eq. (5) will be able to generate the truth table of f_1. This is a contradiction as $f_1 \notin \mathcal{B}_n^{\mathsf{PUF}}$. Thus $F = f_1 \parallel f \notin \mathcal{B}_{n+1}^{\mathsf{PUF}}$. Similar argument works to prove $F = f \parallel f_1 \notin \mathcal{B}_{n+1}^{\mathsf{PUF}}$. □

From Lemma 1 and Theorem 1, it is clear that $\mathcal{B}_n^{\mathsf{PUF}} \subset \mathcal{B}_n$ for $n \geq 2$. In fact we can directly say that if $f \in \mathcal{B}_{n+1}^{\mathsf{PUF}}$ then $f = f_1 \parallel f_2$ where $f_1, f_2 \in \mathcal{B}_n^{\mathsf{PUF}}$. With this we would like to investigate $\mathcal{B}_3^{\mathsf{PUF}}$. Proposition 2 claims that $|\mathcal{B}_2^{\mathsf{PUF}}| = 14$. Now if we prepare a 3-variable Boolean function by concatenating these 14 Boolean functions from $\mathcal{B}_2^{\mathsf{PUF}}$ then we can have maximum 196 Boolean functions. The most natural question is that whether all such Boolean functions belong to $\mathcal{B}_3^{\mathsf{PUF}}$ or not. To answer this, we note the following result.

Proposition 3. *Consider* $f_1 = (1\ 1\ 0\ 1), f_2 = (0\ 1\ 0\ 0) \in \mathcal{B}_2^{\mathsf{PUF}}$ *and* $f = f_1 \parallel f_2$. *The Boolean function* $f \notin \mathcal{B}_3^{\mathsf{PUF}}$.

Proof. We construct a truth table of $f = f_1 \parallel f_2$ for a 3-length PUF, where $f_1 = (1\ 1\ 0\ 1), f_2 = (0\ 1\ 0\ 0) \in \mathcal{B}_2^{\mathsf{PUF}}$. First we consider the following pairs of

C_3	C_2	C_1	$\Delta(C)$	$f = f_1 \parallel f_2$
1	1	1	$\alpha_1 + (\alpha_2 + \beta_1) + (\alpha_3 + \beta_2) + \beta_3 > 0$	1
1	1	-1	$-\alpha_1 + (\alpha_2 + \beta_1) + (\alpha_3 + \beta_2) + \beta_3 > 0$	1
1	-1	1	$-\alpha_1 - (\alpha_2 + \beta_1) + (\alpha_3 + \beta_2) + \beta_3 < 0$	0
1	-1	-1	$\alpha_1 - (\alpha_2 + \beta_1) + (\alpha_3 + \beta_2) + \beta_3 > 0$	1
-1	1	1	$-\alpha_1 - (\alpha_2 + \beta_1) - (\alpha_3 + \beta_2) + \beta_3 < 0$	0
-1	1	-1	$\alpha_1 - (\alpha_2 + \beta_1) - (\alpha_3 + \beta_2) + \beta_3 > 0$	1
-1	-1	1	$\alpha_1 + (\alpha_2 + \beta_1) - (\alpha_3 + \beta_2) + \beta_3 < 0$	0
-1	-1	-1	$-\alpha_1 + (\alpha_2 + \beta_1) - (\alpha_3 + \beta_2) + \beta_3 < 0$	0

equations from the above truth table.

$$\begin{cases} -\alpha_1 + (\alpha_2 + \beta_1) + (\alpha_3 + \beta_2) + \beta_3 > 0 \\ \alpha_1 - (\alpha_2 + \beta_1) - (\alpha_3 + \beta_2) + \beta_3 > 0 \end{cases} \tag{6}$$

$$\begin{cases} -\alpha_1 - (\alpha_2 + \beta_1) + (\alpha_3 + \beta_2) + \beta_3 < 0 \\ \alpha_1 + (\alpha_2 + \beta_1) - (\alpha_3 + \beta_2) + \beta_3 < 0 \end{cases} \tag{7}$$

Table 2. $|\mathcal{B}_n^{\mathsf{PUF}}|$ for different n

n	$|\mathcal{B}_n^{\mathsf{PUF}}|$	n	$|\mathcal{B}_n^{\mathsf{PUF}}|$
1	4	3	104
2	14	4	1882

From Eq. (6) we get $\beta_3 > 0$ and from Eq. (7) we get $\beta_3 < 0$. This is a contradiction. Thus $f = f_1 \parallel f_2 \notin \mathcal{B}_3^{\mathsf{PUF}}$. $\qquad\square$

Proposition 3 shows that even if we take any two Boolean functions f_1, f_2 from $\mathcal{B}_2^{\mathsf{PUF}}$ then $f = f_1 \parallel f_2$ may not belong to $\mathcal{B}_3^{\mathsf{PUF}}$. We have $|\mathcal{B}_1^{\mathsf{PUF}}| = 4$ but $|\mathcal{B}_2^{\mathsf{PUF}}| = 14$. For higher values of n, we have considered the mathematical model of PUF described in Eq. (1) for different values of n and exhaustively searched the Boolean functions which belong to $\mathcal{B}_n^{\mathsf{PUF}}$. For $n = 3, 4$ we have observed that $|\mathcal{B}_3^{\mathsf{PUF}}| = 104 < |\mathcal{B}_2^{\mathsf{PUF}}|^2$ and $|\mathcal{B}_4^{\mathsf{PUF}}| = 1882 < |\mathcal{B}_3^{\mathsf{PUF}}|^2$. We summarize the values of $|\mathcal{B}_n^{\mathsf{PUF}}|$ for different values of n in Table 2.

From this, the following result follows.

Theorem 2. *For any value of n, $|\mathcal{B}_{n+1}^{\mathsf{PUF}}| \leq |\mathcal{B}_n^{\mathsf{PUF}}|^2$. Further, for $n \geq 4$,*
$$\frac{|\mathcal{B}_n^{\mathsf{PUF}}|}{|\mathcal{B}_n|} < \frac{1}{2^{5 \cdot 2^{n-4}}}.$$

Proof. The first result follows from Theorem 1. The next result is initiated from exhaustive experiments, where for different values of delay parameters we have observed that $|\mathcal{B}_4^{\mathsf{PUF}}| = 1882$. Regarding the exhaustive experiment supporting the proof we refer to Algorithm 1 below. If we compute $\frac{|\mathcal{B}_4^{\mathsf{PUF}}|}{|\mathcal{B}_4|} = \frac{1882}{2^{2^4}} < \frac{1}{2^5} = \frac{1}{2^{5 \cdot 2^{4-4}}}$. Assume that the relation holds for $n = k$, for some $k > 4$, i.e., $\frac{|\mathcal{B}_k^{\mathsf{PUF}}|}{|\mathcal{B}_k|} < \frac{1}{2^{5 \cdot 2^{k-4}}}$. For $n = k + 1$, following Theorem 1 we have,

$$\frac{|\mathcal{B}_{k+1}^{\mathsf{PUF}}|}{|\mathcal{B}_{k+1}|} \leq \frac{|\mathcal{B}_k^{\mathsf{PUF}}|^2}{|\mathcal{B}_k|^2} < \left(\frac{1}{2^{5 \cdot 2^{k-4}}}\right)^2 = \left(\frac{1}{2^{5 \cdot 2^{(k+1)-4}}}\right). \tag{8}$$

Hence for $n \geq 4$, $\frac{|\mathcal{B}_n^{\mathsf{PUF}}|}{|\mathcal{B}_n|} < \frac{1}{2^{5 \cdot 2^{n-4}}}$. $\qquad\square$

Although the bound derived in Theorem 2 is not tight, it provides a significant estimation about $\mathcal{B}_n^{\mathsf{PUF}}$. Now the question is how one can obtain $\mathcal{B}_{n+1}^{\mathsf{PUF}}$ exhaustively. One informal way is, consider large number of values varying the delay parameters to construct $(n+1)$ variable PUFs and enumerate the number of distinct ones. However, this cannot be used as a proof but it can be used to find the set $\mathcal{B}_n^{\mathsf{PUF}}$ for small values of n.

Below we provide an iterative way of completely enumerating $\mathcal{B}_{n+1}^{\mathsf{PUF}}$ from $\mathcal{B}_n^{\mathsf{PUF}}$. In Algorithm 1 we consider the mathematical model of $(n+1)$-variable PUF, i.e., $\Delta(C) = \alpha_1 P_0 + (\alpha_2 + \beta_1)P_1 + \cdots + (\alpha_{n+1} + \beta_n)P_n + \beta_{n+1}$, $P_i = \prod_{k=i+1}^{n} C_i$. That is $\Delta(C)$ can be considered as a Boolean function on $C = (C_1, C_2, \ldots, C_{n+1})$, the challenge inputs corresponding to $(n+1)$-length

PUF. Consider any two $f_1, f_2 \in \mathcal{B}_n^{\mathsf{PUF}}$. Let $f = f_1 \parallel f_2$. For $C_{n+1} = 1$ we prepare the system of inequalities involving α_i, β_i, based on the truth table of f_1. Similarly, for $C_{n+1} = -1$ we construct the system of inequalities involving α_i, β_i based on the truth table of f_2. If this system of equations is solvable then we include the Boolean function f in $\mathcal{B}_{n+1}^{\mathsf{PUF}}$ which corresponds to the $(n+1)$-length PUF $\Delta(C)$. If we continue this process for all $f_1, f_2 \in \mathcal{B}_n^{\mathsf{PUF}}$ then we will have $\mathcal{B}_{n+1}^{\mathsf{PUF}}$.

Algorithm 1: Construction of $\mathcal{B}_{n+1}^{\mathsf{PUF}}$ from $\mathcal{B}_n^{\mathsf{PUF}}$

Input : $\mathcal{B}_n^{\mathsf{PUF}}$
Output: $\mathcal{B}_{n+1}^{\mathsf{PUF}}$

1   Assign $\Delta(C) = \alpha_1 P_0 + (\alpha_2 + \beta_1)P_1 + \cdots + (\alpha_{n+1} + \beta_n)P_n + \beta_{n+1}$, $P_i = \prod\limits_{k=i+1}^{n} C_i$;

2   **for** *each* $f_i \in \mathcal{B}_n^{\mathsf{PUF}}$ **do**

3      $F_1 = \{\}$;

4   **if** $C_{n+1} = 1$ **then**

5   **if** $f_i(C_1, \ldots, C_n) = 1$ **then**

6   Construct equation $\Delta(C) > 0$ and include $\Delta(C) > 0$ in F_1;

7   **end**

8   **else**

9   Construct equation $\Delta(C) < 0$ and include $\Delta(C) < 0$ in F_1;

10   **end**

11   **end**

12   **for** *each* $f_j \in \mathcal{B}_n^{\mathsf{PUF}}$ **do**

13          $F_2 = \{\}$;

14   **if** $C_{n+1} = -1$ **then**

15   **if** $f_j(C_1, \ldots, C_n) = 1$ **then**

16   Construct equation $\Delta(C) > 0$ and include $\Delta(C) > 0$ in F_2;

17   **end**

18   **else**

19   Construct equation $\Delta(C) < 0$ and include $\Delta(C) < 0$ in F_2;

20   **end**

21   **end**

22   **if** $F = F_1 \cup F_2$ *is solvable* **then**

23   Construct $f = f_1 \parallel f_2$ and include f in $\mathcal{B}_{n+1}^{\mathsf{PUF}}$;

24   **end**

25   **end**

26   **end**

27   **return** $\mathcal{B}_{n+1}^{\mathsf{PUF}}$;

We have implemented Algorithm 1 in SageMath 9.2 [23] and enumerated $\mathcal{B}_{n+1}^{\mathsf{PUF}}$ for $n = 1, 2, 3$. Algorithm 1 outputs the correct set $\mathcal{B}_{n+1}^{\mathsf{PUF}}$ in 1.891 s, 72.320 s and 2553.546 s for $n = 1, 2, 3$ respectively. For $n = 1, 2$ we have run the experiment in a laptop with processor of 2.80 GHz clock, 16 GB RAM and Linux (Ubuntu 20.04.03) environment. For $n = 3$ we have used multiprocessing in our implementation and the program was executed in a high performance computing machine with processor of 2.30 GHz clock, 72 CPUs, 96 GB RAM and Linux (CentOS 7) environment.

3   On Restricted Autocorrelation of Arbiter PUF

In Sect. 1.3 we have seen that the distribution of Boolean functions and PUFs differs significantly in terms of autocorrelation spectrum. This happens due to the fact that the PUFs depend on multiple device specific parameters and $\mathcal{B}_n^{\mathsf{PUF}} \subset \mathcal{B}_n$ for $n > 2$. Interestingly, if we consider the challenge inputs from $E_{n,k}$ with certain restrictions, then the autocorrelation distributions of random Boolean functions and PUFs become quite close. For measuring this we need to revisit the definition of restricted autocorrelation from Section 1.2.

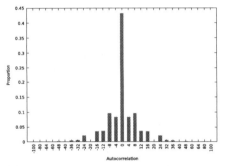
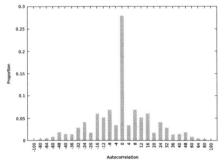

(a) Distribution of the Boolean functions in the restricted domain $E_{6,3}$

(b) Distribution of the randomly chosen PUFs in the restricted domain $E_{6,3}$

Fig. 4. Comparison of the restricted autocorrelation.

As we have discussed, f is an n-variable Boolean function. S_1 and S_2 are two sets defined as $S_1 = \{\mathbf{x} \in E_{n,k} \mid$ u-th bit of $\mathbf{x}$ is $-1\}$, $S_2 = \{\mathbf{x} \in E_{n,k} \mid$ u-th bit of $\mathbf{x}$ is $1\}$. Note that $E_{n,k} = S_1 \cup S_2$ and $S_1 \cap S_2 = \phi$. The restricted autocorrelation of f over $E_{n,k}$ is defined as

$$\mathcal{A}_f^{E_{n,k}} = \sum_{\mathbf{x}_1 \in S_1, \mathbf{x}_2 \in S_2} (-1)^{f(\mathbf{x}_1) \oplus f(\mathbf{x}_2)}.$$

Let us explain the scenario for restricted autocorrelation over the domain $E_{6,3}$. We have classified all the $2^{\binom{6}{3}}$ patterns and computed the distribution of Boolean function corresponding to different restricted autocorrelation values in Fig. 4. Such autocorrelation values are $\{-100, -80, -64, -60, -48, -40, -36, -32, -24, -20, -16, -12, -8, -4, 0, 4, 8, 12, 16, 20, 24, 32, 36, 40, 48, 60, 64, 80, 100\}$. The frequency of all such functions are normalized by dividing with $2^{\binom{6}{3}}$. For 6-length PUFs we have randomly searched with 2^{20} different sets of delay parameters (α_i, β_i) and obtained 14100 such distinct functions. For them we also obtained the same set of distinct autocorrelation values. The normalized frequency distribution is drawn in Fig. 4. A few blocks corresponding to certain autocorrelation values (such as $-100, -80, 80, 100$) in Fig. 4 are not visible due to very small proportion.

From Figs. 3 and 4, it can be observed that the restricted autocorrelation distribution of the PUFs demonstrates same behavior as the set of Boolean functions. That is the differential characteristics related to the bias is not observed for this restricted domain. That is, if the choice of two distinct challenge pairs can be restricted over certain domains (here one from S_1 and another from S_2 given a specific input bit location u), then the cryptographic weakness related to the bias might be avoided. Other than this different larger classes should be explored where such improved properties can be observed. Very simple model of Arbiter PUFs can be used there as cryptographic components with better confidence.

3.1   Theoretical Analysis

We now consider an Arbiter PUF whose inputs are from $E_{n,k}$. Let us divide the complete set $E_{n,k}$ into two subsets S_1 and S_2, where $S_1 = \{\mathbf{x} : \text{MSB of } \mathbf{x} \text{ is } -1\}$ and $S_2 = \{\mathbf{x} : \text{MSB of } \mathbf{x} \text{ is } 1\}$, i.e., the selected input bit is $u = n$.

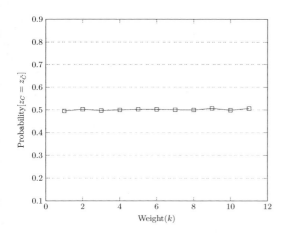

Fig. 5. Distribution of $Pr[z_C = z_{\tilde{C}}]$ in $E_{12,k}$

Table 3. $Pr[z_C = z_{\tilde{C}}]$ in $E_{12,k}$

Weight(k)	$Pr[z_C = z_{\tilde{C}}]$
1	0.495117
2	0.502397
3	0.497111
4	0.499929
5	0.502405
6	0.502307
7	0.500808
8	0.499840
9	0.506651
10	0.498867
11	0.506392

Consider challenge input C from S_1 and $\tilde{C}$ from S_2. For a randomly chosen PUF, let us denote z_C as the output corresponding to C and $z_{\tilde{C}}$ as the output corresponding to $\tilde{C}$. Compute the difference $z_C \oplus z_{\tilde{C}}$ for $C \in S_1$ and $\tilde{C} \in S_2$. If we calculate the average for all the points $C \in S_1$ and $\tilde{C} \in S_2$, then we can estimate the quantity $p_i = Pr[z_C = z_{\tilde{C}}]$. Here p_i denotes the probability corresponding to i-th PUF say. We compute the average of all these probabilities (p_i's) for of all the different cases $E_{12,1}, E_{12,2}, \ldots, E_{12,11}$. The obtained experimental data is presented in Table 3 and the distribution is plotted in Fig. 5. Note that $E_{12,0}$ and $E_{12,12}$ are not considered here as $|E_{12,0}| = |E_{12,12}| = 1$. From this experiment, we observe that the average probability is close to 0.5 for all weights $k = 1, \ldots, 11$. During the experiments, we have also observed that these probabilities do not depend on the choice of input bit t.

We note that this average probability is very close to 0.5 and that motivates us to explore the following theoretical result.

Theorem 3. *Expectation of $\mathcal{A}_f^{E_{n,k}}$ is equal to $\frac{1}{2}$ for $f \in \mathcal{B}_n^{PUF}$.*

Proof. Consider two distinct challenge inputs $C, \tilde{C} \in E_{n,k}$ such that they must differ at location t_1. Here C and $\tilde{C}$ are of the same weight k, hence they will definitely differ at more than one location. Let the m locations where C and $\tilde{C}$ differ be $t_1, t_2, \ldots, t_m$.

Let $\alpha = (\alpha_{t_1+1} + \beta_{t_1})P_{t_1} + (\alpha_{t_1+2} + \beta_{t_1+1})P_{t_1+1} + \ldots + (\alpha_{t_2} + \beta_{t_2-1})P_{t_2-1} + (\alpha_{t_3+1} + \beta_{t_3})P_{t_3} + \ldots + (\alpha_{t_4} + \beta_{t_4-1})P_{t_4-1} + \ldots + (\alpha_{t_m} + \beta_{t_m-1})P_{t_m-1}$ and $X = \Delta(C) - \alpha$. Thus the sign of $\Delta(C)$ corresponding to two challenge inputs $C, \tilde{C}$ will be same if and only if $|\frac{\alpha}{X}| < 1$. Hence the output bits corresponding two inputs C and $\tilde{C}$ will be same if and only if $|\frac{\alpha}{X}| < 1$.

As $\alpha_i, \beta_i \sim \mathcal{N}(0, \sigma)$, the quantity α will follow $\mathcal{N}(0, \sigma_\alpha)$ and X will follow $\mathcal{N}(0, \sigma_X)$, where $\sigma_\alpha = \sigma\sqrt{2[(t_2 - t_1) + (t_4 - t_3) + \ldots + (t_m - t_{m-1})]}$ and $\sigma_X = \sigma\sqrt{2n - 2[(t_2 - t_1) + (t_4 - t_3) + \ldots + (t_m - t_{m-1})]}$. The probability density functions of α and X will be $f_\alpha(y) = \frac{1}{\sqrt{2\pi}\sigma_\alpha}e^{-\frac{y^2}{2\sigma_\alpha^2}}$, $-\infty < y < \infty$ and $f_X(y) = \frac{1}{\sqrt{2\pi}\sigma_X}e^{-\frac{y^2}{2\sigma_X^2}}$, $-\infty < y < \infty$ respectively. Now we consider $Y_1 = \frac{\alpha}{X}$ and $Y_2 = X$. So $\alpha = Y_1 Y_2$. The joint distribution of α, X will be $f_{\alpha,X}(\alpha, x) = \frac{1}{2\pi\sigma_\alpha\sigma_X}e^{-\left(\frac{\alpha^2}{2\sigma_\alpha^2} + \frac{x^2}{2\sigma_X^2}\right)}$. Similarly, the joint distribution of Y_1, Y_2 will be $f_{Y_1,Y_2}(y_1, y_2) = \frac{1}{2\pi\sigma_\alpha\sigma_X}e^{-\left(\frac{y_1^2 y_2^2}{2\sigma_\alpha^2} + \frac{y_2^2}{2\sigma_X^2}\right)}y_2$, where $-\infty < y_1, y_2 < \infty$. The distribution of Y_1 will be $f_{Y_1}(y_1) = \int_{-\infty}^{\infty} f_{Y_1,Y_2}(y_1, y_2)dy_2 = \int_{-\infty}^{\infty} \frac{1}{2\pi\sigma_\alpha\sigma_X}e^{-\left(\frac{y_1^2 y_2^2}{2\sigma_\alpha^2} + \frac{y_2^2}{2\sigma_X^2}\right)}y_2 dy_2 = \frac{1}{\pi}\frac{\frac{\sigma_\alpha}{\sigma_X}}{y_1^2 + \left(\frac{\sigma_\alpha}{\sigma_X}\right)^2}$, where $-\infty < y_1 < \infty$.

We already know that the output bits corresponding to the two inputs C and $\tilde{C}$ will be the same if and only if $|\frac{\alpha}{X}| < 1$. To calculate $Pr[|\frac{\alpha}{X}| < 1]$ we need to calculate $Pr[|Y_1| < 1]$.

$$Pr[|Y_1| < 1] = \left| \int_{-1}^{1} \frac{1}{\pi} \frac{\frac{\sigma_\alpha}{\sigma_X}}{y_1^2 + \left(\frac{\sigma_\alpha}{\sigma_X}\right)^2} dy_1 \right|$$

$$= \frac{1}{\pi} \left| \left\{ \tan^{-1}\left(\frac{1}{\frac{\sigma_\alpha}{\sigma_X}}\right) - \tan^{-1}\left(\frac{-1}{\frac{\sigma_\alpha}{\sigma_X}}\right) \right\} \right|$$

$$= 1 - \frac{2}{\pi} \tan^{-1}\left(\frac{\sigma_\alpha}{\sigma_X}\right)$$

$$= 1 - \frac{2}{\pi} \tan^{-1}\left(\sqrt{\frac{(t_2 - t_1) + (t_4 - t_3) + \ldots + (t_m - t_{m-1})}{n - [(t_2 - t_1) + (t_4 - t_3) + \ldots + (t_m - t_{m-1})]}}\right)$$

$$= 1 - \frac{2}{\pi} \tan^{-1}\sqrt{\frac{t}{n-t}}.$$

Here $t = (t_2 - t_1) + (t_4 - t_3) + \cdots + (t_m - t_{m-1})$. Note that we have selected two distinct challenge inputs $C, \tilde{C}$ from $E_{n,k}$ with the condition that C and $\tilde{C}$ must differ at location t_1. Without loss of generality, we can assume that t_1-th location of C has -1 and t_1-th location of $\tilde{C}$ has 1. Let $S_1 = \{\mathbf{x} \mid \mathbf{x} \in E_{n,k}$ and t_1-th location of $\mathbf{x}$ has $-1\}$, $S_2 = \{\mathbf{x} \mid \mathbf{x} \in E_{n,k}$ and t_1-th location of $\mathbf{x}$ has $1\}$. That is $C \in S_1$, $\tilde{C} \in S_2$ and we have already noted $|S_1| = \binom{n-1}{k-1}$, $|S_2| = \binom{n-1}{k}$. If we consider the average probability for all choices of $C \in S_1$ and $\tilde{C} \in S_2$ then we will get the expectation of $\mathcal{A}_f^{E_{n,k}}$, where f is an n-length Arbiter PUF chosen uniformly at random. Hence,

$$\text{Expectation of } \mathcal{A}_f^{E_{n,k}} = \frac{1}{\binom{n-1}{k} \times \binom{n-1}{k-1}} \times \sum_{C \in S_1} \sum_{\tilde{C} \in S_2} \left[1 - \frac{2}{\pi} \tan^{-1}\sqrt{\frac{t}{n-t}} \right]$$

$$= 1 - \frac{1}{\binom{n-1}{k} \times \binom{n-1}{k-1}} \times \sum_{C \in S_1} \sum_{\tilde{C} \in S_2} \left[\frac{2}{\pi} \tan^{-1}\sqrt{\frac{t}{n-t}} \right].$$

We further simplify this. For every pair of inputs $C \in S_1$ and $\tilde{C} \in S_2$, one can compute $(1 - \frac{2}{\pi} \tan^{-1}\sqrt{\frac{t}{n-t}})$ as follows. Note that for every value of t, $\tan^{-1}\sqrt{\frac{t}{n-t}}$ and $\tan^{-1}\sqrt{\frac{n-t}{t}}$ both term will occur in the summation $\sum_{C \in S_1} \sum_{\tilde{C} \in S_2} \frac{2}{\pi} \tan^{-1}\sqrt{\frac{t}{n-t}}$. That means the above summation will contain the term $\tan^{-1}\sqrt{x} + \tan^{-1}\sqrt{\frac{1}{x}} = \frac{\pi}{2}$, for different values of x. As there are total $\binom{n-1}{k} \times \binom{n-1}{k-1}$ terms in the summation, the final expectation of $\mathcal{A}_f^{E_{n,k}}$ will be equal to $\frac{1}{2}$ for $f \in \mathcal{B}_n^{\text{PUF}}$. This completes our proof. $\square$

Let us provide an example with $n = 9$ and $k = 4$, i.e., $|E_{n,k}| = 126$. Hence $|S_1| = \binom{8}{3} = 56$ and $|S_2| = \binom{8}{4} = 70$. Let $T_i = \{(C, \tilde{C}) \in S_1 \times S_2 : t = i\}$. It can be checked that $|T_i| = |T_{n-i}|$, for $i = 1, \ldots, 8$. In $E_{9,4}$, $|T_1| = |T_8| = 35$, i.e., there are 35 pair of inputs $(C, \tilde{C}) \in S_1 \times S_2$, for which $t = 1$ and another different 35 pairs of inputs $(C, \tilde{C}) \in S_1 \times S_2$, for which $t = 8$. If we add $(1 - \frac{2}{\pi} \tan^{-1}\sqrt{\frac{t}{n-t}})$

128 A. Roy et al.

for all these 70 pairs of distinct inputs, the final value becomes 35. Similarly $|T_2| = |T_7| = 215, |T_3| = |T_6| = 635$ and $|T_4| = |T_5| = 1075$. Hence the final expectation becomes $\frac{1}{{}^8C_3 \times {}^8C_4} \times [35 + 215 + 635 + 1075] = \frac{1}{2}$.

From the result of Theorem 3 it can be observed that if the challenge pairs are chosen with certain restrictions related to the input weights, then there does not exist any bias in the output of the Arbiter PUF. Thus in such restricted scenarios, such simple models of physically unclonable devices might provide acceptable cryptographic parameters.

In a related note, it has been shown [15] that certain cryptographic properties related to the Walsh spectrum of a Boolean function degrades in the restricted domain. Here we show that in the case of Arbiter PUFs, certain kind of autocorrelation property in a restricted sense improves. The proposed notion of restricted autocorrelation might be explored for analyzing the security of FLIP [13] type ciphers under differential attack or related key attack.

4 Conclusion

In this paper, we have studied certain limitations of Arbiter PUFs and shown that the class of Boolean functions constructed using n-length $(n > 1)$ PUFs is a proper subset of the set of all n variable Boolean functions. It is shown that exhaustively varying the delay parameters, the n-length Arbiter PUFs can only generate a negligible portion of Boolean functions. We present several existence and non-existence results in this direction. Further we have looked at autocorrelation in certain restricted sense and presented relevant results in this direction. It is known that the autocorrelation property of Boolean functions generated out of Arbiter PUFs is quite biased in certain cases. Interestingly, here we note that under certain constraints on the weights of inputs, along with the difference in a specific input bit, such biases vanish. That is, such a simple model of Arbiter PUFs provide good cryptographic parameters in terms of differential analysis if certain restrictions on the input challenge pairs are imposed.

Acknowledgments. We would like to thank the anonymous reviewers for their constructive comments and suggestions, which considerably improved the quality of our paper.

References

1. Becker, G.T.: The gap between promise and reality: on the insecurity of XOR arbiter PUFs. In: Güneysu, T., Handschuh, H. (eds.) CHES 2015. LNCS, vol. 9293, pp. 535–555. Springer, Heidelberg (2015). https://doi.org/10.1007/978-3-662-48324-4_27
2. Brzuska, C., Fischlin, M., Schröder, H., Katzenbeisser, S.: Physically uncloneable functions in the universal composition framework. In: Rogaway, P. (ed.) CRYPTO 2011. LNCS, vol. 6841, pp. 51–70. Springer, Heidelberg (2011). https://doi.org/10.1007/978-3-642-22792-9_4

3. Canteaut, A., et al.: Stream ciphers: a practical solution for efficient homomorphic-ciphertext compression. J. Cryptol. **31**(3), 885–916 (2018). https://doi.org/10.1007/s00145-017-9273-9

4. Carlet, C., Méaux, P., Rotella, Y.: Boolean functions with restricted input and their robustness; application to the FLIP cipher. IACR Trans. Symmetric Cryptol. **3**, 192–227 (2017). (presented at FSE 2018)

5. Delvaux, J., Gu, D., Schellekens, D., Verbauwhede, I.: Secure lightweight entity authentication with strong PUFs: mission impossible? In: Batina, L., Robshaw, M. (eds.) CHES 2014. LNCS, vol. 8731, pp. 451–475. Springer, Heidelberg (2014). https://doi.org/10.1007/978-3-662-44709-3_25

6. Devadas, S.: Physical unclonable functions and secure processors. In: Clavier, C., Gaj, K. (eds.) CHES 2009. LNCS, vol. 5747, p. 65. Springer, Heidelberg (2009). https://doi.org/10.1007/978-3-642-04138-9_5

7. Gassend, B.: Physical Random Functions. M.S. thesis, Department of Electrical Engineering Computer Science, Massachusetts Institute of Technology, Cambridge, January 2003. https://citeseerx.ist.psu.edu/viewdoc/download?doi=10.1.1.13.7571&rep=rep1&type=pdf

8. Gassend, B., Clarke, D., Dijk, M.V., Devadas, S.: Silicon physical random functions. In: Proceedings of the 9th ACM Conference on Computer and Communications Security, pp. 148–160. ACM (2002). https://dl.acm.org/citation.cfm?id=586132

9. Hammouri, G., Sunar, B.: PUF-HB: a tamper-resilient HB based authentication protocol. In: Bellovin, S.M., Gennaro, R., Keromytis, A., Yung, M. (eds.) ACNS 2008. LNCS, vol. 5037, pp. 346–365. Springer, Heidelberg (2008). https://doi.org/10.1007/978-3-540-68914-0_21

10. Lee, J.W., Lim, D., Gassend, B., Suh, G.E., Dijk, M.V., Devadas, S.: A technique to build a secret key in integrated circuits for identification and authentication applications. In: 2004 Symposium on VLSI Circuits. Digest of Technical Papers (IEEE Cat. No. 04CH37525), pp. 176–179. IEEE (2004). https://people.csail.mit.edu/devadas/pubs/vlsi-symp-puf.pdf

11. Lim, D.: Extracting Secret Keys from Integrated Circuits. M.Sc. thesis, MIT (2004)

12. Lim, D., Lee, J.W., Gassend, B., Suh, G.E., Dijk, M.V., Devadas, S.: Extracting secret keys from integrated circuits. IEEE Trans. Very Large Scale Integr. (VLSI) Syst. **13**(10), 1200–1205 (2005)

13. Méaux, P., Journault, A., Standaert, F.-X., Carlet, C.: Towards stream ciphers for efficient FHE with low-noise ciphertexts. In: Fischlin, M., Coron, J.-S. (eds.) EUROCRYPT 2016. LNCS, vol. 9665, pp. 311–343. Springer, Heidelberg (2016). https://doi.org/10.1007/978-3-662-49890-3_13

14. Maitra, S., Mandal, B., Martinsen, T., Roy, D., Stănică, P.: Tools in analyzing linear approximation for Boolean functions related to FLIP. In: Chakraborty, D., Iwata, T. (eds.) INDOCRYPT 2018. LNCS, vol. 11356, pp. 282–303. Springer, Cham (2018). https://doi.org/10.1007/978-3-030-05378-9_16

15. Maitra, S., Mandal, B., Martinsen, T., Roy, D., Stănică, P.: Analysis on Boolean function in a restricted (biased) domain. IEEE Trans. Inf. Theory **66**(2), 1219–1231 (2020)

16. Majzoobi, M., Koushanfar, F., Potkonjak, M.: Testing techniques for hardware security. In International Test Conference (ITC), pp. 1–10. IEEE (2008)

17. Mesnager, S., Zhou, Z., Ding, C.: On the nonlinearity of Boolean functions with restricted input. Cryptogr. Commun. **11**(1), 63–76 (2019)

18. Rührmair, U., Busch, H., Katzenbeisser, S.: Strong PUFs: models, constructions, and security proofs. In: Sadeghi, AR., Naccache, D. (eds.) Towards Hardware-Intrinsic Security. ISC, pp. 79–96. Springer, Heidelberg (2010). https://doi.org/10.1007/978-3-642-14452-3_4

19. Rührmair, U., Devadas, S., Koushanfar, F.: Security based on physical unclonability and disorder. In: Tehranipoor, M., Wang, C. (eds.) Introduction to Hardware Security and Trust, pp. 65–102. Springer, New York (2012). https://doi.org/10.1007/978-1-4419-8080-9_4

20. Rührmair, U., Sehnke, F., Sölter, J., Dror, G., Devadas, S., Schmidhuber, J.: Modeling attacks on physical unclonable functions. In: Proceedings of the 17th ACM Conference on Computer and Communications Security, pp. 237–249. ACM (2010)

21. Rührmair, U., Sölter, J., Sehnke, F.: On the Foundations of Physical Unclonable Functions. Cryptology ePrint Archive, p. 277 (2009). https://eprint.iacr.org/2009/277.pdf

22. Rührmair, U., et al.: PUF modeling attacks on simulated and silicon data. IEEE Trans. Inf. Forensics Secur. 8(11), 1876–1891 (2013)

23. SageMath: A free open-source mathematics software. https://www.sagemath.org/

24. Siddhanti, A.A., Bodapati, S., Chattopadhyay, A., Maitra, S., Roy, D., Stănică, P.: Analysis of the strict avalanche criterion in variants of arbiter-based physically unclonable functions. In: Hao, F., Ruj, S., Sen Gupta, S. (eds.) INDOCRYPT 2019. LNCS, vol. 11898, pp. 556–577. Springer, Cham (2019). https://doi.org/10.1007/978-3-030-35423-7_28

MPC for $\mathcal{Q}_2$ Access Structures over Rings and Fields

Robin Jadoul[ID], Nigel P. Smart[(✉)][ID], and Barry Van Leeuwen[ID]

imec-COSIC, KU Leuven, Leuven, Belgium
robin.jadoul@esat.kuleuven.be, {nigel.smart,barry.vanleeuwen}@kuleuven.be

Abstract. We examine Multi-Party Computation protocols in the active-security-with-abort setting for $\mathcal{Q}_2$ access structures over small and large finite fields $\mathbb{F}_p$ and over rings $\mathbb{Z}_{p^k}$. We give general protocols which work for any $\mathcal{Q}_2$ access structure which is realised by a multiplicative Extended Span Program. We generalize a number of techniques and protocols from various papers and compare the different methodologies. In particular we examine the expected communication cost per multiplication gate when the protocols are instantiated with different access structures.

1 Introduction

Secure multiparty computation (MPC) considers the situation where some set of parties $\mathcal{P}$ come together to compute a function, each with their own inputs. The security requirement is that no party is able to learn more than what the output of this computation and their own input would allow them to. From another perspective, this can be seen as a protocol that emulates a perfectly honest, trusted third party that obtains each party's input, performs the computation, and outputs the result.

We can distinguish different security notions based on the power an adversary can have. One axis along which to distinguish is whether the adversary is active or passive. A passive adversary, also sometimes called *honest but curious*, follows the protocol correctly, but tries to obtain more information from the parts of the transcript of the execution it can see. An active adversary on the other hand, is able to arbitrarily deviate from the protocol. In this situation we either require that the honest parties still obtain the correct output from the function, in which case we say that the protocol is robust, or we require that the honest parties abort the protocol with overwhelming probability, in which case we say the protocol is *actively-secure-with-abort*. In this paper we concentrate on protocols which are actively-secure-with-abort, as they are relatively fast and practical in a large number of situations. Those readers who are interested in robust active security should consult [1,8].

Another axis to consider is how many or which subsets of parties the adversary can corrupt. If we have n parties then a full threshold adversary is one who is able to corrupt at most $n-1$ parties. In such a situation we can achieve

R. AlTawy and A. Hülsing (Eds.): SAC 2021, LNCS 13203, pp. 131–151, 2022.
https://doi.org/10.1007/978-3-030-99277-4_7

active-security-with-abort, however this comes at the expense of a costly prepro-cessing phase; see [6,10] for the case of MPC over finite fields, or over finite rings. Simpler protocols can be obtained if one restricts the adversary to corrupt less parties. The classic restriction is that of threshold adversaries who are allowed to corrupt up to $t < n$ parties. When $t < n/2$ very efficient MPC protocols can be realised, using a variety of methodologies to obtain active-security-with-abort. The natural generalisation of the threshold $t < n/2$ case is that of so-called $\mathcal{Q}_2$ adversary structure. A $\mathcal{Q}_2$ adversary structure is one where the union of no two unqualified sets contains the whole set of players $\mathcal{P}$. For threshold structures the set of unqualified sets are all subsets of $\mathcal{P}$ of size t, thus clearly no two sets can contain all of $\mathcal{P}$ when $t < n/2$. In this paper we will focus on $\mathcal{Q}_2$ access structures, again as they are relatively fast and practical in a large number of situations.

A third axis to consider is the underlying field or ring over which the MPC protocol is implemented. Traditionally the focus has been on MPC protocols over fields $\mathbb{F}_p$, either large finite fields or small ones (in particular $\mathbb{F}_2$). However, recently interest has shifted to also considering finite rings such as $\mathbb{Z}_{p^k}$, and in particular $\mathbb{Z}_{2^k}$. In this setting sometimes, to obtain active security, underlying protocols require the players to work in the extended ring $\mathbb{Z}_{2^{k+s}}$, for some security parameter s, and sometimes this is avoided. In this work we will consider all such possibilities.

The final axis to consider is the precise protocol to use. Almost all practical protocols which are actively-secure-with-abort for $\mathcal{Q}_2$ access structures divide the protocol into two, and sometimes three stages. The first stage, called the offline or pre-processing stage, is function independent and generates various forms of correlated randomness amongst the parties. A second stage, called the online stage, uses the pre-processing to compute the output of the function in a secure manner. Sometimes a third stage, called the post-processing stage, is required to ensure active-security.

The investigation of the combination of the second, third and fourth axes forms the basis of this work. We generalize, where needed, prior works in order to investigate as many prior protocol variants as possible, when instantiated over finite rings or fields. We also generalize results from specific $\mathcal{Q}_2$ access struc-tures to general $\mathcal{Q}_2$ access structures so as to obtain a complete smorgasbord of options. We then analyse the different options, as it is unclear in which situation which protocol is to be preferred (even in the case of finite fields).

Prior Related Work: The majority of the literature has focused on the case where the underlying arithmetic is a finite field. These are often based, for gen-eral finite fields and $\mathcal{Q}_2$ access structures, on the classic multiplication protocol of Maurer [16], which works for an arbitrary multiplicative secret sharing scheme. In the case of small finite fields and small numbers of parties, for example $\mathbb{F}_2$ and three players it is common to utilize a multiplication protocol based on repli-cated secret sharing, which originally appeared in the Sharemind software [4]. The generalisation of this specific multiplication protocol to arbitrary fields and

$\mathcal{Q}_2$-access structures implemented by replicated secret sharing [15], the generalization to an arbitrary $\mathcal{Q}_2$ MSP was done in [17]. Both of these multiplication protocols we shall refer to as KRSW. There is a third passively secure multiplication protocol due to Damgård and Nielsen [9], which we shall refer to as DN multiplication. The DN multiplication protocol is often combined with a "king-paradigm" for opening a sharing, this reduces the total amount of data sent at the expense of doubling the number of rounds. As round complexity has often a bigger impact on execution time than data complexity we assume no king paradigm is used in our protocols[1] Thus before one even considers the various protocols, one has (at least) three base passively secure multiplication protocols to consider. In this work we will concentrate on these three, Maurer or KRSW or DN. The one which is more efficient depends on the precise context as we will show. From these, when using multiplication triples, one can derive a third passively secure multiplication triple which we shall call Beaver multiplication.

In more recent works, research has started to focus on MPC over finite rings, such as $\mathbb{Z}_{p^k}$, and $\mathbb{Z}_{2^k}$ in particular. For many cases, this choice is more natural, as it more closely aligns with the bitwise representation of numbers found in standard computing, and it can enable efficient high level operations such as bit-decomposition (which are very useful in practice). For example, working over $\mathbb{Z}_{2^{64}}$ would closely mimic the behaviour we have on most currently used CPUs. The main problem with working with such rings is the presence of zero-divisors.

A method to avoid the problem of zero-divisors in secret sharing schemes over rings with zero-divisors was presented in the SPD$\mathbb{Z}_{2^k}$ protocol of [6]. Originally, this was presented in the case of a full threshold adversary structure, but the basic trick used applies to any access structure. To avoid the problem of zero divisors when working modulo 2^k, the authors extend (for some protocols) the secret sharing to a large modulus 2^{k+s}, for some statistical security parameter s. This idea was extended to the case of simple $\mathcal{Q}_2$ access structures, using a replicated secret sharing schemes, in [11]. With some of the resulting protocols for $n = 3$ and $n = 4$ parties implemented in the MP-SPDZ framework [13].

Across the many papers on $\mathcal{Q}_2$ MPC we identify three forms of actively secure pre-processing used in the literature, which we generalise[2] to an arbitrary setting of p^k. The first, which we denote by $\mathsf{Offline}_1$, uses a passively secure multiplication protocol to obtain $2 \cdot N$ triples. These are then made actively secure using the classic technique of sacrificing (which effectively uses internally a Beaver multiplication), resulting in an output of N triples. This variant has been used in a number of papers, e.g. [17]. A second variant, which we denote by $\mathsf{Offline}_2$, generates N passively secure triples, and then checks these are correct

---

[1] Note the kind-paradigm can be used not only in DN multiplication but in any protocol which involves opening shares to all players, as long as suitable additional checks are performed to ensure active security.

[2] There are a few others which we do not consider, as they do not easily fit into our protocol descriptions below. For example the protocol of [2] looks at threshold structures and uses the multiplication protocol of [9] using a king paradigm.

using a different checking procedure, based on the underlying passively secure multiplication protocol of choice. This variant was used in [11].

A third offline variant, which we shall denote by Offline$_3$, uses a passively secure multiplication protocol to obtain triples in the offline phase. These are then made actively secure using a cut-and-choose method, as opposed to sacrificing. The reason for this is that they are interested in MPC over $\mathbb{F}_2$ and classical sacrificing has a soundness error of one over the field size, and using cut-and-choose allows one to perform an actively secure offline phase without needing to pass to a ring of the form $\mathbb{Z}_{2^k}$. This methodology was presented in [3], and we shall also call this ABF pre-processing. This method seems very well suited to situations when p^k is small as it does not require extending the base ring to $\mathbb{Z}_{p^{k+s}}$.

From these one can derive a number of complete protocol variants. The first variant, which we shall denote Protocol$_1$, exploits the error-detecting properties of a $\mathcal{Q}_2$ access structure to obtain a protocol which uses an actively secure offline phase, and then uses an online phase based on the classical Beaver multiplication method. Active-security-with-abort is achieved using the error detecting properties of the underlying secret sharing scheme. This has been considered in a number of papers in the case of threshold structures with $(n, t) = (3, 1)$, with the generalisation to arbitrary $\mathcal{Q}_2$ structures in the case of large finite fields being done in [17].

In [11] a three party protocol is presented which makes use of a different methodology, which we generalise to arbitrary $\mathcal{Q}_2$ access structures. Here the online phase is executed optimistically using a passively secure multiplication protocol. The multiplications are then checked to be correct at the end of the protocol using a post-processing phase. Depending on the method used to perform this checking, we can either generate auxiliary, passively secure triples in an offline phase, that can be used in a form of sacrificing in the post-processing phase (which we dub Protocol$_2$), or we can completely remove the need for a preprocessing step (which we dub Protocol$_3$).

The paper [3] also uses an optimistic passively secure online phase with a post-processing step, but combines this with an actively secure offline phase. By doing this the post-processing check is always checking possibly incorrect multiplications (from the online phase) against known-to-be-correct multiplications (from the offline phase). This means the post-processing check can be done using a method which is close to that of classical sacrificing, without the need to worry about the small field size. We call this variant Protocol$_4$.

The final protocol variant we consider, which we dub Protocol$_5$, comes from [5]. In this paper the authors dispense with the offline phase, and instead generate a shared MAC-key $[\alpha]$, a bit like in SPDZ, and evaluate the circuit on both $[x]$ and $[\alpha \cdot x]$ using a passively secure multiplication protocol. Thus, in some sense, the circuit is evaluated twice in the online phase. The correctness of the evaluation is then established using the MAC-Check protocol from the SPDZ protocol. Thus there is a post-processing step, but it is relatively light-weight, however the online phase is more expensive than other techniques.

We summarize these in five protocol variants in Table 1 as a means for the reader to maintain a quick overview as they read the paper.

Table 1. Summary of our five protocol variants. A "heavy" post-processing phase denotes a phase akin to sacrificing, where as a "light" post-processing denotes a phase akin to SPDZ-like MAC checking. A Passive online phase refers to an online phase using either Maurer or KRSW multiplication.

	Offline phase		Online	Post-processing	
Protocol	Passive	Active	Phase	Heavy	Light
Protocol$_1$	–	✓	Beaver	–	–
Protocol$_2$	✓	-	Passive	✓	–
Protocol$_3$	–	–	Passive	✓	–
Protocol$_4$	–	✓	Passive	✓	–
Protocol$_5$	–	–	$2 \times$ Passive	–	✓

Our Contribution: In this work we unify all these protocols; in prior work they may have been presented for finite fields, or for rings of the form $\mathbb{Z}_{2^k}$, or for specific access structures. We consider, in all cases, the general case of MPC over rings of the form $\mathbb{Z}_{p^k}$; i.e. where we consider both the case of $k = 1$, large k, small p, and large p in one go. Our methodology applies to all multiplicative $\mathcal{Q}_2$ access structures over such rings. To do so we utilize the language of Extended Span Programs, ESPs, introduced in [12]. This allows us to consider not only replicated access structures, but also access structures coming from Galois Ring constructions. By considering such Galois Ring constructions as an ESP, we can maintain working over $\mathbb{Z}_{p^k}$ without the need to worry about complications arising from the Galois Ring.

We first show how one can create the necessary ESPs for a specific access structure, by constructing an associated MSP over the field $\mathbb{F}_p$ and then lifting it to $\mathbb{Z}_{p^k}$ in a trivial manner. This preserves the access structure, but it does not always preserve multiplicity (see [1] for a relatively contrived counter example). For all "natural" MSPs one might encounter in practice (arising from Shamir or Replicated secret sharing) the lifting does preserve multiplicity. In any case if the resulting ESP over $\mathbb{Z}_{p^k}$ is not multiplicative, it can be extended to a multiplicative ESP in the standard manner[3].

We show that the error-detection properties of [17] apply in this more generalized context of finite rings. This allows us to reduce the communication cost in our protocols for ESPs. Note the error-detection properties exploited in [17] are the precise generalization to arbitrary $\mathcal{Q}_2$ MSPs of the classical check for correctness performed in threshold systems for $(n, t) = (3, 1)$ based on replicated sharing.

---

[3] This is a standard result for MSPs over fields, but it is easily extended to ESPs over finite rings.

We also show that the trick of modulus extension from $\mathbb{Z}_{p^k}$ to $\mathbb{Z}_{p^{k+s}}$ also works in general, and we combine it with other tricks. For example we use Schwarz-Zippel over Galois rings to allow greater batching, and modulus extension even in the case of checking over finite fields. Indeed we show that one can also utilize modulus extension to avoid the problems with sacrificing when $k = 1$ and p is small. However, this comes at the expense of requiring to work modulo p^{k+s} and not working modulo p^k, which may be a problem in some instances (for example in the interesting case of $p^k = 2$). Thus our multiplication checking procedures in Sect. 3 generalise a number of earlier results, and unify various approaches. Note, that depending on the underlying protocol choice such modulus extensions may not be needed.

We finally examine the smorgasbord of options for the offline, online and post-processing which we outlined above in this general context and examine the various benefits and tradeoffs which result. Our cost metrics in this matter are the total number of rounds of communication, as well as the total amount of data sent per multiplication[4]. We consider the case where the user is interested in minimizing the total cost (i.e. the combined cost of all three phases), as well as the case where the user is interested in minimizing the costs of the online and post-processing phases only (i.e. where the user assumes that the offline phase can be done overnight for example and is not an important consideration).

2   Preliminaries

2.1   Notation

We let $\mathbb{F}$ denote a general finite field, and R denote a general finite commutative ring. We let $\mathbb{F}_p$ denote the specific finite field of p elements, and $\mathbb{Z}_{p^k}$ denote the ring of integers modulo p^k. For two sets X, Y we write $X \subset Y$ if X is a proper subset and $X \subseteq Y$ if X is not necessarily proper. For a set B, we denote by $a \leftarrow B$ the process of drawing a from B with a uniform distribution on the set B. For a probabilistic algorithm A, we denote by $a \leftarrow A$ the process of assigning a the output of algorithm A; with the underlying probability distribution being determined by the random coins of A.

For a vector $\mathbf{x}$ we let $\mathbf{x}^{(i)}$ denote it ith component, and for two vectors $\mathbf{x}$ and $\mathbf{y}$ of the same length we let $\langle \mathbf{x}, \mathbf{y} \rangle$ denote the dot-product, unless otherwise noted. We let $M_{n \times m}(K)$, where $K = \mathbb{F}$ or $K = R$, be the set of all matrices with n rows and m columns. For $M \in M_{n \times m}(K)$ denote the transpose by M^T. We let $\ker(M)$ to denote the subspace of K^m which maps to $\mathbf{0}$ under left multiplication by M, and we let $\mathrm{Im}(M)$ to be the subspace of K^n which is the image of all elements in K^n upon left multiplication by M. If V is a subspace of K^r for some r, we let $V^\perp = \{ \mathbf{w} \in K^r \mid \forall \mathbf{v} \in V : \langle \mathbf{w}, \mathbf{v} \rangle = 0 \}$ denote the orthogonal complement. Moreover, we let $\mathbf{0}$ and $\mathbf{1}$ be the all zero and all one vector of appropriate dimension (defined by the context unless explicitly specified) and let

---

[4] Note, as MPC protocols do not usually work *in practice* over arithmetic circuits this is only an approximation of the cost of the various options.

$\mathbf{e}_i$ be the ith canonical basis vector, that is $\mathbf{e}_i^{(j)} = \delta_{i,j}$ where δ is the Kronecker Delta.

2.2   Monotone and Extended Span Programs

As is standard we can associate linear secret sharing schemes over fields with Monotone Span Programs. In [12] these definitions are extended to linear secret sharing schemes over finite rings, such as $\mathbb{Z}_{p^k}$, with the associated structure being called an Extended Span Program. We recap on the relevant definitions here.

Access Structures: The set of parties that the adversary can corrupt is drawn from an access structure (Γ, Δ). The set Γ is the set of all qualified sets, whilst Δ is the set of all unqualified sets. The access/adversary structure is assumed to be monotone, i.e. if $X \subset X'$ and $X \in \Gamma$, then $X' \in \Gamma$ and if $X \subset X'$ and $X' \in \Delta$ then $X \in \Delta$, and we assume $\Gamma \cap \Delta = \emptyset$. We are only interested in this paper in access structures which are $\mathcal{Q}_2$:

Definition 2.1 ($\mathcal{Q}_2$ Access Structure). *Let $\mathcal{P} = \{P_1, \ldots, P_n\}$ be a set of parties, with access structure (Γ, Δ), then (Γ, Δ) is said to be a $\mathcal{Q}_2$ access structure if*

$$P \neq A \cup B \text{ for all } A, B \in \Delta.$$

In other words: An access structure (Γ, Δ) is $\mathcal{Q}_2$, if for any two sets in Δ the union of those sets does not cover $\mathcal{P}$. An access structure is called complete if for any $Q \in \Gamma$ it holds that $\mathcal{P} \backslash Q \in \Delta$ and vice versa. In this paper we will only consider complete access structures.

Monotone Span Programs Over Fields: Using this notation, the definition of a Monotone Span Program follows.

Definition 2.2. *A Monotone Span Program (MSP), denoted $\mathcal{M}$, is a quadruple $(\mathbb{F}, M, \varepsilon, \varphi)$, where $\mathbb{F}$ is a field, $M \in M_{m \times d}(\mathbb{F})$ is a full-rank matrix for some m and $d \leq m$, $\varepsilon \in \mathbb{F}^d$ is an arbitrary non-zero vector called the target vector, and $\varphi : [m] \to \mathcal{P}$ is a surjective map of the rows of M to the parties in $\mathcal{P}$. The size of $\mathcal{M}$ is defined to be m, the number of rows of the matrix M.*

Given a set of parties $\mathcal{S} \subseteq \mathcal{P}$, the submatrix $M_\mathcal{S}$ is the matrix whose rows are indexed by the set $\{i \in [m] : \varphi(i) \in \mathcal{S}\}$. Similarly $\mathbf{s}_\mathcal{S}$ is the vector whose rows are indexed by the same set. We also define the supp-mapping, which maps the rows of a matrix M to a player in $\mathcal{P}$. Formally this is defined as $\mathsf{supp} : \mathbb{F}^d \to 2^{[d]}$ with $\mathbf{s} \mapsto \{i \in [d] : \mathbf{s}^{(i)} \neq 0\}$.

Extended Span Programs Over Rings: In this paper we are not only interested in the Monotone Span Programs, but also their extensions to finite rings, which are known as Extended Span Programs, [12]. An Extended Span Program (ESP) over a ring R is a tuple $\mathcal{M} = (R, M, \varepsilon, \varphi)$ where $M \in M_{m \times d}(R)$ is a full-rank matrix for some m and $d \leq m$, $\varepsilon \in R^d$ is an arbitrary non-zero vector called the target vector, and $\varphi : [m] \rightarrow \mathcal{P}$ is a surjective map of the rows of M to the parties in $\mathcal{P}$.

Definition 2.3. *An ESP $\mathcal{M}$ is to compute an access structure (Γ, Δ) if for every set $A \subset 2^{\mathcal{P}}$ it holds that*

$$A \in \Gamma \Rightarrow \varepsilon \in \mathrm{Im}(M_A^T), \tag{1}$$

$$A \notin \Gamma \Rightarrow \exists \mathbf{v} \in \ker(M_A) \subset R^d : \langle \varepsilon, \mathbf{v} \rangle \in R^*. \tag{2}$$

For the rest of this paper we will only be considering MSPs over finite fields $\mathbb{F}_p$, or ESPs over the finite ring $\mathbb{Z}_{p^k}$. Let $\mathcal{P} = \{P_1, \dots, P_n\}$ be the set of parties involved in our protocols. To implement our MPC functionality over $\mathbb{Z}_{p^k}$ we will utilize an ESP $(\mathbb{Z}_{p^k}, M, \varepsilon, \varphi)$ given by a matrix $M \in \mathbb{Z}^{m \times d}$, such that $M = M$ (mod p) (i.e. the entries of M are in the range $[0, \dots, p)$), such that to share a value $x \in \mathbb{Z}_{p^k}$ one generates a vector $\mathbf{k} \in \mathbb{Z}_{p^k}^d$ such that $\langle \varepsilon, \mathbf{k} \rangle = x$ (mod p^k) and then compute the share values $\mathbf{s} = M \cdot \mathbf{k}$. The entries of $\mathbf{s}$ are passed to the players depending on the value of the function $\varphi : [m] \rightarrow \mathcal{P}$. i.e. player P_i gets $\mathbf{s}^{(j)}$ if $\varphi(j) = i$. Such a sharing $x \in \mathbb{Z}_{p^k}$ of a value will be denoted by $[x]_k$, note the subscript k which will be used to keep track of which ring we are considering at any given point.

2.3 Linear Secret Sharing Schemes Induced from MSPs and ESPs

When you have a Monotone/Extended Span Program it induces a Linear Secret Sharing Scheme (LSSS) using the method in Fig. 1. Recombination works for qualified sets $A \in \Gamma$, since if A is qualified there exists a recombination vector λ_A such that $M_A^T \cdot \lambda_A = \varepsilon$, by requirement (1) of the MSP. Hence

$$\langle \lambda_A, \mathbf{s}_A \rangle = \langle \lambda, \mathbf{s} \rangle = \langle \lambda, M \cdot \mathbf{x} \rangle = \langle M^T \cdot \lambda, \mathbf{x} \rangle = \langle \varepsilon, \mathbf{x} \rangle = s.$$

Conversely, if $A \notin \Gamma$ then A is unqualified, hence by requirement (2) of the ESP, there is no λ that allows for reconstruction. We note that the reconstruction step 2 can be relatively expensive for large MSPs, i.e. those with large m. Thus it is common to only send "just enough" information to each player in order to allow reconstruction. How this is done in a manner which prevents active attacks is discussed in the full version.

Multiplicative Linear Secret Sharing Scheme. A secret sharing scheme induced from a MSP/ESP is by definition linear, i.e. one can compute arbitrary linear functions of secret shared values without interaction. $\mathcal{Q}_2$ access structures are interesting as they allow us to also multiply secret shared values, but using interaction, if the underlying LSSS is multiplicative.

Recall a vector $\mathbf{s} = (s_i) = M \cdot \mathbf{k}$ is some sharing of a value s if we have that $\langle \varepsilon, \mathbf{k} \rangle = s$, with the shares distributed to party P_i being $\mathbf{s}_i = (s_j)_{\varphi(j)=i}$. We let

---

Induced LSSS from an MSP/ESP

Given a Monotone/Extended Span Program, $\mathcal{M} = \{\mathbb{Z}_{p^k}, M, \varepsilon, \varphi\}$ and a secret s, distribution and reconstruction for the associated secret sharing scheme are as follows:

Distribution:

1. Sample $\mathbf{x} \leftarrow \mathbb{Z}_{p^k}^d$ under the condition that $\langle \mathbf{x}, \varepsilon \rangle = s$.
2. Compute $\mathbf{s} = M \cdot \mathbf{x}$, such that $\mathbf{s} = (s_1 s_2 \ldots s_n)$ and distribute each s_i to the party indicated by $\varphi(i)$, such that each party P_j has the vector

$$\mathbf{s}_{P_j} = \begin{cases} s_i & \varphi(i) = P_j \\ 0 & \text{otherwise} \end{cases}$$

Reconstruction: Let $A \in \Gamma$ be a qualified set of players:

1. Define λ_A such that $M_A^T \cdot \lambda_A = \varepsilon$.
2. Each player $P_i \in A$ sends their shares to all other $P_j \in A$ and computes $\mathbf{s}_A = \sum_{P_i \in A} s_{P_i}$.
3. Compute $s^* = \langle \mathbf{s}_Q, \lambda_Q \rangle$.
4. Return s^*.

Fig. 1. Induced LSSS from a Monotone/Extended Span Program.

the total number of shares held by party P_i be given by n_i. The local *Schur product* of two sharings $\mathbf{x}_i$ and $\mathbf{y}_i$ of values x and y for party P_i are the n_i^2 terms given by $\mathbf{x}_i \otimes \mathbf{y}_i$, i.e. the terms $p_{i,j} = \mathbf{x}_i^{(v)} \cdot \mathbf{y}_i^{(v')}$ for $j = 1, \ldots, n_i^2$ and v, v' range over all values for which $\varphi(v) = \varphi(v') = i$. An MSP is said to be *multiplicative* if there are constants $\mu_{i,j}$ for $i = 1, \ldots, n$ and $j = 1, \ldots, n_i^2$ such that

$$x \cdot y = \sum_{i,j} \mu_{i,j} \cdot p_{i,j} \tag{3}$$

for all valid sharings of x and y. By abuse of notation we shall refer to the MSP/ESP being multiplicative, and not just the induced LSSS.

Many "natural" MSPs/ESPs computing $\mathcal{Q}_2$ access structures are multiplicative, i.e. those arising from Shamir secret sharing, or replicated sharing. It is well known, see [7], that when you have an non-multiplicative MSP over a field that computes a $\mathcal{Q}_2$ access structure then it can be made multiplicative with only a small expansion of the dimensions of M. In the full version we prove the following theorem, generalising this result to ESPs over $\mathbb{Z}_{p^k}$,

Theorem 2.1. *There exists an algorithm which, on input of a non-multiplicative ESP $\mathcal{M}$ over $\mathbb{Z}_{p^k}$ computing a $\mathcal{Q}_2$ access structure (Γ, Δ) outputs a multiplicative ESP $\mathcal{M}'$ computing Γ and of size at most $4 \cdot |\mathcal{M}|$. This algorithm is effective if $\ker(M^T)$ admits a basis.*

3   Multiplication Check

We present various protocols which allow one to verify that a set of passively secure multiplications are indeed correct. In the context of generating triples, we note that, we are unable to "lift" a valid triple modulo p^k to a valid triple modulo p^{k+v}. Thus, if one needs to perform a check modulo p^{k+s}, one needs to generate the passively secure multiplication triples modulo the larger modulus first, even if one is only interested in computation modulo p^k.

We assume that the desired security level is 2^κ, i.e. the probability that an adversary can pass off an incorrect passively secure multiplication as correct should be $2^{-\kappa}$. To ensure this we define four (integer) parameters (u, v, w, B) for our protocols defined by, where $B_z = 0$ unless $B \neq 1$ in which case we set $B_z = 1$.

$$u = \lceil (\kappa + B_z)/\log_2 p \rceil$$
$$v = u - 1,$$
$$1 \leq B \leq 1 + (p^w - 1)/2^{\kappa + B_z}.$$

The value u defines the size of the challenge space in our protocols, the value v defines how much bigger a modulus we need to work with, the value w defines the degree of any extension needed to allow the Schwartz-Zippel Lemma to apply, using a set S of size $p^w - 1$, whilst B defines the bucket size of the check (equivalently the degree of the polynomial used in the Schwartz-Zippel Lemma).

Our methods here are a natural generalisation of the methods given in [2,11] which are themselves based on ideas used in [6]. We note for the case of $k = 1$ and a small prime p the following protocols produce more efficient "sacrificing" steps than the "traditional" method of repeating the protocol $\kappa/\log_2 p$ times.

3.1   MultCheck$_1$

The first protocol, often called sacrifice, takes a set of N passively secure multiplication triples $([x_i]_{k+v}, [y_i]_{k+v}, [z_i]_{k+v})$, and checks whether indeed $z_i = x_i \cdot y_i$ (mod p^k), using another set of passively secure multiplication triples $([a_i]_{k+v}, [b_i]_{k+v}, [c_i]_{k+v})$. The "unchecked" triples $([a_i]_{k+v}, [b_i]_{k+v}, [c_i]_{k+v})$ need to be discarded at the end of the protocol (thus the term sacrificing). The output of the protocol is either an abort signal, or a set of N "actively" secure triple $([x_i]_k, [y_i]_k, [z_i]_k)$. The protocol is described in Fig. 2 and is based internally on the Beaver multiplication protocol. For ease of exposition we assume B exactly divides N in the protocol, this can easily be removed.

The number of calls to the procedure OpenToAll($\cdot$), which is the main cost of the protocol is given by $2 \cdot N + N \cdot w/B$, and the number of rounds of communication (for the OpenToAll calls) is bounded by two (if one executes the main j-loop in parallel). This means the communication cost, per output triple, is equal to the communication of $2 + w/B$ executions of OpenToAll($\cdot$). In practice one would try to select w/B to be as small as possible. In such a situation we can treat the cost as two calls to OpenToAll($\cdot$).

The Protocol MultCheck$_1$

Input: $([x_i]_{k+v}, [y_i]_{k+v}, [z_i]_{k+v})_{i=0}^{N-1}$ and $([a_i]_{k+v}, [b_i]_{k+v}, [c_i]_{k+v})_{i=0}^{N-1}$.
Output: abort or $([x_i]_k, [y_i]_k, [z_i]_k)_{i=0}^{N-1}$.

1. Let R denote a degree w Galois ring over $\mathbb{Z}_{p^{k+v}}$.
2. Let S denote the set from the Schwartz-Zippel Lemma of size $p^w - 1$.
3. $t \leftarrow \mathcal{F}_{\text{AgreeRandom}}(\mathbb{Z}_{p^u})$.
4. For $j \in [0, \ldots, N/B)$ do
   (a) $r \leftarrow \mathcal{F}_{\text{AgreeRandom}}(S)$.
   (b) For $i \in [0, \ldots, B)$ do
       i. $[\rho_i]_{k+v} \leftarrow t \cdot [a_{j \cdot B+i}]_{k+v} - [x_{j \cdot B+i}]_{k+v}$.
       ii. $[\sigma_i]_{k+v} \leftarrow [b_{j \cdot B+i}]_{k+v} - [y_{j \cdot B+i}]_{k+v}$.
   (c) $(\rho_i)_{i=0}^{B-1} \leftarrow (\text{OpenToAll}([\rho_i]_{k+v}))_{i=0}^{B-1}$.
   (d) $(\sigma_i)_{i=0}^{B-1} \leftarrow (\text{OpenToAll}([\sigma_i]_{k+v}))_{i=0}^{B-1}$.
   (e) $[\tau]_{k+v} \leftarrow 0$.
   (f) For $i \in [0, \ldots, B)$ do
       i. $[d_i]_{k+v} \leftarrow t \cdot [c_{j \cdot B+i}]_{k+v} - [z_{j \cdot B+i}]_{k+v} - \sigma_i \cdot [x_{j \cdot B+i}]_{k+v} - \rho_i \cdot [y_{j \cdot B+i}]_{k+v} - \sigma_i \cdot \rho_i$.
       ii. $[\tau]_{k+v} \leftarrow [\tau]_{k+v} + r^i \cdot [d_i]_{k+v}$.
   (g) $\tau \leftarrow \text{OpenToAll}([\tau]_{k+v})$
   (h) If $\tau \neq 0 \pmod{p^{k+v}}$ output abort and stop.
5. For $i \in [0, \ldots, N)$ do
   (a) $[x_i]_k \leftarrow [x_i]_{k+v} \pmod{p^k}$, $[y_i]_k \leftarrow [y_i]_{k+v} \pmod{p^k}$, $[z_i]_k \leftarrow [z_i]_{k+v} \pmod{p^k}$.
6. Output $([x]_k, [y]_k, [z]_k)_{i=1}^{N}$.

Fig. 2. The Protocol MultCheck$_1$

In the case of $k = 1$ and a large prime p, the values $w = 1$, $u = 1$, $v = 0$ and $B = 1$ give rise to *exactly* the traditional sacrifice protocol from SPDZ. However, for such large p, we could choose $w = 2$ and allow B to be sufficiently big, without needing an overly large amount of triples to check at once. Thus by utilizing our modified protocol one can achieve an improvement on the classical SPDZ sacrificing protocol. So for large p, for the classical SPDZ sacrifice, we have $w/B = 1$ and hence the cost is three calls to $\text{OpenToAll}(\cdot)$, but for our protocol we can achieve two calls to $\text{OpenToAll}(\cdot)$.

As long as we perform the calls to AgreeRandom only *after* the adversary had a chance to influence the triples, and the adversary is fully committed to any errors introduced in them, we can use the same random values for t and r over all instantiations. The practical advantage of this is that the data cost of these calls can then be amortized over all these executions, and we can consider it negligible. Due to the commit-reveal nature of the AgreeRandom sub-protocol, however, we still need to take a cost of two rounds of communication into account. All invocations of AgreeRandom that we need to generate the required t and r values can be executed in parallel, so the number of rounds we need does not grow as the number of times MultCheck$_1$ is executed grows.

In the full version we prove the following theorem which is an adaption of similar results in [6] (especially Claim 6 in that paper) and the papers [2,11], but we have generalized the method to arbitrary p and also the case of potentially small k.

Lemma 3.1. *In the presence of an active adversary, who can introduce arbitrary additive errors into the input triples, the protocol* MultCheck$_1$ *will output an invalid multiplication triple with probability* $(B-1)/(p^w-1) + p^{-u} \leq 2^{-\kappa}$.

The Protocol MultCheck$_1'$

Input: $([x_i]_k, [y_i]_k, [z_i]_k)_{i=0}^{N-1}$ and $([a_i]_k, [b_i]_k, [c_i]_k)_{i=0}^{N-1}$.
Output: abort or OK.

1. Let R denote a degree w Galois ring over $\mathbb{Z}_{p^k}$.
2. Let S denote the set from the Schwartz-Zippel Lemma.
3. For $j \in [0, \ldots, N/B)$ do
   (a) $r \leftarrow \mathcal{F}_{\text{AgreeRandom}}(S)$.
   (b) For $i \in [0, \ldots, B)$ do
      i. $[\rho_i]_k \leftarrow [a_{j \cdot B + i}]_k - [x_{j \cdot B + i}]_k$.
      ii. $[\sigma_i]_k \leftarrow [b_{j \cdot B + i}]_k - [y_{j \cdot B + i}]_k$.
   (c) $(\rho_i)_{i=0}^{B-1} \leftarrow (\text{OpenToAll}([\rho_i]_k))_{i=0}^{B-1}$.
   (d) $(\sigma_i)_{i=0}^{B-1} \leftarrow (\text{OpenToAll}([\sigma_i]_k))_{i=0}^{B-1}$.
   (e) $[\tau]_k \leftarrow 0$.
   (f) For $i \in [0, \ldots, B)$ do
      i. $[d_i]_k \leftarrow [c_{j \cdot B + i}]_k - [z_{j \cdot B + i}]_k - \sigma_i \cdot [x_{j \cdot B + i}]_k - \rho_i \cdot [y_{j \cdot B + i}]_k - \sigma_i \cdot \rho_i$.
      ii. $[\tau]_k \leftarrow [\tau]_k + r^i \cdot [d_i]_k$.
   (g) $\tau \leftarrow \text{OpenToAll}([\tau]_k)$
   (h) If $\tau \neq 0 \pmod{p^k}$ output abort and stop.
4. Output OK.

Fig. 3. The Protocol MultCheck$_1'$

3.2   MultCheck$_1'$

We will also use the MultCheck$_1$ protocol in the case where we are already guaranteed that the auxiliary triples $([a_i]_k, [b_i]_k, [c_i]_k)_{i=0}^{N-1}$ are correct, and we have $v = 0$ and $u = k$, and we are simply checking whether the passively secure triples $([x_i]_k, [y_i]_k, [z_i]_k)_{i=0}^{N-1}$ are correct. We refer to this special case as MultCheck$_1'$ and it is presented in Fig. 3. The round complexity is the same as that of MultCheck$_1$, except for the output, although now we can operate modulo p^k only, without needing to extend to working modulo p^{k+s}. In this special case we obtain the following result,

Lemma 3.2. *In the presence of an active adversary, who can introduce arbitrary additive errors into the input triples* $([x_i]_k, [y_i]_k, [z_i]_k)_{i=0}^{N-1}$, *but not the input triples* $([a_i]_k, [b_i]_k, [c_i]_k)_{i=0}^{N-1}$, *the protocol* MultCheck$_1'$ *will output* OK *incorrectly with probability* $(B-1)/(p^w - 1) \leq 2^{-(\kappa + B_z)}$.

3.3   MultCheck$_2$

Our third protocol comes from a combination of ideas from [6] and [14]. Instead of consuming previously produced multiplication triples (which themselves require a passively secure multiplication to produce) this second variant makes direct use of a passively secure multiplication protocol PassMult; which can be any of MaurerMult, KRSWMult or DNMult. The protocol, called MultCheck$_2$, is described in Fig. 4. The argument for security is roughly the same as that for protocol MultCheck$_1$. These protocols use a PRSS functionality $\mathcal{F}_{\text{PRSS}}$ which is defined in the full version.

The Protocol MultCheck$_2$

Input: $([x_i]_{k+v}, [y_i]_{k+v}, [z_i]_{k+v})_{i=0}^{N-1}$.
Output: abort or $([x_i]_k, [y_i]_k, [z_i]_k)_{i=0}^{N-1}$.

1. Let R denote a degree w Galois ring over $\mathbb{Z}_{p^{k+v}}$.
2. Let S denote the set from the Schwartz-Zippel Lemma.
3. For $i \in [0, \ldots, N)$ do
   (a) $[a_i]_{k+v} \leftarrow \mathcal{F}_{\text{PRSS}}(k+v)$.
   (b) $[c_i]_{k+v} \leftarrow$ PassMult$([a_i]_{k+v}, [y_i]_{k+v})$.
4. $t \leftarrow \mathcal{F}_{\text{AgreeRandom}}(\mathbb{Z}_{p^u})$.
5. For $j \in [0, \ldots, N/B)$ do
   (a) $r \leftarrow \mathcal{F}_{\text{AgreeRandom}}(S)$.
   (b) For $i \in [0, \ldots, B)$ do
      i. $[\rho_i]_{k+s} \leftarrow t \cdot [x_{j \cdot B + i}]_{k+v} + [a_{j \cdot B + i}]_{k+v}$.
   (c) $(\rho_i)_{i=0}^{B-1} \leftarrow (\text{OpenToAll}([\rho_i]_{k+v}))_{i=0}^{B-1}$.
   (d) $[\tau]_{k+v} \leftarrow 0$.
   (e) For $i \in [0, \ldots, B)$ do
      i. $[\tau]_{k+v} \leftarrow [\tau]_{k+v} + r^i \cdot (t \cdot [z]_{k+v} + [c]_{k+v} - \rho \cdot [y]_{k+v})$.
   (f) $\tau \leftarrow$ OpenToAll$([\tau]_{k+s})$
   (g) If $\tau \neq 0 \pmod{p^{k+v}}$ output abort and stop.
6. For $i \in [0, \ldots, N)$ do
   (a) $[x_i]_k \leftarrow [x_i]_{k+v} \pmod{p^k}$, $[y_i]_k \leftarrow [y_i]_{k+v} \pmod{p^k}$, $[z_i]_k \leftarrow [z_i]_{k+v} \pmod{p^k}$.
7. Output $([x_i]_k, [y_i]_k, [z_i]_k)_{i=0}^{N-1}$.

Fig. 4. The Protocol MultCheck$_2$

3.4 MacCheck

Our final protocol is the generalization of the MacCheck protocol from [10] to our situation. The protocol checks, for an input of a single secret shared value $[\alpha]_{k+v}$ and a series of pairs of secret shared values $([x_i]_{k+v}, [y_i]_{k+v})_{i=0}^{N-1}$, whether we have $y_i = \alpha \cdot x_i \pmod{p^{k+v}}$, or whether y_i is invalid up to an additive error. Note, unlike the MacCheck protocol from [10] we are not checking the MACs of opened values, but checking the consistency of pairs of unopened values with respect to the shared MAC key α, as such it is closer to the verification stage of the protocol in [5]. We note that with the instantiation given in Fig. 5, this checking procedure "burns" the value $[\alpha]_{k+v}$, thus this does not allow for reactive computations. In [5] it is shown how to avoid this problem for *specific* secret sharing schemes. The protocol is given in Fig. 5

The Protocol MacCheck

Input: $[\alpha]_{k+v}$ and $([x_i]_{k+v}, [y_i]_{k+v})_{i=0}^{N-1}$.
Output: abort or OK.

1. For $i \in [0, N)$ do $r_i \leftarrow \mathcal{F}_{\text{AgreeRandom}}(\mathbb{Z}_{p^u})$.
2. $[u] \leftarrow \sum_{i=0}^{N-1} r_i \cdot [x_i]_{k+v}$.
3. $[v] \leftarrow \sum_{i=0}^{N-1} r_i \cdot [y_i]_{k+v}$.
4. $[c]_{k+v} \leftarrow \mathcal{F}_{\text{PRSS}}(k + v)$.
5. $\alpha \leftarrow \text{OpenToAll}([\alpha]_{k+v})$.
6. $[t]_{k+v} \leftarrow [v]_{k+v} - \alpha \cdot [u]_{k+v}$.
7. $[s]_{k+v} \leftarrow \text{PassMult}([t]_{k+v}, [c]_{k+v})$.
8. $s \leftarrow \text{OpenToAll}([s]_{k+v})$.
9. If $s = 0$ then return OK, else return abort.

Fig. 5. The Protocol MacCheck

Lemma 3.3. *Protocol* MacCheck *in Fig. 5 on input of an invalid set of pairs* $([x_i]_{k+v}, [y_i]_{k+v})_{i=0}^{N-1}$ *will return* OK *with probability less than* $2^{-\kappa}$. *Where a pair being invalid means that* $y_i = \alpha \cdot x_i + e_i$, *for an* e_i *known to the adversary with* $e_i \neq 0 \pmod{p^k}$.

3.5 Summary

We summarize the costs of various protocols in Table 2 for a general ESP over $\mathbb{Z}_{p^k}$. These are given in terms of the row m and column d dimensions of the matrix generating the underlying ESP, the number of parties n, and the parameters w and B used in the protocols above. We let $|\mathbf{s}_i|$ denote the share size of player P_i for the given ESP. The data column indicates the total amount of data sent for *all* players[5] as a multiple of the underlying secret shared data size (i.e. either $k \cdot \log_2 p$ or $(k + v) \cdot \log_2 p$); we ignore rounds/data to check the running hash values H as these are amortized over many sub-protocol executions. A $\star$ in the table indicates that the value depends highly on the specific ESP, and thus a formula is hard to present. The cost $\star_1$ of OpenToAll is generally $n \cdot d - m$ for an MSP with no redundancy, but it can be larger than this if the MSP has more redundancy than necessary.

We present three lines corresponding to MultCheck$_2$ and MacCheck depending on whether the underlying passively secure multiplication is Maurer, KRSW or DN based. We assume $\mathcal{F}_{\mathrm{PRSS}}$ is executed non-interactively in all cases, that any calls to $\mathcal{F}_{\mathrm{AgreeRandom}}$ are amortized across many calls to MultCheck$_i$, and that no king-paradigm is used in order to keep the number of rounds to a minimum. As mentioned in the discussion on the multiplication checks, we always consider w/B to be negligibly small.

Table 2. Costs of the base protocols for a general access structures

Protocol	General MSP			
	Rounds	Data	PRSS/PRZS	Triples
Share	1	$m - |\mathbf{s}_i|$	0	0
OpenToOne	1	$m - |\mathbf{s}_i|$	0	0
OpenToAll	1	$\star_1$	0	0
BeaverMult	1	$2 \cdot \star_1$	0	1
MaurerMult	1	$(n - 1) \cdot m$	0	0
KRSWMult	1	$\star_2$	$\star_3$	0
DNMult	1	$n \cdot (n - 1)$	2	0
MacCheck^M	4	$(n - 1) \cdot m + 2 \cdot \star_1$	1	0
MacCheck^K	4	$\star_2 + 2 \cdot \star_1$	$1 + \star_3$	0
MacCheck^D	4	$n \cdot (n - 1) + 2 \cdot \star_1$	3	0
MultCheck$_1$	4	$(2 + w/B) \cdot \star_1$	0	0
MultCheck$_2^M$	5	$(n - 1) \cdot m + (1 + w/B) \cdot \star_1$	1	0
MultCheck$_2^K$	5	$\star_2 + (1 + w/B) \cdot \star_1$	$1 + \star_3$	0
MultCheck$_2^D$	5	$n \cdot (n - 1) + (1 + w/B) \cdot \star_1$	3	0

To provide more concrete values we also give, in the full version, the values for the three different instantiations of threshold sharings for $(n, t) \in \{(3, 1), (5, 2), (10, 4)\}$. The three different sharings have been selected as replicated (for general p^k), standard Shamir (for the case of $p > n$) and Shamir obtained via Galois rings (for the important case of $p = 2$).

---

[5] i.e. not the per-player amount.

4   Offline Preprocessing Protocols

Given the previous components there are a large number of variations one can deploy to obtain an MPC protocol for a $\mathcal{Q}_2$ access structure which is actively secure with abort. In many cases, some form of preprocessing is used to generate multiplication triples. In this section, we aim to give an overview of different methods to generate passive and active multiplication triples, and evaluate the associated cost in terms of their round and data complexity. We give one passively secure offline protocol, and three actively secure variants. To generate actively secure multiplication triples, we generally first generate passively secure triples, and then we check for correctness (against potential additive attacks) in different ways.

Some of these offline protocols inherently require working (internally) with an extension of the modulus p^{k+v}, whilst all can produce triples modulo p^k or p^{k+v} depending on whether the output protocol requires triples modulo p^k or p^{k+v}. Whether the output is modulo p^k or p^{k+v} will depend into which main protocol we will embed the offline protocol. When we want to distinguish these various cases we will write $\mathsf{Offline}_X(p^{\mathsf{output}}, p^{\mathsf{internal}})$ for an offline protocol which outputs triples modulo p^{output}, whilst working internally modulo p^{internal}. Note, if $\mathsf{output} = k + v$ then we must have $\mathsf{internal} = k + v$ as well. In all cases we assume that all PRSS and PRZS operations are performed non-interactively, and all passive secure multiplications will be assumed to be performed using which ever is the best out of KRSW or DN for the specific parameter sets[6].

Offline$_{\mathsf{Pass}}$: When generating N passively secure multiplication triples, we take the approach of first generating $2 \cdot N$ random sharings by performing $2 \cdot N$ calls to PRSS. Following that, we perform a passively secure multiplication protocol N times in parallel to compute the product over pairs of those shares. Since we can perform the N required multiplications in parallel, for the multiplication we only need a single round of communication, with a total data cost of $N \cdot \mathsf{PassMult}_{\mathsf{data}}$, and a corresponding cost of $\mathsf{PassMult}_{\mathsf{data}}$ per triple produced.

Offline$_1$: The first actively secure protocol, Offline$_1$, will follow the ideas presented in [10], in that to generate N actively secure multiplication triples it starts by executing Offline$_{\mathsf{Pass}}$ to produce $2 \cdot N$ triples. Then half of the obtained triples are sacrificed, using MultCheck$_1$, so as to check the remaining half for correctness. The cost of Offline$_1(p^k, p^{k+v})$ and Offline$_1(p^{k+v}, p^{k+v})$ are identical.

Offline$_2$: For the second active offline protocol, Offline$_2$, we follow [11]. First N passively secure triples are generated using Offline$_{\mathsf{Pass}}$. Then these triples are checked to be resistant to additive attacks by running MultCheck$_2$ on the vector of N triples. Again, the cost of Offline$_2(p^k, p^{k+v})$ and Offline$_2(p^{k+v}, p^{k+v})$ are identical.

Offline$_3$: For our third variant of the Offline protocol, which we call Offline$_3$, we use the cut-and-choose methodology of [3, Protocol 3.1]. This is parametrized by

---

[6] These are both cheaper than Maurer in terms of data transfer, although they requires more PRSS and PRZS calls.

four integer parameters (Bk, C, X, L), and it generates $N = (X - C) \cdot L$ triples in each iteration, given input of $T = (N + C \cdot L) \cdot (\mathsf{Bk} - 1) + N$ passively secure triples. The value Bk represents a bucket size for the final checking procedure. The advantage of this version of the Offline protocol is that we achieve active security without needing to extend the ring, i.e. we can work modulo p^k and not work p^{k+v} if we require triples modulo p^k as output.

The statistical security offered by this approach is $1/N^{\mathsf{Bk}-1}$ when used as a standalone offline procedure, or $1/N^{\mathsf{Bk}}$ when used with a specific online procedure (see the third protocol of [3] for the details); note in the latter case one needs to select $C \geq 3$ and that this corresponds to our Protocol 4 below. In [3] the authors, for $p^k = 2$, target a statistical security level of $\kappa = 40$ bits. Thus, they can select $N = 2^{20}$, $\mathsf{Bk} = 2$, $L = 512$ and $C = 3$ to achieve an offline cost of 12 bits per triple when utilized in Protocol 4 below.

To provide a fair comparison between all protocols in this paper we target a statistical security level of $\kappa = 128$. Thus when using $\mathsf{Offline}_3$ in Protocol 1 below we use the parameters $(N, \mathsf{Bk}, L, C) = (2^{22}, 7, 512, 1)$ and when using $\mathsf{Offline}_3$ in Protocol 4 below we use the parameters $(N, \mathsf{Bk}, L, C) = (2^{22}, 6, 512, 3)$.

4.1 Comparing Actively Secure Offline Protocols

Having analysed the three actively secure offline protocols one could compare them theoretically, using the formulae. This is alas however not that illuminative, due to the complexity of the various parameters etc. for $\mathsf{Offline}_3$. Comparing $\mathsf{Offline}_1$ vs $\mathsf{Offline}_2$, is simpler as $\mathsf{Offline}_1$ is better in terms of number of rounds of communication, whereas $\mathsf{Offline}_2$ is better in terms of the amount of data sent per multiplication.

5 Complete Protocols

We now examine the five (main) protocol variants we discussed in the introduction. For each of the following protocols, if an actively secure offline phase is required we can utilize the protocols $\mathsf{Offline}_x$, for x either 1, 2 or 3, given in Sect. 4. There are two basic metrics here that one could be interested in (assuming to a first order approximation we are processing arithmetic circuits over $\mathbb{Z}_{p^k}$), namely, the amount of data transferred per multiplication in the online phase only, or the amount of data transferred per multiplication in the combined online and offline phases. In all cases we assume we are processing an arithmetic circuit with N multiplication gates in a circuit of multiplicative depth d.

Protocol$_1$: This protocol executes an actively secure offline phase to produce N triples in $\mathbb{Z}_{p^k}$, i.e. we execute $\mathsf{Offline}_x(p^k, p^\star)$ for $\star$ being either k or $k+v$, depending on the precise protocol choice x. Note, this means we have three choices for $\mathsf{Protocol}_1$ depending on which offline protocol the main protocol is combined with. The online phase is executed, using these triples, using $\mathsf{BeaverMult}$ as the multiplication procedure. Since the Beaver multiplication is instantiated with actively secure triples the output will also be actively secure, and no post-processing check is necessary. The online cost does not depend on the choice of offline phase. In Table 3 we refer to the three combined costs per multiplication as Total_x, depending on which Offline phase we are utilizing.

Protocol$_2$: In this protocol we optimistically use a passively secure online multiplication protocol PassMult to execute the online phase, and a passively secure Offline protocol to generate N passively secure multiplication triples, all over $\mathbb{Z}_{p^{k+v}}$. These are then checked using a post-processing methodology, based on MultCheck$_1$, to ensure active security. This approach of optimistic, passively secure online multiplication was first suggested in [11].

Protocol$_3$: This proceeds very much as Protocol$_2$ except instead of using an offline phase and the MultCheck$_1$ procedure, one uses the MultCheck$_2$ procedure. As there is no offline phase, online and post-processing costs are the total costs of the protocol. Again all operations needs to be performed over $\mathbb{Z}_{p^{k+v}}$.

Protocol$_4$: This protocol variant follows the pattern from [3] and thus is particularly suited to small values of p^k. It can be applied using any of the actively secure offline protocols, but is better suited (for small p^k) to be used with Offline$_3$.

In the offline phase we generate N actively secure multiplication triples in $\mathbb{Z}_{p^k}$. In the online phase a standard passively secure online phase is executed, using PassMult. Then in the post-processing the triples produced in the offline phase are checked against the 'triples' resulting from the passively secure multiplications, using MultCheck$_1'$. The entire procedure can be executed in $\mathbb{Z}_{p^k}$ without the need to extend to $\mathbb{Z}_{p^{k+v}}$. Again in Table 3 we will refer to the three different combined costs per multiplication as Total_x.

Protocol$_5$: Our final approach is based upon the technique in [5]. At the start of the protocol, in a (very short) offline phase a sharing for an unknown, secret random value $[\alpha]_{k+v}$ is generated. This value is used as an information theoretic MAC key, similar to the SPDZ approach.

In the online phase each wire value x is held as two shared values $\{[x]_{k+v}, [\alpha \cdot x]_{k+v}\}$. To multiply two values x and y we execute a passively secure multiplication twice, once with $[x]_{k+v}$ and $[y]_{k+v}$ to obtain $[x \cdot y]_{k+v}$, and one with $[x]_{k+v}$ and $[\alpha \cdot y]_{k+v}$ to obtain $[\alpha \cdot x \cdot y]_{k+v}$. In a short post-processing phase the MAC values on *all multiplication gates* and *all input and output wires* are checked using the MacCheck procedure. To ensure the security of the MacCheck procedure all computation need to be performed in $\mathbb{Z}_{p^{k+v}}$.

We can now present a summary (in Table 3) of all these options, by way of presenting their respective online and total communications costs (in number of bits communicated per multiplication), for a variety of different scenarios, access structures and base rings. In the table we mark in blue the online variant which is most efficient for a given access structure, ring, and ESP. This is almost always Protocol$_1$. We also mark in gray the most efficient protocol option when one is interested in the total cost. For small rings this is always Protocol$_4$ with Offline$_3$ chosen as the pre-processing, for the others it is Protocol$_5$.

Table 3. Costs of the Full Protocols in number of bits per multiplication, for various access structures; $\kappa = 128$, $p \approx 2^{128}$

Access Structure	Ring	Scheme	Mult	Protocol$_1$				Protocol$_2$		Protocol$_3$	
				Online	Total$_1$	Total$_2$	Total$_3$	Online	Total	Online	Total
(3,1)	$\mathbb{F}_2$	Replicated	KRSW	6	1554	1167	63	1161	1548	1161	1161
(3,1)	$\mathbb{F}_2$	Shamir $\mathbb{Z}_{2^k}$	DN	6	2328	1941	84	1548	2322	1935	1935
(3,1)	$\mathbb{Z}_{2^{128}}$	Replicated	KRSW	768	3840	3072	8067	2304	3072	2304	2304
(3,1)	$\mathbb{Z}_{2^{128}}$	Shamir $\mathbb{Z}_{2^k}$	DN	768	5376	4608	10756	3072	4608	3840	3840
(3,1)	$\mathbb{F}_p$	Replicated	KRSW	768	3840	3072	8067	2304	3072	2304	2304
(3,1)	$\mathbb{F}_p$	Shamir	KRSW	768	3840	3072	8067	2304	3072	2304	2304
(5,2)	$\mathbb{F}_2$	Replicated	KRSW	40	7780	5200	350	6450	7740	5160	5160
(5,2)	$\mathbb{F}_2$	Shamir $\mathbb{Z}_{2^k}$	DN	40	10360	7780	420	7740	10320	7740	7740
(5,2)	$\mathbb{Z}_{2^{128}}$	Replicated	KRSW	5120	20480	15360	44820	12800	15360	10240	10240
(5,2)	$\mathbb{Z}_{2^{128}}$	Shamir $\mathbb{Z}_{2^k}$	DN	5120	25600	20480	53782	15360	20480	15360	15360
(5,2)	$\mathbb{F}_p$	Replicated	KRSW	5120	20480	15360	44820	12800	15360	10240	10240
(5,2)	$\mathbb{F}_p$	Shamir	KRSW	2560	12800	10240	26891	7680	10240	7680	7680
(10,4)	$\mathbb{F}_2$	Replicated	KRSW	1680	231300	122940	12116	223170	229620	121260	121260
(10,4)	$\mathbb{F}_2$	Shamir $\mathbb{Z}_{2^k}$	DN	260	57020	40250	2451	45150	56760	39990	39990
(10,4)	$\mathbb{Z}_{2^{128}}$	Replicated	KRSW	215040	670720	455680	1550803	442880	455680	240640	240640
(10,4)	$\mathbb{Z}_{2^{128}}$	Shamir $\mathbb{Z}_{2^k}$	DN	33280	145920	112640	313735	89600	112640	79360	79360
(10,4)	$\mathbb{F}_p$	Replicated	KRSW	215040	670720	455680	1550803	442880	455680	240640	240640
(10,4)	$\mathbb{F}_p$	Shamir	KRSW	10240	56320	46080	116528	33280	46080	35840	35840

Access Structure	Ring	Scheme	Mult	Protocol$_4$				Protocol$_5$	
				Online	Total$_1$	Total$_2$	Total$_3$	Online	Total
(3,1)	$\mathbb{F}_2$	Replicated	KRSW	9	1557	1170	57	774	774
(3,1)	$\mathbb{F}_2$	Shamir $\mathbb{Z}_{2^k}$	DN	12	2334	1947	78	1548	1548
(3,1)	$\mathbb{Z}_{2^{128}}$	Replicated	KRSW	1152	4224	3456	7299	1536	1536
(3,1)	$\mathbb{Z}_{2^{128}}$	Shamir $\mathbb{Z}_{2^k}$	DN	1536	6144	5376	9988	3072	3072
(3,1)	$\mathbb{F}_p$	Replicated	KRSW	1152	4224	3456	7299	1536	1536
(3,1)	$\mathbb{F}_p$	Shamir	KRSW	1152	4224	3456	7299	1536	1536
(5,2)	$\mathbb{F}_2$	Replicated	KRSW	50	7790	5210	310	2580	2580
(5,2)	$\mathbb{F}_2$	Shamir $\mathbb{Z}_{2^k}$	DN	60	10380	7800	380	5160	5160
(5,2)	$\mathbb{Z}_{2^{128}}$	Replicated	KRSW	6400	21760	16640	39696	5120	5120
(5,2)	$\mathbb{Z}_{2^{128}}$	Shamir $\mathbb{Z}_{2^k}$	DN	7680	28160	23040	48659	10240	10240
(5,2)	$\mathbb{F}_p$	Replicated	KRSW	6400	21760	16640	39696	5120	5120
(5,2)	$\mathbb{F}_p$	Shamir	KRSW	3840	14080	11520	24329	5120	5120
(10,4)	$\mathbb{F}_2$	Replicated	KRSW	1730	231350	122990	10435	12900	12900
(10,4)	$\mathbb{F}_2$	Shamir $\mathbb{Z}_{2^k}$	DN	350	57110	40340	2191	23220	23220
(10,4)	$\mathbb{Z}_{2^{128}}$	Replicated	KRSW	221440	677120	462080	1335642	25600	25600
(10,4)	$\mathbb{Z}_{2^{128}}$	Shamir $\mathbb{Z}_{2^k}$	DN	44800	157440	124160	280432	46080	46080
(10,4)	$\mathbb{F}_p$	Replicated	KRSW	221440	677120	462080	1335642	25600	25600
(10,4)	$\mathbb{F}_p$	Shamir	KRSW	16640	62720	52480	106280	25600	25600

Note, that in the case of Protocol$_4$ and Offline$_3$ the paper [3] obtains a total cost of 21 bits per multiplication operation. As explained earlier this is because they target a statistical security level of $\kappa = 40$, instead of our security level of $\kappa = 128$.

Note that even when Protocol$_1$ is not the most efficient choice, in practice one might still prefer using this protocol as our analysis assumes the only interaction occurs for multiplication. Most MPC protocols make use of OpenToAll executions to open masked data for use in various function specific optimizations. Using Protocol$_1$ enables these protocol specific OpenToAll executions to be merged easily with the OpenToAll executions used in multiplication; thus reducing the total round count. For other online protocols this merging can be more complex.

Acknowledgements. We would like to thank Daniel Escudero and Tim Wood for conversions on aspects of this work whilst it was carried out.

This work has been supported in part by ERC Advanced Grant ERC-2015-AdG-IMPaCT, by the Defense Advanced Research Projects Agency (DARPA) and Space and Naval Warfare Systems Center, Pacific (SSC Pacific) under contract FA8750-19-C-0502, by the FWO under an Odysseus project GOH9718N, and by CyberSecurity Research Flanders with reference number VR20192203.

Any opinions, findings and conclusions or recommendations expressed in this material are those of the author(s) and do not necessarily reflect the views of any of the funders. The U.S. Government is authorized to reproduce and distribute reprints for governmental purposes notwithstanding any copyright annotation therein.

References

1. Abspoel, M., et al.: Asymptotically good multiplicative LSSS over Galois rings and applications to MPC over $\mathbb{Z}/p^k\mathbb{Z}$. In: Moriai, S., Wang, H. (eds.) ASIACRYPT 2020, Part III. LNCS, vol. 12493, pp. 151–180. Springer, Heidelberg, December 2020
2. Abspoel, M., Dalskov, A., Escudero, D., Nof, A.: An efficient passive-to-active compiler for honest-majority MPC over rings. Cryptology ePrint Archive, Report 2019/1298 (2019). https://eprint.iacr.org/2019/1298
3. Araki, T., et al.: Optimized honest-majority MPC for malicious adversaries - breaking the 1 billion-gate per second barrier. In: 2017 IEEE Symposium on Security and Privacy, pp. 843–862. IEEE Computer Society Press, May 2017
4. Bogdanov, D., Laur, S., Willemson, J.: Sharemind: a framework for fast privacy-preserving computations. In: Jajodia, S., Lopez, J. (eds.) ESORICS 2008. LNCS, vol. 5283, pp. 192–206. Springer, Heidelberg (2008). https://doi.org/10.1007/978-3-540-88313-5_13
5. Chida, K., et al.: Fast large-scale honest-majority MPC for malicious adversaries. In: Shacham, H., Boldyreva, A. (eds.) CRYPTO 2018. LNCS, vol. 10993, pp. 34–64. Springer, Cham (2018). https://doi.org/10.1007/978-3-319-96878-0_2
6. Cramer, R., Damgård, I., Escudero, D., Scholl, P., Xing, C.: SPDZ$_{2^k}$: Efficient MPC mod 2^k for Dishonest Majority. In: Shacham, H., Boldyreva, A. (eds.) CRYPTO 2018. LNCS, vol. 10992, pp. 769–798. Springer, Cham (2018). https://doi.org/10.1007/978-3-319-96881-0_26
7. Cramer, R., Damgård, I., Maurer, U.: General secure multi-party computation from any linear secret-sharing scheme. In: Preneel, B. (ed.) EUROCRYPT 2000. LNCS, vol. 1807, pp. 316–334. Springer, Heidelberg (2000). https://doi.org/10.1007/3-540-45539-6_22
8. Cramer, R., Rambaud, M., Xing, C.: Asymptotically-good arithmetic secret sharing over $Z/(p^\ell Z)$ with strong multiplication and its applications to efficient MPC. Cryptology ePrint Archive, Report 2019/832 (2019). https://eprint.iacr.org/2019/832

9. Damgård, I., Nielsen, J.B.: Scalable and unconditionally secure multiparty computation. In: Menezes, A. (ed.) CRYPTO 2007. LNCS, vol. 4622, pp. 572–590. Springer, Heidelberg (2007). https://doi.org/10.1007/978-3-540-74143-5_32

10. Damgård, I., Pastro, V., Smart, N., Zakarias, S.: Multiparty computation from somewhat homomorphic encryption. In: Safavi-Naini, R., Canetti, R. (eds.) CRYPTO 2012. LNCS, vol. 7417, pp. 643–662. Springer, Heidelberg (2012). https://doi.org/10.1007/978-3-642-32009-5_38

11. Eerikson, H., Keller, M., Orlandi, C., Pullonen, P., Puura, J., Simkin, M.: Use your brain! Arithmetic 3PC for any modulus with active security. In: Kalai, Y.T., Smith, A.D., Wichs, D. (eds.) ITC 2020, pp. 5:1–5:24. Schloss Dagstuhl, June 2020

12. Fehr, S.: Span programs over rings and how to share a secret from a module (1998), MSc Thesis, ETH Zurich

13. Keller, M.: MP-SPDZ: A versatile framework for multi-party computation. In: Ligatti, J., Ou, X., Katz, J., Vigna, G. (eds.) ACM CCS 20, pp. 1575–1590. ACM Press, November 2020

14. Keller, M., Orsini, E., Scholl, P.: MASCOT: faster malicious arithmetic secure computation with oblivious transfer. In: Weippl, E.R., Katzenbeisser, S., Kruegel, C., Myers, A.C., Halevi, S. (eds.) ACM CCS 2016, pp. 830–842. ACM Press, October 2016

15. Keller, M., Rotaru, D., Smart, N.P., Wood, T.: Reducing communication channels in MPC. In: Catalano, D., De Prisco, R. (eds.) SCN 2018. LNCS, vol. 11035, pp. 181–199. Springer, Cham (2018). https://doi.org/10.1007/978-3-319-98113-0_10

16. Maurer, U.M.: Secure multi-party computation made simple. Discr. Appl. Math. **154**(2), 370–381 (2006)

17. Smart, N.P., Wood, T.: Error detection in monotone span programs with application to communication-efficient multi-party computation. In: Matsui, M. (ed.) CT-RSA 2019. LNCS, vol. 11405, pp. 210–229. Springer, Cham (2019). https://doi.org/10.1007/978-3-030-12612-4_11

Secret-Key Cryptography: Design and Proofs

Multi-user Security of the Elephant v2 Authenticated Encryption Mode

Tim Beyne[1], Yu Long Chen[1], Christoph Dobraunig[2], and Bart Mennink[3(✉)]

[1] KU Leuven and imec-COSIC, Leuven, Belgium
[2] Lamarr Security Research, Graz, Austria
[3] Radboud University, Nijmegen, The Netherlands
elephant@cs.ru.nl

Abstract. One of the finalists in the NIST Lightweight Cryptography competition is Elephant v2, a parallelizable, permutation-based authenticated encryption scheme. The original first/second-round submission Elephant v1/v1.1 was proven secure against nonce-respecting adversaries in the single-user setting. For the final round, the mode has undergone certain subtle modifications, the most important one being a change in the authentication portion of the mode. These changes require a new dedicated security proof.

In this work, we prove the security of the Elephant v2 mode. First of all, our proof shows that Elephant v2 is indeed a secure authenticated encryption scheme and that its security against nonce-respecting adversaries is on par with that of Elephant v1/v1.1. In addition, our security analysis is in the multi-user setting and demonstrates that Elephant v2 fares well if multiple devices use Elephant v2 with independent keys. Moreover, our proof shows that Elephant v2 even ensures authenticity under nonce misuse.

Keywords: Authenticated encryption · Lightweight · Elephant · Multi-user security · Nonce-misuse

1 Introduction

Authenticated encryption schemes aim to provide confidentiality and authenticity of data. If one aims to prove that a mode achieves these security properties, one typically models an adversary that has access to a single instance of the cryptographic mode (for a single secret key) and aims to break either of these properties. In practice, however, cryptographic modes are rarely used in isolation. Instead, a mode might be used by millions of people worldwide at the same time, with independent keys, and the attacker might aim to attack all instances at the same time.

This particular setting, i.e., where the adversary might attack multiple independent instances at the same time, is called the *multi-user* security setting. Biham [12] observed that recovering one key out of many is much easier than

© The Author(s), under exclusive license to Springer Nature Switzerland AG 2022
R. AlTawy and A. Hülsing (Eds.): SAC 2021, LNCS 13203, pp. 155–178, 2022.
https://doi.org/10.1007/978-3-030-99277-4_8

recovering only one specific key. Intuitively, in general, the adversarial success probability increases by a factor μ if an attacker has μ instead of 1 mode at its disposal. Bellare et al. [4] proved that this μ-factor loss is tight, generically. However, for specific schemes, this μ-factor difference might induce an artificial loss in the security bound and a dedicated analysis might be more accurate. For example, Bellare and Tackmann [5] proved multi-user security of authenticated encryption in the TLS 1.3 protocol, likewise exhibiting a μ-factor loss, but Luykx et al. [22] demonstrated that a more precise analysis yields a better multi-user security bound. Likewise, for permutation-based analysis, Daemen et al. [16] derived a multi-user security bound for the keyed duplex that can, in turn, be used for sponge-based authenticated encryption. Their bound is better than the generic reduction with μ-factor loss, in the sense that their security result precisely indicates which terms in the bound are affected by the availability of multiple keys.

The issue of multi-user security is particularly important in the lightweight setting. One reason is that the internet of things leads to an increase in the number of constrained devices that often interoperate and deal with sensitive information. Another reason is that lightweight cryptographic solutions often use relatively small cryptographic primitives and operate with a smaller security margin. Therefore, an accurate estimation, rather than a rough bound, of the multi-user security of such a scheme is valuable.

In 2018, the US National Institute of Standards and Technology (NIST) initiated a competition for the design of lightweight cryptographic authenticated encryption and hashing [26]. NIST received 57 submissions, the second round covered 32 submissions, and the ongoing final round contains 10 candidates. Some candidates, namely ASCON [19], ISAP [17,18], Sparkle [2,3], and Xoodyak [14,15], are based on the duplex construction and, at least to a certain extent, can rely on the multi-user security of the duplex [16]. Khairallah [21] analyzed multi-user security of GIFT-COFB [1] from a cryptanalytic perspective. We are not aware of other multi-user security analyses of the finalists.

1.1   Elephant

One of the finalists in the NIST Lightweight Cryptography competition is Elephant of Beyne et al. [9]. The mode of Elephant is an encrypt-then-MAC construction, with encryption performed using counter mode and authentication using a variant of the protected counter sum [6,23] MAC function. Elephant is a permutation-based construction, but, unlike sponge-based authenticated encryption, it is *parallelizable*. This way, Elephant is shown [9] to be able to operate using a cryptographic primitive that is significantly smaller than that of its competitors.

The Elephant mode itself has undergone a subtle change in its move to the final round. The original submission (of the first and second round) Elephant v1/v1.1 (henceforth simply referred to as v1) [8] performed authentication using the Wegman-Carter-Shoup [7,28,29] MAC function, but the final-round version Elephant v2 [11] relies on a variant of the protected counter sum [6,23] MAC function. The transition was pre-announced in a status update [10], and was defended by the observation that, while v1 only achieved confidentiality and authenticity in the nonce-respecting setting, v2 *additionally* achieves authenticity under nonce-reuse. We will elaborate on the differences between v1 and v2 in Sect. 4.3.

This change is subtle but the earlier security proof of Elephant v1 [9] is no longer applicable to Elephant v2. In addition, nonce-misuse security is yet unclear. Finally, the earlier proof of Elephant v1 does not consider the multi-user setting.

1.2 Multi-user Security of Elephant v2

In this work, we prove security of Elephant v2 [11]. The proof differs from the one of v1 [9] in that the new authenticator is considered. In addition, our result shows that Elephant v2 indeed achieves authenticity under nonce-misuse. Finally, our new proof is in the multi-user setting.

Due to the similarity between Elephant v1 and v2, the overall structure of the proof is comparable. However, the required changes to the security analysis are non-trivial. As a first step, we investigate the Simplified Masked Even-Mansour (SiM) of [9] and derive a multi-user security bound in Sect. 3. The derived security bound is "tight" in the number of users, in the sense that if one considers a single user, the original bound of [9] is retained. In Sect. 3.2, we highlight how the security analysis of SiM differs in our new proof. The second step is to prove the multi-user security of Elephant v2. The mode is first described in detail in Sect. 4, where we also give a treatment of the differences between v1 and v2. A difficulty in the multi-user security analysis of Elephant v2 is that one considers multiple independently keyed modes, but all these modes *employ* the same underlying cryptographic permutation. By reducing the multi-user security of the Elephant v2 mode to the multi-user security of SiM, which was proven in the first step, we isolate the usage of the same permutation in the modular building block SiM and can consider multi-user security of Elephant v2 as multiple completely independent instantiations. Then, its multi-user security can be upper bounded by the sum of μ single-user instances, where the sum is maximized over any possible distribution of the adversarial complexity over the μ instances. A final change in the security proof is that the proof properly separates Elephant v2 into a nonce-based encryption and a nonce-independent authentication part, where the proof of authenticity subsequently stands under nonce-misuse.

1.3 Outline

We describe basic notation and the multi-user security models for tweakable block ciphers and authenticated encryption schemes in Sect. 2. A multi-user security bound on the Simplified Masked Even-Mansour (SiM) tweakable block cipher is given in Sect. 3. In Sect. 4, we focus on Elephant: a description of Elephant v2 is given in Sect. 4.1, a comparison between Elephant v1 and v2 in Sect. 4.3, and a multi-user security bound for Elephant v2 in Sect. 4.2. The multi-user security proofs of SiM and Elephant v2 are given in Appendix A and Sect. 5, respectively. We conclude the work in Sect. 6.

2   Security Model

For $n \in \mathbb{N}$, $\{0,1\}^n$ denotes the set of n-bit strings and $\{0,1\}^*$ the set of arbitrarily length strings. For $X \in \{0,1\}^*$, we define

$$X_1 \ldots X_\ell \xleftarrow{n} X \tag{1}$$

as the function that partitions X into $\ell = \lceil |X|/n \rceil$ blocks of size n bits, where the last block is padded with 0s. The expression "A ? B : C" equals B if A is true, and equals C if A is false. We denote by $\lfloor x \rfloor_i$ the i leftmost bits of x.

For a finite set $\mathcal{T}$, we denote by $\mathrm{perm}(n)$ the set of all n-bit permutations and by $\mathrm{perm}(\mathcal{T}, n)$ the set of all families of permutations indexed by $T \in \mathcal{T}$. We denote by $\mathrm{func}(n)$ the set of all n-bit to n-bit functions. For a finite set $\mathcal{S}$, we denote by $s \xleftarrow{\$} \mathcal{S}$ the uniform random sampling of an element s from $\mathcal{S}$.

An adversary $\mathcal{A}$ is an algorithm that is given access to one or more oracles $\mathcal{O}$, and after interaction with $\mathcal{O}$ outputs a bit $b \in \{0,1\}$. This event is denoted as $\mathcal{A}^{\mathcal{O}} \to b$. In our work, we will be concerned with computationally unbounded adversaries $\mathcal{A}$; their complexities are only measured by the number of oracle queries. For two randomized oracles $\mathcal{O}$ and $\mathcal{P}$, we denote the advantage of an adversary $\mathcal{A}$ in distinguishing between them by

$$\Delta_{\mathcal{A}} (\mathcal{O} \; ; \; \mathcal{P}) = \left| \mathbf{Pr} \left(\mathcal{A}^{\mathcal{O}} \to 1 \right) - \mathbf{Pr} \left(\mathcal{A}^{\mathcal{P}} \to 1 \right) \right|. \tag{2}$$

Finally, let $k, m, n, t, \mu \in \mathbb{N}$ with $k, m, t \leq n$ throughout.

2.1   Tweakable Block Ciphers

A tweakable block cipher $\widetilde{\mathsf{E}}$ is a function that gets as input a key $K \in \{0,1\}^k$, tweak $T \in \mathcal{T}$,[1] and message $M \in \{0,1\}^n$, and outputs a ciphertext $C \in \{0,1\}^n$. The tweakable block cipher $\widetilde{\mathsf{E}}$ is required to be bijective for any fixed (K, T).

Elephant only uses its underlying primitive in the forward direction. This means that we only need to consider tweakable block ciphers that are secure against adversaries that only have access to $\widetilde{\mathsf{E}}$, and not to $\widetilde{\mathsf{E}}^{-1}$. The tweakable block cipher considered in this work is based on an n-bit permutation P, which is modeled as a random permutation $\mathsf{P} \xleftarrow{\$} \mathrm{perm}(n)$. We will consider the multi-user security of $\widetilde{\mathsf{E}}$, where an adversary can query up to μ instances of the scheme. Specifically, the μ-tprp security of $\widetilde{\mathsf{E}}$ against an adversary $\mathcal{A}$ is defined as

$$\mathbf{Adv}_{\widetilde{\mathsf{E}}}^{\mu\text{-tprp}}(\mathcal{A}) = \Delta_{\mathcal{A}} \left(\left(\widetilde{\mathsf{E}}_{K_j}^{\mathsf{P}} \right)_{j=1}^{\mu}, \mathsf{P}^{\pm} \; ; \; \left(\widetilde{\pi}_j \right)_{j=1}^{\mu}, \mathsf{P}^{\pm} \right), \tag{3}$$

where the randomness is taken over independent $K_1, \ldots, K_\mu \xleftarrow{\$} \{0,1\}^k$, $\mathsf{P} \xleftarrow{\$} \mathrm{perm}(n)$, and $\widetilde{\pi}_1, \ldots, \widetilde{\pi}_\mu \xleftarrow{\$} \mathrm{perm}(\mathcal{T}, n)$.

---

[1] In our application, the tweak space is of a specific form and cannot be conveniently expressed as a set of binary strings.

2.2 Authenticated Encryption

An authenticated encryption scheme AE consists of two algorithms enc and dec. Encryption enc takes a key $K \in \{0,1\}^k$, a nonce $N \in \{0,1\}^m$, associated data $A \in \{0,1\}^*$, and a message $M \in \{0,1\}^*$ as inputs, and it outputs a ciphertext $C \in \{0,1\}^{|M|}$ and a tag $T \in \{0,1\}^t$. Decryption dec takes a key $K \in \{0,1\}^k$, a nonce $N \in \{0,1\}^m$, associated data $A \in \{0,1\}^*$, a ciphertext $C \in \{0,1\}^*$, and a tag $T \in \{0,1\}^t$ as inputs, and it outputs a message $M \in \{0,1\}^{|C|}$ if the tag is correct, or a dedicated $\perp$-sign otherwise. The two functions are required to satisfy

$$\mathsf{dec}(K, N, A, \mathsf{enc}(K, N, A, M)) = M \, .$$

(Note that the output of $\mathsf{enc}(K, N, A, M)$ consists of a tuple (C, T), and hence, dec gets as input a tuple of the form (K, N, A, C, T).)

In our work, the authenticated encryption scheme AE is based on an n-bit permutation P, which is modeled as a random permutation: $\mathsf{P} \xleftarrow{\$} \mathrm{perm}(n)$. We will consider multi-user security of AE, where an adversary can query up to μ versions of the scheme. The multi-user security of AE against an adversary $\mathcal{A}$ is defined as

$$\mathbf{Adv}_{\mathsf{AE}}^{\mu\text{-ae}}(\mathcal{A}) = \Delta_{\mathcal{A}} \left((\mathsf{enc}_{K_j}^{\mathsf{P}}, \mathsf{dec}_{K_j}^{\mathsf{P}})_{j=1}^{\mu}, \mathsf{P}^{\pm} \, ; \, (\mathsf{rand}_j, \perp)_{j=1}^{\mu}, \mathsf{P}^{\pm} \right), \qquad (4)$$

where the randomness is taken over $K_1, \ldots, K_\mu \xleftarrow{\$} \{0,1\}^k$, $\mathsf{P} \xleftarrow{\$} \mathrm{perm}(n)$, and the functions $\mathsf{rand}_1, \ldots, \mathsf{rand}_\mu$ that for each new input (N, A, M) return a random string of size $|M| + t$ bits. The superscript $\pm$ indicates two-sided access by $\mathcal{A}$. The function $\perp$ returns the $\perp$-sign for each query.

The adversary $\mathcal{A}$ is not allowed to relay the output of the encryption oracle (enc_{K_j} in the real world and rand_j in the ideal world) to the decryption oracle (dec_{K_j} in the real world and $\perp$ in the ideal world). Adversary $\mathcal{A}$ is called *nonce-respecting* if it does not make two encryption queries to the same oracle $j \in \{1, \ldots, \mu\}$ for the same nonce.

2.3 Authentication

If we restrict our focus to authentication only of an authenticated encryption scheme, we consider an adversary $\mathcal{A}$ that can query the encryption functionality enc at its discretion, and it wins if it can submit a tuple to dec that (i) succeeds and (ii) was not the result of an earlier encryption query. More formally, for an authenticated encryption scheme AE based on an n-bit permutation P, which is modeled as a random permutation $\mathsf{P} \xleftarrow{\$} \mathrm{perm}(n)$, we will define multi-user authenticity of AE, where an adversary can query up to μ versions of the scheme, as follows:

$$\mathbf{Adv}_{\mathsf{AE}}^{\mu\text{-auth}}(\mathcal{A}) = \mathbf{Pr} \left(\mathcal{A}^{\left(\mathsf{enc}_{K_j}^{\mathsf{P}}, \mathsf{dec}_{K_j}^{\mathsf{P}} \right)_{j=1}^{\mu}, \mathsf{P}^{\pm}} \text{ forges} \right), \qquad (5)$$

where the randomness is taken over $K_1, \ldots, K_\mu \xleftarrow{\$} \{0,1\}^k$ and $\mathsf{P} \xleftarrow{\$} \mathrm{perm}(n)$, and where a successful forgery corresponds to a query to any of the decryption oracles $\mathsf{dec}^\mathsf{P}_{K_j}$ that returned a valid message. The adversary $\mathcal{A}$ is not allowed to relay the output of the encryption oracle enc_{K_j} to the decryption oracle dec_{K_j}. For authenticity, we do not restrict the adversary in its choice of nonce.

3   Simplified Masked Even-Mansour

The Elephant authenticated encryption family uses its underlying permutation in a "Masked Even-Mansour" (MEM) construction [20]: the input to and output of the permutation P are masked using an LFSR (Linear Feedback Shift Register) evaluated on the secret key. To be more precise, Beyne et al. [9] described a simplification, namely "Simplified MEM" (SiM). Their arguments in favor of SiM were that (i) the tweak only consists of the exponents of the LFSRs and the nonce is not a tweak input to SiM, and (ii) Elephant only uses its primitive in the forward direction, which allows for looser conditions on the primitive.

We will describe SiM as introduced by Beyne et al. [9] in Sect. 3.1. In Sect. 3.2, we derive a multi-user security bound on the SiM mode and explain how it differs from the single-user analysis of [9].

3.1   Specification

Let $k, n, z \in \mathbb{N}$. Let $\mathsf{P} \in \mathrm{perm}(n)$ be an n-bit permutation, and let $\varphi_1, \ldots, \varphi_z : \{0,1\}^n \to \{0,1\}^n$ be z LFSRs. Let $\mathcal{T} \subseteq \mathbb{N}^z$ be a finite tweak space. Define the function $\mathsf{mask} : \{0,1\}^k \times \mathcal{T} \to \{0,1\}^n$ as follows:

$$\mathsf{mask}^{a_1, \ldots, a_z}_K = \mathsf{mask}(K, a_1, \ldots, a_z) = \varphi^{a_z}_z \circ \cdots \circ \varphi^{a_1}_1 \circ \mathsf{P}(K \| 0^{n-k}). \quad (6)$$

Define the tweakable block cipher $\mathsf{SiM} : \{0,1\}^k \times \mathcal{T} \times \{0,1\}^n \to \{0,1\}^n$ as

$$\mathsf{SiM}(K, (a_1, \ldots, a_z), M) = \mathsf{P}(M \oplus \mathsf{mask}^{a_1, \ldots, a_z}_K) \oplus \mathsf{mask}^{a_1, \ldots, a_z}_K. \quad (7)$$

3.2   Multi-user Security of SiM

Beyne et al. [9] imposed a restriction on the tweak space $\mathcal{T}$ in order for SiM to be a secure tweakable block cipher, that was in turn taken from Granger et al. [20]. This restriction does not change for the multi-user setting, and we state it for completeness. We say that $\mathcal{T}$ is $2^{-\alpha}$-proper with respect to $(\varphi_1, \ldots, \varphi_z)$ if the function $L \mapsto \varphi^{a_z}_z \circ \cdots \circ \varphi^{a_1}_1(L)$ is $2^{-\alpha}$-uniform and $2^{-\alpha}$-XOR-uniform.

Definition 1. *Let $n, z \in \mathbb{N}$. Let $\varphi_1, \ldots, \varphi_z : \{0,1\}^n \to \{0,1\}^n$ be z LFSRs. The tweak space $\mathcal{T}$ is called $2^{-\alpha}$-proper with respect to $(\varphi_1, \ldots, \varphi_z)$ if the following two properties hold:*

1. For any $Y \in \{0,1\}^n$ and $(a_1, \ldots, a_z) \in \mathcal{T} \cup \{(0, \ldots, 0)\}$,

$$\mathbf{Pr}\left(L \xleftarrow{\$} \{0,1\}^n \ : \ \varphi^{a_z}_z \circ \cdots \circ \varphi^{a_1}_1(L) = Y\right) \leq 2^{-\alpha};$$

2. *For any $Y \in \{0,1\}^n$ and distinct $(a_1, \ldots, a_z), (a'_1, \ldots, a'_z) \in \mathcal{T} \cup \{(0, \ldots, 0)\}$,*

$$\mathbf{Pr}\left(L \xleftarrow{\$} \{0,1\}^n \; : \; \varphi_z^{a_z} \circ \cdots \circ \varphi_1^{a_1}(L) \oplus \varphi_z^{a'_z} \circ \cdots \circ \varphi_1^{a'_1}(L) = Y\right) \leq 2^{-\alpha}.$$

We can now prove that if the tweak space is $2^{-\alpha}$-proper for sufficiently small $2^{-\alpha}$ (note that $2^{-\alpha}$ cannot be smaller than 2^{-n}), then SiM is a *multi-user* secure tweakable block cipher.

Theorem 1. *Let $k, n, z, \mu \in \mathbb{N}$. Let $\varphi_1, \ldots, \varphi_z : \{0,1\}^n \to \{0,1\}^n$ be z LFSRs, and let $\mathcal{T}$ be a $2^{-\alpha}$-proper tweak space with respect to $(\varphi_1, \ldots, \varphi_z)$. Consider SiM of (7) based on a random permutation $\mathsf{P} \xleftarrow{\$} \mathrm{perm}(n)$. For any multi-user adversary $\mathcal{A}$ making at most $q \leq 2^{n-1}$ construction queries (in total to all μ construction oracles) and p primitive queries,*

$$\mathbf{Adv}_{\mathsf{SiM}}^{\mu\text{-tprp}}(\mathcal{A}) \leq \frac{q^2 + 2qp + (\mu - 1)q}{2^\alpha} + \frac{\mu \cdot (2q + p + \frac{\mu-1}{2})}{2^n} + \frac{\mu \cdot (p + \frac{\mu-1}{2})}{2^k}.$$

The main difference with the single-user proof of [9] consists of bad events related to key collisions (details on the differences are given in the proof). Another change is that the analyses of the probability of certain transcripts to occur have changed slightly to facilitate the multi-user setting. When we restrict Theorem 1 to the single-user setting (i.e., $\mu = 1$), the bound of [9] is retained. As the changes compared to the proof of v1 are rather isolated, the proof is given in Appendix A.

4   Elephant Authenticated Encryption

We consider the Elephant v2 authenticated encryption mode as submitted by Beyne et al. to the final round of the NIST Lightweight Cryptography competition [11]. It is described in Sect. 4.1. The main Theorem 2, bounding the multiple-user security of Elephant v2 in terms of the multi-user security of SiM, is given in Sect. 4.2. In Sect. 4.3, we reflect on the differences between Elephant v2 and v1 [8], and explain how the security bound has improved.

4.1   Specification of Elephant v2

Let $k, m, n, t \in \mathbb{N}$ with $k, m, t \leq n$. Let $\mathsf{P} : \{0,1\}^n \to \{0,1\}^n$ be an n-bit permutation, and $\varphi_1 : \{0,1\}^n \to \{0,1\}^n$ be an LFSR. Define $\varphi_2 = \varphi_1 \oplus \mathrm{id}$, where id is the identity function. Define the function $\mathsf{mask} : \{0,1\}^k \times \mathbb{N}^2 \to \{0,1\}^n$ as follows:

$$\mathsf{mask}_K^{a,b} = \mathsf{mask}(K, a, b) = \varphi_2^b \circ \varphi_1^a \circ \mathsf{P}(K \| 0^{n-k}). \tag{8}$$

We next describe the authenticated encryption mode of Elephant v2.

4.1.1   Encryption

Encryption enc takes as input a key $K \in \{0,1\}^k$, a nonce $N \in \{0,1\}^m$, associated data $A \in \{0,1\}^*$, and a message $M \in \{0,1\}^*$, and it outputs a ciphertext $C \in \{0,1\}^{|M|}$ and a tag $T \in \{0,1\}^t$. The description of enc is given in Algorithm 1, and it is depicted in Fig. 1.

Algorithm 1. Elephant v2 encryption algorithm enc

Input: $(K, N, A, M) \in \{0,1\}^k \times \{0,1\}^m \times \{0,1\}^* \times \{0,1\}^*$
Output: $(C, T) \in \{0,1\}^{|M|} \times \{0,1\}^t$
1: $M_1 \ldots M_{\ell_M} \xleftarrow{n} M$
2: **for** $i = 1, \ldots, \ell_M$ **do**
3:     $C_i \leftarrow M_i \oplus \mathsf{P}(N\|0^{n-m} \oplus \mathsf{mask}_K^{i-1,1}) \oplus \mathsf{mask}_K^{i-1,1}$
4: $C \leftarrow \lfloor C_1 \ldots C_{\ell_M} \rfloor_{|M|}$
5: $A_1 \ldots A_{\ell_A} \xleftarrow{n} N\|A\|1$
6: $C_1 \ldots C_{\ell_C} \xleftarrow{n} C\|1$
7: $T \leftarrow A_1$
8: **for** $i = 2, \ldots, \ell_A$ **do**
9:     $T \leftarrow T \oplus \mathsf{P}(A_i \oplus \mathsf{mask}_K^{i-1,0}) \oplus \mathsf{mask}_K^{i-1,0}$
10: **for** $i = 1, \ldots, \ell_C$ **do**
11:     $T \leftarrow T \oplus \mathsf{P}(C_i \oplus \mathsf{mask}_K^{i-1,2}) \oplus \mathsf{mask}_K^{i-1,2}$
12: $T \leftarrow \mathsf{P}(T \oplus \mathsf{mask}_K^{0,0}) \oplus \mathsf{mask}_K^{0,0}$
13: **return** $(C, \lfloor T \rfloor_t)$

4.1.2 Decryption

Decryption dec gets as input a key $K \in \{0,1\}^k$, a nonce $N \in \{0,1\}^m$, associated data $A \in \{0,1\}^*$, a ciphertext $C \in \{0,1\}^*$, and a tag $T \in \{0,1\}^t$, and it outputs a message $M \in \{0,1\}^{|M|}$ if the tag is correct, or a dedicated $\perp$-sign otherwise. The description of dec is given in Algorithm 2.

4.2 Multi-user Security of Elephant v2

We prove security of Elephant v2 of Sect. 4.1 for any $2^{-\alpha}$-proper tweak space.

Theorem 2. *Let* $k, m, n, t, \mu \in \mathbb{N}$ *with* $k, m, t \leq n$. *Let* $\varphi_1, \varphi_2 : \{0,1\}^n \to \{0,1\}^n$ *be LFSRs, and let* $\mathcal{T}$ *be a* $2^{-\alpha}$*-proper tweak space with respect to* (φ_1, φ_2). *Consider* Elephant-v2 $=$ (enc, dec) *of Sect. 4.1 based on random permutation* $\mathsf{P} \xleftarrow{\$} \mathrm{perm}(n)$. *For any multi-user adversary* $\mathcal{A}$ *making at most* $q_e \leq 2^{n-1}$ *construction encryption queries (in total to all* μ *construction oracles) for unique nonces whenever the same oracle is queried,* q_d *construction decryption queries (in total to all* μ *construction oracles), each query at most* ℓ *padded nonce and associated data and message blocks, and in total at most* σ *padded nonce and associated data and message blocks, and* p *primitive queries,*

$$\mathbf{Adv}_{\mathsf{Elephant\text{-}v2}}^{\mu\text{-ae}}(\mathcal{A}) \leq \ell \binom{q_e}{2}/2^n + 3\binom{q_e + q_d}{2}/2^n + q_d/2^t + \mathbf{Adv}_{\mathsf{SiM}}^{\mu\text{-tprp}}(\mathcal{A}'),$$

for some multi-user adversary $\mathcal{A}'$ *that makes* 2σ *construction queries and* p *primitive queries.*

The proof of Theorem 2 is given in Sect. 5 and is significantly different from that of Elephant v1 [9]. In a nutshell, the first change is that the new proof is in the multi-user setting, where the adversary has access to multiple instances, all

Algorithm 2. Elephant v2 decryption algorithm dec

Input: $(K, N, A, C, T) \in \{0,1\}^k \times \{0,1\}^m \times \{0,1\}^* \times \{0,1\}^* \times \{0,1\}^t$
Output: $M \in \{0,1\}^{|C|}$ or $\bot$

1: $C_1 \dots C_{\ell_M} \xleftarrow{n} C$
2: **for** $i = 1, \dots, \ell_M$ **do**
3:     $M_i \leftarrow C_i \oplus \mathsf{P}(N\|0^{n-m} \oplus \mathsf{mask}_K^{i-1,1}) \oplus \mathsf{mask}_K^{i-1,1}$
4: $M \leftarrow \lfloor M_1 \dots M_{\ell_M} \rfloor_{|C|}$
5: $A_1 \dots A_{\ell_A} \xleftarrow{n} N\|A\|1$
6: $C_1 \dots C_{\ell_C} \xleftarrow{n} C\|1$
7: $\bar{T} \leftarrow A_1$
8: **for** $i = 2, \dots, \ell_A$ **do**
9:     $\bar{T} \leftarrow \bar{T} \oplus \mathsf{P}(A_i \oplus \mathsf{mask}_K^{i-1,0}) \oplus \mathsf{mask}_K^{i-1,0}$
10: **for** $i = 1, \dots, \ell_C$ **do**
11:     $\bar{T} \leftarrow \bar{T} \oplus \mathsf{P}(C_i \oplus \mathsf{mask}_K^{i-1,2}) \oplus \mathsf{mask}_K^{i-1,2}$
12: $\bar{T} \leftarrow \mathsf{P}(\bar{T} \oplus \mathsf{mask}_K^{0,0}) \oplus \mathsf{mask}_K^{0,0}$
13: **return** $\lfloor \bar{T} \rfloor_t = T$? M : $\bot$

instantiated with an independent key but with the same underlying permutation. This is resolved by performing a reduction to SiM and therewith ending up with a simplified version of Elephant v2 for which the adversarial μ-user success probability is bounded by a sum of μ single-user success probabilities, maximized over all possible distributions of adversarial complexities. Finally, the authentication of Elephant v2 is different from that of Elephant v1, and a new proof for the authentication portion is given.

A final remark on the security analysis of Theorem 2 is that, although the theorem restricts itself to nonce-respecting adversaries, this nonce-respecting behavior is *only* used for the portion of the proof related to confidentiality. The Elephant v2 mode thus even achieves *authenticity* under nonce-reuse, up to above bound minus $\ell\binom{q_e}{2}/2^n$ (coming from the confidentiality portion of the proof).

Corollary 1. *Let* $k, m, n, t, \mu \in \mathbb{N}$ *with* $k, m, t \leq n$. *Let* $\varphi_1, \varphi_2 : \{0,1\}^n \to \{0,1\}^n$ *be LFSRs, and let* $\mathcal{T}$ *be a* $2^{-\alpha}$-*proper tweak space with respect to* (φ_1, φ_2). *Consider* Elephant-v2 $= (\mathsf{enc}, \mathsf{dec})$ *of Sect. 4.1 based on random permutation* $\mathsf{P} \xleftarrow{\$} \mathrm{perm}(n)$. *For any multi-user adversary* $\mathcal{A}$ *making at most* $q_e \leq 2^{n-1}$ *construction encryption queries (in total to all* μ *construction oracles),* q_d *construction decryption queries (in total to all* μ *construction oracles), each query at most* ℓ *padded nonce and associated data and message blocks, and in total at most* σ *padded nonce and associated data and message blocks, and* p *primitive queries,*

$$\mathbf{Adv}_{\mathsf{Elephant\text{-}v2}}^{\mu\text{-auth}}(\mathcal{A}) \leq 3\binom{q_e + q_d}{2}/2^n + q_d/2^t + \mathbf{Adv}_{\mathsf{SiM}}^{\mu\text{-tprp}}(\mathcal{A}'),$$

for some multi-user adversary $\mathcal{A}'$ *that makes* 2σ *construction queries and* p *primitive queries.*

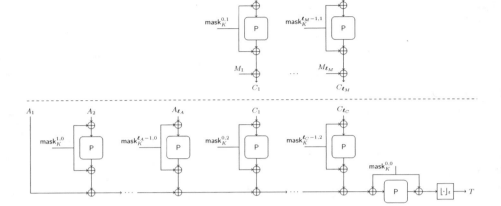

Fig. 1. Depiction of Elephant v2. For the encryption part (top): message is padded as $M_1 \ldots M_{\ell_M} \xleftarrow{n} M$, and ciphertext equals $C = \lfloor C_1 \ldots C_{\ell_M} \rfloor_{|M|}$. For the authentication part (bottom): nonce and associated data are padded as $A_1 \ldots A_{\ell_A} \xleftarrow{n} N\|A\|1$, and ciphertext is padded as $C_1 \ldots C_{\ell_C} \xleftarrow{n} C\|1$.

4.3   Comparison with Elephant v1

We will discuss how Theorem 2 improves over the result of Beyne et al. [9]. Their result was for Elephant v1, which is depicted in Fig. 2.

4.3.1   Comparison Between Elephant v1 and v2

Before discussing Theorem 2 in more detail, we first consider the actual changes between Elephant v1 of Fig. 2 and Elephant v2 of Fig. 1.

The main change is in the authentication. Elephant v1 performed authentication using the Wegman-Carter-Shoup [7,28,29] MAC function. To be precise, the Wegman-Carter-Shoup function is defined as a nonce-based MAC scheme $\mathsf{mac}_{K,L}(N, A, C) = \mathsf{E}_K(N) \oplus \mathsf{H}_L(A, C)$, where E is a block cipher and H a universal hash function. In Elephant v1, the block cipher is instantiated as[2]

$$\mathsf{E}_K(\cdot) = \mathsf{P}(\cdot \oplus \mathsf{mask}_K^{0,2}) \oplus \mathsf{mask}_K^{0,2} \,,$$

and the universal hash function as an XOR of tweakable block cipher evaluations. In Elephant v2, one uses a similar type of universal hash function, but this time, H_L processes all of (N, A, C), where the first data block is not evaluated by a tweakable block cipher but instead added in the clear. The output of H_L is then "protected" with a block cipher call instantiated as

$$\mathsf{E}_K(\cdot) = \mathsf{P}(\cdot \oplus \mathsf{mask}_K^{0,0}) \oplus \mathsf{mask}_K^{0,0} \,.$$

---

[2] As a matter of fact, in Elephant v2, the nonce is smaller than the state size of the permutation and is appended with associated data bits. This does not change the overall argument.

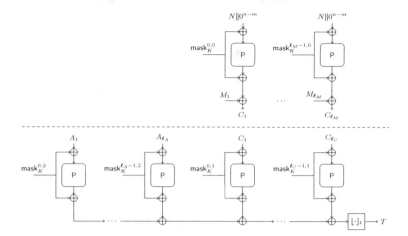

Fig. 2. Depiction of Elephant v1. For the encryption part (top): message is padded as $M_1 \ldots M_{\ell_M} \xleftarrow{n} M$, and ciphertext equals $C = \lfloor C_1 \ldots C_{\ell_M} \rfloor_{|M|}$. For the authentication part (bottom): nonce and associated data are padded as $A_1 \ldots A_{\ell_A} \xleftarrow{n} N\|A\|1$, and ciphertext is padded as $C_1 \ldots C_{\ell_C} \xleftarrow{n} C\|1$.

Concisely written, the resulting MAC scheme is of the form $\mathsf{mac}_{K,L}(N, A, C) = \mathsf{E}_K\big(\mathsf{H}_L(N, A, C)\big)$. The main advantage of the change is that the Wegman-Carter-Shoup construction is nonce-based, meaning that it *requires* the nonce to be unique for each evaluation, but the protected counter sum construction does not rely on a nonce for its security. Concretely, for Elephant v2, this implies that the authenticated encryption scheme guarantees authenticity under nonce-misuse (but no confidentiality).

A second change from Elephant v1 to v2, which is minor, is in the positioning of the masks of the tweakable block cipher calls. In Elephant v2, the roles of the masks are $(\cdot, 0)$ for associated data authentication (used to be encryption), $(\cdot, 1)$ for encryption (used to be ciphertext authentication), and $(\cdot, 2)$ for ciphertext authentication (used to be associated data authentication). This improvement gives a slight efficiency improvement, noting that the finalization, i.e., the "protection" part as mentioned above, can be performed with mask $\mathsf{mask}_K^{0,0}$. This change does not affect the security analysis.

4.3.2   Discussion of Theorem 2

The Elephant v2 submission to the NIST Lightweight Cryptography competition [26] consists of three instances: Dumbo, Jumbo, and Delirium [11]. All three variants process a key of size $k = 128$ bits and a nonce of size $m = 96$ bits. Dumbo uses an $n = 160$-bit permutation and outputs tags of size $t = 64$ bits, Jumbo uses an $n = 176$-bit permutation and outputs tags of size $t = 64$ bits, and Delirium uses an $n = 200$-bit permutation and outputs tags of size $t = 64$ bits. For each of the three variants, the authors have developed an LFSR that defines an 2^{-n}-proper mask function [11].

If we model the permutations underlying Dumbo, Jumbo, and Delirium as random permutations, we can conclude from Theorem 2 and Theorem 1 that the three functions are secure authenticated encryption schemes up to bound

$$\ell\binom{q_e}{2}/2^n + 3\binom{q_e + q_d}{2}/2^n + q_d/2^t$$
$$+ \frac{4\sigma^2 + 4\sigma p + (\mu - 1)2\sigma + \mu \cdot (4\sigma + p + \frac{\mu-1}{2})}{2^n} + \frac{\mu \cdot (p + \frac{\mu-1}{2})}{2^k},$$

against any nonce-respecting adversary that makes at most q_e encryption queries and q_d decryption queries, all of maximum length ℓ blocks and in total of length at most σ blocks, and that makes at most p evaluations of the random primitive P. Note that the dominating term in the bound is $4\sigma p/2^n$. By capping $\sigma \leq 2^{n-114}$, this term is less than 1 as long as $p \leq 2^{112}$. Likewise, by capping $\sigma \leq 2^{n-130}$, this term is less than 1 as long as $p \leq 2^{128}$. To put these numbers in perspective, Beyne et al. aimed to achieve around 112-bit security for Dumbo and close to 128-bit security for Jumbo and Delirium. However, one also needs to take the other terms of the bound into account. Most of the terms are negligible compared to $4\sigma p/2^n$, and are covered by taking a slightly stricter condition on σ. There is one exception to these negligible terms, namely the factor $p/2^k$ for Jumbo and Delirium: it equals 1 for $p = 2^{128}$. This term thus accounts for a factor 2 loss in the security strength of Jumbo and Delirium. In conclusion, we obtain that Dumbo is secure as long as $p \ll 2^{112}$ and $\sigma \ll 2^{50}/(n/8) < 2^{46}$, that Jumbo is secure as long as $p \ll 2^{127}$ and $\sigma \ll 2^{50}/(n/8) < 2^{46}$, and that Delirium is secure as long as $p \ll 2^{127}$ and $\sigma \ll 2^{74}/(n/8) < 2^{70}$. This is exactly in line with the security claims of the developers of Elephant v2 [11], and also confirms that the change from v1 to v2 has not induced an extra security loss.

In conclusion, we remark that in the above bound the term μ only appears in the minor terms and thus only plays a small role. To be precise, the complexity p is solely determined by the offline power of the adversary whereas μ (just like q_e, q_d, ℓ, σ) is determined by the actual system that the adversary aims to attack. This means that, in practice, $\mu \ll p$. Likewise, $\mu \ll \sigma$ as σ counts the *total* complexity in blocks to all oracles. From this, we can conclude that all terms involving μ are negligible compared to $4\sigma p/2^n$.

5   Proof of Theorem 2 (on Elephant)

Let $K_1, \ldots, K_\mu \xleftarrow{\$} \{0,1\}^k$, $P \xleftarrow{\$} \text{perm}(n)$, and $\text{rand}_1, \ldots, \text{rand}_\mu$ be functions that for each input $(N, A, M) \in \{0,1\}^m \times \{0,1\}^* \times \{0,1\}^*$ return a random string of size $|M| + t$ bits. Consider a deterministic computationally unbounded multi-user adversary $\mathcal{A}$ that tries to distinguish $\mathcal{O} := ((\text{enc}^P_{K_j}, \text{dec}^P_{K_j})^\mu_{j=1}, P^\pm)$ from $\mathcal{P} := ((\text{rand}_j, \bot)^\mu_{j=1}, P^\pm)$:

$$\mathbf{Adv}^{\mu\text{-ae}}_{\text{Elephant-v2}}(\mathcal{A}) = \Delta_{\mathcal{A}}\left(\left(\text{enc}^P_{K_j}, \text{dec}^P_{K_j}\right)^\mu_{j=1}, P^\pm \; ; \; \left(\text{rand}_j, \bot\right)^\mu_{j=1}, P^\pm\right). \quad (9)$$

5.1   First Step: Isolating SiM

As a first step, we will describe an alternative authenticated encryption scheme AE' based on tweakable permutations $\widetilde{\pi}_1, \ldots, \widetilde{\pi}_\mu \xleftarrow{\$} \mathrm{perm}(\mathcal{T}, n)$, where $\mathcal{T}$ is $2^{-\alpha}$-proper with respect to LFSRs (φ_1, φ_2). Its encryption function $\overline{\mathsf{enc}}$ and decryption function $\overline{\mathsf{dec}}$ are given in Algorithms 3 and 4, respectively, for any function $\widetilde{\pi} \in \{\widetilde{\pi}_1, \ldots, \widetilde{\pi}_\mu\}$. Unlike the original functions enc and dec of Algorithms 1 and 2, the functions $\overline{\mathsf{enc}}$ and $\overline{\mathsf{dec}}$ are not explicitly keyed by $K_1, \ldots, K_\mu$, but are instead implicitly keyed by the use of random secret tweakable permutations $\widetilde{\pi}_1, \ldots, \widetilde{\pi}_\mu$.

Algorithm 3. encryption $\overline{\mathsf{enc}}$	**Algorithm 4.** decryption $\overline{\mathsf{dec}}$
Input: (N, A, M)	**Input:** (N, A, C, T)
Output: (C, T)	**Output:** M or $\bot$
1: $M_1 \ldots M_{\ell_M} \xleftarrow{n} M$	1: $C_1 \ldots C_{\ell_M} \xleftarrow{n} C$
2: **for** $i = 1, \ldots, \ell_M$ **do**	2: **for** $i = 1, \ldots, \ell_M$ **do**
3: $C_i \leftarrow M_i \oplus \widetilde{\pi}((i-1, 1), N\|0^{n-m})$	3: $M_i \leftarrow C_i \oplus \widetilde{\pi}((i-1, 1), N\|0^{n-m})$
4: $C \leftarrow \lfloor C_1 \ldots C_{\ell_M} \rfloor_{|M|}$	4: $M \leftarrow \lfloor M_1 \ldots M_{\ell_M} \rfloor_{|C|}$
5: $A_1 \ldots A_{\ell_A} \xleftarrow{n} N\|A\|1$	5: $A_1 \ldots A_{\ell_A} \xleftarrow{n} N\|A\|1$
6: $C_1 \ldots C_{\ell_C} \xleftarrow{n} C\|1$	6: $C_1 \ldots C_{\ell_C} \xleftarrow{n} C\|1$
7: $T \leftarrow A_1$	7: $\bar{T} \leftarrow A_1$
8: **for** $i = 2, \ldots, \ell_A$ **do**	8: **for** $i = 2, \ldots, \ell_A$ **do**
9: $T \leftarrow T \oplus \widetilde{\pi}((i-1, 0), A_i)$	9: $\bar{T} \leftarrow \bar{T} \oplus \widetilde{\pi}((i-1, 0), A_i)$
10: **for** $i = 1, \ldots, \ell_C$ **do**	10: **for** $i = 1, \ldots, \ell_C$ **do**
11: $T \leftarrow T \oplus \widetilde{\pi}((i-1, 2), C_i)$	11: $\bar{T} \leftarrow \bar{T} \oplus \widetilde{\pi}((i-1, 2), C_i)$
12: $T \leftarrow \widetilde{\pi}((0, 0), T)$	12: $\bar{T} \leftarrow \widetilde{\pi}((0, 0), \bar{T})$
13: **return** $(C, \lfloor T \rfloor_t)$	13: **return** $\lfloor \bar{T} \rfloor_t = T$? M : $\bot$

By a simple hybrid argument, we obtain for the distance of (9):

$$(9) \leq \Delta_{\mathcal{A}} \left((\mathsf{enc}^{\mathsf{P}}_{K_j}, \mathsf{dec}^{\mathsf{P}}_{K_j})_{j=1}^{\mu}, \mathsf{P}^{\pm} \; ; \; (\overline{\mathsf{enc}}^{\mathsf{SiM}^{\mathsf{P}}_{K_j}}, \overline{\mathsf{dec}}^{\mathsf{SiM}^{\mathsf{P}}_{K_j}})_{j=1}^{\mu}, \mathsf{P}^{\pm} \right)$$

$$+ \Delta_{\mathcal{A}} \left((\overline{\mathsf{enc}}^{\mathsf{SiM}^{\mathsf{P}}_{K_j}}, \overline{\mathsf{dec}}^{\mathsf{SiM}^{\mathsf{P}}_{K_j}})_{j=1}^{\mu}, \mathsf{P}^{\pm} \; ; \; (\overline{\mathsf{enc}}^{\widetilde{\pi}_j}, \overline{\mathsf{dec}}^{\widetilde{\pi}_j})_{j=1}^{\mu}, \mathsf{P}^{\pm} \right)$$

$$+ \Delta_{\mathcal{A}} \left((\overline{\mathsf{enc}}^{\widetilde{\pi}_j}, \overline{\mathsf{dec}}^{\widetilde{\pi}_j})_{j=1}^{\mu}, \mathsf{P}^{\pm} \; ; \; (\mathsf{rand}_j, \bot)_{j=1}^{\mu}, \mathsf{P}^{\pm} \right). \qquad (10)$$

The first distance of (10) equals 0 by design of AE'. The second distance of (10) is at most $\Delta_{\mathcal{A}'} \left((\mathsf{SiM}^{\mathsf{P}}_{K_j})_{j=1}^{\mu}, \mathsf{P}^{\pm} \; ; \; (\widetilde{\pi}_j)_{j=1}^{\mu}, \mathsf{P}^{\pm} \right) = \mathbf{Adv}^{\mu\text{-tprp}}_{\mathsf{SiM}}(\mathcal{A}')$, where $\mathcal{A}'$ is a multi-user adversary that makes 2σ construction queries (in total to all μ construction oracles) and p primitive queries in order to simulate $\mathcal{A}$'s oracles. For the third distance of (10), access to P does not help the adversary, and the oracle can be dropped. We obtain from (10):

$$(9) \leq \mathbf{Adv}^{\mu\text{-tprp}}_{\mathsf{SiM}}(\mathcal{A}') + \Delta_{\mathcal{A}} \left((\overline{\mathsf{enc}}^{\widetilde{\pi}_j}, \overline{\mathsf{dec}}^{\widetilde{\pi}_j})_{j=1}^{\mu} \; ; \; (\mathsf{rand}_j, \bot)_{j=1}^{\mu} \right). \qquad (11)$$

Due to the independence of the oracles for $j = 1, \ldots, \mu$, the remaining distance in (11) can be upper bounded by the sum of the distances for the j oracles, maximized over any choice of adversaries $\mathcal{A}_1, \ldots, \mathcal{A}_\mu$ whose accumulated query complexity is at most that of $\mathcal{A}$:

$$(9) \leq \mathbf{Adv}_{\mathsf{SiM}}^{\mu\text{-tprp}}(\mathcal{A}') + \max_{\mathcal{A}_1, \ldots, \mathcal{A}_\mu} \sum_{j=1}^{\mu} \Delta_{\mathcal{A}_j} \left(\overline{\mathsf{enc}}^{\widetilde{\pi}_j}, \overline{\mathsf{dec}}^{\widetilde{\pi}_j} \; ; \; \mathsf{rand}_j, \perp \right), \qquad (12)$$

where the query complexity of adversary $\mathcal{A}_j$ (for $j = 1, \ldots, \mu$) is parametrized by $q_{e,j}$, $q_{d,j}$, and σ_j, and where $\sum_{j=1}^{\mu} q_{e,j} = q_e$, $\sum_{j=1}^{\mu} q_{d,j} = q_d$, and $\sum_{j=1}^{\mu} \sigma_j = \sigma$. Here, we recall that complexity parameter ℓ denotes the maximum length of a single query, and it stays the same for each adversary.

The authenticated encryption scheme AE' can be seen as a generic encrypt-then-MAC construction, and more specifically as the N2 construction of Nam-prempre et al. [24], where encryption is done in counter mode and message authentication using a variant of the protected counter sum [6,23] MAC function. We describe a dedicated security proof that is more compact and gives a better bound.

5.2   Second Step: Simplifying Authentication

The simplification of (12) allows us to focus on a single-user instance, and in this step, we drop the subscript j of the oracles for readability. Nevertheless, we keep the subscript j for $\mathcal{A}$ and for its complexities for clarity. In other words, this second step is about bounding

$$\Delta_{\mathcal{A}_j} \left(\overline{\mathsf{enc}}^{\widetilde{\pi}}, \overline{\mathsf{dec}}^{\widetilde{\pi}} \; ; \; \mathsf{rand}, \perp \right) \qquad (13)$$

for $\widetilde{\pi} \xleftarrow{\$} \mathrm{perm}(\mathcal{T}, n)$ and rand a function that for each input $(N, A, M) \in \{0,1\}^m \times \{0,1\}^* \times \{0,1\}^*$ returns a random string of length $|M| + t$ bits. The query complexity of the adversary is measured by parameters $q_{e,j}$, $q_{d,j}$, ℓ, and σ_j.

Let ρ be a random function that for each input $(N, A, C) \in \{0,1\}^m \times \{0,1\}^* \times \{0,1\}^*$ returns a random string of length n bits. We describe an alternative authenticated encryption scheme AE'' based on tweakable permutation $\widetilde{\pi}$ and on ρ. Its encryption function $\overline{\overline{\mathsf{enc}}}$ and decryption function $\overline{\overline{\mathsf{dec}}}$ are given in Algorithms 5 and 6, respectively.

Algorithm 5. encryption $\overline{\mathsf{enc}}$	**Algorithm 6.** decryption $\overline{\mathsf{dec}}$
Input: (N, A, M)	**Input:** (N, A, C, T)
Output: (C, T)	**Output:** M or $\perp$
1: $M_1 \ldots M_{\ell_M} \xleftarrow{n} M$	1: $C_1 \ldots C_{\ell_M} \xleftarrow{n} C$
2: **for** $i = 1, \ldots, \ell_M$ **do**	2: **for** $i = 1, \ldots, \ell_M$ **do**
3: $\quad C_i \leftarrow M_i \oplus \widetilde{\pi}((i-1, 1), N\|0^{n-m})$	3: $\quad M_i \leftarrow C_i \oplus \widetilde{\pi}((i-1, 1), N\|0^{n-m})$
4: $C \leftarrow \lfloor C_1 \ldots C_{\ell_M} \rfloor_{|M|}$	4: $M \leftarrow \lfloor M_1 \ldots M_{\ell_M} \rfloor_{|C|}$
5: $A_1 \ldots A_{\ell_A} \xleftarrow{n} N\|A\|1$	5: $A_1 \ldots A_{\ell_A} \xleftarrow{n} N\|A\|1$
6: $C_1 \ldots C_{\ell_C} \xleftarrow{n} C\|1$	6: $C_1 \ldots C_{\ell_C} \xleftarrow{n} C\|1$
7: $T \leftarrow \rho(N, A, C)$	7: $\bar{T} \leftarrow \rho(N, A, C)$
8: **return** $(C, \lfloor T \rfloor_t)$	8: **return** $\lfloor \bar{T} \rfloor_t = T$? M : $\perp$

Proceeding from (13):

$$(13) \leq \Delta_{\mathcal{A}_j}\left(\overline{\mathsf{enc}}^{\widetilde{\pi}}, \overline{\mathsf{dec}}^{\widetilde{\pi}} \; ; \; \overline{\overline{\mathsf{enc}}}^{\widetilde{\pi},\rho}, \overline{\overline{\mathsf{dec}}}^{\widetilde{\pi},\rho}\right)$$

$$+ \Delta_{\mathcal{A}_j}\left(\overline{\overline{\mathsf{enc}}}^{\widetilde{\pi},\rho}, \overline{\overline{\mathsf{dec}}}^{\widetilde{\pi},\rho} \; ; \; \overline{\overline{\mathsf{enc}}}^{\widetilde{\pi},\rho}, \perp\right)$$

$$+ \Delta_{\mathcal{A}_j}\left(\overline{\overline{\mathsf{enc}}}^{\widetilde{\pi},\rho}, \perp \; ; \; \mathsf{rand}, \perp\right). \tag{14}$$

We will analyze the three distances of (14) separately.

First Distance of (14). Define the function $h : \{0,1\}^m \times \{0,1\}^* \times \{0,1\}^* \to \{0,1\}^n$ as

$$h^{\widetilde{\pi}}(N, A, C) = A_1 \oplus \left(\bigoplus_{i=2}^{\ell_A} \widetilde{\pi}((i-1, 0), A_i)\right) \oplus \left(\bigoplus_{i=1}^{\ell_C} \widetilde{\pi}((i-1, 2), C_i)\right),$$

where $A_1 \ldots A_{\ell_A} \xleftarrow{n} N\|A\|1$ and $C_1 \ldots C_{\ell_C} \xleftarrow{n} C\|1$. This function is $(2^n - 1)^{-1}$-uniform: for any distinct $(N, A, C) \neq (N', A', C')$, the probability over the drawing of $\widetilde{\pi} \xleftarrow{\$} \mathrm{perm}(\mathcal{T}, n)$ that $h^{\widetilde{\pi}}(N, A, C) = h^{\widetilde{\pi}}(N', A', C')$ is at most $(2^n - 1)^{-1}$.

Next, define $f : \{0,1\}^m \times \{0,1\}^* \times \{0,1\}^* \to \{0,1\}^n$ as

$$f^{\widetilde{\pi}}(N, A, C) = \widetilde{\pi}((0, 0), h^{\widetilde{\pi}}(N, A, C)).$$

In $\overline{\mathsf{enc}}^{\widetilde{\pi}}$ and $\overline{\mathsf{dec}}^{\widetilde{\pi}}$ the tag (before truncation) is computed as $f^{\widetilde{\pi}}(N, A, C)$, whereas in $\overline{\overline{\mathsf{enc}}}^{\widetilde{\pi},\rho}$ and $\overline{\overline{\mathsf{dec}}}^{\widetilde{\pi},\rho}$ it is computed as $\rho(N, A, C)$. Therefore, the first distance of (14) is at most $\Delta_{\mathcal{A}'_j}\left(f^{\widetilde{\pi}} \; ; \; \rho\right)$, where $\mathcal{A}'_j$ is an adversary that makes $q_{e,j} + q_{d,j}$ construction queries, each query at most ℓ padded nonce and associated data and ciphertext blocks. Here, we make use of the fact that $f^{\widetilde{\pi}}$ only evaluates its tweakable permutation for tweaks $(\cdot, 0)$ and $(\cdot, 2)$, these tweaks do not occur elsewhere in the encryption and decryption function, and thus $\mathcal{A}'_j$ can properly simulate $\mathcal{A}_j$'s oracles.

Looking inside $f^{\widetilde{\pi}}$, it consists of an independent composition of $h^{\widetilde{\pi}}$, that never evaluates its primitive for tweak $(0, 0)$, and $\widetilde{\pi}((0, 0), \cdot)$. We replace $\widetilde{\pi}((0, 0), \cdot)$ with a random function $\tau \xleftarrow{\$} \text{func}(n)$, which by the PRP-PRF switching lemma comes at a cost of $\binom{q_{e,j}+q_{d,j}}{2}/2^n$:

$$\Delta_{\mathcal{A}'_j}\left(f^{\widetilde{\pi}} ; \rho\right) \leq \Delta_{\mathcal{A}'_j}\left(\tau \circ h^{\widetilde{\pi}} ; \rho\right) + \binom{q_{e,j}+q_{d,j}}{2}/2^n.$$

The function $\tau \circ h^{\widetilde{\pi}}$ is perfectly indistinguishable from ρ as long as no two inputs to $h^{\widetilde{\pi}}$ collide. As $h^{\widetilde{\pi}}$ is $(2^n - 1)^{-1}$-uniform, we in turn have

$$\Delta_{\mathcal{A}'_j}\left(\tau \circ h^{\widetilde{\pi}} ; \rho\right) \leq \binom{q_{e,j}+q_{d,j}}{2}(2^n - 1)^{-1}.$$

Concluding, we obtain for the first distance of (14):

$$\Delta_{\mathcal{A}_j}\left(\overline{\text{enc}}^{\widetilde{\pi}}, \overline{\text{dec}}^{\widetilde{\pi}} ; \overline{\text{enc}}^{\widetilde{\pi},\rho}, \overline{\text{dec}}^{\widetilde{\pi},\rho}\right) \leq 3\binom{q_{e,j}+q_{d,j}}{2}/2^n. \tag{15}$$

Second Distance of (14). The adversary $\mathcal{A}_j$ can only distinguish both worlds if it ever makes a non-trivial evaluation to $\overline{\overline{\text{dec}}}^{\widetilde{\pi},\rho}$ that succeeds. Consider any forgery attempt (N, A, C, T). If the tuple (N, A, C) occurred in an earlier encryption query, then necessarily the tag T must differ and the forgery will not succeed. Otherwise, ρ has never been evaluated on (N, A, C) before, and $\lfloor \rho(N, A, C) \rfloor_t = T$ with probability $1/2^t$. By summing over all $q_{d,j}$ forgery attempts, we obtain for the second distance of (14):

$$\Delta_{\mathcal{A}_j}\left(\overline{\overline{\text{enc}}}^{\widetilde{\pi},\rho}, \overline{\overline{\text{dec}}}^{\widetilde{\pi},\rho} ; \overline{\overline{\text{enc}}}^{\widetilde{\pi},\rho}, \bot\right) \leq q_{d,j}/2^t. \tag{16}$$

Third Distance of (14). We remark that every query is made for a unique nonce, and in more detail:

- The ith block of ciphertext equals $\widetilde{\pi}((i-1, 1), N) \oplus M_i$, where M_i is the ith block of plaintext;
- The tag equals $\rho(N, A, C)$.

The tweakable permutation $\widetilde{\pi}$ is independent for different tweaks, but two different inputs for the same tweak never collide. Therefore, this third distance of (14) is upper bounded by the probability that any two out of $q_{e,j}$ evaluations of rand collide in any of the ℓ blocks, or more detailed:

$$\Delta_{\mathcal{A}_j}\left(\overline{\overline{\text{enc}}}^{\widetilde{\pi},\rho}, \bot ; \text{rand}, \bot\right) \leq \ell\binom{q_{e,j}}{2}/2^n. \tag{17}$$

Conclusion. Proceeding from (14) and the individual bounds of (15), (16), and (17), we obtain:

$$(13) \leq 3\binom{q_{e,j}+q_{d,j}}{2}/2^n + q_{d,j}/2^t + \ell\binom{q_{e,j}}{2}/2^n. \tag{18}$$

5.3 Third Step: Conclusion

Recall that in the second step, we dropped the subscripts and focused on a single-user case, as inspired by (12). We have to sum the bound of (18) over $j = 1, \ldots, \mu$, and maximize over the choice of $q_{e,j}$ and $q_{d,j}$ such that $\sum_{j=1}^{\mu} q_{e,j} = q_e$ and $\sum_{j=1}^{\mu} q_{d,j} = q_d$. As (18) is convex in $q_{e,j}$ and $q_{d,j}$, we obtain from (12):

$$(9) \leq \mathbf{Adv}_{\mathsf{SiM}}^{\mu\text{-tprp}}(\mathcal{A}') + 3\binom{q_e + q_d}{2}/2^n + q_d/2^t + \ell\binom{q_e}{2}/2^n,$$

and this completes the proof of Theorem 2.

6 Conclusion

We proved multi-user security of Elephant v2, one of the finalists in the NIST Lightweight Cryptography competition, under the assumption that the keys of all instances are mutually independent and under the assumption that the underlying permutation is random. From our observations in Sect. 4.3, we can conclude that the change from Elephant v1 to Elephant v2 has improved its security, with the most important change that Elephant v2 even achieves authenticity under nonce-misuse. In addition, from our analysis, we show that no unexpected things happen when moving to multiple users.

Acknowledgments. This work was supported in part by the Research Council KU Leuven: GOA TENSE (C16/15/058). Tim Beyne and Yu Long Chen are supported by a Ph.D. Fellowship from the Research Foundation - Flanders (FWO). Christoph Dobraunig is supported by the Austrian Science Fund (FWF): J 4277-N38. Bart Mennink is supported by the Netherlands Organisation for Scientific Research (NWO) under grant VI.Vidi.203.099.

A Proof of Theorem 1 (on SiM)

The proof closely follows Granger et al. [20], just like that of Beyne et al. [9] did, and is performed using the H-coefficient technique [13,27]. The main difference is in the fact that we consider multi-user security, where the adversary can query $\mu \geq 1$ construction oracles.

Let $K_1, \ldots, K_\mu \xleftarrow{\$} \{0,1\}^k$, $\mathsf{P} \xleftarrow{\$} \mathrm{perm}(n)$, and $\widetilde{\pi}_1, \ldots, \widetilde{\pi}_\mu \xleftarrow{\$} \mathrm{perm}(\mathcal{T}, n)$, where $\mathcal{T}$ is $2^{-\alpha}$-proper with respect to LFSRs $(\varphi_1, \ldots, \varphi_z)$. Consider a computationally unbounded adversary $\mathcal{A}$ that tries to distinguish $\mathcal{O} := ((\widetilde{\mathsf{E}}_{K_j}^{\mathsf{P}})_{j=1}^{\mu}, \mathsf{P}^{\pm})$ from $\mathcal{P} := ((\widetilde{\pi}_j)_{j=1}^{\mu}, \mathsf{P}^{\pm})$. Without loss of generality, we can consider it to be deterministic: for any probabilistic adversary there exists a deterministic one that has at least the same success probability. The interaction of $\mathcal{A}$ with its oracle ($\mathcal{O}$ or $\mathcal{P}$) is gathered in a view ν. Denote by $D_{\mathcal{O}}$ (resp., $D_{\mathcal{P}}$) the probability distribution of views in interaction with $\mathcal{O}$ (resp., $\mathcal{P}$). Denote by $\mathcal{V}$ the set of "attainable views", i.e., views ν such that $\mathbf{Pr}\left(D_{\mathcal{P}} = \nu\right) > 0$.

Lemma 1 (H-coefficient technique). *Consider a partition $\mathcal{V} = \mathcal{V}_{\text{good}} \cup \mathcal{V}_{\text{bad}}$ of the set of views into "good" and "bad" views. Let $\varepsilon \in [0,1]$ be such that $\frac{\mathbf{Pr}(D_{\mathcal{O}}=\nu)}{\mathbf{Pr}(D_{\mathcal{P}}=\nu)} \geq 1 - \varepsilon$ for all $\nu \in \mathcal{V}_{\text{good}}$. Then,*

$$\Delta_{\mathcal{A}}(\mathcal{O} \; ; \; \mathcal{P}) \leq \varepsilon + \mathbf{Pr}(D_{\mathcal{P}} \in \mathcal{V}_{\text{bad}}) . \tag{19}$$

For view $\nu = \{(x_1, y_1), \ldots, (x_q, y_q)\}$ consisting of q input/output tuples, we denote by $\mathcal{O} \vdash \nu$ the event that oracle $\mathcal{O}$ satisfies that $\mathcal{O}(x_i) = y_i$ for all $i = \{1, \ldots, q\}$.

The remainder of the proof is structured as follows. We specify the views of an adversary in Sect. A.1 and define the bad views in Sect. A.2. The probability of bad views is analyzed in Sect. A.3 and the probability ratio for good views is considered in Sect. A.4. Section A.5 concludes the proof.

A.1   Views

The adversary can make q construction queries to $(\widetilde{\mathsf{E}}^{\mathsf{P}}_{K_j})^{\mu}_{j=1}$ or $(\widetilde{\pi})^{\mu}_{j=1}$, all *in forward direction only*. Each such query is made for user index $j_i \in \{1, \ldots, \mu\}$, some tweak $\bar{a}_i = (a_1, \ldots, a_z)_i$, and message input M_i, and results in an output C_i. The q queries are summarized in a view

$$\nu_c = \{(j_1, \bar{a}_1, M_1, C_1), \ldots, (j_q, \bar{a}_q, M_q, C_q)\} .$$

The adversary can make p primitive queries to $\mathsf{P}^{\pm}$, and these are likewise summarized in a view

$$\nu_p = \{(X_1, Y_1), \ldots, (X_p, Y_p)\} .$$

After the conversation of $\mathcal{A}$ with its oracle, but before it makes its final decision, we reveal the key material used in the interaction. This can be done without loss of generality; it only improves the adversarial success probability. The first values that are revealed are values $K_1, \ldots, K_{\mu}$. In the real world, these are the keys $K_1, \ldots, K_{\mu} \xleftarrow{\$} \{0,1\}^k$ that are actually used by the construction oracle; in the ideal world, these are dummy keys $K_1, \ldots, K_{\mu} \xleftarrow{\$} \{0,1\}^k$. The second values that are revealed are values $L_1, \ldots, L_{\mu} \in \{0,1\}^n$. In the real world, these are the values $L_j = \mathsf{P}(K_j \| 0^{n-k})$ for $j = 1, \ldots, \mu$; in the ideal world, these are dummy keys $L_1, \ldots, L_{\mu} \xleftarrow{\$} \{0,1\}^n$.[3] The revealed data is summarized in a view

$$\nu_k = \{(K_1, L_1), \ldots, (K_{\mu}, L_{\mu})\}.$$

(Note that in the single-user setting, where $\mu = 1$, ν_k is a singleton.) The complete view is defined as $\nu = (\nu_c, \nu_p, \nu_k)$. We assume that the adversary never makes any duplicate query, hence ν_c and ν_p contain no duplicate elements.

---

[3] In the original analysis of MEM [20] (that was about single-user security only), the mask involves a computation $\mathsf{P}(K \| N)$ for nonce N. This not only complicates the values that have to be revealed; it also results in a larger view and hence a higher collision probability among tuples in the view.

A.2   Definition of Good and Bad Views

In the real world, all tuples in ν_p define exactly one input-output pair for P. Likewise, the tuples in ν_k are input-output pairs for P. Using these tuples, one can observe that any tuple $(j_i, \bar{a}_i, M_i, C_i) \in \nu_c$ also defines an input-output pair for P, namely

$$\left(M_i \oplus \bar{\varphi}^{\bar{a}_i}(L_{j_i}), C_i \oplus \bar{\varphi}^{\bar{a}_i}(L_{j_i}) \right),$$

see (7), where we define $\bar{\varphi}^{\bar{a}_i} := \varphi_z^{a_{zi}} \circ \cdots \circ \varphi_1^{a_{1i}}$ for brevity. If among all these $q + p + \mu$ input-output pairs defined by ν, there are two that have colliding input or output values, we consider ν to be a bad view. Formally, ν is called "bad" if one of the following conditions is satisfied, where we recall that the user index j in a tuple in ν_c determines which key tuple from ν_k has to be used:

$$\begin{aligned}
\mathrm{bad}_{c,c} : \ &\text{for some distinct } (j, \bar{a}, M, C), (j', \bar{a}', M', C') \in \nu_c: \\
&\bar{\varphi}^{\bar{a}}(L_j) \oplus \bar{\varphi}^{\bar{a}'}(L_{j'}) \in \{M \oplus M', C \oplus C'\}, \\
\mathrm{bad}_{c,p} : \ &\text{for some } (j, \bar{a}, M, C) \in \nu_c \text{ and } (X, Y) \in \nu_p: \\
&\bar{\varphi}^{\bar{a}}(L_j) \in \{M \oplus X, C \oplus Y\}, \\
\mathrm{bad}_{c,k} : \ &\text{for some } (j, \bar{a}, M, C) \in \nu_c \text{ and } (K, L) \in \nu_k: \\
&\bar{\varphi}^{\bar{a}}(L_j) \in \{M \oplus K \| 0^{n-k}, C \oplus L\}, \\
\mathrm{bad}_{p,k} : \ &\text{for some } (X, Y) \in \nu_p \text{ and } (K, L) \in \nu_k: \\
&X = K \| 0^{n-k} \text{ or } Y = L, \\
\mathrm{bad}_{k,k} : \ &\text{for some distinct } (K, L), (K', L') \in \nu_k: \\
&K = K' \text{ or } L = L'.
\end{aligned}$$

We write $\mathrm{bad} = \mathrm{bad}_{c,c} \vee \mathrm{bad}_{c,p} \vee \mathrm{bad}_{c,k} \vee \mathrm{bad}_{p,k} \vee \mathrm{bad}_{k,k}$.

The definition of bad events differs from the single-user analysis of Beyne et al. [9] in the adjustment of bad events $\mathrm{bad}_{c,k}$ and $\mathrm{bad}_{p,k}$ and the addition of the bad event $\mathrm{bad}_{k,k}$. The events $\mathrm{bad}_{c,k}$ and $\mathrm{bad}_{p,k}$ have been adjusted as construction or permutation queries may now collide with μ different key tuples. The addition of the new bad event $\mathrm{bad}_{k,k}$ come from the fact that different key tuples might collide.

A.3   Probability of Bad View in Ideal World

Our goal is to bound $\mathbf{Pr}\,(D_{\mathcal{P}} \in \mathcal{V}_{\mathrm{bad}})$, the probability of a bad view in the ideal world $\mathcal{P} = ((\tilde{\pi}_j)_{j=1}^{\mu}, \mathsf{P}^{\pm})$. For brevity, denote by $D_{\mathcal{P}} \propto \mathrm{bad}$ the event that $D_{\mathcal{P}}$ satisfies bad. By the union bound,

$$\begin{aligned}
\mathbf{Pr}\,(D_{\mathcal{P}} \propto \mathrm{bad}) &= \mathbf{Pr}\,(D_{\mathcal{P}} \propto \mathrm{bad}_{c,c} \vee \mathrm{bad}_{c,p} \vee \mathrm{bad}_{c,k} \vee \mathrm{bad}_{p,k} \vee \mathrm{bad}_{k,k}) \\
&\leq \mathbf{Pr}\,(D_{\mathcal{P}} \propto \mathrm{bad}_{c,c}) + \mathbf{Pr}\,(D_{\mathcal{P}} \propto \mathrm{bad}_{c,p}) + \mathbf{Pr}\,(D_{\mathcal{P}} \propto \mathrm{bad}_{c,k}) \\
&\quad + \mathbf{Pr}\,(D_{\mathcal{P}} \propto \mathrm{bad}_{p,k}) + \mathbf{Pr}\,(D_{\mathcal{P}} \propto \mathrm{bad}_{k,k}). \quad (20)
\end{aligned}$$

We will analyze the five probabilities separately, thereby noticing that (i) K_1, $\ldots, K_\mu \xleftarrow{\$} \{0,1\}^k$ and $L_1, \ldots, L_\mu \xleftarrow{\$} \{0,1\}^n$ are random variables in the ideal world, and (ii) as the adversary only makes forward construction queries, each tuple $(j, \bar{a}, M, C) \in \nu_c$ satisfies that C is randomly drawn from a set of size at least $2^n - q$.

Event $\mathrm{bad}_{c,c}$. For $\mathrm{bad}_{c,c}$, let $(j, \bar{a}, M, C), (j', \bar{a}', M', C') \in \nu_c$ be any two distinct tuples. If $j = j'$ and $\bar{a} = \bar{a}'$, then necessarily $M \neq M'$ and $C \neq C'$, and $\mathrm{bad}_{c,c}$ holds with probability 0. Otherwise, if $j = j'$ but $\bar{a} \neq \bar{a}'$, we can deduce from $2^{-\alpha}$-properness of $\mathcal{T}$, namely property 2 of Definition 1, that event $\mathrm{bad}_{c,c}$ holds with probability at most $2/2^\alpha$. Finally, if $j \neq j'$, the subkeys $L_j, L_{j'}$ are independent and we can likewise deduce from $2^{-\alpha}$-properness of $\mathcal{T}$, namely property 1 of Definition 1, that event $\mathrm{bad}_{c,c}$ holds with probability at most $2/2^\alpha$. Thus, summing over all $\binom{q}{2}$ possible choices of queries,

$$\mathbf{Pr}\left(D_\mathcal{P} \propto \mathrm{bad}_{c,c}\right) \leq \frac{q(q-1)}{2^\alpha}.$$

Event $\mathrm{bad}_{c,p}$. For $\mathrm{bad}_{c,p}$, let $(j, \bar{a}, M, C) \in \nu_c$ and $(X, Y) \in \nu_p$ be any two tuples. We can deduce from $2^{-\alpha}$-properness of $\mathcal{T}$, namely property 1 of Definition 1, that event $\mathrm{bad}_{c,p}$ holds with probability at most $2/2^\alpha$. Thus, summing over all qp possible choices of queries,

$$\mathbf{Pr}\left(D_\mathcal{P} \propto \mathrm{bad}_{c,p}\right) \leq \frac{2qp}{2^\alpha}.$$

Event $\mathrm{bad}_{c,k}$. For $\mathrm{bad}_{c,k}$, let $(j, \bar{a}, M, C) \in \nu_c$ and $(K, L) \in \nu_k$ be any two tuples. We consider the two equations of $\mathrm{bad}_{c,k}$ separately. For the first equation,

$$\bar{\varphi}^{\bar{a}}(L_j) = M \oplus K \| 0^{n-k},$$

we will use that $L_j \xleftarrow{\$} \{0,1\}^n$ is a randomly generated value independent of K. We can deduce from $2^{-\alpha}$-properness of $\mathcal{T}$, namely property 1 of Definition 1, that this equation holds with probability at most $1/2^\alpha$.

For the second equation,

$$\bar{\varphi}^{\bar{a}}(L_j) = C \oplus L,$$

it might be that $L = L_j$, and we cannot rely on Definition 1. Instead, we will use that all construction queries are made in the forward direction, and that C is randomly drawn from a set of size at least $2^n - q$ elements. The above equation thus holds with probability at most $1/(2^n - q)$.

Thus, summing over all μq possible choices of queries,

$$\mathbf{Pr}\left(D_\mathcal{P} \propto \mathrm{bad}_{c,k}\right) \leq \frac{\mu q}{2^\alpha} + \frac{\mu q}{2^n - q}.$$

Event $\mathrm{bad}_{p,k}$. For $\mathrm{bad}_{p,k}$, let $(X, Y) \in \nu_p$ and $(K, L) \in \nu_k$ be any two tuples. As $K \xleftarrow{\$} \{0,1\}^k$ and $L \xleftarrow{\$} \{0,1\}^n$, the tuples set $\mathrm{bad}_{p,k}$ with probability at most $1/2^k + 1/2^n$. Thus, summing over all μp possible choices of queries,

$$\mathbf{Pr}\left(D_{\mathcal{P}} \propto \mathrm{bad}_{p,k}\right) \leq \frac{\mu p}{2^k} + \frac{\mu p}{2^n}.$$

Event $\mathrm{bad}_{k,k}$. For $\mathrm{bad}_{k,k}$, let $(K, L), (K', L') \in \nu_k$ be any two distinct tuples. As $K, K' \xleftarrow{\$} \{0,1\}^k$ and $L, L' \xleftarrow{\$} \{0,1\}^n$, the tuples set $\mathrm{bad}_{k,k}$ with probability at most $1/2^k + 1/2^n$. Thus, summing over all $\binom{\mu}{2}$ possible choices of queries,

$$\mathbf{Pr}\left(D_{\mathcal{P}} \propto \mathrm{bad}_{k,k}\right) \leq \frac{\mu(\mu - 1)}{2^{k+1}} + \frac{\mu(\mu - 1)}{2^{n+1}}.$$

Conclusion. Concluding, we obtain for (20):

$$\mathbf{Pr}\left(D_{\mathcal{P}} \propto \mathrm{bad}\right) \leq \frac{q^2 + 2qp + (\mu - 1)q}{2^\alpha} + \frac{\mu \cdot (2q + p + \frac{\mu-1}{2})}{2^n} + \frac{\mu \cdot (p + \frac{\mu-1}{2})}{2^k}, \tag{21}$$

using that $2^n - q \geq 2^{n-1}$.

A.4   Probability Ratio for Good Views

Consider any good view $\nu \in \mathcal{V}_{\mathrm{good}}$. We will prove the inequality $\mathbf{Pr}\left(D_{\mathcal{O}} = \nu\right) \geq \mathbf{Pr}\left(D_{\mathcal{P}} = \nu\right)$. The proof is a direct generalization of that of Granger et al. [20], noting that in our case, we consider multi-user security. The proof is included for completeness.

Real World. In the real world $\mathcal{O} = ((\widetilde{\mathsf{E}}^{\mathsf{P}}_{K_j})^\mu_{j=1}, \mathsf{P}^\pm)$, goodness of the view means that $\nu = (\nu_c, \nu_p, \nu_k)$ defines exactly $q + p + \mu$ input-output pairs for P, and no two of them collide on the input or output, and ν_k consists of random values $K_1, \ldots, K_\mu \xleftarrow{\$} \{0,1\}^k$. Therefore, we obtain:

$$\mathbf{Pr}\left(D_{\mathcal{O}} = \nu\right) = \mathbf{Pr}\left(K'_1, \ldots, K'_\mu \xleftarrow{\$} \{0,1\}^k \; : \; K'_1 = K_1 \wedge \cdots \wedge K'_\mu = K_\mu\right) \cdot$$

$$\mathbf{Pr}\left(\mathsf{P} \xleftarrow{\$} \mathrm{perm}(n) \; : \; (\widetilde{\mathsf{E}}^{\mathsf{P}}_{K_j})^\mu_{j=1} \vdash \nu_c \wedge \mathsf{P} \vdash \nu_p \wedge \mathsf{P} \vdash \nu_k\right)$$

$$= \frac{1}{2^{k\mu}} \cdot \frac{(2^n - (q + p + \mu))!}{2^n!}. \tag{22}$$

Ideal World. In the ideal world $\mathcal{P} = ((\widetilde{\pi}_j)^\mu_{j=1}, \mathsf{P}^\pm)$, the view $\nu = (\nu_c, \nu_p, \nu_k)$ consists of three lists of independent tuples: ν_c defines exactly q input-output pairs for $\widetilde{\pi}_j$, ν_p defines exactly p input-output pairs for P, and ν_k consists of μ random tuples $(K_1, L_1), \ldots, (K_\mu, L_\mu) \xleftarrow{\$} \{0,1\}^k \times \{0,1\}^n$. For counting, it is convenient to group the tuples in ν_c depending on the user index j and tweak value $\bar{a}$. For $J \in \{1, \ldots, \mu\}$ and $T \in \mathcal{T}$, define

$$q_{J,T} = |\{(j, \bar{a}, M, C) \in \nu_c \mid j = J \wedge \bar{a} = T\}|,$$

where $\sum_{(J,T) \in \{1,\ldots,\mu\} \times \mathcal{T}} q_{J,T} = q$. We obtain:

$$
\begin{aligned}
\mathbf{Pr}\left(D_{\mathcal{P}} = \nu\right) &= \mathbf{Pr}\left(K_1', \ldots, K_\mu' \xleftarrow{\$} \{0,1\}^k \ : \ K_1' = K_1 \wedge \cdots \wedge K_\mu' = K_\mu\right) \cdot \\
&\quad \mathbf{Pr}\left(L_1', \ldots, L_\mu' \xleftarrow{\$} \{0,1\}^n \ : \ L_1' = L_1 \wedge \cdots \wedge L_\mu' = L_\mu\right) \cdot \\
&\quad \mathbf{Pr}\left(\tilde{\pi}_1, \ldots, \tilde{\pi}_\mu \xleftarrow{\$} \mathrm{perm}(\mathcal{T}, n) \ : \ (\tilde{\pi}_j)_{j=1}^\mu \vdash \nu_c\right) \cdot \\
&\quad \mathbf{Pr}\left(\mathsf{P} \xleftarrow{\$} \mathrm{perm}(n) \ : \ \mathsf{P} \vdash \nu_p\right) \\
&= \frac{1}{2^{(k+n)\mu}} \cdot \prod_{\substack{J \in \{1,\ldots,\mu\} \\ T \in \mathcal{T}}} \frac{(2^n - q_{J,T})!}{2^n!} \cdot \frac{(2^n - p)!}{2^n!} \\
&= \frac{1}{2^{k\mu}} \cdot \left(\frac{(2^n - 1)!}{2^n!}\right)^\mu \cdot \prod_{\substack{J \in \{1,\ldots,\mu\} \\ T \in \mathcal{T}}} \frac{(2^n - q_{J,T})!}{2^n!} \cdot \frac{(2^n - p)!}{2^n!} \\
&\leq \frac{1}{2^{k\mu}} \cdot \frac{(2^n - (q + p + \mu))!}{2^n!}, \tag{23}
\end{aligned}
$$

using that for any $\sigma + \tau \leq 2^n$ we have $\frac{(2^n - \sigma)!}{2^n!} \cdot \frac{(2^n - \tau)!}{2^n!} \leq \frac{(2^n - (\sigma + \tau))!}{2^n!}$.

Conclusion. Combining (22) and (23), we obtain that for any good view $\nu \in \mathcal{V}_{\mathrm{good}}$:

$$\frac{\mathbf{Pr}\left(D_{\mathcal{O}} = \nu\right)}{\mathbf{Pr}\left(D_{\mathcal{P}} = \nu\right)} \geq 1. \tag{24}$$

A.5   Conclusion

By the H-coefficient technique (Lemma 1), we directly obtain from (21) and (24):

$$\mathbf{Adv}_{\tilde{\mathsf{E}}}^{\mu\text{-tprp}}(\mathcal{A}) \leq 0 + \frac{q^2 + 2qp + (\mu - 1)q}{2^\alpha} + \frac{\mu \cdot (2q + p + \frac{\mu-1}{2})}{2^n} + \frac{\mu \cdot (p + \frac{\mu-1}{2})}{2^k}.$$

References

1. Banik, S., et al.: GIFT-COFB v1.1. submission to NIST Lightweight Cryptography (2021)
2. Beierle, C., et al.: Schwaemm and Esch: lightweight authenticated encryption and hashing using the sparkle permutation family. Submission to NIST Lightweight Cryptography (2021)
3. Beierle, C., et al.: Lightweight AEAD and hashing using the sparkle permutation family. IACR Trans. Symmetric Cryptol. **2020**(S1), 208–261 (2020)
4. Bellare, M., Boldyreva, A., Micali, S.: Public-key encryption in a multi-user setting: security proofs and improvements. In: Preneel, B. (ed.) EUROCRYPT 2000. LNCS, vol. 1807, pp. 259–274. Springer, Heidelberg (2000). https://doi.org/10.1007/3-540-45539-6_18
5. Bellare, M., Tackmann, B.: The multi-user security of authenticated encryption: AES-GCM in TLS 1.3. In: Robshaw, M., Katz, J. (eds.) CRYPTO 2016. LNCS, vol. 9814, pp. 247–276. Springer, Heidelberg (2016). https://doi.org/10.1007/978-3-662-53018-4_10
6. Bernstein, D.J.: How to stretch random functions: the security of protected counter sums. J. Cryptol. **12**(3), 185–192 (1999)
7. Bernstein, D.J.: Stronger security bounds for Wegman-Carter-Shoup authenticators. In: Cramer, R. (ed.) EUROCRYPT 2005. LNCS, vol. 3494, pp. 164–180. Springer, Heidelberg (2005). https://doi.org/10.1007/11426639_10
8. Beyne, T., Chen, Y.L., Dobraunig, C., Mennink, B.: Elephant v1.1. Submission to NIST Lightweight Cryptography (2019)
9. Beyne, T., Chen, Y.L., Dobraunig, C., Mennink, B.: Dumbo, Jumbo, and Delirium: parallel authenticated encryption for the lightweight circus. IACR Trans. Symmetric Cryptol. **2020**(S1), 5–30 (2020)
10. Beyne, T., Chen, Y.L., Dobraunig, C., Mennink, B.: Status update on Elephant. Note at NIST Lightweight Cryptography (2020)
11. Beyne, T., Chen, Y.L., Dobraunig, C., Mennink, B.: Elephant v2. Submission to NIST Lightweight Cryptography (2021)
12. Biham, E.: How to decrypt or even substitute DES-encrypted messages in 2^{28} steps. Inf. Process. Lett. **84**(3), 117–124 (2002)
13. Chen, S., Steinberger, J.P.: Tight security bounds for key-alternating ciphers. In: Nguyen and Oswald [25], pp. 327–350
14. Daemen, J., Hoffert, S., Peeters, M., Van Assche, G., Van Keer, R.: Xoodyak, a lightweight cryptographic scheme. IACR Trans. Symmetric Cryptol. **2020**(S1), 60–87 (2020)
15. Daemen, J., Hoffert, S., Peeters, M., Van Assche, G., Van Keer, R., Mella, S.: Xoodyak, a lightweight cryptographic scheme. Submission to NIST Lightweight Cryptography (2021)
16. Daemen, J., Mennink, B., Van Assche, G.: Full-state keyed duplex with built-in multi-user support. In: Takagi, T., Peyrin, T. (eds.) ASIACRYPT 2017. LNCS, vol. 10625, pp. 606–637. Springer, Cham (2017). https://doi.org/10.1007/978-3-319-70697-9_21
17. Dobraunig, C., et al.: ISAP v2.0. IACR Trans. Symmetric Cryptol. **2020**(S1), 390–416 (2020)
18. Dobraunig, C., et al.: ISAP v2. Submission to NIST Lightweight Cryptography (2021)

19. Dobraunig, C., Eichlseder, M., Mendel, F., Schläffer, M.: Ascon v1.2. Submission to NIST Lightweight Cryptography (2021)
20. Granger, R., Jovanovic, P., Mennink, B., Neves, S.: Improved masking for tweakable blockciphers with applications to authenticated encryption. In: Fischlin, M., Coron, J.-S. (eds.) EUROCRYPT 2016, Part I. LNCS, vol. 9665, pp. 263–293. Springer, Heidelberg (2016). https://doi.org/10.1007/978-3-662-49890-3_11
21. Khairallah, M.: Weak keys in the rekeying paradigm: application to COMET and mixFeed. IACR Trans. Symmetric Cryptol. **2019**(4), 272–289 (2019)
22. Luykx, A., Mennink, B., Paterson, K.G.: Analyzing multi-key security degradation. In: Takagi, T., Peyrin, T. (eds.) ASIACRYPT 2017, Part II. LNCS, vol. 10625, pp. 575–605. Springer, Cham (2017). https://doi.org/10.1007/978-3-319-70697-9_20
23. Luykx, A., Preneel, B., Tischhauser, E., Yasuda, K.: A MAC mode for lightweight block ciphers. In: Peyrin, T. (ed.) FSE 2016. LNCS, vol. 9783, pp. 43–59. Springer, Heidelberg (2016). https://doi.org/10.1007/978-3-662-52993-5_3
24. Namprempre, C., Rogaway, P., Shrimpton, T.: Reconsidering Generic Composition. In: Nguyen and Oswald [25], pp. 257–274 (2014)
25. Nguyen, P.Q., Oswald, E. (eds.) EUROCRYPT 2014. LNCS, vol. 8441, pp. 257–274. Springer, Heidelberg (2014). https://doi.org/10.1007/978-3-642-55220-5_15
26. NIST: Lightweight Cryptography, February 2019. https://csrc.nist.gov/Projects/Lightweight-Cryptography
27. Patarin, J.: The "coefficients H" technique. In: Avanzi, R.M., Keliher, L., Sica, F. (eds.) SAC 2008. LNCS, vol. 5381, pp. 328–345. Springer, Heidelberg (2009). https://doi.org/10.1007/978-3-642-04159-4_21
28. Shoup, V.: On fast and provably secure message authentication based on universal hashing. In: Koblitz, N. (ed.) CRYPTO 1996. LNCS, vol. 1109, pp. 313–328. Springer, Heidelberg (1996). https://doi.org/10.1007/3-540-68697-5_24
29. Wegman, M.N., Carter, L.: New hash functions and their use in authentication and set equality. J. Comput. Syst. Sci. **22**(3), 265–279 (1981)

Designing S-Boxes Providing Stronger Security Against Differential Cryptanalysis for Ciphers Using Byte-Wise XOR

Yosuke Todo[✉] and Yu Sasaki

NTT Social Informatics Laboratories, Tokyo 180-8585, Japan
{yosuke.todo.xt,yu.sasaki.sk}@hco.ntt.co.jp

Abstract. In this paper, we develop an S-box designing method by considering an interplay between an S-box and a linear layer, which enhances security against differential cryptanalysis. The basic idea can be found in bitslice-friendly ciphers such as Serpent and bit-permutation ciphers such as PRESENT. In those designs, S-boxes were chosen so that the branch number is not too small, which rapidly diffuses differences. We apply a similar analysis to other constructions. The first target is extended generalized Feistel networks (EGFN) and its instance Lilliput, which has an XOR layer after the standard GFN. We show that security of EGFN can be enhanced by using an S-box that does not allow any difference Δ to be mapped to the same Δ with a high probability, say 2^{-2} for a 4-bit S-box. The second target is AES-like ciphers that use a binary matrix in MixColumns. We focus on the chain of differences $\Delta A \to \Delta B \to \Delta C \to \cdots$ over the S-box, where each transition occurs with a high probability. We show that security of such AES-like ciphers can be enhanced if the maximum length of the chains is short. As a proof-of-concept, we evaluate Lilliput, Midori, and SKINNY with the new S-box satisfying the property.

Keywords: S-box · Design · SPN · EGFN · Differential cryptanalysis

1 Introduction

Primitive designers are required to evaluate security against various cryptanalyses, particularly differential cryptanalysis [1,2] and linear cryptanalysis [3,4]. For a block cipher with a substitution-permutation network (SPN), a popular approach is to design an S-box that has a small maximum differential probability (MDP) and a linear layer that ensures a large number of differentially active S-boxes as represented by the wide trail strategy [5]. Let $minAS$ be the minimum number of differentially active S-boxes. Then, the probability to satisfy any differential characteristic is upper-bounded by $(MDP)^{minAS}$.

An advantage of this method is simplicity. It enables to search for an S-box and a linear layer independently. A disadvantage is that an effect derived by an

© The Author(s), under exclusive license to Springer Nature Switzerland AG 2022
R. AlTawy and A. Hülsing (Eds.): SAC 2021, LNCS 13203, pp. 179–199, 2022.
https://doi.org/10.1007/978-3-030-99277-4_9

interplay between the S-box and the linear layer can be overlooked. Our goal is to develop an S-box-designing method that takes into account such an interplay.

Bitslice-Friendly Ciphers and SbPN Ciphers. The interplay between the S-box and the linear layers has already been considered for ciphers in which one block computation can be processed efficiently in a bitslice manner such as Serpent [6], Noekeon [7], LS-designs [8], and Rectangle [9]. In those designs, an internal state is divided into several slices, then a linear function is applied for each slice and an S-box is applied over multiple slices. To increase security, the following (4-bit) S-box criteria were introduced.

A) S-box differential branch number of 3
B) MDP of 2^{-2} (best possible for 4-bit S-box)

The differential branch number of an S-box S is the minimum value of $hw(x \oplus y) + hw(S(x) \oplus S(y))$ for any distinct x and y, where hw is the Hamming weight.

PRESENT [10] adopts the SPN structure where the linear layer is a simple bit-permutation. We denote ciphers with this structure by "SbPN ciphers." Both criteria A and B are important for SbPN ciphers. In fact, the PRESENT S-box was designed to satisfy both. After a while, two SbPN ciphers GIFT [11] and TRIFLE-BC [12] refined those criteria. In TRIFLE-BC, criterion A was relaxed: an input difference of weight 1 can propagate to an output difference of weight 1 if its probability is 2^{-3}. [1] GIFT relaxed both criteria A and B. First, MDP of the S-box is $2^{-1.4}$, while GIFT ensures $hw(x \oplus y) + hw(S(x) \oplus S(y)) \geq 4$ for any differential transitions with probability 2^{-2} or higher. Second, GIFT introduced a new criterion called BOGI. In short, it classifies the bit positions into good or bad depending on whether a single-bit difference on this bit can propagate with probability 2^{-2} or not. Then, the bit-permutation is chosen to map bad outputs (BO) to good inputs (GI).

To sum up, the branch number of the S-box is important for bitslice-friendly and SbPN ciphers to increase the number of active S-boxes. GIFT and TRIFLE-BC considered the interplay between the S-box and the linear layer, particularly by forcing a small probability for differential transitions with a small weight.

Challenges for Other Constructions. To the best of our knowledge, other constructions do not use S-boxes that are considered the interplay with the linear layer. One reason is that important S-box criteria, corresponding to the branch number for the bitslice-friendly and the SbPN ciphers, are non-trivial for other linear layers. In fact, for AES, it is difficult to exploit the property of the linear layer to give a more accurate evaluation than $(MDP)^{minAS}$.

1.1 Our Contributions

In this paper, we tackle the above-mentioned challenge[2]. We first identify input and output differences of the linear layer that result in a small number of active

---

[1] Unfortunately, the choices of the S-box and the bit-permutation of TRIFLE-BC derived a bad interplay, which resulted in an efficient attack [13,14].

[2] In this paper, we mainly focus on differential cryptanalysis. The same idea can be applied to linear cryptanalysis, and we will discuss it in Sect. 5.

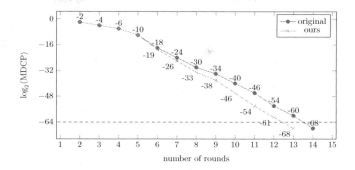

Fig. 1. Results of Lilliput

S-boxes. We then design an S-box so that the identified differences for the linear layer cannot be satisfied with a high probability. In such a manner, we reveal a property of an S-box that is imposed by a linear layer. For convenience, we call the property "attention-required property (ARP)" in this paper.

The goal of this paper is to design S-boxes by taking into account the ARP of the linear layer for several ciphers other than the bitslice-friendly and the SbPN ciphers. We search for S-boxes for several existing schemes and show that the resistance against differential cryptanalysis can be improved by replacing the existing S-box with new ones.

Extended Generalized Feistel Network. We start our discussion from an extended generalized Feistel network (EGFN) proposed at SAC2013 [15] because this is a typical example where the interplay between the S-box and linear layers can significantly increase the resistance against differential cryptanalysis.

We observe that the differential characteristic probability of Lilliput tends to be high when the S-box has identity-differential transition, i.e. an input difference Δ is mapped to the same difference Δ via active S-boxes. In fact, Lilliput's S-box maps the difference 0x6 to 0x6 with probability 2^{-2} and this appears many times in the best differential characteristic. From this observation, we define that the ARP of Lilliput is identity-differential transitions with MDP. Then, we modify Lilliput's S-box so that any identity-differential transition occurs with probability 2^{-3}. To confirm the impact of our modification, we evaluate the maximum differential characteristic probability with the new S-box. We show that the number of rounds to guarantee 2^{-64} is reduced by 1 round as shown in Fig. 1. Note that the new S-box is obtained only by swapping the LSB and the second LSB of the original S-box, thus implementation overhead is negligible.

AES-bMC Ciphers. Our next target is AES-like ciphers in which MixColumns applies the multiplication by a binary matrix. We call such ciphers "AES-bMC ciphers." AES-bMC ciphers are popular for lightweight cryptography. Midori [16], SKINNY [17], MANTIS [17], and CRAFT [18] are examples of AES-bMC Ciphers.

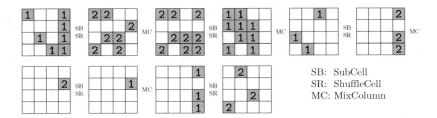

Fig. 2. Best differential characteristic for 5-round Midori64. Numbers in gray cells represent the difference in the hexadecimal, and there are no differences in white cells.

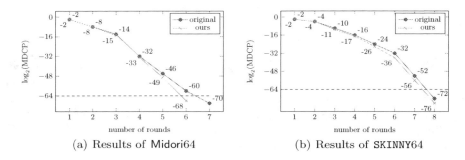

(a) Results of Midori64   (b) Results of SKINNY64

Fig. 3. Results of Midori64 and SKINNY64

We observe that the ARP of the AES-bMC ciphers is completely different from that of the EGFN. As an example, Fig. 2 shows the best differential characteristic for 5-round Midori64. The 1st round uses differential transitions 0x1 → 0x2 with MDP, and the 2nd round uses differential transitions 0x2 → 0x1. We call such a chain of differential transitions "high-probability chain ". We define the ARP of AES-bMC ciphers as the maximum length of the high-probability chain. Then, we observe that the differential characteristic probability can be lowered by choosing an S-box that only allows short high-probability chains.

We then need to find S-boxes that satisfy the ARP. Regarding 4-bit S-boxes, we can exhaustively check all S-boxes belonging to the 16 classes available in the previous works [19, 20]. As a result, we find S-boxes where the maximum length of the high-probability chain is the shortest of S-boxes belonging to the 16 classes.

To demonstrate the effect, we replaced the original S-boxes of Midori64 and SKINNY64 with our S-box without modifying their diffusion parts. Figure 3 shows comparisons of their maximum differential characteristic probabilities (MDCPs). Our S-box reduces the number of rounds to reach 2^{-64} by one for Midori64.

Regarding 8-bit S-boxes, exhaustive check is impossible and we need to reduce the search space by introducing some heuristic. In the appendix, we show a SKINNY-like S-box whose high-probability chain is at most 2. The comparison of the MDCP with the new S-box and SKINNY128 is shown in the full version of this paper.

2 Preliminaries

2.1 Basic Knowledge About S-Boxes

The differential probability between input difference Δ_{in} and output difference Δ_{out} of an S-box S is expressed as

$$DP_S[\Delta_{in}, \Delta_{out}] = \frac{\#\{x \in \{0,1\}^n | S(x) \oplus S(x \oplus \Delta_{in}) = \Delta_{out}\}}{2^n}.$$

Let MDP be the maximum probability of DP_S for all possible pairs of $(\Delta_{in}, \Delta_{out})$ excluding $(\Delta_{in}, \Delta_{out}) = (0,0)$. The smaller the MDP, the more secure an S-box is against differential cryptanalysis. Therefore, many cryptographers have studied the design methods of such S-boxes [21,22]. When n is odd, S-boxes whose MDP is 2^{-n+1} can be designed [21]. However, the problem is generally open when n is even. Only for $n = 6$, an S-box whose MDP is 2^{-5} is known [22].

The affine-equivalent class is useful to understand the property of S-boxes.

Definition 1. *Let M_{in} and M_{out} be two invertible matrices and c_{in} and c_{out} be two vectors. Then, the S-box S' defined by two affine transformations as*

$$S'(x) = M_{out} \times S(M_{in} \times x \oplus c_{in}) \oplus c_{out}$$

is affine equivalent with the S-box S.

c_{in} and c_{out} do not affect the differential probability. Moreover, $DP_{S'}[\Delta_{in}, \Delta_{out}]$ is equal to $DP_S[M_{in} \times \Delta_{in}, M_{out}^{-1} \times \Delta_{out}]$. Therefore, the affine-equivalent S-box preserves not only the MDP but also the frequency that each probability appears because M_{in} and M_{out} are invertible.

Cryptographers' main interest is 8-bit and 4-bit S-boxes, where 8-bit S-boxes are widely applied to various block ciphers such as AES [23] and 4-bit S-boxes are applied to many lightweight block ciphers. It was already proven by exhaustive analysis that the best possible 4-bit S-box has an MDP of 2^{-2} [19,24]. The number of 4-bit S-boxes is $2^4! \approx 2^{44.25}$, but the number of affine-inequivalent S-boxes is 302 [20]. Among them, 16 classes also achieve the highest security against linear cryptanalysis [19,20].

A differential branch number of S-boxes is also one of the well-known design criteria. It is commonly used in bitslice-friendly ciphers such as Serpent [6] or SbPN ciphers such as PRESENT [10]. Note that the branch number of S-boxes is not useful for block ciphers whose linear layer consists of byte-wise XOR such as SKINNY or Midori, which are the main focus in our paper, because it never divides the output of one S-box into each bit.

2.2   Basic Knowledge About Linear Layers

Some ciphers adopt a multiplication with a matrix to diffuse outputs of several S-boxes. Let $M \in (\mathbb{F}_{2^n})^{m \times m}$ be a diffusion matrix, and m outputs of n-bit S-boxes denoted as $x \in (\mathbb{F}_{2^n})^m$ are diffused as $y = M \times x$. We say that the branch number of M is d when the sum of input and output non-zero n-bit differences is at least d for any non-zero Δx.

In this paper, we focus on the linear layer consisting of byte-wise XOR, i.e., entries of M are 0 or 1. Such a matrix is often used to design lightweight block ciphers [16–18]. For example, Midori diffuses four bytes as

$$
\begin{pmatrix} y_0 \\ y_1 \\ y_2 \\ y_3 \end{pmatrix} = \begin{pmatrix} 0\ 1\ 1\ 1 \\ 1\ 0\ 1\ 1 \\ 1\ 1\ 0\ 1 \\ 1\ 1\ 1\ 0 \end{pmatrix} \times \begin{pmatrix} x_0 \\ x_1 \\ x_2 \\ x_3 \end{pmatrix} = \begin{pmatrix} x_1 \oplus x_2 \oplus x_3 \\ x_0 \oplus x_2 \oplus x_3 \\ x_0 \oplus x_1 \oplus x_3 \\ x_0 \oplus x_1 \oplus x_2 \end{pmatrix},
$$

and the branch number of this matrix is 4. We call such a matrix binary matrix.

2.3   Differential Characteristics and Their Probabilities

We often evaluate differential characteristics and their probabilities. Block cipher E_k is composed of an iteration of round functions as $E_k := F_r \circ \cdots \circ F_1$. The probability of a differential characteristic denoted as $(\Delta_0, \Delta_1, \ldots, \Delta_r)$ is defined as $\prod_{i=1}^{r} DP_{F_i}[\Delta_{i-1}, \Delta_i]$. Designers of block ciphers must guarantee that the *maximum differential characteristic probability (MDCP)* will be sufficiently low so that attackers cannot distinguish the cipher from an ideal one.

The so-called "differential" is used to consider multiple differential characteristics with fixed Δ_0 and Δ_r. If there are multiple differential characteristics from Δ_0 to Δ_r, the total probability is the sum of them. We call this the *differential effect* to avoid confusion.

2.4   How to Search for the Best Differential Characteristic

There are many known techniques to search for the differential characteristic with the MDCP, i.e., the best differential characteristic. One of the most famous methods is the so-called branch-and-bound algorithm [4], which was used to show the best differential and linear characteristics on DES.

After the proposal of the MILP-based method by Mouha et al. [25], the recent trend is turning to the method aided by solvers such as MILP, SAT, or CP. The method by Mouha et al. can show the lower bound of the number of active S-boxes but it does not always give the tight bound. Namely, found characteristics are not always used for attacks directly. Sun et al. [26,27] proposed a rigorous algorithm to search for the differential characteristics with consideration of differential transitions of active S-boxes. It enables us to show the tight bound of the minimum number of active S-boxes. On the other hand, the differential characteristic with the minimum number of active S-boxes does not always yield the best differential characteristic. Evaluating differential characteristic probability is also important. They also showed how to evaluate the differential characteristic probability rather than the number of active S-boxes, but it was not efficient. A more practical algorithm was shown in [28]. They decomposed a differential distribution table (DDT) into several tables for every probability and constraints are generated for every table. This method allows us to evaluate the MDCP for given ciphers.

The focus of our paper is to design S-boxes lowering differential characteristic probability. After designing such S-boxes, to demonstrate the effect, we replace the original S-boxes of Lilliput, SKINNY, and Midori64 with ours, and re-evaluate the MDCP by using the method shown in [28].

3   Designing S-Boxes Suited for EGFN

The upper bound $(MDP)^{minAS}$ can be tight only when the probability of the differential transition is MDP in all active S-boxes. However, the choice of differential transitions with MDP is limited.

Therefore, when differential characteristics with $minAS$ (and close to $minAS$) always involve low-probability transitions in active S-boxes as many as possible, the MDCP can be lower than $(MDP)^{minAS}$.

We start concrete discussion from the extended generalized Feistel network (EGFN). It is an easy example to demonstrate why considering high- and low-probability transitions are significant.

3.1   Extended Generalized Feistel Network

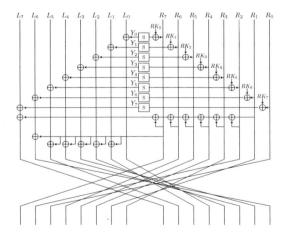

Fig. 4. Round function of Lilliput

An EGFN, which was proposed in [15], is an extension of the block-shuffle generalized Feistel network [29]. It has an additional linear layer to diffuse active bytes more quickly. Later, Lilliput was proposed as a concrete substantiation of the EGFN in [30]. Figure 4 shows the round function, where there is the additional linear layer between the S-box layer and the permutation layer.

Table 1. The maximum differential characteristic probability of Lilliput. The experiment continued until the number of rounds when the probability is lower than 2^{-64}.

# of rounds		8	9	10	11	12	13	14
	$minAS$ [31]	15	17	19	22	24	25	28
Original	MDCP	2^{-30}	2^{-34}	2^{-40}	2^{-46}	2^{-54}	2^{-60}	2^{-68}
S-box	AS	15	17	20	23	27	30	34
Modified	MDCP	2^{-33}	2^{-38}	2^{-46}	2^{-54}	2^{-61}	2^{-68}	–
S-box	AS	15	17	21	25	25	28	–

–AS: The number of active S-boxes in the differential characteristic with MDCP. Remark: this is not the minimum number of active S-boxes. This information is provided for reference only, and the large-or-small about these values are not important.

Our goal is to design an S-box suited to this network, and we show the original S-box of Lilliput as a reference.

$$S = \{0x4, 0x8, 0x7, 0x1, 0x9, 0x3, 0x2, 0xE, 0x0, 0xB, 0x6, 0xF, 0xA, 0x5, 0xD, 0xC\}.$$

Table 1 summarizes the minimum number of active S-boxes and MDCP when the original S-box is used. The minimum number of active S-boxes has been discussed in [31], but the evaluation of the MDCP has not been reported yet. We evaluated the MDCP by using a SAT/SMT solver. As shown in Table 1, differential characteristics with $minAS$ do not lead to the best differential characteristic in 10 rounds and later.

3.2 Identity-Differential Transitions

To reveal the attention-required property (ARP) of this network, we first analyze the condition that differential transitions lead to the best differential characteristic. A notable fact derived from Table 1 is that the minus log base 2 of the probability of the best differential characteristics is always double the number of active S-boxes in the corresponding characteristics. In other words, the best differential characteristics use only transitions with 2^{-2} in all active S-boxes.

Figure 5 shows the DDT of the S-box and the best 13-round differential characteristic. In all active S-boxes, the input and output differences are always 0x6, and all XORes of two active differences are inactive. Here, we observe an interesting property, particularly in the EGFN. Unlike SP networks, the input difference of S-boxes transits to the next round directly. To cancel two active differences

	Δ_{out}															
	0	1	2	3	4	5	6	7	8	9	A	B	C	D	E	F
0	16	0	0	0	0	0	0	0	0	0	0	0	0	0	0	0
1	0	2	0	0	0	0	2	0	0	2	2	2	4	0	0	2
2	0	0	0	2	2	0	2	2	0	4	0	2	0	2	0	0
3	0	2	0	0	0	2	2	2	2	0	0	0	0	2	0	4
4	0	0	0	2	0	0	2	0	0	0	0	2	4	0	2	2
5	0	4	2	2	0	2	0	2	0	2	2	0	0	0	0	0
6	0	0	2	0	0	0	4	2	0	0	2	0	2	2	2	0
7	0	0	0	2	2	2	2	0	2	0	4	0	2	0	0	0
8	0	2	2	4	2	0	2	0	0	0	0	0	0	0	2	2
9	0	0	0	2	0	0	0	2	4	2	0	0	2	0	2	2
A	0	0	2	0	2	0	0	4	2	0	2	2	0	0	0	2
B	0	2	0	0	2	2	0	2	0	0	0	2	2	0	4	0
C	0	2	0	0	2	0	0	0	2	2	2	0	0	4	2	0
D	0	2	4	2	0	0	0	0	2	0	0	2	2	2	0	0
E	0	0	2	0	4	2	0	0	0	2	0	0	2	2	0	2
F	0	0	2	0	0	4	2	0	2	2	0	2	0	0	2	0

round	ΔL	ΔR	ΔY
0	66660600	00000600	00600000
1	06000000	00006606	60660000
2	06600006	66000606	60600066
3	66660000	06006660	06660060
4	06060066	60600000	00000606
5	60006000	06000060	06000060
6	00006060	60600066	66000606
7	60606060	06060060	06006060
8	00006660	06000060	60000060
9	00660000	00006600	00660000
10	06000006	00000000	00000000
11	00000000	00060006	60006000
12	00600600	00000060	06000000
13	00000060	66006006	

Fig. 5. DDT of Lilliput S-box (left) and the best 13-round characteristic (right)

	Δ_{out}															
	0	1	2	3	4	5	6	7	8	9	A	B	C	D	E	F
0	16	0	0	0	0	0	0	0	0	0	0	0	0	0	0	0
1	0	0	2	0	0	2	0	0	0	2	2	2	4	0	0	2
2	0	0	0	0	2	2	2	0	2	0	0	4	2	0	0	2
3	0	0	2	0	0	2	2	2	2	0	0	0	0	0	2	4
4	0	0	0	2	0	0	2	0	0	2	0	4	0	2	2	2
5	0	2	4	2	0	0	2	2	0	2	2	0	0	0	0	0
6	0	2	0	0	0	4	0	2	0	2	0	0	2	2	2	0
7	0	0	0	2	2	2	0	2	4	0	2	0	0	0	0	0
8	0	2	2	4	2	2	0	0	0	0	0	0	0	2	0	2
9	0	0	0	2	0	0	0	2	4	0	2	0	2	2	0	2
A	0	2	0	0	2	0	0	4	2	2	0	2	0	0	0	2
B	0	0	2	0	2	0	2	2	0	0	2	2	4	0	0	0
C	0	0	2	0	2	0	0	0	2	2	2	0	0	2	4	0
D	0	4	2	2	0	0	0	0	2	0	0	2	2	0	2	0
E	0	2	0	0	4	0	2	0	0	0	2	0	2	0	2	2
F	0	2	0	0	0	2	4	0	2	0	2	2	0	2	0	0

round	ΔL	ΔR	ΔY
0	a50eeee4	e0000040	0b000004
1	e0000040	0e000000	00000040
2	000e0000	00000000	00000000
3	00000000	00000e00	00f00000
4	0e000000	ef000000	00000054
5	e00f0000	1eb4eee0	011eddff
6	1e0eb4ee	00efc0c0	0e0eb400
7	0000efcc	00ee0000	0000ef00
8	0000ee00	00cc0000	0000ee00
9	0000cc00	00000000	00000000
10	00000000	0000c0c0	0e0e0000
11	000000cc	00000e0e	40400000
12	0ee00000	a4cc0000	

Fig. 6. DDT of modified S-box (left) and the best 12-round characteristic (right)

by XORing in the additional linear layer, the input difference should transit to the same difference via S-boxes. Thus, we expect that ARP of this network is identity-differential transitions with MDP, such as 0x6 → 0x6 with probability 2^{-2}. Assuming that a replaced S-box has 0x1 → 0x1 as such a transition instead of 0x6 → 0x6, there always exist characteristics whose all non-zero differences are replaced from 0x6 to 0x1. Therefore, avoiding identity-differential transitions with MDP is at least necessary to lower the 13-round differential characteristic probability of Lilliput from the original.

3.3 Replacing S-Box

We now modify the specification of the 4-bit S-box to avoid identity-differential transitions with MDP. To avoid degradation of implementation efficiency, we search for S-boxes belonging to the same bit-permutation equivalent class as the original S-box. The following modified S-box

$$S' = \{\texttt{0x4}, \texttt{0x8}, \texttt{0x7}, \texttt{0x2}, \texttt{0xA}, \texttt{0x3}, \texttt{0x1}, \texttt{0xD}, \texttt{0x0}, \texttt{0xB}, \texttt{0x5}, \texttt{0xF}, \texttt{0x9}, \texttt{0x6}, \texttt{0xE}, \texttt{0xC}\},$$

in which the LSB and the second LSB of the output of the original S-box are swapped, successfully avoids identity-differential transitions with MDP (see Fig. 6).

We finally use a solver-aided method to evaluate the MDCP of Lilliput using the modified S-box to confirm the validity of our replacement. The row labeled "modified" in Table 1 shows the MDCP when the modified S-box is used. The best 12-round differential characteristic is shown in Fig. 6. It is clear that this best differential characteristic is more complicated than the original one in which all non-zero transitions are $\texttt{0x6} \rightarrow \texttt{0x6}$.

We finally stress the impact on this replacement. The probability of the 12-round best differential characteristic is 2^{-61}, which is almost the same as the 13-round MDCP in the original. Besides, the new 13-round MDCP is lower than 2^{-64}. Roughly, the gain of about 1 round can be achieved only by swapping the LSB and the 2nd LSB in the output of the S-box.

4   Designing S-Boxes Suited for AES-bMC Ciphers

Unlike the case of EGFN, avoiding the identity high-probability differential transitions is not significant for the AES-bMC ciphers. We introduce a new S-box design criterion called *high-probability chain* as the ARP for AES-bMC ciphers. We show that using S-boxes with shorter high-probability chain length plays a critical role to lower the MDCP.

4.1   Definition of AES-bMC Ciphers

Intuitively, AES-bMC ciphers are AES-like ciphers that apply a binary matrix during the MixColumns operation. The state of AES-bMC ciphers can be composed of several cells of c bits, typically $c = 4$ or $c = 8$, and cells are arranged in an $n \times m$ 2-dimensional array. For example, $n = m = 4$ and $c = 8$ for SKINNY128 and $n = m = 4$ and $c = 4$ for Midori64. In each round, the AES-bMC ciphers operate the following computations to update the state.

SubCell(SB). A c-bit to c-bit S-box is applied to each cell in the state.
ShuffleCell(SR). Cell positions in each row is permuted.
MixColumn(MC). Each column is multiplied with a binary matrix.
AddRoundKey(AK). A subkey of $n \times m \times c$ bits is XORed to the state.

We regard that all subkeys are different and distributed uniformly at random.

4.2   High-Probability Chain

The strategy to reveal ARP is the same as the case for EGFN. We focus on high-probability transitions of S-boxes and design S-boxes such that characteristics with $minAS$ (and close to $minAS$) become invalid when only the high-probability transitions are used.

The number of active S-boxes of AES-bMC ciphers can be small when output differences from two active S-boxes cancel each other by the XOR in the MC operation. Considering that cell-positions move to different columns by the SR operation, the number of active S-boxes tends to be small when all the active S-boxes in every round propagate from the same input difference to the same output difference, as shown in Fig. 2.

It is impossible to avoid that all the active S-boxes in a certain single round propagate from the same input difference to the same output difference with MDP, say $\Delta A \rightarrow \Delta B$ in round i. An efficient differential characteristic appears when the same event also occurs in subsequent rounds, say $\Delta B \rightarrow \Delta C$ with MDP in round $i + 1$, $\Delta C \rightarrow \Delta D$ with MDP in round $i + 2$, and so on. In particular, if such a chain makes a loop after a certain number of rounds, say $\Delta A \rightarrow \Delta B \rightarrow \Delta C \rightarrow \Delta D \rightarrow \cdots \rightarrow \Delta A$, a high-probability differential characteristic may occur for a large (or infinite) number of rounds. We call such a chain of the differential transitions with MDP *high-probability chain*. Then, ARP of the multiplication by a binary matrix in AES-bMC ciphers can be defined as the maximum length of the high-probability chain.

Definition 2 (High-probability chain length). *We say that an S-box has a high-probability chain of length L when there exists a set of differences $(\Delta_0, \Delta_1, \ldots, \Delta_L)$ such that $\Delta_i \rightarrow \Delta_{i+1}$ is a high-probability transition on the S-box for all $i \in \{0, 1, \ldots, L - 1\}$. We also define "the maximum high-probability chain length" as the longest high-probability chain length among all high-probability chains.*

If there exists a high-probability chain such that $\Delta_0 = \Delta_L$, we say that this chain has the iterative property, or the chain length is infinite. Figure 7 shows the DDT

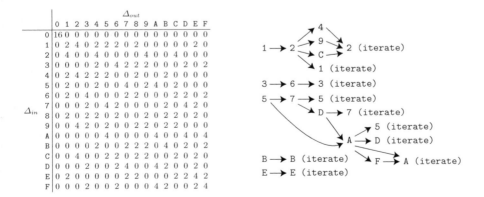

Fig. 7. DDT of S-box of Midori64 and its high-probability chain

of Midori64's S-box and its high-probability chain. Many high-probability chains have the iterative property, i.e., the maximum high-probability chain length of Midori64's S-box is infinite.

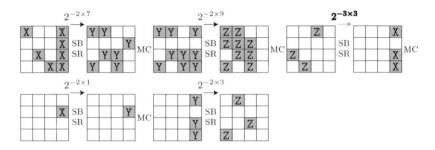

Fig. 8. 5-round differential characteristic with $minAS$ for Midori64 with S-box such that the maximum high-probability chain length is 2

To demonstrate the effect of the high-probability chain, we recall the 5-round differential characteristic shown in Fig. 2 with 23 active S-boxes. In this characteristic, all the active cells in a state have the same difference, i.e. 0x1 at the input and 0x2 after the first SB operation, and so on. Differences are preserved before and after the MC operation because of the property of the binary matrix. With Midori's S-box, all the active S-boxes can be bypassed with probability 2^{-2} which results in probability $2^{-2 \times 23} = 2^{-46}$ for the entire characteristic. This is because the maximum high-probability chain length of Midori64's S-box is infinite. In contrast, suppose that we can adopt an S-box whose maximum high-probability chain length is 2. Then, at least one out of three rounds require 2^{-3} to be bypassed. For example, in Fig. 8, three active S-boxes in the 3rd round require 2^{-3}, thus the entire probability decreases to $2^{-23 \times 2-3} = 2^{-49}$. Note that this impact is as big as increasing the number of active S-boxes by 1.

We assume that differences are preserved before and after the MC operation in the best differential characteristics as shown in this example. Of course, it does not always hold. We emphasize that the high-probability chain is still meaningful enough even if differences are not preserved before and after all the MC operations. This is because we can still expect that differences are preserved before and after most of the MC operations.

4.3 Design of 4-Bit S-Boxes with Shortest High-Probability Chains

We discuss how to design S-boxes with the shortest maximum high-probability chain length. We focus on 16 classes of 4-bit S-boxes. We first introduce useful properties of S-boxes related to high-probability chain lengths.

Property 1. Two S-boxes S and S' with the relation $S'(x) = M^{-1} \times S(M \times x \oplus c_{in}) \oplus c_{out}$ have the same high-probability chain length.

Table 2. Maximum high-probability chain lengths of 20160 S-boxes belonging to each affine-equivalent class

ID	Maximum high-probability chain lengths											
	1	2	3	4	5	6	7	8	9	10	11	∞
G_0	0	0	0	32	16	0	8	24	0	0	0	20080
G_1	0	0	0	0	0	0	0	0	8	0	0	20152
$G_2 \sim G_0^{-1}$	0	0	0	32	16	0	8	24	0	0	0	20080
G_3	0	0	0	0	0	0	0	0	0	0	0	20160
G_4	0	0	8	240	408	608	448	200	64	32	0	18152
G_5	0	0	0	0	0	0	0	0	0	0	0	20160
G_6	0	0	8	204	504	584	396	160	80	16	0	18208
G_7	0	10	180	765	580	535	230	95	0	0	0	17765
G_8	0	0	16	112	112	24	40	0	0	0	0	19856
G_9	0	0	0	9	52	100	124	120	68	20	0	19667
G_{10}	0	0	0	8	54	130	160	86	20	0	0	19702
G_{11}	0	10	170	560	730	590	210	70	10	0	0	17810
G_{12}	0	20	160	320	820	680	350	80	20	0	0	17710
G_{13}	0	0	0	14	170	287	365	335	240	139	32	18578
G_{14}	0	0	0	13	48	76	114	98	49	12	0	19750
$G_{15} \sim G_{14}^{-1}$	0	0	0	13	48	76	114	98	49	12	0	19750

Proof. Let us consider the DDTs of S and S'. Since two constants c_{in} and c_{out} do not affect the differential distribution table (DDT), they are independent of the high-probability chain. Next, the sequence of operations corresponding to a high-probability chain can be written as

$$\cdots \to S \to M^{-1} \to M \to S \to M^{-1} \to M \to \cdots$$

Since M^{-1} and M are always cancelled out, these two S-boxes clearly have the same high-probability chain length. Note that assuming the high-probability chain length of S is 1, the high-probability chain length of S' is also 1. This is because, if it is 2, the high-probability chain length of S is 2. $\qquad\square$

In other words, Property 1 implies that S-boxes belonging to the same affine equivalent class have the same high-probability chain length when $M_{out} = M_{in}^{-1}$.

Property 2. If for any non-zero δ_{in} (resp. δ_{out}), there exist δ_{out} (resp. δ_{in}) such that the transition $\delta_{in} \to \delta_{out}$ is high-probability, the high-probability chain length is always infinite.

Proof. Let us focus on one high-probability transition $\delta_{in} \to \delta_{out}$. When Property 2 holds, we always continue high-probability transitions from δ_{out} (resp, to δ_{in}). Therefore, the high-probability chain length is infinite. $\qquad\square$

We call that high-probability transitions are uniformly distributed in the DDT when the DDT fulfills Property 2.

Property 3. If the S-box is an involution, i.e., $S(S(x)) = x$ for any x, the high-probability chain length is always infinite.

Proof. In any involution S-box, when an input difference Δ_{in} propagates to Δ_{out} with high probability, Δ_{out} also propagates to Δ_{in} with high probability. Therefore, the high-probability chain length is always infinite. □

Table 3. Forty S-boxes with the shortest high-probability chain lengths

G_7	G_{11}	G_{12}	
0x042BAC985FD3716E	0x062D15F3A9E87CB4	0x052D9EFB1A63478C	0x03D6C2B19874AE5F
0x041FD8EC6BA37259	0x065B12E4C8F97AD3	0x042EBDC9187356AF	0x03E7F291BA658D4C
0x0147D839B62EFA5C	0x026DC8BA3975E1F4	0x0576CE1BF4D8A239	0x0D1B59A437F2EC68
0x0247AC3EF519BD68	0x056BA9DC4872F1E3	0x0467FD19C5EA823B	0x0E194B8536C2DF7A
0x01A629C857DEF4B3	0x028FC67415B9E3DA	0x06913C8A4EBD2F75	0x086D97BFC32A4E51
0x02D51E8C67A9B4F3	0x059EA67312D8F4BC	0x07B13FA85D9E2C64	0x0A7EB69CF3285D41
0x0A1F29E3754C6DB8	0x095E48B132F6DA7C	0x06FB5C4A8217E9D3	0x0AD216FC95E4378B
0x0D2B1E9376485AFC	0x082F39D145E6BC7A	0x07C94F58A216DBE3	0x08E217CFB4D536A9
0x0AD54389BF2C617E	0x098745FCA6B2D3E1	0x02BF814356CE79DA	0x0DCF8934AEB67125
0x0DA643CEFB185279	0x089732EAC6D5B4F1	0x029CA15347FD6BE8	0x0EFCAB358D976124

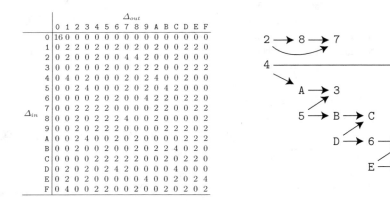

Fig. 9. DDT of S-box described in Example 1 and its high-probability chain

Property 1 implies that the exhaustive evaluation is not difficult. The number of invertible 4×4 matrices is 20160, and the search space is only 16×20160 for the exhaustive evaluation of 16 classes. We evaluated all S-boxes belonging to 16 classes, and each maximum high-probability chain length is summarized in Table 2. Since high-probability transitions are uniformly distributed in G_3 and G_5, there is no S-box whose high-probability chain length is finite because of Property 2. As a result, the shortest maximum high-probability chain length is 2, and we can find 10, 10, and 20 S-boxes in G_7, G_{11}, and G_{12}, respectively. Table 3 summarizes these 40 S-boxes. Note that all S-boxes with the form $M^{-1} \times S(M \times x \oplus c_{in}) \oplus c_{out}$ have the shortest maximum high-probability chain length 2 when S is chosen from 40 S-boxes listed in Table 3.

Example 1 (Example of S-boxes with maximum high-probability chain length 2). The following S-box

$$\{0xA, 0x4, 0xD, 0x5, 0x7, 0x3, 0xE, 0xF, 0x0, 0x6, 0x8, 0x2, 0x1, 0xC, 0x9, 0xB\}$$

belongs to class G_7, and the maximum high-probability chain length is 2. Figure 9 shows the DDT and its high-probability chain. Note that this S-box is generated as $M^{-1} \times S(M \times x \oplus 0x5) \oplus 0x3$, where S-box S and (bijective) linear transformation M are specified as

$$S = \{0x0, 0x4, 0x2, 0xB, 0xA, 0xC, 0x9, 0x8, 0x5, 0xF, 0xD, 0x3, 0x7, 0x1, 0x6, 0xE\},$$
$$M = \{0x0, 0x5, 0xE, 0xB, 0xC, 0x9, 0x2, 0x7, 0xA, 0xF, 0x4, 0x1, 0x6, 0x3, 0x8, 0xD\}.$$

4.4   Case Study with Midori64

Specification of Midori64. Midori64 is an SPN block cipher. The block size is 64 bits and the state is denoted as a 4×4 nibble array as follows.

$$\begin{pmatrix} s_0 & s_4 & s_8 & s_{12} \\ s_1 & s_5 & s_9 & s_{13} \\ s_2 & s_6 & s_{10} & s_{14} \\ s_3 & s_7 & s_{11} & s_{15} \end{pmatrix}$$

The round function applies the following four operations to the state.

SubCell: A 4-bit to 4-bit S-box is applied to 16 nibbles.
ShuffleCell: Each cell of the state is permuted as follows:
$(s_0, s_1, \ldots, s_{15}) \leftarrow (s_0, s_{10}, s_5, s_{15}, s_{14}, s_4, s_{11}, s_1, s_9, s_3, s_{12}, s_6, s_7, s_{13}, s_2, s_8)$.
MixColumn: Four nibbles in each column are multiplied by the binary matrix, where all entries except for the first diagonal take 1.
KeyAdd: A round key is XORed to some of the nibbles of the state. We omit their details because these operations do not have any impact on MDCP.

Tight MDCP on Original Midori64. The designers of Midori evaluated the minimum number of active S-boxes, and it reaches 35 after 7 rounds. Then, the upper bound of the MDCP given by the minimum number of active S-boxes is lower than 2^{-64} because MDP of the S-box is 2^{-2}. The tightness of the upper bound was reported in [32].

Replacing S-Box. We replace the original S-box of Midori64 with that described in Example 1 and evaluate the tight MDCP.

Table 4. The maximum differential characteristic probabilities of Midori64

# of rounds			1	2	3	4	5	6
# of active S-boxes			1	4	7	16	23	30
Upper bound			2^{-2}	2^{-8}	2^{-14}	2^{-32}	2^{-46}	2^{-60}
S-box	Chain length							
Original	∞	MDCP	2^{-2}	2^{-8}	2^{-14}	2^{-32}	2^{-46}	2^{-60}
Example 1	2	MDCP	2^{-2}	2^{-8}	2^{-15}	2^{-33}	2^{-49}	2^{-68}
0xA4D573EF06821C9B		gain	0	0	1	1	3	8

-gain is computed from $-\log_2((\text{Original MDCP})/(\text{MDCP in the modified S-box}))$

Table 4 shows the detail of the result. To evaluate the MDCP, we used the SAT/SMT solver STP [33]. Our modeling is based on the method shown by CryptoSMT [34], but the modeling for the S-box is replaced with that for our designed S-box. As described above, the upper bounds of the MDCP given by the minimum number of active S-boxes are always tight in the original S-box of Midori64. However, when the S-box shown in Example 1 is used, the MDCP becomes lower than the original from three rounds because the high-probability chain length is at most 2. Moreover, we can see significant gain in 6 rounds because the chain is disconnected in two out of six rounds. While the original 6-round Midori64 is insufficient to prove that the MDCP is lower than 2^{-64}, 6 rounds are enough to prove it when our designed S-box is adopted.[3]

4.5   Case Study with SKINNY

We applied the same 4-bit S-box with SKINNY64, and its result is summarized in Fig. 3. To apply the same idea to SKINNY128, we need to design an 8-bit S-box whose high-probability chain length is short. We also investigate such S-boxes and applied to SKINNY128. The result is shown in the full version of this paper in detail.

4.6   Remark for Implementation Performance

Unlike the case of Lilliput, our S-box with the shortest high-probability chain does not satisfy the original criteria of Midori and SKINNY regarding the implementation performance. Therefore, we do not claim that our S-box is better than the original, though our S-box enhances security against differential cryptanalysis. Our goal of those demonstrations is to show the proof-of-concept about the possibility of enhancing security against differential cryptanalysis by considering the interplay between S-boxes and the linear layer even in AES-bMC ciphers. We believe that the approach we present should be taken into consideration for future designs.

---

[3] Since the S-box of Midori64 is designed such that its energy consumption is minimized, we do not claim that our S-box is clearly better than the original one.

5   Discussion and Conclusion

5.1   Evaluation of Differential Effect

Our S-boxes lower the MDCP, but a more accurate probability should be estimated by considering the differential effect. For example, even if the MDCP is lower, the differential probability including the differential effect could be higher if the number of characteristics with the MDCP is relatively larger. Unfortunately, it is difficult to predict the differential effect in advance.

Table 5. Differential effect on 6-round Midori64 with our modified S-box

Probability	2^{-68}	2^{-69}	2^{-70}	2^{-71}	2^{-72}	2^{-73}	2^{-74}
Number of characteristics	4	0	47	103	173	609	1698
Total	2^{-66}	2^{-66}	$2^{-64.0227}$	$2^{-63.1608}$	$2^{-62.6985}$	$2^{-62.1304}$	$2^{-61.5906}$

As an exercise to understand the differential effect of our S-box, we compared the original S-box and our one by evaluating the differential effect on the 6-round Midori64. The differential effect of the original Midori64 was discussed in [32]. The differential effect is extremely strong, which increases the probability from 2^{-60} to $2^{-48.36}$. Thus, the gain is $2^{11.64} = 2^{-48.36}/2^{-60}$. Similarly to [32], we evaluated the differential effect of 6-round Midori64 using our S-box. The best differential characteristic of the original Midori64 no longer leads to the highest probability when our S-box is used. Instead, the following input and output differences

$$\begin{pmatrix} E\,0\,0\,0 \\ E\,0\,0\,E \\ E\,E\,0\,0 \\ E\,0\,E\,0 \end{pmatrix} \xrightarrow{\text{6 rounds}} \begin{pmatrix} 0\,3\,3\,3 \\ 0\,3\,0\,3 \\ 0\,3\,3\,0 \\ 0\,0\,3\,3 \end{pmatrix}$$

include the best differential characteristic with probability 2^{-68}, where the last ShuffleCell and MixColumn are removed in the last round. Table 5 summarizes the differential effect of this input/output differences. While the MDCP is 2^{-68}, the probability increases to about 2^{-61} due to the differential effect. Thus, the gain is about $2^5 = 2^{-61}/2^{-66}$. Compared to the gain $2^{11.64}$ in the original Midori64, the gain 2^5 in ours is relatively small.

5.2   On Application to Linear Cryptanalysis

Linear cryptanalysis is also an important method similarly to differential cryptanalysis. Therefore, we observe the case of linear cryptanalysis.

Corresponding to the DDT of differential cryptanalysis, the linear approximation table (LAT) is constructed in linear cryptanalysis. The LAT also includes transition with both high and low correlations. Thus, our idea can be also applied to linear cryptanalysis conceptually by focusing on the ARP and transitions with the highest correlation in the LAT.

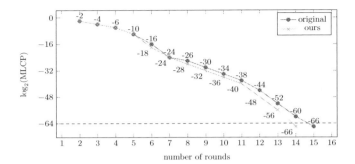

Fig. 10. Results of Lilliput for linear cryptanalysis

The number of transitions with the highest correlation in the LAT tends to be more than that in the DDT. However, avoiding the identity high-correlation transitions is still possible. We discuss the case of the EGFN in the full version of this paper and show that our S-box is useful for linear cryptanalysis too. Figure 10 shows our result of Lilliput for the linear cryptanalysis. While 15 rounds are necessary to lower the probability to less than 2^{-64} in the original, 14 rounds are enough in ours. Unfortunately, avoiding infinite chain length is more difficult due to more high-correlation transitions, and application to AES-bMC ciphers looks difficult. In practice, when we evaluated high-probability chain lengths for LAT, all S-boxes belonging to the sixteen 4-bit S-box classes have infinite high-probability chains. On the other hand, considering the SKINNY-like 8-bit S-box, the maximum (linear) high-probability chain length can be 3: 0x04 → 0x40 → 0x08 → 0x01 and 0x20 → 0x02 → 0x80 → 0x10.

5.3   Concluding Remarks

In this paper, we applied a method of designing S-boxes to take care of the ARP of the linear layer for EGFN and AES-bMC ciphers. We observed that ARP of the EGFN ciphers is the identity-differential transition with MDP. For its instance Lilliput, we showed that such a property can be avoided only by swapping the two bits of the S-box output, which imposes negligible performance overhead. By replacing Lilliput's S-box with the new one, we show that the number of rounds to ensure 2^{-64} can be reduced. We then observed that ARP of the AES-bMC ciphers is the length of the high-probability chain. We list 4-bit S-boxes achieving the maximum chain length of 2. The effect of using such S-boxes is demonstrated by replacing the original S-box of Midori64 and SKINNY with the new ones.

We aimed to show that it would be possible to go beyond the simple bound of $(MDP)^{minAS}$ by designing the S-box considering the crucial property of the linear layer. Applications of AES-bMC ciphers and EGFN ciphers are just the first step in this direction, and we believe that the same idea can be extended to more structures. We hope that this paper will provide useful knowledge for future block cipher designers.

References

1. Biham, E., Shamir, A.: Differential cryptanalysis of DES-like cryptosystems. In: Menezes, A.J., Vanstone, S.A. (eds.) CRYPTO 1990. LNCS, vol. 537, pp. 2–21. Springer, Heidelberg (1991). https://doi.org/10.1007/3-540-38424-3_1
2. Biham, E., Shamir, A.: Differential cryptanalysis of DES-like cryptosystems. J. Cryptol. **4**(1), 3–72 (1991). https://doi.org/10.1007/BF00630563
3. Matsui, M.: Linear cryptanalysis method for DES cipher. In: Helleseth, T. (ed.) EUROCRYPT 1993. LNCS, vol. 765, pp. 386–397. Springer, Heidelberg (1994). https://doi.org/10.1007/3-540-48285-7_33
4. Matsui, M.: On correlation between the order of S-boxes and the strength of DES. In: De Santis, A. (ed.) EUROCRYPT 1994. LNCS, vol. 950, pp. 366–375. Springer, Heidelberg (1995). https://doi.org/10.1007/BFb0053451
5. Daemen, J., Rijmen, V.: The wide trail design strategy. In: Honary, B. (ed.) Cryptography and Coding 2001. LNCS, vol. 2260, pp. 222–238. Springer, Heidelberg (2001). https://doi.org/10.1007/3-540-45325-3_20
6. Biham, E., Anderson, R., Knudsen, L.: Serpent: a new block cipher proposal. In: Vaudenay, S. (ed.) FSE 1998. LNCS, vol. 1372, pp. 222–238. Springer, Heidelberg (1998). https://doi.org/10.1007/3-540-69710-1_15
7. Daemen, J., Peeters, M., Assche, G.V., Rijmen, V.: Nessie proposal: the block cipher NOEKEON. Nessie submission (2000). http://gro.noekeon.org/
8. Grosso, V., Leurent, G., Standaert, F.-X., Varıcı, K.: LS-designs: bitslice encryption for efficient masked software implementations. In: Cid, C., Rechberger, C. (eds.) FSE 2014. LNCS, vol. 8540, pp. 18–37. Springer, Heidelberg (2015). https://doi.org/10.1007/978-3-662-46706-0_2
9. Zhang, W.T., Bao, Z.Z., Lin, D.D., Rijmen, V., Yang, B.H., Verbauwhede, I.: Sci. China Inf. Sc. **58**(12), 1–15 (2015). https://doi.org/10.1007/s11432-015-5459-7
10. Bogdanov, A., et al.: PRESENT: an ultra-lightweight block cipher. In: Paillier, P., Verbauwhede, I. (eds.) CHES 2007. LNCS, vol. 4727, pp. 450–466. Springer, Heidelberg (2007). https://doi.org/10.1007/978-3-540-74735-2_31
11. Banik, S., Pandey, S.K., Peyrin, T., Sasaki, Yu., Sim, S.M., Todo, Y.: GIFT: a small present. In: Fischer, W., Homma, N. (eds.) CHES 2017. LNCS, vol. 10529, pp. 321–345. Springer, Cham (2017). https://doi.org/10.1007/978-3-319-66787-4_16
12. Datta, N., Ghoshal, A., Mukhopadhyay, D., Patranabis, S., Picek, S., Sadhukhan, R.: Trifle. NIST lightweight cryptography submission (2019). https://csrc.nist.gov/CSRC/media/Projects/Lightweight-Cryptography/documents/round-1/spec-doc/trifle-spec.pdf
13. Liu, F., Isobe, T.: Iterative differential characteristic of TRIFLE-BC. In: Paterson, K.G., Stebila, D. (eds.) SAC 2019. LNCS, vol. 11959, pp. 85–100. Springer, Cham (2020). https://doi.org/10.1007/978-3-030-38471-5_4
14. Sarkar, S., Sasaki, Yu., Sim, S.M.: On the design of bit permutation based ciphers. In: Aoki, K., Kanaoka, A. (eds.) IWSEC 2020. LNCS, vol. 12231, pp. 3–22. Springer, Cham (2020). https://doi.org/10.1007/978-3-030-58208-1_1
15. Berger, T.P., Minier, M., Thomas, G.: Extended generalized Feistel networks using matrix representation. In: Lange, T., Lauter, K., Lisoněk, P. (eds.) SAC 2013. LNCS, vol. 8282, pp. 289–305. Springer, Heidelberg (2014). https://doi.org/10.1007/978-3-662-43414-7_15
16. Banik, S., et al.: Midori: a block cipher for low energy. In: Iwata, T., Cheon, J.H. (eds.) ASIACRYPT 2015. LNCS, vol. 9453, pp. 411–436. Springer, Heidelberg (2015). https://doi.org/10.1007/978-3-662-48800-3_17

17. Beierle, C., et al.: The SKINNY family of block ciphers and its low-latency variant MANTIS. In: Robshaw, M., Katz, J. (eds.) CRYPTO 2016. LNCS, vol. 9815, pp. 123–153. Springer, Heidelberg (2016). https://doi.org/10.1007/978-3-662-53008-5_5

18. Beierle, C., Leander, G., Moradi, A., Rasoolzadeh, S.: CRAFT: lightweight tweakable block cipher with efficient protection against DFA attacks. IACR Trans. Symmetric Cryptol. **2019**(1), 5–45 (2019)

19. Leander, G., Poschmann, A.: On the classification of 4 bit S-boxes. In: Carlet, C., Sunar, B. (eds.) WAIFI 2007. LNCS, vol. 4547, pp. 159–176. Springer, Heidelberg (2007). https://doi.org/10.1007/978-3-540-73074-3_13

20. Cannière, C.D.: Analysis and design of symmetric encryption algorithms. Ph.D. thesis, Katholieke Universiteit Leuven (2007)

21. Nyberg, K.: On the construction of highly nonlinear permutations. In: Rueppel, R.A. (ed.) EUROCRYPT 1992. LNCS, vol. 658, pp. 92–98. Springer, Heidelberg (1993). https://doi.org/10.1007/3-540-47555-9_8

22. Browning, K., Dillon, J., McQuistan, M., Wolfe, A.: An APN permutation in dimension six. In: The 9th International Conference on Finite Fields and Their Applications FQ'9. Volume 518 of Contemporary Mathematics, pp. 33–42 (2010)

23. Daemen, J., Rijmen, V.: The Design of Rijndael: AES - The Advanced Encryption Standard. ISC, Springer, Heidelberg (2002). https://doi.org/10.1007/978-3-662-04722-4

24. Nyberg, K.: Perfect nonlinear S-boxes. In: Davies, D.W. (ed.) EUROCRYPT 1991. LNCS, vol. 547, pp. 378–386. Springer, Heidelberg (1991). https://doi.org/10.1007/3-540-46416-6_32

25. Mouha, N., Wang, Q., Gu, D., Preneel, B.: Differential and linear cryptanalysis using mixed-integer linear programming. In: Wu, C.-K., Yung, M., Lin, D. (eds.) Inscrypt 2011. LNCS, vol. 7537, pp. 57–76. Springer, Heidelberg (2012). https://doi.org/10.1007/978-3-642-34704-7_5

26. Sun, S., Hu, L., Wang, P., Qiao, K., Ma, X., Song, L.: Automatic security evaluation and (related-key) differential characteristic search: application to SIMON, PRESENT, LBlock, DES(L) and other bit-oriented block ciphers. In: Sarkar, P., Iwata, T. (eds.) ASIACRYPT 2014. LNCS, vol. 8873, pp. 158–178. Springer, Heidelberg (2014). https://doi.org/10.1007/978-3-662-45611-8_9

27. Sun, S., et al.: Automatic enumeration of (related-key) differential and linear characteristics with predefined properties and its applications. IACR Cryptol. ePrint Arch. **2014**, 747 (2014)

28. Abdelkhalek, A., Sasaki, Y., Todo, Y., Tolba, M., Youssef, A.M.: MILP modeling for (large) s-boxes to optimize probability of differential characteristics. IACR Trans. Symmetric Cryptol. **2017**(4), 99–129 (2017)

29. Suzaki, T., Minematsu, K.: Improving the generalized Feistel. In: Hong, S., Iwata, T. (eds.) FSE 2010. LNCS, vol. 6147, pp. 19–39. Springer, Heidelberg (2010). https://doi.org/10.1007/978-3-642-13858-4_2

30. Berger, T.P., Francq, J., Minier, M., Thomas, G.: Extended generalized Feistel networks using matrix representation to propose a new lightweight block cipher: Lilliput. IEEE Trans. Comput. **65**(7), 2074–2089 (2016)

31. Sasaki, Y., Todo, Y.: Tight bounds of differentially and linearly active S-boxes and division property of Lilliput. IEEE Trans. Comput. **67**(5), 717–732 (2018)

32. Ankele, R., Kölbl, S.: Mind the gap - a closer look at the security of block ciphers against differential cryptanalysis. In: Cid, C., Jacobson, M., Jr. (eds.) SAC 2018. LNCS, vol. 11349, pp. 163–190. Springer, Cham (2018). https://doi.org/10.1007/978-3-030-10970-7_8

33. Ganesh, V., Hansen, T., Soos, M., Liew, D., Govostes, R.: Simple Theorem Prover (STP). https://github.com/stp/stp
34. Kölbl, S.: CryptoSMT: An easy to use tool for cryptanalysis of symmetric primitives https://github.com/kste/cryptosmt

Parallel Verification of Serial MAC and AE Modes

Kazuhiko Minematsu[1]([envelope])[iD], Akiko Inoue[1][iD], Katsuya Moriwaki[2],
Maki Shigeri[2], and Hiroyasu Kubo[2]

[1] NEC, Kawasaki, Japan
{k-minematsu,a_inoue}@nec.com
[2] NEC Solution Innovators, Hokuriku, Japan
{m-shigeri_pb,h-kubo}@nec.com

Abstract. A large number of the symmetric-key mode of operations, such as classical CBC-MAC, have serial structures. While a serial mode gives an implementation advantage in terms of required memory or footprint compared to the parallel counterparts, it wastes the capability of parallel process even when it is available. The problem is becoming more relevant as lightweight cryptography is going to be deployed in the real world. In this article, we propose an alternative implementation strategy for serial MAC modes and serial authenticated encryption (AE) modes that allows 2-block parallel operation for verification/decryption. Our proposal maintains the original functionality and security. It is simple yet novel, and generally applicable to a wide range of existing modes including two NIST recommendations, CMAC and CCM. We demonstrate the effectiveness of our proposal by showing several case studies with software implementations.

Keywords: Mode of operation · MAC · Authenticated encryption · Parallel verification · CMAC · CCM · Romulus

1 Introduction

Lightweight cryptography is a subfield of symmetric-key cryptography that aims at designing cryptographic functions that perform well under constrained environments where standards might not perform well or not be implementable at all. One of the major directions is lightweight cryptographic primitives, such as block ciphers [10,19,21], tweakable block ciphers [9,12], and cryptographic permutations [15,25,28]. As well as the primitives, the modes for encryption, authentication or authenticated encryption (AE) have been actively studied from the viewpoint of lightweight cryptography.

The hardware implementation size is an important metric for lightweight modes. When one wants to design a mode with small implementation size, the *state memory* (memory for keeping the internal chaining value or precomputed secret values) can occupy a significant amount in the total size compared to the

R. AlTawy and A. Hülsing (Eds.): SAC 2021, LNCS 13203, pp. 200–219, 2022.
https://doi.org/10.1007/978-3-030-99277-4_10

core cryptographic logics. Parallelizable modes allow to process input blocks in parallel, however this imposes some additional state memory blocks, which is disadvantageous in terms of size. From this reason, making the mode entirely serial is quite effective and deemed as a common strategy for lightweight modes. This is illustrated by the ongoing NIST Lightweight Cryptography project for standardizing lightweight authenticated encryption (hereafter NIST LWC) [1], where a large fraction of proposals are serial. However, losing parallelizability means losing performance gain even when parallel processing is available. This can occur in practice, *e.g.*, when lots of tiny sensor devices are connected to the edge server – which is typically much more powerful than sensors – that aggregates information from the sensors. This exhibits a dilemma for lightweight cryptographic schemes.

In this paper, we propose a new simple implementation strategy for serial modes. More specifically we consider serial MAC (authentication) modes and AE modes, where each input block must be serially processed in the original specifications. Our strategy allows to process two input blocks in parallel in the verification of MAC modes and the (authenticated) decryption of AE modes. The idea, which we call *pincer verification*, is to process the input message from the top and the bottom, and performs the verification check at the middle of the message. It is quite intuitive and simple, yet to our knowledge never studied in the literature. The easiest example is the plain CBC-MAC with message $M = (M[1], \ldots, M[m])$ and tag T, where $|M[i]| = |T| = n$. The pincer verification performs the regular CBC-MAC computation from $M[1], M[2], \ldots$, using the block cipher encryption E_K. At the same time, it performs the "backward" computation from T, $M[m], M[m-1], \ldots$, using the block cipher decryption E_K^{-1}, and verifies at the middle. The idea may look almost trivial, however, to deal with more complex modes of operations, we need an abstract model to clarify when and how such implementation is possible. In addition we extend the idea to AE modes. When we emphasize that the target is AE we may call it *pincer decryption*[1]. For both MAC and AE modes, the functional equivalence needs to be maintained. We clarify the condition that enables pincer verification that maintains the original functionality. More precisely, the result of pincer verification (*i.e.*, a binary verification result for a MAC mode, and a decrypted plaintext for an AE mode when verification is successful) is always the same as the original. Thus, we can use pincer verification without any security loss. We look into the current MAC and AE modes, and show that pincer verification is applicable to a wide variety of them. In particular it is applicable to the most of known CBC-MAC based MAC modes, including the NIST recommendation, CMAC [3]. Regarding AE, pincer verification is applicable to some of the state-of-the-art serial AE modes including some submissions to NIST LWC [1]. Finally, although the structure is not fully serial, the NIST recommendation CCM [2] also allows a variant of pincer decryption (see below). Parallelizability of our proposal is limited, still it doubles the verification performance in theory. Considering that

---

[1] We use the term pincer verification to cover both MAC and AE modes. Note that pincer verification for AE is in fact authenticated decryption, not just verification.

no further fundamental speedup is not possible for single message, our proposal pushes the performance limit of serial modes and can play a meaningful role in practice.

We show three case studies to demonstrate the utility of pincer verification. Pincer verification is generally useful for software on multi-core processors. That is, one core for the forward direction starting at the first message block and the other for the backward direction starting at the last message block and the tag. We basically assume that the verification routine takes the entire input kept in memory. Although it is a limitation, this assumption holds for the typical API of cryptographic library.

Our first case study follows the aforementioned basic implementation scenario. The target algorithm is Romulus [27,29], a finalist of the NIST LWC. The target platform is a low-end 32-bit dual-core microcontroller ESP32[2], which is one of the common choices for IoT applications, for its built-in Wifi and Bluetooth. We show that even on this constrained device the pincer decryption can double the performance for a reasonable length of message. The advantage of ESP32's dual-core operation was explored in the post-quantum cryptography [45], however to our knowledge no concrete application has been shown in the symmetric-key literature.

Our second case study takes CMAC[3], which is the standard MAC mode recommended by NIST. On x86 platforms equipped with AES instruction set (AES-NI), the pincer verification doubles the performance utilizing the pipeline as in the same manner to the parallelizable (e.g., CTR) modes. An important remark is that our code runs on *single core*. It runs about 1.65 cycles per byte for 1024-byte message where the regular implementation runs at 3.35. Thus, we double the verification performance of CMAC per core from the straightforward (but previously the fastest) implementation.

Our third case study is CCM, a NIST-recommended AE mode based on AES. It has been quite widely deployed, such as TLS, IPSec, Wifi (WPA2) and so on. CCM composes CBC-MAC and CTR mode in a similar way to the MAC-then-encrypt generic composition. As mentioned earlier, CCM does not perfectly fall into our framework since it is not fully serial, however it still benefits from pincer verification technique due to its complete serial MAC part (CBC-MAC). We show that, on x86 platforms with AES-NI, a variant of pincer verification can halve the computation cost of decryption from the previous fastest implementation strategy (e.g., OpenSSL[4]) that interleaves CBC-MAC and CTR decryption. Our concrete implementation achieves 1.78 cycles per byte for CCM decryption. It is faster than the previous one by a factor of two. See Sects. 6, 7 and 8 for more details of these case studies.

Organization. This paper is organized as follows. After the introduction at Sect. 1, Sect. 2 describes some technical backgrounds. Section 3 describes the

---

[2] https://www.espressif.com/en/products/socs/esp32.

[3] CMAC is a generic mode for 128-bit block ciphers. This paper assumes AES-128 as the underlying block cipher for CMAC. The same applies to CCM.

[4] https://www.openssl.org/.

basic idea of pincer verification for MAC modes, and Sect. 4 extends it to
AE modes. Section 5 shows the applicability of pincer verification to existing
MAC/AE modes. We provide three case studies with concrete implementation
results at Sects. 6, 7, 8, and conclude at Sect. 9.

1.1 Related Work

Bitslice introduced by Biham [17] is a general technique to boost the software
performance of serial symmetric-key algorithms by block-wise parallelization. It
has been initially developed for DES, but it is also applicable to other primitives,
such as tweakable block ciphers [33] and cryptographic permutations. Bitslicing
AES has been extensively studied [8,35,44]. Matsuda and Moriai [34] showed
how lightweight block ciphers can run fast with bitslicing on x86/x64 platforms.
It also highlights the practical importance of fast, parallel implementation at
the server side in the context of Internet-of-Things (IoT). The original form of
bitslice assumes multiple input blocks, which can be few to n for n-bit block
cipher.

The implementation strategy proposed by Bogdanov *et al.* [20] can be interpreted as bitslicing at the mode level. In principle it is applicable to any mode.
For example, Bogdanov *et al.* reports 0.84 cycles per byte for CMAC on an Intel
Haswell processor. However, it requires a certain number of multiple messages
that processed at one time, which does not fit the typical interface of popular
cryptographic libraries. Also the performance will be affected by the distribution
of message length.

2 Preliminaries

Let $\{0,1\}^*$ be the set of all bit strings. For $x \in \{0,1\}^*$, $|x|$ denotes its bit length
and $|x|_n$ for some positive integer n denotes $\lceil |x|/n \rceil$. The encryption function of
a tweakable block cipher (TBC) is a function $E : \mathcal{K} \times \mathcal{T}_w \times \mathcal{M} \to \mathcal{M}$, where $\mathcal{K}$
is the key space, $\mathcal{T}_w$ is the tweak space, and $\mathcal{M}$ is the message space. The key
is a secret value, and the tweak is typically used as a public value that may be
determined by the users. We require that $E(K,T,*)$ for any $(K,T) \in \mathcal{K} \times \mathcal{T}_w$ is
a permutation over $\mathcal{M}$. We may write $E(K,T,*)$ as $E_K^T(*)$ or $E_K(T,*)$. A block
cipher is a TBC with $\mathcal{T}_w$ being a singleton, and in that case we drop $\mathcal{T}_w$ from the
notation. The decryption function is denoted by $E^{-1} : \mathcal{K} \times \mathcal{T}_w \times \mathcal{M} \to \mathcal{M}$ such
that $E_K^{-1}(T, E_K(T,M)) = M$ for any $(K,T,M) \in \mathcal{K} \times \mathcal{T}_w \times \mathcal{M}$. For $M \in \{0,1\}^*$,
$(M[1], \ldots, M[m]) \xleftarrow{n} M$ for some positive integer n means a parsing of M into n-
bit blocks, *i.e.*, $|M[i]| = n$ for $i = 1, \ldots, m-1$ and $|M[m]| \leq n$, where $m = |M|_n$.

MAC and AE. We follow the standard syntax of MAC and AE schemes [13,18,
30]. Let MAC be a deterministic MAC scheme. It consists of a tagging function
MAC.$\mathcal{T} : \mathcal{K} \times \mathcal{M} \to \mathcal{T}$ and a verification function MAC.$\mathcal{V} : \mathcal{K} \times \mathcal{M} \times \mathcal{T} \to \{\top, \bot\}$,
where $\mathcal{K}$ is the key space and $\mathcal{M}$ is the message space and $\mathcal{T}$ is the tag space.

The tagging function is to compute the tag $T \in \mathcal{T}$ using key $K \in \mathcal{K}$ (which is shared by the prover and the verifier) and message $M \in \mathcal{M}$, and written as $T \leftarrow \mathsf{MAC}.\mathcal{T}_K(M)$. The prover sends the tuple (M, T) to the verifier. Once (M', T') is received (which may be tampered by the adversary), the verifier performs the verification function $\mathsf{MAC}.\mathcal{V}_K$, which first computes $\widehat{T} = \mathsf{MAC}.\mathcal{T}_K(M')$ and returns $\top$ (meaning verification success) if $T' = \widehat{T}$ and $\bot$ otherwise.

Let AE be a nonce-based AE scheme[5]. It consists of an encryption function $\mathsf{AE}.\mathcal{E} : \mathcal{K} \times \mathcal{N} \times \mathcal{A} \times \mathcal{M} \to \mathcal{M} \times \mathcal{T}$ and a decryption function $\mathsf{AE}.\mathcal{D} : \mathcal{K} \times \mathcal{N} \times \mathcal{A} \times \mathcal{M} \times \mathcal{T} \to \mathcal{M} \cup \{\bot\}$. Here, $\mathcal{K}$ is the key space, $\mathcal{N}$ is the nonce space (which is the value that never repeats at encryption), $\mathcal{M}$ is the message space, $\mathcal{A}$ is the associated data (AD) space, and $\mathcal{T}$ is the tag space. AD is a part of input that is not encrypted but authenticated, for example the protocol header or the receiver address.

For encrypting $M \in \mathcal{M}$ with $A \in \mathcal{A}$ and $N \in \mathcal{N}$ and $K \in \mathcal{K}$, we compute $(C, T) \leftarrow \mathsf{AE}.\mathcal{E}_K(N, A, M)$ and send (N, A, C, T) to the receiver. After receiving the tuple (N', A', C', T') (which may be a tampered version of (N, A, C, T)), the receiver performs decryption by computing $\mathsf{AE}.\mathcal{D}_K(N', A', C', T')$ and if it returns $M' \neq \bot$ the receiver decides that the tuple is authenticated with the decrypted plaintext M'. Otherwise the receiver decides that the verification fails.

We omit the corresponding security notions defined with certain games, as they are less relevant to our work. Refer to [13, 18, 30] for them.

3   Pincer Verification of MAC Modes

Let $\mathsf{MAC} = (\mathsf{MAC}.\mathcal{T}, \mathsf{MAC}.\mathcal{V})$ be a deterministic MAC scheme. Let $M \in \mathcal{M}$ be a message and $\mathcal{S}$ be a internal state space of MAC. We require $\mathcal{S} = \mathcal{T}$. Suppose $\mathsf{MAC}.\mathcal{T}$ can be decomposed into two functions: $F : \mathcal{K} \times \mathcal{M} \times \mathcal{S} \to \mathcal{S}$ and $G : \mathcal{K} \times \mathcal{M} \times \mathcal{S} \to \mathcal{T}$ and an initial constant $\mathtt{init} \in \mathcal{S}$, such that

$$\mathsf{MAC}.\mathcal{T}_K(M) = G_K(M_2, F_K(M_1, \mathtt{init})), \tag{1}$$

where $M_1 \parallel M_2 = M$ determined by a certain parsing function $f : \mathcal{M} \to \mathcal{M} \times \mathcal{M}$. We write $(M_1, M_2) \xleftarrow{f} M$ to mean this parsing. The specification of f depends on how pincer verification is applied. Typically $|M_1|$ and $|M_2|$ are similar and $|M_1|$ is a multiple of n for the block length n. For simplicity we only consider such messages, however in practice this may not hold true (e.g., a single-block message for CBC-MAC). We can fall back to the normal verification procedure if the parsing is not possible. To implement pincer verification, we require that $G(K, M_2, *)$ is a TBC with tweak M_2 (and message space $\mathcal{S}$). The inverse of G is denoted by $G^{-1} : \mathcal{K} \times \mathcal{M} \times \mathcal{T} \to \mathcal{S}$. We emphasize that we do not require a secure TBC for G: we just require $G(K, M_2, *)$ is a permutation for any (K, M_2).

---

[5] Our proposal covers AE schemes that do not necessarily require nonce, such as deterministic AE. We focus on nonce-based AE for simplicity.

Algorithm MAC.$\mathcal{T}_K(M)$	Algorithm MAC.$\mathcal{V}_K(M, T^*)$	Algorithm MAC.$\mathcal{PV}_K(M, T^*)$
1. $(M_1, M_2) \leftarrow f(M)$	1. $(M_1, M_2) \leftarrow f(M)$	1. $(M_1, M_2) \leftarrow f(M)$
2. $S \leftarrow F(K, M_1, \mathtt{Init})$	2. $S \leftarrow F(K, M_1, \mathtt{Init})$	2. $S \leftarrow F(K, M_1, \mathtt{Init})$
3. $T \leftarrow G(K, M_2, S)$	3. $T \leftarrow G(K, M_2, S)$	3. $S^* \leftarrow G^{-1}(K, M_2, T^*)$
4. **return** T	4. **return** $\top$ **if** $T = T^*$	4. **return** $\top$ **if** $S = S^*$
	5. **return** $\bot$ **otherwise**	5. **return** $\bot$ **otherwise**

Fig. 1. (Left) tagging of a MAC function MAC. (Middle) regular verification. (Right) Pincer Verification.

When (M, T^*)[6] is received, the normal MAC verification is to check if $T :=$ MAC.$\mathcal{T}_K(M)$ is identical to T^*. Then, for $M = M_1 \| M_2$, we compute $S \leftarrow F(K, M_1, \mathtt{Init})$ and $S^* \leftarrow G^{-1}(K, M_2, T^*)$ and check if $S = S^*$. Note that both F and G^{-1} can be computed in parallel, and the parsing function f determines which point to be matched in the entire MAC computation. To maximize the gain of parallelizability, this would be typically determined by the difference of computation costs of F and G^{-1}.

The soundness of pincer verification described above is simply shown by the following proposition.

Proposition 1. *If the above requirement holds for MAC, the normal verification (the middle of Fig. 1) and the pincer verification (the right of Fig. 1) are equivalent, that is, MAC.$\mathcal{V}_K(M, T^*) = $ MAC.$\mathcal{PV}_K(M, T^*)$ for any (K, M, T^*).*

Proof. When (M, T^*) is given, let $S = F_K(M_1, \mathtt{Init})$, $T = G_K(M_2, S)$ and $S^* = G_K^{-1}(M_2, T^*)$, where $M_1 \| M_2 \xleftarrow{f} M$. The normal verification accepts iff $T = T^*$ and the pincer verification accepts iff $S = S^*$. Since G is a TBC, the event $[T = T^*]$ is equivalent to $[G_K^{-1}(M_2, T) = G_K^{-1}(M_2, T^*)]$ which is identical to $[S = S^*]$ (Fig. 2). □

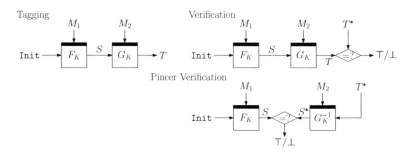

Fig. 2. MAC subroutines. The black rectangles in the boxes denote tweaks.

---

[6] We write (M, T^*) instead of (M', T') written at Sect. 2: this is convenient and intuitive to understand the data flow of pincer verification.

4   Pincer Verification of AE Modes

The idea of pincer verification is also extended to serial AE modes with some modifications. For this purpose we introduce an abstract model for serial AE. The idea is based on COFB [23]. For simplicity, we only consider the case that the matching point for the pincer decryption is in the ciphertext and not in the AD. First we define a component of (our abstraction of) serial AEs.

Definition 1. *Let* $\widehat{E} : \mathcal{K} \times \mathcal{T}_w \times \mathcal{S} \to \mathcal{B} \times \mathcal{S}$ *and* $\mathcal{T}_w = \mathcal{W} \times \mathcal{B}$, *for some finite sets* $\mathcal{K}$, $\mathcal{W}$, $\mathcal{B}$ *and* $\mathcal{S}$. *We say* $\widehat{E}$ *is a TBC with auxiliary output (TBC-AO) if there exist two functions,* $\widehat{E}_f^{-1}, \widehat{E}_b^{-1} : \mathcal{K} \times \mathcal{T}_w \times \mathcal{S} \to \mathcal{B} \times \mathcal{S}$ *such that, for any* $(K, T_w = (W, B)), B', S, S')$ *fulfilling* $\widehat{E}(K, T_w, S) = (B', S')$,

$$\widehat{E}_f^{-1}(K, T_w', S) = (B, S') \ and \ \widehat{E}_b^{-1}(K, T_w', S') = (B, S) \tag{2}$$

hold, where $T_w' = (W, B')$.

The functions $\widehat{E}$, $\widehat{E}_f^{-1}$ and $\widehat{E}_b^{-1}$ are required for encryption, (regular) decryption, and pincer decryption respectively. Equation (2) implies that, (T_w', S, S') is a tuple of (tweak, plaintext, ciphertext) of a TBC whose encryption and decryption routines are obtained by ignoring the first output elements of $\widehat{E}_f^{-1}$ and $\widehat{E}_b^{-1}$. As in the case of MAC, Definition 1 does not require any security property for TBC-AO.

Definition 2. *Let* $\mathcal{T}_w = \mathcal{W} \times \mathcal{B}$, $\mathcal{W} = \mathcal{N} \times \mathcal{A}$, $\mathcal{B} = \mathcal{M}$ *and* $\mathcal{S} = \{0,1\}^n$ *for nonce space* $\mathcal{N}$, *AD space* $\mathcal{A}$, *and message space* $\mathcal{M}$. *Let* SerialAE = (SerialAE.$\mathcal{E}$, SerialAE.$\mathcal{D}$) *be an AE scheme that can be decomposed into two TBC-AOs[7]* $F, G : \mathcal{K} \times \mathcal{T}_w \times \mathcal{S} \to \mathcal{M} \times \mathcal{S}$ *as shown in Fig. 3 together with a parsing function* f.

Let us briefly explain Fig. 3. The encryption SerialAE.$\mathcal{E}$ first parses M to M_1 and M_2 and encrypts M_1 to C_1 by F_K taking tweak $T_w = (N, A, M_1)$ and a constant Init as the initial state. The auxiliary output S is then used as the state input to G_K for encrypting M_2 to C_2 and producing the tag T. For (regular) decryption, SerialAE.$\mathcal{D}$ first parses C to C_1 and C_2 and applies $F_{f,K}^{-1}$ to recover M_1 and the intermediate state S. This S is used as the state input to $G_{f,K}^{-1}$ to recover M_2 and the locally computed tag T to be checked.

For the sake of generality we consider both F and G take the nonce N and the entire AD A, however in the real schemes this is not necessary, say G may ignore A (which is the case of COFB).

The pincer decryption of SerialAE is derived in a similar manner to the case of MAC. When (N, A, C, T^*) is received, the pincer decryption routine SerialAE.$\mathcal{PD}$ first parses C, and performs the forward computation in the same manner to the regular decryption using F_f^{-1} and the backward computation using G_b^{-1} in

---

[7] More precisely we only need F_f^{-1} for F.

Algorithm SerialAE.$\mathcal{E}(K, N, A, M)$	Algorithm SerialAE.$\mathcal{D}(K, N, A, C, T^*)$	Algorithm SerialAE.$\mathcal{PD}(K, N, A, C, T^*)$
1. $(M_1, M_2) \leftarrow f(M)$	1. $(C_1, C_2) \leftarrow f(C)$	1. $(C_1, C_2) \leftarrow f(C)$
2. $(C_1, S) \leftarrow F_K((N, A, M_1), \mathrm{Init})$	2. $(M_1, S) \leftarrow F_{f,K}^{-1}((N, A, C_1), \mathrm{Init})$	2. $(M_1, S) \leftarrow F_{f,K}^{-1}((N, A, C_1), \mathrm{Init})$
3. $(C_2, T) \leftarrow G_K((N, A, M_2), S)$	3. $(M_2, T) \leftarrow G_{f,K}^{-1}((N, A, C_2), S)$	3. $(M_2, S^*) \leftarrow G_{b,K}^{-1}((N, A, C_2), T^*)$
4. $C \leftarrow (C_1 \,\|\, C_2)$	4. If $T = T^*$	4. If $S = S^*$
5. return (C, T)	5. $M \leftarrow (M_1 \,\|\, M_2)$	5. $M \leftarrow (M_1 \,\|\, M_2)$
	6. return M	6. return M
	7. Else return $\perp$	7. Else return $\perp$

Fig. 3. Algorithms of serial AE scheme SerialAE.

parallel. See Fig. 3. As well as the case of MAC, the parsing function f determines which point to be matched, so it should be determined by considering the efficiency gap between F_f^{-1} and G_b^{-1}.

Any SerialAE allows a pincer decryption, as follows.

Proposition 2. *The regular decryption and the pincer decryption (the middle and the right of Fig. 3) are equivalent for any SerialAE, that is, SerialAE.$\mathcal{D}$ (K, N, A, C, T^*) $=$ SerialAE.$\mathcal{PD}(K, N, A, C, T^*)$ for any (K, N, A, C, T^*).*

Proof. The proof is basically the same as that of Proposition 1. We use the same notations as Fig. 3. Given (N, A, C, T^*) with key K, the derivations of S are identical for both SerialAE.$\mathcal{D}$ and SerialAE.$\mathcal{PD}$. We observe that $[T = T^*]$ is equivalent to $[S = S^*]$ as $G_{f,K}^{-1}$ and $G_{f,K}^{-1}$ is a pair of forward and backward permutation evaluations specified by (N, A, C_2) and K. Thus the verification result is always identical. If the verification successes, the decrypted plaintext $(M \leftarrow M_1 \,\|\, M_2)$ is identical; for M_1 it is trivial and for M_2, from Eq. (2), whenever $G_{f,K}^{-1}$ maps (C_2, S) to (M_2, T), with additional tweak variables (N, A), $G_{b,K}^{-1}$ maps (C_2, T) to (M_2, S). This concludes the proof.

5 Applications

5.1 MAC Modes

Pincer verification is applicable to any MAC scheme that can be interpreted as Eq. (1). This covers a wide range of MAC modes. Intuitively, one can apply when an internal chaining state of a MAC mode is computable from the tag. This requires that the tag is untruncated, which is usually a part of the specification; hereafter we assume untruncated tags when it is allowed in the specification. Most notably this applies to the classical CBC-MAC and CMAC, and their variants (See the last of Sect. 5). However, there are some exceptions because of their non-invertible state update (*e.g.*, GCBC [40]).

For parallel MAC modes, even if the pincer verification is applicable, the advantage is generally small because of their inherent parallelizability for regular verification. This applies to PMAC [42] or Carter-Wegman MACs (assuming a parallelizable universal hash function), such as GMAC [4] or Poly1305 [14]. Still some practical benefit is expected when the message is too short to gain the benefit of parallelizability. For example, PMAC for two message blocks essentially reduces to a variant of CBC-MAC and pincer verification will make it to two parallel block cipher calls instead of two serial calls. The main component of GMAC is the polynomial hash function over $\mathrm{GF}(2^n)$, which is defined as $\mathrm{poly}_K(M) = \sum_{i=1,\ldots,m} M[i] \cdot K^{m-i+1}$ for m-block message $M = (M[1],\ldots,M[m])$. This can be easily parallelized by pre-computing $K^2,\ldots,K^{s+1}$ so that s blocks are processed in parallel [26]. The choice of s will depend on the platform and implementation of multiplication over $\mathrm{GF}(2^n)$. For $s = 2$, the pincer verification allows a 2-parallel evaluation of $\mathrm{poly}_K(M)$ without caching K^2. The benefit would be small though.

Sponges. A cryptographic permutation is also a popular primitive to build a MAC. The typical MAC construction is (keyed) Sponge, such as KMAC [5]. Unfortunately Sponge-based MAC usually truncates the tag to ensure security, as otherwise the adversary is able to derive the internal state that can be used to create a forgery. In case the permutation is used to instantiate an Even-Mansour (EM) cipher and that EM is used to built a MAC in a serial MAC mode, we generally do not need to truncate and pincer verification may be possible. Chaskey [37] is one such example.

5.2 AE Modes

Small-state nonce-based AE has been very actively studied in the context of lightweight cryptography. CLOC [31] is a CAESAR submission that explicitly claims their small state of $2n$ bits as one of their advantages (when n-bit block cipher is used, and we exclude the memory for the key). It needs two block cipher calls per one input block (rate 1/2). COFB [23,24] is the first rate-1 block cipher mode for AE with a small state size of $1.5n$ bits. SAEB [38] further pushes the limit of state size to just n bits, which is the minimum. Its rate is effectively 1/2. To achieve these small state size, COFB and SAEB adopt serial structures. For AE based on TBC, Romulus [29] and PFB [39] achieve the smallest state size, *i.e.*, the state size is what is needed to implement TBC itself. More precisely, the state size is $n + t$ bits, for a TBC of n-bit block and t-bit tweak (again we exclude the key).

As we have shown, pincer decryption is possible whenever the AE scheme is interpreted as SerialAE of Definition 1. We investigated state-of-the-art small-state modes mentioned above.

COFB. Figure 4 shows an abstract, general structure of COFB and the related designs. Details are different by designs, but this figure is enough to discuss. The core component is the (keyless) state update function $\rho : \{0,1\}^n \times \{0,1\}^n \to \{0,1\}^n \times \{0,1\}^n$. The n-bit block TBC $\widetilde{E}_K$ takes distinct tweaks for each call, and in case of COFB it is instantiated by a block cipher with a mask derived by a nonce, a key, and a block index. The ρ function is defined as $\rho(S, M) \to (S', C)$ (where the first argument corresponds to the state value) such that

$$S' = \mathsf{G}(S) \oplus M, \text{ and } C = M \oplus S \tag{3}$$

using an $n \times n$ binary matrix G (Fig. 5). The function ρ is used to update the internal state (S) and to encrypt a plaintext block (M). When AD is processed, the first argument of ρ is an AD block and the second output is ignored (See Fig. 4). In the regular decryption we need to recover (S', M) from (S, C). This is possible irrespective of G by ρ_f^{-1}, which we call *forward ρ inversion*, defined as $\rho_f^{-1}(S, C) = (C \oplus S \oplus \mathsf{G}(S), C \oplus S)$. The correctness of the scheme is trivial to see, while we need some conditions on G to make it secure.

To make pincer verification possible for COFB, we need to recover (S, M) from (S', C). We call this procedure *backward ρ inversion*. It requires that $(\mathsf{G} + \mathsf{I})$ is regular, where I denotes the identity matrix. If this holds the pincer verification is implemented by using ρ_b^{-1} defined as

$$\rho_b^{-1}(S', C) = ((\mathsf{G} + \mathsf{I})^{-1}(C \oplus S'), (\mathsf{G} + \mathsf{I})^{-1}(C \oplus S') \oplus C).$$

The right hand side of the above equation coincides with (S, M). The specifications of COFB shown at [23] and [24] qualify the regularity of $(\mathsf{G} + \mathsf{I})$, and hence meet the condition of Definition 2. One can simply confirm this by backtracking the decryption algorithm from the tag, which involves (tweakable) block cipher decryption and ρ_b^{-1} in an alternating manner. However, the version that was submitted to NIST LWC, called GIFT-COFB [11], uses a simple G such that $\mathsf{G} + \mathsf{I}$ has rank $n - 1$. We stress that this does not harm its provable security; the security claim requires that the ranks of G and $\mathsf{G} + \mathsf{I}$ are high but not necessarily n.

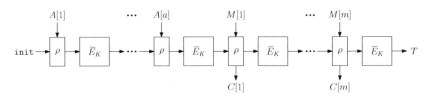

Fig. 4. General structure of COFB and the related designs, where ρ is the state update function. The second output of ρ is ignored while processing AD. $\widetilde{E}_K$ is a TBC possibly instantiated by a block cipher.

SAEB and SAEAES. SAEB [38] cannot use pincer decryption since the scheme is essentially identical to duplex sponge [16], which is a variant of CFB with an additional chaining state (rate part). The backtracking the internal state from the tag requires the knowledge of the plaintext rather than the ciphertext. A NIST LWC 2nd-round candidate SAEAES is an instantiation of SAEB, hence pincer decryption is not possible for it.

Romulus and PFB. Romulus [29] and PFB [39] share the general design shown at Fig. 4. They use TBCs. Their ρ functions have different structures from that of COFB (Eq. (3)). However, they allow the backward ρ inversion ρ_b^{-1}, hence pincer decryption is possible. The case of PFB is rather obvious, for its plaintext-feedback structure. The case of Romulus is bit more complex. Section 6 will give more details together with actual implementation results.

Summary of Applicability. We list MAC and AE modes that allow pincer verification/decryption as follows. We stress that the list is not exhaustive as it is not possible to list all the known modes in the literature. For CCM, we refer to Sect. 8.

- MAC modes: CMAC [3,30], CBC-MAC, EMAC [22], ECBC, FCBC, XCBC [18], TMAC [32], CBCR [46], PC-MAC [36], Chaskey [37]
- AE modes: CCM [2], Versions of COFB [23,24], Romulus [29], PFB [39]

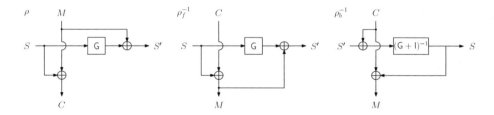

Fig. 5. The state update functions of COFB.

6   Case Study 1: Romulus

6.1   Pincer Verification of Romulus

We show a pincer decryption implementation for Romulus on microcontrollers. First we need to show that pincer decryption is indeed possible. In this paper, we focus on the nonce-based variant of Romulus, Romulus-N, which is the main variant of the NIST LWC submission. It uses SKINNY TBC [12]. We skip the details and focus on its ρ. For simplicity we only show the case that the last message block is n bits, but this can be extended to the case that the last block is less than n bits. As mentioned, the definition of ρ is different from Eq. (3). We have

$$\rho(S, M) = (S', C), \text{ such that } S' = S \oplus M, C = M \oplus \mathsf{G}(S)$$

for some $n \times n$ binary matrix G (see Fig. 6). The regular decryption is done by ρ_f^{-1}, which corresponds to ρ^{-1} defined as $\rho_f^{-1}(S, C) = (\mathsf{G}(S) \oplus C \oplus S, \mathsf{G}(S) \oplus C)$.

To make pincer decryption possible, we need ρ_b^{-1} that recovers (S, M) given (S', C), and it can be defined as

$$\rho_b^{-1}(S', C) := ((\mathsf{G} + \mathsf{I})^{-1}(S' \oplus C), (\mathsf{G} + \mathsf{I})^{-1}(S' \oplus C)) \oplus S'$$

if $\mathsf{G} + \mathsf{I}$ is regular. The ρ of Romulus fulfills this condition.

6.2 ESP32

We chose ESP32 for our implementation target, which is a very popular low-cost 32-bit microcontroller with buit-in Wi-Fi and Bluetooth. It is widely used for IoT applications. It shipments reached 100-Million at 2017 [7] and a report in 2018 showed that ESP became a leader in the embedded WiFi chip market sector [6]. ESP32 uses Tensilica's Xtensa LX6 microprocessor and is available in dual-core and single-core versions. We took Sipeed's Maixduino[8] which contains a dual-core ESP32 running at 240 MHz. This board was also used by a comprehensive microcontroller benchmark of NIST LWC candidates including Romulus, conducted by Renner, Pozzobon, and Mottok [41] (see also https://lwc.las3.de/).

The ESP32 chip used in our implementation has two cores, CPU0 and CPU1. Normally, the user application task runs on CPU1, while the system task runs on CPU0. The ESP32 runs FreeRTOS built in, and this allows tasks to run on different cores with a small overhead. CPU1 and CPU0 share the same memory space. Therefore, by accessing the same memory address in the task on CPU1 and the task on CPU0, coordinated processing can be performed between tasks running on multiple cores.

6.3 Implementation Details

In our implementation, the decryption routine first parses C into C_1 and C_2 and runs CPU1 to compute the forward direction of pincer decryption taking C_1, and CPU0 to compute the backward direction taking C_2 and the received tag T^*. For simplicity, we let C_1 and C_2 have (almost) equal number of blocks, thus the check is done at the midpoint of message, and assume the empty associated data. The information necessary for a task on CPU0 to operate is achieved by passing the memory location where the information is stored when the task starts. This keeps the API of decryption as normal (single-core) decryption, hence users are not required to change the outer code.

Due to the overhead of task switch (*i.e.*, invoking another task at CPU1 while CPU0 runs a main task), the pincer decryption is disadvantageous when the message is too short. In our environment, a task switch requires around 9,000 cycles. As we will see later, this makes pincer decryption effective for messages longer than 4 blocks (64 bytes). We wrote a C code and complied it with `xtensa-esp32-elf-gcc 5.2.0`.

---

[8] https://maixduino.sipeed.com/en/.

Implementation Results. Table 1 shows our implementation results on ESP32. When messages are long enough (1,536 bytes in our case), pincer decryption roughly halves the cycles from the regular decryption, showing pincer decryption performs ideally at this setting. The performance of encryption is mostly the same as the regular decryption. Since our purpose is to show the feasibility, we adopt a fast, table-based implementation for SKINNY. If cache-timing attacks are concern one can adopt a constant-time implementation, such as [8]. Other implementation details of SKINNY will be shown in an extended version.

Table 1. Comparison of regular decryption and pincer decryption of Romulus, measured by cycles per byte.

Message length (byte)	16	64	128	256	512	1024	1536
Regular decryption	1418	705	586	526	500	485	480
Pincer decryption	1427	615	425	330	283	261	254

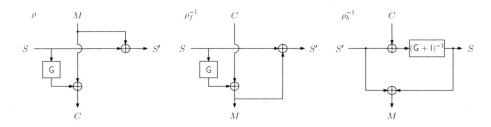

Fig. 6. The state update functions of Romulus.

7 Case Study 2: CMAC

The second case study takes CMAC on x86 CPUs with AES-NI. We implemented the regular and the pincer verifications of CMAC showed in Fig. 7. The regular one was implemented in the (trivial) serial manner, and the pincer one was implemented by parallelizing the lines 3–5 and the lines 6–12. In detail, we perform one-block encryption and one-block decryption of AES-128 by interleaving `aesenc` and `aesdec` instructions. This effectively parallelizes two-block computations, so we can process one-block encryption and decryption with the cycles to process one-block encryption/decryption. The technique is common for parallelizable modes, however previous implementations interleave multiple `aesenc` *or* `aesdec` instructions. The benchmark environment is as follows:

- OS: Linux version 4.15.0-128-generic
- Distribution: Ubuntu 18.04.5 LTS
- Processor: Intel Xeon Silver 4114 (2.2 GHz Skylake), Turboboost off
- Language: C with intrinsics

– Compiler: gcc 7.5.0

Table 2 shows the results of our implementations. Note that both results were taken on single core. In our environment, each AES instruction has latency 4 and throughput 1, in cycles. It shows that the cycle per byte (cpb) of the pincer verification converges to the half of that of the regular verification when the message is long enough. For a long message, the regular verification performance is almost identical to the that of single AES call. The use of intrinsics and some C function calls in our code introduced some overhead for both implementations, which could be improved by the use of assembly language. In any case, the important point is that we halved the verification time on single core.

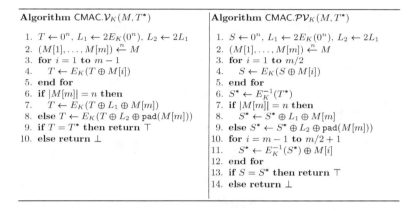

Algorithm CMAC.$\mathcal{V}_K(M, T^*)$

1. $T \leftarrow 0^n$, $L_1 \leftarrow 2E_K(0^n)$, $L_2 \leftarrow 2L_1$
2. $(M[1], \ldots, M[m]) \xleftarrow{n} M$
3. **for** $i = 1$ **to** $m - 1$
4. $T \leftarrow E_K(T \oplus M[i])$
5. **end for**
6. **if** $|M[m]| = n$ **then**
7. $T \leftarrow E_K(T \oplus L_1 \oplus M[m])$
8. **else** $T \leftarrow E_K(T \oplus L_2 \oplus \mathsf{pad}(M[m]))$
9. **if** $T = T^*$ **then return** $\top$
10. **else return** $\bot$

Algorithm CMAC.$\mathcal{PV}_K(M, T^*)$

1. $S \leftarrow 0^n$, $L_1 \leftarrow 2E_K(0^n)$, $L_2 \leftarrow 2L_1$
2. $(M[1], \ldots, M[m]) \xleftarrow{n} M$
3. **for** $i = 1$ **to** $m/2$
4. $S \leftarrow E_K(S \oplus M[i])$
5. **end for**
6. $S^* \leftarrow E_K^{-1}(T^*)$
7. **if** $|M[m]| = n$ **then**
8. $S^* \leftarrow S^* \oplus L_1 \oplus M[m]$
9. **else** $S^* \leftarrow S^* \oplus L_2 \oplus \mathsf{pad}(M[m]))$
10. **for** $i = m - 1$ **to** $m/2 + 1$
11. $S^* \leftarrow E_K^{-1}(S^*) \oplus M[i]$
12. **end for**
13. **if** $S = S^*$ **then return** $\top$
14. **else return** $\bot$

Fig. 7. (Left) Regular verification of CMAC. (Right) Pincer verification of CMAC. The padding is $\mathsf{pad}(x) = x \parallel 10^{n-|x|-1}$ when $0 \le |x| < n$ and $\mathsf{pad}(x) = x$ when $|x| = n$. $2L$ denotes $\mathrm{GF}(2^n)$ multiplication by the constant x. The pincer verification assumes even m for simplicity.

Table 2. Comparison of regular verification and pincer verification of CMAC, measured by cycle per byte. Measurements were taken on single core.

Message length (byte)	64	128	192	256	512	1024
Regular verification	2.00	2.34	2.68	2.85	3.10	3.35
Pincer verification	1.84	1.52	1.66	1.63	1.65	1.65

8   Case Study 3: CCM

We show how pincer verification technique is applied to CCM, which is one of the two NIST recommended AE modes based on AES (Fig. 9). It is widely deployed by major protocols and products (TLS, IPSec, WPA2, and lots of cryptographic library). Compared with another NIST recommendation GCM, its efficiency is generally inferior on modern desktop/mobile platforms. However, CCM does not need a 128-bit multiplier that is used by GCM, hence it enables a simpler implementation with a small code. This makes CCM useful on constrained devices.

The overall structure of CCM is MAC-then-Encrypt, where MAC is a plain CBC-MAC and encryption is CTR mode. While CTR mode is parallelizable it can be seen as SerialAE[9], and pincer verification is possible. Suppose we decrypt a tuple (N, A, C, T^*) with CCM, where $|A|_n = a$ and $|C|_n = m$ and $n = 128$, the normal procedure is to first decrypt C by CTR mode decryption to obtain the (unverified) plaintext M, and compute the candidate tag T by CBC-MAC taking (N, A, M) and check if $T = T^*$. CTR decryption and CBC-MAC are performed over m and $a + m$ blocks, hence we need $a + 2m$ block cipher calls in total. We also need 2 or 3 more calls depending on the parameters.

Pincer Decryption of CCM. Suppose we can process s blocks of AES computations in parallel, how fast CCM can decrypt? The trivial solution (which we call plain parallel) is to first perform CTR decryption in s-parallel, and perform CBC-MAC in serial. It costs $\lceil m/s \rceil + a + m$ parallel AES calls for a AD blocks and m ciphertext blocks. A more advanced solution is to interleave CTR decryption and CBC-MAC, which we call (plain) interleave. It reduces the latency of CTR decryption and has been employed by OpenSSL[10]. Our proposal is to combine interleaving and pincer verification of CBC-MAC. Depending on s, we derive two strategies. The first one (Option 1) interleaves CTR decryption and (the plain, forward direction of) CBC-MAC, and once CTR decryption is done, continues the pincer verification for the remaining CBC-MAC inputs. The second one (Option 2) performs "pincer decryption" of CTR, that is, from the first ciphertext block (forward direction) and from the last ciphertext block (backward direction), and at the same time performs the pincer verification of CBC-MAC. The latter is possible as above CTR decryption gives necessary input blocks. When CTR decryption is done, it continues the pincer verification for the remaining CBC-MAC blocks. See Fig. 8 for an illustration of Option 2. Option 1 works when $s \geq 2$, while Option 2 is faster but needs $s \geq 4$: two for pincer CTR decryption and two for pincer verification of CBC-MAC. Clearly $s = 4$ is optimal and achieves about $\lceil (a + m)/2 \rceil$ calls (Table 3). When $s = 4$, (plain parallel, interleave, pincer verification option 1, pincer verification option 2) needs about $(a + 5m/4, a + m, a/2 + 2m/3, (a + m)/2)$ calls, and when $s = 8$, $(a + 9m/8, a + m, a/2 + 4m/7, (a + m)/2)$ calls.

Table 4 shows the implementation results of CCM with AES-NI, using the same environment as Sect. 7. We set $s = 4$ as the best choice from the latency figures of AES-NI on our platform. We set 64-bit nonce and empty AD. The results showed the same trend as CMAC (Sect. 7): for a long message the pincer

---

[9] Strictly speaking it is not, because of the specification of `encode`, however this difference is not critical.

[10] https://github.com/openssl/openssl/blob/master/crypto/aes/asm/aesni-x86_64.pl.

decryption (Option 2) halves the computation cost from the previously known strategy (interleave).

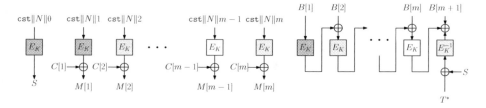

Fig. 8. Pincer decryption (Option 2) for CCM with $s = 4$ and empty AD. $B[1]$ involves N, and $B[i] = M[i-1]$ for $i > 1$. After the green boxes are computed, 4 light yellow boxes consisting of 3 E_K and 1 E_K^{-1} are computed in parallel. (Color figure online)

Table 3. Comparison of CCM decryption costs for a AD blocks, m ciphertext blocks, using parallel computation of s AES blocks. We ignore constant overhead.

Plain parallel	Interleave	Pincer decrypt (Opt. 1)	Pincer decrypt (Opt. 2)
$\lceil m/s \rceil + a + m$	$a + m$	$\lceil (a + m + \lceil m/(s-1) \rceil)/2 \rceil$	$\lceil (a+m)/2 \rceil$

Table 4. Comparison of regular decryption (which implements interleaving of CTR decryption and CBC-MAC) and pincer decryption (Option 2 with $s = 4$) for CCM, measured by cycle per byte. Measurements were taken on single core.

Message length (byte)	64	128	192	256	512	1024
Regular decryption	3.97	3.28	3.29	3.30	3.30	3.51
Pincer decryption	3.59	2.53	2.24	2.11	1.90	1.78

9   Conclusion

This article presented a new parallel implementation strategy, pincer verification, for verification/decryption routines of serial MAC and AE modes. The core idea is pretty simple, yet to our knowledge it has not been proposed in the literature. Although it is intuitive for the case of simple mode such as CBC-MAC, to deal with more complex mode we provided a formalization to see when and how pincer verification is possible that maintains the original functionality

Algorithm CCM.$\mathcal{E}_K(N, A, M)$	Algorithm CCM.$\mathcal{D}_K(N, A, C, T^*)$
1. $B \leftarrow \text{encode}(N, A, M)$	1. $M \leftarrow \text{CTR}[E_K](N, C)$
2. $U \leftarrow \text{CBC-MAC}[E_K](B)$	2. $B \leftarrow \text{encode}(N, A, M)$
3. $C \leftarrow \text{CTR}[E_K](N, M)$	3. $U \leftarrow \text{CBC-MAC}[E_K](B)$
4. $T \leftarrow E_K(\text{cst} \| N \| \langle 0 \rangle_{8\lambda}) \oplus U$	4. $T \leftarrow E_K(\text{cst} \| N \| \langle 0 \rangle_{8\lambda}) \oplus U$
5. return (C, T)	5. if $T = T^*$ then return M
	6. else return $\perp$
Algorithm CBC-MAC$[E_K](X)$	**Algorithm CTR$[E_K](N, X)$**
1. $S \leftarrow 0^n$	1. $(X[1], \ldots, X[x]) \xleftarrow{n} X$
2. $(X[1], \ldots, X[x]) \xleftarrow{n} X$	2. for $i = 1$ to x
3. for $i = 1$ to x	3. $Y[i] \leftarrow E_K(\text{cst} \| N \| \langle i \rangle_{8\lambda}) \oplus X[i]$
4. $S \leftarrow E_K(S \oplus X[i])$	4. $Y \leftarrow Y[1] \| \ldots \| Y[x]$
5. return S	5. return Y

Fig. 9. Algorithms of CCM. encode is an encoding function, cst is a byte determined by λ, and λ determines the maximum message length. $\langle i \rangle_j$ denotes the j-bit encoding of integer $i > 0$. Nonce is $15 - \lambda$ bytes, where $n = 128$. See [2] for details.

and security. Our case studies demonstrated its practicality. Notably it improves the verification/decryption performance of two NIST recommendations (CMAC and CCM) for x86 CPUs by a factor of 2.

We list some final remarks for future research. For CMAC and CCM, experiments with 64-bit ARM CPUs with AES instructions will be interesting from a practical point of view. The applicability of pincer decryption can be extended to some more generic-composition-like AE schemes, such as SIV [43], but whether it is effective or not depends on the MAC and Encryption parts. Although dual/multi-core microcontrollers are becoming popular, the implementation is still bit tricky and needs ad-hoc analysis to get the best performance. Finally, it would be interesting to consider if bitslice is combined with pincer verification, to improve performance on single core. Bitslice is usually for encryption of parallel blocks, however if encryption and decryption routines have a great similarity (e.g., Feistel), it may be possible to bitslice one encryption and one decryption of a cipher in an efficient manner.

Acknowledgements. The authors would like to thank the anonymous reviewers for their insightful comments, and thank Thomas Peyrin and Mustafa Khairallah for feedback.

References

1. NIST Lightweight Cryptography. https://csrc.nist.gov/projects/lightweight-cryptography. National Institute of Standards and Technology
2. Recommendation for Block Cipher Modes of Operation: The CCM Mode for Authentication and Confidentiality. NIST Special Publication 800-38C (2004). National Institute of Standards and Technology

3. Recommendation for Block Cipher Modes of Operation: the CMAC Mode for Authentication. NIST Special Publication 800-38B (2005). National Institute of Standards and Technology

4. Recommendation for Block Cipher Modes of Operation: Galois/Counter Mode (GCM) and GMAC. NIST Special Publication 800-38D (2007). National Institute of Standards and Technology

5. SHA-3 Derived Functions: cSHAKE, KMAC, TupleHash and ParallelHash. NIST Special Publication 800-185 (2016). National Institute of Standards and Technology

6. Wireless connectivity market analysis. TSR report (2018). www.t-s-r.co.jp/e/report/4543.html

7. Espressif milestones (2019). www.espressif.com/en/company/about-us/milestones

8. Adomnicai, A., Peyrin, T.: Fixslicing AES-like ciphers. IACR TCHES **2021**(1), 402–425 (2021). https://doi.org/10.46586/tches.v2021.i1.402-425. https://tches.iacr.org/index.php/TCHES/article/view/8739

9. Avanzi, R.: The QARMA block cipher family. IACR Trans. Symm. Cryptol. **2017**(1), 4–44 (2017). https://doi.org/10.13154/tosc.v2017.i1.4-44

10. Banik, S., et al.: Midori: a block cipher for low energy. In: Iwata, T., Cheon, J.H. (eds.) ASIACRYPT 2015. LNCS, vol. 9453, pp. 411–436. Springer, Heidelberg (2015). https://doi.org/10.1007/978-3-662-48800-3_17

11. Banik, S., et al.: GIFT-COFB. Submission to NIST Lightweight Cryptography (2019)

12. Beierle, C., et al.: The SKINNY family of block ciphers and its low-latency variant MANTIS. In: Robshaw, M., Katz, J. (eds.) CRYPTO 2016. LNCS, vol. 9815, pp. 123–153. Springer, Heidelberg (2016). https://doi.org/10.1007/978-3-662-53008-5_5

13. Bellare, M., Namprempre, C.: Authenticated encryption: relations among notions and analysis of the generic composition paradigm. In: Okamoto, T. (ed.) ASIACRYPT 2000. LNCS, vol. 1976, pp. 531–545. Springer, Heidelberg (2000). https://doi.org/10.1007/3-540-44448-3_41

14. Bernstein, D.J.: The Poly1305-AES message-authentication code. In: Gilbert, H., Handschuh, H. (eds.) FSE 2005. LNCS, vol. 3557, pp. 32–49. Springer, Heidelberg (2005). https://doi.org/10.1007/11502760_3

15. Bernstein, D.J., et al.: GIMLI: a cross-platform permutation. In: Fischer, W., Homma, N. (eds.) CHES 2017. LNCS, vol. 10529, pp. 299–320. Springer, Cham (2017). https://doi.org/10.1007/978-3-319-66787-4_15

16. Bertoni, G., Daemen, J., Peeters, M., Van Assche, G.: Duplexing the sponge: single-pass authenticated encryption and other applications. In: Miri, A., Vaudenay, S. (eds.) SAC 2011. LNCS, vol. 7118, pp. 320–337. Springer, Heidelberg (2012). https://doi.org/10.1007/978-3-642-28496-0_19

17. Biham, E.: A fast new DES implementation in software. In: Biham, E. (ed.) FSE 1997. LNCS, vol. 1267, pp. 260–272. Springer, Heidelberg (1997). https://doi.org/10.1007/BFb0052352

18. Black, J., Rogaway, P.: CBC MACs for arbitrary-length messages: the three-key constructions. J. Cryptol. **18**(2), 111–131 (2005). https://doi.org/10.1007/s00145-004-0016-3

19. Bogdanov, A., et al.: PRESENT: an ultra-lightweight block cipher. In: Paillier, P., Verbauwhede, I. (eds.) CHES 2007. LNCS, vol. 4727, pp. 450–466. Springer, Heidelberg (2007). https://doi.org/10.1007/978-3-540-74735-2_31

20. Bogdanov, A., Lauridsen, M.M., Tischhauser, E.: Comb to pipeline: fast software encryption revisited. In: Leander, G. (ed.) FSE 2015. LNCS, vol. 9054, pp. 150–171. Springer, Heidelberg (2015). https://doi.org/10.1007/978-3-662-48116-5_8

21. Borghoff, J., et al.: PRINCE – a low-latency block cipher for pervasive computing applications. In: Wang, X., Sako, K. (eds.) ASIACRYPT 2012. LNCS, vol. 7658, pp. 208–225. Springer, Heidelberg (2012). https://doi.org/10.1007/978-3-642-34961-4_14

22. Bosselaers, A., Preneel, B. (eds.): Integrity Primitives for Secure Information Systems. LNCS, vol. 1007. Springer, Heidelberg (1995). https://doi.org/10.1007/3-540-60640-8

23. Chakraborti, A., Iwata, T., Minematsu, K., Nandi, M.: Blockcipher-based authenticated encryption: how small can we go? In: Fischer, W., Homma, N. (eds.) CHES 2017. LNCS, vol. 10529, pp. 277–298. Springer, Cham (2017). https://doi.org/10.1007/978-3-319-66787-4_14

24. Chakraborti, A., Iwata, T., Minematsu, K., Nandi, M.: Blockcipher-based authenticated encryption: how small can we go? J. Cryptol. **33**(3), 703–741 (2019). https://doi.org/10.1007/s00145-019-09325-z

25. Dobraunig, C., Eichlseder, M., Mendel, F., Schläffer, M.: Ascon. Submission to NIST Lightweight Cryptography (2019)

26. Gueron, S., Kounavis, M.E.: Efficient implementation of the Galois Counter Mode using a carry-less multiplier and a fast reduction algorithm. Inf. Process. Lett. **110**(14–15), 549–553 (2010)

27. Guo, C., Khairallah, M., Minematsu, K., Peyrin, T.: Romulus v1.3. Submission to NIST Lightweight Cryptography (2021)

28. Hoffert, J.D.S., Peeters, M., Assche, G.V., Keer, R.V., Mella, S.: Zoodyak. Submission to NIST Lightweight Cryptography (2019)

29. Iwata, T., Khairallah, M., Minematsu, K., Peyrin, T.: Duel of the titans: the Romulus and Remus families of lightweight AEAD algorithms. IACR Trans. Symm. Cryptol. **2020**(1), 43–120 (2020). https://doi.org/10.13154/tosc.v2020.i1.43-120

30. Iwata, T., Kurosawa, K.: OMAC: one-key CBC MAC. In: Johansson, T. (ed.) FSE 2003. LNCS, vol. 2887, pp. 129–153. Springer, Heidelberg (2003). https://doi.org/10.1007/978-3-540-39887-5_11

31. Iwata, T., Minematsu, K., Guo, J., Morioka, S.: CLOC: authenticated encryption for short input. In: Cid, C., Rechberger, C. (eds.) FSE 2014. LNCS, vol. 8540, pp. 149–167. Springer, Heidelberg (2015). https://doi.org/10.1007/978-3-662-46706-0_8

32. Kurosawa, K., Iwata, T.: TMAC: two-key CBC MAC. In: Joye, M. (ed.) CT-RSA 2003. LNCS, vol. 2612, pp. 33–49. Springer, Heidelberg (2003). https://doi.org/10.1007/3-540-36563-X_3

33. Liskov, M., Rivest, R.L., Wagner, D.: Tweakable block ciphers. In: Yung, M. (ed.) CRYPTO 2002. LNCS, vol. 2442, pp. 31–46. Springer, Heidelberg (2002). https://doi.org/10.1007/3-540-45708-9_3

34. Matsuda, S., Moriai, S.: Lightweight cryptography for the cloud: exploit the power of Bitslice implementation. In: Prouff, E., Schaumont, P. (eds.) CHES 2012. LNCS, vol. 7428, pp. 408–425. Springer, Heidelberg (2012). https://doi.org/10.1007/978-3-642-33027-8_24

35. Matsui, M.: How far can we go on the x64 processors? In: Robshaw, M. (ed.) FSE 2006. LNCS, vol. 4047, pp. 341–358. Springer, Heidelberg (2006). https://doi.org/10.1007/11799313_22

36. Minematsu, K., Tsunoo, Y.: Provably secure MACs from differentially-uniform permutations and AES-based implementations. In: Robshaw, M. (ed.) FSE 2006. LNCS, vol. 4047, pp. 226–241. Springer, Heidelberg (2006). https://doi.org/10.1007/11799313_15

37. Mouha, N., Mennink, B., Van Herrewege, A., Watanabe, D., Preneel, B., Verbauwhede, I.: Chaskey: an efficient MAC algorithm for 32-bit microcontrollers. In: Joux, A., Youssef, A. (eds.) SAC 2014. LNCS, vol. 8781, pp. 306–323. Springer, Cham (2014). https://doi.org/10.1007/978-3-319-13051-4_19

38. Naito, Y., Matsui, M., Sugawara, T., Suzuki, D.: SAEB: a lightweight blockcipher-based AEAD mode of operation. IACR TCHES **2018**(2), 192–217 (2018). https://doi.org/10.13154/tches.v2018.i2.192-217. https://tches.iacr.org/index.php/TCHES/article/view/885

39. Naito, Y., Sugawara, T.: Lightweight authenticated encryption mode of operation for tweakable block ciphers. IACR TCHES **2020**(1), 66–94 (2019). https://doi.org/10.13154/tches.v2020.i1.66-94. https://tches.iacr.org/index.php/TCHES/article/view/8393

40. Nandi, M.: Fast and secure CBC-type MAC algorithms. In: Dunkelman, O. (ed.) FSE 2009. LNCS, vol. 5665, pp. 375–393. Springer, Heidelberg (2009). https://doi.org/10.1007/978-3-642-03317-9_23

41. Renner, S., Pozzobon, E., Mottok, J.: A hardware in the loop benchmark suite to evaluate NIST LWC ciphers on microcontrollers. In: Meng, W., Gollmann, D., Jensen, C.D., Zhou, J. (eds.) ICICS 2020. LNCS, vol. 12282, pp. 495–509. Springer, Cham (2020). https://doi.org/10.1007/978-3-030-61078-4_28

42. Rogaway, P.: Efficient instantiations of tweakable blockciphers and refinements to modes OCB and PMAC. In: Lee, P.J. (ed.) ASIACRYPT 2004. LNCS, vol. 3329, pp. 16–31. Springer, Heidelberg (2004). https://doi.org/10.1007/978-3-540-30539-2_2

43. Rogaway, P., Shrimpton, T.: A provable-security treatment of the key-wrap problem. In: Vaudenay, S. (ed.) EUROCRYPT 2006. LNCS, vol. 4004, pp. 373–390. Springer, Heidelberg (2006). https://doi.org/10.1007/11761679_23

44. Schwabe, P., Stoffelen, K.: All the AES you need on Cortex-M3 and M4. In: Avanzi, R., Heys, H. (eds.) SAC 2016. LNCS, vol. 10532, pp. 180–194. Springer, Cham (2017). https://doi.org/10.1007/978-3-319-69453-5_10

45. Wang, B., Gu, X., Yang, Y.: Saber on ESP32. In: Conti, M., Zhou, J., Casalicchio, E., Spognardi, A. (eds.) ACNS 2020. LNCS, vol. 12146, pp. 421–440. Springer, Cham (2020). https://doi.org/10.1007/978-3-030-57808-4_21

46. Zhang, L., Wu, W., Zhang, L., Wang, P.: CBCR: CBC MAC with rotating transformations. Sci. China Inf. Sci. **54**(11), 2247–2255 (2011)

Secret-Key Cryptography:
Cryptanalysis

Related-Tweak Impossible Differential Cryptanalysis of Reduced-Round TweAES

Chao Niu[1,2], Muzhou Li[1,2], Meiqin Wang[1,2,3(✉)], Qingju Wang[4],
and Siu-Ming Yiu[5]

[1] Key Laboratory of Cryptologic Technology and Information Security,
Ministry of Education, Shandong University, Jinan, China
{niuchao,muzhouli}@mail.sdu.edu.cn, mqwang@sdu.edu.cn
[2] School of Cyber Science and Technology, Shandong University, Qingdao, China
[3] Quan Cheng Shandong Laboratory, Jinan, China
[4] SnT, University of Luxembourg, L-4364 Esch-sur-Alzette, Luxembourg
[5] Department of Computer Science, The University of Hong Kong,
Hong Kong 999077, China
smyiu@cs.hku.hk

Abstract. We consider the related-tweak impossible differential cryptanalysis of TweAES. It is one of the underlying primitives of Authenticated Encryption with Associated Data (AEAD) scheme ESTATE which was accepted as one of second-round candidates in the NIST Lightweight Cryptography Standardization project. Firstly, we reveal several properties of TweAES, which show what kinds of distinguishers are more effective in recovering keys. With the help of automatic solver Simple Theorem Prover (STP), we achieve many 5.5-round related-tweak impossible differentials with fixed input differences and output differences that just have one active byte. Then, we implement 8-round key recovery attacks against TweAES based on one of these 5.5-round distinguishers. Moreover, another 5.5-round distinguisher that has four active bytes at the end is utilized to mount a 7-round key recovery attack against TweAES, which needs much lower attack complexities than the 6-round related-tweak impossible differential attack of TweAES in the design document. Our 8-round key recovery attack is the best one against TweAES in terms of the number of rounds and complexities so far.

Keywords: TweAES · Tweakable block ciphers · Related-tweak · Impossible differential cryptanalysis

1 Introduction

TweAES is one of the underlying primitives of Authenticated Encryption with Associated Data (AEAD) scheme ESTATE [7], which was accepted as one of second-round candidates in the NIST Lightweight Cryptography Standardization project. As a tweakable variant of AES-128 [11], TweAES is explicitly designed for efficient processing of small tweaks of 4 bits and the tweak is used to provide domain separation. More specifically, TweAES is identical to AES-128 except that it injects a tweak value at an interval of every two rounds.

After two decades of cryptanalysis, various attacks have been carried out on AES-128 [1,4,5,9,10,12,15,18,19]. Among all these attacks, the best attack against it in the single-key setting only reaches 7 out of 10 rounds, and the best-known attack so far is either an impossible differential attack [1,5,15], or a meet-in-the-middle attack [4,9,10]. Moreover, a known-key attack against full AES-128 is proposed in [12]. With the extra freedom brought by the 4-bit tweak, the security of TweAES compared to AES-128 is worthy of further study. In [7], designers of TweAES evaluated its security against differential, impossible differential and boomerang attacks in the chosen-tweak setting. Among all of them, the most effective attack is the impossible differential attack, where the data and time complexity are both 2^{127} while the memory complexity is 2^{96}.

Here, we give the first third-party cryptanalytic result on TweAES utilizing impossible differentials under related tweaks, which is also the best key recovery attack in terms of the number of rounds and complexities according to our knowledge.

Motivations and Contributions. A tweakable block cipher has the advantages of easier to prove models of operation based on it, and respond to the high demand, many tweakable block ciphers have been proposed [3,13,14]. As a tweakable block cipher, TweAES provides a more efficient way to process the demand of domain separation when encrypting a short message. Although the AEAD scheme ESTATE does not enter the finalist of the NIST competition, the security of the newly designed TweAES is still worth noticing.

In this paper, we firstly reveal several interesting properties of TweAES, which show that the related-tweak impossible differential attack on 8-round cipher proposed in the design document [7] is not valid actually. In their attack, same data sets are used under 2^7 different tweak differences trying to filter out wrong keys. However, as shown in Sect. 2.3, different tweak differences will lead to different involved key bits used before and after this distinguisher. With these facts, their data complexity is corrected as 2^{131}, and then the time complexity of their attack is at least 2^{131} 8-round TweAES encryptions. Thus, their attack is invalid due to the time complexity exceeding the exhaustively search.

To evaluate the security of TweAES against impossible differential, we use the automatic solver STP to search for more effective distinguishers aiming to achieve more rounds in key recovery attacks. As a result, we achieve many 5.5-round distinguishers with fixed input and tweak differences, and the output differences only have one active byte. Then, we implemented 8-round key recovery attack against TweAES based on one of these 5.5-round related-tweak impossible differential distinguishers shown in Sect. 4. Moreover, we use the 5.5-round impossible differential that has four active bytes at the end to mount a 7-round key recovery attack against TweAES in Sect. 5 with much lower attack complexities than the 6-round attack proposed in the design document [7].

Our attacks along with others on TweAES are shown in Table 1, from which one can see that our 8-round key recovery attack is the best one against TweAES in terms of the number of rounds and complexities so far.

Table 1. Summary of attacks against TweAES. The time complexity is measured by the unit of encryptions, and the memory complexity is measured in bits.

#Round	Data	Time (EN)	Memory (Bits)	#TK	Attack Type	Ref.
5	2^5 CP	2^{26}	$2^{28.58}$	2	Trunc. Diff.	[7]
6	2^5 KP	2^{45}	$negl.$	2^4	Integral	[7]
6	2^{119} CP	2^{119}	$2^{78.17}$	2	RTID	[7]
7	2^{99} CP	2^{100}	2^{70}	2	RTID	Sect. 5
$8^\dagger$	2^{131} CP	$>2^{131}$	$2^{112.58}$	2^4	RTID	[7]
8	$2^{124.28}$ CP	$2^{124.36}$	$2^{118.81}$	2	RTID	Sect. 4

CP: chosen plaintext;   KP: known plaintext;   #TK: the number of tweak used;
RTID: related-tweak impossible differential;
† After correction, the time complexity exceeds the exhaustive search,
which makes it invalid.

Outline. In Sect. 2, we briefly recall the specification of TweAES and reveal several interesting properties of it. With these properties, the attack complexity of related-tweak impossible differential attack in [7] has been corrected. Then an automatic search algorithm with STP for finding a key recovery conducive impossible differential and a new 8-round key recovery attack with 5.5-round related-tweak impossible differential is proposed in Sect. 3 and Sect. 4, respectively. Moreover, in Sect. 5, we mount a key recovery attack against 7-round TweAES with much lower complexities than the 6-round attack in the design document. Finally Sect. 6 concludes this work.

2   Preliminaries

TweAES, one of the underlying primitives of the AEAD scheme ESTATE [7], is a tweakable variant of AES-128 [11]. In this section, we first recall the specification of TweAES. Then, we reveal several properties of it, which cause the 8-round attack in [7] to be illusive. Actual complexities of this attack are evaluated in the end of this section.

2.1   Specification of TweAES

TweAES is a 128-bit tweakable block cipher with a 4-bit tweak and a 128-bit key, which is a tweakable variant of AES-128. More specifically, TweAES is identical to AES-128 except that it injects a tweak value at an interval of every two rounds.

Fig. 1. 4×4 (left) and 1×16 (right) byte indexing of 128-bit data block of TweAES

A 128-bit plaintext states are commonly treated as byte matrices of size 4×4, as shown in Fig. 1.

The round function of TweAES is composed of five operations, which are implemented sequentially, and we detail them as follows:

- **SubByte** (SB): TweAES uses the same 8-bit Sbox as AES-128. One can refer to [11] for more details.
- **ShiftRows** (SR): The bytes in the i-th row are cyclically shifted by i place to the left.
- **MixColumn** (MC): Multiply each column with a constant 4×4 matrix

$$\begin{bmatrix} 2 & 3 & 1 & 1 \\ 1 & 2 & 3 & 1 \\ 1 & 1 & 2 & 3 \\ 3 & 1 & 1 & 2 \end{bmatrix}$$

over the finite field $\mathbb{F}_8$, where the irreducible polynomial is $x^8 + x^4 + x^3 + x + 1$.
- **AddKey** (AK): XOR the state with a 128-bit subkey, which is generated from the 128-bit master key according to the key schedule of AES-128.
- **AddTweak** (AT): The 4-bit tweak is first expanded to an 8-bit value using a linear code, and then the 8-bit value is XORed to the state at an interval of every two rounds. To be specific, let us denote r as the r-th round with $1 \le r \le 10$, $r \in \mathbb{Z}$, then the AT operation is only applied when r is odd.

Note that, all the operations except for the AT, are identical to that of AES-128 including the key schedule. The detail of AT is shown as follows. At first, the 4-bit tweak expanded to an 8-bit value using a linear code. Define (T_0, T_1, T_2, T_3) as the 4-bit tweak, and

$$T_\oplus = T_0 \oplus T_1 \oplus T_2 \oplus T_3.$$

Then for each $i \in \{0, 1, 2, 3\}$, we have

$$T_{i+4} \leftarrow T_i \oplus T_\oplus.$$

Afterwards, the 8-bit expanded tweak $(T_0, T_1, T_2, T_3, T_4, T_5, T_6, T_7)$ is XORed into the least significant bit of each byte in first two rows of the state. The values of expanded tweak are the same for each AT operation.

2.2   Notations and Definitions

The following notations are utilized throughout the rest of this paper.

X_i: state before SB in round i
Y_i: state before SR in round i
Z_i: state before MC in round i
W_i: state before AK in round i
T: the four-bit tweak
T_i: the i-th bit of T
K_i: the subkey in round i
ET: the eight-bit expanded tweak
ΔX: the difference in a state X
$X_i[m]$: the mth byte of a state X in round i, where $0 \leq m \leq 15$
$X_i[p, \ldots, r]$: bytes from p^{th} to r^{th} of state X in round i, where $0 \leq p, r \leq 15$

2.3   Properties of TweAES

Some interesting properties of TweAES that were utilized during our attacks are described as follows:

1. The linear expand code of the 4-bit tweak make sure that the number of the active columns of the state caused by the tweak difference is at least three after the AT operation and one AES round.
2. After the inverse AT operation and one inverse AES round, the tweak difference propagates to the whole state when the active number of tweak bits is odd or 1111_2.
3. Recall that the TweAES has a 4-bit tweak, and this 4-bit tweak has 15 kinds of nonzero differences. With the insert of tweak difference and propagation of difference before and after the distinguisher, key bytes involved are different in the key recovery attack.

In general, multi distinguishers can be used to mount a key recovery attack only when the involved key bits in the process are the same. By exploiting the involved key bits when appending one round before and after the distinguisher, we can determine that one cannot use a different tweak difference in the key recovery because of the different involved key bits. Under the 15 different nonzero tweak differences, involved key bits are shown in Table 2. Here, we omit the MC operation in the appending round after the distinguisher.

We utilize the following proposition in our attacks, which is also exploited in [10].

Proposition 1 *(Differential Property of Sbox [10]). Given the nonzero input and output difference pair $(\Delta_{in}, \Delta_{out})$ of an Sbox S, there exists one solution y on average, for which the equation, $S(y) \oplus S(y \oplus \Delta_{in}) = \Delta_{out}$, holds true.*

Table 2. The involved key bits under different non-zero tweak differences, where $*$ denotes the key bits involved, and 0 denotes the key bits not involved. The byte order of the involved key is shown in Fig. 1.

Tweak Diff.	Expanded Tweak Diff.	Before	After
0001_2	$(0001\ 1110)_2$	**** **** **** ****	000* **0* 0000 0000
0010_2	$(0010\ 1101)_2$	**** **** **** ****	00*0 *0** 0000 0000
0100_2	$(0100\ 1011)_2$	**** **** **** ****	0*00 0*** 0000 0000
1000_2	$(1000\ 0111)_2$	**** **** **** ****	*000 ***0 0000 0000
1110_2	$(1110\ 0001)_2$	**** **** **** ****	***0 00*0 0000 0000
1101_2	$(1101\ 0010)_2$	**** **** **** ****	**0* 0*00 0000 0000
1011_2	$(1011\ 0100)_2$	**** **** **** ****	*0** *000 0000 0000
0111_2	$(0111\ 1000)_2$	**** **** **** ****	0*** 000* 0000 0000
0011_2	$(0011\ 0011)_2$	00** *00* **00 0**0	00** 0**0 0000 0000
0110_2	$(0110\ 0110)_2$	0**0 00** *00* **00	0**0 **00 0000 0000
1100_2	$(1100\ 1100)_2$	**00 0**0 00** *00*	**00 *00* 0000 0000
1001_2	$(1001\ 1001)_2$	*00* **00 0**0 00**	*00* 00** 0000 0000
0101_2	$(0101\ 0101)_2$	0*0* *0*0 0*0* *0*0	0*0* *0*0 0000 0000
1010_2	$(1010\ 1010)_2$	*0*0 0*0* *0*0 0*0*	*0*0 0*0* 0000 0000
1111_2	$(1111\ 1111)_2$	**** **** **** ****	**** **** 0000 0000

2.4   Impossible Differential Attack on TweAES Proposed by Designers

In [7], designers proposed a key recovery attack on 8-round TweAES utilizing a 6-round related-tweak impossible differential, which is depicted in Appendix A. By adding one round before and after it, they claimed that 8-round TweAES can be attacked (see Appendix B). However, there are two main points one should notice.

The first one comes from the properties described in Property 3. As we can see, different tweak differences will lead to different involved key bits. In their attack [7], tweak difference is set to be 1100_2. Thus, there are only $2^2 \times 2^2 \times \frac{1}{2} = 2^3$ tweak pairs satisfying this difference. However, they exploited 2^7 tweak pairs to filter out wrong keys which is not achievable. And then, the attack procedure of [7] in Step 3 will obtain about $2^{3+64+64-96} = 2^{35}$ pairs rather than 2^{39} pairs. Hence, in Step 5, for filtering the wrong key, they need repeat 2^{63} times from the first step to obtain $2^{35+63} = 2^{98}$ wrong-key candidates. The data complexity is $2^4 \times 2^{64} \times 2^{63} = 2^{131}$ chosen plaintexts. And then the time complexity of this attack is at least 2^{131} 8-round TweAES encryptions.

The second one is that to recover the master key, the attack needs much higher complexity than the exhaustive search. In the attack [7], after filtering the wrong key candidates, the remaining key space of the involved 12 bytes becomes $2^{96} \times (1 - 2^{-96})^{2^{98}} \approx 2^{96} \times e^{-2} \approx 2^{90.2}$. Due to the complicated key schedule of TweAES, the reduced factor of 5.77-bit subkey information cannot be used to recover 5.77-bit master key information. To recover the master key, we should exhaustively search the subkey candidates and the left eight bytes of K_1. Then, the time complexity for recovering the master key is $2^{90.2} \times 2^{64} \approx 2^{154.2}$ 8-round encryption units, which costs much higher than the exhaustively search of 128-bit master key.

3 STP-Based Automatic Searching Algorithm for Related-Tweak Impossible Differential

Recently, many cryptanalytic results have been improved with the advent of various automated tools. Among all of them, the Boolean Satisfiability (SAT) [8] and Satisfiability Modulo Theories (SMT) problem [2] solver STP[1] has been playing an important role. The application of STP in cryptanalysis is firstly proposed by Mouha and Preneel [17]. It is a decision procedure to check if there is a solution to a set of equations. These equations must follow the rule of input language parsed by STP[2].

When searching for related-tweak impossible differentials, differences on the input state is often set to be canceled by tweak differences in the first round, as shown in [20], which can lead to longer distinguishers. Moreover, to make them effective when mounting key recovery attacks, the number of active bytes of input and output differences is usually restricted to be as small as possible. And position of active bytes shall be chosen carefully. Motivated by this kind of strategy, we try to find distinguishers that cancel the state difference with tweak at the beginning, but remain one active byte at the end.

With the help of automatic tools, we can accurately characterize the propagation of the difference. More specifically, in the search algorithm, differential propagation properties of operations should be represented by some equations and precisely depicted. In addition to these propagation properties, equations representing the condition for related-tweak impossible differential are also included. Whether these equations have a solution or not can directly help us to confirm whether the expected impossible differential exists.

In practice, if we aim at finding an r-round related-tweak impossible differential, we describe the difference propagation through the round function and tweak schedule (in the case of TweAES, the same tweak is used in each round). These constraint equations can be divided into two parts. Part 1 contains equations depicting propagation properties between input and output difference of operations in the round function and the tweak schedule. In Part 2, we describe equations representing the condition we used for related-tweak impossible differentials.

Part 1. Equations for Basic Operations in Block Cipher

In the first part of the model, we describe equations of XOR and branching operations for differential propagation [16]. Then, we give equations to describe the ideal Sbox and confusion layer. For clarity, differential propagation of XOR and branching operations are illustrated in Fig. 2.

---

[1] http://stp.github.io/.

[2] STP supports two kinds of input languages, here we use the CVC one. For more information about the CVC, please refer to https://stp.readthedocs.io/en/latest/cvc-input-language.html.

Fig. 2. XOR and branching

Property 1 (**XOR**[16]). Let Δ_1 and Δ_2 represent two input differences for the operation XOR, and output difference is Δ_{out}. Then the relation between them is $\Delta_{out} = \Delta_1 \oplus \Delta_2$.

Property 2 (**Three-Branch**[16]). Let Δ_{in} denote input difference, and output difference to be decided are Δ_1 and Δ_2. Then the relation between them are $\Delta_{in} = \Delta_1 = \Delta_2$.

In our search model, we explicitly described the linear layer in the bit level. For the Sbox operation, we assume that the AES Sbox can map a nonzero input difference to any nonzero output difference. Under this assumption, when we found an impossible differential, it will still hold for real ciphers since contradictions occur at the bit-level linear layer.

Property 3 (**Ideal Sbox**). Let S be the Sbox used in the round function of the target cipher. The input difference is Δ_{in}, and the corresponding output difference is denoted as Δ_{out}. Then we have $\Delta_{out} = 0$ if $\Delta_{in} = 0$. Otherwise, $\Delta_{out} \neq 0$.

The linear layer of many block ciphers can be represented as matrix multiplication. Then, we have the following property.

Property 4 (**Confusion Matrix**). Let A denote the confusion matrix, $\vec{\Delta}_{in}$ and $\vec{\Delta}_{out}$ represent the column-wise input and output difference, respectively. Then, we have $\vec{\Delta}_{out} = A \cdot \vec{\Delta}_{in}$.

Part 2. Equations Depicting the Related-Tweak Impossible Differential Condition

The original impossible differential cryptanalysis usually derives the differential propagation in the forward and backward directions, and finds the contradiction in the middle. Our search model is at the bit level, and we just need to add constraints at the beginning and the end of the model. Then, STP will detect the contradiction in the whole model. Note that, the active state or the active bytes of input and output state are heuristically determined. In our search strategy, we restrict the input difference at the beginning of the state equal to the tweak difference. At the end of the state, we remain only one active byte. In the actual search, we found that the less the number of non-zero differences in the output is limited, the longer distinguisher we can get.

Algorithm 1: Search RTID $(R, \Delta_T, \Delta_0, \Delta_R)$

Input: R : Number of rounds covered by the expected distinguisher
       Δ_T : Active state of tweak difference
       Δ_0 : Active state of input difference in the state
       Δ_R : Active state of output difference in the state
Output: R-round related-tweak impossible differential or "No solution"

1 **forall the** *considered difference on the 4-bit tweak* **do**
2 | **forall the** *considered position of active output difference byte* **do**
       /* Equations in Part 1 describing state update   */
3   **for** $r \leftarrow 0$ *to* $R - 1$ **do**
4 | Use Property $1 \sim 4$ to construct equations for the r-th round function;
       /* Equations in Part 2 describing the related-tweak impossible differential condition   */
5   Construct equations describing the active state of the difference on tweak, input and output according to Δ_T, Δ_0 and Δ_R;
6   Input all these equations into STP and let it solve;
7   **if** *STP return "Invalid"* **then**
8 | Output $(\Delta_T, \Delta_0, \Delta_R)$ as a related-tweak impossible differential;

9 **return** "No Solution";

Given all these properties, the searching algorithm for related-tweak impossible differential is listed in Algorithm 1.

One thing we have to mention is that this algorithm can also be used to search for related-tweak impossible differentials under different strategies of choosing input and output differences, by simply modifying equations in Part 2.

4   Key Recovery Attack on 8-Round TweAES

After revealing that the related-tweak impossible differential distinguisher in [7] cannot perform valid key recovery attacks, we try to find a new related-tweak impossible differential distinguisher and perform a key recovery attack against TweAES. Before the attack is explained, we introduce some more notations which are borrowed from [6]. Suppose an impossible differential $(\Delta X \nrightarrow \Delta Y)$ has been constructed for r_Δ rounds under a pair of related tweaks, and is used to attack $r_{in} + r_\Delta + r_{out}$ rounds. Through r_{in} and r_{out}, ΔX and ΔY propagate to Δ_{in} and Δ_{out} with probability one, respectively. Let c_{in} (resp. c_{out}) denote the number of bit-conditions that have to be verified to obtain ΔX from Δ_{in} (resp. ΔY from Δ_{out}).

4.1 The 5.5-Round Related-Tweak Impossible Differential Distinguisher of TweAES

With the help of Algorithm 1, we can find lots of 5.5-round impossible differential distinguishers which have only one active byte at the end. These distinguishers are shown in Table 3. To clarify, we visualize the contradiction leading to the impossible differential property in Fig. 3 for D_{11} with the 12-th byte of the output difference. To illustrate the contradiction that leads to the impossible differential, we depict the propagation of the difference through the encryption data path. First, we derive the difference propagation in the forward direction. Recall the AT operation in the specification of TweAES, the 4-bit tweak is firstly expanded to an 8-bit value using a linear code, and the 8-bit value is XORed to the least significant bit of each byte in the first two rows of state. For canceling the difference on the state with a tweak difference, we set the difference on the $W_2[0, 1, 4, 5]$ equal to the active one-bit tweak difference, which means the least significant bit of each byte has an active difference, along with other bits a zero difference. Hence, the difference on each byte of $W_2[0, 1, 4, 5]$ is fixed 0x01. Since the tweak of TweAES is XORed every two rounds, after the difference canceling occurs at the beginning of the distinguisher, the zero difference will propagate through two rounds to W_4.

Table 3. Tweak differences and corresponding possible active byte of the output difference. The active byte index at the end is shown as a list $[0, ..., 15]$.

Dist.	Tweak Diff.	Expanded Tweak Diff.	Active Byte Index
D_1	0001_2	$(0001\ 1110)_2$	$[0, 1, 3, 4, 5, 6, 7, 8, 9, 10, 11, 12, 13, 14, 15]$
D_2	0010_2	$(0010\ 1101)_2$	$[0, 2, 3, 4, 5, 6, 7, 8, 9, 10, 11, 12, 13, 14, 15]$
D_3	0100_2	$(0100\ 1011)_2$	$[1, 2, 3, 4, 5, 6, 7, 8, 9, 10, 11, 12, 13, 14, 15]$
D_4	1000_2	$(1000\ 0111)_2$	$[0, 1, 2, 4, 5, 6, 7, 8, 9, 10, 11, 12, 13, 14, 15]$
D_5	1110_2	$(1110\ 0001)_2$	$[0, 1, 2, 4, 5, 6, 7, 8, 9, 10, 11, 12, 13, 14, 15]$
D_6	1101_2	$(1101\ 0010)_2$	$[0, 1, 3, 4, 5, 6, 7, 8, 9, 10, 11, 12, 13, 14, 15]$
D_7	1011_2	$(1011\ 0100)_2$	$[0, 2, 3, 4, 5, 6, 7, 8, 9, 10, 11, 12, 13, 14, 15]$
D_8	0111_2	$(0111\ 1000)_2$	$[1, 2, 3, 4, 5, 6, 7, 8, 9, 10, 11, 12, 13, 14, 15]$
D_9	0011_2	$(0011\ 0011)_2$	$[0, 1, 2, 3, 4, 5, 6, 7, 8, 9, 10, 11, 12, 13, 14, 15]$
D_{10}	0110_2	$(0110\ 0110)_2$	$[0, 1, 2, 3, 4, 5, 6, 7, 8, 9, 10, 11, 12, 13, 14, 15]$
D_{11}	1100_2	$(1100\ 1100)_2$	$[0, 1, 2, 3, 4, 5, 6, 7, 8, 9, 10, 11, 12, 13, 14, 15]$
D_{12}	1001_2	$(1001\ 1001)_2$	$[0, 1, 2, 3, 4, 5, 6, 7, 8, 9, 10, 11, 12, 13, 14, 15]$
D_{13}	0101_2	$(0101\ 0101)_2$	$[4, 5, 6, 7, 8, 9, 10, 11, 12, 13, 14, 15]$
D_{14}	1010_2	$(1010\ 1010)_2$	$[4, 5, 6, 7, 8, 9, 10, 11, 12, 13, 14, 15]$
D_{15}	1111_2	$(1111\ 1111)_2$	$[4, 5, 6, 7, 8, 9, 10, 11, 12, 13, 14, 15]$

After the AT operation, the tweak difference inserts into the state. Hence, the difference of $X_5[0, 1, 4, 5]$ has an active difference on the least significant bit of each byte with other bits a zero difference. Then, after SB operation, SR operation, and MC operation, we get the active status of the state W_5 where the third column of it is an inactive difference.

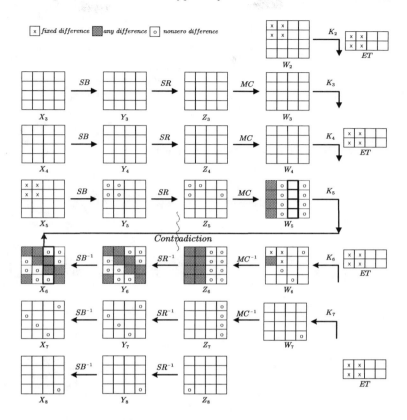

Fig. 3. 5.5-round distinguisher of TweAES with tweak difference 1100_2

Next, we will derive the difference propagation in the back direction. At the end of the distinguisher, we set $Z_8[12]$ to be an active byte. After inverse SR operation and inverse SB operation, the difference propagates to $W_7[15]$. Then, the active byte is propagating to the state $X_7[3, 4, 9, 14]$ after one inverse AES round. After the AT operation, the difference propagates to $W_6[0, 1, 3, 4, 5, 9, 14]$. Then, after one inverse AES round, the third column of state X_6 has at least two active bytes.

Due to the inactiveness of the second column of W_5, the contradiction occurs in the third column of state W_5 and state X_6.

As shown in Table 3, the end of the distinguisher D_{11} can be any byte of Z_8. Hence, the active byte of W_7 can be anyone of the four bytes of the fourth column. Moreover, we can easily derive that the active column of state Z_7 can also be anyone of the four-column.

Remarks.

1. The beginning of distinguisher D_{11} shows that the possible difference has only one value that equals the expanded tweak difference.
2. The distinguisher D_{11} shows that, in key recovery attacks, anyone of the four bytes in the first column of ΔZ_8 can be used to recover the same key bytes, which means there are $(2^8 - 1) \times \binom{4}{1} \approx 2^{10}$ possible values.

4.2   The Key Recovery Attack on 8-Round TweAES

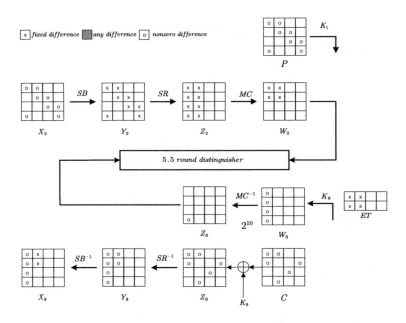

Fig. 4. Key recovery attack on 8-round TweAES

By appending one round on the top and another one round at the bottom of the distinguisher D_{11} where one of the four bytes in the first column of Z_8 is active, as illustrated in Fig. 3, we mount a key recovery attack on 8-round TweAES. As usual, we omit the last round MC operation in the reduced-round version of TweAES. Before the attack is explained, we instantiate the notation mentioned before for better comprehension. Here, r_Δ covers 5.5-round, r_{in} and r_{out} are both one round, $c_{in} = |\Delta_{in}| = 64$, $c_{out} = 8 \times (6 - 1) - 2 = 38$, $|\Delta_{out}| = 8 \times 6 = 48$ and $|k_{in} \cup k_{out}| = 8 \times (8 + 6) = 112$. In our attack, the number of keys that can be eliminated by one qualified plaintext pair is denoted as 2^{elim}. Then, we have the sieved wrong key with probability $2^{elim}/2^{|k_{in} \cup k_{out}|} = 1/2^{c_{in}+c_{out}} = 2^{-102}$.

The attack procedure is briefly described in Algorithm 2 and illustrated in Fig. 4. Detailed attack procedure is shown as follows.

Data Collection. Consider a pair of structures S_1 and S_2, where, each structure consists of $2^{|\Delta_{in}|} = 2^{64}$ plaintexts, and for each plaintext pair $P_1 \in S_1$ and $P_2 \in S_2$, $P_1 \oplus P_2 = (\, * * 0\,0\,|\,0\, * * 0\,|\,0\,0\, * * \,|\, * \,0\,0\, * \,)$, where $*$ denotes any byte value. The total number of possible plaintext pairs is $2^{2 \times |\Delta_{in}|} = 2^{128}$. Choose T and $T^{'}$, where $T \oplus T^{'} = 1100_2$. Encrypt the pool S_1 under T and the pool S_2 under $T^{'}$ to obtain the corresponding ciphertexts. For each ciphertext pair, check whether $n - |\Delta_{out}| = 80$ bits, i.e., $\Delta C[2, 3, 5, 6, 8, 9, 11, 12, 14, 15] = 0$ or not, and discard it if false. Generate 2^N such pair of structures and repeat this for each pair of structures. In total, we will get about $M = 2^{N + |\Delta_{in}| \times 2 - n + |\Delta_{out}|} = 2^{N + 64 \times 2 - (128 - 8 \times 6)} = 2^{N + 48}$ pairs. This step requires a total of $2^{N + |\Delta_{in}| + 1} = 2^{N + 65}$ encryptions.

Key Recovery. For each one of these M pairs, do the following steps:

1. As mentioned by the Note in the end of Sect. 4.1, there is only one possible value of $\Delta W_2[0, 1, 4, 5]$ where differences on these four bytes are all 0x01. By inverse MC and inverse SR operation, we can deduce the difference of $\Delta Y_2[0, 1, 5, 6, 10, 11, 12, 15]$. Note that, the value of ΔY_2 is also fixed. Considering that we can get $\Delta X_2[0, 1, 5, 6, 10, 11, 12, 15]$ from ΔP. Then, by using Proposition 1, we can deduce the value of $X_2[0, 1, 5, 6, 10, 11, 12, 15]$. So we can get one possible value of $K_1[0, 1, 5, 6, 10, 11, 12, 15]$ as $K_1 = P \oplus X_2$. This step has a time complexity of $M \cdot 1$ one-round encryptions.

2. As mentioned by the Note in Sect. 4.1, there are 2^{10} possible values of $\Delta W_8[0, 4, 8, 12]$. For each possible value of $\Delta W_8[0, 4, 8, 12]$, by a AT operation, we can deduce the difference $\Delta X_9[0, 1, 4, 5, 8, 12]$. Considering that we can get $\Delta Y_9[0, 1, 4, 5, 8, 12]$ from ΔC, by using Proposition 1, we can deduce the value of $Y_9[0, 1, 4, 5, 8, 12]$. So we can get 10-bit information of $K_9[0, 1, 4, 5, 8, 12]$ as $K_9 = SR(Y_9) \oplus C$. Then 10-bit information of K_9 is obtained. These obtained keys are wrong ones since they fulfill the impossible differential distinguisher. Hence, one pair of M can eliminate $2^{elim} = 2^{10}$ keys. This step has a time complexity of $M \cdot 2^{elim}$ one-round encryptions.

3. We can use the above steps to filter out the wrong subkey values.

The time complexity of analyzing M pairs is $M \cdot 2^{elim}$, and the total number of subkey left is:

$$K_{rem} = 2^{|k_{in} \cup k_{out}|} \times (1 - 2^{elim}/2^{|k_{in} \cup k_{out}|})^M = 2^{112} \times (1 - 2^{-102})^{2^{N+48}} \quad (1)$$

Suppose $(1 - 2^{elim - |k_{in} \cup k_{out}|})^M = 2^{-g}$, where $1 < g \leq |k_{in} \cup k_{out}|$. It means that g-bit key information is recovered, then we have $M = 2^{|k_{in} \cup k_{out}| - elim} g \ln 2$ since $(1 - 2^{elim - |k_{in} \cup k_{out}|})^M \approx e^{-M2^{|k_{in} \cup k_{out}| - elim}}$. Moreover we know $M = 2^{N + |\Delta_{in}| \times 2 - n + |\Delta_{out}|}$, thus $2^N = 2^{|k_{in} \cup k_{out}| - elim - |\Delta_{in}| \times 2 + n - |\Delta_{out}|} \times g \ln 2$. Finally the data complexity is $D = 2^{N + |\Delta_{in}| + 1} = 2^{|k_{in} \cup k_{out}| - elim + n + 1 - |\Delta_{in}| - |\Delta_{out}|} g \ln 2$.

Brute Force. For the subkey candidates that remain, we guess the left key bytes of $K_1[2, 3, 4, 7, 8, 9, 13, 14]$ (8 bytes), and exhaustively search the $K_{rem} \times 2^{8 \times 8} =$

$2^{112-g+64} = 2^{176-g}$ keys. For every guessed K_1, deduce the master key using key schedule, and verify this master key by one pair of plaintext and ciphertext.

Algorithm 2: Key Recovery Attack on 8-Round TweAES

```
/* Data collection                                              */
```
1 **for** 2^N *pairs of structures* **do**
2   Choose (T, T'), where $T \oplus T' = 1100_2$;
3   Choose $P_1 \in S_1$, $P_2 \in S_2$, $P_1 \oplus P_2 = (* * 0 0 | 0 * * 0 | 0 0 * * | * 0 0 *)$;
4   **forall the** $2^{|\Delta_{in}|}$ *plaintext* P_1 *in* S_1 **do**
5        $C \leftarrow$ Encrypt P_1 under (T, K);
6   **forall the** $2^{|\Delta_{in}|}$ *plaintext* P_2 *in* S_2 **do**
7        $C' \leftarrow$ Encrypt P_2 under (T', K);
8   **forall the** $2^{2|\Delta_{in}|}$ *pairs* **do**
9        $\Delta C \leftarrow C \oplus C'$;
10   **if** $\Delta C = (* * 0 0 | * 0 0 * | 0 0 * 0 | 0 * 0 0)$ **then**
11   Remain the pair of (P_1, T, C) and (P_2, T', C');
           /* Sieve 2^{N+48} remaining pairs finally   */

```
/* Key recovery                                                 */
```
12 **forall the** 2^{N+48} *remaining pairs* **do**
13     $\Delta X_2 = \Delta P$, $\Delta Y_2 = SR^{-1} \circ MC^{-1}(\Delta W_2)$;
14   Using Proposition 1, $X_2 \leftarrow (\Delta X_2, \Delta Y_2)$;
15     $K_1 \leftarrow (X_2 \oplus P \oplus ET)$;
16   **forall the** 2^{10} *possible* ΔW_8 **do**
17        $\Delta X_9 = \Delta W_8 \oplus \Delta ET$, $\Delta Y_9 = SR^{-1}(\Delta C)$;
18   Using Proposition 1, $Y_9 \leftarrow (\Delta X_9, \Delta Y_9)$;
19        $K_9 \leftarrow (SR(Y_9) \oplus C)$;

```
/* Exhaustively search the candidate and the remaining key bits */
```
20 **for** 2^{64} *left key bits of* K_1 **do**
21   **forall the** *remaining key candidates* K_{rem} **do**
22   Compute the master key MK from K_1 and K_{rem} using key schedule;
23   Get a random new pair of (P, C);
24        $C' \leftarrow$ encrypt P under MK;
25   **if** $C' = C$ **then**
26   Output the MK as the right key.

Complexity Computation. The attack described above requires a data complexity of

$$D = 2^{|k_{in} \cup k_{out}| - elim + n + 1 - |\Delta_{in}| - |\Delta_{out}|} g \ln 2 = 2^{-elim + n + 1} g \ln 2 = 2^{119} g \ln 2$$

chosen plaintexts. The total time complexity is the summation of the time consumption of all the steps:

$$T = D + M \cdot 2^{elim} + K_{rem} \times 2^{64}.$$

The memory complexity is the storage for one structure and wrong keys. We set $g = 56$, then $D = 2^{124.28}$, $M \cdot 2^{10} = 2^{117.28}$, $K_{rem} \times 2^{64} = 2^{120}$, $T = 2^{124.36}$ 8-round encryption, and the memory complexity is $2^{112} \times 112 \approx 2^{118.81}$ bits.

5 The Key Recovery Attack on 7-Round TweAES

In this section, we evaluate the security of 7-round TweAES under related-tweak impossible differential attacks. Moreover, this 7-round attack needs much lower attack complexity than 6-round attack [7] of TweAES in design document. This shows that, the security of the cipher needs to be further studied. Our result shows that the security strength of AES-128 will decrease after adding 4-bit tweak in this cipher.

5.1 The 5.5-Round Impossible Differential with Tweak Difference 1001_2

Applying the automatic search algorithm introduced in Sect. 3, we can find a 5.5-round related-tweak impossible distinguisher of TweAES which is shown in Fig. 5. We visualize the contradiction leading to the impossible differential property.

As before, we depict the propagation of the differential with the tweak difference 1001_2. First, we derive the difference propagation in the forward direction. For canceling the difference on the state with a tweak difference, we set the difference on the $W_2[0, 3, 4, 7]$ equal to the active one-bit tweak difference, which means the least significant bit of each byte has an active difference, along with other bits a zero difference. Hence, the difference on each byte of $W_2[0, 3, 4, 7]$ is fixed as 0x01. Since the tweak of TweAES is XORed every two rounds, after the difference canceling occurs at the beginning of the distinguisher, the zero difference will propagate through two rounds to W_4.

After the AT operation, the tweak difference inserts to the state. Hence, the difference of $X_5[0, 3, 4, 7]$ has an active difference on the least significant bit of each byte with other bits a zero difference. Then, after SB operation, SR operation, and MC operation, we get the active status of W_5 where the second column of it is an inactive difference. Next, after the SB operation and SR operation we get that the difference on the third column of Z_6 have at most three nonzero bytes.

Then, we will derive the difference propagation in the back direction. At the end of distinguisher, we set the difference on $Z_8[0, 7, 10, 13]$ to be any value. After the inverse SR operation and inverse SB operation, the difference propagates to $W_7[0, 4, 8, 12]$. Then, the difference propagates to the state $X_7[0, 5, 10, 15]$ after one inverse AES round. After the AT operation, the difference propagates to

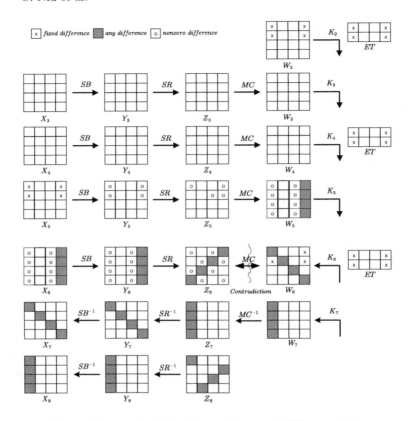

Fig. 5. 5.5-round distinguisher with tweak difference 1001_2

$W_6[0, 3, 4, 5, 7, 10, 15]$. The difference on third column of W_6 has at most one nonzero byte. Since the AES operation Mixcolumns has the branch number as 5, the contradiction occurs on the third column of Z_6 and W_6.

Remarks. The active column of W_7 can be one of the four-column. It's easy to verify that there are still contradictions existing, but the indices of active bytes in Z_8 change.

5.2   The Key Recovery Attack on 7-Round TweAES

By appending one round on the top of the distinguisher described in Sect. 5.1, we mount a key recovery attack on 7-round TweAES. Here, r_Δ covers 5.5-round, r_{in} is one round while $r_{out} = 0$, $c_{in} = |\Delta_{in}| = 64$, $c_{out} = 0$, $|\Delta_{out}| = 0$ and $|k_{in} \cup k_{out}| = 8 \times (8 + 0) = 64$.

The attack process is briefly described in Algorithm 3 and illustrated in Fig. 6. Detailed attack procedures are as follows.

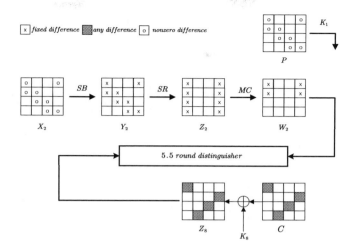

Fig. 6. 7-round key recovery attack of `TweAES`

1. Construct 2^N structure such that each structure is made up of 2^{64} plaintexts. In each structure, we set $\Delta P[0, 3, 4, 5, 9, 10, 14, 15]$ the eight active bytes.
2. Choose a pair of (T, T') such that the tweak difference is fixed 1001_2. Encrypt the plaintexts under two tweaks and only choose the ciphertexts pairs satisfying $\Delta Z_8[1, 2, 3, 4, 5, 6, 8, 9, 11, 12, 14, 15] = 0$ which is one of the 4 cases mentioned in Sect. 5.1.
   In total, we will get about $2^{N+64\times2-8\times12} \times \binom{4}{1} = 2^{N+34}$ pairs.

   For each of the remaining pairs, do the following steps:
3. As mentioned before, $\Delta W_2[0, 3, 4, 7]$ is fixed `0x01` on each byte, after the inverse MC and SR operation, we can deduce $\Delta Y_2[0, 3, 4, 5, 9, 10, 14, 15]$. Note the value of ΔY_2 is also fixed.
   Considering that we can get $\Delta X_2[0, 3, 4, 5, 9, 10, 14, 15]$ from ΔP. Then, by using Proposition 1, we can deduce the value of $X_2[0, 3, 4, 5, 9, 10, 14, 15]$.
   So we can get one possible value of $K_1[0, 3, 4, 5, 9, 10, 14, 15]$ as $K_1 = P \oplus X_2$.
4. We can use the above steps to filter out the wrong key values and then exhaustively search the left key bits.
5. For the subkey candidates that remain, guess the left key bytes of K_1 (8 bytes), and exhaustively search the $K_{rem} \times 2^{64}$ keys. For every guessed K_1, deduce the master key using key schedule, and verify this master key by one plaintext and ciphertext pair.

Complexity Computation. In total, the number of deduced key bytes is 8, i.e., 64 bits information of the key. In this case, each pair can eliminate only one value of the 64-bit guessed key information. Then, we choose $N = 35$, and the remaining candidate key is $K_{rem} = 2^{64} \times (1 - 1/2^{64})^{2^{N+34}} \approx 2^{17.8}$.

The memory for storing the key bits is $2^{64}64 \approx 2^{70}$ bit. The data complexity is $2^{35+64} = 2^{99}$ plaintexts under one pair of tweaks, which is 2^{100} chosen plaintexts.

The time complexity of Step 2 for encrypting the plaintexts is $2 \times 2^{35+64} = 2^{100}$. In Step 3, the total number of guesses is $2^{N+34} = 2^{69}$, which is equivalent to $2^{69} \times 8/16 \times 1/7 \times 2 \approx 2^{66.2}$ 7-round encryption. The time complexity of exhaustively search left key candidate and the left key bits of K_1 is $K_{rem} \times 2^{64} = 2^{17.8} \times 2^{64} = 2^{81.8}$. Thus the time complexity is approximately 2^{100} 7-round encryptions.

6 Conclusions

In this paper, we firstly reveal several properties of TweAES, which show what kinds of distinguishers are more effective in key recovery phase. Then, we use the automatic solver STP to search more effective related-tweak impossible differentials. As a result, we achieved many 5.5-round distinguishers with fixed input differences and output differences that only have one active byte. Then, based on one of these 5.5-round distinguishers, we implemented 8-round key recovery attack against TweAES. Moreover, another 5.5-round distinguisher that has four active bytes at the end is utilized to mount a 7-round key recovery attack against TweAES, which needs much lower attack complexities than 6-round attack [7] of TweAES in the design document. Our 8-round key recovery attack is the best one against TweAES in terms of the number of rounds and complexities so far.

As a tweakable variant of AES-128, TweAES is identical to AES-128 except for the addition of the 4-bit tweak. Compared to AES-128, the security of TweAES against impossible differential has dropped due to the extra freedom brought from the 4-bit tweak discussed in our work. Moreover, the best attack against AES-128 is meet-in-the-middle attack or impossible differential. With the addition of the 4-bit tweak, the security of TweAES against the meet-in-the-middle attack deserves further evaluation.

Acknowledgements. We thank the anonymous reviewers for their valuable comments and suggestions to improve the quality of the paper. This work is supported by the National Natural Science Foundation of China (Grant No. 62032014), the National Key Research and Development Program of China (Grant No. 2018YFA0704702), the Major Basic Research Project of Natural Science Foundation of Shandong Province, China (Grant No. ZR202010220025). Qingju Wang is funded by Huawei Technologies Co., Ltd (Agreement No.: YBN2020035184).

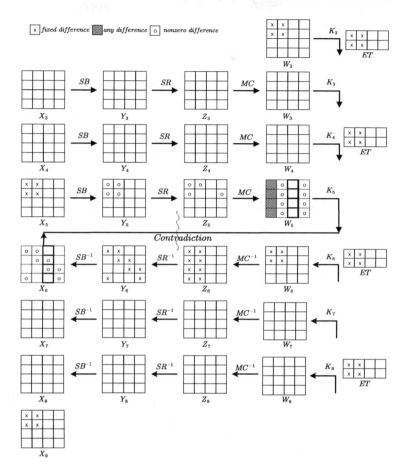

Fig. 7. 6-round related-tweak impossible distinguisher of TweAES [7]

A   Related-Tweak Impossible Differential Distinguisher of TweAES in Design Document [7]

B   8-Round Key Recovery Attack on TweAES in Design Document [7]

By appending one round at the beginning and the end of the distinguisher (Fig. 7), they can perform an 8-round key recovery attack. The attack differential is shown in Fig. 8. The key recovery attack procedure is as follows.

1. Choose all tweak values denoted by T^i where $i = 0, 1, ..., 2^4 - 1$.

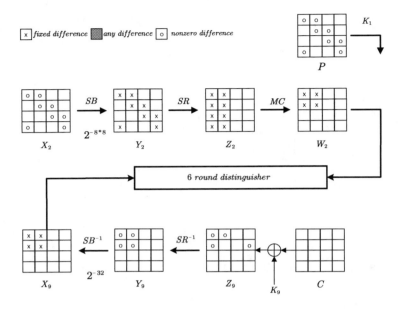

Fig. 8. Key recovery attack against 8-round `TweAES` in [7]

2. For each of T^i, fix the value of inactive 8 bytes at the input, choose all 8-byte values at the active byte positions of the input state. Query those 2^{64} values to get the corresponding outputs. Those outputs are stored in the list L^i where $i = 0, 1, ..., 2^4 - 1$.

3. For all $\binom{2^4}{2} \approx 2^7$ pairs of L^i and L^j with $i \neq j$, find the pairs that do not have difference in 12 inactive bytes of the output state. About $2^{7+64+64-96} = 2^{39}$ pairs will be obtained.

4. For each of the obtained pairs, the tweak difference is fixed and the differences at the input and output states are also fixed. Those fix both of input and output differences of each Sbox in the first round and the last round. Hence, each pair suggests a wrong key.

5. Repeat the procedure 2^{59} times from the first step by changing the inactive byte values at the input. After this step, $2^{39+59} = 2^{98}$ wrong-key candidates (including overlaps) will be obtained. The remaining key space of the involved 12 bytes becomes $2^{96} \times (1 - 2^{-96})^{2^{98}} \approx 2^{96} \times e^{-2} \approx 2^{90.2}$. Hence, the key space for the 8 bytes of K_1 and 4 bytes of K_9 will be reduced by a factor of $2^{5.77}$.

The data complexity is $2^4 \times 2^{64} \times 2^{59} = 2^{127}$. The time complexity is also 2^{127} memory accesses. The memory complexity is to record the wrong keys of the 12 bytes, which is 2^{96}.

C   The Algorithm for The Key Recovery Attack on 7-Round `TweAES`

Algorithm 3: Key Recovery Attack on 7-Round `TweAES`

```
/* Data collection                                                    */
```
1 **for** 2^N *pairs of structures* **do**
2   Choose (T, T'), where $T \oplus T' = 1001_2$;
3   Choose $P_1 \in S_1$, $P_2 \in S_2$, $P_1 \oplus P_2 = (**00 | 0**0 | 00** | *00*)$;
4   **forall the** $2^{|\Delta_{in}|}$ *plaintext* P_1 *in* S_1 **do**
5         $C \leftarrow$ Encrypt P_1 under (T, K);
6   **forall the** $2^{|\Delta_{in}|}$ *plaintext* P_2 *in* S_2 **do**
7         $C' \leftarrow$ Encrypt P_2 under (T', K);
8   **forall the** $2^{2|\Delta_{in}|}$ *pairs* **do**
9         $\Delta C \leftarrow C \oplus C'$;
10   **if** $\Delta C = (**00 | *00* | 0000 | 0000)$ **then**
11   Remain the pair of (P_1, T, C) and (P_2, T', C');
```
            /* Seive 2^{N+32} remaining pairs finally;             */
```

```
/* Key recovery                                                       */
```
12 **forall the** 2^{N+32} *remaining pairs* **do**
13    $\Delta X_2 = \Delta P$, $\Delta Y_2 = SR^{-1} \circ MC^{-1}(\Delta W_2)$;
14   Using Proposition 1, $X_2 \leftarrow (\Delta X_2, \Delta Y_2)$;
15    $K_1 \leftarrow (X_2 \oplus P \oplus ET)$;

```
/* Exhaustively search the candidate and the remaining key bits    */
```
16 **for** 2^{64} *left key bits of* K_1 **do**
17   **for** *Remaining key candidates* K_{rem} **do**
18   Deduce the master key using key schedule;
19   Verify this master key by one plaintext and ciphertext pair.

References

1. Bahrak, B., Aref, M.R.: Impossible differential attack on seven-round AES-128. IET Inf. Secur. **2**(2), 28–32 (2008)
2. Barrett, C.W., Sebastiani, R., Seshia, S.A., Tinelli, C.: Satisfiability modulo theories. In: Biere, A., Heule, M., van Maaren, H., Walsh, T. (eds.) Handbook of Satisfiability, Frontiers in Artificial Intelligence and Applications, vol. 185, pp. 825–885. IOS Press (2009)
3. Beierle, C., et al.: The SKINNY family of block ciphers and its low-latency variant MANTIS. In: Robshaw, M., Katz, J. (eds.) CRYPTO 2016. LNCS, vol. 9815, pp. 123–153. Springer, Heidelberg (2016). https://doi.org/10.1007/978-3-662-53008-5_5
4. Bonnetain, X., Naya-Plasencia, M., Schrottenloher, A.: Quantum security analysis of AES. IACR Trans. Symmetric Cryptol. **2019**(2), 55–93 (2019)
5. Boura, C., Lallemand, V., Naya-Plasencia, M., Suder, V.: Making the impossible possible. J. Cryptol. **31**(1), 101–133 (2018)
6. Boura, C., Naya-Plasencia, M., Suder, V.: Scrutinizing and improving impossible differential attacks: applications to CLEFIA, Camellia, LBlock and SIMON. In: Sarkar, P., Iwata, T. (eds.) ASIACRYPT 2014. LNCS, vol. 8873, pp. 179–199. Springer, Heidelberg (2014). https://doi.org/10.1007/978-3-662-45611-8_10
7. Chakraborti, A., Datta, N., Jha, A., Mancillas-López, C., Nandi, M., Sasaki, Y.: ESTATE: a lightweight and low energy authenticated encryption mode. IACR Trans. Symmetric Cryptol. **2020**(S1), 350–389 (2020)
8. Cook, S.A.: The complexity of theorem-proving procedures. In: Harrison, M.A., Banerji, R.B., Ullman, J.D. (eds.) Proceedings of the 3rd Annual ACM Symposium on Theory of Computing, 3–5 May 1971, Shaker Heights, Ohio, USA, pp. 151–158. ACM (1971)
9. Demirci, H., Selçuk, A.A.: A meet-in-the-middle attack on 8-round AES. In: Nyberg, K. (ed.) FSE 2008. LNCS, vol. 5086, pp. 116–126. Springer, Heidelberg (2008). https://doi.org/10.1007/978-3-540-71039-4_7
10. Derbez, P., Fouque, P.-A., Jean, J.: Improved key recovery attacks on reduced-round, in the single-key setting. In: Johansson, T., Nguyen, P.Q. (eds.) EUROCRYPT 2013. LNCS, vol. 7881, pp. 371–387. Springer, Heidelberg (2013). https://doi.org/10.1007/978-3-642-38348-9_23
11. Dworkin, M., Barker, E., Nechvatal, J., Foti, J., Bassham, L., Roback, E., Dray, J.: Advanced encryption standard (aes), 26 November 2001. https://doi.org/10.6028/NIST.FIPS.197
12. Gilbert, H.: A simplified representation of AES. In: Sarkar, P., Iwata, T. (eds.) ASIACRYPT 2014. LNCS, vol. 8873, pp. 200–222. Springer, Heidelberg (2014). https://doi.org/10.1007/978-3-662-45611-8_11
13. Jean, J., Nikolić, I., Peyrin, T.: Tweaks and keys for block ciphers: the TWEAKEY framework. In: Sarkar, P., Iwata, T. (eds.) ASIACRYPT 2014. LNCS, vol. 8874, pp. 274–288. Springer, Heidelberg (2014). https://doi.org/10.1007/978-3-662-45608-8_15
14. Jérémy Jean, I.N., Peyrin., T.: Deoxys v1.41. Submission to CAESAR (2016). https://competitions.cr.yp.to/round3/deoxysv141.pdf
15. Leurent, G., Pernot, C.: New representations of the AES key schedule. In: Canteaut, A., Standaert, F.-X. (eds.) EUROCRYPT 2021. LNCS, vol. 12696, pp. 54–84. Springer, Cham (2021). https://doi.org/10.1007/978-3-030-77870-5_3

16. Liu, Y., et al.: STP models of optimal differential and linear trail for s-box based ciphers. IACR Cryptol. ePrint Arch. **2019**, 25 (2019)
17. Mouha, N., Preneel, B.: Towards finding optimal differential characteristics for arx: Application to salsa20. Cryptology ePrint Archive, Report 2013/328 (2013). https://eprint.iacr.org/2013/328
18. Sun, S., et al.: Analysis of AES, skinny, and others with constraint programming. IACR Trans. Symmetric Cryptol. **2017**(1), 281–306 (2017)
19. Tiessen, T.: Polytopic cryptanalysis. In: Fischlin, M., Coron, J.-S. (eds.) EUROCRYPT 2016. LNCS, vol. 9665, pp. 214–239. Springer, Heidelberg (2016). https://doi.org/10.1007/978-3-662-49890-3_9
20. Zong, R., Dong, X.: Milp-aided related-tweak/key impossible differential attack and its applications to qarma, joltik-bc. IEEE Access **7**, 153683–153693 (2019)

Improved Attacks on GIFT-64

Ling Sun[1,2,3], Wei Wang[1,3], and Meiqin Wang[1,3(✉)]

[1] Key Laboratory of Cryptologic Technology and Information Security,
Ministry of Education, Shandong University, Jinan, China
{lingsun,weiwangsdu,mqwang}@sdu.edu.cn
[2] State Key Laboratory of Cryptology, P. O. Box 5159, Beijing 100878, China
[3] School of Cyber Science and Technology, Shandong University, Qingdao, China

Abstract. One of the well-known superiorities of GIFT-64 over PRESENT lies in the correction of the strong linear hull effect. However, apart from the investigation of the 9-round linear hull effect in the design document, we find no linear attack result on GIFT-64. Although we do not doubt the security of GIFT-64 regarding the linear cryptanalysis, the actual resistance of the cipher to the linear attack should be evaluated since it promotes a comprehensive perception of the soundness of GIFT-64. Motivated by this observation, we implement an automatic search and find a 12-round linear distinguisher whose dominating trail is an optimal linear characteristic. Following that, the first 19-round linear attack is launched by utilising the newly identified distinguisher. On the other side, we notice that the previous differential attack of GIFT-64 covering 20 rounds claims the entire codebook. To reduce the data complexity of the 20-round attack, we apply the automatic method to exhaustively check 13-round differential trails with probabilities no less than 2^{-64} and identify multiple 13-round differentials facilitating 20-round attacks without using the full codebook. One of the candidate differentials with the maximum probability and the minimum number of guessed subkey bits is then employed to realise the first 20-round differential attack without relying on the complete codebook. Given the newly obtained results, we conjecture that the resistances of GIFT-64 against differential and linear attacks do not have a significant gap. Also, we note that the attack results in this paper are far from threatening the security of GIFT-64.

Keywords: Linear cryptanalysis · Differential cryptanalysis · GIFT-64

1 Introduction

GIFT [4] is a lightweight block cipher motivated by the PRESENT [10] design strategy. The comprehensive treatment on the linear layer and the S-box makes it one of the most energy-efficient ciphers as of today. It outperforms even SIMON [5] and SKINNY [6] for round-based implementations. Another bonus of the wise organisation is the significantly reduced linear hull effect [14], which constitutes the weak point of PRESENT.

R. AlTawy and A. Hülsing (Eds.): SAC 2021, LNCS 13203, pp. 246–265, 2022.
https://doi.org/10.1007/978-3-030-99277-4_12

Because of the good performance in hardware and software implementations, GIFT acted as the underlying primitives of many lightweight designs, such as GIFT-COFB [3], HyENA [12], LOTUS-AEAD and LOCUS-AEAD [11], and SUNDAE-GIFT [2]. Notably, GIFT-COFB has been selected as one of the ten finalists of the ongoing NIST Lightweight Cryptography standardisation project[1]. Thus, evaluating the security level of GIFT is essential.

When we investigate the security of GIFT-64, which is one version of GIFT with the 64-bit block size, an interesting phenomenon is identified. Many results are focusing on the differential attack [7] of GIFT-64. As in Table 1, Chen et al. [13] proposed 20-round and 21-round differential attacks with the full codebook. To reduce the data requirement, they utilised multiple differentials and provided a 20-round attack without using the full codebook. However, few works consider the security of the cipher regarding the linear attack [21]. To be precise, apart from the study of the 9-round linear hull effect in the design document [4], we find no linear attack result on GIFT-64. Although we do not doubt the security of GIFT-64 regarding the linear cryptanalysis, the actual resistance of the cipher to the linear attack should be evaluated since it promotes a comprehensive perception of the soundness of GIFT-64. This observation drives the work in this paper.

1.1   Contributions

This paper focuses on the security of GIFT-64 regarding the linear and differential attacks. The search of distinguishers is accomplished with the automatic method in [29], which is realised via the Boolean Satisfiability Problem (SAT). The contributions are fourfold.

Estimations for Expected Linear Potentials of All 12-Round Linear Approximations with Dominating Trails Being the Optimal Ones. After discovering 5120 optimal 12-round linear trails with the SAT solver, we perceive that all of them can launch valid 19-round linear attacks. However, in order to identify relatively good distinguishers among these candidates, we turn attention to the expected linear potentials of the 5120 linear approximations containing the 5120 trails. We exhaustively search for all trails belonging to the linear approximations with correlations larger than 2^{-40} and generate rough estimations for the expected linear potentials of the 5120 linear approximations. The estimations facilitate the selection of linear distinguisher in the attack.

The First 19-Round Linear Attack Result on GIFT-64. Among the 5120 candidate distinguishers, we choose one linear approximation maintaining the minimum number of guessed subkey bits in the subkey enumeration phase. This linear approximation is then exploited to drive a 19-round attack. The data complexity is $2^{62.96}$ known plaintexts, the time complexity is $2^{127.11}$ 19-round of encryptions, and the memory complexity is about $2^{60.00}$. As far as we know, this is the first linear attack result on GIFT-64.

---

[1] https://csrc.nist.gov/projects/lightweight-cryptography.

Estimations for Probabilities of 2392 Differentials Facilitating 20-Round Differential Attacks. We check all 13-round differential trails with probabilities more significant than 2^{-64} and notice that none can perform valid 20-round differential attacks for the considerable time complexities. Thus, we manage to study trails with probabilities being 2^{-64}. With the SAT solver, we discover 92768 trails with probabilities being 2^{-64} and identify 2392 differentials having the possibility to actualise valid 20-round differential attacks. Then, in order to get approximate evaluations for the probabilities of the 2392 differentials, we apply the SAT solver to search for all differential trails within each differential with probabilities being larger than 2^{-71}. The experimental results guide the decision of the distinguisher in the differential attack.

The First 20-Round Differential Attack Without Using the Full Codebook. We notice that the previous 20-round differential attack in [13] demanded the full codebook. To reduce the data complexity of the 20-round attack, we detect a new 13-round distinguisher with the maximum differential probability and the minimum number of guessed subkey bits. Based on this distinguisher, we realise the first 20-round differential attack without relying on the entire codebook. The data complexity is $2^{62.58}$ chosen plaintexts, the time complexity is $2^{125.50}$ 19-round of encryptions, and the memory complexity is about $2^{62.58}$. A summary of cryptanalytic results on GIFT-64 to date can be found in Table 1.

Table 1. Summary of cryptanalytic results on GIFT-64.

Round	Method	Setting	Time	Data	Memory	Ref.
14	Integral	SK	$2^{97.00}$	$2^{63.00}$	–	[4]
15	MITM	SK	$2^{120.00}$	$2^{64.00}$	–	[4]
15	MITM	SK	$2^{112.00}$	–	–	[23]
19	Differential	SK	$2^{112.0}$	$2^{63.00}$	–	[32]
19	**Linear**	**SK**	$\mathbf{2^{127.11}}$⊛	$\mathbf{2^{62.96}}$	$\mathbf{2^{60.00}}$	**Sect. 3**
20	**Differential**	**SK**	$\mathbf{2^{125.50}}$	$\mathbf{2^{62.58}}$	$\mathbf{2^{62.58}}$	**Sect. 4**
20	Differential	SK	$2^{101.68}$*	$2^{64.00}$	$2^{96.00}$	[13]
21	Differential	SK	$2^{107.61}$*	$2^{64.00}$	$2^{96.00}$	[13]
20	Multiple differential	SK	$2^{112.68}$*	$2^{62.00}$	$2^{112.00}$	[13]
23	Boomerang	RK	$2^{126.60}$	$2^{63.30}$	–	[19]
24	Rectangle	RK	$2^{106.00}$	$2^{63.78}$	$2^{64.10}$	[16]
25	Rectangle	RK	$2^{120.92}$	$2^{63.78}$	$2^{64.10}$	[16]
26	Differential	RK	$2^{123.23}$	$2^{60.96}$	$2^{102.86}$	[30]

* Attacks in [13] only computed the time complexity in the subkey enumeration phase.
⊛ The success probability of the attack is 60%.

Outline of the Paper. In Sect. 2, the structure of GIFT-64, the utilised automatic approach, and the methods to compute the complexities are recalled. Section 3 presents the first 19-round linear attack on the cipher. The first 20-round differential attack on GIFT-64 without using the full codebook is proposed in Sect. 4. Section 5 concludes the paper. All details are provided in the full version of the paper [31].

2 Preliminaries

In this section, we first review the objective primitive of this work. Then, the automatic method utilised to search for differential and linear distinguishers is briefly introduced. At last, the methods to evaluate the complexities in the differential and linear attacks are recalled.

2.1 Description of GIFT-64

GIFT [4] is a family of lightweight block ciphers composed of two versions. The version with the 64-bit block size is denoted as GIFT-64 in this paper. GIFT-64 is a 28-round Substitution-Permutation Network (SPN) cipher and has a key length of 128-bit. The plaintext is presented as $b_0 b_1 \cdots b_{63}$, where b_0 stands for the most significant bit. We use $K = k_0 \| k_1 \| \cdots \| k_7$ to represent the 128-bit key, where k_i's are 16-bit words. Each round of GIFT-64 consists of three steps: SubCells, PermBits, and AddRoundKey.

SubCells. An invertible 4-bit S-box GS, provided in the following, is applied to every nibble of the cipher state.

x	0x0	0x1	0x2	0x3	0x4	0x5	0x6	0x7	0x8	0x9	0xa	0xb	0xc	0xd	0xe	0xf
$GS(x)$	0x1	0xa	0x4	0xc	0x6	0xf	0x3	0x9	0x2	0xd	0xb	0x7	0x5	0x0	0x8	0xe

PermBits. The bit permutation operation maps the i-th bit of the cipher state to the $P(i)$-th bit, i.e., $b_{P(i)} \leftarrow b_i$, $i \in \{0, 1, \ldots, 63\}$. The specification of P is given as follows.

i	0	1	2	3	4	5	6	7	8	9	10	11	12	13	14	15
$P(i)$	48	1	18	35	32	49	2	19	16	33	50	3	0	17	34	51
i	16	17	18	19	20	21	22	23	24	25	26	27	28	29	30	31
$P(i)$	52	5	22	39	36	53	6	23	20	37	54	7	4	21	38	55
i	32	33	34	35	36	37	38	39	40	41	42	43	44	45	46	47
$P(i)$	56	9	26	43	40	57	10	27	24	41	58	11	8	25	42	59
i	48	49	50	51	52	53	54	55	56	57	58	59	60	61	62	63
$P(i)$	60	13	30	47	44	61	14	31	28	45	62	15	12	29	46	63

AddRoundKey. This step includes adding the round key and the round constant. Since adding the round constant does not alter validities of attacks in this paper, we do not introduce it.

As for the adding round key operation, after extracting a 32-bit round key RK from the key state, we split it into two 16-bit words as $RK = U\|V = u_0 u_1 \cdots u_{15}\|v_0 v_1 \cdots v_{15}$. Then, U and V are XORed with the cipher state as $b_{4\cdot i+2} \leftarrow b_{4\cdot i+2} \oplus u_i$, $b_{4\cdot i+3} \leftarrow b_{4\cdot i+3} \oplus v_i$, $i \in \{0, 1, \ldots, 15\}$.

The key schedule of `GIFT-64` is carefully created so that the hardware and software implementations of the cipher are optimised.

Key schedule. Before updating the key state, the round key is first extracted from the key state as $RK = U\|V = k_6\|k_7$. Then, the key state is updated as $k_0\|k_1\| \cdots \|k_7 \leftarrow (k_6 \ggg 2)\|(k_7 \ggg 12)\|k_0\| \cdots \|k_4\|k_5$.

Note that we only recall the necessary message about the cipher. For more details, please refer to [4].

2.2   Searching for Differential and Linear Distinguishers of `GIFT-64`

The cornerstones in differential and linear attacks are distinguishers exhibiting non-random cryptanalytic features. In this work, we exploit the automatic method in [29] to accomplish the search of differential and linear distinguishers. The underlying mathematical problem that facilitates the automatic search is the Boolean Satisfiability Problem (SAT), which studies the satisfiability of a given Boolean formula. A SAT problem is said satisfiable if there exists an assignment of Boolean values to variables so that the formula is evaluated to be `True`. Although the SAT problem is proved to be NP-complete [15], modern SAT solvers can handle practical problems with millions of variables.

Almost all existing SAT solvers accept Boolean formulas in Conjunctive Normal Form (CNF) as inputs. That is, the Boolean formula in question should be expressed as a conjunction ($\wedge$) of one or more clauses, where a clause is a disjunction ($\vee$) of (possibly negated) Boolean variables. Thus, in cryptanalysis, the automatic search is realised by converting the distinguisher searching problem into SAT problems in CNF.

In the following, we take the search of differential distinguisher for `GIFT-64` as an illustration and remind readers that the distinguisher searching in the linear setting can be implemented likewise.

We start with the search for differential trails. According to the functionality, the Boolean expressions in the SAT problem can be partitioned into two groups. The first group is used to track the differential propagation, and the second one characterises the differential probability of the trail.

Group 1: Propagating Differences Inside the Cipher. As the PermBits operation only alters the positions of bits in the cipher state, depicting the differential propagation across the cipher comes down to the description of the S-box GS. Let $\boldsymbol{x} \in \mathbb{F}_2^4$ and $\boldsymbol{y} \in \mathbb{F}_2^4$ be the input and output differences of GS, respectively.

The entries in the differential distribution table (DDT) of GS have five possible evaluations, which are 0, 2, 4, 6, and 16. Correspondingly, the range of differential probabilities is $\{0, 2^{-3}, 2^{-2}, 2^{-1.415}, 1\}$. As in [29], for each S-box, four more Boolean variables ρ_0, ρ_1, ρ_2, and ε are introduced to encode the information about the probability. For a differential propagation with nonzero probability p, the value of $\rho_0 \| \rho_1 \| \rho_2 \| \varepsilon$ meets the following rule

$$
\rho_0 \| \rho_1 \| \rho_2 \| \varepsilon = \begin{cases} 1110, & \text{if } p = 2^{-3} \\ 0110, & \text{if } p = 2^{-2} \\ 0011, & \text{if } p = 2^{-1.415} \\ 0000, & \text{if } p = 1 \end{cases}.
$$

Note that the opposite number of the binary logarithm of p equals $\rho_0 + \rho_1 + \rho_2 + 0.415 \cdot \varepsilon$. Next, we define a 12-bit Boolean function $f(\boldsymbol{x} \| \boldsymbol{y} \| \rho_0 \| \rho_1 \| \rho_2 \| \varepsilon)$ as

$$
f(\boldsymbol{x} \| \boldsymbol{y} \| \rho_0 \| \rho_1 \| \rho_2 \| \varepsilon) = \begin{cases} 1, & \begin{array}{l} \text{if } \boldsymbol{x} \to \boldsymbol{y} \text{ is a possible propagation} \\ \text{with } -\log_2(p) = \sum\limits_{i=0}^{2} \rho_i + 0.415 \cdot \varepsilon \end{array} \\ 0, & \text{otherwise} \end{cases}.
$$

After simplifying the expression of f with the off-the-shelf software Logic Friday [22], we obtain a set of Boolean equations that draws the relation among $\boldsymbol{x}$, $\boldsymbol{y}$, ρ_0, ρ_1, ρ_2, and ε. Please refer to [29] for more details.

Group 2: Monitoring the Differential Probability of Trail. Suppose that we aim at r-round trails. Denote the auxiliary variables for the j-th S-box in the i-th round as $\rho_k^{(i,j)}$ and $\varepsilon^{(i,j)}$, where $0 \leqslant i \leqslant r-1$, $0 \leqslant j \leqslant 15$, and $0 \leqslant k \leqslant 2$. The weight, which equals the opposite number of the binary logarithm of the probability, of the differential trail should be $\sum\limits_{i=0}^{r-1} \sum\limits_{j=0}^{15} \sum\limits_{k=0}^{2} \rho_k^{(i,j)} + 0.415 \cdot \left(\sum\limits_{i=0}^{r-1} \sum\limits_{j=0}^{15} \varepsilon^{(i,j)} \right)$, and we call the first and second terms in this formula the *integral* and *decimal parts* of the differential probability, respectively. In theory, given a prospective value $\omega \in \mathbb{R}^2$ for the weight of the trail, the automatic search should fulfil the search of trails with

$$
\sum_{i=0}^{r-1} \sum_{j=0}^{15} \sum_{k=0}^{2} \rho_k^{(i,j)} + 0.415 \cdot \left(\sum_{i=0}^{r-1} \sum_{j=0}^{15} \varepsilon^{(i,j)} \right) \leqslant \omega. \tag{1}
$$

However, as the SAT problem is oriented to binary variables, we do not find a feasible method to interpret decimal arithmetics with Boolean expressions. Thus, we transform the original restriction in Eq. (1) into two inequalities oriented to integers. To be specific, the predicted value ω is expressed as $\omega = \omega_{\mathrm{I}} + 0.415 \cdot$

---

[2] $\mathbb{R}$ stands for the rational number field.

ω_D with ω_I and ω_D being two non-negative integers. Accordingly, the objective function of the SAT problem consists of the following two inequalities

$$\sum_{i=0}^{r-1}\sum_{j=0}^{15}\sum_{k=0}^{2}\rho_k^{(i,j)} \leqslant \omega_I \text{ and } \sum_{i=0}^{r-1}\sum_{j=0}^{15}\varepsilon^{(i,j)} \leqslant \omega_D.$$

Note that these two restrictions are cardinality constraints of the form $\sum_{i=0}^{n-1} x_i \leqslant k$, where k is a non-negative integer.

$\diamond$ If $k = 0$, this constraint is equivalent to the following n Boolean expressions

$$\overline{x_i} = 1, \quad 0 \leqslant i \leqslant n-1.$$

$\diamond$ In the case of $k > 0$, according to the method in [20], this kind of constraint can be converted into Boolean expressions with the sequential encoding method [25]. Precisely, after introducing $(n-1) \cdot k$ auxiliary Boolean variables $v_{i,j}$ ($0 \leqslant i \leqslant n-2, 0 \leqslant j \leqslant k-1$), the following clauses should be satisfied simultaneously if the relation $\sum_{i=0}^{n-1} x_i \leqslant k$ holds

$$\overline{x_0} \vee v_{0,0} = 1$$
$$\overline{v_{0,j}} = 1, \ 1 \leqslant j \leqslant k-1$$
$$\left.\begin{array}{l}\overline{x_i} \vee v_{i,0} = 1 \\ \overline{v_{i-1,0}} \vee v_{i,0} = 1 \\ \left.\begin{array}{l}\overline{x_i} \vee \overline{v_{i-1,j-1}} \vee v_{i,j} = 1 \\ \overline{v_{i-1,j}} \vee v_{i,j} = 1\end{array}\right\} 1 \leqslant j \leqslant k-1 \\ \overline{x_i} \vee \overline{v_{i-1,k-1}} = 1\end{array}\right\} 1 \leqslant i \leqslant n-2$$
$$\overline{x_{n-1}} \vee \overline{v_{n-2,k-1}} = 1$$

For now, we complete the creation of SAT problems for the search of differential trails with the desired probability, and the search for linear characteristics can be realised similarly. The solver utilised in this work is CryptoMiniSat5 [28].

Lastly, we note that there might be trails with the same input and output differences (resp., masks), and the distinguishers operating in attacks are differentials (resp., linear approximations) comprising all trails sharing the same input and output differences (resp., masks). Thus, after fixing the input and output differences (resp., masks) in the differential (resp., linear) distinguisher, the differential (resp., linear hull) effect is also evaluated by applying the SAT solver to search for more trails within the differential (resp., linear approximation). Please find in [1,17,20,27,29] for more information.

The source codes regarding the search in this paper are publicly available at https://github.com/SunLing134340/Improved_Attacks_GIFT64.

2.3   Complexity Analysis of the Differential Attack

Let $\Delta_{\text{in}} \rightarrow \Delta_{\text{out}}$ be an r-round differential of an iterated block cipher. According to the Markov cipher theory [18], the probability of a differential is calculated as the sum of probabilities regarding all trails sharing the same input and output differences with the differential. Denote the probability of the r-round differential as p_0 and the number of plaintext pairs utilised in the attack as N_{D}. Thus, under the right key guess, the counter memorising the number of pairs validating the differential follows a binomial distribution of parameters (N_{D}, p_0). On the other side, suppose that the probability of a pair fulfilling the differential under a wrong key guess is p. Consequently, the counter follows a binomial distribution of parameters (N_{D}, p). We fix the threshold in the attack as τ_{D}, and the key guess will be accepted if the counter of right pairs is no less than τ_{D}.

The statistical cryptanalysis is always faced with two errors, and we denote by α the non-detection error probability and β the false alarm error probability. Therefore, the success probability P_S of the attack equals $1-\alpha$. With the analysis in [8], when N_{D} is sufficiently large, the following approximations hold

$$\alpha \approx \frac{(1-p) \cdot \sqrt{\tau_{\text{D}}/N_{\text{D}}}}{(\tau_{\text{D}}/N_{\text{D}} - p) \cdot \sqrt{2 \cdot \pi \cdot N_{\text{D}} \cdot (1 - \tau_{\text{D}}/N_{\text{D}})}} \cdot \exp\left[-N_{\text{D}} \cdot D\left(\frac{\tau_{\text{D}}}{N_{\text{D}}} \middle\| p\right)\right],$$

$$\beta \approx \frac{p_0 \cdot \sqrt{1 - (\tau_{\text{D}} - 1)/N_{\text{D}}}}{(p_0 - (\tau_{\text{D}} - 1)/N_{\text{D}}) \cdot \sqrt{2 \cdot \pi \cdot (\tau_{\text{D}} - 1)}} \cdot \exp\left[-N_{\text{D}} \cdot D\left(\frac{\tau_{\text{D}} - 1}{N_{\text{D}}} \middle\| p_0\right)\right],$$

where $D(p\|q) \triangleq p \cdot \ln\left(\frac{p}{q}\right) + (1-p) \cdot \ln\left(\frac{1-p}{1-q}\right)$ is the Kullback-Leibler divergence between two Bernoulli probability distributions with parameters respectively being p and q.

2.4   Complexity Analysis of the Linear Attack

Denote $\Gamma_{\text{in}} \rightarrow \Gamma_{\text{out}}$ an r-round linear approximation of an iterated block cipher with n-bit block size. Suppose that the absolute value of the correlation regarding the dominating linear characteristic $\mu = (\mu_0, \mu_1, \cdots, \mu_r)$ with $\mu_0 = \Gamma_{\text{in}}$ and $\mu_r = \Gamma_{\text{out}}$ of this approximation is c. The expected linear potential $ELP(\Gamma_{\text{in}}, \Gamma_{\text{out}})$ of the approximation is the quadratic sum of correlations for all characteristics belonging to it.

In the linear attack implemented with this approximation, we evaluate its empirical correlation by performing partial encryption and decryption with the guessed values for some subkeys. The key candidate is accepted if its empirical correlation is greater than the predetermined value of the threshold τ_{L}. Since the linear attack belongs to the statistical cryptanalysis, the two errors under the differential attack setting also exist in the linear attack setting. Let a be the advantage [24] of the attack. Then, the proportion of keys that survives after the subkey enumeration phase equals 2^{-a}. Equivalently, we have $\beta = 2^{-a}$.

Suppose that N_L known plaintexts participate in the key-recovery attack. With the method in [9], if we set the threshold as

$$\tau_L = \sqrt{1/N_L} \cdot \Phi^{-1}\left(1 - 2^{-(a+1)}\right),$$

and N_L is sufficiently large, the success probability of the attack is approximated by

$$P_S \approx \Phi\left(\frac{c \cdot \sqrt{N_L} - \Phi^{-1}\left(1 - 2^{-(a+1)}\right) \cdot \sqrt{1 + N_L \cdot 2^{-n}}}{\sqrt{1 + N_L \cdot \left(ELP(\Gamma_{\text{in}}, \Gamma_{\text{out}}) - c^2\right)}}\right), \tag{2}$$

where $\Phi(\cdot)$ signifies the cumulative distribution function of the standard normal distribution.

3   19-Round Linear Attack on GIFT-64

This section first states the selection phase of the linear distinguisher. After that, the first linear attack on GIFT-64 is proposed.

3.1   Selecting Linear Distinguishers

With the experimental result in [30], the maximum absolute value of the correlation for 13-round linear characteristics is 2^{-34}. Given the weak linear hull effect of GIFT-64, we conjecture that there is no 13-round linear approximation with the expected linear potential more significant than 2^{-64}. Thus, we manage to apply 12-round linear approximations to launch key-recovery attacks. Considering that GIFT-64 achieves the full diffusion after three rounds [4], we expect to append three and four rounds before and after the distinguisher, respectively.

Note that the maximum correlation of 12-round linear characteristics is 2^{-31}. We first apply the SAT solver to exhaustively search for all 12-round linear trails with correlations being 2^{-31} and obtain 5120 trails in total. Then, the possibilities of implementing $19(= 3 + 12 + 4)$-round linear attacks with these trails are evaluated. Denote GSB_L the number of subkey bits involved in the subkey enumeration phase. The distribution for the number of linear trails with distinct values of GSB_L is provided in Fig. 1. A rough estimation indicates that all 5120 trails have the potentials to launch valid key-recovery attacks. Hence, we turn attention to the ELP's of the 5120 linear approximations containing the 5120 trails because the value of ELP affects the data requirement, which acts as a crucial criterion for the performance of the linear attack. Due to the considerable number of linear approximations, we can only exhaustively search for all trails with correlations larger than 2^{-40} and give approximate estimations for the ELP's. The distribution for the number of linear approximations with different features is presented in Table 4 of the full version [31].

The experimental results narrow the range of candidate distinguishers to 32 linear approximations, which are provided in Table 5 of the full version [31]. If we aim at linear attacks with lower data requirements, the group of 16 linear approximations L00 - L15 with $ELP = 2^{-61.607}$ and $\text{GSB}_\text{L} = 101$ is preferred. The group of 16 linear approximations L16 - L31 with $ELP = 2^{-61.611}$ and $\text{GSB}_\text{L} = 91$ is suitable for linear attacks with lower time complexities. In the following 19-round attack, we employ L16 as the distinguisher.

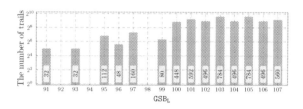

Fig. 1. Distribution for the number of 12-round linear trails with correlations 2^{-31}.

3.2   19-Round Linear Attack on GIFT-64

The 12-round linear approximation L16 is exploited to launch a 19-round attack. To improve the accuracy of the ELP of the distinguisher, we apply the SAT solver to exhaustively search for all trails with correlations being larger than 2^{-46}, which takes about 10 hours on one processor of a server with AMD EPYC 7302 16-Core Processor. Finally, the ELP of L16 is $2^{-61.607}$. Please refer to Appendix C of the full version [31] for more details about L16.

In the attack, we append three and four rounds before and after the linear distinguisher, respectively. The key-recovery attack is illustrated in Fig. 2, where X^i and Y^i denote the 64-bit input and output of the SubCells operation in the i-th round ($0 \leqslant i \leqslant 19$), EY^i represents the 64-bit state $P^{-1}(X^{i+1})$, RK^i stands for the i-th round key, and EK^i is referred to as the equivalent round key $P^{-1}(RK^i)$. In the following, we use $X^i[j]$ to represent the j-th bit of X^i.

Suppose that the number of required plaintext-ciphertext pairs is N_L. The attack is realised with the following steps.

$\text{S}_\text{L}1$ Allocate a counter $C_1^\text{L}[z_1]$ for each of 2^{60} possible values of

$$z_1 = X^{17}[32, 34\text{-}36, 38\text{-}40, 43, 44, 46, 47] \| EY^{17}[0\text{-}31, 48\text{-}63] \| t_1,$$

where $t_1 = X^3[20] \oplus X^3[21] \oplus X^3[28] \oplus X^3[29] \oplus X^{17}[42]$. Then, for each possible 60-bit subkey value

$$RK^0[16\text{-}31] \| RK^1[12\text{-}15, 28\text{-}31] \| EK^{17}[17, 18, 21, 22] \| EK^{18}[0\text{-}31],$$

we compute the value of z_1 and update $C_1^\text{L}[z_1]$ with $C_1^\text{L}[z_1] + 1$. In this step, the time mainly spends on the GS operation, the XOR operation, and the memory access. Following the method in [26], we view one memory access to a large table as one 19-round of encryption. Thus, the dominant time complexity is $N_\text{L} \cdot 2^{60}$ memory accesses to a table with 2^{60} elements.

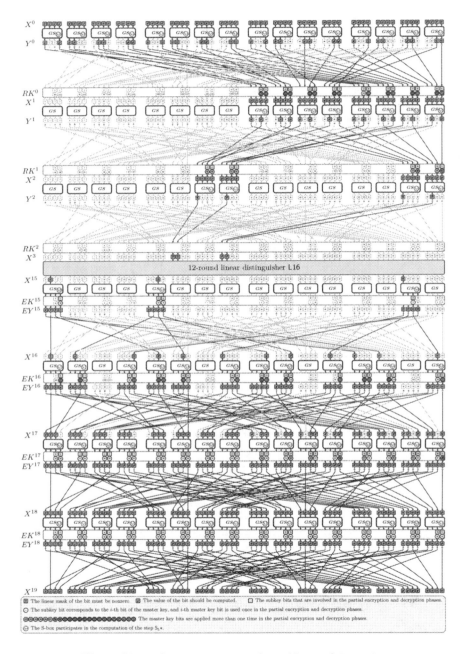

Fig. 2. Linear key-recovery attack on 19-round GIFT-64.

S_L2 Allocate a counter $C_2^L[z_2]$ for each of 2^{56} possible values of

$$z_2 = X^{17}[32, 34\text{-}36, 38\text{-}40, 43, 44, 46\text{-}49, 51\text{-}53, 55\text{-}57, 59\text{-}61, 63]\|EY^{17}[0\text{-}31]\|t_1.$$

For each possible 4-bit subkey value $EK^{17}[25, 26, 29, 30]$, we compute the value of z_2 and update $C_2^L[z_2]$ as $C_2^L[z_2] + C_1^L[z_1]$. Similarly to the case in S_L1, the dominant time complexity of this step is $2^{60} \cdot 2^{60} \cdot 2^4 = 2^{124}$ memory accesses to a table with 2^{56} elements.

S_L3 Allocate a counter $C_3^L[z_3]$ for each of 2^{50} possible values of

$$z_3 = X^{17}[\text{Index}^{S_L3}(X^{17})]\|EY^{17}[0\text{-}3, 8\text{-}19, 24\text{-}31]\|t_2,$$

where $\text{Index}^{S_L3}(X^{17})$ is an index set containing the bit positions that should be memorised,

$$\text{Index}^{S_L3}(X^{17}) = \{4, 6, 21, 23, 32, 34\text{-}36, 38, 40, 43, 44, 46\text{-}49, 51, 53, 55\text{-}57, 59\text{-}61, 63\},$$

and $t_2 = t_1 \oplus X^{16}[18]$. For each possible 4-bit subkey value $EK^{17}[2, 3, 10, 11]$, we compute the value of z_3 and update $C_3^L[z_3]$ as $C_3^L[z_3] + C_2^L[z_2]$. The dominant time complexity of this step is $2^{56} \cdot 2^{64} \cdot 2^4 = 2^{124}$ memory accesses to a table with 2^{50} elements.

S_L4 Allocate a counter $C_4^L[z_4]$ for each of 2^{44} possible values of

$$z_4 = X^{16}[22, 28]\|X^{17}[\text{Index}^{S_L4}(X^{17})]\|EY^{17}[0\text{-}3, 8\text{-}19, 24\text{-}31]\|t_2,$$

where

$$\text{Index}^{S_L4}(X^{17}) = \{32, 34, 35, 40, 43, 44, 46\text{-}49, 51, 56, 57, 59\text{-}61, 63\}.$$

For each possible 2-bit subkey value $EK^{16}[11, 14]$, we compute the value of z_4 and update $C_4^L[z_4]$ as $C_4^L[z_4] + C_3^L[z_3]$. The dominant time complexity of this step is $2^{50} \cdot 2^{68} \cdot 2^2 = 2^{120}$ memory accesses to a table with 2^{44} elements.

S_L5 Allocate a counter $C_5^L[z_5]$ for each of 2^{33} possible values of

$$z_5 = X^{16}[22, 28, 35, 39]\|X^{17}[\text{Index}^{S_L5}(X^{17})]\|EY^{17}[0\text{-}3, 12\text{-}19, 28\text{-}31]\|t_3,$$

where $\text{Index}^{S_L5}(X^{17}) = \{32, 34, 35, 44, 46\text{-}49, 51, 60, 61, 63\}$ and $t_3 = t_2 \oplus X^{16}[45]$. For each possible 5-bit subkey value $EK^{16}[19]\|EK^{17}[4, 5, 12, 13]$, we compute the value of z_5 and update $C_5^L[z_5]$ as $C_5^L[z_5] + C_4^L[z_4]$. The dominant time complexity of this step is $2^{44} \cdot 2^{70} \cdot 2^5 = 2^{119}$ memory accesses to a table with 2^{33} elements.

S_L6 Allocate a counter $C_6^L[z_6]$ for each of 2^{22} possible values of

$$z_6 = X^{16}[22, 28, 35, 39, 48, 52, 62]\|X^{17}[32, 34, 35, 48, 49, 51]\|EY^{17}[0\text{-}3, 16\text{-}19]\|t_3.$$

For each possible 6-bit subkey value $EK^{16}[27, 30]\|EK^{17}[6, 7, 14, 15]$, we compute the value of z_6 and update $C_6^L[z_6]$ as $C_6^L[z_6] + C_5^L[z_5]$. The dominant time complexity of this step is $2^{33} \cdot 2^{75} \cdot 2^6 = 2^{114}$ memory accesses to a table with 2^{22} elements.

S_L7 Allocate a counter $C_7^L[z_7]$ for each of 2^8 possible values of

$$z_7 = X^{16}[5, 22, 28, 35, 39, 48, 52, 62]\|t_4,$$

where $t_4 = t_3 \oplus X^{16}[1] \oplus X^{16}[15]$. For each possible 6-bit subkey value $EK^{16}[3, 6]\|EK^{17}[0, 1, 8, 9]$, we compute the value of z_7 and update $C_7^L[z_7]$ as $C_7^L[z_7] + C_6^L[z_6]$. The number of memory accesses in this step is $2^{22} \cdot 2^{81} \cdot 2^6 = 2^{109}$. As the number of counters is relatively small, the time complexity of this step is not dominated by memory accesses. However, note that the number of GS operations and the number of XOR operations are about $\mathcal{O}(2^{109})$. Therefore, the time complexity of this step is bounded by 2^{109} 19-round of encryptions.

S_L8 Initialise a counter Σ_L. For each possible 4-bit subkey value $EK^{15}[1, 8, 9, 28]$, we compute the value of $t_5 = t_4 \oplus X^{15}[1] \oplus X^{15}[18] \oplus X^{15}[46]$. If t_5 equals zero, we update Σ_L as $\Sigma_L + C_7^L[z_7]$. With a similar analysis as in S_L7, the time complexity of this step is bounded by $2^8 \cdot 2^{87} \cdot 2^4 = 2^{99}$ 19-round of encryptions.

S_L9 We set the threshold as τ_L. The key guess will be accepted as a candidate if the counter Σ_L validates the condition $|\Sigma_L/N_L - 0.5| > \tau_L$. Then, all master keys that are compatible with the guessed 91 subkey bits are tested exhaustively against a maximum of two plaintext-ciphertext pairs.

Complexity Analysis. We set the advantage of the attack as $a = 1.40$ and the number of pairs N_L as $2^{62.96}$. So, the data complexity of this attack is $2^{62.96}$. With Eq. (2), the success probability is $P_S = 60.00\%$. The time complexity in each step between S_L1 and S_L6 depends on the number of accesses to the memory. Following the method in [26], we consider one memory access to the largest counter $C_1^L[z_1]$ as one 19-round of encryption. The time complexity of steps S_L1 - S_L6 is bounded by $(N_L \cdot 2^{60} + 2^{124} + 2^{124} + 2^{120} + 2^{119} + 2^{114})$ 19-round of encryptions. The time complexity of S_L9 is about $2^{128} \cdot 2^{-a} \cdot (1 + 2^{-64})$ 19-round of encryptions. Then, the time complexity of the attack is about $2^{127.11}$ 19-round of encryptions. Since $C_1^L[z_1]$ constitutes the most remarkable memory, the memory complexity is roughly 2^{60}. Given that the time complexity of the 19-round linear attack is $2^{127.11}$, we claim that the success probability of the attack is 60.00%, and it cannot be improved by repeating the entire work as the time complexity will go beyond 2^{128}.

4　Differential Attack Without Using the Full Codebook

In [13], Chen et al. proposed a 20-round differential attack on GIFT-64 with the full codebook. We aim at improving this cryptanalytic result in this section.

4.1　Selecting Differential Distinguishers

A common countermeasure to reduce the data complexity in the differential attack is to construct structures. Since GIFT-64 does not employ any whitening key at the input, we can create structures at the output of the first SubCells operation. Given the full diffusion of GIFT-64 with three rounds, we infer that the maximum number of rounds annexed before the differential distinguisher in the attack is three. On the other side, note that the 20-round attack in [13] attached four rounds after the distinguisher. Therefore, we also expect to append at least four rounds after the distinguisher.

In the selection phase of differential distinguishers, we first set the objective probability as a relatively high value and obtain candidate trails with the SAT solver. Then, we check the possibility of using the trail at hand to launch a valid attack. If none of the existing trails actualises a feasible attack, we lower the objective probability in the automatic search and repeat the abovementioned procedures. The selection task terminates until we identify at least one proper distinguisher.

Based on previous analyses on GIFT-64 [13,30], we know that the longest differential trail that can be utilised in attacks covers 13-round, and the probability of the optimal 13-round trail achieves 2^{-62}. Hence, we first fix the objective differential probability in the automatic search as 2^{-62} and discover 288 trails possessing the maximum probability. However, when these trails are exploited to launch $20(= 3 + 13 + 4)$-round differential attacks, the time complexities go beyond 2^{128} for the extensively involved subkey bits in the subkey enumeration phase. In the following, we use GSB_D to stand for the number of subkey bits involved in the subkey enumeration phase of the differential attack. Next, we reduce the objective differential probability and discover no trial with probability being $2^{-62.415}$ or $2^{-62.83}$. Further, the objective probability is turned down to 2^{-63}, and the SAT solver returns 5184 trails. Again, after checking all the 5184 trails, we find that none of them facilitates a valid 20-round attack for the considerable time complexity. Subsequently, we get 6272 trails with probabilities being $2^{-63.415}$ and also notice that all the 6272 trails face the risk of enormous time complexity. Since the SAT solver does not identify any trail with probability being $2^{-63.83}$, we lower the objective probability to 2^{-64}. 92768 trails are returned, and the distribution for the number of trails with different values of GSB_D is exhibited in Fig. 3. A rough investigation shows that the 3096 trails with $GSB_D < 112$ are qualified for 20-round valid differential attacks.

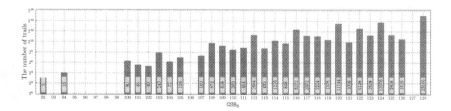

Fig. 3. Distribution for the number of differential trails with probabilities 2^{-64}.

After controlling the time complexity of the attack, we focus on the data complexity, which is affected by the probability of the distinguisher. Before evaluating the probability of the distinguisher, we notice that some of the 3096 candidate trails share the same input and output differences, and the number of distinct differentials is 2392. In order to obtain approximate evaluations for the probabilities of the 2392 differentials, we use the SAT solver to search for all differential trails within each differential with probabilities being larger than 2^{-71}. The distribution for the number of differentials with distinct probabilities can be found in Table 2. Then, we narrow the range of candidate distinguishers to the 32 differentials with probabilities being $2^{-61.313}$, which are listed in Table 7 of the full version [31]. Among the 32 differentials, 16 differentials D00 - D15 satisfy $\mathtt{GSB_D} = 107$, and the remaining 16 ones D16 - D31 validate $\mathtt{GSB_D} = 110$.

In this work, we employ D03 as the distinguisher for the following 20-round attack and remind readers that the performances of using D00 - D15 are similar. Lastly, we remark that the differential D27 was identified in [13]. Nevertheless, the authors did not exploit it in the 20-round differential attack.

Table 2. Distribution for 2392 differentials with different probabilities.

Probability	#{Differentials}	Probability	#{Differentials}	Probability	#{Differentials}
$2^{-61.313}$	32	$2^{-62.093}$	64	$2^{-62.678}$	112
$2^{-61.461}$	32	$2^{-62.105}$	64	$2^{-62.771}$	8
$2^{-61.625}$	8	$2^{-62.142}$	48	$2^{-62.791}$	32
$2^{-61.715}$	64	$2^{-62.272}$	144	$2^{-62.830}$	32
$2^{-61.791}$	64	$2^{-62.430}$	32	$2^{-62.871}$	32
$2^{-61.810}$	64	$2^{-62.574}$	456	$2^{-62.913}$	32
$2^{-62.063}$	24	$2^{-62.608}$	144	$2^{-62.956}$	904

4.2 20-Round Differential Attack on GIFT-64

The 13-round differential D03 is utilised to realise a 20-round attack. To ensure the accuracy of the probability, we apply the SAT solver to implement a more thorough search for trails belonging to the differential. All trails with probabilities being more significant than 2^{-92} are identified, and the number of trails with different probabilities is illustrated in Fig. 4. Three dominating trails with probabilities being 2^{-64} can be found in Table 8 of the full version [31].

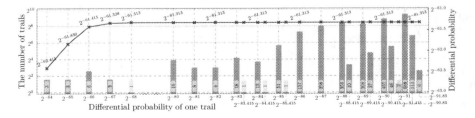

Fig. 4. Distribution of trails belonging to the 13-round differential D03.

In the attack, we append three and four rounds before and after the distinguisher, respectively. The key-recovery attack is demonstrated in Fig. 6 of the full version [31]. Since there is no whitening key at the input, we can construct structures at the position of Y^0. In each structure, the 16 bits

$$Y^0[1, 6, 11, 12, 17, 22, 27, 28, 33, 38, 43, 44, 49, 54, 59, 60]$$

with the difference being zero are fixed, and the values of the remaining 48 bits are traversed. Then, according to the 4-bit value $Y^0[32, 37, 40, 45]$, the elements in the structure are further partitioned into 16 groups $\mathcal{G}_{0x0}$, $\mathcal{G}_{0x1}$, ... $\mathcal{G}_{0xf}$, and all elements Y^0 in $\mathcal{G}_i$ validate the equation $Y^0[32, 37, 40, 45] = \text{i}$. After that, one pair is generated by respectively drawing one element from two groups $\mathcal{G}_i$ and $\mathcal{G}_j$ with $\text{i} \oplus \text{j} = \text{0xf}$. Thus, 2^{91} pairs can be created with one structure composed of 2^{48} elements.

In the attack, we prepare $\mathcal{S}$ structures and obtain $N_1 = \mathcal{S} \cdot 2^{91}$ pairs. In this way, the data complexity of the attack is $\mathcal{S} \cdot 2^{48}$. For each pair (Y^0, Y'^0), we compute the values of the plaintexts (P, P') by applying GS^{-1} to every nibble of the two states (Y^0, Y'^0). By querying the oracle, we obtain the corresponding values of the ciphertexts (C, C'). To minimise the time complexity in the subsequent subkey enumeration phase, we also consider the property of the key schedule.

In the first step, we guess the value of $RK^0[10, 11]$ and check whether the 4-bit difference validates $\overline{\Delta Y^1[16]} = \Delta Y^1[17] = \Delta Y^1[18] = \Delta Y^1[19] = 0$. The remaining $N_1 \cdot 2^{-4}$ pairs will participate in the following processes. We repeat this guess-and-check procedure for the remaining 28-bit of $RK^0[8, 9, 12\text{-}31] \| RK^1[18\text{-}23]$ involved in the partial encryption phase. The time complexity and the number of remaining pairs in steps $\mathsf{S_D}1\text{--}\mathsf{S_D}42$ illustrated in Fig. 6 of the full version [31] are detailed in Table 3. After enumerating the related bits in RK^0 and RK^1, we obtain $N_D \triangleq N_1 \cdot 2^{-44}$ pairs that match the input difference of the 13-round distinguisher. Then, we turn to the tail of the distinguisher. The order to enumerate the subkey is selected in order to filter out the pairs that cannot result in the right pairs as soon as possible.

We set a counter to record the number of right pairs that validate the input and output differences of the 13-round distinguisher. With the analysis in Table 3, for random key guesses, the number of right pairs is about $N_1 \cdot 2^{-108}$. For the right key guess, the number of right pairs is expected to be $N_1 \cdot 2^{-44} \cdot 2^{-61.31} = 2^{-105.31}$. Thus, the number of right pairs follows a binomial distribution with parameters $(N_D, p_0 = 2^{-61.31})$ in the case of the good key and $(N_D, p_1 = 2^{-64})$ otherwise. The threshold is fixed as τ_D, and the key guess will be accepted as a candidate if the counter of right pairs is no less than τ_D. For all surviving candidates for the 107-bit subkey involved in the subkey enumeration phase, we exhaustively search for the value of the remaining 21-bit with at most two plaintext-ciphertext pairs.

Complexity Analysis. From Table 3, we know the time complexity T_1 regarding the subkey enumeration phase is about $N_1 \cdot 2^{23.53} \cdot \frac{1}{20 \cdot 16} \approx N_1 \cdot 2^{15.21}$ 20-round

Table 3. Detailed computation of complexity.

Step	Guessed subkey bits	Condition on the difference of the state	#{Remaining pairs}	Time complexity (GS operations)
S_b1	$RK^0[10,11]$	$\Delta Y^1[16] = \Delta Y^1[17] = \Delta Y^1[18] = \Delta Y^1[19] = 0$	$N_1 \cdot 2^{-4}$	$2 \cdot N_1 \cdot 2^2$
S_b2	$RK^0[26,27]$	$\Delta Y^1[52] = \Delta Y^1[53] = \Delta Y^1[54] = \Delta Y^1[55] = 0$	$N_1 \cdot 2^{-4} \cdot 2^{-4}$	$2 \cdot N_1 \cdot 2^{-4} \cdot 2^2 \cdot 2^2$
S_b3	$RK^0[16,17]$	$\Delta Y^1[32] = \Delta Y^1[33] = \Delta Y^1[34] = 0$	$N_1 \cdot 2^{-8} \cdot 2^{-3}$	$2 \cdot N_1 \cdot 2^{-8} \cdot 2^4 \cdot 2^2$
S_b4	$RK^0[18,19]$	$\Delta Y^1[37] = \Delta Y^1[38] = \Delta Y^1[39] = 0$	$N_1 \cdot 2^{-11} \cdot 2^{-3}$	$2 \cdot N_1 \cdot 2^{-11} \cdot 2^6 \cdot 2^2$
S_b5	$RK^0[20,21]$	$\Delta Y^1[40] = \Delta Y^1[42] = \Delta Y^1[43] = 0$	$N_1 \cdot 2^{-14} \cdot 2^{-3}$	$2 \cdot N_1 \cdot 2^{-14} \cdot 2^8 \cdot 2^2$
S_b6	$RK^0[22,23]$	$\Delta Y^1[44] = \Delta Y^1[45] = \Delta Y^1[47] = 0$	$N_1 \cdot 2^{-17} \cdot 2^{-3}$	$2 \cdot N_1 \cdot 2^{-17} \cdot 2^{10} \cdot 2^2$
S_b7	$RK^0[20,21]$	$\Delta Y^2[40] = \Delta Y^2[41] = \Delta Y^2[42] = \Delta Y^2[43] = 0$	$N_1 \cdot 2^{-20} \cdot 2^{-4}$	$2 \cdot N_1 \cdot 2^{-20} \cdot 2^{12} \cdot 2^2$
S_b8	$RK^0[8,9]$	$\Delta Y^1[16] = \Delta Y^1[17] = \Delta Y^1[18] = 0$	$N_1 \cdot 2^{-24} \cdot 2^{-3}$	$2 \cdot N_1 \cdot 2^{-24} \cdot 2^{14} \cdot 2^2$
S_b9	$RK^0[14,15]$	$\Delta Y^1[28] = \Delta Y^1[29] = \Delta Y^1[31] = 0$	$N_1 \cdot 2^{-27} \cdot 2^{-3}$	$2 \cdot N_1 \cdot 2^{-27} \cdot 2^{16} \cdot 2^2$
S_b10	$RK^0[24,25]$	$\Delta Y^1[48] = \Delta Y^1[49] = \Delta Y^1[50] = 0$	$N_1 \cdot 2^{-30} \cdot 2^{-3}$	$2 \cdot N_1 \cdot 2^{-30} \cdot 2^{18} \cdot 2^2$
S_b11	$RK^0[30,31]$	$\Delta Y^1[60] = \Delta Y^1[61] = \Delta Y^1[63] = 0$	$N_1 \cdot 2^{-33} \cdot 2^{-3}$	$2 \cdot N_1 \cdot 2^{-33} \cdot 2^{20} \cdot 2^2$
S_b12	$RK^0[12,13]$	$\Delta Y^1[24] = \Delta Y^1[25] = \Delta Y^1[26] = \Delta Y^1[27] = 0$	$N_1 \cdot 2^{-36} \cdot 2^{-2}$	$2 \cdot N_1 \cdot 2^{-36} \cdot 2^{22} \cdot 2^2$
S_b13	$RK^0[28,29]$	$\Delta Y^1[56] = \Delta Y^1[57] = \Delta Y^1[58] = \Delta Y^1[59] = 0$	$N_1 \cdot 2^{-38} \cdot 2^{-2}$	$2 \cdot N_1 \cdot 2^{-38} \cdot 2^{24} \cdot 2^2$
S_b14	$RK^0[18,19]$	$\Delta Y^2[36] = \Delta Y^2[37] = \Delta Y^2[38] = \Delta Y^2[39] = 0$	$N_1 \cdot 2^{-40} \cdot 2^{-2}$	$2 \cdot N_1 \cdot 2^{-40} \cdot 2^{26} \cdot 2^2$
S_b15	$RK^0[22,23]$	$\Delta Y^2[44] = \Delta Y^2[45] = \Delta Y^2[46] = \Delta Y^2[47] = 0$	$N_1 \cdot 2^{-42} \cdot 2^{-2}$	$2 \cdot N_1 \cdot 2^{-42} \cdot 2^{28} \cdot 2^2$
S_b16	$EK^{18}[0,1]\|EK^{19}[0,1,8,9,16,17,24,25]$	$\Delta X^{18}[1] = \Delta X^{18}[3] = 0$	$N_1 \cdot 2^{-44} \cdot 2^{-2}$	$2 \cdot N_1 \cdot 2^{-44} \cdot 2^{30} \cdot 2^{10} \cdot 5$
S_b17	$EK^{18}[2,3]$	$\Delta X^{18}[5] = \Delta X^{18}[7] = 0$	$N_1 \cdot 2^{-48} \cdot 2^{-2}$	$2 \cdot N_1 \cdot 2^{-48} \cdot 2^{40} \cdot 2^2$
S_b18	$EK^{18}[4,5]$	$\Delta X^{18}[9] = \Delta X^{18}[11] = 0$	$N_1 \cdot 2^{-48} \cdot 2^{-2}$	$2 \cdot N_1 \cdot 2^{-48} \cdot 2^{42} \cdot 2^2$
S_b19	$EK^{18}[6,7]$	$\Delta X^{18}[13] = \Delta X^{18}[15] = 0$	$N_1 \cdot 2^{-50} \cdot 2^{-2}$	$2 \cdot N_1 \cdot 2^{-50} \cdot 2^{44} \cdot 2^2$
S_b20	$EK^{18}[8,9]\|EK^{19}[2,3,10,11,18,19,26,27]$	$\Delta X^{18}[16] = \Delta X^{18}[18] = 0$	$N_1 \cdot 2^{-52} \cdot 2^{-2}$	$2 \cdot N_1 \cdot 2^{-52} \cdot 2^{46} \cdot 2^{10} \cdot 5$
S_b21	$EK^{18}[10,11]$	$\Delta X^{18}[20] = \Delta X^{18}[22] = 0$	$N_1 \cdot 2^{-54} \cdot 2^{-2}$	$2 \cdot N_1 \cdot 2^{-54} \cdot 2^{56} \cdot 2^2$
S_b22	$EK^{18}[12,13]$	$\Delta X^{18}[24] = \Delta X^{18}[26] = 0$	$N_1 \cdot 2^{-56} \cdot 2^{-2}$	$2 \cdot N_1 \cdot 2^{-56} \cdot 2^{58} \cdot 2^2$
S_b23	$EK^{18}[14,15]$	$\Delta X^{18}[28] = \Delta X^{18}[30] = 0$	$N_1 \cdot 2^{-58} \cdot 2^{-2}$	$2 \cdot N_1 \cdot 2^{-58} \cdot 2^{60} \cdot 2^2$
S_b24	$EK^{18}[16,17]\|EK^{19}[4,5,12,13,20,21,28,29]$	$\Delta X^{18}[33] = \Delta X^{18}[35] = 0$	$N_1 \cdot 2^{-60} \cdot 2^{-2}$	$2 \cdot N_1 \cdot 2^{-60} \cdot 2^{62} \cdot 2^{10} \cdot 5$
S_b25	$EK^{18}[18,19]$	$\Delta X^{18}[37] = \Delta X^{18}[39] = 0$	$N_1 \cdot 2^{-62} \cdot 2^{-2}$	$2 \cdot N_1 \cdot 2^{-62} \cdot 2^{72} \cdot 2^2$
S_b26	$EK^{18}[20,21]$	$\Delta X^{18}[41] = \Delta X^{18}[43] = 0$	$N_1 \cdot 2^{-64} \cdot 2^{-2}$	$2 \cdot N_1 \cdot 2^{-64} \cdot 2^{74} \cdot 2^2$
S_b27	$EK^{18}[22,23]$	$\Delta X^{18}[45] = \Delta X^{18}[47] = 0$	$N_1 \cdot 2^{-66} \cdot 2^{-2}$	$2 \cdot N_1 \cdot 2^{-66} \cdot 2^{76} \cdot 2^2$
S_b28	$EK^{18}[28,29]\|EK^{19}[6,7,14,15,22,23,30,31]$	$\Delta X^{18}[56] = \Delta X^{18}[58] = 0$	$N_1 \cdot 2^{-68} \cdot 2^{-2}$	$2 \cdot N_1 \cdot 2^{-68} \cdot 2^{78} \cdot 2^{10} \cdot 5$
S_b29	$EK^{18}[19]$	$\Delta X^{17}[36] = \Delta X^{17}[37] = \Delta X^{17}[38] = \Delta X^{17}[39] = 0$	$N_1 \cdot 2^{-70} \cdot 2^{-2}$	$2 \cdot N_1 \cdot 2^{-70} \cdot 2^{88} \cdot 2^1$
S_b30	$EK^{18}[26,27]$	$\Delta X^{18}[52] = \Delta X^{18}[54] = 0$	$N_1 \cdot 2^{-74} \cdot 2^{-2}$	$2 \cdot N_1 \cdot 2^{-74} \cdot 2^{89} \cdot 2^2$
S_b31	$EK^{17}[11]$	$\Delta X^{17}[20] = \Delta X^{17}[21] = \Delta X^{17}[23] = 0$	$N_1 \cdot 2^{-76} \cdot 2^{-3}$	$2 \cdot N_1 \cdot 2^{-76} \cdot 2^{91} \cdot 2^1$
S_b32	$EK^{18}[30,31]$	$\Delta X^{18}[60] = \Delta X^{18}[62] = 0$	$N_1 \cdot 2^{-79} \cdot 2^{-2}$	$2 \cdot N_1 \cdot 2^{-79} \cdot 2^{92} \cdot 2^2$
S_b33	$EK^{17}[27]$	$\Delta X^{17}[53] = \Delta X^{17}[54] = \Delta X^{17}[55] = 0$	$N_1 \cdot 2^{-81} \cdot 2^{-3}$	$2 \cdot N_1 \cdot 2^{-81} \cdot 2^{93} \cdot 2^1$
S_b34	$EK^{17}[24,25]$	$\Delta X^{18}[48] = \Delta X^{18}[50] = 0$	$N_1 \cdot 2^{-84} \cdot 2^{-2}$	$2 \cdot N_1 \cdot 2^{-84} \cdot 2^{95} \cdot 2^2$
S_b35	$EK^{17}[2,3]$	$\Delta X^{17}[4] = \Delta X^{17}[6] = \Delta X^{17}[7] = 0$	$N_1 \cdot 2^{-86} \cdot 2^{-3}$	$2 \cdot N_1 \cdot 2^{-86} \cdot 2^{97} \cdot 2^1$
S_b36	-	$\Delta X^{16}[16] = \Delta X^{16}[17] = \Delta X^{16}[18] = \Delta X^{16}[19] = 0$	$N_1 \cdot 2^{-89} \cdot 2^{-2}$	$2 \cdot N_1 \cdot 2^{-89} \cdot 2^{99}$
S_b37	$EK^{17}[6,7]$	$\Delta X^{17}[12] = \Delta X^{17}[15] = 0$	$N_1 \cdot 2^{-92} \cdot 2^{-2}$	$2 \cdot N_1 \cdot 2^{-92} \cdot 2^{99} \cdot 2^2$
S_b38	$EK^{17}[14,15]$	$\Delta X^{17}[28] = \Delta X^{17}[29] = 0$	$N_1 \cdot 2^{-94} \cdot 2^{-2}$	$2 \cdot N_1 \cdot 2^{-94} \cdot 2^{101} \cdot 2^2$
S_b39	$EK^{17}[22,23]$	$\Delta X^{17}[45] = \Delta X^{17}[46] = 0$	$N_1 \cdot 2^{-96} \cdot 2^{-2}$	$2 \cdot N_1 \cdot 2^{-96} \cdot 2^{103} \cdot 2^2$
S_b40	$EK^{17}[30,31]$	$\Delta X^{17}[62] = \Delta X^{17}[63] = 0$	$N_1 \cdot 2^{-98} \cdot 2^{-2}$	$2 \cdot N_1 \cdot 2^{-98} \cdot 2^{105} \cdot 2^2$
S_b41	-	$\Delta X^{16}[48] = \Delta X^{16}[49] = \Delta X^{16}[50] = \Delta X^{16}[51] = 0$	$N_1 \cdot 2^{-100} \cdot 2^{-4}$	$2 \cdot N_1 \cdot 2^{-100} \cdot 2^{107}$
S_b42	-	$\Delta X^{16}[52] = \Delta X^{16}[53] = \Delta X^{16}[54] = \Delta X^{16}[55] = 0$	$N_1 \cdot 2^{-104} \cdot 2^{-4}$	$2 \cdot N_1 \cdot 2^{-104} \cdot 2^{107}$
Total	-	-	-	$N_1 \cdot 2^{23.53}$

of encryptions. The time complexity T_2 to exhaustively check the value of the remaining 21-bit master key is $2^{128} \cdot \beta \cdot (1 - 2^{-64})$ 20-round of encryptions. We set the threshold as $\tau_D = 1$ and the number of structures as $\mathcal{S} = 2^{14.58}$. So, the data requirement of the attack is $2^{62.58}$ chosen plaintexts. With the method recalled in Sect. 2.3, the time complexity of this attack is $2^{125.50}$, and the success probability is $P_S = 70.00\%$. Since we should memorise the right pairs, the memory complexity of this attack is roughly $2^{62.58}$.

5   Conclusion

This work is motivated by filling the vacancy of the linear attack on GIFT-64. Firstly, we apply the automatic method to search for linear approximations of the cipher and discover several 12-round linear distinguishers involving the minimum number of subkey bits in the subkey enumeration phase. One of these linear approximations is utilised to launch a 19-round linear attack, which is the first linear attack result on GIFT-64. In parallel, we notice that the previous differential attack of GIFT-64 covering 20 rounds claims the full codebook. To reduce the data complexity of the 20-round attack, we apply the automatic method to exhaustively check 13-round differential trails with probabilities no less than 2^{-64}. A group of 32 differentials with the maximum probability is identified. One of the candidate differentials involving the minimum number of guessed subkey bits in the subkey enumeration phase is employed to realise the first 20-round differential attack without relying on the entire codebook. Given the newly proposed results, we conjecture that the resistances of GIFT-64 against differential and linear attacks do not have a significant gap.

Acknowledgements. The authors would like to thank the shepherd Kalikinkar Mandal and the anonymous reviewers for their valuable comments and suggestions to improve the quality of the paper. The authors also would like to thank Yong Fu for the kind discussion. The research leading to these results has received funding from the National Natural Science Foundation of China (Grant No. 62002201, Grant No. 62032014), the National Key Research and Development Program of China (Grant No. 2018YFA0704702), the Major Scientific and Technological Innovation Project of Shandong Province, China (Grant No. 2019JZZY010133), the Major Basic Research Project of Natural Science Foundation of Shandong Province, China (Grant No. ZR202010220025), and the Qingdao Postdoctor Application Research Project (Grant No. 61580070311101).

References

1. Ankele, R., Kölbl, S.: Mind the gap - a closer look at the security of block ciphers against differential cryptanalysis. In: Selected Areas in Cryptography - SAC 2018 - 25th International Conference, Calgary, AB, Canada, 15–17 August 2018, Revised Selected Papers, pp. 163–190. Springer, Cham (2018). https://doi.org/10.1007/978-3-030-10970-7_8
2. Banik, S., et al.: SUNDAE-GIFT. Submission to Round 1 (2019)
3. Banik, S., et al.: GIFT-COFB. IACR Cryptol. ePrint Arch. **2020**, 738 (2020). https://eprint.iacr.org/2020/738
4. Banik, S., Pandey, S.K., Peyrin, T., Sasaki, Yu., Sim, S.M., Todo, Y.: GIFT: a small present. In: Fischer, W., Homma, N. (eds.) CHES 2017. LNCS, vol. 10529, pp. 321–345. Springer, Cham (2017). https://doi.org/10.1007/978-3-319-66787-4_16
5. Beaulieu, R., Shors, D., Smith, J., Treatman-Clark, S., Weeks, B., Wingers, L.: The SIMON and SPECK families of lightweight block ciphers. IACR Cryptol. ePrint Arch. **2013**, 404 (2013)

6. Beierle, C., et al.: The SKINNY family of block ciphers and its low-latency variant MANTIS. In: Robshaw, M., Katz, J. (eds.) CRYPTO 2016. LNCS, vol. 9815, pp. 123–153. Springer, Heidelberg (2016). https://doi.org/10.1007/978-3-662-53008-5_5

7. Biham, E., Shamir, A.: Differential cryptanalysis of DES-like cryptosystems. In: Menezes, A.J., Vanstone, S.A. (eds.) CRYPTO 1990. LNCS, vol. 537, pp. 2–21. Springer, Heidelberg (1991). https://doi.org/10.1007/3-540-38424-3_1

8. Blondeau, C., Gérard, B., Tillich, J.: Accurate estimates of the data complexity and success probability for various cryptanalyses. Des. Codes Cryptogr. 59(1–3), 3–34 (2011). https://doi.org/10.1007/s10623-010-9452-2

9. Blondeau, C., Nyberg, K.: Joint data and key distribution of simple, multiple, and multidimensional linear cryptanalysis test statistic and its impact to data complexity. Des. Codes Cryptogr. 82(1), 319–349 (2016). https://doi.org/10.1007/s10623-016-0268-6

10. Bogdanov, A., et al.: PRESENT: an ultra-lightweight block cipher. In: Paillier, P., Verbauwhede, I. (eds.) CHES 2007. LNCS, vol. 4727, pp. 450–466. Springer, Heidelberg (2007). https://doi.org/10.1007/978-3-540-74735-2_31

11. Chakraborti, A., Datta, N., Jha, A., Lopez, C.M., Nandi, M., Sasaki, Y.: LOTUS-AEAD and LOCUS-AEAD. Submission to the NIST Lightweight Cryptography project (2019)

12. Chakraborti, A., Datta, N., Jha, A., Nandi, M.: HYENA. Submission to the NIST Lightweight Cryptography project (2019)

13. Chen, H., Zong, R., Dong, X.: Improved differential attacks on GIFT-64. In: Zhou, J., Luo, X., Shen, Q., Xu, Z. (eds.) ICICS 2019. LNCS, vol. 11999, pp. 447–462. Springer, Cham (2020). https://doi.org/10.1007/978-3-030-41579-2_26

14. Cho, J.Y.: Linear cryptanalysis of reduced-round PRESENT. In: Pieprzyk, J. (ed.) CT-RSA 2010. LNCS, vol. 5985, pp. 302–317. Springer, Heidelberg (2010). https://doi.org/10.1007/978-3-642-11925-5_21

15. Cook, S.A.: The complexity of theorem-proving procedures. In: Proceedings of the 3rd Annual ACM Symposium on Theory of Computing, Shaker Heights, Ohio, USA, 3–5 May 1971, pp. 151–158 (1971). https://doi.org/10.1145/800157.805047

16. Ji, F., Zhang, W., Zhou, C., Ding, T.: Improved (related-key) differential cryptanalysis on GIFT. In: Dunkelman, O., Jacobson, Jr., M.J., O'Flynn, C. (eds.) SAC 2020. LNCS, vol. 12804, pp. 198–228. Springer, Cham (2021). https://doi.org/10.1007/978-3-030-81652-0_8

17. Kölbl, S., Leander, G., Tiessen, T.: Observations on the SIMON block cipher family. In: Gennaro, R., Robshaw, M. (eds.) CRYPTO 2015. LNCS, vol. 9215, pp. 161–185. Springer, Heidelberg (2015). https://doi.org/10.1007/978-3-662-47989-6_8

18. Lai, X., Massey, J.L., Murphy, S.: Markov ciphers and differential cryptanalysis. In: Davies, D.W. (ed.) EUROCRYPT 1991. LNCS, vol. 547, pp. 17–38. Springer, Heidelberg (1991). https://doi.org/10.1007/3-540-46416-6_2

19. Liu, Y., Sasaki, Yu.: Related-key boomerang attacks on GIFT with automated trail search including BCT effect. In: Jang-Jaccard, J., Guo, F. (eds.) ACISP 2019. LNCS, vol. 11547, pp. 555–572. Springer, Cham (2019). https://doi.org/10.1007/978-3-030-21548-4_30

20. Liu, Y., Wang, Q., Rijmen, V.: Automatic search of linear trails in ARX with applications to SPECK and Chaskey. In: Manulis, M., Sadeghi, A.-R., Schneider, S. (eds.) ACNS 2016. LNCS, vol. 9696, pp. 485–499. Springer, Cham (2016). https://doi.org/10.1007/978-3-319-39555-5_26

21. Matsui, M.: Linear cryptanalysis method for DES cipher. In: Helleseth, T. (ed.) EUROCRYPT 1993. LNCS, vol. 765, pp. 386–397. Springer, Heidelberg (1994). https://doi.org/10.1007/3-540-48285-7_33

22. Rickmann, S.: Logic Friday (version 1.1. 3) [bibcomputer software] (2011)

23. Sasaki, Yu.: Integer linear programming for three-subset meet-in-the-middle attacks: application to GIFT. In: Inomata, A., Yasuda, K. (eds.) IWSEC 2018. LNCS, vol. 11049, pp. 227–243. Springer, Cham (2018). https://doi.org/10.1007/978-3-319-97916-8_15

24. Selçuk, A.A.: on probability of success in linear and differential cryptanalysis. J. Cryptol. **21**(1), 131–147 (2007). https://doi.org/10.1007/s00145-007-9013-7

25. Sinz, C.: Towards an optimal CNF encoding of Boolean cardinality constraints. In: van Beek, P. (ed.) CP 2005. LNCS, vol. 3709, pp. 827–831. Springer, Heidelberg (2005). https://doi.org/10.1007/11564751_73

26. Soleimany, H., Nyberg, K.: Zero-correlation linear cryptanalysis of reduced-round LBlock. Des. Codes Cryptogr. **73**(2), 683–698 (2014). https://doi.org/10.1007/s10623-014-9976-y

27. Song, L., Huang, Z., Yang, Q.: Automatic differential analysis of ARX block ciphers with application to SPECK and LEA. In: Liu, J.K., Steinfeld, R. (eds.) ACISP 2016. LNCS, vol. 9723, pp. 379–394. Springer, Cham (2016). https://doi.org/10.1007/978-3-319-40367-0_24

28. Soos, M., Nohl, K., Castelluccia, C.: Extending SAT solvers to cryptographic problems. In: Kullmann, O. (ed.) SAT 2009. LNCS, vol. 5584, pp. 244–257. Springer, Heidelberg (2009). https://doi.org/10.1007/978-3-642-02777-2_24

29. Sun, L., Wang, W., Wang, M.: More accurate differential properties of LED64 and Midori64. IACR Trans. Symmetric Cryptol. **2018**(3), 93–123 (2018). https://doi.org/10.13154/tosc.v2018.i3.93-123

30. Sun, L., Wang, W., Wang, M.: Accelerating the search of differential and linear characteristics with the SAT method. IACR Trans. Symmetric Cryptol. **2021**(1), 269–315 (2021). https://doi.org/10.46586/tosc.v2021.i1.269-315

31. Sun, L., Wang, W., Wang, M.: Improved attacks on GIFT-64. IACR Cryptol. ePrint Arch., 1179 (2021). https://eprint.iacr.org/2021/1179

32. Zhu, B., Dong, X., Yu, H.: MILP-based differential attack on round-reduced GIFT. In: Matsui, M. (ed.) CT-RSA 2019. LNCS, vol. 11405, pp. 372–390. Springer, Cham (2019). https://doi.org/10.1007/978-3-030-12612-4_19

A Simpler Model for Recovering Superpoly on Trivium

Stéphanie Delaune[1], Patrick Derbez[1], Arthur Gontier[1(✉)],
and Charles Prud'homme[2]

[1] Univ Rennes, CNRS, IRISA, Rennes, France
{stephanie.delaune,patrick.derbez,arthur.gontier}@irisa.fr
[2] TASC, IMT-Atlantique, LS2N-CNRS, 44307 Nantes, France
charles.prudhomme@imt-atlantique.fr

Abstract. The cube attack is a powerful cryptanalysis technique against symmetric primitives, especially for stream ciphers. One of the key step in a cube attack is recovering the superpoly. The division property has been introduced to cube attacks with the aim first to identify variables/monomials that are *not* involved in the superpoly. Recently, some improved versions of this technique allowing the recovery of the exact superpoly have been developed and applied on various stream ciphers [13,15].

In this paper, we propose a new model to recover the exact superpoly of a stream cipher given a cube. We model the polynomials involved in the stream cipher as a directed graph. It happens that this structure handles some of the monomial cancellations more easily than those based on division property, and this leads to better timing results. We propose two implementations of our model, one in MILP and one in CP, which are up to 10 times faster than the original division property-based model from Hao *et al.* [13], and consistently 30 to 60 times faster than the monomial prediction-based model from Hu *et al.* [15].

Keywords: Stream cipher · Cube attack · Division property · Trivium · MILP · CP

1 Introduction

Generic solvers as Gurobi [12] or Choco [17] are nowadays very common tools for cryptographers. They allow cryptographers to describe the problems they want to solve with high-level codes, making implementation faster and results much easier to verify. This approach has been very successful so far as generic solvers were used to find a large variety of attacks and distinguishers. On the one hand, Gurobi was used to search for integral distinguishers based on division property [23], differential characteristics [1], advanced meet-in-the-middle attacks [19] and cube attacks [13] by solving Mixed-Integer Linear Programming (MILP) models. On the other hand, Constraint Programming (CP) solvers as

© The Author(s), under exclusive license to Springer Nature Switzerland AG 2022
R. AlTawy and A. Hülsing (Eds.): SAC 2021, LNCS 13203, pp. 266–285, 2022.
https://doi.org/10.1007/978-3-030-99277-4_13

Choco were mainly used for highly non-linear problems as instantiating truncated differential characteristics [5, 11]. Furthermore, some works combine both approaches as in [6] where a MILP model is first used to search for best truncated boomerang characteristics followed by a call to Choco to find the best instantiations and clusters.

Given a cryptographic problem, there are most often many ways to model it in MILP or CP and determining the best one is a hard task. It is commonly assumed that smaller the model is, faster it can be solved and many works were dedicated to decrease the number of constraints required to describe cryptographic problems. For instance, Abdelkhalek *et al.* used both the Quine-McCluskey and Espresso algorithms to reduce the number of inequalities required to model the Difference Distribution Table (DDT) of 8-bit Sboxes [1]. Similarly, Boura *et al.* proposed new techniques to represent any subset of $\{0, 1\}^n$ with a small number of inequalities [3]. However this approach has its limits and sometimes adding redundant constraints may improve the running times. For instance, Delaune *et al.* found that adding the constraints related to minimal number of active Sboxes into their model dedicated to boomerang characteristics greatly improves it [6].

Another approach used to decrease the overall running time consists in dividing the problem into two (or more) subproblems much easier to solve. In [25], Zhou *et al.* showed that to search for best truncated differential characteristics against Substitution-Permutation Network (SPN) it was much faster to split the whole model according to the number of active Sboxes on some of the internal states. The intuition is that best truncated differential characteristics will have several internal states with very few active Sboxes. Similarly, in [13], Hao *et al.* proposed MILP models to recover the superpolies of several stream ciphers using division property. To speed-up the resolution and reach reasonable running times they had to compute all the possible monomials at the half of the initialisation process (from the output bit) and then solve the problem for each of them.

Our Contributions. In this paper, we propose a new model to recover the superpoly of a stream cipher given a cube. We illustrate it on TRIVIUM but the approach is generic and could be applied to other stream ciphers. Our idea is to model the polynomials involved in the initialisation process as a directed graph for which nodes are the state variables and edges the monomials. The main advantage of our model regarding the one of Hao *et al.* [13] based on division property is that it is much easier to handle some of the monomial cancellations and thus much faster to solve large instances. We then propose two implementations of this model, one in MILP and one in CP, which are up to 10 times faster than the original division property-based model from Hao *et al.* [13]. We also compare our approach to the *monomial prediction* technique introduced by Hu *et al.* in [15] and found our models are consistently 30 to 60 times faster to solve. Finally, regarding the MILP model, we show how to improve the strategy deployed by Gurobi without relying on a divide-and-conquer strategy.

2   Some Background

2.1   Cube Attacks

Cube attacks, introduced by Dinur and Shamir at EUROCRYPT in 2009 [7], has become a general tool for evaluating the security of cryptographic primitives, and has been successfully applied against various stream ciphers, e.g. [2,7,9].

Roughly, the output bit of a cipher is seen as an unknown Boolean polynomial $f(\boldsymbol{k}, \boldsymbol{v})$ where $\boldsymbol{k}$ is a vector of secret input variables, and $\boldsymbol{v}$ is a vector of public input variables. Given a monomial t_I which is the product of public variables in $I = \{i_1, \dots, i_d\}$, i.e. $t_I = v_{i_1} \cdot \dots \cdot v_{i_d}$, the function f can be represented as:

$$f(\boldsymbol{k}, \boldsymbol{v}) = t_I \cdot p_I + q(\boldsymbol{k}, \boldsymbol{v})$$

where the polynomial $q(\boldsymbol{k}, \boldsymbol{v})$ only contains terms which are not supersets of I. The polynomial p_I is called the *superpoly* of I in f. The set $I = \{i_1, \dots, i_d\}$ determines a specific structure called *cube*, denoted as C_I, containing 2^d values where variables in $\{v_{i_1}, \dots, v_{i_d}\}$ take all possible combinations of values.

Then, the main idea behind a cube attack (and its variants) is the fact that the sum of the polynomials $f(\boldsymbol{k}, \boldsymbol{v})$ considering all the possible values for the cube, and assuming that the other ones are fixed, is exactly the superpoly p_I.

$$\bigoplus_{C_I} f(\boldsymbol{k}, \boldsymbol{v}) = \bigoplus_{C_I} \left(t_I \cdot p_I(\boldsymbol{k}, \boldsymbol{v}) + q(\boldsymbol{k}, \boldsymbol{v}) \right) = p_I(\boldsymbol{k}, \boldsymbol{v})$$

Thus, being able to determine the superpoly allows either to distinguish the cipher from a random function (if $p_I = 0$) or to retrieve some information on the key. The goal of the adversary is then to find the best trade-off between the size of the cube, the number of key bits involved in the superpoly and how far is the superpoly from a balanced function.

The mainly used methods to retrieve the superpoly are currently all based on the division property without unknown subsets.

2.2   Division Property

The division property is a generic technique to search for integral distinguishers. It was originally proposed by Todo *et al.* at Eurocrypt 2015 [20] and has been widely applied to many ciphers, e.g. [22]. In [21], division property was used to search for cube attacks against stream ciphers but authors made two assumptions on superpolies which turned out to be wrong [24]. Thus, at Eurocrypt 2020, Hao *et al.* introduced the *exact* division property and showed the technique allows one to fully recover the superpoly of several round-reduced stream ciphers [13]. Basically, this technique allows one to track a monomial through the successive applications of a round function relying on the notion of trails.

We illustrate this on a simple example.

Example 1. Consider the functions f and g defined as follows:

$$(y_1, y_2) = f(x_1, x_2, x_3) = (x_1 + x_3,\ x_1 x_2 + x_1)$$
$$(z_1, z_2) = \quad g(y_1, y_2) \quad = (y_1 y_2,\ y_1 + y_2)$$

Assume that our cipher is given by $g \circ f$. We can compute the ANF (Algebraic Normal Form) of the entire cipher to determine the monomials that compose this function but performing this computation is not possible on real ciphers. Here, we have that:

$$(z_1, z_2) = (g \circ f)(x_1, x_2, x_3) = (x_1 + x_1 x_2 + x_1 x_3 + x_1 x_2 x_3,\ x_3 + x_1 x_2)$$

Instead of computing the ANF, we may represent the propagation of the different monomials through a table. The tables below represent respectively the behaviours of the functions f and g.

x_1	x_2	x_3	y_1	y_2
0	0	0	0	0
1	0	0	1	0
0	0	1	1	0
1	0	0	0	1
1	1	0	0	1
1	1	0	1	1
1	0	0	1	1
1	1	1	1	1
1	0	1	1	1

y_1	y_2	z_1	z_2
0	0	0	0
0	1	0	1
1	0	0	1
1	1	1	0
0	0	1	1

For instance, the 4 last lines of the first table represent the fact $x_1 x_2$, x_1, $x_1 x_2 x_3$, and $x_1 x_3$ are monomials occurring in $y_1 y_2$. Consulting this first table, we can also see that the monomial x_1 is present in y_1 (2nd line), in y_2 (4th line) and also in $y_1 y_2$ (7th line) .

Now, if we want to study whether the monomial x_1 occurs for instance in the first component of the ANF of the function $g \circ f$, we have to look for the existence of some trails starting from $(1, 0, 0)$ which represents x_1 to $(z_1, z_2) = (1, 0)$. Reading the tables, we have that: $(1, 0, 0) \rightarrow (1, 0)$, $(1, 0, 0) \rightarrow (0, 1)$ and $(1, 0, 0) \rightarrow (1, 1)$ in the table representing f. Each of these trails can be completed with a line from the table representing g, leading to the following trails:

$$(1, 0, 0) \rightarrow (1, 0) \rightarrow (0, 1)$$
$$(1, 0, 0) \rightarrow (0, 1) \rightarrow (0, 1)$$
$$(1, 0, 0) \rightarrow (1, 1) \rightarrow (1, 0)$$

The last line represents the fact that the monomial x_1 occurs in $y_1 y_2$, and thus in z_1. Regarding, the two first lines, we can see that we have two trails starting from $(1, 0, 0)$ and ending with $(0, 1)$. The first one indicates that the monomial x_1 occurs in y_1, and thus in z_2 (since y_1 occurs in z_2). The second one indicates that the monomial x_1 occurs in y_2, and thus in z_2 (since y_2 occurs also in z_2). These two occurrences cancel each other, and thus at the end, x_1 does not occur in z_2. Therefore to accurately decide whether a given monomial occurs in the ANF, it is important to count the number of trails: an even number means that the monomial does not occur, whereas an odd number means that it is indeed present.

Relying on this technique, we are therefore looking for trails starting with a given vector representing a particular monomial and leading to a specific vector indicating the presence of the monomial in the ANF after a number of iterations of the round function. The difficulty of the search procedure depends on many parameters as the round function, the state size, the number of rounds. However, for real ciphers computing the whole propagation table of the round function may be infeasible or requires too many inequalities to be described. Hence, in most of the cases, propagation rules are added for each basic operator of the cipher (xor, and, copy).

Several algorithms have been developed to evaluate the propagation of the division property on ciphers. Some are based on the so-called breadth-first search algorithm [20,22] whereas some others implement this search using the mixed integer linear programming (MILP) method [13].

The downside of all these approaches is that we can hardly add new properties to strengthen the model as a global view on the problem we are trying to solve is missing.

3   A Graph-Based Model for Superpoly Recovery

In this section, we present a novel and simple graph-based model dedicated to recovering the superpoly of a stream cipher for a given cube. It is fully equivalent to the last version of division property since it can recover the exact superpoly, but has the main advantage of being much easier to understand and manipulate. We represent all the intermediate variables and monomials using a directed graph G. A node of G represents a variable and an edge from x to y indicates that y appears in the ANF of x. The possible transitions from a node to its child nodes are described by the monomials of the round function. This results in an automaton which defines the set of outgoing edge of each node of G.

Example 2. Let get back to Example 1. We have the equations:

$$y_1 = x_1 \oplus x_3 \qquad\qquad z_1 = y_1 y_2$$
$$y_2 = x_1 x_2 \oplus x_1 \qquad\qquad z_2 = y_1 \oplus y_2$$

This system of equations can be expressed as a graph $G = (V, E)$ where :

- $V = \{x_1, x_2, x_3, y_1, y_2, z_1, z_2\}$ is the set of nodes,
- $E = \{(y_1, x_1), (y_1, x_3), (y_2, x_1), (y_2, x_2), (z_1, y_1), (z_1, y_2), (z_2, y_1), (z_2, y_2)\}$ is the set of edges.

We call *trail* any collection of edges $\mathcal{T}$ representing a monomial together with the process to obtain it by developing the polynomial expressions of the root nodes. For the above system it means that $\mathcal{T}$ has to satisfy the following extra constraints:

- $(y_1, x_1) \in \mathcal{T} \implies (y_1, x_3) \notin \mathcal{T}$ – $(z_1, y_1) \in \mathcal{T} \iff (z_1, y_2) \in \mathcal{T}$
- $(y_1, x_3) \in \mathcal{T} \implies (y_1, x_1) \notin \mathcal{T}$ – $(z_2, y_1) \in \mathcal{T} \implies (z_2, y_2) \notin \mathcal{T}$
- $(y_2, x_2) \in \mathcal{T} \implies (y_2, x_1) \in \mathcal{T}$ – $(z_2, y_2) \in \mathcal{T} \implies (z_2, y_1) \notin \mathcal{T}$

It is interesting to compare our model to the model based on division property with basic propagation rules. In that case the system would be rewritten as:

$$(x_{11}, x_{12}, x_{13}) = \mathrm{copy}(x_1)$$
$$y_1 = \mathrm{xor}(x_{11}, x_3)$$
$$a = \mathrm{and}(x_{12}, x_2)$$
$$y_2 = \mathrm{xor}(a, x_{13})$$
$$(y_{11}, y_{12}) = \mathrm{copy}(y_1)$$
$$(y_{21}, y_{22}) = \mathrm{copy}(y_2)$$
$$z_1 = \mathrm{and}(y_{11}, y_{21})$$
$$z_2 = \mathrm{xor}(y_{12}, y_{22})$$

It now contains 15 variables, 4 copy-constraints, 3 xor-constraints and 2 and-constraints, which seems much more complex than our model with 8 variables (the edges) and 6 constraints. However we have to add extra constraints to our model to ensure that if an edge $(\cdot, a)$ belongs to $\mathcal{T}$ then either a is a leaf or an edge $(a, \cdot)$ also belongs to $\mathcal{T}$. For complex polynomials this can be tricky and force us to use the same intermediate variables than above to simplify the constraints.

Interestingly, and most importantly, both models have exactly the same solutions. This means that there is a one-to-one mapping between the possible trails $\mathcal{T}$ and the possible solutions of the division property-based model. Hence, the main advantage of our model relies on the ease of adding extra constraints to remove false (even) trails and deploying branch-and-cut strategies.

Example on Trivium

TRIVIUM [4] is an NFSR-based stream cipher. Its internal state is represented by a 288-bit state $(s_1, s_2, \ldots, s_{288})$ distributed on three registers A, B, and C. The 80-bit secret key K is loaded to register A, and the 80-bit initialisation vector IV is loaded to register B. The other state bits are set to 0 except the last three bits in register C. Namely, the initial state bits are represented as:

$$s_1, \ldots, s_{80}, s_{81}, \ldots, s_{93} \leftarrow K[1], \ldots, K[80], 0, \ldots, 0$$
$$s_{94}, \ldots, s_{174}, s_{175}, s_{176}, s_{177} \leftarrow IV[1], \ldots, IV[80], 0, 0, 0, 0$$
$$s_{178}, \ldots, s_{285}, s_{286}, s_{287}, s_{288} \leftarrow 0, \ldots, 0, 1, 1, 1$$

At each round, we first compute t_1, t_2, and t_3 as:

$$t_1 \leftarrow s_{66} + s_{91}s_{92} + s_{93} + s_{171}$$
$$t_2 \leftarrow s_{162} + s_{175}s_{176} + s_{177} + s_{264}$$
$$t_3 \leftarrow s_{243} + s_{286}s_{287} + s_{288} + s_{69}$$

Then, the three registers are updated as follows:

$$\mathsf{A} \leftarrow t_3, s_1, \ldots, s_{92} \quad \mathsf{B} \leftarrow t_1, s_{94}, \ldots, s_{176} \quad \mathsf{C} \leftarrow t_2, s_{178}, \ldots, s_{287}$$

The state is updated 1152 times and then, at each new round, an output bit is produced: $z \leftarrow s_{66} + s_{93} + s_{162} + s_{177} + s_{243} + s_{288}$. Figure 1 depicts graphically transitions of the TRIVIUM stream cipher.

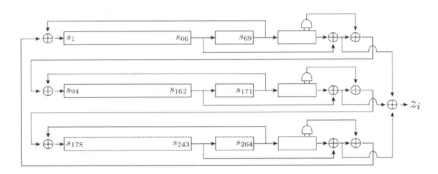

Fig. 1. The Trivium cipher.

Figure 2 depicts the Deterministic Finite Automaton (DFA) deduced from the description of TRIVIUM. Note that the DFA develops TRIVIUM backwards: from the output bit to first round. There are four possible transitions to go from one register (A, B or C) to its successors: three of them are simple, and one is doubling ($\Longrightarrow$). In the following, the three simple transitions will be named the looping ($\cdots\!\!\rightarrow$), the short ($--\!\rightarrow$), and the long ($\longrightarrow$) one.

One may have noticed that the DFA relies only on the first bit of each register. Indeed, for the other bits, the application of the round function simply consists of shifting them to the left. The value of the shifted bits only changes when they turn back to the first position of a register. Moreover, none of these shifted bits are a result of a round function, so they have no use in the DFA. In summary, the DFA already simplifies all the shifted bits at each round on each register to focus on the one produced in the corresponding round function (t_1, t_2, and t_3). The node A (resp. B, C) represents the first bit of register A (resp. B, C). Whenever a transition is taken, the generated bit will have to be shifted k times to be on the first position again. For example, if the bit at the first position of register A is set to 1 at round R, then it can be propagated to register C or A. If A is selected, then the first bit of A will be activated at round $R - 69$, that is $k = 69$. Otherwise, if C is selected, there are two scenarios. Either a simple transition is taken (short or long), which corresponds to the activation of the the first bit of C at either round $R - 66$ or $R - 111$. Or the doubling transition is picked and the first bit of the register C will be activated at round $R - 110$ and $R - 109$.

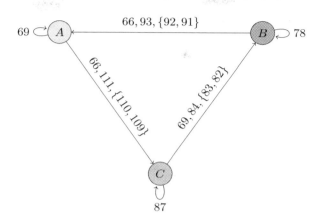

Fig. 2. A DFA that encodes possible transitions for the Trivium cipher.

Now we will present the way to build a graph modelling a division trail based on the DFA (Fig. 2), using a breadth-first search algorithm. The node corresponding to the output bit z at round R is created first and pushed into a queue. This triggers a loop that ends when the queue is empty. A node is popped from the queue and marked as visited. If the node has a positive R value, its child nodes described by the DFA are lazily created, added to the queue and used edges are created. Creating a node requires to know its round R: anytime a transition is visited, the number of shifts that label it is subtracted from the R value of its parent node. If a popped node has a negative R value, which corresponds to the first state of the cipher, no action is performed. When the loop stops, the graph of all possibilities is declared.

Such a graph is not very deep but it is very wide since any node has potentially five child nodes. However, each node in a solution has only one or two outgoing edges. Figure 3 shows a graph solution for TRIVIUM 672 with the starter node s_{243}, i.e. the 66th bit of register C. Therefore, the source node is labelled by C with $R = 672 - 66 = 606$ since the bit at position 66 in register C has to be shifted 66 times to be on the first position. The blue nodes are the cube bits and the red ones are the key bits. Double-line edges ($\Longrightarrow$) stand for doubling transitions, plain-line edges ($\longrightarrow$) for long transitions, dashed-line edges ($--\rightarrow$) for short transition, and dotted-line edges ($\cdots\cdots\rightarrow$) for looping transitions. This solution represents one trail for the superpoly monomial x_{16}.

Once we have formalised our problem as a graph problem, we can rely on a MILP solver (e.g. Gurobi) or a CP solver (e.g. Choco) to enumerate all the solutions.

In the following we chose Gurobi [12] as the solver for the MILP model because it already showcased its efficiency on division property and Choco [17] as a constraint programming (CP) solver for comparison but also because it natively supports constraints over graph variables [8].

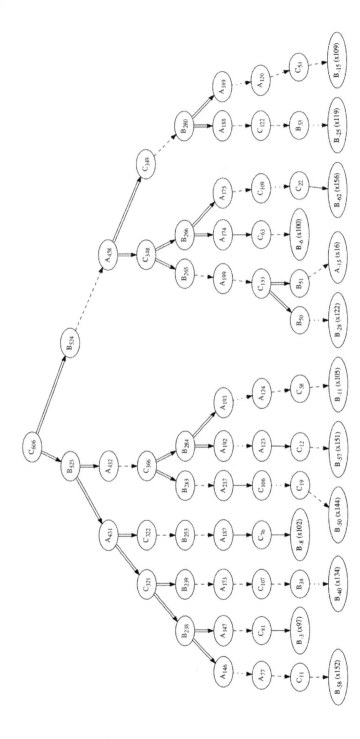

Fig. 3. A solution for TRIVIUM 672 considering s_{243} (66th bit of register C) as starter node. Blue nodes are the cube bits; the red one is the key bit. Double-line edges are for doubling transitions, plain-line edges for long transitions, dashed-line edges for short transition and dotted-line edges for looping transitions. (Color figure online)

4   Strengthening the Graph-Based Model

The graph-based model is equivalent to the more classical model based on trails, but its global structure eases new constraints like the following ones.

4.1   Constrain the Doubling Paths

To retrieve the superpoly we need to enumerate all the trails and count how many trails there are for one given monomial. Indeed, a monomial with an even number of trails will cancel itself in the superpoly.

In the graph-based representation, a doubling path is a pair of distinct sub-graphs connecting a given set of nodes to another given set of nodes (the leaves). If a trail uses one sub-graph of a doubling path, then the trail using the other sub-graph will produce the same monomial. Therefore, preventing doubling paths to exist in the graph will reduce the number of trails that cancel each other out. We identified several doubling paths for TRIVIUM.

Pattern 1 (Long-Double). Between each register there is the long transition with a given number of shifts p, and the doubling transition with $p-1$ and $p-2$ shifts. Therefore, if the doubling edge is followed by two long edges, we will get the same leaves than taking the long edge first and the doubling edge after, as depicted on Fig. 4.

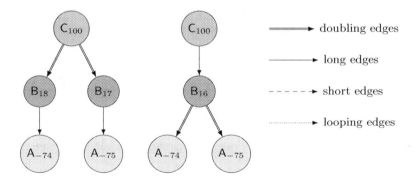

Fig. 4. Long-double pattern

To discard this pattern, we have to take care that the intermediate nodes, here B_{16}, B_{17}, and B_{18}, are not used in any other part of the trail.

Pattern 2 (3 Consecutive Bits). An other doubling pattern is when three bits are at consecutive rounds on the same register as depicted on Fig. 5. For example on the nodes C_{97}, C_{98}, and C_{99}. If the doubling edges are taken on C_{97} and C_{99}, the long and the doubling edges of the middle bit can then be removed because these two choices lead to the same output nodes $(B_{14},B_{15},B_{16},B_{17})$.

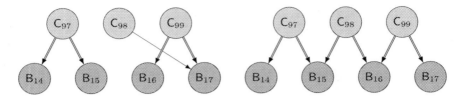

Fig. 5. 3 consecutive bits pattern

Pattern 3 (Looping). When a looping transition is taken *i.e.*, the bit stays on the same register, and if all the outgoing edges of the looping register return to the same register at least once in the trail, then a similar result can be obtained by not taking the first looping transition but taking it on each outgoing edges as shown on Fig. 6.

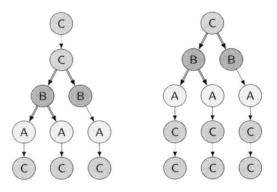

Fig. 6. Looping pattern

Pattern 4 (Simple Cycle). A cycle pattern is completed whenever the path returns to the first register without doubling, then taking any different edge of the cycle after is a doubling pattern. Indeed, any edge after the cycle could be taken before the cycle as shown on Fig. 7.

By considering all these patterns, it seems possible to reduce the number of even solutions and save some useless trail explorations without changing the parity of each solution. However we faced many problems. First adding the constraints for all these patterns slows down the solvers and finding the right trade-off between solution space reduction and time consumption is not easy. Second, we have to ensure a doubling pattern does not interfere with another one. More precisely, let (p_1, p_2) be a doubling pattern. We may have an issue if it is possible to reach a trail containing p_1 while it is impossible to reach p_2 because of another doubling pattern. There are several ways of taking this into account. One option is to apply a constraint if and only if all the nodes involved

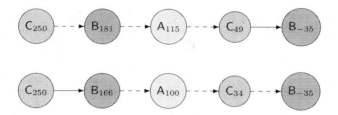

Fig. 7. Simple cycle pattern

in a doubling pattern are not reached by other edges than the ones from the pattern. But in practice doing so highly limits the number of times doubling patterns are applied. As a result of our experimentation, we decided to take into account pattern 2 only.

Thus selecting the right patterns to add to the model is still an open and interesting question.

4.2 Use an Arity Approximation

The idea of approximating the number of cube bits reachable for each bit of the cipher was explored in [16] and we propose to use it to reduce the search space in our graph-based model.

The reasoning on arity is as follows. Starting from the bits of the initialisation vector and going back to the active bit, each intermediate node aggregates an over-approximation of the number of bits of the cube that it would allow to reach if we took it. This value is called arity and is built by consulting all or part of its descendants. Under certain conditions between the arity of a node and that of its predecessors or successors it is possible to deduce whether it may belong to a trail or not.

As shown in [16], an approximation regarding the arity can be computed by recursively taking two consecutive transitions into account, and by propagating the arity from the cube to the output bit.

Example 3. Consider the case where one wants to compute the arity of register C at round 100 and the doubling transitions is selected.

$$ar(C_{100}) = ar(B_{18}) + ar(B_{17}) \tag{1}$$

These terms are developed as follows:

$$ar(B_{18}) = \max(ar(B_{-60}), ar(A_{-48}), ar(A_{-75}), ar(A_{-74}) + ar(A_{-73})) \tag{2}$$
$$ar(B_{17}) = \max(ar(B_{-61}), ar(A_{-49}), ar(A_{-76}), ar(A_{-75}) + ar(A_{-74})) \tag{3}$$

Suppose now that arity of registers with negative round are all equal to the same value, say the value 1. Then (2) and (3) can be simplified to:

$$ar(B_{18}) = ar(A_{-74}) + ar(A_{-73}) \tag{4}$$
$$ar(B_{17}) = ar(A_{-75}) + ar(A_{-74}) \tag{5}$$

By mapping the (4) and (5) in (1), we remark that the arity of A_{-74} is counted twice. In the graph representation, the node labelled A_{-74} will be reachable multiple time from C_{100}. Such an over-approximation would be accumulated along way to the output bit.

For a given node, the approximation of its arity has to take into account all the child cases of the doubling edges and take the maximum of their arity to better approximate the arity of the source. Note that a similar reasoning can also be applied to compute the minimum arity of a node.

This approximation of the arity can then be used as a strategy for a MILP solver or as a constraint for a CP solver. Since the goal is to find the superpoly, it is expected that a significant part of the graph will be cut from the search because of a too low arity.

5   Implementations

In this section we present two implementations of our graph model and discuss our results on TRIVIUM. The first implementation is in Mixed Integer Linear Programming with a relaxed flow problem and the second implementation is in Constraint Programming with a graph variable.

The results presented in this section and in particular the MILP and CP models are publicly available[1].

5.1   MILP

Mixed Integer Linear Programming aims at solving problems described with linear constraints. The MILP graph model is written as a relaxed flow problem. A flow problem is usually defined with the conservation of flows constraint. This constraint states that anything that enter a node must leave it. In our case, this is relaxed because multiple incoming transitions are possible. Having multiple incoming transitions means that a variable is in the monomial multiple times. Regardless of the incoming number of edges, if it is reached, then the out transition is either simple or doubling.

In the following, $Pred(i)$ gives all the predecessors of the node i and $Succ(i)$ gives all the linear successors and one of the doubling successor. The functions $brother_1(i)$ and $brother_2(i)$ gives the two doubling sons of i.

First all the edges are declared as Boolean variables:

$$X_{i,j} = \begin{cases} 1 & \text{if the edge } (i,j) \text{ is in the trail} \\ 0 & \text{otherwise} \end{cases}$$

---

[1] https://gitlab.inria.fr/agontier/trivium-superpoly.

To implement the graph model of TRIVIUM, we add the following constraints:

$$\sum_{j \in Pred(i)} X_{j,i} \geq \sum_{j \in Succ(i)} X_{i,j} \qquad \forall i \in V \qquad (6)$$

$$\sum_{j \in Pred(i)} X_{j,i} \leq |Pred(i)| \sum_{j \in Succ(i)} X_{i,j} \qquad \forall i \in V \qquad (7)$$

$$X_{i,brother_1(i)} = X_{i,brother_2(i)} \qquad \forall i \in V \qquad (8)$$

$$\sum_{j \in Succ(i)} X_{i,j} \leq 1 \qquad \forall i \in V \qquad (9)$$

The constraints (6) and (7) are the conservation of flows constraints while (8) and (9) are related to the edges outputting a node (and thus dedicated to TRIVIUM). The cube and the output bit are constrained in the solution by the following:

$$\sum_{j \in Pred(i)} X_{j,i} \geq 1 \qquad \forall i \in cube \qquad (10)$$

$$\sum_{j \in Pred(i)} X_{j,i} = 0 \qquad \substack{\forall i \in leaves, \\ i \notin cube, \ i \notin key, \\ i \notin non\text{-}zero\text{-}constants} \qquad (11)$$

The key bits are free as well as the non-zero constants because they can also appear in the superpoly.

Constraints for Doubling Patterns. The MILP model can be strengthened with constraints to discard the doubling patterns. Let P a set of doubling patterns (p_1, p_2) with p_1, p_2 sub-graphs with the same sources and the same leaves.

We used only Pattern 2 for which both the sub-graphs p_1 and p_2 are composed of respectively 5 and 6 edges of the form:

- $p_1 = \{(x_1, y_1), (x_1, y_2), (x_2, y_4), (x_3, y_3), (x_3, y_4)\}$
- $p_2 = \{(x_1, y_1), (x_1, y_2), (x_2, y_2), (x_2, y_3), (x_3, y_3), (x_3, y_4)\}$

Thanks to the equalities of doubling edges we can simplify both p_1 and p_2 such that:

- $p_1 = \{(x_1, y_2), (x_2, y_4), (x_3, y_4)\}$
- $p_2 = \{(x_1, y_2), (x_2, y_2), (x_3, y_4)\}$

Because (x_2, y_4) and (x_2, y_2) cannot be active both at the same time, we can add the inequality $X_{(x_1,y_2)} + X_{(x_2,y_2)} + X_{(x_2,y_4)} + X_{(x_3,y_4)} \leq 2$ to remove both p_1 and p_2. However a problem occurs if the node x_4 consecutive to x_3 is active and reaches y_4. Indeed, the configuration for which the 4 consecutive nodes follow the doubling edges would be removed twice. Thus we modified the inequalitie into:

$$2X_{(x_1,y_2)} + 2X_{(x_2,y_2)} + X_{(x_2,y_4)} + 2X_{(x_3,y_4)} - X_{(x_4,y_4)} \leq 4$$

We verified that adding this inequality to all consecutive nodes leads to the right ANF. In more details, this inequality forbids 3 consecutive nodes to all take the doubling edge and forbids x_2 to take the long edge if x_4 does not take the doubling edge.

Strategy. In both [13] and [15], authors used a divide-and-conquer strategy together with their MILP models. Basically they developed the polynomial of the root node for several hundreds of rounds (between 200 and 400) and then applied their models on each monomial of the polynomial. Without this strategy the solving times are much higher, making unfeasible to retrieve the superpoly in reasonable time. This shows that Gurobi fails to identify the right variables to branch on. While Gurobi does not allow the user to fully control the branch-and-cut strategy, it offers several options to modify it and we mainly used two of them:

- **BranchPriority:** With this option it is possible to give to each variable of the model a priority during the selection of the next variable to branch on. We tried several strategies and it seems that the best choice is to sort the variable according to their arity. More precisely, given an edge (x, y), we chose to:
   1. set a negative priority if $ar(y) \leq 0$, i.e. if the variable y cannot lead to any cube variable;
   2. set the priority to zero for all simple edges, based on the idea that we have to focus on doubling edges;
   3. set the priority to $ar(x)$ for all doubling edges, to focus on the edges which can reach the most cube variables.
- **VarHintVal:** With this option we can tell Gurobi that we think the value of a variable will be in a solution. We chose to set to 0 all simple edges, again to focus on doubling edges.

Using both those options it became unnecessary to use the divide-and-conquer strategy as we reach approximately the same running times with and without it. However we believe there is still room for improvements. First the **BranchPriority** is static while a dynamic approach would be much better. Second, both the options above apply to variables only while we may want to use them on linear combinations of variables. The problem is that if we create a new variable x and add a constraint $x = y + z$, x will be removed from the model during the presolve and it seems Gurobi does not keep its branch priority.

5.2 CP

Constraint programming [18] is a technique for solving combinatorial problems, like MILP. Unlike the latter, it is not necessary to express the rules solely in terms of linear constraints. In addition, CP solves a problem in a way similar to branch-and-bound except that it eliminates, by *filtering*, impossible states or combinations. CP techniques have already been successfully applied to cryptanalytic problems [5, 10, 11].

The CP graph uses a directed graph variable G. A graph variable G has a domain defined by a graph interval $[\underline{G}, \overline{G}]$. $\underline{G}$ is the lower bound of G and defines nodes and edges that must appear in any solution. In our case, it is declared with the mandatory nodes of the cube. $\overline{G}$ is the upper bound of G

and defines nodes and edges that can appear in any solution. In our case, it is the total graph developed from the automaton defined is Sect. 3. A solution is found when $\overline{G} = \underline{G}$. The solving processes by adding nodes or edges from $\underline{G}$ or by removing nodes or edges from $\overline{G}$. Such modifications are triggered by constraints defining properties on G that need to be satisfied in any solution.

In the following, D is a view of G which only contains doubling edges and the endpoint nodes; L is another view of G wich only contains the long edges and the endpoint nodes; K stores leaf nodes of G. The functions $pred_X(n)$ and $succ_X(n)$ give the predecessors and the successors of a node n in the (sub-)graph X.

The graph model is declared as $(12) \wedge ((13) \vee (14)) \wedge (15) \wedge (16)$ where:

$$|pred_G(n)| > 0 \qquad \forall n \in \underline{G},\ n \neq source \qquad (12)$$
$$|succ_G(n)| = 1 \wedge (n, s) \notin D \qquad \forall n \in \underline{G},\ n \notin K, \forall s \in succ_G(n) \qquad (13)$$
$$|succ_G(n)| = 2 \wedge (n, s) \in D \qquad \forall n \in \underline{G},\ n \notin K, \forall s \in succ_G(n) \qquad (14)$$
$$(n, s_1) \in \underline{G} \iff (n, s_2) \in \underline{G} \qquad \forall n \in \underline{G},\ (n, s_1) \in D, (n, s_2) \in D \qquad (15)$$
$$(n, s_1) \notin \overline{G} \iff (n, s_2) \notin \overline{G} \qquad \forall n \in \underline{G},\ (n, s_1) \in D, (n, s_2) \in D \qquad (16)$$

The constraint (12) ensures that each node selected in a solution, but the source node, has at least one predecessor. Constraints (13) and (14) maintain the number of successors of each node but the leaf ones. If a given node takes a simple transition then it has exactly one successor; if it takes a doubling transition then it has exactly two successors. The two conditions cannot hold simultaneously. Finally, constraints (15) and (16) ensures that either a single edge or a pair of doubling edges is selected.

The doubling constraints of Sect. 4.1 are added to the CP model in the form of clauses expressed on the disjoint membership of edges in G and are propagated using a SAT-like constraint. The algorithm for estimating the degree of TRIVIUM-like ciphers [16] can directly be integrated in the graph model as an additional constraint as presented in Sect. 4.2. Without going into too much details, it imposes to declare RIV (for Reachable Initialisation Vector) additional integer variables. An integer variable v has a domain $[\underline{v}, \overline{v}]$ where $\underline{v}$ (resp. $\overline{v}$) denotes the smallest (resp. the largest) value it can be assigned to. The RIV variables stores, for each node in $\underline{G}$, an approximation of the number of nodes of the cube it can reach. The algorithm [16] is directly applied dynamically to refine bounds of each RIV_i variable associated to node i, based on RIV_j, $\forall j \in succ_G(i)$. It is important to note that RIV variables are bounded as long as the involved nodes and edges are in $\overline{G}$. When a RIV domain is emptied or is inconsistent with those of its neighbours then the corresponding node is removed from $\overline{G}$.

Strategy. Unlike Gurobi, we can fully control the strategy deployed by Choco. However, this solver is inherently sequential and thus we decided to apply the divide-and-conquer strategy to run several instances in parallel. The main issue we faced is that only few instances are hard to solve and thus we regularly need to redivide models in order to maximize the use of available cores.

5.3   Results

We ran our new models together with the ones from both [13] and [15] on our server, limiting the number of available cores to 32. Results are given on Tables 1 and 2 while the cubes used to perform our experiments are detailed on Table 3.

Table 1. Results on Trivium

Model	Monomial prediction [15]	Division property [13]	MILP graph	CP graph
$R = 675$	3 m	1m	3 s	15 s
$R = 735$	4 m	2m	10 s	31 m
$R = 840/1$	472 m	269 m	10 m	>24 h
$R = 840/2$	316 m	91 m	10 m	
$R = 840/3$	351 m	108 m	6 m	
$R = 841$	956 m	282 m	19 m	
$R = 842$	>24 h	990 m	182 m	

We see that the graph model of TRIVIUM performs better with the MILP implementation and the Gurobi solver. One explanation might be that TRIVIUM is not highly combinatorial. Indeed, the round function of TRIVIUM has only one nonlinear case and it is a simple product. Our graph model implemented in MILP is consistently much faster than the models from Hu *et al.* based on monomial prediction and from Hao *et al.* based on division property.

Regarding the number of trails outputted by our model, it is reduced by a factor between 2 and 4 which shows how useful are the doubling patterns described in Sect. 4. But as we explained, we were not able to use all of them. Checking a posteriori the trails for Trivium-842 shows that taking into account all the doubling patterns could remove much more trails. We believe this is an interesting research direction for a future work.

Table 2. Number of solutions

Graph solver	$R = 840/1$	$R = 841$	$R = 842$
Without doubling constraints	12 909	30 177	3 188 835
With Pattern 2	5 953	18 929	720 779

Table 3. Cubes used in our experiments for TRIVIUM

Rounds	Cube indices
675	3, 14, 21, 25, 38, 43, 44, 47, 54, 56, 58, 68
735	2, 5, 9, 12, 13, 14, 19, 28, 36, 38, 40, 47, 49, 51, 52, 53, 55, 57, 63, 64, 66, 73, 79
840 /1	$IV \setminus \{34, 47\}$
840 /2	$IV \setminus \{71, 73, 75, 77, 79\}$
840 /3	$IV \setminus \{73, 75, 77, 79\}$
841	$IV \setminus \{9, 79\}$
842	$IV \setminus \{19, 35\}$

6   Conclusion

In this paper, we proposed a graph-based model to recover the exact superpoly of a stream cipher given a cube. Unlike the division property, our graph model is a convenient mathematical object that allows one the use of cipher specific constraints like doubling paths and arity approximation. We show that this graph model can be implemented in MILP and CP. By taking into account some doubling patterns in our model and refining the branch-and-cut strategy, our MILP implementation is faster than existing MILP implementations based on division property [13], or monomial prediction [15] for TRIVIUM and we expect similar results on other stream ciphers.

We opened new research directions and working further on Gurobi strategy may lead to significant improvements of all MILP models used in cryptography as searching for differential characteristics or integral distinguishers. We also believe that our new graph-oriented model can improve the recent work of Hebborn *et al.* [14] regarding lower bounds on the degree of block ciphers.

Acknowledgements. The work presented in this article was funded by the French National Research Agency as part of the DeCrypt project (ANR- 18-CE39-0007). The authors would like to express their very great appreciation to Dr Marie Euler from DGA-MI for her valuable and constructive suggestions during the development of this research work.

References

1. Abdelkhalek, A., Sasaki, Y., Todo, Y., Tolba, M., Youssef, A.M.: MILP modeling for (Large) S-boxes to optimize probability of differential characteristics. IACR Trans. Symmetric Cryptol. **2017**(4), 99–129 (2017)
2. Aumasson, J.-P., Dinur, I., Meier, W., Shamir, A.: Cube testers and key recovery attacks on reduced-round MD6 and trivium. In: Dunkelman, O. (ed.) FSE 2009. LNCS, vol. 5665, pp. 1–22. Springer, Heidelberg (2009). https://doi.org/10.1007/978-3-642-03317-9_1

3. Boura, C., Coggia, D.: Efficient MILP modelings for Sboxes and linear layers of SPN ciphers. IACR Trans. Symmetric Cryptol. **2020**(3), 327–361 (2020)
4. Cannière, C.D., Preneel, B.: Trivium. In: Robshaw, M.J.B., Billet, O. (eds.) New Stream Cipher Designs - The eSTREAM Finalists, Lecture Notes in Computer Science, vol. 4986, pp. 244–266. Springer (2008). https://doi.org/10.1007/978-3-540-68351-3
5. Delaune, S., Derbez, P., Huynh, P., Minier, M., Mollimard, V., Prud'homme, C.: Efficient methods to search for best differential characteristics on SKINNY. In: Sako, K., Tippenhauer, N.O. (eds.) ACNS 2021. LNCS, vol. 12727, pp. 184–207. Springer, Cham (2021). https://doi.org/10.1007/978-3-030-78375-4_8
6. Delaune, S., Derbez, P., Vavrille, M.: Catching the fastest boomerangs - application to SKINNY. IACR Trans. Symmetric Cryptol. **2020**(4), 104–129 (2020)
7. Dinur, I., Shamir, A.: Cube attacks on tweakable black box polynomials. In: Joux, A. (ed.) EUROCRYPT 2009. LNCS, vol. 5479, pp. 278–299. Springer, Heidelberg (2009). https://doi.org/10.1007/978-3-642-01001-9_16
8. Fages, J.-G.: On the use of graphs within constraint-programming. Constraints **20**(4), 498–499 (2015). https://doi.org/10.1007/s10601-015-9223-9
9. Fouque, P.-A., Vannet, T.: Improving key recovery to 784 and 799 rounds of trivium using optimized cube attacks. In: Moriai, S. (ed.) FSE 2013. LNCS, vol. 8424, pp. 502–517. Springer, Heidelberg (2014). https://doi.org/10.1007/978-3-662-43933-3_26
10. Gérault, D., Lafourcade, P., Minier, M., Solnon, C.: Computing AES related-key differential characteristics with constraint programming. Artif. Intell. **278**, 103183 (2020)
11. Gérault, D., Minier, M., Solnon, C.: Using constraint programming to solve a cryptanalytic problem. In: Sierra, C. (ed.) 26th International Joint Conference on Artificial Intelligence (IJCAI 2017), pp. 4844–4848. ijcai.org (2017)
12. Gurobi Optimization, LLC: Gurobi Optimizer Reference Manual (2021). https://www.gurobi.com
13. Hao, Y., Leander, G., Meier, W., Todo, Y., Wang, Q.: Modeling for three-subset division property without unknown subset. In: Canteaut, A., Ishai, Y. (eds.) EUROCRYPT 2020. LNCS, vol. 12105, pp. 466–495. Springer, Cham (2020). https://doi.org/10.1007/978-3-030-45721-1_17
14. Hebborn, P., Lambin, B., Leander, G., Todo, Y.: Lower bounds on the degree of block ciphers. In: Moriai, S., Wang, H. (eds.) Advances in Cryptology - ASIACRYPT 2020 - 26th International Conference on the Theory and Application of Cryptology and Information Security, Daejeon, South Korea, December 7-11, 2020, Proceedings, Part I. Lecture Notes in Computer Science, vol. 12491, pp. 537–566. Springer (2020). https://doi.org/10.1007/978-3-030-64837-4_18, https://doi.org/10.1007/978-3-030-64837-4_18
15. Hu, K., Sun, S., Wang, M., Wang, Q.: An algebraic formulation of the division property: revisiting degree evaluations, cube attacks, and key-independent sums. In: Moriai, S., Wang, H. (eds.) ASIACRYPT 2020. LNCS, vol. 12491, pp. 446–476. Springer, Cham (2020). https://doi.org/10.1007/978-3-030-64837-4_15
16. Liu, M.: Degree evaluation of NFSR-based cryptosystems. In: Katz, J., Shacham, H. (eds.) CRYPTO 2017. LNCS, vol. 10403, pp. 227–249. Springer, Cham (2017). https://doi.org/10.1007/978-3-319-63697-9_8
17. Prud'homme, C., Fages, J., Lorca, X.: Choco solver documentation. TASC, INRIA Rennes, LINA CNRS UMR 6241 (2016)
18. Rossi, F., van Beek, P., Walsh, T. (eds.): Handbook of Constraint Programming, Foundations of Artificial Intelligence, vol. 2. Elsevier (2006)

19. Sun, S., et al.: Analysis of AES, SKINNY, and others with constraint programming. IACR Trans. Symmetric Cryptol. **2017**(1), 281–306 (2017)
20. Todo, Y.: Structural evaluation by generalized integral property. In: Oswald, E., Fischlin, M. (eds.) EUROCRYPT 2015. LNCS, vol. 9056, pp. 287–314. Springer, Heidelberg (2015). https://doi.org/10.1007/978-3-662-46800-5_12
21. Todo, Y., Isobe, T., Hao, Y., Meier, W.: Cube attacks on non-blackbox polynomials based on division property. In: 37th Annual International Cryptology Conference on Advances in Cryptology (CRYPTO 2017). Lecture Notes in Computer Science, vol. 10403. Springer (2017)
22. Todo, Y., Morii, M.: Bit-based division property and application to SIMON family. In: Peyrin, T. (ed.) FSE 2016. LNCS, vol. 9783, pp. 357–377. Springer, Heidelberg (2016). https://doi.org/10.1007/978-3-662-52993-5_18
23. Xiang, Z., Zhang, W., Bao, Z., Lin, D.: Applying MILP method to searching integral distinguishers based on division property for 6 lightweight block ciphers. In: Cheon, J.H., Takagi, T. (eds.) 22nd International Conference on the Theory and Application of Cryptology and Information Security (ASIACRYPT 2016). Lecture Notes in Computer Science, vol. 10031, pp. 648–678 (2016)
24. Ye, C., Tian, T.: Revisit division property based cube attacks: Key-recovery or distinguishing attacks? IACR Trans. Symmetric Cryptol. **2019**(3), 81–102 (2019)
25. Zhou, C., Zhang, W., Ding, T., Xiang, Z.: Improving the MILP-based security evaluation algorithm against differential/linear cryptanalysis using a divide-and-conquer approach. IACR Trans. Symmetric Cryptol. **2019**(4), 438–469 (2019)

Automated Truncation of Differential Trails and Trail Clustering in ARX

Alex Biryukov[1], Luan Cardoso dos Santos[1], Daniel Feher[1],
Vesselin Velichkov[2(✉)], and Giuseppe Vitto[1]

[1] University of Luxembourg, Esch-sur-Alzette, Luxembourg
{alex.biryukov,luan.cardoso,daniel.feher,giuseppe.vitto}@uni.lu
[2] University of Edinburgh, Edinburgh, UK
vvelichk@ed.ac.uk

Abstract. We propose a tool for automated truncation of differential trails in ciphers using modular addition, bitwise rotation, and XOR (ARX). The tool takes as input a differential trail and produces as output a set of truncated differential trails. The set represents all possible truncations of the input trail according to certain predefined rules. A linear-time algorithm for the exact computation of the differential probability of a truncated trail that follows the truncation rules is proposed. We further describe a method to merge the set of truncated trails into a compact set of non-overlapping truncated trails with associated probability and we demonstrate the application of the tool on block cipher SPECK64.

We have also investigated the effect of clustering of differential trails around a fixed input trail. The best cluster that we have found for 15 rounds has probability $2^{-55.03}$ (consisting of 389 unique output differences) which allows us to build a distinguisher using 128 times less data than the one based on just the single best trail, which has probability 2^{-62}. Moreover, we show examples for SPECK64 where a cluster of trails around a suboptimal (in terms of probability) input trail results in higher overall probability compared to a cluster obtained around the best differential trail.

Keywords: Symmetric-key · Block ciphers · Differential cryptanalysis · Truncated differentials · ARX · SPECK

1 Introduction

Truncated differential cryptanalysis (TC) is a technique for analysing symmetric-key cryptosystems proposed in [11]. It is a variant of differential cryptanalysis (DC) [4] and has been used successfully against a number of cryptographic algorithms such as IDEA, SKIPJACK and SALSA20 among others. Similarly to

This work was supported by the Luxembourg National Research Fund (FNR) projects FinCrypt (C17/IS/11684537) and SP² (PRIDE15/10621687/SPsquared).

differential cryptanalysis, truncated cryptanalysis traces the propagation of differences through multiple rounds of a cipher. In contrast to DC, TC does not analyse full but *truncated* differences. A truncated difference is one in which only some of the bits are specified i.e. fixed to given value 0 or 1, while the rest are truncated i.e. not specified. A truncated bit is typically denoted by a ∗ symbol implying that it may take any value.

In differential cryptanalysis a sequence of differences through several rounds of a cipher is called a *differential trail* (or differential characteristic). When only the input and output differences (and not the intermediate differences) of a differential trail are specified the resulting object is called a *differential*. The analogous concepts in truncated differential cryptanalysis are *truncated differential trails* and *truncated differentials*, both being composed of *truncated* differences.

As in DC, the objective of TC is to find a truncated differential (trail) with a sufficiently high probability p over R rounds. The latter is called a *distinguisher* as it distinguishes the cipher from a random permutation, which has probability lower than p. In its most general form, the attack principle of TC is the same as in DC. Namely, the distinguisher is used to attack $R + r$ rounds for some value of r, by guessing the last r round keys, inverting the permutation and checking if the output truncated difference after R rounds matches the one computed after the inversion under the guessed key/s. The success and complexity of a TC attack crucially depends on the ability to find high probability truncated trails and differentials.

ARX (standing for Addition-Rotation-XOR) is a class of cryptographic algorithms designed using three simple arithmetic operations: modular addition, bitwise rotation and XOR. These algorithms are typically easy to describe and implement and are very efficient, especially in software. At the same time they have been notoriously difficult to analyse due to intricate dependencies between the various operations [12]. As a result a significant body of research has been dedicated to the development of tools and techniques for the automated analysis of ARX.

One of the first automated techniques for constructing differential trails for ARX-based designs is due to De Cannière *et al.* [8]. It uses the idea of generalized bit conditions to find collisions in the hash function SHA1. A few related automated techniques have been subsequently proposed by Leurent [13], Stevens [21] and Mendel *et al.* [18]. Similarly, all of them have been applied to hash functions. Dedicated tools for searching for differential paths in (pure) ARX ciphers have been proposed by Liu *et al.* [17], Huang *et al.* [10] and Biryukov *et al.* [6,7]. Finally, several authors have modelled the differential search problem in terms of Boolean satisfiability or mixed-integer linear programming and have proposed the use of off-the-shelf SAT or MILP solvers to find solutions in an automated way. Some results in this direction are by Mouha *et al.* [19], Fu *et al.* [9], Sun *et al.* [22,23,23] and Song *et al.* [20]. The problem of clustering of differential characteristics has been researched in [2,5,20], where the authors apply SMT solvers or dedicated tools to enumerate characteristics belonging to a given differential.

In this paper we extend the set of existing tools for analysis of ARX. More specifically, we propose a new automated tool for constructing truncated differential trails for ARX from existing non-truncated ones and computing their exact probability. The main idea is to truncate every bit from the input non-truncated trail (i.e. transforming all 0 and 1 bits into a *), according to certain predefined propagation rules. The rules ensure that the truncated * bit will propagate until the last round of the input trail so that the resulting truncated trail will remain valid and of non-zero probability for *any* assignment of the *. As a result, from an input trail we obtain a set of trails represented by a single truncated trail that has probability at least as high as the probability of the initial trail. In addition, we propose a method to construct a cluster of non-overlapping truncated trails composed of all possible truncations of the input (up to the propagation rules) together with its associated probability. In contrast to [2,5,20] the trails in the constructed clusters do not necessarily belong to the same differential. They have compact representation due to which the analyst is able to trace the propagation of multiple trails at the same time.

We propose two sets of truncation rules: simple rules (Sect. 3) and relaxed rules (Sect. 6). The simple rules do not consider dependencies between consecutive bits within the same round (i.e. within the same modular addition operation). Consequently, with the simple rules, truncated bits with different labels are independent from each other and can take values 0 and 1 with equal probability. In contrast, the relaxed rules are a generalization of the simple rules that is applicable also in cases in which bits within the same round are dependent on each other. In that case truncated bits with different labels are dependent on each other (often in complex ways) and may take values 0 and 1 with different probability.

Both for the simple and for the relaxed truncation rules the only assumption we rely on is the Markov assumption i.e. treating rounds as independent. In particular, we do *not* assume that individual non-truncated trails belonging to the same truncated trail have equal probability. Indeed, in general they don't and this is taken care of by the proposed tool.

The tool is useful for constructing truncated differential distinguishers which have lower data complexity than the traditional ones based on the best non-truncated trail. Its application is demonstrated on block cipher SPECK64, for which we report clusters of truncated trails produced from the optimal non-truncated trails on up to 15 rounds. The latter is the highest number of rounds covered by a single trail with probability 2^{-62} higher than random 2^{-64}. For 15 rounds in particular, we report a set of 24 truncated trails, encoding 135 non-truncated trails, the top 22 of which have probability $\geq 2^{-64}$ and cumulative probability $2^{-59.05}$. The latter improves the probability of the single optimal trail by a factor of about 8 at the expense of considering multiple trails. A summary of those results is given in Table 1.

In the context of the existing tools mentioned earlier, the proposed tool bears similarity to the generalized conditions idea introduced in [8] and extended in [13]. Indeed the set of truncated and fixed bits is a subset of the full set of (extended) generalized conditions. Several features set our tool apart from [8, 13]. First, by limiting ourselves to just a very small subset of the generalized conditions we are able to compute the exact probability of a single truncated trail in linear time in its length. Second, due to the same reason we are also able to transform a set of overlapping truncated trails into a set of disjoint truncated trails. The latter is critical for being able to compute the probability of a cluster of truncated trails, which on its turn is critical in estimating the data complexity of an attack. Finally, ours is a dedicated tool for finding truncated trails, while the mentioned tools have been applied in the context of collision search in hash functions.

The source code of the tool for the simple rules (Sect. 3, 4 and 5) will be made publicly available as part of the YAARX Toolkit [1].

Table 1. Truncation of optimal trails for SPECK64. Legend: R number of rounds; Δ_{in} (#) input differences to the ADD at first round (# number of trails with such input); $\#T_{tr}$ number of truncated trails produced by the tool; $\#T_{ntr}$ number of non-truncated trails in the truncated cluster T_{tr} (in brackets are the number of trails with $\Pr \geq 2^{-64}$); P_{min} and P_{max} resp. minimum and maximum trail Pr in the set T_{ntr} ($\log_2$ scale); P_{tr} total Pr of the truncated cluster ($\log_2$ scale); $\log_2(S/N) = 64 - |\log_2(P_{tr})| - \log_2(\#T_{ntr})$; Numbers in brackets in col. 7,8 based on top trails in T_{ntr} with $\Pr \geq 2^{-64}$. The columns mat.S/N and mat.P_{tr} are the signal-noise and probabilities of the optimal truncation, approximated with a Matsui-search tool, whose probability limit was chosen in such a way as to make computation time feasible on a small scale server PC with a few hours of computation.

R	Δ_{in} (#)	$\#T_{tr}$	$\#T_{ntr}$	P_{min} ($\log_2$)	P_{max} ($\log_2$)	P_{tr} ($\log_2$)	S/N ($\log_2$)	mat.S/N ($\log_2$)	mat.P_{tr} ($\log_2$)
5	02000012 02000002 (1)	3	20	-15	-10	-7.58	52.10	33.13	-3.70
6	00008202 00001202 (1)	6	48	-23	-15	-12.02	46.40	32.31	-6.46
6	00401042 00400240 (1)	3	20	-20	-15	-12.58	47.10	33.37	-8.92
7	92400040 10420040 (1)	3	40	-27	-21	-18.00	40.68	24.42	-13.10
7	40924000 40104200 (1)	6	48	-29	-21	-18.02	40.40	24.47	-13.05
7	C0924000 40104200 (1)	6	48	-29	-21	-18.02	40.40	24.49	-13.06
8	00008202 00001202 (2)	6	144	-42	-29	-25.00	31.83	20.94	-16.63
8	92400040 10420040 (3)	28	576	-40	-29	-23.37	31.46	21.28	-16.23
8	40924000 40104200 (3)	25	544	-41	-29	-23.40	31.51	21.28	-16.23
9	00008202 00001202 (1)	3	48	-44	-34	-30.65	27.76	20.25	-23.33
9	80240000 00040080 (1)	3	20	-39	-34	-31.58	28.10	20.87	-27.39
9	80208080 00048080 (1)	2	12	-43	-34	-32.24	28.18	20.93	-28.85
9	00802400 80000400 (1)	6	30	-46	-34	-31.58	27.51	20.86	-27.33
10	80208080 00048080 (1)	6	30	-50	-38	-35.58	23.51	20.35	-32.69
11	00000090 00000010 (1)	3	5	-45	-42	-40.75	20.93	20.19	-40.00
12	00000090 00000010 (1)	5	24	-53	-46	-43.60	15.81	11.07	-40.12
12	00008202 00001202 (1)	3	5	-49	-46	-44.75	16.93	11.59	-42.35
13	00008202 00001202 (1)	5	24	-57	-50	-47.60	11.81	10.22	-45.57
14	20200008 20200001 (1)	6	48	-64	-56	-53.02	5.40	5.06	-51.07
14	00008202 00001202 (1)	15	112 (99)	-67	-56	(-52.41)	(4.79)	4.70	-50.68
14	92400040 10420040 (1)	6	24	-63	-56	-53.60	5.81	5.70	-51.37
14	40924000 40104200 (1)	5	24	-63	-56	-53.60	5.81	4.97	-52.06
15	92400040 10420040 (1)	24	135 (22)	-74	-62	(-59.05)	(0.49)	0.37	-58.54
15	40924000 40104200 (1)	15	112 (22)	-73	-62	(-59.05)	(0.49)	0.37	-58.54
15	00040924 20040104 (1)	6	48 (16)	-70	-62	(-59.42)	(0.58)	0.50	-58.79

The outline of the paper is as follows. We begin with preliminaries in Sect. 2, followed by exposition of the rules for truncation in Sect. 3. In Sect. 4 and Sect. 5 is presented respectively a tool for automated truncation of differential trails in

ARX and a tool for merging a set of truncated trails into a set of non-overlapping truncated trails. A set of relaxed truncation rules is described in Sect. 6. Results from the application of those tools to block cipher SPECK64 are given in Sect. 7. Statistical analysis of the distinguishing advantage using truncated distinguishers is given in Sect. 8. In Sect. 9 we discuss an improved truncated distinguisher for 15 rounds of SPECK64. The exposition concludes with Sect. 10. Notations and abbreviations are listed in Table 2.

Table 2. Symbols and notation.

Symbol	Meaning
n	Word size in bits
$\boxplus$ or ADD	Addition modulo 2^n
$\lll$, $\ggg$	Left, right bitwise rotation
$\wedge$, $\vee$	Logical AND, OR
$\overline{x}$ or $\neg x$	Logical NOT
$\oplus$	Binary exclusive-OR (XOR)
α, β, γ	n-bit XOR or truncated differences
α_i	The i-th bit of α (α_0 is LSB, α_{n-1} is MSB)
$(\alpha\beta\gamma)_i$	The i-th bits of α, β, γ as 3-bit string
$*$	Truncated bit (can be both 0 and 1)
$\tilde{*}$	Dependent truncated bit (can be both 0 and 1)
$\cdot$	Fixed bit (can be either 0 or 1)
T, τ	Truncated trail
$\mathfrak{T}, t$	Sets of truncated trails
$\#\mathfrak{T}$ or $|\mathfrak{T}|$	Size of the set $\mathfrak{T}$
Pr	Probability
DP	Differential probability
S/N	Signal-to-Noise Ratio

2 Preliminaries

In this section we present notations, definitions and theorems that are relevant to the subsequent parts of the paper.

By $\mathbf{xdp}^+$ is denoted the XOR differential probability (DP) of ADD and is defined below.

Definition 1. $\mathbf{xdp}^+$ *is the probability with which input XOR differences* α, β *propagate to output XOR difference* γ *through the operation ADD, computed over all n-bit inputs a, b:*

$$\mathbf{xdp}^+(\alpha, \beta, \gamma) = 2^{-2n} \, \#\{(a,b) : ((a \oplus \alpha) + (b \oplus \beta)) \oplus (a + b) = \gamma\} \,. \quad (1)$$

The following lemma provides the condition under which $\mathbf{xdp}^+$ is non-zero:

Lemma 1 (Lemma 3 [16]). *The probability* $\mathbf{xdp}^+(\alpha, \beta, \gamma)$ *is non-zero if:*

$$\alpha_i \oplus \beta_i \oplus \gamma_i = \begin{cases} 0 & \text{if} \quad (i = 0) \,, \\ \alpha_{i-1} & \text{if} \quad (\alpha_{i-1} = \beta_{i-1} = \gamma_{i-1}) \wedge (i > 0) \end{cases} . \tag{2}$$

Proof. Lemma 3 [16].

The next theorem provides a formula for the computation of $\mathbf{xdp}^+$.

Theorem 1 (Algorithm 2 [16]). *If* $\mathbf{xdp}^+(\alpha, \beta, \gamma)$ *is non-zero then its exact value is computed according to the following formula:*

$$\mathrm{xdp}^+(\alpha, \beta, \gamma) = 2^{-n+k+1} : \ k = \#\{i \geq 1 : \ (\alpha_{i-1} = \beta_{i-1} = \gamma_{i-1})\} \,. \tag{3}$$

Proof. Algorithm 2 [16].

Theorem 1 essentially states that the probability $\mathbf{xdp}^+$ decreases by a factor of $1/2$ for every bit position i at which the three bits of the differences α_i, β_i and γ_i are *not* equal, excluding the most significant bit (MSB) (hence the $+1$ in the power).

A bit in a truncated differential trail can either be *fixed*, denoted by the dot symbol · or *truncated*, denoted by the star symbol $*$. A fixed bit has value either 0 or 1. A truncated bit can take on both values 0 and 1. More precisely, if a bit in a truncated differential trail is truncated, then the trail is valid (i.e. of non-zero probability) for both assignments of this bit.

3   Rules for Truncation

Truncation is performed according to three simple rules. They make truncation feasible over multiple rounds of a cipher, where the ARX operations are sequentially applied one after another. We describe those rules next, together with the rationale behind them.

Rule 1. Let (α, β, γ) be a differential through ADD. Allow at most one truncated bit in $(\alpha\beta\gamma)_i$ at all bit positions i except the least significant bit (LSB) and allow no truncated bits at the LSB:

$$(\alpha\beta\gamma)_i \in \begin{cases} \{(\cdot \cdot \cdot)\} & , \ i = 0 \,, \\ \{(\cdot \cdot \cdot), (\cdot \cdot *), (\cdot * \cdot), (* \cdot \cdot)\} & , \ n > i > 0 \end{cases} . \tag{4}$$

The rationale behind Rule 1 is to make truncation feasible over multiple ADD operations iterated in sequence as in an ARX algorithm. If we allow more than one truncated bit per bit position in Rule 1 then the number of $*$ bits quickly explodes in the number of rounds. Consequently it becomes infeasible to keep track of the truncated bits across multiple rounds i.e. to maintain information as to which $*$ bit at round r is related to which $*$ bit/s at round $r-1$. Note that the final goal is to end up with a truncated differential trail which results in non-zero probability non-truncated trail for *any* assignment of the $*$ bits. Finally and most importantly due to Rule 1 it is possible to efficiently (in linear time) compute the differential probability of a truncated differential through a single ADD.

Rule 2. Let (α, β, γ) be input/output differences through XOR so that $\alpha \oplus \beta = \gamma$. Allow at most one truncated bit in $(\alpha\beta)_i$ at all bit positions:

$$(\alpha\beta)_i \in \{(\cdot\cdot), (\cdot*), (*\cdot)\} : \ n > i \geq 0 . \tag{5}$$

Similarly to Rule 1, the rationale behind Rule 2 is to make it feasible to keep track of the dependency between $*$ bits over sequences of XOR operations. For example if $\alpha_i = \cdot$ and $\beta_i = *$ then the output of XOR is $\alpha_i \oplus * = *$. Thus the output star $*$ is either equal to the input star $*$ or to its negation depending on the value of α_i which is fixed. In contrast, if both input bits are truncated i.e. $\alpha_i = *$ and $\beta_i = *$ then the output is a $*$ bit that is dependent on the inputs in a (relatively) complex way.

Rule 3. Let (α, β, γ) be a truncated differential through ADD respecting Rule 1. If, at position $i-1$, two bits are fixed and equal while the third is truncated or all three bits are fixed and equal to each other, then all bits at position i must be fixed:

$$((\alpha_{i-1} = \beta_{i-1} = \cdot) \wedge (\gamma_{i-1} = *)) \vee$$
$$((\beta_{i-1} = \gamma_{i-1} = \cdot) \wedge (\alpha_{i-1} = *)) \vee$$
$$((\alpha_{i-1} = \gamma_{i-1} = \cdot) \wedge (\beta_{i-1} = *)) \vee$$
$$(\alpha_{i-1} = \beta_{i-1} = \gamma_{i-1} = \cdot) \implies (\alpha\beta\gamma)_i = (\cdot\cdot\cdot) . \tag{6}$$

Rule 3 is a consequence of the $\mathbf{xdp^+}$ non-zero condition (Lemma 1). It ensures that a non-zero probability differential (trail) remains of non-zero probability for all assignments of the $*$ bits after truncation. More specifically, if e.g. $\alpha_{i-1} = \beta_{i-1} = \cdot$ and $\gamma_{i-1} = *$ then we treat the $*$ value of γ_{i-1} as being equal to α_{i-1} in order to check that this is a valid truncation i.e. that the differential remains of non-zero Pr for both assignments of γ_{i-1}. This is the case only if $\alpha_i \oplus \beta_i \oplus \gamma_i \oplus \alpha_{i-1} = 0$, otherwise the truncation is invalid (cf. Lemma 1).

The described rules allow stars in all bit positions (even several stars per round) and in all rounds, except in the input differences. In practice however a star at a given position, for example round j, bit i, might violate one of the rules as it propagates to the last round. If that is the case, then bit (j, i) remains fixed. As a result the number of $*$ bits is relatively small. Another related consequence is that more stars appear in the last rounds since at those positions there is smaller chance to break any of the rules.

Rule 1, Rule 2 and Rule 3, when used in combination, make it possible to compute the DP of a truncated differential trail in linear time in the length of the trail.

We note that the proposed rules can be relaxed in several directions. In particular, one may relax Rule 2 by allowing two $*$ bits to enter the XOR operation. Rule 3 can be relaxed to allow a $*$ bit at a position that follows a position with equal fixed bits. Indeed we describe such a set of relaxed rules in Sect. 6. Such relaxations naturally allow to capture more signal (larger cluster of differential trails) at the expense of added complexity for keeping track of $*$ dependencies across rounds.

4   Differential Trail Truncation

The truncation algorithm takes a non-truncated trail as input and produces as output all its truncated variants that comply to Rules 1, 2 and 3. The input trail can be found by using one of the existing tools mentioned earlier e.g. [7,10,17].

Denote the input trail by τ. The i-th bit at round j is denoted τ_i^j for $0 \leq i < n$, $0 \leq j < R$ and it can either be truncated or not. The algorithm explores both possibilities recursively in a depth-first search manner. Once a bit is truncated i.e. $\tau_i^j \leftarrow *$, it is propagated to the last round of the trail. The propagation through the ADD and XOR operations is performed according to Rules 1, 2, 3. Propagation through the bitwise rotation operation is done by simply rotating the $*$ bit by the corresponding rotation amount. If propagation fails for a given bit (i.e. a rule is violated), the algorithm backtracks and explores the next possibility or the next bit position. Full pseudocode for the simple rules is available as part of the YAARX Toolkit[1].

The differential probability (DP) of a truncated differential trail that follows Rules 1, 2, 3 through a single ADD operation can be computed in linear time. The procedure represents a slight modification of the one for $\mathbf{xdp}^+$ (Theorem 1) and is outlined next.

Let (α, β, γ) be a differential through ADD. In the non-truncated case the probability p of this differential decreases by a factor of $1/2$ for every bit position i at which $\alpha_{i-1} = \beta_{i-1} = \gamma_{i-1}$ does *not* hold (cf. Theorem 1). The modification of this rule concerns the cases in which there is a $*$ at some bit positions. Let $i-1$ be such a position other than the MSB i.e. $(\alpha\beta\gamma)_{i-1} \in \{(\cdot\cdot*), (\cdot*\cdot), (*\cdot\cdot)\}$ and $i \neq n$. Without loss of generality assume that $(\alpha\beta\gamma)_{i-1} = (*\cdot\cdot)$ i.e. $\alpha_{i-1} = *$. By Rule 3 it is ensured that the bits at the next position are all fixed i.e. $(\alpha\beta\gamma)_i = (\cdot\cdot\cdot)$. Two cases are possible. In the first case $\beta_{i-1} = \gamma_{i-1}$ and the probability is multiplied by 1 if $\alpha_{i-1} = \beta_{i-1}$ and by $1/2$ if $\alpha_{i-1} \neq \beta_{i-1}$ Therefore the total probability p is multiplied by $1 + 1/2 = 3/2$ in this case. In the second case $\beta_{i-1} \neq \gamma_{i-1}$ and the probability decreases by $1/2$ for both values of α_{i-1}. Thus the total probability p is multiplied by $1/2 + 1/2 = 1$ (i.e. p remains unchanged) in this case. When $i = n$ and there is a $*$ at $i - 1$ (MSB), the probability p is multiplied by 2 as the value at the MSB does not change the (non-truncated) DP (cf. Theorem 1).

The differential probability of a truncated trail that follows Rules 1, 2, 3 can be computed in linear time in the length of the trail. Consider a conceptual

---

[1] https://github.com/vesselinux/yaarx/blob/master/txt/arxtrunc.pdf .

ARX cipher with round function composed of a single ADD operation followed by a linear part composed of XOR-s and bitwise rotations. Let $\tau = (\tau^0 \ldots \tau^{R-1})$ be a truncated differential trail over R rounds such that the differential transition at round $0 \leq j < R$ represents input/output differences to ADD i.e. $\tau^j = (\alpha^j, \beta^j, \gamma^j)$. The DP of a single non-truncated differential $(\alpha^j, \beta^j, \gamma^j)$ at round j can be computed bitwise with bit i conditioned on bit $i-1$ using Theorem 1 as follows:

$$\mathbf{xdp}^+(\alpha^j, \beta^j, \gamma^j) = p_0^j \prod_{i=1}^{n-1} p_i^j \; : \; p_i^j = \mathsf{DP}[(\alpha\beta\gamma)_i^j \mid (\alpha\beta\gamma)_{i-1}^j] \; , \qquad (7)$$

where $p_0^j = \mathsf{DP}[(\alpha\beta\gamma)_0^j]$. Therefore, under the Markov assumption, the probability of the trail τ is computed as $\mathsf{DP}[\tau] = \prod_{j=0}^{R-1} p_0^j \prod_{i=1}^{n-1} p_i^j$.

Notice that the probabilities p_i^j in the expression for $\mathsf{DP}[\tau]$ can be computed in any order (for a fixed τ). When computing the DP of a truncated trail τ, we are ordering the terms p_i^j by the dependency of the $*$ bits in consecutive rounds. Then we compute each term for both possible values 0 and 1 of the $*$ bit denoted resp. $(p_i^j)_0$ and $(p_i^j)_1$ and we sum the two products.

For example suppose that $\tau_r^k = *$ for some round k and bit r and that this $*$ bit propagates to subsequent rounds, up to the final one, at positions τ_s^{k+1}, ..., τ_t^{R-1}. Suppose also that these are the only $*$ bits in τ. The truncated DP of τ then is computed as:

$$\prod_{\substack{(i,j) \notin \\ \{(k,r),(k+1,s)\ldots(R-1,t)\}}} p_i^j \left((p_r^k)_0 (p_s^{k+1})_0 \cdots (p_t^{R-1})_0 + (p_r^k)_1 (p_s^{k+1})_1 \cdots (p_t^{R-1})_1 \right) \quad (8)$$

In Eq. (8), we are essentially splitting the trail τ into bitwise subtrails, where each subtrail contains $*$ bits that are directly dependent on each other. Note that Rules 1, 2, 3 ensure that there are no dependencies between the $*$ bits belonging to different subtrails. In other words, if a $*$ bit is part of a given subtrail, then it can not be part of other subtrails.

5   Merging of Truncated Trails

In the general case an input non-truncated trail may have more than one possible truncation. Therefore the set of all possible (up to Rules 1, 2, 3) truncated trails produced from a given non-truncated trail may contain duplicate non-truncated trails. In this section we describe a method to transform this set into a set of truncated trails that are disjoint i.e. do not contain any duplicates.

As described earlier, a truncated difference (TD) α represents a set of non-truncated differences defined by the $*$ bit positions in its truncated representation. We say that two TD α and α' are *disjoint*, denoted as $\alpha \cap \alpha' = \emptyset$, if their corresponding sets are disjoint i.e. if they do not have any common non-truncated differences. Note that α and α' are disjoint if there is at least one bit that is fixed and of opposite value in each TD i.e. $\exists i : 0 \leq i < n : (\alpha_i = \cdot) \wedge (\alpha'_i = \cdot) \wedge (\alpha_i \neq \alpha'_i)$.

If the set represented by α is fully contained in the set represented by α' then we say that α is a *subset* of α' denoted as $\alpha \subset \alpha'$. If α and α' are not subsets of each other and are not disjoint i.e. if $(\alpha \not\subset \alpha') \wedge (\alpha \not\supset \alpha')$ and $\alpha \cap \alpha' \neq \emptyset$ then we say that α and α' are *partially overlapping* (PO). The latter implies that some, but strictly not all, differences that are in α are also in α' and vice versa. Note that if α and α' are PO then there exists at least one bit position i at which $(\alpha_i = *) \wedge (\alpha'_i = \cdot)$ and there exists at least one bit position j at which $(\alpha_j = \cdot) \wedge (\alpha'_j = *)$, where clearly $i \neq j$.

The terms *disjoint*, *subset* and *partially overlapping* have analogous meaning for the cases of truncated differentials through ADD (α, β, γ) and of truncated trails $\tau = ((\alpha^0, \beta^0, \gamma^0), (\alpha^1, \beta^1, \gamma^1) \ldots)$ composed of ADD truncated differentials.

The merging algorithm takes as input a set $\mathfrak{T}$ of truncated trails T that are all pairwise disjoint and a truncated trail τ to be merged with $\mathfrak{T}$. The output is an updated set $\mathfrak{T}$ composed of disjoint truncated trails and containing all (non-truncated) trails from τ that were not initially in $\mathfrak{T}$. For each truncated trail T in $\mathfrak{T}$, the algorithm checks three cases. If τ is already in T i.e. $\tau \subset$ T then output $\mathfrak{T}$ and terminate. If τ and T are disjoint i.e. $\tau \cap$ T $= \emptyset$ then move on to the next trail in $\mathfrak{T}$ or add τ to $\mathfrak{T}$ if all trails in $\mathfrak{T}$ have been processed. Finally, if T is a subset of τ i.e. T $\subset \tau$ or if T and τ are partially overlapping, then split τ into a set of truncated trails t (explained below). The set t is such that all its elements are pairwise disjoint and each trail from t is disjoint to T. With this the procedure is finished for the trail T and moves on to the next trail in $\mathfrak{T}$ where it performs the same steps for each trail in the set t. The process terminates either when the set t becomes empty (i.e. the initial trail τ has been fully absorbed into $\mathfrak{T}$) or when all trails from $\mathfrak{T}$ have been processed, in which case the set t is added to $\mathfrak{T}$. In both cases the updated set $\mathfrak{T}$ is returned.

A step that needs clarification in the described procedure is how the trail τ is split into pairwise disjoint trails t that are also disjoint to T. Let T $= ((\alpha^0, \beta^0, \gamma^0), (\alpha^1, \beta^1, \gamma^1) \ldots)$ and $\tau = ((a^0, b^0, c^0), (a^1, b^1, c^1) \ldots)$. By design we know that either T $\subset \tau$ or T, τ: PO. In either case there must be at least one bit position i and round j for which the bit in T is fixed and the same bit in τ is truncated. Let α_i^j be one such bit i.e. $(\alpha_i^j = \cdot) \wedge (a_i^j = *)$. We construct a new trail τ' by setting a_i^j to the opposite value of α_i^j i.e. $a_i^j = 1 \oplus \alpha_i^j$. Note that this makes τ' disjoint from T since it differs in one fixed bit. We add τ' to t and we discard the original trail τ. By doing so we don't lose any information since τ for $a_i^j = \alpha_i^j$ is already in T and τ for the opposite value $a_i^j = 1 \oplus \alpha_i^j$ is in t. If T and τ happen to differ also in another bit, say $(\beta_l^k = \cdot) \wedge (b_l^k = *)$ then we set a_i^j to the value in T: $a_i^j = \alpha_i^j$ and we set b_l^k to the negated value in T: $b_l^k = 1 \oplus \beta_l^k$. We add this new trail τ'' to t. Now t contains τ' and τ'' which are pairwise disjoint since they differ in a_i^j. At the same time they are also disjoint from T since they differ from T respectively in a_i^j and b_l^k. This procedure is executed iteratively for all positions in which τ is fixed and T is truncated. Its complexity is quadratic in $\max(\#\mathfrak{T}, \#\mathsf{t})$, where $\#\mathfrak{T}$ is the number of truncated trails in $\mathfrak{T}$ and $\#\mathsf{t}$ is the number of non-truncated trails in τ.

6 Relaxed Rules

In this Section we will generalize the truncation rules provided in Sect. 3 by allowing truncations with dependent truncated bits $\tilde{*}$, i.e. bits whose value depends (non-linearly) on previous bits' assignments and for which Lipmaa-Moriai conditions are automatically satisfied.

Rule 1 naturally generalizes to this setting by allowing at most one dependent truncated bit per bit position except for the LSB. Other truncation rules are as follows.

Rule 4. Let (α, β, γ) be input/output differences through XOR so that $\alpha \oplus \beta = \gamma$. Then

$$\alpha\beta_i = (\cdot\cdot) \implies (\gamma_i = \cdot)$$
$$\alpha\beta_i = \{(\cdot*), (*\cdot), (**), (\tilde{*}*), (*\tilde{*}), (\tilde{*}\tilde{*})\} \implies (\gamma_i = \tilde{*})$$

where, in the latter case the dependent truncate bit $\gamma_i = \tilde{*}$ is equal to $\alpha_i \oplus \beta_i$.

Rule 5. Let (α, β, γ) be a truncated differential through ADD respecting Rule 1. If, at position $i-1$ and i two bits are fixed and not equal, then we can freely truncate the remaining third bit at position i:

$$\left((\alpha_{i-1} \neq \beta_{i-1} = \cdot) \vee (\alpha_{i-1} \neq \gamma_{i-1} = \cdot) \vee (\beta_{i-1} \neq \gamma_{i-1} = \cdot) \right) \wedge$$
$$\left((\alpha_i \neq \beta_i = \cdot) \vee (\alpha_i \neq \gamma_i = \cdot) \vee (\beta_i \neq \gamma_i = \cdot) \right) \wedge (\gamma_i = \cdot)$$
$$\implies (\alpha\beta\gamma)_i = \{(\cdot\cdot*), (\cdot*\cdot), (*\cdot\cdot)\} .$$

Rule 5 is a consequence of the $\mathbf{xdp}^+$ non-zero condition (Lemma 1), i.e. there are no conflicts at position i if at position $i-1$ and i two bits are not equal.

Rule 6. Let (α, β, γ) be a truncated differential through ADD respecting Rule 1. If, at position $i-1$, two bits are fixed and equal while the third is truncated, then at position i we allow the truncation of bit γ_i:

$$((\alpha_{i-1} = \beta_{i-1} = \cdot) \wedge (\gamma_{i-1} = \{*, \tilde{*}\})) \vee ((\beta_{i-1} = \gamma_{i-1} = \cdot) \wedge (\alpha_{i-1} = \{*, \tilde{*}\})) \vee$$
$$((\alpha_{i-1} = \gamma_{i-1} = \cdot) \wedge (\beta_{i-1} = \{*, \tilde{*}\})) \implies (\alpha\beta\gamma)_i = (\cdot\cdot\tilde{*})$$

Rule 6 is a consequence of the $\mathbf{xdp}^+$ non-zero condition (Lemma 1). To make explicit the dependence relation we assume, without loss of generality that $((\alpha_{i-1} = \beta_{i-1} = \cdot) \wedge (\gamma_{i-1} = *))$ and $(\alpha\beta\gamma)_i = \{(\cdot\cdot\tilde{*})$. Hence the truncated bit γ_i depends on the value of the truncated bit γ_{i-1} as

$$\gamma_i = * \cdot (\alpha_{i-1} \oplus \gamma_{i-1}) \oplus \alpha_i \oplus \beta_i \oplus \alpha_{i-1} \tag{9}$$

where $*$ represents a (new) independent truncated bit. Recalling that a transition is impossible if and only if $(\alpha_{i-1} = \beta_{i-1} = \gamma_{i-1}) \wedge (\alpha_i \oplus \beta_i \oplus \gamma_i \oplus \alpha_{i-1}) = 1$, two alternatives are possible when we expand Eq. 9:

- $\gamma_{i-1} = \alpha_{i-1}$: then $(\alpha_{i-1} \oplus \gamma_{i-1}) = 0$ and $(\alpha_i \oplus \beta_i \oplus \gamma_i \oplus \alpha_{i-1}) = 0$;
- $\gamma_{i-1} \neq \alpha_{i-1}$: then $(\alpha_{i-1} \oplus \gamma_{i-1}) = 1$ and $\gamma_i = *$, in accordance to Rule 5.

Fixed bits and truncated bit assignments can be modelled as outputs of multivariate Boolean functions $f(x_0, .., x_m) \in \mathbb{F}_2[x_0, ..x_m]$. More precisely, fixed bits $\cdot$ are represented by constant functions $f(x_0, .., x_m) = 0, 1$, an independent $*$ bit can be seen as the output of a degree-one monomial $f(x_0, .., x_m) = x_i$, while $\tilde{*}$ bits correspond in general to non-linear functions, e.g. $f(x_0, .., x_m) = x_0 x_1 x_2 + x_3 + 1$. Within this model, relaxed truncation rules allow to compute Boolean function $f_{\alpha_i}, f_{\beta_i}, f_{\gamma_i}$ representations of the (fixed or truncated) bits $\alpha_i, \beta_i, \gamma_i$.

However there are some technicalities: i) the Boolean polynomial ring in which truncated bit functions are defined $\mathbb{F}_2[x_0, ..x_m]$ should have enough variables to truncate (independently) all bits in the input trail, hence, in general, we assume $m = \frac{(\#\text{of rounds}) \times (\text{block-size})}{2} - 1$; ii) when a bit is truncated with a $*$ or we need a new independent $*$ bit like in Rule 6, to ensure independence of their assignments, the corresponding Boolean function representing such truncated bit is set to be equal to a never-used independent variable x_i with $0 \leq i \leq m$.

From now on we will refer to bits by meaning the corresponding Boolean multivariate function representing its assignment. Thus, XOR and AND operations used in above rules naturally map to addition and multiplications of Boolean functions.

Differential Probability Computation. Since different bit assignments for truncated bits are represented by unique solutions to a multivariate system of equations, in order to correctly compute the overall accumulated weight of non-truncated trails obtained by expanding a truncated one, we need to compute the truth tables of each Boolean functions and filter out duplicate solutions. Then, we can compute the weight as usual by using the Lipmaa-Moriai algorithm. This results in an $O(n \cdot 2^{m_0})$ space-time algorithm for computing the accumulated weight of all expanded non-truncated trails given a truncated one where n is the number of unique Boolean functions appearing in the truncated representation and m_0 is the number of independent variables appearing in all such functions (in fact, the working polynomial ring can, without loss of generality, be the smaller $\mathbb{F}_2[x_0, ..x_{m_0}]$).

Implementation and Experimental Results. We implemented the relaxed rules in C++ and we were able to truncate in few seconds all trails reported in Table 1 except 2 cases with 15 rounds due to memory limitations. For some of these input trails, we expanded all obtained truncations and we computed, using the above algorithm, the accumulated weight of each corresponding non-truncated trails cluster. We then identified the best and the worst truncation in terms of its corresponding cluster weight and we computed the accumulated probability of all unique trails given by expanding all truncations available (we note that different truncated trails, when expanded, may overlap in some non-truncated trails). Some experimental results can be found in Table 3.

Table 3. Trail clustering obtained by truncating trails for SPECK64 using relaxed rules. R denotes the number of rounds; Δ_{in} denotes the input difference of the truncated optimal weight trail seed; $\#T_{tr}$ denotes the number of different truncations obtained; $\#T_{ntr}$ denotes the number of unique non-truncated trails obtained by expanding all $\#T_{tr}$ truncations; $\#B_{ntr}$ denotes the number of unique non-truncated trails obtained by expanding the best truncation in terms of cumulative weight; $P_{\min}$ and $P_{\max}$ are the cumulative probability of the worst and best truncated trail among all $\#T_{tr}$ truncations (here $P_{\max}$ correspond to the cumulative weight of all; P_{ntr} denotes the cumulative weight of all $\#T_{ntr}$ non-truncated trails; Finally, the last column is the S/N ratio of the best truncated trail, i.e. $S/N = 64 - \log_2(\#B_{ntr}) + P_{\max}$.

R	Δ_{in}	$\#T_{\text{tr}}$	$\#T_{\text{ntr}}$	$\#B_{\text{ntr}}$	$P_{\min}$ ($\log_2$)	$P_{\max}$ ($\log_2$)	$P_{B_{\text{ntr}}}$ ($\log_2$)	S/N ($\log_2$)
6	00008202 00001202	8823	7437	5589	−15	−10	−9.8	42.5
6	00401042 00400240	3102	2772	2310	−15	−11	−10.9	41.8
9	80240000 00040080	1281	1246	1127	−34	−30	−29.9	23.8
10	80208080 00048080	2745	2670	2415	−38	−34	−33.9	18.7

Comparison with Simple Rules (Sect. 3). The simple truncation rules described in Sect. 3 allow for linear-time computation of the DP of a truncated trail. This comes at the expense of missing much of the signal (many trails are not captured by the truncation). In comparison, the relaxed rules capture a significantly larger portion of the signal, but the computation of the DP in this case has exponential complexity in the number of truncated bits. Therefore one may use either the simple or the advanced rules depending on the available computational resources.

7   Application to SPECK64

SPECK is a family of lightweight block ciphers proposed in [3]. The family has five members corresponding resp. to the block sizes $32, 48, 64, 96$ and 128 bits and denoted by SPECKN, where $N/2$ is the word size in bits. In the remaining part of this exposition we shall be concerned with SPECK64 i.e. the variant with 32-bit words. SPECK64 has two variants: 96-bit key and 26 rounds, and 128-bit key and 27 rounds.

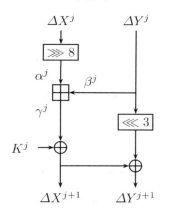

ΔX^j ΔY^j

$\ggg 8$

α^j β^j

γ^j

$\lll 3$

K^j

ΔX^{j+1} ΔY^{j+1}

Fig. 1. The round function of SPECK64 with differential inputs.

Denote by X^j and Y^j the left and right 32-bit input words to the j-th round of SPECK64 ($0 \leq j \leq R$) and by K^j the 32-bit round key applied at round j ($0 \leq j < R$). The output X^{j+1}, Y^{j+1} from round j is computed as follows:

$$X^{j+1} = ((X^j \ggg 8) \boxplus Y^j) \oplus K^j , \quad (10)$$
$$Y^{j+1} = (Y^j \lll 3) \oplus X^{j+1} , \quad (11)$$

where $\boxplus$ denotes addition modulo 2^n for $n = N/2 = 32$. The round function of SPECK64 with differential inputs is shown in Fig. 1.

We have applied the tool for automated truncation and merging of truncated trails to the optimal (non-truncated) differential trails of SPECK64 for up to 15 rounds. The results are shown in Table 1. Explanation and analysis of the data in the table follows.

The first column of Table 1 gives the number of rounds R. The second column shows the input difference Δ_{in} of the input optimal trail followed by the number of such trails with this input difference (in brackets). From the input trail/s[2], a set of $\#T_{tr}$ non-overlapping truncated trails (column 3) is computed by applying all possible truncations (up to Rules 1, 2, 3) and merging them. The set T_{tr} contains $\#T_{ntr}$ number of distinct non-truncated trails (column 4) with probabilities ranging from P_{max} and P_{min} (columns 5, 6). The total probability of the truncated set T_{tr} is P_{tr} (column 7). The last column of Table 1 shows the $\log_2$ of the signal-to-noise ratio (S/N) computed as $\log_2(S/N) = 64 - |\log_2(P_{tr})| - \log_2(\#T_{ntr})$ (we elaborate further on this parameter below). Numbers in brackets in the $\#T_{ntr}$ column show the number of trails in the set T_{ntr} that have $\Pr \geq 2^{-64}$ (the probability of a random output difference). Correspondingly, the numbers in brackets in the last two columns are based on this subset of trails of T_{ntr} (as opposed to the full set T_{ntr}).

The S/N ratio shown in the last column of Table 1 is the ratio between the probability of the truncated set distinguisher P_{tr} and the probability of choosing at random a ciphertext difference that belongs to the set T_{ntr}: $\#T_{ntr} \cdot 2^{-64}$. Note that all ciphertext differences composing the distinguisher are unique. To ensure this, trails with the same output difference are "merged" in one and their probabilities are summed. The S/N ratio is an indicator of the strength of the truncated differential set distinguisher. In particular, when S/N > 1 the distinguisher can be used to distinguish the cipher from a random permutation.

The data in Table 1 indicates that the probability of the truncated differential set P_{tr} is strictly higher than the probability of the underlying optimal non-truncated trail P_{max}. Consequently a truncated differential set distinguisher built

---

[2] There can be more than one input trail, provided that they share the same input difference.

around the optimal non-truncated trail is better than just single optimal trail in most cases (see next) in terms of data complexity.

The above conclusion has to be applied with caution. In particular, one has to be careful when the probability of the truncated distinguisher approaches the probability of the random event i.e. when $\mathrm{Pr}_{\mathrm{tr}} \approx \#T_{\mathrm{ntr}} \cdot 2^{-64}$ as then the S/N can easily drop below 1. This indeed happens in the case of the 15 round truncated distinguishers for SPECK64 (see Table 1). If the full truncated sets are used as distinguishers in those cases, the corresponding three S/N ratios are $2^{-1.42}$, $2^{-1.21}$ and $2^{-0.60}$ all of which are below 1. To increase them, one has to consider only those non-truncated trails from the sets that have probability $\geq 2^{-64}$. For the three 15 round distinguishers from the table, these are the top 22, 22 and 16 trails respectively (as indicated by the numbers in brackets in the T_{ntr} column). By discarding all trails with $\mathrm{Pr} < 2^{-64}$ in those cases, the S/N ratios are increased respectively to $2^{0.49}$, $2^{0.49}$ and $2^{0.59}$ as shown in the table.

Another observation from the data in Table 1 is that some input trails have higher truncation rate (more number of truncated bits) than others. The reason for this is the specific structure of the trails with respect to Rules 1, 2 and 3. More specifically, for some trails the rules are contradicted in smaller number of bit positions (higher truncation rate) than in others.

For example from the input trail on 11 rounds, 3 truncated trails are produced containing (only) 5 non-truncated ones. At the same time the first input trail on 12 rounds (starting with the same input difference as the 11 round one) is truncated into a set of 5 truncated trails containing 24 non-truncated. Upon inspection we could see that the trail on 11 rounds has a very *thick* (i.e. low probability) transition at round 5 (counting from 0) that costs 2^{-13}, followed by *thin* (i.e. high probability) transitions until the end. So one explanation of the mentioned effect is that the thick transition breaks all rules up to round 5, while the following thin transitions don't offer many options for truncation. Interestingly the trail on 12 rounds is an extension of the one on 11 and the better truncation rate there is due to the extra round added at the end.

In the following section we provide a more detailed statistical analysis of the distinguishing advantage of distinguishers built from clusters of differential trails.

8   Distinguishing Advantage

Distinguishing from Random. In this section we provide a probabilistic model for distinguishers for SPECK built from clusters of trails. In this setting, the attacker does some pre-processing by analysing the cipher (i.e. collects trails, computes their differential weights and clusters them by weights) and then queries an oracle black-box, that can either be a `speck-box`, which returns SPECK encryptions for a uniformly chosen key, or a `random-box`, which returns random values.

Assume that in the pre-processing phase the attacker has collected **disjoint** clusters of trails $\{C_i\}_{i=0,...,l}$ where C_i has weight w_i (i.e. probability 2^{-w_i}) so that a random trail belongs to it with probability p_{C_i}.

Thus, if we're in

- random-box then $p_{C_i} = \frac{|C_i|}{2^{64}}$;
- speck-box then $p_{C_i} = |C_i| \cdot 2^{-w_i} = |C_i| \cdot 2^{-(w_0+i)}, i = 0, 1, \ldots, l$, where w_0 is the weight of the best differential trail.[3] We consider trails with weight increasing from the optimal one. Thus we express trail weights w_i as $w_i = w_0 + i$ where w_0 is the optimal weight and i ranges from 0 to a given bound.

The probability p to hit at least 1 ciphertext in a collection of clusters after 2^N queries to the oracle is then equal to

$$p = 1 - \Pr(\text{none of the ciphertexts is in any cluster}) = 1 - \left(1 - \sum_{i=0}^{l} p_{C_i}\right)^{2^N}$$

By approximating $\left(1 - \frac{1}{x}\right)^n \approx e^{-n/x}$, we can rewrite this probability as

$$1 - \left(1 - \sum_{i=0}^{l} p_{C_i}\right)^{2^N} = 1 - \left(\frac{1}{e}\right)^{2^{N+\log_2\left(\sum_{i=0}^{l} p_{C_i}\right)}} = 1 - \left(\frac{1}{e}\right)^{2^{N+k}}$$

Where for the speck-box we have

$$k_{speck} \doteq \log_2\left(\sum_{i=0}^{l} p_{C_i}\right) = -w_0 + \log_2\left(\sum_{i=0}^{l} |C_i| \cdot 2^{-i}\right)$$

while for the random-box we have

$$k_{rand} \doteq \log_2\left(\sum_{i=0}^{l} p_{C_i}\right) = \log_2\left(\sum_{i=0}^{l} |C_i|\right) - 64$$

It follows that if the attacker wants to hit with probability p a ciphertext in any cluster, he then needs to make 2^N queries, where N is equal to

$$N = \log_2\left(-\log(1-p)\right) - k$$

and k is either k_{speck} or k_{rand} depending on his guess for the oracle box.

Note that both models random-box and speck-box are similar and differ only in their terms k_*: in fact, the more these two values differ, the easier would be to distinguish points belonging to one model or the other. We then define

$$k_{speck} - k_{rand} = -w_0 + \log_2\left(\sum_{i=0}^{l} |C_i| \cdot 2^{-i}\right) - \log_2\left(\sum_{i=0}^{l} |C_i|\right) + 64 = S/N$$

(which corresponds to the S/N definition we introduced in previous Sections) and the higher this value is, the better we distinguish the two boxes. We assume that there exists at least one trail of weight less than 64 for the reduced SPECK64

---

[3] In practical attacks the differential effect would increase these probabilities and make the distinguisher better.

(i.e. $w_0 < 64$) and in order for the distinguisher to work we require $S/N > 1$ thus:

$$S/N_l \doteq 64 - w_0 + \log_2 \left(\sum_{i=0}^{l} |C_i| \cdot 2^{-i} \right) - \log_2 \left(\sum_{i=0}^{l} |C_i| \right) > 1$$

From this inequality and given the histogram of cluster sizes $|C_i|$ we can derive the optimal l up to which we can grow our collection of signal ciphertexts. The main criteria for the attacker is to minimize the amount of data for the distinguisher, i.e. minimizing $N = \log_2 \left(- \log(1 - p) \right) - k_{speck}$ (which is equivalent to maximizing the collection weight l), while keeping $S/N = k_{\text{speck}} - k_{\text{rand}} > 1$. The larger the gap $64 - w_0$ the higher l the attacker can afford.

Statistical Distinguisher. Here we provide a statistical test to distinguish with a certain confidence level α if the queried box is the random-box or the speck-box. We can model our experiments using geometric distribution of parameter p, i.e. $X_{rand}, X_{speck} \approx Geo(p)$.[4]

The two statistical alternative hypothesis can be then formulated as follows:

- H_0: $p = p_{speck} = \sum_i |C_i| \cdot 2^{-w_i}$, i.e. encryptions come from the speck-box.
- H_1: $p = p_{rand} = \sum_i |C_i| \cdot 2^{-64}$, i.e. encryptions come from the random-box.

Given a certain confidence level α (e.g. $\alpha = 0.05$) we want to compute a threshold t_α so that if the first matching ciphertext is found after $X_* = 2^N$ encryptions, we accept H_0 if $2^N \le t_\alpha$, otherwise if $2^N > t_\alpha$ we accept H_1. We then have the following

$$\Pr(\text{Reject } H_0 \,|\, H_0) \;=\; \Pr(X > t_\alpha \,|\, p = p_{speck}) \;=\; \sum_{k=t_\alpha+1}^{\infty} (1 - p_{speck})^{k-1} p_{speck}$$

$$= (1 - p_{speck})^{t_\alpha} p_{speck} \cdot \sum_{l=0}^{\infty} (1 - p_{speck})^l \;=\; (1 - p_{speck})^{t_\alpha}$$

By requiring $\Pr(\text{Reject } H_0 \,|\, H_0) \le \alpha$, we have at least

$$t_\alpha = \left\lceil \frac{\ln \alpha}{\ln (1 - p_{speck})} \right\rceil$$

Thus, given such threshold t_α, the probability of accepting H_0 while being in H_1 would then be equal to

$$\Pr(\text{Accept } H_0 \,|\, H_1) \;=\; \Pr(X \le t_\alpha \,|\, p = p_{rand}) \;=\; 1 - (1 - p_{rand})^{t_\alpha}$$

Best Distinguishing Confidence Level α. We are interested in achieving the highest distinguishing power possible within the statistical model outlined above. In

---

[4] For Speck, this is a consequence of the assumed Markov assumption.

practice, for a given distinguisher with probabilities p_{rand}, p_{speck}, we would like to choose a confidence level α which maximizes

$$f(\alpha) = \Pr(\text{Accept } H_0 \,|\, H_0) - \Pr(\text{Accept } H_0 \,|\, H_1)$$

where we assume at least $f(\alpha) > 0$. By expanding this definition, we get

$$f(\alpha) = (1 - p_{rand})^{t_\alpha} - (1 - p_{speck})^{t_\alpha} = (1 - p_{rand})^{\frac{\ln \alpha}{\ln (1 - p_{speck})}} - \alpha = \alpha^c - \alpha$$

where $c = \frac{\ln(1 - p_{rand})}{\ln(1 - p_{speck})}$. So, a solution for $f'(\alpha) = 0$, would then be $\alpha = \left(\frac{1}{c}\right)^{\frac{1}{c-1}}$ and this is a local maximum if $f''(\alpha) = c \cdot (c - 1)\alpha^{c-2} < 0$. Thus, since $c > 0$, $\alpha = c^{\frac{1}{1-c}}$ is a local maximum when $c < 1$ or, equivalently, when $p_{speck} > p_{rand}$.

Experimental Verification. We have experimentally verified the above probabilistic and statistical model. More precisely, we have run a distinguishing attack on Speck32 reduced to 9 rounds. We have collected a cluster of differentials with the input difference (0211, 0a04) with a cumulative probability of at least $2^{-25.4}$. These were gathered by first finding optimal full trails until weight 32, of which there were 30 unique input/output pairs, and then calculating all the possible trails until weight 40 on these input/output pairs to accommodate for the differential effect. This resulted in a S/N ratio of 1.7. Then, using the formula from the previous section we can calculate the highest distinguishing α, which in this case is $\alpha = 0.1825$, which results in the threshold $t_\alpha = 2^{26.16}$. Using t_α we can also calculate the probability of false positives for the random permutation box given t_α samples, i.e. $\Pr(\text{Accept } H_0 \,|\, H_1)$, which is equal to 0.408. The distinguishing gap is $0.8175 - 0.408 = 0.4095$ which is clearly significant.

In our experiment we have used two boxes (Speck32 with 9 rounds and the random permutation). For the test with the Speck box, we encrypt t_α random input pairs with the fixed input difference, and record a success if any of the output differences is equal to one specified by our differentials. For the random box we use Speckey32 with 40 rounds (as that should emulate a random permutation), and similarly we encrypt t_α pairs of samples with the same input difference, and record a success if any of the two differences are in our set of output differences.

We ran both the Speck32 and the random experiment 1000 times, and received 892 successes for Speck32 (hinting at an even higher real differential probability), and 404 successes for the random variant, verifying our statistical model.

9   Best Distinguisher for SPECK64

In this Section we will discuss the best distinguisher we have found for 15 rounds of SPECK64. Aiming at finding the most suitable one, we considered 4 optimal trails of weight -62 found with Matsui's search with input differences $\Delta_0 = (\Delta x_0, \Delta y_0)$ equal to (40004092, 10420040), (04092400, 20040104), (92400040, 40104200), (924000c0, 40104200), respectively.

Given an optimal 15 rounds trail, we split it in $n + k$ rounds; by iteratively setting $k = 3, 4, 5$ we compute the best feasible approximation of the differential probability for the first n rounds while maximizing the S/N ratio obtained from freely varying the difference transitions in the last k rounds.

Since computing the differential probability over $n = 12, 11, 10$ rounds (depending on the value of k set) quickly becomes prohibitive as the minimum trail weight limit decreases, we split the first n rounds in two chunks of j and $n - j$ rounds, respectively. Hence, by iteratively setting $j = 3, \ldots, n - 3$ we independently compute the two differential probabilities of these two chunks and we select the best index j so that $\Pr(\Delta_0 \to \Delta_j) + \Pr(\Delta_j \to \Delta_n)$ is minimum.

In order to approximate the differential probability of the two sub-trails $\Delta_0 \to \Delta_j$ and $\Delta_j \to \Delta_n$, we use an SMT solver to find all trails with such input/output differences and weight exceeding at most -25 with respect to their optimal weight.

The trail that performed better within this framework has parameters $k = 3$, $n = 12$ and $j = 3$. More precisely, for the differential $\Delta_0 \to \Delta_3$ we found 6 trails of total probability -10.954, while for $\Delta_3 \to \Delta_{12}$ we found 21022 trails of total probability -37.418. Thus

$$\Pr(\Delta_0 \to \Delta_{12}) \geq 2^{-48.372}$$

We then proceed by collecting all possible $k = 3$ rounds trails with input difference equal to Δ_{12} and weight less equal -12, as long as the total S/N remains greater than 0: for $\Delta_{12} = (00080000, 00080000)$ we obtained 389 unique Δ_{15} of weight at least -16 with total weight -6.731 and $S/N = 0.361$. We further slightly improve the total weight to -6.657 by computing the differential probability of each 3 round trail found $\Delta_{12} \to \Delta_{15}$.

This, gives us a distinguisher of probability $p_{speck} = 2^{-48.372-6.657} = 2^{-55.029}$ consisting of 389 unique ciphertexts.

Given that $p_{rand} = \frac{389}{2^{64}} = 2^{-55.396}$, in light of the previous section, we obtain the best confidence level $\alpha = c^{\frac{1}{1-c}} = 0.322$ with $c = \frac{\ln(1-p_{rand})}{\ln(1-p_{speck})} = 0.775$ which in turn correspond to a distinguishing threshold $t_\alpha = 2^{55.576}$ and distinguishing gap of 0.094, small but non-negligible.

Best Cluster Around Sub-optimal Trail. It is natural to use the best trail as a starting point for a trail cluster. However one may wonder if it always produces the cluster with the highest total probability for a given S/N ratio. Interestingly the answer is "no". In some cases the cluster around sub-optimal trail will have higher distinguishing power than the one starting from the best trail. For example, we have seen this behaviour for clusters collected for SPECK64 reduced to 11 and 14 rounds. For 11 rounds there is one best trail and there are numerous sub-optimal trails with better clusters. For 14 rounds there are three best trails and there are two sub-optimal trails which are better than two of them and very close to the very best cluster. For 15 rounds sub-optimal trails always have weaker clusters but the four available best trails differ significantly. This fact has helped us to build the best distinguisher for 15 rounds SPECK64 described above.

These results were obtained by exploring sub-optimal trails up to certain weight bound beyond the best trail. This analysis shows that when deciding on a number of rounds of a cipher it might be important to consider not only the best differential, but the best differential cluster.

10 Conclusion

In this paper we described a new tool for the automated truncation of differential trails in ARX. The tool generates all possible truncations of an input non-truncated trail (up to certain pre-defined rules) and outputs a set of non-overlapping truncated trails with associated probability. The latter is strictly greater than the probability of the input trail. The proposed tool is useful for constructing truncated differential distinguishers which have lower data complexity than the traditional ones based on the best non-truncated differential. Interestingly, in some cases differential cluster around sub-optimal trail gives better resulting distinguisher then when starting from the best trail.

The application of the tool was demonstrated on block cipher SPECK64. More specifically, truncated differential set distinguishers based on the optimal trail/s on up to 15 (out of 24) rounds were reported. A natural future direction is the application of the tool to other ARX algorithms. Beside other ciphers, the tool could potentially be used in the area of ARX-based hash functions and sponge permutations. In particular, it may be worth exploring its use in an initial pre-processing phase that would facilitate the subsequent application of advanced collision search tools such as e.g. [14, 15, 18, 21].

Acknowledgements. The authors thank the anonymous reviewers for their time and for the insightful comments and corrections. Luan Cardoso dos Santos was supported by the Luxembourg National Research Fund project SP^2 (PRIDE15/ 10621687/SPsquared). Daniel Feher and Giuseppe Vitto were supported by the Luxembourg National Research Fund project FinCrypt (C17/IS/11684537).

Alex Biryukov, Luan Cardoso dos Santos and Vesselin Velichkov have significant contribution to the sections on the simple rules for truncation (Sect. 3), probability computation using simple rules (Sect. 4) and merging of differential trails produced with simple rules (Sect. 5). Daniel Feher and Giuseppe Vitto have significant contribution to the sections on relaxed rules for truncation (Sect. 6), the statistical analysis of the distinguishing advantage (Sect. 8) and on the best distinguisher for SPECK64 (Sect. 9).

References

1. YAARX: Yet Another Toolkit for Analysis of ARX Cryptographic Algorithms (2012–2018). Source code: https://github.com/vesselinux/yaarx. Documentation: https://vesselinux.github.io/yaarx/index.html

2. Ankele, R., Kölbl, S.: Mind the gap - a closer look at the security of block ciphers against differential cryptanalysis. In: Cid, C., Jacobson, M., Jr. (eds.) Selected Areas in Cryptography - SAC 2018. LNCS, vol. 11349, pp. 163–190. Springer, Cham (2018). https://doi.org/10.1007/978-3-030-10970-7_8

3. Beaulieu, R., Shors, D., Smith, J., Treatman-Clark, S., Weeks, B., Wingers, L.: The SIMON and SPECK Families of Lightweight Block Ciphers. Cryptology ePrint Archive, Report 2013/404

4. Biham, E., Shamir, A.: Differential cryptanalysis of DES-like cryptosystems. J. Cryptol. **4**, 3–72 (1991)

5. Biryukov, A., Roy, A., Velichkov, V.: Differential analysis of block ciphers SIMON and SPECK. In: Cid, C., Rechberger, C. (eds.) FSE 2014. LNCS, vol. 8540, pp. 546–570. Springer, Heidelberg (2015). https://doi.org/10.1007/978-3-662-46706-0_28

6. Biryukov, A., Velichkov, V.: Automatic search for differential trails in ARX ciphers. In: Benaloh, J. (ed.) CT-RSA 2014. LNCS, vol. 8366, pp. 227–250. Springer, Cham (2014). https://doi.org/10.1007/978-3-319-04852-9_12

7. Biryukov, A., Velichkov, V., Le Corre, Y.: Automatic search for the best trails in ARX: application to block cipher SPECK. In: Peyrin, T. (ed.) FSE 2016. LNCS, vol. 9783, pp. 289–310. Springer, Heidelberg (2016). https://doi.org/10.1007/978-3-662-52993-5_15

8. De Cannière, C., Rechberger, C.: Finding SHA-1 characteristics: general results and applications. In: Lai, X., Chen, K. (eds.) ASIACRYPT 2006. LNCS, vol. 4284, pp. 1–20. Springer, Heidelberg (2006). https://doi.org/10.1007/11935230_1

9. Fu, K., Wang, M., Guo, Y., Sun, S., Hu, L.: MILP-based automatic search algorithms for differential and linear trails for speck. In: Peyrin, T. (ed.) FSE 2016. LNCS, vol. 9783, pp. 268–288. Springer, Heidelberg (2016). https://doi.org/10.1007/978-3-662-52993-5_14

10. Huang, M., Wang, L.: Automatic tool for searching for differential characteristics in ARX ciphers and applications. In: Hao, F., Ruj, S., Sen Gupta, S. (eds.) INDOCRYPT 2019. LNCS, vol. 11898, pp. 115–138. Springer, Cham (2019). https://doi.org/10.1007/978-3-030-35423-7_6

11. Knudsen, L.R.: Truncated and higher order differentials. In: Preneel, B. (ed.) FSE 1994. LNCS, vol. 1008, pp. 196–211. Springer, Heidelberg (1995). https://doi.org/10.1007/3-540-60590-8_16

12. Leurent, G.: Analysis of differential attacks in ARX constructions. In: Wang, X., Sako, K. (eds.) ASIACRYPT 2012. LNCS, vol. 7658, pp. 226–243. Springer, Heidelberg (2012). https://doi.org/10.1007/978-3-642-34961-4_15

13. Leurent, G.: Construction of differential characteristics in ARX designs - application to skein. IACR Cryptol. ePrint Arch. **2012**, 668 (2012)

14. Leurent, G.: Construction of differential characteristics in ARX designs application to skein. In: Canetti, R., Garay, J.A. (eds.) CRYPTO 2013. LNCS, vol. 8042, pp. 241–258. Springer, Heidelberg (2013). https://doi.org/10.1007/978-3-642-40041-4_14

15. Leurent, G., Peyrin, T.: SHA-1 is a shambles: first chosen-prefix collision on SHA-1 and application to the PGP web of trust. In: USENIX (2020)

16. Lipmaa, H., Moriai, S.: Efficient algorithms for computing differential properties of addition. In: Matsui, M. (ed.) FSE 2001. LNCS, vol. 2355, pp. 336–350. Springer, Heidelberg (2002). https://doi.org/10.1007/3-540-45473-X_28

17. Liu, Z., Li, Y., Jiao, L., Wang, M.: A new method for searching optimal differential and linear trails in ARX ciphers. Cryptology ePrint Archive, Report 2019/1438

18. Mendel, F., Nad, T., Schläffer, M.: Finding SHA-2 characteristics: searching through a minefield of contradictions. In: Lee, D.H., Wang, X. (eds.) ASIACRYPT 2011. LNCS, vol. 7073, pp. 288–307. Springer, Heidelberg (2011). https://doi.org/10.1007/978-3-642-25385-0_16

19. Mouha, N., Wang, Q., Gu, D., Preneel, B.: Differential and linear cryptanalysis using mixed-integer linear programming. In: Wu, C.-K., Yung, M., Lin, D. (eds.) Inscrypt 2011. LNCS, vol. 7537, pp. 57–76. Springer, Heidelberg (2012). https://doi.org/10.1007/978-3-642-34704-7_5

20. Song, L., Huang, Z., Yang, Q.: Automatic differential analysis of ARX Block ciphers with application to SPECK and LEA. In: Liu, J.K., Steinfeld, R. (eds.) ACISP 2016. LNCS, vol. 9723, pp. 379–394. Springer, Cham (2016). https://doi.org/10.1007/978-3-319-40367-0_24

21. Stevens, M.: New collision attacks on SHA-1 based on optimal joint local-collision analysis. In: Johansson, T., Nguyen, P.Q. (eds.) EUROCRYPT 2013. LNCS, vol. 7881, pp. 245–261. Springer, Heidelberg (2013). https://doi.org/10.1007/978-3-642-38348-9_15

22. Sun, S., et al.: Towards finding the best characteristics of some bit-oriented block ciphers and automatic enumeration of (related-key) differential and linear characteristics with predefined properties. Cryptology ePrint Archive, Report 2014/747

23. Sun, S., Hu, L., Wang, M., Yang, Q., Qiao, K., Ma, X., Song, L., Shan, J.: Extending the applicability of the mixed-integer programming technique in automatic differential cryptanalysis. In: Lopez, J., Mitchell, C.J. (eds.) ISC 2015. LNCS, vol. 9290, pp. 141–157. Springer, Cham (2015). https://doi.org/10.1007/978-3-319-23318-5_8

Quantum Cryptanalysis

Improved Quantum Algorithms for the k-XOR Problem

André Schrottenloher[✉]

Cryptology Group, CWI, Amsterdam, The Netherlands
andre.schrottenloher@m4x.org

Abstract. The k-XOR problem can be generically formulated as the following: given many n-bit strings generated uniformly at random, find k distinct of them which XOR to zero. This generalizes collision search (two equal elements) to a k-tuple of inputs.

This problem has become ubiquitous in cryptanalytic algorithms, including variants in which the XOR operation is replaced by a modular addition (k-SUM) or other non-commutative operations (e.g., the composition of permutations). The case where a single solution exists on average is of special importance.

At EUROCRYPT 2020, Naya-Plasencia and Schrottenloher defined a class of *quantum merging algorithms* for the k-XOR problem, obtained by combining quantum search. They represented these algorithms by a set of *merging trees* and obtained the best ones through linear optimization of their parameters.

In this paper, we give a simplified representation of merging trees that makes their analysis easier. We give better quantum algorithms for the Single-solution k-XOR problem by relaxing one of the previous constraints, and making use of quantum walks. Our algorithms subsume or improve over all previous quantum algorithms for Single-solution k-XOR. For example, we give an algorithm for 4-XOR (or 4-SUM) in quantum time $\widetilde{\mathcal{O}}(2^{7n/24})$.

Keywords: Quantum algorithms · Merging algorithms · k-XOR · k-SUM · Bicomposite search

1 Introduction

The *collision search problem* for a random function can be formulated as follows: given a random $h : \{0,1\}^n \rightarrow \{0,1\}^n$, find a pair of distinct inputs (x, y) such that $h(x) = h(y)$. This problem is ubiquitous in cryptography and collision search algorithms have been well studied. It is well known that, as formulated here, it can be solved in about $\mathcal{O}(2^{n/2})$ classical queries to h and time. Using Floyd's cycle-finding algorithm, we need only polynomial memory.

Part of this work was done while the author was at Inria, France.

A possible generalization would be to look for more than two elements having the same image: the problem (*multicollision* search) then becomes harder. Another would be to have *more than two elements collide* in the sense that they sum to zero, or that their combination satisfies some constraint. This leads to the *Generalized Birthday Problem*, or k-XOR for us, formulated by Wagner [25]:

> Given k lists of random n-bit strings: $\mathcal{L}_1, \ldots, \mathcal{L}_k$ which can be extended at will, find a k-tuple $(y_1, \ldots, y_k) \in (\mathcal{L}_1 \times \ldots \times \mathcal{L}_k)$ such that $y_1 \oplus \ldots \oplus y_k = 0$.

In [25], Wagner gave an algorithm to solve k-XOR for any k, based on the *merging* building block. Although the idea of merging had been around for a longer time, with examples like [9], this was the first generic k-list merging algorithm. Later on, many works have either pursued the generic direction [11,22], or the optimization of more specific algorithms. For example, the best algorithms for randomized instances of subset-sum [3,6,15] actually solve k-list problems with additional constraints, and use *merging* as an algorithmic subroutine.

Quantum k-XOR Algorithms. Obviously, *quantum* k-XOR algorithms can be used as replacements for classical ones in the context of quantum cryptanalysis. But our need for understanding the quantum speedups for k-XOR goes further, as quantum k-list algorithms of similar shapes have played a role in generic decoding [16] or in lattice sieving [17]. Knowing and improving the "generic" advantage of k-XOR algorithms may help for further improvements in these specific settings.

Grassi et al. [13] tackled the Many-solutions case (the case initially studied by Wagner) for a generic k. A more complete picture was obtained in [21]. Quantum algorithms for k-XOR were extended to a whole family derived from classical merging strategies, among which some appear to be optimal. These *quantum merging algorithms* were represented syntactically as *merging trees*, with some parameters to optimize linearly. Besides, this was the first study of the Single-solution case for a generic k.

Contrary to what occurs classically, the Single-solution k-XOR problem has a quantum time complexity advantage when k increases. For example, the Single-solution 2-XOR problem has a quantum time complexity $\widetilde{\mathcal{O}}(2^{n/3})$ [1], and an algorithm of time complexity $\widetilde{\mathcal{O}}(2^{0.3n})$ for the 4-XOR problem has been given in [5]. In [21], a closed formula for the time complexity exponent, depending on k, was obtained. Though the algorithms differed from [5] (as they did not use quantum walks), their complexity exponent also reached 0.3 at best.

Contributions. In this paper we give a simplified definition of *merging trees*, with a better emphasis on the correspondence between classical and quantum merging algorithms. In the Many-solutions case, we recover the algorithms of [21] and obtain simpler proofs of their optimality in the class of merging trees. In the Single-solution case, we simplify the presentation of [21] and modify one of its constraints. We obtain a new closed formula with a convergence towards 2/7 instead of 0.3. Finally, we introduce *quantum walks* as a new building block in these algorithms. They allow to reduce further the exponents, although not below $2/7$. In particular, we solve 4-SUM in quantum time $\widetilde{\mathcal{O}}(2^{7n/24})$, below the previous $\widetilde{\mathcal{O}}(2^{0.3n})$ [5].

Organization of the Paper. We define the problem and present *classical* merging algorithms in Sect. 2. In Sect. 3, we give some brief preliminaries of quantum computing. In Sect. 4, we introduce our new definition of *merging trees*. In Sect. 5, we explain how the trees are extended to the Single-solution case, and we give some of our new results. Next, in Sect. 6, we show how to obtain our best exponents with quantum walk algorithms for claw-finding.

2   Classical Algorithms for Many-Solutions k-XOR

In this paper, we use the term "k-XOR" to refer to a simple variant of Wagner's Generalized Birthday Problem, where the data is generated by a single random function h. Note that, since h is random, a solution might not exist. We include this as a case of failure in our algorithms, as we only require them to succeed on average. We name "k-SUM" the problem where the n-bit bitwise XOR ($\oplus$) is replaced by addition modulo 2^n ($+$). Other extensions are possible provided that *merging* is properly defined, as shown by Wagner [25].

Problem 1 (Many-solutions k-XOR). Given oracle access to a random function $h : \{0,1\}^n \rightarrow \{0,1\}^n$, find distinct inputs $(x_1, \ldots, x_k)$ such that $h(x_1) \oplus \ldots \oplus h(x_k) = 0$.

We will assume that *quantum* access to h is given. By restricting the domain of h to $\{0,1\}^{n/k}$, we obtain the *Single-solution* case (a single solution on average). Here having quantum access to h is not a strong restriction, because the time complexity of the best algorithms will exceed $2^{n/k}$, so we can query the whole function classically, store its table, and emulate quantum access to its contents.

Query Complexity. The classical query complexity of the k-XOR problem, Single- or Many-solutions, is $\Omega(2^{n/k})$. The quantum query complexity was determined to be $\Omega(2^{n/(k+1)})$ by Belovs and Spalek [4] in the Single-solution case and by Zhandry [26] in the Many-solutions case.

Time Complexity. The time complexity of the k-XOR problem is also exponential in k. We will write it in the form $\widetilde{\mathcal{O}}(2^{\alpha_k n})$ or $\mathcal{O}(2^{\alpha_k n})$ where the exponent α_k depends only on k. The polynomial factors will be constant or logarithmic. All the quantum algorithms that we will present are composing Grover's quantum search algorithm [14] and MNRS quantum walks [19], which achieve at most a quadratic speedup. So this is the best we can expect.

2.1   Classical Merging

We adopt the following conventions: lists named $\mathcal{L}_i$ have corresponding sizes $L_i = 2^{\ell_i n}$ (up to a constant). We write for simplicity that $\mathcal{L}_i$ "has size ℓ_i". All these parameters ℓ_i are constants.

Let $\mathcal{L}_1$ and $\mathcal{L}_2$ be two lists of n-bit strings selected uniformly and independently at random, of respective sizes $L_1 \simeq 2^{\ell_1 n}$ and $L_2 \simeq 2^{\ell_2 n}$. We assume that they are sorted. We select a prefix t of un bits ($u < 1$), where un is approximated to an integer. By *merging $\mathcal{L}_1$ and $\mathcal{L}_2$ with prefix t*, we say that we compute the *join* list $\mathcal{L}_1 \bowtie_t \mathcal{L}_2$ of pairs (x_1, x_2) such that $x_1 \in \mathcal{L}_1, x_2 \in \mathcal{L}_2, x_1 \oplus x_2 = t|*$. We say that such x_1 and x_2 *partially collide* on un bits. The join list is expected to keep track of the values of x_1 and x_2 that led to $x_1 \oplus x_2$, but we omit them for clarity.

Until Sect. 4 included, the prefixes will have arbitrary values. In that case, we care only about the parameter u and we use the notation $\bowtie_u$. The notation $\bowtie_t$, with the actual value of the prefix, will be used in Sect. 5 and Sect. 6.

The merging operation is efficiently computed by iterating through the lists to retrieve the partial collision pairs. The result is a list of *average* size $\frac{L_1 L_2}{2^{un}}$. Indeed, when $x_1 \in \mathcal{L}_1$ and $x_2 \in \mathcal{L}_2$ are selected uniformly at random, then $\Pr(x_1 \oplus x_2 = t|*) = 2^{-un}$. By linearity of the expectation, the average time complexity of algorithms based on merging is easy to compute. The variance is a more difficult problem, which was first studied by Minder and Sinclair [20, Section 4].

In this paper, we consider the following heuristic, which is enough to ensure the correctness of our algorithms. We show how to remove it from our algorithms in the XOR case, up to a polynomial increase in time, in the full version of the paper [24].

Heuristic 1. *If $\mathcal{L}_1$ and $\mathcal{L}_2$ have uniformly random elements, then so does the join $\mathcal{L}_u$ (with the constraint on un bits).*

Lemma 1 (Classical merging, adapted from [25]). *The join list $\mathcal{L}_u = \mathcal{L}_1 \bowtie_u \mathcal{L}_2$ can be computed in time $\max(\ell_1 + \ell_2 - u, \min(\ell_1, \ell_2))$ (in $\log_2$). This list is of size L_u, which has an expectation: $\mathbb{E}(L_u) = \frac{L_1 L_2}{2^{un}}$. Under Heuristic 1, the deviation from $\mathbb{E}(L_u)$ is exponentially small.*

2.2   Wagner's Algorithm

Wagner's algorithm starts from lists of pairs $(x, h(x))$ for many arbitrary values of x, and merges recursively the lists pairwise with increasing zero-prefixes, until a tuple of k elements with a full-zero sum of images is found. This *merging strategy* is best represented as a *merging tree*. It is a binary tree where each node represents an intermediate list of ℓ-tuples with a given size and prefix constraint on the sum. The example of $k = 4$ is given in Fig. 1.

We name *merging algorithms* the class of classical algorithms that are represented by valid merging trees. That is, the root node should have prefix length n and expected size 1, and all intermediate nodes have parameters constrained by the formula of Lemma 1. For any merging tree, there exists a k-XOR algorithm with time and memory complexities equal to the maximum of list sizes in the tree.

In the context of Wagner's algorithm, if k is not a power of 2, $k - 2^{\lfloor \log_2(k) \rfloor}$ degrees of freedom are left unused. The tree has $2^{\lfloor \log_2(k) \rfloor}$ prefixless leaves of size

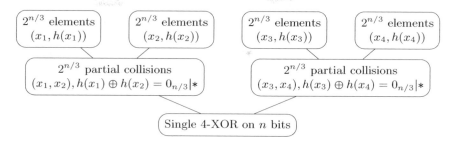

Fig. 1. Structure of Wagner's 4-XOR tree.

$2^{\frac{n}{\lceil \log_2(k) \rceil + 1}}$ (single elements obtained by querying h). At subsequent levels, lists are merged pairwise on $\frac{n}{\lceil \log_2(k) \rceil + 1}$ bits, so they remain of size $2^{\frac{n}{\lceil \log_2(k) \rceil + 1}}$. The final level merges on $\frac{2n}{\lceil \log_2(k) \rceil + 1}$ bits to obtain a single solution on average. The total complexity exponent is $\frac{1}{\lceil \log_2(k) \rceil + 1}$.

3   Quantum Preliminaries

In this paper, we assume basic knowledge of quantum computing, such as qubits, quantum states, ket notations $|\cdot\rangle$. However, we stress that we will only use well-known algorithmic tools such as quantum search in a black-box way (especially since we consider asymptotic complexities).

Aside from a few exceptions, the known quantum speedups for k-XOR [13, 21], including those of this paper, require some *quantum RAM* (qRAM) model. We will use:

- Classical memory with quantum random-access (QRACM): it contains classical data, but *superposition access* is allowed. Assuming that the data bits are indexed by $1 \leq i \leq 2^m - 1$, a unit cost qRAM gate is given:

$$|i\rangle |y\rangle \xmapsto{\text{qRAM}} |i\rangle |y \oplus M_i\rangle \quad , \text{ where } M_i \text{ is the data at index } i.$$

That is, all memory cells can be accessed simultaneously in superposition.
- Quantum memory with quantum random-access (QRAQM): it also allows superposition access, but the data can be a quantum state:

$$|i\rangle |y\rangle |M_0 \cdots M_{2^m-1}\rangle \xmapsto{\text{qRAM}} |i\rangle |y \oplus M_i\rangle |M_0 \cdots M_{2^m-1}\rangle \quad .$$

The QRACM/QRAQM terminology is borrowed from [18], and corresponds to QACM/QAQM in [21]. Both are ubiquitous in quantum algorithms, although QRACM is often regarded as much more reasonable than QRAQM [18]. The qRAM gate is defined in [1, Section 6.1]. We will also briefly consider algorithms *without* qRAM, using purely classical storage instead. A memory of size M is then accessed in time $\mathcal{O}(M)$ using a sequential circuit.

Quantum Search. Grover's quantum search [14] is one of the most well-known quantum algorithms. We will actually make use of Amplitude Amplification, a powerful generalization proposed by Brassard et al. [7]. It speeds up the search for a "good" output of *any* probabilistic algorithm.

Theorem 1 ([7], Theorem 2). *Let $\mathcal{A}$ be a quantum algorithm that uses no intermediate measurements, let $f : X \rightarrow \{0,1\}$ be a boolean function that tests if an output of $\mathcal{A}$ is "good" and assume that a quantum oracle O_f for f is given:* $|x\rangle |0\rangle \xrightarrow{O_f} |x\rangle |f(x)\rangle$. *Let $\theta_a = \arcsin \sqrt{a}$. Then there exists an algorithm running in time:* $\left\lfloor \frac{\pi}{4\theta_a} \right\rfloor (2|\mathcal{A}| + |O_f| + \mathcal{O}(\log |X|))$ *that obtains a good result with success probability greater than* $\max(1 - a, a)$.

We can define a *quantum sampling* black-box, analogous to a classical algorithm which would sample uniformly at random from some well-defined set. We use the **Sample** keyword to write down such quantum algorithms in a simple way, by using recursively the conversion given by Theorem 1. We just have to define a search space and a testing function (the inside of the **Sample** block, which may itself contain another **Sample**).

Definition 1. *Let X be a set. A quantum sampling algorithm for X (denoted qSample(X)) is a quantum algorithm that takes no input and creates the uniform superposition of elements of X (that is, of basis states uniquely representing the elements of X).*

4 Quantum Algorithms for Many-Solutions k-XOR

The representation of Wagner's algorithm as a *merging tree* does not make any assumption on the *order* in which the algorithm computes the lists. The tree can be traversed breadth-first, in which case the merging algorithm computes all leaves, then all nodes of depth $\lfloor \log_2(k) \rfloor - 1$, then all nodes of depth $\lfloor \log_2(k) \rfloor - 2$, *etc.*. A more interesting option is to traverse it *depth-first*. This well-known technique reduces the storage from $2^{\lfloor \log_2(k) \rfloor}$ to $\lfloor \log_2(k) \rfloor$ lists.

This depth-first traversal actually rewrites the k-XOR algorithm as a sequence of classical Sample procedures. If the list $\mathcal{L}$ is a leaf node, then Sample($\mathcal{L}$) consists in making an arbitrary query to h and returning $(x, h(x))$. Otherwise, we use recursively a result equivalent to Lemma 1:

Lemma 2. *Let $\mathcal{L}_1$ and $\mathcal{L}_2$ be two lists of respective sizes $2^{\ell_1 n}$ and $2^{\ell_2 n}$, with $\mathcal{L}_2$ stored in memory, and $\mathcal{L}_u = \mathcal{L}_1 \bowtie_u \mathcal{L}_2$ be the join list with an arbitrary prefix of un bits. Let Sample($\mathcal{L}_1$) be a sampling algorithm for $\mathcal{L}_1$. Then there exists a sampling algorithm Sample($\mathcal{L}_u$) with average complexity:*

$$\mathsf{T}_c(\mathsf{Sample}(\mathcal{L}_u)) = \mathsf{T}_c(\mathsf{Sample}(\mathcal{L}_1) + \mathcal{O}(n)) \cdot \max(2^{(u-\ell_2)}, 1) \ . \tag{1}$$

Proof. The algorithm consists in sampling $x_1 \in \mathcal{L}_1$, and searching an element $x_2 \in \mathcal{L}_2$ such that $x_1 \oplus x_2$ has the right prefix. We repeat this until such an element is found. $\qquad\square$

Although this rewriting does not change the classical time complexity, nor the correctness of the algorithm, it leads to the definition of *quantum merging algorithms* in [21]: each Sample can be replaced by a quantum algorithm qSample, using quantum search. Now, any merging tree does not only represent a classical algorithm for k-XOR, but also a quantum one. Unfortunately, the trees defined in [21] are multiary and more complex than those used classically. We will provide in Sect. 4.2 a simpler definition that goes back to these binary trees.

4.1 Merging in the Quantum Setting

Quantum merging algorithms are based on a result analogous to Lemma 2: if the list $\mathcal{L}_2$ is given, then from a quantum algorithm that samples from the list $\mathcal{L}_1$, we can create another that samples from $\mathcal{L}_u$.

Lemma 3 (Quantum merging). *Let t be an arbitrary prefix of un bits. Let $\mathcal{L}_1$ and $\mathcal{L}_2$ be two lists of respective sizes $2^{\ell_1 n}$ and $2^{\ell_2 n}$. Assume that $\mathcal{L}_2$ is stored either in QRACM or in classical memory.*

Assume that we are given a quantum sampling algorithm qSample$(\mathcal{L}_1)$ *for $\mathcal{L}_1$. Then there exists a quantum sampling for $\mathcal{L}_u = \mathcal{L}_1 \bowtie_u \mathcal{L}_2$ with quantum time complexity:*

$$
\mathsf{T_q}(\mathsf{qSample}(\mathcal{L}_u)) = \begin{cases} (\mathsf{T_q}(\mathsf{qSample}(\mathcal{L}_1)) + \mathcal{O}(n)) \cdot \max(2^{\frac{(u-\ell_2)}{2}n}, 1) \ with \ QRACM \\ (\mathsf{T_q}(\mathsf{qSample}(\mathcal{L}_1)) + 2^{\ell_2 n}) \cdot \max(2^{\frac{(u-\ell_2)}{2}n}, 1) \ without \end{cases}
$$
(2)

in qRAM *gates and n-qubit register operations.*

Proof. We use an Amplitude Amplification, where the amplified algorithm consists in sampling $\mathcal{L}_1$, finding whether there is a match of the given prefix in $\mathcal{L}_2$, and returning the pair if it exists. Using Heuristic 1 ensures an exponentially low error for the full procedure. Indeed, this error depends on the difference between the average number of solutions (which dictates the number of search iterations) and the actual one.

To obtain the time complexity, we separate two cases: if $u > \ell_2$, then the amplification really needs to take place, and it has $2^{(u-\ell_2)n/2}$ iterations up to a constant. Each iteration calls qSample$(\mathcal{L}_1)$ and queries the memory. Without QRACM, we use a circuit that performs a sequence of $2^{\ell_2 n}$ classically controlled comparisons (hence the additional term).

If $u < \ell_2$, then a given element $x_1 \in \mathcal{L}_1$ will have on average exponentially many $x_2 \in \mathcal{L}_2$ such that $x_1 \oplus x_2 = t|*$. It is possible to return the superposition of them at no greater time cost, by organizing the QRACM in a radix tree. □

Because we are now using quantum search, the balanced trees such as Wagner's are not suitable anymore, and we must re-optimize the parameters. The example of 4-XOR, which reaches a time complexity $\mathcal{O}(2^{n/4})$, is displayed in Fig. 2. In this algorithm, we first built the two intermediate lists of size $2^{n/4}$, then find the 4-XOR with an exhaustive search in the $2^{n/2}$-sized leaf list. This list

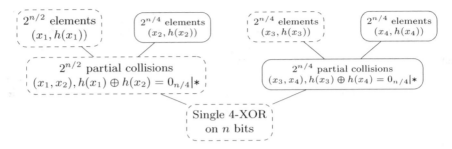

Fig. 2. Re-optimization of 4-XOR merging (from [21]). Plain lines indicate the lists actually stored in QRACM.

is not written down, as it only corresponds to a search space efficiently sampled. Given a random $(x, h(x))$, we find a partial collision with the first intermediate list, moving to the next level. Then we try to match against the second intermediate list. Both operations require memory access to the lists, which becomes QRACM access when the search is done quantumly.

4.2   Definition of Merging Trees

The goal of *merging trees* is to represent quantum merging strategies for k-XOR in a purely syntactical way. Though we use the same name as [21], our definition will largely differ.

Definition 2 (Merging trees). *A k-merging tree $\mathcal{T}_k$ is a binary tree defined recursively as follows:*

- *A node is either labeled "Sample" (S-node) or "List" (L-node)*
- *If $k = 1$, this is a leaf node $\mathcal{T}_1$*
- *If $k > 1$, $\mathcal{T}_k$ has two children: an S-node $\mathcal{T}_{k_l}$ and an L-node $\mathcal{T}_{k_r}$, where $k_l + k_r = k$.*

It follows inductively that a k-merging tree has k leaf nodes. Intuitively, an S-node represents a procedure that samples from a given list and an L-node represents a list stored in memory, constructed with exponentially many samples.

By convention, we draw Sample nodes (dashed) on the left and List nodes (plain) on the right, as in Fig. 2. To each node $\mathcal{T}$ corresponds a list $\mathcal{L}$ which is either *built* or *sampled*. Since the trees are binary, we adopt a simple numbering of lists $\mathcal{L}_i^j$. The root node, at level 0 in the tree, is $\mathcal{L}_0^0$, and the two children of $\mathcal{L}_i^j$ are numbered respectively $\mathcal{L}_{2i}^{j+1}$ for the sampled one and $\mathcal{L}_{2i+1}^{j+1}$ for the list one. We label a node with the following variables describing $\mathcal{L}_i^j$:

- The *width* k_i^j
- The number u_i^j of bits set to zero (relatively to n)
- The size ℓ_i^j of this list: by our conventions, ℓ_i^j represents a size of $2^{\ell_i^j n}$

Thus, $\mathcal{L}_i^j$ is a list of k_i^j-tuples $(x_1, \ldots, x_{k_i^j})$ such that $x_1 \oplus \ldots \oplus x_{k_i^j} = 0_{u_i^j n}|*$, of size $2^{\ell_i^j n}$, which is only stored in memory if i is odd, and otherwise, represents a *search space*.

Merging Strategy and Constraints. We constrain the variables ℓ_i^j and u_i^j in order to represent a valid merging strategy. First, we want a solution to the k-XOR problem.

Constraint 1 (Root node). *At the root node:* $u_0^0 = 1$ *and* $\ell_0^0 = 0$.

As each node results from the merging of its two children, the number of zeros increases. Furthermore, two siblings shall have the same number of zeros: $u_{2i}^j = u_{2i+1}^j$. Otherwise, we could reduce this parameter to $\min(u_{2i}^j, u_{2i+1}^j)$.

Constraint 2 (Zero-prefixes). $\forall i, j \geq 1, u_{2i}^j = u_{2i+1}^j$ *and* $u_i^{j-1} \geq u_{2i}^j$.

Finally, the size of a list is constrained by the sizes of its predecessors and the new constraint $((u_i^{j-1} - u_{2i+1}^j)n$ more bits to put to zero).

Constraint 3 (Size of a list). $\forall i, j \geq 1, \ell_i^{j-1} = \ell_{2i}^j + \ell_{2i+1}^j - (u_i^{j-1} - u_{2i+1}^j)$.

Possible extensions of this framework are discussed in [21]. None of the classical techniques of [2,11,12,20,22] seem to bring further improvements to the k-XOR problem in the quantum setting.

4.3 From Trees to Algorithms

We attach to each node another parameter t, which represents the *sample time*. Our intuition is that the time to sample from the list $\mathcal{L}_i^j$ represented by this node will be $\tilde{\mathcal{O}}(2^{nt})$.

Constraint 4 (Sampling). *Let* T_i^j *be a node in the tree, either an S-node or an L-node. If* T_i^j *is a leaf,* $t_i^j = \frac{u_i^j}{2}$. *Otherwise,* T_i^j *has an S-child* T_{2i}^{j+1} *and an L-child* T_{2i+1}^{j+1}, *and:*

$$t_i^j = \begin{cases} t_{2i}^{j+1} + \frac{1}{2}\max\left(u_i^j - u_{2i}^{j+1} - \ell_{2i+1}^{j+1}, 0\right) & \text{with QRACM} \\ \max(t_{2i}^{j+1}, \ell_{2i+1}^{j+1}) + \frac{1}{2}\max\left((u_i^j - u_{2i}^{j+1} - \ell_{2i+1}^{j+1}, 0\right) & \text{without} \\ t_{2i}^{j+1} + \max\left(u_i^j - u_{2i}^{j+1} - \ell_{2i+1}^{j+1}, 0\right) & \text{classically} \end{cases} \quad (3)$$

If the node is a leaf, then we simply run Grover's algorithm multiple times. Equation (3) is simply a translation of (2) in the case of a specific node. The third option needs to be added when QRACM is not available, in order to model a situation where the best thing to do is to sample the list classically. If we do that, then the whole branch (from this node to the root) becomes classical. Next, we can deduce the time complexity exponent of a tree.

Definition 3. *Let $\mathcal{T}_k$ be a k-merging tree. We define $\mathsf{T_q}(\mathcal{T}_k)$ and $\mathsf{M}(\mathcal{T}_k)$ as:*

$$\mathsf{T_q}(\mathcal{T}_k) = \max\left(\max_{List\ nodes}\left(t_i^j + \ell_i^j\right), t_0^0\right) \text{ and } \mathsf{M}(\mathcal{T}_k) = \max_{List\ nodes}\left(\ell_i^j\right).$$

It should be noted that the list size of Sample nodes plays only a role in the structural constraints, not in the time complexity. They should simply have a size sufficient to ensure the existence of a solution in the tree. Thanks to Lemma 3, we can prove that to any merging tree satisfying the constraints, there corresponds a quantum merging algorithm.

Theorem 2 (Quantum merging strategies). *Let $\mathcal{T}_k$ be a k-merging tree and $\mathsf{T_q}(\mathcal{T}_k)$ computed as in Definition 3. Then there exists a quantum merging algorithm that, given access to a quantum oracle for h, finds a k-XOR.*

Under Heuristic 1, this algorithm succeeds with probability more than $1 - e^{-an}$ for some constant $a > 0$. It runs in time $\mathcal{O}\left(n2^{\mathsf{T_q}(\mathcal{T}_k)n}\right)$, makes the same number of queries to h. It requires only $\mathcal{O}(n)$ computing qubits. It uses a memory $\mathcal{O}\left(2^{\mathsf{M}(\mathcal{T}_k)n}\right)$, counted in n-bit registers (either classical or QRACM).

Proof. We define recursively the correspondence $\mathcal{T}_k \overset{\mathcal{A}}{\longmapsto} \mathcal{A}(\mathcal{T}_k)$ from a merging tree $\mathcal{T}_k$ to a k-XOR algorithm $\mathcal{A}(\mathcal{T}_k)$. The complexities follow from Lemma 3 and simplifying $\mathcal{O}(2^{\alpha n}) + \mathcal{O}(2^{\beta n}) = \mathcal{O}(2^{\max(\alpha,\beta)n})$. A global factor $\mathcal{O}(n)$ comes from the memory operations.

Let $N(k, u, \ell)$ be the root node of $\mathcal{T}_k$ and $S(k', u', \ell')$ and $L(k'', u'', \ell'')$ its two children, if they exist.

- If it is a Sample leaf, then $\mathcal{A}(\mathcal{T}_k)$ simply consists in running Grover's algorithm in time $\mathcal{O}\left(2^{un/2}\right)$.
- Otherwise, if it is a Sample: • we sample from the child L with $\mathcal{A}(L)$, and build the list in time $\mathcal{O}\left(2^{(\mathsf{T_q}(L)+\ell'')n}\right)$. • we apply Lemma 3, using $\mathcal{A}(S)$ as a sample for the child S.
- If it is a List, the situation is the same, except that we repeat the operation exponentially many times. $\square$

4.4   Optimal Trees for Many-Solutions k-XOR

Now that we have defined the set of merging trees, we can explore this space to search for the trees $\mathcal{T}_k$ that minimize $\mathsf{T_q}(\mathcal{T}_k)$.

Given a tree $\mathcal{T}_k$, its time and memory complexity exponents $\mathsf{T_q}(\mathcal{T}_k)$ and $\mathsf{M}(\mathcal{T}_k)$ are defined as the maximums of linear combinations of the parameters ℓ_i^j, u_i^j. Thus, there exists a choice of these parameters that minimizes $\mathsf{T_q}(\mathcal{T}_k)$, under Constraint 1, 2, 3 and 4. As remarked in [21], this is a linear problem, solvable with Mixed Integer Linear Programming (MILP). Given k, we try all possible tree structures and find the optimal one. Note that thanks to our new definition of merging trees, we have a much smaller set of tree shapes to explore than in [21].

There always exists an optimal tree $\mathcal{T}_k$ that achieves the best time complexity exponent. For a given k, there is sometimes more than one, but we find that it is reached by a family of *balanced* trees T_k. When k is a power of 2, T_k is Wagner's balanced binary tree.

Definition 4 (Trees T_k). *If $k = 1$, then T_k is simply a leaf node. If $k = 2k'$, then the "Sample" child of T_k is $T_{k'}$ and the "List" child is $T_{k'}$. If $k = 2k' + 1$, then the "Sample" child of T_k is $T_{k'+1}$ and the "List" child is $T_{k'}$.*

When QRACM is available, the authors of [21] find a complexity exponent $\alpha_k = \frac{2^\kappa}{(1+\kappa)2^\kappa + k}$ for any k, where $\kappa = \lfloor \log_2(k) \rfloor$. When QRACM is not available, and $k \geq 8$, they find $\beta_k = \frac{1}{\kappa+1}$ if $k < 2^\kappa + 2^{\kappa-1}$ and $\beta_k = \frac{2}{2\kappa+3}$ if $k \geq 2^\kappa + 2^{\kappa-1}$. In the latter case, the strategies for 2, 3, 5, 7 reach respectively $\beta_2 = \frac{2}{5}$ (see [10]), $\beta_3 = \frac{5}{14}$ (see [13]), $\beta_5 = \frac{14}{45}$ and $\beta_7 = \frac{2}{7}$. Thanks to our rewriting of the constraints, we are able to improve to $\beta_5 = \frac{40}{129}$ and $\beta_7 = \frac{15}{53}$. Our new optimality proofs are given in the full version of the paper [24].

5 Quantum Algorithms for Single-Solution k-XOR

The algorithms of Sect. 4 solve the Many-solutions case (Problem 1). Following again the study in [21], we extend the merging trees to target the Single-solution case. In this section, we assume QRAQM.

When only a few solutions are to be found, *merging* does not seem to help at first sight, since it puts more constraints on the solution tuples. However, an interesting idea is to merge with arbitrary constraints, e.g., by choosing a prefix t, and to repeat this for every value of t. Obviously, the set of all merging trees obtained by looping on the value of t contains all k-tuples of elements, so the solution cannot be missed.

This is the core idea of Schroeppel and Shamir's 4-SUM algorithm [23] and more generally, the *Dissection* algorithms of [12, Section 3]. In the quantum setting, it encompasses some proposed algorithms such as the element distinctness (Single-solution 2-XOR) algorithm of [8].

The classical algorithms are intended to decrease the memory usage while keeping the time equal or close to the classical birthday bound $\mathcal{O}(2^{n/2})$. In contrast, the quantum algorithms allow to *decrease* the time complexity with respect to the quantum birthday bound $\mathcal{O}(2^{n/3})$, as shown in [5,21].

5.1 Extended Merging Trees

The *extended merging trees* that we use in this paper subsume those given in [21], with a technical trick that will allow smaller complexities. The optimal strategies turn out to have a very simple description. Thus, we defer their derivation in the full version of the paper [24], and we focus here on the actual algorithms.

A merging tree is now extended with *repetition loops*. We make the selection of some arbitrary prefixes, or more generally, sublists of list nodes. This choice defines *a subset of the merging tree*. We complete the merging process. If a solution is obtained, then this choice of subset was good. These repetition loops are performed with quantum searches.

Note that in Sect. 4, we only needed QRACM, as all intermediate lists could be written down classically, and quantum access was only necessary to sample their elements. Here, we need to write down lists *under a quantum search*, which is why QRAQM is necessary.

Remark 1 (Amending the constraints). Our improved complexities with respect to [21] rely on the following idea. A subtree $\mathcal{T}^j$ of width k^j can cost 0 inside the repetitions if a global cost $2^{\frac{k^j}{k}n}$ (in time and memory) has been already paid. Indeed, when $\mathcal{T}^j$ is of width 1, a full lookup table of h can be prepared beforehand and reused instead of having to rebuild the tree in each search iteration. Likewise, we can prepare the sorted list of all k^j-tuples (which is of size $\left(2^{\frac{n}{k}}\right)^{k^j}$) in order to retrieve quickly those having a wanted prefix.

5.2 New Results for Single-Solution k-XOR

Remark 1 allows us to reach better exponents than [21], and to break the previous lower bound of 0.3 for k-list merging.

Theorem 3 (New trees for single-solution k-XOR). *Let $k > 2$ be an integer. The best extended merging tree (with our definition) finds a k-XOR in time $\mathcal{O}(2^{\gamma_k n})$ where:*

$$\gamma_k = \frac{k + \lfloor \frac{k+6}{7} \rfloor + \lfloor \frac{k+1}{7} \rfloor - \lfloor \frac{k}{7} \rfloor}{4k} . \tag{4}$$

In particular, γ_k converges towards a minimum $\frac{2}{7}$, reached by multiples of 7.

The proof of this optimality is given in the full version of the paper [24]. The formula of Theorem 3 comes from the reduction of the constraints to a simple linear optimization problem with two integer variables. These variables are sufficient to describe the shape of the corresponding tree.

Optimal Trees. For $k \leq 5$, the results of Theorem 3 and [21] coincide and we can refer to [21]. The novelty of Theorem 3 appears with Algorithm 1 (Fig. 3), whose total time complexity is, up to a constant:

$$\underbrace{2^{2n/7}}_{\substack{\text{Building } \mathcal{L}_{34} \\ \text{and } \mathcal{L}_{67}}} + \underbrace{2^{n/7}}_{\text{Search of } s} \left(\underbrace{2^{n/7}}_{\text{Computing } \mathcal{L}_{567}} + \underbrace{2^{n/7}}_{\text{Search in } \mathcal{L}_{12}} \right) = \mathcal{O}\left(2^{2n/7}\right) .$$

It benefits from computing some products of lists *outside the loops*. Interestingly, this also modifies the memory requirements: only $2^{n/7}$ QRAQM is required, in order to hold $\mathcal{L}_{567}$, and $2^{2n/7}$ QRACM is needed for $\mathcal{L}_{34}$ and $\mathcal{L}_{67}$.

Algorithm 1. New Single-solution 7-XOR algorithm. As a quantum algorithm, each **Sample** becomes a quantum search.

> **Input:** 7 lists $\mathcal{L}_i$ of size $2^{n/7}$
> **Output:** a 7-tuple $(x_i) \in \prod_i \mathcal{L}_i$ that XORs to 0
> 1: Build $\mathcal{L}_{67} = \mathcal{L}_6 \bowtie_0 \mathcal{L}_7$ (all sums between these two lists)
> 2: Build $\mathcal{L}_{34} = \mathcal{L}_3 \bowtie_0 \mathcal{L}_4$ (all sums between these two lists)
> 3: **Sample** $s \in \{0,1\}^{2n/7}$ ▷ $2^{n/7}$ quantum search iterates
> 4:   Build $\mathcal{L}_{567} = \mathcal{L}_5 \bowtie_s \mathcal{L}_{67}$ ▷ Time $2^{n/7}$, which is the size of the list
> 5:   **Sample** $x \in \mathcal{L}_1 \times \mathcal{L}_2$ ▷ $2^{n/7}$ quantum search iterates
> 6:   Find $y \in \mathcal{L}_{34}$ such that $x \oplus y = s|*$
> 7:   Find $z \in \mathcal{L}_{567}$ such that $x \oplus y \oplus z = 0_{3n/7}|*$
> 8:   **return** "good" if $x \oplus y \oplus z = 0$, "not good" otherwise
> 9:   **EndSample**
> 10:   **return** "good" if there is a solution x, "not good" otherwise
> 11: **EndSample**

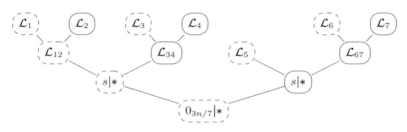

Fig. 3. Single-solution 7-XOR merging tree of Algorithm 1.

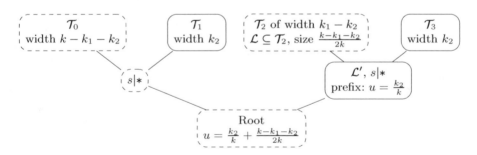

Fig. 4. Generic merging tree that reaches the optimal complexity for single-solution k-XOR (see Algorithm 2).

Algorithm 2. Generic Single-solution k-XOR algorithm. As a quantum algorithm, each **Sample** becomes a quantum search.

Input: k lists $\mathcal{L}_i$ of size $2^{n/k}$
Output: a k-tuple $(x_i) \in \prod_i \mathcal{L}_i$ that XORs to 0
1: Select k_1, k_2 by Equation 5
2: Build $\mathcal{T}_1$ and $\mathcal{T}_3$, each with the product of k_2 lists
3: **Sample** $s \in \{0,1\}^{\frac{k_2}{k}n}$
4:     **Sample** Sublists $\mathcal{L}$ of $\mathcal{T}_2$ of size $\frac{k-k_1-k_2}{2k}$
5:        Merge $\mathcal{L}$ with $\mathcal{T}_3$ to obtain a list $\mathcal{L}'$ with prefix s and size $\frac{k-k_1-k_2}{2k}$
6:        **Sample** $x \in \mathcal{T}_0$ $\triangleright$ $2^{\frac{k-k_1-k_2}{2k}n}$ quantum search iterates
7:           Find $y \in \mathcal{T}_1$ such that $x \oplus y = s|*$
8:           **return** "good" if there is a collision with $\mathcal{L}'$, "not good" otherwise
9:        **EndSample**
10:        **return** "good" if there is a solution, "not good" otherwise
11:     **EndSample**
12:     **return** "good" if there is a solution, "not good" otherwise
13: **EndSample**

The optimal strategy for a bigger k actually mimics the 7-XOR example. We introduce two integer variables k_1 and k_2 with the values:

$$k_1 = \left\lfloor \frac{3k}{7} \right\rceil , \qquad k_2 = \left\lfloor \frac{2k}{7} \right\rfloor - \left\lfloor \frac{k-1}{7} \right\rfloor + \left\lfloor \frac{k-2}{7} \right\rfloor , \qquad (5)$$

where $\left\lfloor \frac{3k}{7} \right\rceil$ is the integer closest to $\frac{3k}{7}$, and we perform Algorithm 2. The tree structure (Fig. 4) is overly simple: there are four subtrees, each of which is a trivial product of lists (a merge with empty prefixes). There is only a single repetition loop, and the whole algorithm contains only two levels of quantum search. Intuitively, the subtrees end up being "trivial" because enforcing a prefix of length un would induce a new quantum search loop with $2^{un/2}$ iterates (all prefixes must be searched). Instead, a better strategy is to forget the prefix and pay the cost $2^{un/2}$ later on, when sampling the parent. A formal proof is given in the full version of the paper [24]. The fact that this choice of structure matches the complexity given by Theorem 3 also follows from it.

Memory Complexity. Our algorithms for single-solution k-XOR reach the best time complexity $\mathcal{O}(2^{2n/7})$ when k is a multiple of 7, but at these points, they require a QRACM of size $2^{2n/7}$. This is suboptimal with respect to the time-memory product. By optimizing for it, we obtained the same results as [21]. The experiments suggest that the list sizes in the tree never exceed $2^{n/k}$ in that case. For trees with a list size fixed to $2^{n/k}$, we observe that the best time-memory product decreases for small k, reaches a minimum at $k = 17$ with $\widetilde{\mathcal{O}}(2^{\frac{7}{17}n})$, and increases again later, as it behaves like $(k - \mathcal{O}(\sqrt{k}))/2$. More details are provided in the full version of the paper [24].

On Memory Models. The balance between QRACM and QRAQM is interesting here, since in general, we will use more QRACM than QRAQM. An interesting question is whether we can completely eliminate QRAQM. In this setting, the best procedure remains to cut the lists in three complete products of equal size, and do a quantum search on two groups for a match on the third one. This converges towards $\widetilde{\mathcal{O}}(2^{n/3})$ and this complexity is reached for multiples of 3.

6 Extension with Quantum Walks

The algorithms presented so far are the best ones achievable *in the restricted model of quantum merging trees*. One of the open questions left in [21] was whether it was possible to improve generically the time complexity using quantum walks. We find that this is the case, yielding a better curve than Theorem 3 that we will now explicit. In particular, we obtain the first 4-SUM algorithm with complexity below $\mathcal{O}(2^{0.3n})$ (obtained in [5] with a quantum walk).

Theorem 4 (Single-solution k-XOR with quantum walks). *Let $k > 2$ be an integer. There exists a quantum Single-solution k-XOR algorithm running in time $\widetilde{\mathcal{O}}(2^{\gamma_k n})$ where:*

$$\gamma_k = \frac{2k - \lfloor \frac{k}{7} \rfloor - \lfloor \frac{k+3}{7} \rfloor}{6k} . \tag{6}$$

In particular, γ_k converges towards a minimum $\frac{2}{7}$, reached by multiples of 7.

6.1 Preliminaries

In this paper, we only need quantum walks to solve the following problem.

Problem 2 (Single claw-finding). Let f, g be two functions of different domains $\{0,1\}^{\ell_1 n}, \{0,1\}^{\ell_2 n}$, that we can query quantumly, with the promise that there exists either a single *claw* (x, y) such that $f(x) = g(y)$, or none. Determine the case and find the claw.

This is an extension of the *element distinctness* problem, or Single-solution 2-XOR, and it can be solved by similar algorithms. In particular, we will consider Ambainis' algorithm [1] which is a quantum walk for element distinctness running in time $\mathcal{O}(2^{2\ell n/3})$ when $\ell_1 = \ell_2 = \ell$. We will give some high-level ideas and refer to [1,5,16] for applications of quantum walks to k-SUM algorithms.

When there is a single function h, Ambainis' algorithm is a walk on a *Johnson graph*, where a vertex represents a subset of 2^{nr} elements, for some parameter r. We move randomly on the walk by replacing elements, until the vertex contains the wanted collision. The classical time complexity of such a random walk (up to a logarithmic factor) is: $\left(2^{rn} + \frac{2^{2\ell n}}{2^{2rn}}(2^{rn})\right)$, where $\frac{2^{2\ell n}}{2^{2rn}}$ is the number of "walk steps" that one should do classically before finding a marked vertex, and 2^r is the number of vertex updates before arriving to a new uniformly random vertex. The corresponding quantum walk algorithm, either in the specific

example of Ambainis [1], or the more generic MNRS framework [19], achieves:
$2^{rn} + \sqrt{\frac{2^{2\ell n}}{2^{2rn}}} \left(\sqrt{2^{rn}} \right)$, using a quantum memory (QRAQM) of size 2^{rn} and the
same number of quantum queries to h.

When there are two functions f, g with domains of different size, we will use a
random walk on a *product Johnson graph*, as in [16]. We choose two parameters
r_1, r_2; the vertices now contain $2^{r_1 n}$ elements queried to f and $2^{r_2 n}$ elements
queried to g, with $r_1 \leq \ell_1$ and $r_2 \leq \ell_2$. The quantum time complexity becomes:

$$2^{r_1 n} + 2^{r_2 n} + \sqrt{\frac{2^{(\ell_1 + \ell_2)n}}{2^{(r_1 + r_2)n}}} \left(2^{r_1 n/2} + 2^{r_2 n/2} \right) .$$

By symmetry between r_1 and r_2, we can choose $r_1 = r_2 = r$ and restrict ourselves
to a single parameter.

Theorem 5 (Adaptation of [1,16]). *There exists a quantum algorithm solving
the single claw-finding problem with domains $\ell_1 n$ and $\ell_2 n$, in time $\widetilde{\mathcal{O}}(2^{\tau n})$ and
memory $\mathcal{O}(2^{rn})$, where: $\tau = \max\left(r, \frac{\ell_1 + \ell_2 - r}{2}\right)$, for any r such that $r \leq \ell_1, r \leq \ell_2, r \geq 0$.*

This algorithm succeeds with constant probability. Up to a polynomial factor,
it can be boosted to any probability exponentially close to 1, and thus, used as
a subroutine in a quantum search.

6.2 Using Quantum Walks in a Merging Tree

Since we did not include quantum walks in our merging tree framework, it
remains an open question whether the algorithms obtained here are the best
possible. Our goal is merely to improve on what we presented above, using Theorem 5 as a building block.

We reuse the tree structure of Fig. 4, where $\mathcal{T}_0$ to $\mathcal{T}_3$ are the nodes at level
2, which are products of base lists. Thus, we reuse most of the structure of
Algorithm 2, except that the parameters will be re-optimized and that the two
innermost **Sample** loops are replaced by a single call to **Claw-finding**. This is
why we reach an improved time complexity. The new choice of k_1 and k_2 is:

$$k_1 = \begin{cases} \lfloor \frac{k+1}{7} \rfloor + \lfloor \frac{k+4}{7} \rfloor + \lfloor \frac{k+6}{7} \rfloor \text{ for } k \geq 4 \\ 1, 1, 2 \text{ for } k = 2, 3, 4 \text{ respectively} \end{cases} \quad , \quad k_2 = \lfloor \frac{k}{7} \rfloor + \lfloor \frac{k+4}{7} \rfloor . \quad (7)$$

The key idea of Algorithm 3 is that the knowledge of $\mathcal{T}_1$ and $\mathcal{T}_3$, and the constraints of merging, make sure that we can run the quantum walk as expected.
That is, we can query $\mathcal{T}_0 \bowtie_s \mathcal{T}_1$ and $\mathcal{T}_2 \bowtie_s \mathcal{T}_3$ in time $\mathcal{O}(1)$.

By definition of k_1 and k_2, the product lists $\mathcal{T}_0, \mathcal{T}_1, \mathcal{T}_2, \mathcal{T}_3$ have respective
widths $(k - k_1 - k_2)$, k_2, $(k_1 - k_2)$, k_2. Thus, taking into account the quantum
search on the right prefix s, and using Theorem 5, we compute the following
time complexity for Algorithm 3:

$$2^{\frac{k_2}{2k}n} \left(2^{rn} + 2^{\left(\frac{k-k_1-k_2}{2k} + \frac{k_1-k_2}{2k} - r \right)n} \times 2^{rn/2} \right) + 2^{\frac{k_2}{k}n} , \quad (8)$$

Algorithm 3. Single-solution k-XOR algorithm with a quantum walk.

Input: k lists $\mathcal{L}_i$
Output: a k-tuple $(x_i) \in \prod_i \mathcal{L}_i$ that XORs to 0
1: Select k_1, k_2 by Equation (7)
2: Build $\mathcal{T}_1$ and $\mathcal{T}_3$, each with the product of k_2 lists
3: **Sample** $s \in \{0,1\}^{\frac{k_2}{k}n}$
4:    Apply **Claw-finding** between the lists $\mathcal{T}_0 \bowtie_s \mathcal{T}_1$ and $\mathcal{T}_2 \bowtie_s \mathcal{T}_3$
5:    **return** "good" if a claw is found, "not good" otherwise
6: **EndSample**

---

where r is the parameter specifying the size of the vertex. The corresponding QRACM used is $2^{\frac{k_2}{k}n}$, the corresponding QRAQM (for the walks) is 2^{rn}, and the total memory is the maximum between both.

Thus, when k_1, k_2 are free, the time complexity exponent t of Algorithm 3 is solution to the following optimization problem:

$$(\text{C1}) \; t \geq \tfrac{k_2}{2k} + r \qquad (\text{C2}) \; t \geq \tfrac{k_2}{k} \qquad (\text{C3}) \; t \geq \tfrac{k-k_2}{2k} - \tfrac{r}{2}$$
$$(\text{C4}) \; r \leq \tfrac{k-k_1-k_2}{k} \qquad (\text{C5}) \; r \leq \tfrac{k_1-k_2}{k}$$

Here (C1) and (C3) correspond to the walks, (C2) to the computation of lists $\mathcal{L}_1$ and $\mathcal{L}_3$ *outside* the main loop. (C4) and (C5) are the constraints imposed on our choice of r. Solving this optimization problem gives us the choice of k_1 and k_2 specified by Eq. (7), and the time complexity exponent of Theorem 4.

6.3   Results

In Fig. 5, we compare Algorithm 3 with the previous work of [21] (where the formula was $\gamma_k = \frac{1}{k}\frac{k+\lceil k/5 \rceil}{4}$) and to the intermediate result of Theorem 3. Numerical results are given in the full version of the paper [24]. Our curve improves or subsumes all previous works on k-XOR (including the special cases of Ambainis' algorithm for $k = 2$ and [5] for 4-SUM).

The algorithm for 4-SUM is very simple. We start from 4 lists. Two of them are stored in QRACM. Then, we do a quantum search over a prefix of $\frac{n}{4}$ bits. In order to find the good one, we search for a claw between the two level-1 lists of size $2^{\frac{n}{4}}$. Thus the complexity is of order: $\sqrt{2^{\frac{n}{4}}} \times 2^{\frac{n}{4} \times \frac{2}{3}} = 2^{7n/24}$.

6.4   Applications

Similarly as those of [21], the algorithms of this paper apply to the class of *bicomposite* problems studied by Dinur et al. [12]. This correspondence is actually easier to see than in [21], because our algorithms have a simple description.

A prominent example of bicomposite search is multiple-encryption, where we search for the key used by a block cipher made of a sequential composition of independent block ciphers.

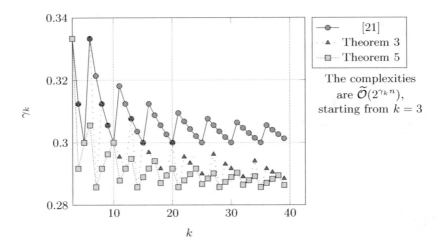

Fig. 5. Single-solution k-XOR time complexity, and comparison with [21].

Problem 3 (r-encryption). Let $E^1, \ldots, E^r$ be r random block ciphers on n bits, indexed by key spaces of the same size 2^n. Assume that we are given r plaintext-ciphertext pairs (p_i, c_i), encrypted by the composition of the E^i under a sequence of independent keys $k_1, \ldots, k_r$:

$$\forall i, c_i = \left(E^r_{k_r} \circ \ldots \circ E^1_{k_1} \right)(p_i), \quad \text{then retrieve } k_1, \ldots, k_r.$$

Theorem 6. *For any* $r \geq 2$, *let* γ_r *be the time complexity exponent given by Theorem 4. Then there exists a quantum algorithm for r-encryption, of time complexity* $\mathcal{O}(2^{\gamma_r rn})$.

In particular, we obtain an algorithm for 4-encryption (Algorithm 4) that runs in time $\widetilde{\mathcal{O}}(2^{7n/6})$ for $4n$ bits of key, improving the previous $\widetilde{\mathcal{O}}(2^{5n/4})$ [21].

Algorithm 4. 4-encryption algorithm.

    Input: 4 plaintext-ciphertext pairs (p_i, c_i)
    Output: the sequence of 4 keys k_1, k_2, k_3, k_4
1: Build the list $\mathcal{L}_1$: $\{E^1_{k_1}(p_1), k_1 \in \{0,1\}^n\}$
2: Build the list $\mathcal{L}_4$: $\{(E^4_{k_4})^{-1}(c_4), k_4 \in \{0,1\}^n\}$
3: **Sample** $s \in \{0,1\}^n$
4:     Define: $\mathcal{L}_{12}$ the list of all (k_1, k_2) such that $E^1_{k_1}(p_1) = (E^2_{k_2})^{-1}(s)$
                 ▷ It is easy to sample from $\mathcal{L}_{12}$, by taking a random key k_2, computing
    $(E^2_{k_2})^{-1}(s)$, and looking in $\mathcal{L}_1$ for a match
5:     Define: $\mathcal{L}_{34}$ the list of all (k_3, k_4) such that $E^3_{k_3}(s) = (E^4_{k_4})^{-1}(c_4)$
6:     Search a claw between $\mathcal{L}_{12}$ and $\mathcal{L}_{34}$, if it exists: a pair $(k_1, k_2), (k_3, k_4)$ such that all p_i encrypt to all c_i
7:     **return** "good" if a claw exists, "not good" otherwise
8: **EndSample**

---

7   Conclusion

In this paper, we simplified the analysis of quantum k-XOR algorithms and improved the previous results for the single-solution case, leading to the best known quantum algorithms for *bicomposite search* and multiple-encryption.

We have found significant advantage in combining *merging trees* and *quantum walks*, such as improving the previous best algorithm for 4-SUM. However, this advantage vanishes in the long run, and both methods converge towards the same exponent $\frac{2}{7}$. For now, a problem that can be reduced to k-SUM for any k (such as subset-sum) does not see any improvement from using walks.

It is possible, although we have not attempted, to define a bigger class of merging tree algorithms built entirely over quantum walks, possibly with nested walks. This would be much more technical, and it is difficult to estimate whether one would gain a significant advantage. Whether this might improve the exponent $\frac{2}{7}$ is an interesting open question.

Acknowledgement. The author would like to thank André Chailloux and María Naya-Plasencia for many discussions and comments on intermediate versions of this work, as well as Pierre Briaud, Johanna Loyer and the anonymous reviewers of SAC for their comments. This work has been supported by the European Union's H2020 project No. 714294 (QUASYModo) and by ERC-ADG-ALGSTRONGCRYPTO (project 740972).

References

1. Ambainis, A.: Quantum walk algorithm for element distinctness. SIAM J. Comput. **37**(1), 210–239 (2007)
2. Bai, S., Galbraith, S.D., Li, L., Sheffield, D.: Improved combinatorial algorithms for the inhomogeneous short integer solution problem. J. Cryptol. **32**(1), 35–83 (2019)
3. Becker, A., Coron, J.-S., Joux, A.: Improved generic algorithms for hard knapsacks. In: Paterson, K.G. (ed.) EUROCRYPT 2011. LNCS, vol. 6632, pp. 364–385. Springer, Heidelberg (2011). https://doi.org/10.1007/978-3-642-20465-4_21
4. Belovs, A., Spalek, R.: Adversary lower bound for the k-SUM problem. In: ITCS, pp. 323–328. ACM (2013)
5. Bernstein, D.J., Jeffery, S., Lange, T., Meurer, A.: Quantum algorithms for the subset-sum problem. In: Gaborit, P. (ed.) PQCrypto 2013. LNCS, vol. 7932, pp. 16–33. Springer, Heidelberg (2013). https://doi.org/10.1007/978-3-642-38616-9_2
6. Bonnetain, X., Bricout, R., Schrottenloher, A., Shen, Y.: Improved classical and quantum algorithms for subset-sum. In: Moriai, S., Wang, H. (eds.) ASIACRYPT 2020. LNCS, vol. 12492, pp. 633–666. Springer, Cham (2020). https://doi.org/10.1007/978-3-030-64834-3_22
7. Brassard, G., Hoyer, P., Mosca, M., Tapp, A.: Quantum amplitude amplification and estimation. Contemp. Math. **305**, 53–74 (2002)
8. Buhrman, H., et al.: Quantum algorithms for element distinctness. SIAM J. Comput. **34**(6), 1324–1330 (2005)
9. Camion, P., Patarin, J.: The Knapsack Hash Function proposed at Crypto'89 can be broken. In: Davies, D.W. (ed.) EUROCRYPT 1991. LNCS, vol. 547, pp. 39–53. Springer, Heidelberg (1991). https://doi.org/10.1007/3-540-46416-6_3

10. Chailloux, A., Naya-Plasencia, M., Schrottenloher, A.: An efficient quantum collision search algorithm and implications on symmetric cryptography. In: Takagi, T., Peyrin, T. (eds.) ASIACRYPT 2017. LNCS, vol. 10625, pp. 211–240. Springer, Cham (2017). https://doi.org/10.1007/978-3-319-70697-9_8

11. Dinur, I.: An algorithmic framework for the generalized birthday problem. Des. Codes Cryptogr. **87**(8), 1897–1926 (2018). https://doi.org/10.1007/s10623-018-00594-6

12. Dinur, I., Dunkelman, O., Keller, N., Shamir, A.: Efficient dissection of composite problems, with applications to cryptanalysis, knapsacks, and combinatorial search problems. In: Safavi-Naini, R., Canetti, R. (eds.) CRYPTO 2012. LNCS, vol. 7417, pp. 719–740. Springer, Heidelberg (2012). https://doi.org/10.1007/978-3-642-32009-5_42

13. Grassi, L., Naya-Plasencia, M., Schrottenloher, A.: Quantum algorithms for the k-xor problem. In: Peyrin, T., Galbraith, S. (eds.) ASIACRYPT 2018. LNCS, vol. 11272, pp. 527–559. Springer, Cham (2018). https://doi.org/10.1007/978-3-030-03326-2_18

14. Grover, L.K.: A fast quantum mechanical algorithm for database search. In: STOC, pp. 212–219. ACM (1996)

15. Howgrave-Graham, N., Joux, A.: New generic algorithms for hard knapsacks. In: Gilbert, H. (ed.) EUROCRYPT 2010. LNCS, vol. 6110, pp. 235–256. Springer, Heidelberg (2010). https://doi.org/10.1007/978-3-642-13190-5_12

16. Kachigar, G., Tillich, J.-P.: Quantum information set decoding algorithms. In: Lange, T., Takagi, T. (eds.) PQCrypto 2017. LNCS, vol. 10346, pp. 69–89. Springer, Cham (2017). https://doi.org/10.1007/978-3-319-59879-6_5

17. Kirshanova, E., Mårtensson, E., Postlethwaite, E.W., Moulik, S.R.: Quantum algorithms for the approximate k-list problem and their application to lattice sieving. In: Galbraith, S.D., Moriai, S. (eds.) ASIACRYPT 2019. LNCS, vol. 11921, pp. 521–551. Springer, Cham (2019). https://doi.org/10.1007/978-3-030-34578-5_19

18. Kuperberg, G.: Another subexponential-time quantum algorithm for the dihedral hidden subgroup problem. In: TQC. LIPIcs, vol. 22, pp. 20–34. Schloss Dagstuhl - Leibniz-Zentrum für Informatik (2013)

19. Magniez, F., Nayak, A., Roland, J., Santha, M.: Search via quantum walk. SIAM J. Comput. **40**(1), 142–164 (2011)

20. Minder, L., Sinclair, A.: The extended k-tree algorithm. J. Cryptol. **25**(2), 349–382 (2012)

21. Naya-Plasencia, M., Schrottenloher, A.: Optimal merging in quantum k-xor and k-sum algorithms. In: Canteaut, A., Ishai, Y. (eds.) EUROCRYPT 2020. LNCS, vol. 12106, pp. 311–340. Springer, Cham (2020). https://doi.org/10.1007/978-3-030-45724-2_11

22. Nikolić, I., Sasaki, Yu.: Refinements of the k-tree algorithm for the generalized birthday problem. In: Iwata, T., Cheon, J.H. (eds.) ASIACRYPT 2015. LNCS, vol. 9453, pp. 683–703. Springer, Heidelberg (2015). https://doi.org/10.1007/978-3-662-48800-3_28

23. Schroeppel, R., Shamir, A.: A $t = \mathcal{O}(2^{n/2}), s = \mathcal{O}(2^{n/4})$ algorithm for certain np-complete problems. SIAM J. Comput. **10**(3), 456–464 (1981)

24. Schrottenloher, A.: Improved quantum algorithms for the k-XOR problem. IACR Cryptol. ePrint Arch. **2021**, 407 (2021)

25. Wagner, D.: A generalized birthday problem. In: Yung, M. (ed.) CRYPTO 2002. LNCS, vol. 2442, pp. 288–304. Springer, Heidelberg (2002). https://doi.org/10.1007/3-540-45708-9_19

26. Zhandry, M.: How to record quantum queries, and applications to quantum indifferentiability. In: Boldyreva, A., Micciancio, D. (eds.) CRYPTO 2019. LNCS, vol. 11693, pp. 239–268. Springer, Cham (2019). https://doi.org/10.1007/978-3-030-26951-7_9

Quantum Boomerang Attacks and Some Applications

Paul Frixons[1,2], María Naya-Plasencia[2], and André Schrottenloher[3(✉)]

[1] Orange Labs, Caen, France
[2] Inria, Paris, France
{paul.frixons,maria.naya_plasencia}@inria.fr
[3] Cryptology Group, CWI, Amsterdam, The Netherlands
andre.schrottenloher@m4x.org

Abstract. In this paper, we study quantum key-recovery attacks on block ciphers. While it is well known that a quantum adversary can generically speed up an exhaustive search of the key, much less is known on how to use specific vulnerabilities of the cipher to accelerate this procedure. In this context, we show how to convert classical boomerang and mixing boomerang attacks into efficient quantum key-recovery attacks. In some cases, we can even obtain a quadratic speedup, the same as simple differential attacks. We apply this technique to a 5-round attack on SAFER++.

Keywords: Boomerang attack · Post-quantum security · Mixing boomerang attack · SAFER++ · AES

1 Introduction

In symmetric cryptography, cryptanalysis is the base of the confidence we have in the primitives we use. In order to consider a primitive secure, we need to constantly evaluate it with respect to all known attack families. One of the most well known families of attacks is boomerang attacks, introduced by Wagner in [28]. They are a particular type of differential attacks that, instead of considering a long differential trail in the primitive (a propagation of differences from the plaintext through the ciphertext), combine several short ones that have high individual probabilities. While differential attacks usually consider pairs of plaintexts having a certain difference, boomerang attacks use quartets instead. They have shown to be effective (or the most effective known attacks) against several primitives like [3,16], and have seen many improvements, like recently [11].

The quantum security of symmetric primitives has attracted an increasing interest in the last few years. Some works have targeted the security of generic constructions, for example [21–23], while others have studied the security of actual designs [5,7,20]. Many have proposed quantum versions of popular classical attacks, like for instance [6,21].

R. AlTawy and A. Hülsing (Eds.): SAC 2021, LNCS 13203, pp. 332–352, 2022.
https://doi.org/10.1007/978-3-030-99277-4_16

In this paper, as in most of these previous works, we consider key-recovery attacks in the single secret-key setting. Here it is well-known that Grover's quantum search algorithm [19] can be used to quadratically speed up the exhaustive search of the key. However, when the design under study admits some vulnerability (e.g., a classical attack exists), a faster quantum key-recovery procedure might exist. Designing such procedures from classical design patterns is often a non-trivial task. It is known that if a classical attack can be represented as a sequence of nested exhaustive searches, then it can be converted into a sequence of quantum searches: this framework was applied in [7] to Square [12,17] and DS Meet-in-the-Middle attacks [13,14]. But not all attacks can be covered this way, and many of them still seem difficult to translate.

Boomerang Attacks. In this paper, we consider Boomerang attacks, which form a particular type of differential attacks introduced by Wagner in [28]. We study how to build an efficient quantum version of boomerang attacks and of mixing boomerang attacks [15] recently introduced in the context of AES. We propose, for the first time, efficient *quantum boomerang attacks*, and we apply them to several reduced-round versions of well known ciphers.

The quantum attacks studied in this paper are also based on quantum search. One should note that, since quantum search always provides a quadratic speedup, our procedures admit a quadratic speedup at best. By comparing with the quadratic speedup of exhaustive key search, it follows that we will not be able to attack more rounds than in the classical setting: any quantum attack in our framework can be converted back into a valid classical attack. Though this result can seem rather negative at first sight, our new attacks, like previous works with similar conclusions [7,21], tend to show that block ciphers should be assumed to retain half of their bits of classical security against quantum adversaries, even when this security has been reduced with respect to the generic key search.

Outline. In Sect. 2, we give a broad introduction to the boomerang attacks we will quantize later and detail the quantum tools that we use within this paper. In Sect. 3, we present quantum algorithms for boomerang distinguishers, last-round attacks and mixing boomerang attacks. In Sect. 4, we show an attack on 5 rounds of the block cipher SAFER++ (where the best classical attack reaches 5.5 rounds). In Sect. 5 we study a related-key attack against AES-256, with more details given in the full version of the paper [18]. We conclude the paper in Sect. 6.

2   Preliminaries

In this section, we introduce the classical Boomerang attack from [28] and the Mixing Boomerang attack from [15]. We give generic formulas for their time complexity depending on the parameters of the cipher attacked. Next, we introduce our quantum tools. We stress that knowledge of quantum computing is not required to understand our work, as we will use standard quantum algorithms (such as Grover search) as black-box components, and design our attacks from a rather abstract perspective.

Throughout this paper, we consider an n-bit block cipher E, with unknown key k. Standard block ciphers (SPNs or Feistel schemes) are built by iterating a round function, and we will sometimes decompose E into subciphers, e.g., $E = E_2 \circ E_1$ where E_1 forms the r_1 first rounds and E_2 the r_2 last rounds.

Boomerang cryptanalysis is a subset of differential cryptanalysis, which studies the propagation of differences in a cipher. Given a cipher (or subcipher) E, and a pair of differences $(\Delta_{in}, \Delta_{out})$, we say that $\Delta_{in} \to \Delta_{out}$ is a *differential* for E of probability:

$$\Pr\left(\Delta_{in} \xrightarrow{E} \Delta_{out}\right) = \Pr_X(E(X \oplus \Delta_{in}) \oplus E(X) = \Delta_{out}) \ .$$

Since E is a keyed function, the probability of a differential depends on the choice of key. In the analysis, it is usually computed on average over the key. When running an attack, we consider a black box with a fixed given key. We then assume that the differential probability is equal to the analyzed average (even if there is a small variation in practice, we may run the attack again with another estimate – this is valid for classical as well as quantum attacks).

2.1   The Classical Boomerang Attack

We briefly describe the *boomerang distinguisher* introduced in [28] and the last-round key-recovery attack that can be based on it. The notation that we introduce here $(E, p, q, \alpha, \ldots)$ will be kept throughout the paper.

Boomerang Distinguisher. As above, let E be a block cipher of block size n and key size k, that can be decomposed into: $E = E_2 \circ E_1$. We assume that each part has a high-probability differential: $\alpha \to \beta$ for E_1 and $\delta \to \gamma$ for E_2^{-1}.

$$\Pr\left(\alpha \xrightarrow{E_1} \beta\right) = p_\downarrow, \quad \Pr\left(\beta \xrightarrow{E_1^{-1}} \alpha\right) = p_\uparrow, \quad \Pr\left(\delta \xrightarrow{E_2^{-1}} \gamma\right) = q \ .$$

The distinguisher is given in Algorithm 1. It uses $\frac{4}{p_\downarrow p_\uparrow q^2}$ encryptions, decryptions, and negligible memory. We can check its correctness as follows (see also Fig. 1 for the notations):

Step 3: using the differential on E_1; with probability $p_\downarrow$, $E_1(P_1) \oplus E_1(P_2) = \beta = E_2^{-1}(C_1) \oplus E_2^{-1}(C_2)$

Step 4: using the differential on E_2^{-1}; with probability q^2, $E_2^{-1}(C_3) \oplus E_2^{-1}(C_1) = \gamma$ and $E_2^{-1}(C_4) \oplus E_2^{-1}(C_2) = \gamma$. Thus, by summing these equations: $E_2^{-1}(C_3) \oplus E_2^{-1}(C_4) = E_2^{-1}(C_1) \oplus E_2^{-1}(C_2) = \beta$.

Step 5: since we have established $E_2^{-1}(C_1) \oplus E_2^{-1}(C_2) = \beta$ with probability $p_\downarrow q^2$, it remains to satisfy the differential on E_1^{-1}, and we obtain $P_3 \oplus P_4 = \alpha$ with probability $p_\uparrow \times p_\downarrow q^2$.

Then, the full path is satisfied with probability $(p_\downarrow p_\uparrow q)^2$ instead of 2^{-n} for a random permutation, and making $1/(p_\downarrow p_\uparrow q)^2$ trials is enough to determine the case. Usually, we also have $p_\downarrow = p_\uparrow = p$ and this formula simplifies into $(pq)^2$.

Algorithm 1. Boomerang Distinguisher

> **Input:**   oracle access to $E = E_2 \circ E_1$, and its inverse (or a random permutation)
> **Output:**   "E" or "Random"
> 1: **Repeat** $(p_\uparrow p_\downarrow q)^{-2}$ **times**   ▷ (probability of success of $\frac{1}{2}$)
> 2:   Select P_1 at random and set $P_2 = P_1 \oplus \alpha$
> 3:   Encrypt: $C_1 = E(P_1)$ and $C_2 = E(P_2)$
> 4:   Compute: $C_3 = C_1 \oplus \delta$ and $C_4 = C_2 \oplus \delta$
> 5:   Decrypt: $P_3 = E^{-1}(C_3)$ and $P_4 = E^{-1}(C_4)$
> 6:   **if** $P_4 = P_3 \oplus \alpha$ **then return** "E"
> 7: **EndRepeat**
> 8: **return** "Random"

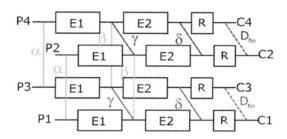

Fig. 1. Last-round key recovery

Key Recovery on the Last Round. We now explain how to build a key-recovery attack using this boomerang distinguisher.

We append one (or more) additional rounds R to the cipher, which is now $E = R \circ E_2 \circ E_1$ (if the additional round is at the beginning, consider E^{-1}). Let D_{fin} denote the set of differences that can be obtained from δ after the additional rounds, p_{out} the probability that we get δ back from an element in D_{fin} by computing the last rounds backwards, and k_{out} the number of key bits involved in these additional rounds. We need D_{fin} to be a vector space. This is usually the case as most of the time, non-zero components of δ become unknown after a passage through an S-Box. This property is used to make data *structures* of the form $\{X \oplus \Delta / \Delta \in D_{\text{fin}}\}$, from which we can extract quadratically many pairs with differences in D_{fin}: $\forall \Delta_1, \Delta_2, (X \oplus \Delta_1) \oplus (X \oplus \Delta_2) = \Delta_1 \oplus \Delta_2 \in D_{\text{fin}}$.

To simplify for now, we assume that $\frac{1}{\sqrt{p_{out}}pq} < |D_{\text{fin}}|$, in which case a single structure is needed. Otherwise when $\frac{1}{\sqrt{p_{out}}pq} \geq |D_{\text{fin}}|$, we will actually generate multiple structures with $|D_{\text{fin}}|$ ciphertexts each, so that they form a total of $\frac{1}{p_{out}(pq)^2}$ pairs.

Algorithm 2 detects a good guess of the k_{out} key bits using the boomerang distinguisher. We will now explain its correctness and compute its average time complexity (up to a constant factor).

We start by generating a structure S of $\frac{1}{\sqrt{p_{out}}pq}$ ciphertexts with differences in D_{fin}. This first step costs a time and memory: $\frac{1}{\sqrt{p_{out}}pq}$.

Algorithm 2. Boomerang last-round attack

Input: oracle access to $E = R \circ E_2 \circ E_1$
Output: guess of partial key K_{out} involved in the round(s) R
1: Generate a *structure* S of $\frac{1}{\sqrt{p_{\text{out}}pq}}$ ciphertexts of the form: $S \subseteq \{X \oplus \Delta, \Delta \in D_{\text{fin}}\}$
2: $L_{\text{pairs}} \leftarrow \emptyset$
3: Compute all the $C' = E(E^{-1}(C) \oplus \alpha)$ for all $C \in S$, sort S by values of C'
4: **ForEach** pair C'_i, C'_j such that $C'_i \oplus C'_j \in D_{\text{fin}}$
5:      $L_{\text{pairs}} \leftarrow L_{\text{pairs}} \cup \{(C_i, C_j, C'_i, C'_j)\}$
6: **EndFor** ▷ Here $|L_{\text{pairs}}| = \frac{|D_{\text{fin}}|}{2^n} \frac{1}{p_{\text{out}}(pq)^2}$
▷ Note that S being sorted, these pairs are computed efficiently
7: $L_{\text{triplets}} \leftarrow \emptyset$
8: **ForEach** pair $C_i, C_j, C'_i, C'_j \in L_{\text{pairs}}$
9:      **ForEach** possible value K_{out} of the k_{out} bits of key
▷ $2^{k_{\text{out}}}$ trials, $2^{k_{\text{out}}}p_{\text{out}}^2$ solutions
10:         If both (C_i, C_j) and (C'_i, C'_j) lead to a difference δ through R^{-1} under K_{out}
11:         $L_{\text{triplets}} \leftarrow L_{\text{triplets}} \cup \{(C_i, C_j, K_{\text{out}})\}$
12:      **EndFor**
13: **EndFor** ▷ Here $|L_{\text{triplets}}| = \frac{|D_{\text{fin}}|}{2^n} \frac{1}{(pq)^2} 2^{k_{\text{out}}}p_{\text{out}}$
14: **return** all guesses of K_{out} in the triplet list

Now we will partially decrypt these ciphertexts and obtain pairs with difference δ. Among the $\frac{1}{p_{\text{out}}(pq)^2}$ pairs (C_i, C_j) in S, we expect $\frac{1}{(pq)^2}$ of them to be such that $R^{-1}(C_i) \oplus R^{-1}(C_j) = \delta$, where R involves the actual partial key K_{out} used in the last rounds. Then we define $C'_i = E(E^{-1}(C_i) \oplus \alpha)$ and $C'_j = E(E^{-1}(C_j) \oplus \alpha)$. By the boomerang property, with probability $(pq)^2$, we will have $R^{-1}(C'_i) \oplus R^{-1}(C'_j) = \delta$. This difference gets then mapped to D_{fin} with probability 1. Obtaining the list L_{pairs} costs $\frac{2}{\sqrt{p_{\text{out}}pq}}$ data and memory and $\frac{1}{\sqrt{p_{\text{out}}pq}} \log\left(\frac{1}{\sqrt{p_{\text{out}}pq}}\right)$ computations for sorting the C'_i (since D_{fin} is a vector space, we can sort according to its cosets). This sorting allows to extract efficiently the pairs C'_i, C'_j such that $C'_i \oplus C'_j \in D_{\text{fin}}$ at Step 4 of Algorithm 2.

There are enough quartets (C_i, C_j, C'_i, C'_j) in L_{pairs} to ensure that, for the good key guess of K_{out}, one of them is an actual boomerang quartet. Let C_{out} be the time complexity to obtain all valid keys K_{out} for a given pair (C_i, C_j) (Step 9 in Algorithm 2 is the naive way to do so, but there is usually a better algorithm). Since we expect on average $2^{k_{\text{out}}}p_{\text{out}}^2$ such keys, we have $C_{\text{out}} \geq 2^{k_{\text{out}}}p_{\text{out}}^2$.

After having obtained the list L_{pairs} of size $\frac{|D_{\text{fin}}|}{2^n} \frac{1}{p_{\text{out}}(pq)^2}$, we find all possible key guesses for each of these pairs, that is, all possible K_{out} such that (C_i, C_j) and (C'_i, C'_j) lead to a difference δ through R^{-1} (in which case they form a boomerang quartet). This costs a time $\frac{|D_{\text{fin}}|}{2^n} \frac{1}{p_{\text{out}}(pq)^2} C_{\text{out}}$. The list of triplets obtained is of size: $\frac{|D_{\text{fin}}|}{2^n} \frac{2^{k_{\text{out}}}p_{\text{out}}}{(pq)^2}$, and we know that the actual key K_{out} occurs in one of these triplets, because one of the pairs went through the boomerang. Thus, if we have: $\frac{|D_{\text{fin}}|}{2^n} \frac{2^{k_{\text{out}}}p_{\text{out}}}{(pq)^2} \leq 2^{k_{\text{out}}}$, we have reduced the number of possibilities for K_{out}.

We perform an exhaustive search over the remaining $k - k_{\text{out}}$ bits of key. We obtain a key-recovery attack of total time complexity:

$$\frac{1}{\sqrt{p_{\text{out}}}pq} \log\left(\frac{1}{\sqrt{p_{\text{out}}}pq}\right) + \frac{|D_{\text{fin}}|}{2^n} \frac{1}{p_{\text{out}}(pq)^2} \left(C_{\text{out}} + p_{\text{out}}^2 2^k\right) \ , \qquad (1)$$

in number of queries to E and E^{-1} or evaluations of the cipher. Note that C_{out} is counted relatively to the cost of an evaluation of E. The memory used is: $\max\left(\frac{2}{\sqrt{p_{\text{out}}}pq}, \frac{|D_{\text{fin}}|}{2^n} \frac{2^{k_{\text{out}}} p_{\text{out}}}{(pq)^2}\right)$. The data used is: $\frac{2}{\sqrt{p_{\text{out}}}pq}$.

Remark 1. Another situation commonly encountered in Boomerang attacks is when two (or more) boomerang pairs occur within the trials. In that case, it is possible to recognize immediately the good guess of K_{out}, as the only one that appears in two (or more) triples in the list L_{triplets}.

2.2   Mixing Boomerang Attacks

This variant of boomerang attacks [15] is related to mixture distinguishers.

Distinguisher. As in Sect. 2.1, the cipher is decomposed as $E = E_2 \circ E_1$ and we assume that a good (truncated) differential $\alpha \to \beta$ exists on E_1 with probability $p_\downarrow$ forwards and with probability $p_\uparrow$ backwards. We further assume that E_2 can be divided into a "left" and a "right" part $E_2 = (E_{2,L}, E_{2,R})$ (see the notations on Fig. 2).

The distinguisher relies on the independence of $E_{2,L}$ and $E_{2,R}$. It requires $\frac{4}{p_\downarrow p_\uparrow}$ encryptions-decryptions, operations and negligible memory. We repeat:

1. Select P_1 at random, set $P_2 = P_1 \oplus \alpha$ and encrypt $C_1 = E(P_1)$ and $C_2 = E(P_2)$
2. Compute $C_3 = (C_{1,L}, C_{2,R})$ and $C_4 = (C_{2,L}, C_{1,R})$
3. Decrypt: $P_3 = E^{-1}(C_3)$ and $P_4 = E^{-1}(C_4)$

Indeed, in Step 1 we have $E_1(P_1) \oplus E_1(P_2) = \beta$ with probability $p_\downarrow$. By definition of E, $E_1(P_i) = E_2^{-1}(C_i)$, so in Step 2, we know that $E_2^{-1}(C_1) \oplus E_2^{-1}(C_2) = \beta$. If we separate $\beta = \beta_L \| \beta_R$, this rewrites:

$$\begin{cases} E_{2,L}^{-1}(C_{1,L}) \oplus E_{2,L}^{-1}(C_{2,L}) = \beta_L \\ E_{2,R}^{-1}(C_{1,R}) \oplus E_{2,R}^{-1}(C_{2,R}) = \beta_R \end{cases} . \qquad (2)$$

Thus, by definition of C_3, C_4, we also have $E_2^{-1}(C_3) \oplus E_2^{-1}(C_4) = \beta$. Finally in Step 3, with probability $p_\uparrow$, β gets mapped to α. After $(p_\downarrow p_\uparrow)^{-1}$ iterations, we obtain a valid quartet with probability $1/2$.

Attack on First Round. We append one or more additional rounds R before those covered by the distinguisher. Similarly as before, we write $E = E_2 \circ E_1 \circ R$. We let D_{start} denote the set of differentials that can lead to α for the additional rounds R, p_{in} the probability to get α from an element of D_{start} and k_{in} the number of bits of the key involved in the additional rounds.

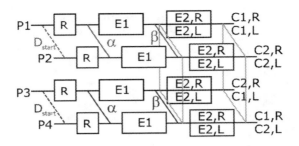

Fig. 2. First-round mixing boomerang attack.

Step 1: Generating Pairs. We generate a list of $\frac{1}{p_{\mathrm{in}}p_{\downarrow}p_{\uparrow}}$ pairs of plaintexts (P_1, P_2) such that their difference is in D_{start}. Again, there can be one or multiple structures, but as the term $\frac{1}{p_{\mathrm{in}}p_{\downarrow}p_{\uparrow}}$ (the number of pairs) will appear in the complexity, there is no difference between these two cases.

For each pair (P_1, P_2) we compute:

$$(C_1 = E(P_1), C_2 = E(P_2)), \quad (C_3 = (C_{1,L}, C_{2,R}), C_4 = (C_{2,L}, C_{1,R}),$$
$$(P_3 = E^{-1}(C_3), P_4 = E^{-1}(C_4)) . \quad (3)$$

For each pair, we have $R(P_1) \oplus R(P_2) = \alpha$ with probability p_{in}. Then, $(E_2 \circ E_1)^{-1}(C_3) \oplus (E_2 \circ E_1)^{-1}(C_4) = \alpha$ with probability $p_{\downarrow}p_{\uparrow}$. Thus, we expect that one pair satisfies the boomerang distinguisher; by decrypting through R we fall back on D_{start}.

Thus, we keep only the pairs (P_1, P_2) such that $P_3 \oplus P_4 \in D_{\mathrm{start}}$, among which the pair that went through the boomerang must remain. We get a list of $\frac{|D_{\mathrm{start}}|}{2^n} \frac{1}{p_{\mathrm{in}}p_{\downarrow}p_{\uparrow}}$ pairs at a cost of $\frac{4}{p_{\mathrm{in}}p_{\downarrow}p_{\uparrow}}$ computations and data.

Step 2: Sieving Key Bits. For each one of the kept pairs (P_1, P_2), we determine the values of K_{in} (the k_{in} bits of key that intervene in R) such that P_1, P_2 and P_3, P_4 both lead to a difference α through R. The average expected number of possible values for K_{in} for each pair is thus $2^{k_{\mathrm{in}}}(p_{\mathrm{in}})^2$. We let C_{in} denote the cost of finding all these possible values.

At a cost of $\frac{|D_{\mathrm{start}}|}{2^n} \frac{1}{p_{\mathrm{in}}p_{\downarrow}p_{\uparrow}}C_{\mathrm{in}}$ computations, we get a list of $\frac{|D_{\mathrm{start}}|}{2^n} \frac{1}{p_{\downarrow}p_{\uparrow}}2^{k_{\mathrm{in}}}p_{\mathrm{in}}$ elements $(P_1, P_2, K_{\mathrm{in}})$. If we have:

$$\frac{|D_{\mathrm{start}}|}{2^n} \frac{1}{p_{\downarrow}p_{\uparrow}}2^{k_{\mathrm{in}}}p_{\mathrm{in}} < 2^{k_{\mathrm{in}}} , \quad (4)$$

then we have reduced the number of possible values for K_{in} and we do an exhaustive search of the remaining $k - k_{\mathrm{in}}$ bits of key. The attack has a total time complexity:

$$\frac{1}{p_{\mathrm{in}}p_{\downarrow}p_{\uparrow}} + \frac{|D_{\mathrm{start}}|}{2^n} \frac{1}{p_{\mathrm{in}}p_{\downarrow}p_{\uparrow}} \left(C_{\mathrm{in}} + p_{\mathrm{in}}^2 2^k\right) , \quad (5)$$

in number of queries to E and E^{-1} or evaluations of the cipher. Note that C_{in} is counted relatively to the cost of an evaluation of E.

2.3   Quantum Tools

In this paper, we consider quantum algorithms written in the *quantum circuit model* (see [27] for an introduction). A quantum circuit starts with a pool of qubits initialized in a basis state. The state is modified through the application of *quantum gates*. The *time complexity* is the number of gates of the circuit. The memory complexity is the width of the circuit, or the number of qubits.

Complexity Estimations. A quantum procedure qualifies as an attack if it runs with a lower time complexity than the corresponding quantum generic procedure (in this paper, key-recovery via Grover's algorithm). Since we only need to perform comparisons, we can use as cost metric the evaluation of the primitive that is attacked. In our case, the time is counted in evaluations of the cipher E as a *quantum circuit*, and the memory in multiples of its block size n.

Quantum RAM. We shall specify whether or not our algorithms require the *quantum RAM* model, which can be seen as the quantum counterpart of classical random-access. In this model, a "qRAM" gate of cost 1 allows to perform memory lookups in superposition (see [2]).

Amplitude Amplification. We will use as a black-box the Amplitude Amplification framework of [8], which generalizes Grover's quantum search [19].

Theorem 1 ([8], Theorem 2 and 4). *Let $\mathcal{A}$ be a quantum algorithm that uses no intermediate measurements, let $f : X \to \{0,1\}$ be a boolean function that tests if an output of $\mathcal{A}$ is "good". Let a be the success probability of $\mathcal{A}$. Let $\theta_a = \arcsin\sqrt{a}$ and $0 < \theta_a \leq \frac{\pi}{2}$. There exists a quantum algorithm* Amplify$(\mathcal{A}, f)$ *that runs in time:* $\left\lfloor \frac{\pi}{4\theta_a} \right\rfloor (2T_\mathcal{A} + T_f + \mathcal{O}(\log_2|X|))$ *, where $T_\mathcal{A}$ is the time complexity of $\mathcal{A}$ and T_f is the time complexity of a quantum algorithm for f. Measuring the output of* Amplify$(\mathcal{A}, f)$ *yields a "good" output of $\mathcal{A}$ with probability* $\max(1-a, a)$. *If a is known exactly, then the probability of success can be brought to 1.*

We will neglect the term $\mathcal{O}(\log_2|X|)$ since our complexity is expressed in quantum circuits for the attacked cipher, usually much more expensive. The memory consumed by the procedure itself is also usually negligible with respect to the memory of $\mathcal{A}$ and f.

To the quantum procedure Amplify$(\mathcal{A}, f)$, there corresponds a *classical* exhaustive search procedure with about $\left(\lfloor \pi/(4\theta_a) \rfloor \right)^2$ iterations, which consists in a **Repeat** loop that calls $\mathcal{A}$ and tests its output until it satisfies the constraint f. Since $\mathcal{A}$ in Theorem 1 can be *any* quantum algorithm, especially another quantum search, there is a recursive correspondence between classical procedures made of such **Repeat** loops and quantum procedures made of nested quantum searches [7]. It follows that many quantum attacks, including the ones of this paper, can be first described classically.

More precisely, we will write down our algorithms using a **Repeat** block which specifies a number of iterations. Inside, we run a randomized algorithm

$\mathcal{A}$ followed by a test f (**If** block) that checks if the current state is "good" or "bad". It is then expected that, if a good state exists, it is found after the specified number of iterations. Using Theorem 1, we make this algorithm correspond to Amplify$(\mathcal{A}, f)$. If a solution exists, then Amplify$(\mathcal{A}, f)$ produces it (or a superposition of possible solutions).

Searching for Collisions. We will also need to solve the following problem: given access to a random function $f : \{0, 1\}^n \to \{0, 1\}^m$, where $n \geq \frac{m}{2}$, find a pair (x, y) such that $f(x) = f(y)$. This can be done classically by sorting $\mathcal{O}\left(2^{m/2}\right)$ queries to f. In the quantum setting, we can either use quantum search among the pairs (x, y), for a time $\mathcal{O}\left(2^{m/2}\right)$ and a negligible memory, or *quantum collision search*. In that case we use Ambainis' algorithm [2], which works even in the worst case $n = \frac{m}{2}$ (where a single collision exists on expectation). It requires the qRAM model. The precise analysis made in [10] gives a number of $\left(\frac{\pi}{2}\right)^2 2^{m/3}$ queries in our case for an overwhelming success. These queries are the dominant term. Note that the lower bound on quantum collision search for random functions [1,29] prevents the existence of a more efficient algorithm

2.4 On Quantum Scenarios

In quantum symmetric cryptanalysis, there exist two scenarios that depend on the capabilities of the attacker. • the Q1 setting allows an attacker to perform quantum computations, but he can only use classical queries to black-box primitives (in this paper, an encryption oracle in the secret-key model). • the Q2 setting allows the attacker to query the black-box as a *quantum* oracle instead of a classical oracle. Although the latter is much more powerful, it remains nontrivial. Besides, as shown in [7], when attacks requires low data, it is sometimes possible to replace Q2 queries by Q1. Thus, when following classical design patterns to perform quantum key-recoveries, like in [7], it seems more suitable to consider the Q2 model by default and then see if they can be avoided afterwards. Note that it is not unusual for quantum attacks to require superposition queries, as it is the case of many attacks in [21].

3   Quantum Boomerang Attacks

In this section, we adapt the attacks presented in Sect. 2 to the quantum setting.

3.1 Quantum Boomerang Distinguisher

Similarly to the differential attacks from [21], the boomerang distinguisher of Algorithm 1 can be accelerated *in the Q2 setting* (Algorithm 3). The **Repeat** loop becomes a quantum search with $\frac{\pi}{4}(pq)^{-1}$ iterations looking for an element P_1 such that $P_1, P_1 \oplus \alpha$ forms a boomerang pair. If E satisfies the expected property, such a P_1 will be found, otherwise measuring the result will give us an invalid pair. We make in total $\frac{\pi}{4}(pq)^{-1} \times 8$ queries to E and E^{-1} (each query is made twice for reversibility), which are in superposition since the quantum search space is on the value P_1.

Algorithm 3. Quantum Boomerang Distinguisher

> **Input:** *superposition* oracle access to $E = E_2 \circ E_1$, or a random permutation
> **Output:** "E" or "Random"
> 1: **Repeat** $\frac{\pi}{4}(pq)^{-1}$ **times**
> 2:   Select P_1 at random
> 3:   **If** $E^{-1}(E(P_1) \oplus \delta) = E^{-1}(E(P_1 \oplus \alpha) \oplus \delta) \oplus \alpha$ **then**
> 4:   the state (P_1) is "good" **Else** the state (P_1) is "bad"
> 5: **EndRepeat**
> 6: Measure and check if a solution was found
> 7: **If** it was found **return** "E" **Else Return** "Random"

3.2   Quantum Boomerang Last-Rounds Attack

Recall that the last-rounds attack of Sect. 2.1 is in two phases: first, we use the boomerang property to sieve the k_{out} bits that intervene in the last rounds R. Second, we perform an exhaustive search on the $k - k_{\text{out}}$ remaining key bits.

For now, let us put aside the small constant factors. We count all quantum times in evaluations of E or E^{-1} and consider a Q2 query to E or E^{-1} to cost the same. The generic key-recovery is Grover's exhaustive search, with a time $2^{k/2}$ and a negligible number of Q1 queries. Our first idea is to go below that using the sieve on the k_{out} bits of key that the Boomerang property gives. If we can produce the superposition of valid K_{out} with a time complexity below $2^{(k-k_{\text{out}})/2}$, and if there are strictly less than $2^{k_{\text{out}}}$ elements in this superposition, then we can do better than Grover search: we Amplify an algorithm that first samples a K_{out}, then tries to complete the key in time $2^{(k-k_{\text{out}})/2}$.

In order to produce a possible value of K_{out}, we look for a pair C_1, C_2 such that: • $C_1 \oplus C_2 \in D_{\text{fin}}$ and $C_1' \oplus C_2' \in D_{\text{fin}}$, where $C_i' = E(E^{-1}(C_i) \oplus \alpha)$; • there exists a subkey K_{out} such that (C_1, C_2) and (C_1', C_2') decrypt to the difference δ through R^{-1} under K_{out}.

Finding a valid pair C_1, C_2 is a collision search problem, solved with Ambainis' algorithm[1]. Let us assume that $D_{\text{fin}} \geq 2^{n/3}$, which corresponds to the case where a single structure is enough. A structure contains $|D_{\text{fin}}|^2$ pairs, and the constraint $C_1' \oplus C_2' \in D_{\text{fin}}$ selects a proportion $\frac{|D_{\text{fin}}|}{2^n}$ of them. Thus there is at least one solution.

We now check the number of iterations in the loops of Algorithm 4.

Step 1: the number of iterations to perform depends on the probability that a subkey guess K_{out}, obtained with the procedure in the loop, is the good one. In the classical analysis of the procedure, we obtained a list of $\frac{|D_{\text{fin}}|}{2^n} \frac{2^{k_{\text{out}}} p_{\text{out}}}{(pq)^2}$ tuples $(C_1, C_2, C_1', C_2', K_{\text{out}})$, and we took the key K_{out} from one of these tuples. We know that the good one is in one of these tuples. The computation inside the **Repeat** loop is the same, so the probability of success (the full key is found) is $\frac{2^n}{|D_{\text{fin}}|} \frac{(pq)^2}{2^{k_{\text{out}}} p_{\text{out}}}$ and the number of iterations follows.

---

[1] If there are many solutions, an alternative is the BHT algorithm [9].

Algorithm 4. Quantum Last-rounds Key-recovery

Input: *superposition* oracle access to E and E^{-1}

Output: the full key

1: **Repeat** $(\frac{|D_{\text{fin}}|}{2^n} \frac{2^{k_{\text{out}}} p_{\text{out}}}{(pq)^2})$ **times**

2:     Sample a subkey guess K_{out} using:

3:     **Repeat** $(\frac{1}{2^{k_{\text{out}}} p_{\text{out}}^2})$ **times**

4:         Use Ambainis' algorithm to find a valid pair (C_1, C_2, C_1', C_2')

5:         **Repeat** $2^{k_{\text{out}}}$ **times**

6:             Sample a guess of K_{out}

7:             **If** $R^{-1}(C_1) \oplus R^{-1}(C_2) = \delta = R^{-1}(C_1') \oplus R^{-1}(C_2')$ then K_{out} is "good"

8:         **EndRepeat**

9:         **If** we obtained a valid K_{out} then (C_1, C_2, C_1', C_2') is "good"

10:     **EndRepeat**

11:     Given this subkey guess K_{out}:

12:     **Repeat** $2^{(k-k_{\text{out}})}$ **times**

13:         Sample a choice of the $k - k_{\text{out}}$ other key bits, check if the full K matches

14:     **EndRepeat**

15:     **If** we obtained a valid full key K then K_{out} is "good"

16: **EndRepeat**

17: Measure K_{out}, recompute K and return it

Step 3: here, we are iterating on tuples (C_1, C_2, C_1', C_2') until we find a key candidate. The probability that a tuple yields a key candidate is $2^{k_{\text{out}}} p_{\text{out}}^2$, thus there are $\max(1, \frac{1}{\sqrt{2^{k_{\text{out}}} p_{\text{out}}^2}})$ iterations. We will assume $2^{k_{\text{out}}} p_{\text{out}}^2 \leq 1$. Note that the key candidate (actually the superposition of all possible candidates for the given pair) is obtained by exhaustive search, but a more involved procedure could likely be applied in order to reduce the time complexity.

Step 12: having obtained a candidate for K_{out}, it remains to try it: for this, we perform a simple Grover search over the remaining $k - k_{\text{out}}$ bits.

By changing the loops into nested quantum searches, the *quantum* time complexity of Algorithm 4 is:

$$\sqrt{\frac{|D_{\text{fin}}|}{2^n} \frac{2^{k_{\text{out}}} p_{\text{out}}}{(pq)^2}} \left(\frac{1}{\sqrt{2^{k_{\text{out}}} p_{\text{out}}^2}} \left(\left(\frac{2^n}{|D_{\text{fin}}|}\right)^{1/3} + 2^{k_{\text{out}}/2} \right) + 2^{(k-k_{\text{out}})/2} \right)$$

$$= \underbrace{\sqrt{\frac{|D_{\text{fin}}|}{2^n} \frac{2^{k_{\text{out}}} p_{\text{out}}}{(pq)^2}}}_{<2^{k_{\text{out}}/2} \text{ by the classical analysis}} \left(\frac{2^{n/3}}{2^{k_{\text{out}}/2} p_{\text{out}} |D_{\text{fin}}|^{1/3}} + \frac{1}{p_{\text{out}}} + \underbrace{2^{(k-k_{\text{out}})/2}}_{\text{Exhaustive search}} \right).$$

The algorithm requires Q2 queries to E and E^{-1}, and uses $(2^n/|D_{\text{fin}}|)^{1/3}$ qRAM due to the use of Ambainis' algorithm (or BHT) to find valid pairs. However, if we can replace the factor $(2^n/|D_{\text{fin}}|)^{1/3}$ by $(2^n/|D_{\text{fin}}|)^{1/2}$, then we can use a Grover search instead of Ambainis' algorithm, and the algorithm will now require a small number of qubits only.

Making the Attack Q1. Recall that the attack requires only a structure of $\frac{1}{\sqrt{p_{\text{out}}(pq)}}$ ciphertexts. For each of these, we will have to compute $E(E^{-1}(C) \oplus \alpha) := f(C)$. Thus, all the queries made to E and E^{-1} asked during the attack fall actually in a set of size $\frac{1}{\sqrt{p_{\text{out}}(pq)}}$. If we have $\frac{1}{\sqrt{p_{\text{out}}(pq)}} < 2^{k/2}$, then we can *make all the queries classically beforehand* and store the results in a quantum RAM of size $\frac{1}{\sqrt{p_{\text{out}}(pq)}}$. Inside Algorithm 4, we replace the on-the-fly computation of f by a memory lookup.

3.3   Quantum Mixing Boomerang Distinguisher

We now study the Mixing Boomerang attacks presented in Sect. 2.2. Since the distinguisher is a single loop similar to Algorithm 1, it can be replaced by a quantum search of a valid pair $(P_1, P_1 \oplus \alpha)$ with about $1/\sqrt{p_\downarrow p_\uparrow}$ iterations, with Q2 queries and negligible memory.

Quantum First-round Mixing Attack. The attack will work similarly as the quantum last-round attack of Algorithm 4. The main difference is that we do not need a collision search algorithm to filter out the valid pairs (P_1, P_2) such that $P_3 \oplus P_4 \in D_{\text{start}}$.

We analyze the time complexity of Algorithm 5, when translated into nested Amplitude Amplifications.

Step 1: here, the number of iterations depends on the number of possible keys K_{in} obtained in the sieving step. From the classical analysis, we know that there will be $\frac{|D_{\text{start}}|}{2^n} \frac{1}{p_\uparrow p_\downarrow} 2^{k_{\text{in}}} p_{\text{in}} < 2^{k_{\text{in}}}$ tuples $(P_1, P_2, P_3, P_4, K_{\text{in}})$ obtained, among which the good subkey K_{in} appears (at least once). Thus there are at most $\left(\frac{|D_{\text{start}}|}{2^n} \frac{1}{p_\uparrow p_\downarrow} 2^{k_{\text{in}}} p_{\text{in}} \right)^{1/2}$ iterations.

Step 3: from a valid quadruple (P_1, P_2, P_3, P_4), i.e., one that satisfies $P_1 \oplus P_2 \in D_{\text{start}}$ and $P_3 \oplus P_4 \in D_{\text{start}}$, the probability that we obtain a subkey guess is $2^{k_{\text{in}}} p_{\text{in}}^2$. This gives the number of iterations.

Step 5: the probability for a given pair to be valid is simply $\frac{|D_{\text{start}}|}{2^n}$.

Step 16: similarly to Algorithm 4, we complete the quantum search for the key.

The total quantum time complexity of Algorithm 5 is given by:

$$\sqrt{\frac{|D_{\text{start}}|}{2^n} \frac{2^{k_{\text{in}}} p_{\text{in}}}{p_\uparrow p_\downarrow}} \left(\frac{1}{\sqrt{2^{k_{\text{in}}} p_{\text{in}}^2}} \left(\sqrt{\frac{2^n}{|D_{\text{start}}|}} + 2^{k_{\text{in}}/2} \right) + 2^{(k-k_{\text{in}})/2} \right)$$
$$= \sqrt{\frac{|D_{\text{start}}|}{2^n} \frac{2^{k_{\text{in}}} p_{\text{in}}}{p_\uparrow p_\downarrow}} \left(\frac{2^{n/2}}{2^{k_{\text{in}}/2} p_{\text{in}} |D_{\text{start}}|^{1/2}} + \frac{1}{p_{\text{in}}} + 2^{(k-k_{\text{in}})/2} \right) . \quad (6)$$

The baseline algorithm does not use quantum RAM and requires only a small number of qubits, but it also relies on Q2 queries. Depending on the amount of data required, it may be possible to make it Q1: for this, we query all the $\frac{1}{p_{\text{in}} p_\uparrow p_\downarrow}$ pairs required by the classical attack, and store the tuples P_1, P_2, P_3, P_4 in a quantum RAM. This can only work if $\frac{1}{p_{\text{in}} p_\uparrow p_\downarrow} < 2^{k/2}$.

Algorithm 5. Quantum first-rounds key-recovery

    Input: *superposition* oracle access to E and E^{-1}
    Output: the full key
1: **Repeat** $\frac{|D_{\text{start}}|}{2^n} \frac{1}{p_\uparrow p_\downarrow} 2^{k_{\text{in}}} p_{\text{in}}$ **times**
2:    Sample a subkey guess K_{in} using:
3:    **Repeat** $1/(2^{k_{\text{in}}} p_{\text{in}}^2)$ **times**
4:        Sample a valid (P_1, P_2) using:
5:        **Repeat** $\frac{2^n}{|D_{\text{start}}|}$ **times**
6:            Sample a pair $P_1, P_2 = P_1 \oplus \alpha$, compute P_3, P_4 as in the distinguisher
7:            **If** $P_3 \oplus P_4 = \alpha$, then (P_1, P_2) is "good"
8:        **EndRepeat**
9:        **Repeat** $2^{k_{\text{in}}}$ **times**
10:          Sample a guess of K_{in}
11:          **If** $R(P_1) \oplus R(P_2) = \alpha = R(P_3) \oplus R(P_4)$, then K_{in} is "good"
12:        **EndRepeat**
13:        **If** there is a valid K_{in}, then $(P_1, P_2, K_{\text{in}})$ is "good"
14:    **EndRepeat**
15:    Given this subkey guess K_{in}:
16:    **Repeat** $2^{k-k_{\text{in}}}$ **times**
17:        Sample a choice of the $k - k_{\text{in}}$ other key bits, check if the full K matches
18:    **EndRepeat**
19:    If the valid full key K was obtained, K_{in} is good
20: **EndRepeat**
21: Measure K_{in}, recompute the full K and return it

---

4   Application to SAFER

SAFER is a family of block ciphers (Substitution-Permutation Networks) that dates back to the SAFER K-64 proposal of [24]. SAFER-K-64 was a block cipher of 64 bits. A new version SAFER+, with 128-bit blocks, was a candidate of the AES competition organized by the NIST [25]. Finally, another variant, SAFER++, was submitted to the NESSIE project [26]. Here, we focus on SAFER++ and more precisely, on the boomerang attack presented in [3]. It reaches 5.5 rounds out of 7 total rounds.

4.1   Description of the Cipher

We use $\boxplus$ and $\boxminus$ to denote addition and subtraction modulo 2^8. We consider the version of SAFER++ with a 128-bit key (and 128-bit blocks), which has 7 rounds. The round function (see or Fig. 1 in [3]) consists of key additions, a nonlinear layer and a linear layer. The state and the round keys are represented as 16 bytes numbered from 0 to 15, partitioned into $S_1 = \{0, 3, 4, 7, 8, 11, 12, 15\}$ and $S_2 = \{1, 2, 5, 6, 9, 10, 13, 14\}$. A single round performs the following steps:

Upper key addition: bytes in S_1 of the 16-byte round key are XORed to the corresponding bytes of the block and the others are added modulo 2^8.

Nonlinear layer: it uses two functions X and L:

$$X(a) = (45^a \bmod 257) \bmod 256, \quad L(a) = \log_{45}(a) \bmod 257 \text{ and } L(0) = 128, \tag{7}$$

where L is the inverse of X. Bytes in S_1 go through X and bytes in S_2 go through L.

Lower key addition: another 16-byte round key is added to the state, using modular addition in S_1 and XOR in S_2.

Linear layer: it repeats twice the following: a permutation of the bytes, followed by a Pseudo Hadamard Transform to groups of 4 bytes. This linear layer contains a total of 48 modular additions of individual bytes and can be described by the matrix given in [3].

4.2   5-Round Classical Boomerang Attack

We present the attack from [3]. It relies on a boomerang distinguisher on 4.5 rounds of SAFER++. If A denotes the linear layer and S the nonlinear layer (X and L), the distinguisher works against a sequence $A_0 S_1 A_1 - S_2 - A_2 S_3 A_3 S_4 A_4$. It would work against 4 rounds if any S-Boxes were used, but it reaches an additional 0.5 round thanks to the following property of the inverse-based S-Boxes in SAFER++:

$$\forall a, X(a) \boxplus X(a \boxplus 128) = 1 \bmod 256 \ . \tag{8}$$

The top part of the boomerang starts with pairs of plaintexts having difference $\alpha = (0, x, 0, 0, x, x, 0, 0, 0, 0, 0, -4x, 0, 0, x, -x)$. This difference is such that it maps to a single active byte after A_0, and up to 16 active bytes after $A_1 \circ S_1$.

The difference added to ciphertexts is:

$$\delta = (0, 0, 128, 0, 128, 128, 0, 0, 0, 0, 0, 0, 128, 0, 0, 0) \ .$$

After $S_4^{-1} \circ A_4^{-1}$, it maps to a difference $(0, 0, 0, 0, 0, x, -x, 0, \ldots)$ with probability 2^{-7} (not 2^{-8} because the difference 128 maps to odd differences through X). Then after A_3^{-1}, bytes 3, 9, 11 and 14 are active.

In order to traverse the middle S-Box, the authors observe that if the byte-differences coming both from the top and the bottom part of the boomerang are 128, then the boomerang traverses this S-Box layer for free. Indeed, if we encrypt $P_1, P_2 = P \boxplus 128$ through X, we obtain $X(P), 1 \boxminus X(P)$, i.e., two values that sum to 1. If the difference coming from the bottom part is 128, then the second pair of ciphertexts $C_3, C_4 = C_1 \boxplus 128, C_2 \boxplus 128$ still sums to 1. Thus, by going through X^{-1}, they get mapped to a difference 128 with probability 1.

Boomerang Attack. The full differential path of the classical 5-round boomerang attack of [3] is reproduced in Fig. 3. We use $S_0 A_0 S_1 A_1 - S_2 - A_2 S_3 A_3 S_4 A_4$ to denote the whole construction. The total probability for the boomerang to occur is: $(2^{-7-30.4})^2 2^{-40-8} = 2^{-122.8}$.

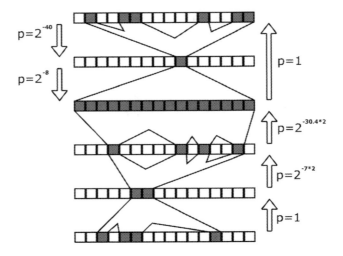

Fig. 3. Classical boomerang attack on SAFER++ (reproduction of Fig. 4 in [3])

Top boomerang: At the top, the difference is active in 6 bytes in positions 1, 4, 5, 11, 14, 15. This difference propagates to a single active byte after one round $(A_0 \circ S_0)$ with probability 2^{-40}, as there are 5 byte-conditions to meet. This difference is then mapped to a single active byte of difference 128 after the next nonlinear layer S_1, with probability 2^{-8}, and with probability 1, we obtain a difference 128 in bytes $0, 1, 2, 3, 8, 9, 11, 13, 14, 15$ after A_1. All other bytes are inactive.

Bottom boomerang: In the lower part of the boomerang, we start with a difference 128 (changing one bit) in the 4 bytes at positions 2, 4, 5, 12. By decrypting through $S_4 A_4$, this yields a difference $x, -x$ in bytes 5 and 6 with probability 1. By decrypting through $S_3 A_3$, this yields a difference active in bytes $3, 9, 11, 14$ with probability 2^{-7}. Then, by decrypting through A_2, we can obtain a difference 128 in all bytes except 2, 4, 9, 12 with probability $2^{-30.4}$.

Middle: In the middle, the S-Box trick allows to traverse the layer S_2 with probability 1. When going backwards from this middle to the top, everything propagates with probability 1.

We recall the attack procedure from [3] in Algorithm 6. It requires 2^{78} encryptions.

From a pool of 2^{48} plaintexts, we get approximately 2^{95} pairs, which have to satisfy an 80-bit condition, so we get 2^{15} pairs in Step 4. The probability that the structure contains a boomerang is approximately $2^{-27.8}$, so by using 2^{29} structures, we can expect two boomerang quartets to occur among the 2^{44} filtered quartets.

Algorithm 6. Classical attack on 5-round SAFER++ (adapted from [3], Sec. 6.3).

Input: access to E and E^{-1}
1: Prepare 2^{29} structures of 2^{48} plaintexts P_i that take all values in bytes 1, 4, 5, 11, 14 and 15 and are constant in the others
2: For each structure, obtain the ciphertexts $C_i = E(P_i)$
3: For each structure, add the difference δ (one bit in bytes 2, 4, 5, 12) to the C_i and decrypt: obtain $Q_i = E^{-1}(C_i \oplus \delta)$
4: For each structure, the Q_i on the values of the bytes that are constant in the P_i and keep the pairs Q_i, Q_j that have zero difference on these ten bytes
   $\triangleright$ We search for a difference after the S-Box of the form $(0, x, 0, 0, x, x, 0, 0, 0, 0, -4x, 0, 0, x, -x)$
5: For each possible quartet (P_j, P_k, Q_j, Q_k), search for the upper key bytes $K_0^4, K_0^{11}, K_0^{14}, K_0^{15}$ such that after the first S-Box layer, we have a difference $(x, -4x, x, -x)$ (x odd) between P_j and P_k and between Q_j and Q_k. The quartets are kept with their partial key and the observed x.
6: For each quartet, search for the key bytes K_0^1 and $K_{0'}^2$ (upper and lower key addition in byte 0) such that the difference after the first S-Box is the right one. Repeat this for K_0^5 and $K_{0'}^6$.
7: Find a suggestion of the 8 key bytes that appears twice, and run exhaustive search on the remaining bytes.

Next, we guess 4 bytes of the first upper round key $(K_0^4, K_0^{11}, K_0^{14}, K_0^{15})$ to remove wrong quartets. For each guess, we have a 25-bit condition on both pairs. Thus, 50 bits of restriction on the quartets. At this point, we obtain $2^{44} \times 2^{32} \times 2^{-50} = 2^{26}$ valid quartets and key guesses. Note that this already yields a valid key-recovery attack, as we have been able to reduce the number of possible $K_0^4, K_0^{11}, K_0^{14}, K_0^{15}$ from 2^{32} to 2^{26}.

For the next 4 key bytes guessed at Step 6, there is approximately one choice for each valid quartet currently kept. Thus, at this point, we have 2^{26} guesses of 8 bytes of the key, among which we expect the good one to occur. If we ran immediately an exhaustive search for the remaining 8 bytes, we would obtain a complexity $2^{26} \times 2^{8 \times 8} = 2^{90}$.

However, there are two valid boomerang pairs: one of the key guesses occurs twice. As the key guesses are 8 bytes and there are 2^{26} of them, we can expect that random collisions are not likely to occur, and the only key guess occurring twice is the good one. Thus exhaustive search is ran only once. The bottleneck of the complexity lies in encrypting and decrypting the 2^{29} structures, for a total of 2^{78} time and queries.

Extension. Another half round can be added at the end, by making 30 bits of additional key guess and running Algorithm 6 2^{30} times.

4.3   Quantum Boomerang Attack

Our quantum attack on 5-round SAFER++ uses the framework of Algorithm 4, adapted to the setting of the classical attack (Algorithm 6). We will first explain its time complexity, and show how it goes below Grover's exhaustive search in time 2^{64}. Recall that the time complexity is counted in number of evaluations of SAFER++.

Algorithm 7. Attack on 5-round SAFER++.

    Input: superposition access to E and E^{-1}
    Output: the full key
1: **Repeat** 2^{26} **times**
2:      Sample a guess for $K_0^4, K_0^{11}, K_0^{14}, K_0^{15}, K_0^1, K_{0'}^2, K_0^5, K_{0'}^6$ using:
3:      **Repeat** 2^{18} **times**   ▷ a valid quartet yields a key guess with prob. 2^{-18}
4:          Find a valid quartet
                     ▷ Either using Ambainis' algorithm, or quantum search
         ▷ We need the same number of quartets as classically: 2^{78} plaintexts in total
5:          **Repeat** 2^{32} **times**   ▷ at most one solution
6:              Pick a key guess $K_0^4, K_0^{11}, K_0^{14}, K_0^{15}$
7:              Check if this key guess yields the good difference $(x, -4x, x, -x)$ for both
     pairs of the quartet
8:          **EndRepeat**
9:          If a solution was found, return it (and the quartet)
10:      **EndRepeat**
11:      Search exhaustively for $K_0^1, K_{0'}^2$ and $K_{0'}^6$ (keep at most one value)
         ▷ there is on average one value; sometimes there can be more; but we only need
     this to work for the actual boomerang quartet
12:      Given the current guess of 8 bytes of key, complete the key by Grover search
13: **EndRepeat**
14: Measure and return the full key

Assuming that we use Grover search at Step 4 (instead of collision search), the attack *would* run in approximately:

$$\sqrt{2^{26}} \left(\sqrt{2^{18}} \left(\underbrace{\sqrt{2^{80}}}_{\text{Step 4}} + \underbrace{\sqrt{2^{32}} + 2 \cdot 2^{16}}_{\text{Step 11}} \right) + \underbrace{\sqrt{2^{64}}}_{\text{Step 12}} \right) \tag{9}$$

calls to SAFER++ and its inverse. The dominating term comes from the search for quartets satisfying the partial collision condition on 10 bytes. Indeed, the classical attack can sample these quartets very easily using structures. If we use classical search in Algorithm 7, we can obtain an attack running with polynomial memory in little less time than 2^{128}. However, in the quantum setting, additional factors from Amplitude Amplification will prevent that, so we must resort to quantum collision search in Step 4.

Since a structure is of size 2^{48} and we need 80 bits of collision, we can use Ambainis' algorithm to produce a superposition of colliding pairs (thus valid quartets) in about $(\pi/2)^2 2^{80/3} \simeq 2^{28.3}$ calls to E and E^{-1} in superposition.

Assuming that the numbers of iterations are exact, but putting the additional factors of quantum search, we obtain:

$$2\left\lfloor\frac{\pi}{4}2^{13}\right\rfloor\left(2\left\lfloor\frac{\pi}{4}2^9\right\rfloor\left(\underbrace{2^{28.3}\times 4}_{\text{Step 4}}+\underbrace{2\left\lfloor\frac{\pi}{4}2^{16}\right\rfloor+4\cdot2^{16}}_{\text{Step 11}}\right)+\underbrace{\left\lfloor\frac{\pi}{4}2^{32}\right\rfloor\times 4}_{\text{Step 12}}\right)$$

$$\simeq 2^{13.65}\left(2^{9.65}(2^{30.3}+2^{16.65}+2^{19})+2^{33.65}\right)\simeq 2^{53.6}<2^{64}\quad(10)$$

where the time is counted in computations of SAFER++ and its inverse, and we assume that a black-box (quantum) query costs the same. In the last step (quantum exhaustive search over 8 key bytes), we match against two given plaintext-ciphertext pairs.

In Step 12, we know that there is exactly one solution (or none) in a search space of size 2^{64}. Thus, we can run *exact* Amplitude Amplification with $\left\lfloor\frac{\pi}{4}2^{32}\right\rfloor$ iterations and succeed with probability 1 (either we find the solution, or prove that there is none). For the other loops, we can ensure a high probability of success by making a few assumptions on the *classical* attack: • the number of valid quartets for each structure is close to the average (this ensures that Ambainis' algorithm works as intended; if necessary we make multiple copies of it); • the actual boomerang pair yields only a single value at Step 11, and our algorithm does not lose it; • the probability, for a given guess of 8 key bytes sampled at Step 2, to be the good one, is close to 2^{-26}.

The attack requires 2^{27} registers of 256 qubits to store the values of P_i and $E^{-1}(E(P_i)\oplus\delta)$ for each P_i, and $2^{53.6}$ superposition queries to E and E^{-1}.

5   Application to Related-Key AES

In the full version of the paper [18], we detail the quantum version of a classical related-key attack on AES-256 from [4]. The classical attack recovers the key in time $2^{99.5}$ using a tuple of 4 related keys. With the same configuration, our quantum attack runs in time $2^{96.4}$ (counted in evaluations of the cipher, forwards and backwards), which is rather a minor improvement compared to what we could do with SAFER++.

The reason for this is that the structure of the attack is different from the framework of Sect. 3. Here, we are looking among the quartets (and all the key guesses that they generate) for a key guess that appears at least three times. With high probability, there is only one such guess, which corresponds to the three valid boomerang quartets that should exist in the search space.

Classically, it takes time N to examine N objects and find the one that appears three times. This *3-distinctness* problem can be solved quantumly with a generalization of Ambainis' element distinctness algorithm [2], but it will take time $\mathcal{O}\left(N^{3/4}\right)$, which is far from a square-root speedup. This is the core reason why this attack does not perform well.

In the quantum setting, it is a much better strategy to discriminate the right key guess by checking exhaustively the remaining bits of key (e.g., Step 12 in Algorithm 4). In the attack on AES-256, using the path of [4], this is not possible because there are too many bits remaining. There probably exists a more suitable path, which would yield a more efficient quantum procedure. We leave this as an open question.

6   Conclusion

In this paper we proposed an efficient quantum boomerang attack, as well as a variant for mixing boomerang attacks. We proposed several improvements for different cases, as reducing the quantum RAM need or making Q2 attacks work in Q1 under certain circumstances. In some cases, our attacks reach a quadratic speed up with respect to classical attacks. This shows that boomerang attacks are also performant cryptanalysis tools for the post-quantum world, that will be needed for correctly determining the best security margins.

Acknowledgment. This work has been supported by the European Union's H2020 project No. 714294 (QUASYModo) and by the ERC Advanced Grant ALGSTRONGCRYPTO (project 740972).

References

1. Aaronson, S., Shi, Y.: Quantum lower bounds for the collision and the element distinctness problems. J. ACM **51**(4), 595–605 (2004)
2. Ambainis, A.: Quantum walk algorithm for element distinctness. SIAM J. Comput. **37**(1), 210–239 (2007)
3. Biryukov, A., De Cannière, C., Dellkrantz, G.: Cryptanalysis of SAFER++. In: Boneh, D. (ed.) CRYPTO 2003. LNCS, vol. 2729, pp. 195–211. Springer, Heidelberg (2003). https://doi.org/10.1007/978-3-540-45146-4_12
4. Biryukov, A., Khovratovich, D.: Related-Key cryptanalysis of the full AES-192 and AES-256. In: Matsui, M. (ed.) ASIACRYPT 2009. LNCS, vol. 5912, pp. 1–18. Springer, Heidelberg (2009). https://doi.org/10.1007/978-3-642-10366-7_1
5. Bonnetain, X., Jaques, S.: Quantum period finding against symmetric primitives in practice. IACR Trans. Cryptogr. Hardw. Embed. Syst. **2022**(1), 1–27 (2022)
6. Bonnetain, X., Naya-Plasencia, M., Schrottenloher, A.: On quantum slide attacks. In: Paterson, K.G., Stebila, D. (eds.) SAC 2019. LNCS, vol. 11959, pp. 492–519. Springer, Cham (2020). https://doi.org/10.1007/978-3-030-38471-5_20
7. Bonnetain, X., Naya-Plasencia, M., Schrottenloher, A.: Quantum security analysis of AES. IACR Trans. Symmetric Cryptol. **2019**(2), 55–93 (2019)
8. Brassard, G., Hoyer, P., Mosca, M., Tapp, A.: Quantum amplitude amplification and estimation. Contemp. Math. **305**, 53–74 (2002)

9. Brassard, G., HØyer, P., Tapp, A.: Quantum cryptanalysis of hash and claw-free functions. In: Lucchesi, C.L., Moura, A.V. (eds.) LATIN 1998. LNCS, vol. 1380, pp. 163–169. Springer, Heidelberg (1998). https://doi.org/10.1007/BFb0054319
10. Childs, A.M., Eisenberg, J.M.: Quantum algorithms for subset finding. Quantum Inf. Comput. **5**(7), 593–604 (2005)
11. Cid, C., Huang, T., Peyrin, T., Sasaki, Yu., Song, L.: Boomerang connectivity table: a new cryptanalysis tool. In: Nielsen, J.B., Rijmen, V. (eds.) EUROCRYPT 2018. LNCS, vol. 10821, pp. 683–714. Springer, Cham (2018). https://doi.org/10.1007/978-3-319-78375-8_22
12. Daemen, J., Rijmen, V.: AES proposal: Rijndael. Submission to NIST AES competition (1999)
13. Demirci, H., Selçuk, A.A.: A meet-in-the-middle attack on 8-round AES. In: Nyberg, K. (ed.) FSE 2008. LNCS, vol. 5086, pp. 116–126. Springer, Heidelberg (2008). https://doi.org/10.1007/978-3-540-71039-4_7
14. Derbez, P., Fouque, P.-A., Jean, J.: Improved key-recovery attacks on reduced-round AES, in the single-key setting. In: Johansson, T., Nguyen, P.Q. (eds.) EUROCRYPT 2013. LNCS, vol. 7881, pp. 371–387. Springer, Heidelberg (2013). https://doi.org/10.1007/978-3-642-38348-9_23
15. Dunkelman, O., Keller, N., Ronen, E., Shamir, A.: The retracing Boomerang attack. In: Canteaut, A., Ishai, Y. (eds.) EUROCRYPT 2020. LNCS, vol. 12105, pp. 280–309. Springer, Cham (2020). https://doi.org/10.1007/978-3-030-45721-1_11
16. Dunkelman, O., Keller, N., Shamir, A.: A practical-time related-key attack on the KASUMI cryptosystem used in GSM and 3G telephony. J. Cryptol. **27**(4), 824–849 (2014)
17. Ferguson, N., et al.: Improved cryptanalysis of Rijndael. In: Goos, G., Hartmanis, J., van Leeuwen, J., Schneier, B. (eds.) FSE 2000. LNCS, vol. 1978, pp. 213–230. Springer, Heidelberg (2001). https://doi.org/10.1007/3-540-44706-7_15
18. Frixons, P., Naya-Plasencia, M., Schrottenloher, A.: Quantum boomerang attacks and some applications. IACR Cryptol. ePrint Arch. p. 060 (2022). https://eprint.iacr.org/2022/060
19. Grover, L.K.: A fast quantum mechanical algorithm for database search. In: STOC, pp. 212–219. ACM (1996)
20. Hosoyamada, A., Sasaki, Yu.: finding hash collisions with quantum computers by using differential trails with smaller probability than birthday bound. In: Canteaut, A., Ishai, Y. (eds.) EUROCRYPT 2020. LNCS, vol. 12106, pp. 249–279. Springer, Cham (2020). https://doi.org/10.1007/978-3-030-45724-2_9
21. Kaplan, M., Leurent, G., Leverrier, A., Naya-Plasencia, M.: Quantum differential and linear cryptanalysis. IACR Trans. Symmetric Cryptol. **2016**(1), 71–94 (2016)
22. Kuwakado, H., Morii, M.: Quantum distinguisher between the 3-round Feistel cipher and the random permutation. In: ISIT, pp. 2682–2685. IEEE (2010)
23. Kuwakado, H., Morii, M.: Security on the quantum-type even-mansour cipher. In: ISITA, pp. 312–316. IEEE (2012)
24. Massey, J.L.: SAFER K-64: a byte-oriented block-ciphering algorithm. In: Anderson, R. (ed.) FSE 1993. LNCS, vol. 809, pp. 1–17. Springer, Heidelberg (1994). https://doi.org/10.1007/3-540-58108-1_1
25. Massey, J.L., Khachatrian, G.H., Kuregian, M.K.: Nomination of SAFER+ as candidate algorithm for the advanced encryption standard (AES) (1998)
26. Massey, J.L., Khachatrian, G.H., Kuregian, M.K.: Nomination of SAFER++ as candidate algorithm for the new European schemes for signatures, integrity, and encryption (NESSIE) (2000)

27. Nielsen, M.A., Chuang, I.: Quantum computation and quantum information (2002)
28. Wagner, D.: The Boomerang attack. In: Knudsen, L. (ed.) FSE 1999. LNCS, vol. 1636, pp. 156–170. Springer, Heidelberg (1999). https://doi.org/10.1007/3-540-48519-8_12
29. Zhandry, M.: A note on the quantum collision and set equality problems. Quantum Inf. Comput. **15**(7&8), 557–567 (2015). http://www.rintonpress.com/xxqic15/qic-15-78/0557-0567.pdf

Post-quantum Cryptography

MAYO: Practical Post-quantum Signatures from Oil-and-Vinegar Maps

Ward Beullens[✉]

imec-COSIC, KU Leuven, Leuven, Belgium
Ward.beullens@esat.kuleuven.be

Abstract. The Oil and Vinegar signature scheme, proposed in 1997 by Patarin, is one of the oldest and best understood multivariate quadratic signature schemes. It has excellent performance and signature sizes but suffers from large key sizes on the order of 50 KB, which makes it less practical as a general-purpose signature scheme. To solve this problem, this paper proposes MAYO, a variant of the UOV signature scheme whose public keys are two orders of magnitude smaller. MAYO works by using a UOV map $\mathcal{P} : \mathbb{F}_q^n \to \mathbb{F}_q^n$ with an unusually small oil space, which makes it possible to represent the public key very compactly. The usual UOV signing algorithm fails if the oil space is too small, but MAYO works around this problem by "whipping up" the oil and vinegar map $\mathcal{P}$ into a larger map $\mathcal{P}^\star : \mathbb{F}_q^{kn} \to \mathbb{F}_q^m$, that does have a sufficiently large oil space. With parameters targeting NISTPQC security level I, MAYO has a public key size of only 614 Bytes and a signature size of 392 Bytes. This makes MAYO more compact than state-of-the-art lattice-based signature schemes such as Falcon and Dilithium. Moreover, we can choose MAYO parameters such that, unlike traditional UOV signatures, signatures provably only leak a negligible amount of information about the private key.

1 Introduction

The Oil and Vinegar signature scheme, introduced by Patarin in 1997, is a simple and seemingly well understood signature scheme in Multivariate Quadratic (MQ) cryptography. This scheme is based on a trapdoored multivariate map $\mathcal{P} : \mathbb{F}_q^n \to \mathbb{F}_q^m$, which consists of m multivariate quadratic polynomials in n variables. The trapdoor is a secret m-dimensional linear subspace O of $\mathbb{F}_q^n$, called the *oil space*, on which $\mathcal{P}$ vanishes. (I.e., $\mathcal{P}(\mathbf{o}) = 0$ for all $\mathbf{o}$ in O.) Knowledge of this oil space allows a user to efficiently sample preimages for $\mathcal{P}$. This trapdoor can be converted into a post-quantum signature scheme with the Full Domain Hash approach: to sign a message M, the signer produces a preimage $\mathbf{x}$ such that $\mathcal{P}(\mathbf{x}) = H(M)$, where H is a hash function that outputs elements of $\mathbb{F}_q^m$.

This work was supported by CyberSecurity Research Flanders with reference number VR20192203 and the Research Council KU Leuven grant C14/18/067 on Cryptanalysis of post-quantum cryptography. Ward Beullens is funded by a Junior Postdoctoral Fellowship from the Research Foundation - Flanders (FWO), FWO fellowship 1S95620N.

Clearly, the security of the scheme relies on the assumption that given $\mathcal{P}$, it is hard to find the oil space $O \subset \mathbb{F}_q^n$ on which $\mathcal{P}$ vanishes. Not surprisingly, if we increase n for fixed $m = \dim(O)$, then finding O becomes more difficult. Initially Patarin proposed to use $n = 2m$, but Kipnis and Shamir showed that in this case O can be found in polynomial time. Their attack runs in time $\tilde{O}(q^{n-m})^1$, so the attack quickly becomes infeasible if n is sufficiently larger than $2m$. This is why Kipnis et al. proposed to use UOV with $n = 3m$. Despite recent progress in key recovery algorithms [1] (which breaks a parameter set with $n = 2.4m$), the $n = 3m$ proposal still seems secure today.

The main drawback of the UOV scheme is that the public keys are large. A public key consists of a list of m multivariate quadratic polynomials in n variables, which requires $\mathcal{O}(mn^2 \log q)$ bits to represent. For example, conservative parameters targeting NIST security level 1 are $m = 53, n = 3m, q = 31$, which results in a key size of 421 KB. Petzoldt et al. [10] realized that it is possible to generate a large part of the public key with a PRNG and choose the remaining part such that $\mathcal{P}$ vanishes on a secret space O. This technique allows to reduce the key size from $\mathcal{O}(mn^2 \log q)$ to $O(m^3 \log q)$, which is a significant reduction. For the previous example, this reduces the key size from 421 KB to 48 KB. However, the public key remains large compared to other post-quantum signature schemes.

Contributions. For the UOV trapdoor to work, the dimension of the oil space needs to be at least as large as the number of polynomials m. In this paper, we propose a signing algorithm that uses a UOV map with $o = \dim(O) < m$, which has two immediate benefits:

- By reducing $\dim(O)$, the complexity of key recovery attacks increases, which allows us to choose smaller parameters.
- If $\dim(O)$ is smaller, the constraint that $\mathcal{P}$ vanishes on O becomes weaker, so we can generate a larger part of $\mathcal{P}$ pseudo-randomly with the technique of Petzoldt et al. [10]. This reduces the overall key size significantly. We get a key size of $O(mo^2 \log q)$ instead of $O(m^3 \log q)$.

To achieve this, we show how to "whip up" the oil and vinegar: given a UOV map $\mathcal{P} : \mathbb{F}_q^n \to \mathbb{F}_q^m$ that vanishes on some unknown oil space of dimension o, one can construct a larger map $\mathcal{P}^\star : \mathbb{F}_q^{kn} \to \mathbb{F}_q^m$ that vanishes on a space of dimension ko. A simple example of such a map is given by $\mathcal{P}^\star(\mathbf{x}_1, \ldots, \mathbf{x}_k) = \mathcal{P}(\mathbf{x}_1) + \cdots + \mathcal{P}(\mathbf{x}_k)$, although we will see that this choice of $\mathcal{P}^\star$ will not result in a secure signature scheme. Using this technique, the signature scheme is simple: The public key is a UOV map $\mathcal{P} : \mathbb{F}_q^n \to \mathbb{F}_q^m$ with an oil space of dimension $o < m$. Both the signer and the verifier locally whip up this map to get the larger map $\mathcal{P}^\star$ with an oil space of size $ko \geq m$, which they use as if it was a standard UOV trapdoor.

The case where $k = 1$ (no whipping) and $o = m$ is equivalent to the standard UOV signature scheme, but choosing larger k allows us to reduce o to $\lceil m/k \rceil$, so that we achieve the advantages mentioned earlier.

---

[1] The $\tilde{O}$-notation ignores polynomial factors.

In this paper, we analyze the security of this construction. We formulate two hard problems, and we show if these problems are indeed hard, then the MAYO scheme is EUF-CMA secure in the random oracle model. Since one of the hardness assumptions is new, this security reduction itself provides little to no evidence for the security of MAYO. However, we hope that by carefully formulating our assumptions, we can help others to understand and cryptanalyze our scheme.

We propose parameter sets aiming for NIST security level I, III, and V. For example, targeting NIST security level I, we propose and implement the parameter set $q = 31, n = 62, m = 60, o = 6$, and $k = 10$. This results in a signature size of 420 bytes, and a public key size of only 803 bytes, which is two orders of magnitude smaller than classic UOV public keys, and even more compact than lattice-based signature schemes such as Falcon [11] and Dilithium [9]. With our implementation, the signing operation takes roughly 1 ms and the verification operation takes 0.5 ms on an intel i5-8400H CPU. Our hope is that the good communication sizes and performance numbers of MAYO will motivate external cryptanalysis of our scheme.

2 Preliminaries

Notation. We denote by $\mathbb{F}_q$ the finite field of q elements. If X is a finite set, we write $x \leftarrow X$ to denote sampling an element from X uniformly at random and assigning the result to x. If A is a (possibly probabilistic) algorithm, we write $y \leftarrow A(x)$ to denote running the algorithm A on input x, and assigning the output to y. We denote the n-by-n identity matrix by $\mathbf{I}_n$. For a square matrix $\mathbf{A} = \{a_{ij}\}_{1 \leq i,j \leq n}$, we denote by $\mathsf{Upper}(\mathbf{A})$ the upper diagonal matrix that is equal to $\mathbf{A}$ up to the addition of an anti-symmetric matrix, i.e., $\mathsf{Upper}(\mathbf{A}) = \{b_{ij}\}_{\leq i,j \leq n}$, where $b_{ij} = a_{ij} + a_{ji}$ if $i \leq j$, $b_{ij} = a_{ij}$ if $i = j$ or $b_{ij} = 0$ otherwise. We say a function $f(\lambda) : \mathbb{N} \to \mathbb{R}$ is negligible if for every $c > 0$, there exits λ_0 such that $|f(\lambda)| < \lambda^{-c}$ for all $\lambda > \lambda_0$.

Multivariate Quadratic Maps. The central object in Multivariate Quadratic cryptography is the multivariate quadratic map. A multivariate quadratic map $\mathcal{P}$ over $\mathbb{F}_q$ with n variables and m components is a sequence $p_1(\mathbf{x}), \cdots, p_m(\mathbf{x})$ of m multivariate quadratic polynomials in n variables $\mathbf{x} = (x_1, \cdots, x_n)$, with coefficients in a finite field $\mathbb{F}_q$. We denote the set of multivariate quadratic maps over $\mathbb{F}_q^n$ with n variables and m components by $\mathsf{MQ}_{n,m,q}$.

To evaluate a map $\mathcal{P} \in \mathsf{MQ}_{n,m,q}$ at a value $\mathbf{a} \in \mathbb{F}_q^n$, we simply evaluate each of its component polynomials in $\mathbf{a}$ to get a vector $\mathbf{b} = (b_1 = p_1(\mathbf{a}), \cdots, b_m = p_m(\mathbf{a}))$ of m output elements. We denote this by $\mathcal{P}(\mathbf{a}) = \mathbf{b}$.

MQ Problem. The main source of computational hardness for multivariate cryptosystems is the Multivariate Quadratic (MQ) problem. Given a multivariate quadratic map $\mathcal{P} \in \mathsf{MQ}_{n,m,q}$, and given a target $\mathbf{t} \in \mathbb{F}_q^m$, the MQ problem asks to find a solution $\mathbf{s}$ such that $\mathcal{P}(\mathbf{s}) = \mathbf{t}$. This problem is NP-hard, and even though it can be solved in polynomial time if $m \geq n(n+1)/2$ or $n \geq m(m+1)$, it is believed to be exponentially hard on average if $n \sim m$, even for quantum algorithms. Currently, the best algorithms to solve instances of this problem (for cryptographically relevant parameters) are algorithms such as F_4/F_5 or XL that use a Gröbner-basis-like approach [4,6].

Polar Forms. To a homogeneous multivariate quadratic polynomial $p(\mathbf{x})$, we can associate the symmetric bilinear form

$$p'(\mathbf{x}, \mathbf{y}) := p(\mathbf{x} + \mathbf{y}) - p(\mathbf{x}) - p(\mathbf{y}),$$

which is called the *polar form* of $p(\mathbf{x})$. Similarly, we define the polar form of a multivariate quadratic map $\mathcal{P}(\mathbf{x}) = p_1(\mathbf{x}), \cdots, p_m(\mathbf{x})$, to be $\mathcal{P}'(\mathbf{x}, \mathbf{y}) = p'_1(\mathbf{x}, \mathbf{y}), \cdots, p'_m(\mathbf{x}, \mathbf{y})$.

3   The UOV Signature Scheme

As mentioned in the introduction, the Oil and Vinegar signature scheme is based on an elegant multivariate quadratic trapdoor function $\mathcal{P} : \mathbb{F}_q^n \to \mathbb{F}_q^m$. This trapdoor function is converted into a signature scheme with the Full Domain Hash approach: The public key is a description of the trapdoor function $\mathcal{P} \in \mathrm{MQ}_{n,m,q}$, the secret key contains the trapdoor information, and a signature on a message M is simply an input $\mathbf{s}$ such that $\mathcal{P}(\mathbf{s}) = \mathcal{H}(M\|\mathsf{salt})$, where $\mathcal{H}$ is a cryptographic hash function that outputs elements in the range of $\mathcal{P}$ and where salt is a bit string of length 2λ, chosen at random when the signature is generated. Therefore, to understand the UOV signature scheme, we only need to understand how the UOV trapdoor function works.

3.1   UOV Trapdoor Function

The UOV trapdoor function is a multivariate quadratic map $\mathcal{P} : \mathbb{F}_q^n \to \mathbb{F}_q^m$ that vanishes on a secret linear subspace $O \subset \mathbb{F}_q^n$ of dimension $\dim(O) = m$, i.e.

$$\mathcal{P}(\mathbf{o}) = 0 \quad \text{for all } \mathbf{o} \in O.$$

The trapdoor information is nothing more than a basis for O. To generate the trapdoor function one first picks the subspace O uniformly at random and then one picks $\mathcal{P}$ uniformly at random from the set of multivariate quadratic maps with m components in n variables that vanish on O. Note that on top of the q^m "artificial" zeros in the subspace O, we expect roughly q^{n-m} "natural" zeros that do not lie in O.

Given a target $\mathbf{t} \in \mathbb{F}_q^m$, how do we use this trapdoor to find $\mathbf{x} \in \mathbb{F}_q^n$ such that $\mathcal{P}(\mathbf{x}) = \mathbf{t}$? To do this, one picks a vector $\mathbf{v} \in \mathbb{F}_q^n$ and solves the system $\mathcal{P}(\mathbf{v} + \mathbf{o}) = \mathbf{t}$ for a vector $\mathbf{o} \in O$. This can simply be done by solving a linear system for $\mathbf{o}$, because

$$\mathcal{P}(\mathbf{v} + \mathbf{o}) = \underbrace{\mathcal{P}(\mathbf{v})}_{\text{fixed by choice of } \mathbf{v}} + \underbrace{\mathcal{P}(\mathbf{o})}_{=0} + \underbrace{\mathcal{P}'(\mathbf{v}, \mathbf{o})}_{\text{linear function of } \mathbf{o}} = \mathbf{t}.$$

With probability roughly $1 - 1/q$ over the choice of $\mathbf{v}$ the linear map $\mathcal{P}'(\mathbf{v}, \cdot)$ will be non-singular, in which case the linear system $\mathcal{P}(\mathbf{v} + \mathbf{o}) = \mathbf{t}$ has a unique solution. If this is not the case, one can simply pick a new value for $\mathbf{v}$ and try again.

Oil Space Can have Basis of the Form $(\mathbf{O}\ \mathbf{I_0})^{\top}$. In practice, we choose O as the row space of a random matrix of the form $(\mathbf{O}\ \mathbf{I}_o) \in \mathbb{F}_q^{o \times n}$. Since most o-dimensional subspaces can be represented in this form, this restriction does not affect the security of the scheme much.

Last m Entries of $\mathbf{v}$ Can be Zero. In the original Oil and Vinegar signature scheme the vector $\mathbf{v}$ is not chosen uniformly at random, but the last m entries are fixed to zero. This is slightly more efficient, and it does not affect the output distribution of the signing algorithm. To see why this is the case, notice that adding a vector $\mathbf{o}^{\star} \in O$ to the choice for $\mathbf{v}$ does not affect the output of the signing algorithm: If $\mathbf{o}$ was the solution to $\mathcal{P}(\mathbf{v} + \mathbf{o}) = \mathbf{t}$, then $\mathbf{o} - \mathbf{o}^{\star}$ is the solution to $\mathcal{P}(\mathbf{v} + \mathbf{o}^{\star} + \mathbf{o}') = \mathbf{t}$, so the signing algorithm outputs $\mathbf{v} + \mathbf{o}$ if it started from $\mathbf{v}$, or it outputs $(\mathbf{v} + \mathbf{o}^{\star}) + (\mathbf{o} - \mathbf{o}^{\star})$ if it starts from $\mathbf{v} + \mathbf{o}^{\star}$. Either way, the output is the same. Therefore, since every $\mathbf{v} \in \mathbb{F}_q^n$ can be written as $\mathbf{v}' + \mathbf{o}$, where the last m entries of $\mathbf{v}'$ are zero, it follows that the last m entries of $\mathbf{v}$ can be fixed at zero without affecting the distribution of the signatures.

4   Key Recovery Attacks Against UOV

A straightforward approach to attack the UOV signature scheme is to completely ignore the existence of the oil subspace and directly try to solve the system $\mathcal{P}(\mathbf{s}) = \mathcal{H}(M\|\mathsf{salt})$ to produce a signature for the message M. This can be done with a Gröbner basis-like approach such as XL or F_4/F_5 [4,6]. This is called a direct attack.

More interestingly, the attacker can first try to find the oil space O. After O is found, the attacker can sign any message as if he was a legitimate signer. It was shown by Kipnis and Shamir [8], that O can be found in polynomial time if $n = 2m$, which was the cased for the original oil and vinegar proposal. That is why the current proposals use $n > 2m$, which is known as the Unbalanced Oil and Vinegar (UOV) signature scheme. The conservative recommendation is to use $n = 3m$ or even $n = 4m$, and with these choices there are no known attacks that outperform a direct attack.

In the remainder of this section we summarize the known algorithms for recovering a linear subspace O of dimension o, given a multivariate quadratic map $\mathcal{P} : \mathbb{F}_q^n \to \mathbb{F}_q^m$ that vanishes on this subspace O. Usually, these algorithms are specialized to $o = m$, since this corresponds to the UOV signature use-case. Here, we will generalize the attacks to the case where o is not necessarily equal to m because this is relevant for MAYO. The presentation of the attacks is mostly borrowed from Beullens [1], with slight modifications to generalize to the $o \leq m$ case.

4.1   Reconciliation Attack

The reconciliation attack was developed by Ding *et al.*. as a stepping stone towards the Rainbow Band Separation (RBS) attack against the Rainbow signature scheme [5].

The attack tries to find a number of vectors $\mathbf{o}_1, \mathbf{o}_2, \ldots$ in O, until a complete basis for O is found. To find the first vector $\mathbf{o}_1$ we simply try to find a solution to the system $\mathcal{P}(\mathbf{o}_1) = 0$. By assumption, this system of equations has a o-dimensional linear space of solutions, so if we impose o affine constraints on the entries of $\mathbf{o}_1$, we expect a unique solution $\mathbf{o}_1 \in O$ such that $\mathcal{P}(\mathbf{o}_1) = 0$. This step amounts to finding a solution to a system of m equations in $n - o$ variables, because we can use the o affine constraints to eliminate o variables in the system.

Once the first vector $\mathbf{o}_1 \in O$ is found, it becomes easier to find additional vectors, because the second vector $\mathbf{o}_2$ satisfies $\mathcal{P}(\mathbf{o}_2) = 0$, as well as $\mathcal{P}'(\mathbf{o}_1, \mathbf{o}_2) = 0$, which for fixed $\mathbf{o}_1$ is a set of m linear equations in the entries of $\mathbf{o}_2$. Therefore, after imposing o additional affine constraints, the second step amounts to solving a system of m quadratic equations in $n - m - o$ variables. Compared to the first step, the number of variables is reduced by m, which makes the second step much more efficient. Similarly, finding subsequent vectors $\mathbf{o}_i \in O$ amounts to finding a solution to the system

$$\begin{cases} \mathcal{P}(\mathbf{o}_i) = 0 \\ \mathcal{P}'(\mathbf{o}_1, \mathbf{o}_i) = 0 \\ \ldots \\ \mathcal{P}'(\mathbf{o}_{i-1}, \mathbf{o}_i) = 0 \end{cases},$$

which after imposing o additional affine constraints and eliminating variables amounts to solving a system of m quadratic equations in $n - (i - 1)m - o$ variables. If $n < (i - 1)m + o$, then we can ignore the quadratic equations and just solve a system of linear equations to find $\mathbf{o}_i$.

The attack does not work as described if $n - o > m$, because in this case the first system $\mathcal{P}(\mathbf{o}_1) = 0$ is underdetermined, and the system has $O(q^{n-o-m})$ solutions, only one of which lies in O. If you start with a solution $\mathbf{o}_1 \notin O$, the subsequent steps will fail to find additional vectors $\mathbf{o}_2, \ldots, \mathbf{o}_o$. In this case one can enumerate all the solutions $\mathcal{P}(\mathbf{o}_1) = 0$, or solve the system

$$\begin{cases} \mathcal{P}(\mathbf{o}_1) = 0 \\ \mathcal{P}(\mathbf{o}_2) = 0 \\ \mathcal{P}'(\mathbf{o}_1, \mathbf{o}_2) = 0 \end{cases},$$

to find $\mathbf{o}_1$ and $\mathbf{o}_2$ simultaneously. In this paper, we will only use UOV maps with $n - o \le m$, so this more complicated attack is not relevant for us.

If $n - o \le m$, then the complexity of the attack is dominated by the complexity of finding the first oil vector $\mathbf{o}_1$, which is the complexity of solving a system of m quadratic equations in $n - o$ variables.

4.2   Kipnis-Shamir Attack

Historically, the first attack on the OV signature scheme was given by Kipnis and Shamir [8]. The basic version of this attack works when $n = 2o$, which was the case for the parameter sets initially proposed by Patarin.

Attack if n = 2o. The attack looks at the m components of $\mathcal{P}'(\mathbf{x}, \mathbf{y})$. Each component $p_i'(\mathbf{x}, \mathbf{y}) = p_i(\mathbf{x} + \mathbf{y}) - p_i(\mathbf{x}) - p_i(\mathbf{y})$, defines a matrix M_i such that $p_i'(\mathbf{x}, \mathbf{y}) = \mathbf{x}^\top M_i \mathbf{y}$. Kipnis and Shamir observed the following useful property of M_i.

Lemma 1. *For each $i \in \{1, \cdots, m\}$, we have that $M_i O \subset O^\perp$. That is, each M_i sends O into its own orthogonal complement $O^\perp$.*

Proof. For any $\mathbf{o}_1, \mathbf{o}_2 \in O$ we need to prove that $\langle \mathbf{o}_2, M_i \mathbf{o}_1 \rangle = 0$. This follows from the assumption that p_i vanishes on O:

$$\langle \mathbf{o}_2, M_i \mathbf{o}_1 \rangle = \mathbf{o}_2^\top M_i \mathbf{o}_1 = p_i'(\mathbf{o}_1, \mathbf{o}_2) = p_i(\mathbf{o}_1 + \mathbf{o}_2) - p_i(\mathbf{o}_1) - p_i(\mathbf{o}_2) = 0. \quad \square$$

If $n = 2o$, then $\dim(O^\perp) = n - o = o$, so if M_i is nonsingular (which happens with high probability if q is odd), then Lemma 1 turns into an equality $M_i O = O^\perp$. This means that for any pair of invertible M_i, M_j, we have that $M_j^{-1} M_i O = O$, i.e. that O is an invariant subspace of $M_j^{-1} M_i$. It turns out that finding a common invariant subspace of a large number of linear maps can be done in polynomial time, so this gives an efficient algorithm for finding O. For more details we refer to [8].

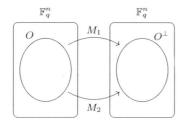
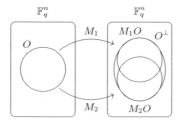

Fig. 1. Behavior of O under M_1 and M_2, in case $n = 2o$ (on the left) and $2o < n < 3o$ (on the right).

Attack if n > 2o. If $n > 2o$, then it is still the case that M_i sends O into $O^\perp$, but because $\dim(O^\perp) = n - o > o$ the equality $M_i O = M_j O$ may no longer hold. Therefore, $M_i^{-1} M_j$ is no longer guaranteed to have O as an invariant subspace and the basic attack fails. However, even though in general $M_i O \neq M_j O$, they still have an unusually large intersection (see Fig. 1): $M_i O$ and $M_j O$ are both subspaces of $O^\perp$, so their intersection has dimension at least $\dim(M_i O) + \dim(M_j O) - \dim(O^\perp) = 3o - n$. Kipnis *et al.* [7] realized that this means that vectors in O are more likely to be eigenvectors of $M_j^{-1} M_i$.

Heuristically, for $\mathbf{x} \in O$, the probability that it gets mapped by M_i to some point in the intersection $M_i O \cap M_j O$ is approximately

$$\frac{|M_i O \cap M_j O|}{|M_i O|} = q^{2o-n}.$$

If this happens, then the probability that M_j^{-1} maps $M_i \mathbf{x}$ back to a multiple of $\mathbf{x}$ is expected to be $(q-1)/|O| \approx q^{1-o}$. Therefore, we can estimate that the probability that a vector in O is an eigenvector of $M_j^{-1} M_i$ is approximately q^{1+o-n}, and the expected number of eigenvectors in O is therefore q^{1+2o-n}.

The same analysis holds when you replace M_i and M_j by arbitrary invertible linear combinations of the M_i. The attacker can repeatedly compute the eigenvectors of $F^{-1}G$, where F and G are random invertible linear combinations of the M_i. After q^{n-2o} attempts he can expect to find a vector in O (he can verify whether a given eigenvector $\mathbf{x}$ is in O by checking that $\mathcal{P}(\mathbf{x}) = 0$). The complexity of the attack is $\tilde{O}(q^{n-2o})$, so the attack runs in polynomial time if $n = 2o$, but quickly becomes infeasible for unbalanced instances of the OV construction. For more details on the attack, we refer to [7].

4.3   Intersection Attack

The intersection attack, introduced by Beullens [1], is a generalisation of the reconciliation attack which uses the ideas behind the Kipnis-Shamir attack. After choosing k matrices $M_1, \ldots, M_k$ as in the Kipnis-Shamir attack, the attacker tries to find a vector $\mathbf{x}$ in the intersection $M_1 O \cap \cdots \cap M_k O$. This intersection has dimension at least $ko - (k-1)(n-o)$, so the attacker chooses k such that this is strictly positive. If a vector $\mathbf{x}$ is in this intersection, then $M_i^{-1} \mathbf{x} \in O$ for all $i \in \{1, \ldots, k\}$, which means that $\mathbf{x}$ satisfies the following system of equations:

$$\begin{cases} \mathcal{P}(M_i^{-1}\mathbf{x}) = 0 & \forall i \in \{1, \ldots, k\} \\ \mathcal{P}'(M_i^{-1}\mathbf{x}, M_j^{-1}\mathbf{x}) & \forall i < j \in \{1, \ldots, k\}^2 \end{cases} . \tag{1}$$

The attacker uses a Gröbner-basis-like algorithm to find a solution $\mathbf{x}$ to this system, and recovers k vectors $M_1^{-1}\mathbf{x}, \ldots, M_k^{-1}\mathbf{x}$ in O. Extending these to a basis of O can be done efficiently, as described in Sect. 4.1.

The complexity of the intersection attack is dominated by the complexity of solving a system of $\binom{k+1}{2}m - 2\binom{k}{2}$ linearly independent multivariate quadratic equations (the $\binom{k+1}{2}m$ equations in (1) are linearly dependent) in $n - \dim(M_1 O \cap \cdots \cap M_k O) = kn - (2k-1)o$ variables. For more details, we refer to [1].

5   Whipping Oil and Vinegar

In this section we introduce a "whipping" transformation, that turns a multivariate quadratic map $\mathcal{P} : \mathbb{F}_q^n \to \mathbb{F}_q^m$ into a larger map $\mathcal{P}^\star : \mathbb{F}_q^{kn} \to \mathbb{F}_q^m$ for an integer $k > 1$. Our whipping transformation has the property that if $\mathcal{P}(\mathbf{x})$ vanishes on a subspace $O \subset \mathbb{F}_q^n$, then $\mathcal{P}^\star$ vanishes on $O^k \subset \mathbb{F}_q^{kn}$. This allows us to transform a useless UOV map with $o < m$ into a more useful map that vanishes on a space of dimension at least m.

First Attempt. A first attempt is to simply use

$$\mathcal{P}^\star(\mathbf{x}_1, \ldots, \mathbf{x}_k) = \mathcal{P}(\mathbf{x}_1) + \cdots + \mathcal{P}(\mathbf{x}_k).$$

If $\mathcal{P}$ vanishes on O, then clearly this $\mathcal{P}^\star$ vanishes on O^k. However, it turns out that this $\mathcal{P}^\star$ is not preimage resistant for $k > 1$, so we can not use this construction for our signature scheme. To illustrate the problem, suppose $k \geq 2$ and suppose there exists $\alpha \in \mathbb{F}_q$ such that $\alpha^2 = -1$. Then the attacker can choose $\delta \in \mathbb{F}_q^n$ at random, put $\mathbf{x}_2 = \alpha\mathbf{x}_1 + \delta$, and put $\mathbf{x}_i = 0$ for $i > 2$. Then we have

$$\begin{aligned}
\mathcal{P}^\star(\mathbf{x}_1, \ldots, \mathbf{x}_k) &= \mathcal{P}(\mathbf{x}_1) + \mathcal{P}(\alpha\mathbf{x}_1 + \delta) \\
&= \mathcal{P}(\mathbf{x}_1) + \mathcal{P}(\alpha\mathbf{x}_1) + \mathcal{P}(\delta) + \mathcal{P}'(\alpha\mathbf{x}_1, \delta) \\
&= \mathcal{P}(\delta) + \mathcal{P}'(\alpha\mathbf{x}_1, \delta),
\end{aligned}$$

where we have used that $\mathcal{P}$ is homogeneous, such that $\mathcal{P}(\alpha\dot{\mathbf{x}}_1) = -\mathcal{P}(\mathbf{x}_1)$. What remains is linear in $\mathbf{x}_1$, so an attacker can efficiently solve for $\mathbf{x}_1$ such that $\mathcal{P}^\star(\mathbf{x}_1, \alpha\mathbf{x}_1 + \delta, 0, \ldots, 0) = \mathbf{t}$.

Second Attempt. The first attempt resulted in a whipped up map that could be made to collapse into a linear map. To fix this problem, we will add some "emulsifier" maps to the mix.[2] Concretely, for the second attempt we choose k invertible linear m-by-m matrices $\mathbf{E}_1, \ldots, \mathbf{E}_k$ at random and set

$$\mathcal{P}^\star(\mathbf{x}_1, \ldots, \mathbf{x}_k) = \mathbf{E}_1\mathcal{P}(\mathbf{x}_1) + \cdots + \mathbf{E}_k\mathcal{P}(\mathbf{x}_k).$$

This blocks attacks of the type that broke our first attempt: Suppose the attacker sets $\mathbf{x}_i = \alpha_i\mathbf{x}_1 + \delta_i$, for $i > 1$ and for some $\alpha_i \in \mathbb{F}_q$ and $\delta_i \in \mathbb{F}_q^n$, then the quadratic part of $\mathcal{P}^\star(\mathbf{x}_1, \ldots, \mathbf{x}_k)$ becomes

$$\left(\mathbf{E}_1 + \sum_{i=2}^{k} \alpha_i^2\mathbf{E}_i\right)\mathcal{P}(\mathbf{x}_1).$$

If the $\mathbf{E}_i$ are chosen at random, then for each choice of α_i, the probability that the quadratic terms vanish is q^{-m^2}, so a union bound says that the probability that there exist α_i such that the quadratic part vanishes is at most q^{k-1-m^2}, which can be made negligibly small by choosing the parameters appropriately. However, the attacker can still take advantage of α_i such that $\mathbf{E}_1 + \sum_{i=2}^{k} \alpha_i^2\mathbf{E}_i$ has low rank. Therefore, we choose the $\mathbf{E}_i$ from a set of q^m matrices such that any non-zero linear combination of these matrices has full rank. We use the set of matrices that correspond to multiplication by elements of $\mathbb{F}_{q^m}$. In the following, we fix an embedding of $\mathbb{F}_{q^m}$ in the algebra of m-by-m matrices over $\mathbb{F}_q$, and

---

[2] An emulsifier is a chemical that stabilizes an emulsion. An example is Lecithin, which is found in egg yolks, and which can stabilize a foam of oil droplets in an oil and vinegar mixture to form mayonnaise.

with a mild abuse of notation, we will identify the elements of $\mathbb{F}_{q^m}$ with the corresponding matrices. With this choice of "emulsifier maps", the probability that there exists a linear combination $\mathbf{E}_1 + \sum_{i=2}^{k} \alpha_i^2 \mathbf{E}_i$ with rank lower than n (i.e. rank 0) is at most q^{k-1-m}, which can still be made negligible.[3]

However, there is still a different issue. Since $\mathcal{P}^\star$ is the sum of k functions with independent inputs the problem of finding a preimage for $\mathcal{P}^\star$ reduces to a k-SUM problem. The attacker constructs k lists of evaluations of $\mathbf{E}_i(\mathcal{P}(\mathbf{x}))$ respectively, and searches for one value in each list such that their sum is $\mathbf{t}$. This can be done in time $O(q^{m/\lfloor \log_2(k) \rfloor})$ with Wagner's k-tree algorithm [14]. For moderately large values of k (e.g. $k = 8$) this attack will be more efficient than the other known attacks against our signature scheme, so it is worthwhile to choose a different $\mathcal{P}^\star$ that is not susceptible to this attack.

Final Construction. To avoid the k-tree attacks, we finally propose to use the following construction: Let q be odd, choose invertible linear matrices $\mathbf{E}_{i,j}$ for all (i, j) with $1 \le i \le j \le n$ (still representing multiplication by an element of $\mathbb{F}_{q^m}$), and let

$$\mathcal{P}^\star(\mathbf{x}_1, \ldots, \mathbf{x}_k) = \sum_{1 \le i \le j \le n} \mathbf{E}_{i,j}(\mathcal{P}(\mathbf{x}_i + \mathbf{x}_j)).$$

Remark 2. Note that in characteristic 2, the $\mathbf{E}_{ii}\mathcal{P}(\mathbf{x}_i + \mathbf{x}_i)$ terms vanish, so it would be slightly more natural to consider the maps $\mathcal{P}^\star(\mathbf{x}_1, \ldots, \mathbf{x}_k) = \sum_i \mathbf{E}_{ii}\mathcal{P}(\mathbf{x}_i) + \sum_{i<j} \mathbf{E}_{ij}\mathcal{P}(\mathbf{x}_i + \mathbf{x}_j)$. Both definitions are equivalent for odd q, so to keep the notation (and the implementation of our scheme) as simple as possible, we have chosen to use the simpler definition, and to let q be odd.

The probability that there exist α_i such that the quadratic part of $\mathcal{P}^\star(\mathbf{x}_1, \alpha_2\mathbf{x}_2 + \delta_2, \ldots, \alpha_k\mathbf{x}_1 + \delta_1)$ is still bounded by q^{k-1-m}. Moreover, the cross-terms in $\mathbf{E}_{i,j}\mathcal{P}(\mathbf{x}_i + \mathbf{x}_j)$ prevent the list-sum attack, because in general $\mathcal{P}^\star(0, \ldots, \mathbf{x}_i, \ldots, 0) + \mathcal{P}^\star(0, \ldots, \mathbf{x}_j, \ldots, 0) \ne \mathcal{P}^\star(0, \ldots, \mathbf{x}_i, \ldots, \mathbf{x}_j, \ldots, 0)$.

6   Mayo Signatures

In this section we introduce our new signature scheme that uses UOV maps with $o < m$. Recall that in the $o = m$ case, the signature generation algorithms proceeds by picking a random salt of length 2λ and a random vector $\mathbf{v} \in \mathbb{F}_q^n$, and solving for $\mathbf{o} \in O$ such that $\mathcal{P}(\mathbf{v} + \mathbf{o}) = \mathsf{Hash}(M \| \mathsf{salt})$, which is a linear system of equations. If $o < m$ the same strategy fails because the linear system has m equations, but only $o < m$ degrees of freedom, such that with large probability the system will not have any solutions. To solve this problem, we fix some k such that $ko \ge m$ and we let the signer whip up $\mathcal{P}(\mathbf{x})$ into a larger map $\mathcal{P}^\star(\mathbf{x}_1, \ldots, \mathbf{x}_k)$ with the method from the previous section (with random

---

[3] For odd q we can get a slightly better bound of $\left(\frac{q+1}{2}\right)^{k-1} q^{-m}$, because each α_i^2 can only take $(q + 1)/2$ distinct values.

emulsifier maps $\{\mathbf{E}_{ij}\}_{1 \leq i \leq j \leq k}$ obtained by hashing $M\|\mathsf{salt}$). Now the signer can choose $(\mathbf{v}_1, \ldots, \mathbf{v}_k) \in \mathbb{F}_q^{kn}$, and solve for $(\mathbf{o}_1, \ldots, \mathbf{o}_k) \in O^k$ such that $\mathcal{P}(\mathbf{v}_1 + \mathbf{o}_1, \ldots, \mathbf{v}_k + \mathbf{o}_k) = \mathbf{t}$. This amounts to solving a system of m linear equations with $ko \geq m$ degrees of freedom, so solutions can be found with large probability. The signature consists of the salt, and the preimage $\{\mathbf{s}_i = \mathbf{v}_i + \mathbf{o}_i\}_{i \in [k]}$. Note that, as in the original UOV signature algorithm, we can let the last o entries of the $\mathbf{v}_i$ be zero to speed up the signing algorithm without affecting its output distribution.

To verify a signature, the verifier simply hashes $M\|\mathsf{salt}$ to obtain $\{\mathbf{E}_{ij}\}_{1 \leq i \leq j \leq k}$ and $\mathbf{t}$, and accepts the signature if and only if $\mathcal{P}^\star(\mathbf{s}_i) = \mathbf{t}$.

To generate a key-pair, a user first chooses a random oilspace by sampling a uniformly random o-by-$(n - o)$ matrix $\mathbf{O}$, and letting O be the rowspace of $(\mathbf{O}\, \mathbf{I}_o)$, where $\mathbf{I}_o$ is the identity matrix of size o. Then the user generates a random multivariate quadratic map $\mathcal{P}(\mathbf{x})$ that vanishes on O. Recall that every multivariate quadratic polynomial $p_i(\mathbf{x})$ of the public key can be represented with an upper triangular matrix $\mathbf{P}_i$ such that

$$p_i(\mathbf{x}) = \mathbf{x}^\top \mathbf{P}_i \mathbf{x} = \mathbf{x}^\top \begin{pmatrix} \mathbf{P}_i^{(i)} & \mathbf{P}_i^{(2)} \\ 0 & \mathbf{P}_i^{(3)} \end{pmatrix} \mathbf{x},$$

where $\mathbf{P}_i^{(1)}$ and $\mathbf{P}_i^{(3)}$ are square upper triangular matrices of size $n - o$ and o respectively, and where $\mathbf{P}_i^{(2)}$ is rectangular of size $(n - o)$-by-o. To reduce the size of the public key, we choose the matrices $\mathbf{P}_i^{(i)}$ and $\mathbf{P}_i^{(2)}$ pseudo-randomly from a random seed value $\mathsf{seed} \in \{0, 1\}^\lambda$. Then we solve for $\mathbf{P}_i^{(3)}$ such that p_i vanishes on O. The polynomial $p_i(\mathbf{x})$ vanishes on O if

$$(\mathbf{O}\, \mathbf{I}_o) \begin{pmatrix} \mathbf{P}_i^{(i)} & \mathbf{P}_i^{(2)} \\ 0 & \mathbf{P}_i^{(3)} \end{pmatrix} (\mathbf{O}\, \mathbf{I}_o)^\top = \mathbf{O}\mathbf{P}_i^{(1)}\mathbf{O}^\top + \mathbf{O}\mathbf{P}_i^{(2)} + \mathbf{P}_i^{(3)} = 0,$$

so it suffices to set $\mathbf{P}_i^{(3)}$ to be $\mathsf{Upper}(-\mathbf{O}\mathbf{P}_i^{(1)}\mathbf{O}^\top - \mathbf{O}\mathbf{P}_i^{(2)})$. Note that taking Upper does not influence the quadratic polynomial represented by $\mathbf{P}_i$.

The key generation, signing and verification algorithms are described in more detail in Fig. 2.

The following lemma says the probability that the signing algorithm needs to restart is small if $ok \geq m$. The proof is not particularly interesting, so in the interest of space we put it in Appendix A.

Lemma 3. *Let $O, \mathcal{P}, \{\mathbf{E}_{ij}\}$, and $\{\mathbf{v}_i\}_{i \in [k]}$ in $\mathbb{F}_q^{n-m} \times \{0\}^m$ be chosen at random as during the key-generation and signing algorithms of the MAYO signature scheme with parameters n, m, o, k, q. Then as a function of $\{\mathbf{o}_i\}_{i \in [k]} \in O$ the affine map*

$$\mathcal{P}^\star(\mathbf{v} + \mathbf{o}) = \sum_{ij} \mathbf{E}_{ij} \mathcal{P}(\mathbf{v}_i + \mathbf{v}_j + \mathbf{o}_i + \mathbf{o}_k)$$

has full rank except with probability bounded by $\frac{1}{q^m - 1} + \frac{q^{k-(n-o)}}{q-1} + \frac{q^{m-ko}}{q-1}$.

KeyGen():

1: $\mathbf{O} \leftarrow \mathbb{F}_q^{o \times (n-o)}$
2: seed $\leftarrow \{0,1\}^{\lambda}$
3: **for** i from 1 to m **do**
4:     $\mathbf{P}_i^{(1)} \leftarrow \mathsf{Expand}(\mathsf{seed}||\mathsf{P1}||i)$ ▷ Upper triangular $(n-o)$-by-$(n-o)$ matrix.
5:     $\mathbf{P}_i^{(2)} \leftarrow \mathsf{Expand}(\mathsf{seed}||\mathsf{P2}||i)$ ▷ o-by-$(n-o)$ matrix.
6:     $\mathbf{P}_i^{(3)} \leftarrow \mathsf{Upper}(-\mathbf{O}\mathbf{P}_i^{(1)}\mathbf{O}^{\top} - \mathbf{O}\mathbf{P}_i^{(2)})$
7: **return** $(\mathsf{pk}, \mathsf{sk}) = ((\mathsf{seed}, \{\mathbf{P}_i^{(3)}\}_{i \in \{i,\dots,m\}}), (\mathsf{seed}, \mathbf{O}))$.

Sign(M, sk):

1: $(\mathsf{seed}, \mathbf{O}) \leftarrow \mathsf{sk}$
2: salt $\leftarrow \{0,1\}^{2\lambda}$
3: $(\{\mathbf{E}_{ij}\}_{1 \leq i \leq j \leq k}, \mathbf{t}) \leftarrow \mathsf{Hash}(M||\mathsf{salt})$
4: $\mathcal{P}^*(\mathbf{x}_1, \dots \mathbf{x}_k) \leftarrow \sum_{1 \leq i \leq j \leq k} \mathbf{E}_{ij}\mathcal{P}(\mathbf{x}_i + \mathbf{x}_j)$
5: $\mathbf{v}_i \leftarrow \mathbb{F}_q^{n-m} \times \{0\}^m$
6: If $\mathcal{P}^*(\mathbf{v}_1 + \mathbf{o}_1, \dots, \mathbf{v}_k + \mathbf{o}_k)$ does not have full rank, return to step 2.
7: Solve $\mathcal{P}^*(\mathbf{v}_1 + \mathbf{o}_1, \dots, \mathbf{v}_k + \mathbf{o}_k) = \mathbf{t}$ for $\mathbf{o}_1, \dots, \mathbf{o}_k \in \mathrm{RowSpace}((\mathbf{O}\,\mathbf{I}_o))$.
8: **return** $\sigma = (\mathsf{salt}, \{\mathbf{x}_i = \mathbf{v}_i + \mathbf{o}_i\}_{i \in [k]})$

Verify(M, pk, σ):

1: $(\mathsf{salt}, \{\mathbf{x}_i\}_{i \in [k]}) \leftarrow \sigma$
2: $(\{\mathbf{E}_{ij}\}_{1 \leq i \leq j \leq k}, \mathbf{t}) \leftarrow \mathsf{Hash}(M||\mathsf{salt})$
3: $\mathbf{t}' \leftarrow \sum_{1 \leq i \leq j \leq k} \mathbf{E}_{ij}\mathcal{P}(\mathbf{x}_i + \mathbf{x}_j)$
4: **return** accept if $\mathbf{t} = \mathbf{t}'$ and reject otherwise.

Fig. 2. The key generation, signing, and verification algorithms of the MAYO signature scheme.

7 Security Analysis

Traditional MQ signature algorithms usually rely on ad-hoc assumptions, which makes it impossible to prove security reductions from well-established hardness assumptions.[4] The MAYO signature scheme is no exception. However, we will still formally define two assumptions based on which our scheme can be proven to be secure. Since one of the assumptions is new, this security reduction itself does not provide any kind of guarantee for the security of the scheme. Still, we hope the security reduction is valuable for cryptanalysts to understand what is necessary to attack our scheme. Most notably, we prove that if ko is sufficiently larger than m, each signature only leaks a negligible amount of information about the secret key.

Our first hardness assumption says that it is hard to distinguish a random multivariate quadratic map that vanishes on a random linear subspace from a uniformly random quadratic map.

Definition 4 (UOV problem). *For $\mathbf{O} \in \mathbb{F}_q^{o \times (n-o)}$, we let $\mathsf{MQ}_{n,m,q}(\mathbf{O})$ denote the set of $\mathcal{P} \in \mathsf{MQ}_{n,m,q}$ that vanish on the rowspace of $(\mathbf{O}\ \mathbf{I}_o)$. The UOV problem*

---

[4] Signature schemes such as MQDSS [3,12] and MUDFISH [2] that do not make use of trapdoors are an exception because they enjoy security reductions from the one-wayness of a system of uniformly random multivariate quadratic equations.

asks to distinguish a random multivariate quadratic map $\mathcal{P} \in \mathsf{MQ}_{n,m,q}$, from a random multivariate quadratic map in $\mathsf{MQ}_{n,m,q}(\mathbf{O})$ for a random $\mathbf{O} \in \mathbb{F}_q^{o \times (n-o)}$.

Let $\mathcal{A}$ be a UOV distinguisher algorithm. We say the distinguishing advantage of $\mathcal{A}$ is

$$\mathsf{Adv}^{\mathsf{UOV}}_{n,m,o,q}(\mathcal{A}) = \left| \Pr\left[\mathcal{A}(\mathcal{P}) = 1 \middle| \mathcal{P} \leftarrow \mathsf{MQ}_{m,n,q}\right] \right.$$

$$\left. - \Pr\left[\mathcal{A}(\mathcal{P}) = 1 \middle| \begin{array}{c} \mathbf{O} \leftarrow \mathbb{F}_q^{o \times (n-o)} \\ \mathcal{P} \leftarrow \mathsf{MQ}_{n,m,q}(\mathbf{O}) \end{array}\right] \right|.$$

The UOV problem has been studied since the invention of the UOV signature scheme in 1997 and seems relatively well understood. In contrast, our second hardness assumption is tailored to the MAYO signature scheme and is therefore a new assumption. This assumption says that picking a random multivariate quadratic map $\mathcal{P} \in \mathsf{MQ}_{n,m,q}$, and whipping it up to a larger map $\mathcal{P}^* \in \mathsf{MQ}_{kn,m,q}$ results in a preimage resistant function on average.

Definition 5 (Whipped MQ problem). *Given random $\mathcal{P} \in \mathsf{MQ}_{n,m,q}$, $\{\mathbf{E}_{ij}\}_{1 \leq i \leq j \leq k} \in \mathbb{F}_{q^m}$ and $\mathbf{t} \in \mathbb{F}_q^m$, the whipped MQ problem asks to compute $\mathbf{s}_1, \ldots, \mathbf{s}_k$, such that $\sum_{i,j} \mathbf{E}_{ij} \mathcal{P}(\mathbf{s}_i + \mathbf{s}_j) = \mathbf{t}$.*

Let $\mathcal{A}$ be an adversary. We say that the advantage of $\mathcal{A}$ against the whipped MQ problem is

$$\mathsf{Adv}^{\mathsf{WMQ}}_{n,m,k,q}(\mathcal{A}) = \Pr\left[\sum_{i,j} \mathbf{E}_{ij} \mathcal{P}(\mathbf{s}_i + \mathbf{s}_j) = \mathbf{t} \middle| \begin{array}{c} \mathcal{P} \leftarrow \mathsf{MQ}_{n,m,q} \\ \{\mathbf{E}_{ij}\}_{1 \leq i \leq j \leq k} \leftarrow \mathbb{F}_{q^m} \\ \mathbf{t} \leftarrow \mathbb{F}_q^m \\ (\mathbf{s}_1, \ldots, \mathbf{s}_k) \leftarrow \mathcal{A}(\mathcal{P}, \{\mathbf{E}_{ij}\}_{i,j}, \mathbf{t}) \end{array}\right].$$

Finally, we state the standard EUF-CMA and EUF-KOA security definition for digital signature algorithms in the random oracle model.

Definition 6 (EUF-CMA/EUF-KOA security). *Let $\mathcal{O}$ be a random oracle, and let $\mathcal{A}$ be an adversary. We say the advantage of $\mathcal{A}$ gainst the EUF-CMA game of a signature scheme $S = (KeyGen, Sign^{\mathcal{O}}, Verify^{\mathcal{O}})$ in the random oracle model is*

$$\mathsf{Adv}^{\mathsf{EUF\text{-}CMA}}_S(\mathcal{A}) = \Pr\left[\begin{array}{c} Verify^{\mathcal{O}}(\mathsf{pk}, m, \sigma) = 1, \\ and\ Sign^{\mathcal{O}}(\mathsf{sk}, \cdot)\ was \\ not\ queried\ on\ input\ m \end{array} \middle| \begin{array}{c} (\mathsf{pk}, \mathsf{sk}) \leftarrow KeyGen() \\ (m, \sigma) \leftarrow \mathcal{A}^{\mathcal{O}, Sign^{\mathcal{O}}(\mathsf{sk}, \cdot)}(\mathsf{pk}) \end{array}\right].$$

The EUF-KOA advantage $\mathsf{Adv}^{\mathsf{EUF\text{-}KOA}}_S(\mathcal{A})$ is defined in the same way, except that $\mathcal{A}$ does not have access to the signing oracle $Sign^{\mathcal{O}}(\mathsf{sk}, \cdot)$.

With these definitions out of the way we can formulate our security theorem.

Theorem 7. *Let $\mathcal{A}$ be an EUF-CMA adversary that runs in time T against the MAYO signature in the random oracle model with parameters n, m, o, k, q,* and which makes Q_s signing queries and Q_h queries to the random oracle. Let $\mathsf{B} = \frac{1}{q^m-1} + \frac{q^{k-(n-o)}}{q-1} + \frac{q^{m-ko}}{q-1}$ be the bound on the restarting probability from Lemma 3 and suppose $Q_s\mathsf{B} < 1$, then there exist adversaries $\mathcal{A}_{\mathsf{UOV}}$ and $\mathcal{A}_{\mathsf{WMQ}}$ against the $UOV_{n,m,o,q}$ and $WMQ_{n,m,k,q}$ assumptions respectively, that run in time $T + (Q_s + Q_h + 1) \cdot poly(n, m, k, q)$ such that

$$\mathsf{Adv}_{n,m,o,k,q}^{\mathsf{EUF-CMA}}(\mathcal{A}) \leq \left(\mathsf{Adv}_{n,m,o,q}^{\mathsf{UOV}}(\mathcal{B}) + Q_h\mathsf{Adv}_{n,m,k,q}^{\mathsf{WMQ}}(\mathcal{B}') + q^{-m}\right)(1 - Q_s\mathsf{B})^{-1}$$
$$+ (Q_h + Q_s)Q_s 2^{-2\lambda}.$$

We prove the theorem with two lemmas. The first lemma reduces the EUF-CMA security of the MAYO signature scheme to its EUF-KOA, by showing that we can simulate a signing oracle if ko is sufficiently larger than m. The second lemma then finishes the proof by giving a reduction from the UOV and WMQ problems to the EUF-KOA security game. The reduction from the WMQ problem loses a factor Q_h in advantage, because the reduction programs the random oracle to output the WMQ instance for one of the Q_h random oracle queries, and succeeds only if the adversary forges a signature for that particular query. The proofs of Lemmas 8 and 9 can be found in Appendices B and C respectively.

Lemma 8. *If there exists an adversary $\mathcal{A}$, that runs in time T against the* EUF-CMA *security of the MAYO signature in the random oracle model with parameters n, m, o, k, q, with $k < (n-o)$, and which makes Q_h queries to the random oracle and Q_s queries to the signing oracle. Let $\mathsf{B} = \frac{1}{q^m-1} + \frac{q^{k-(n-o)}}{q-1} + \frac{q^{m-ko}}{q-1}$ be the bound on the restarting probability from Lemma 3 and suppose $Q_s\mathsf{B} < 1$, then there exists an adversary $\mathcal{B}$ against the* EUF-KOA *security of the MAYO signature scheme, that runs in time $T + O((Q_h + Q_s)poly(n, m, k, q))$ such that*

$$\mathsf{Adv}_{n,m,o,k,q}^{\mathsf{EUF-CMA}}(\mathcal{A}) \leq \mathsf{Adv}_{n,m,o,q}^{\mathsf{EUF-KOA}}(\mathcal{B})(1 - Q_s\mathsf{B})^{-1}$$
$$+ (Q_h + Q_s)Q_s 2^{-2\lambda}.$$

Lemma 9. *Let $\mathcal{A}$ be an* EUF-KOA *adversary that runs in time T against the MAYO signature in the random oracle model with parameters n, m, o, k, q, and which makes Q_h queries to the random oracle. Then there exists an adversary $\mathcal{B}$ against the $UOV_{n,m,o,q}$ problem, and an adversary $\mathcal{B}'$ against the $WMQ_{n,m,k,q}$ problem, that run in time $T + O((1 + Q_h)poly(n, m, k, q))$ such that*

$$\mathsf{Adv}_{n,m,o,k,q}^{\mathsf{EUF-KOA}}(\mathcal{A}) \leq \mathsf{Adv}_{n,m,o,q}^{\mathsf{UOV}}(\mathcal{B}) + (1 + Q_h)\mathsf{Adv}_{n,m,k,q}^{\mathsf{WMQ}}(\mathcal{B}') + q^{-m}.$$

8   Parameter Selection and Implementation

In this section, we choose some parameter sets for the MAYO signature scheme. A parameter set consists of five values $n, m, o, k,$ and q (as well as the length of the salt, which we choose to be $256, 384$ or 512 bits long for NIST security levels I, III, and V respectively.) The only requirement for the correctness of the signature scheme is that $ko \geq m$ because otherwise, the signing algorithm will fail with high probability. For security, we need to choose n, m, o, k and q such that the UOV and WMQ problems are hard. The best known attacks against the UOV assumption are summarized in Sect. 3. Since we are not aware of attacks that exploit the whipping structure, we estimate that the hardness of the WMQ problem is the same as the hardness of breaking the preimage resistance of a uniformly random multivariate quadratic map $\mathcal{P} \in \mathsf{MQ}_{kn,m,q}$. These systems are very underdetermined, so we can use the technique of Thomae and Wolf [13] to reduce the problem of finding a solution to a system in $\mathsf{MQ}_{kn,m,q}$, to a system in $\mathsf{MQ}_{n',m',q}$, where $n' = m' = \lceil m + 1 - \frac{nk}{m} \rceil$. To achieve NISTPQC security levels I, III, or V we choose parameters such that finding such a solution with the Hybrid XL algorithm, or breaking the UOV assumption costs at least $2^{143}, 2^{207}$, or 2^{272} bit operations respectively. The fact that all known attacks require frequently accessing large amounts of memory provides a comfortable security margin. Table 1 contains the proposed parameter sets. Estimates of the bit complexity of known attacks against these parameter sets are given in Table 2.

Our security reduction has a factor Q_h advantage loss for the reduction from the WMQ problem, where Q_h is the number of random oracle queries that the adversary is allowed to make. Therefore, if one wanted the reduction to guarantee l bits of security, we would have to pick parameters such that the WMQ problem has $2l$ bits of hardness. We choose not to do this because it would come at a significant cost in performance and communication size, and we are not aware of any attacks that exploit the looseness in the reduction. E.g., for our parameters, there do not appear to exist multi-target attacks on the WMQ problem that meaningfully outperform single-target attacks. (This is also the case for the standard MQ problem.)

Information-theoretically, UOV signatures (and variants such as Rainbow) leak information about the secret key. Although it seems hard to exploit this leakage in an attack, one might want to stop this leakage altogether. For the UOV scheme, it would be possible to stop the leakage by choosing $o > m$, but this would come at a very significant cost in terms of performance. For the MAYO signatures, it is much cheaper to prevent the leakage, because we only need $ko > m$. Table 1 proposes two parameter sets per NIST security level: a first parameter set that does not attempt to prevent leakage, and a second parameter set that satisfies $\mathsf{B} \leq 2^{-65}$, such that Lemma 8 gives a tight reduction from EUF-KOA security to EUF-CMA security for adversaries that are allowed to make up to 2^{64} signature queries. Figure 3 shows the signature size and public key size of a variety of MAYO parameter sets (with and without leaky signatures), compared to the key and signature sizes of the three finalist signature schemes in the NISTPQC process. We see that by choosing the parameters, we can make a trade-off between signature size and public key size. We also see that the cost of making the signatures statistically close to random is small.

Table 1. Parameter sets for the MAYO signature scheme.

SL	No leakage	Parameters					|pk| (Bytes)	|sig| (Bytes)
		n	m	o	k	q		
I	✗	74	76	6	13	7	614	392
	✓	76	78	7	15	7	835	459
III	✗	111	117	6	20	7	937	880
	✓	112	117	7	20	7	1244	888
V	✗	148	152	8	20	7	2068	1174
	✓	149	157	7	26	7	1664	1516

Table 2. Estimated complexities (log_2 of number of bit operations) of known attacks against MAYO parameter sets.

SL	No leakage	Parameters	Direct	KS	Recon.	Inters.
		$n\ m\ o\ k\ q$				
I	✗	74, 76, 6, 13, 7	145	190	143	245
	✓	76, 78, 7, 15, 7	145	190	144	245
III	✗	111, 117, 6, 20, 7	210	296	208	374
	✓	112, 117, 7, 20, 7	209	292	208	370
V	✗	148, 152, 8, 20, 7	273	390	272	486
	✓	149, 157, 7, 26, 7	273	398	272	498

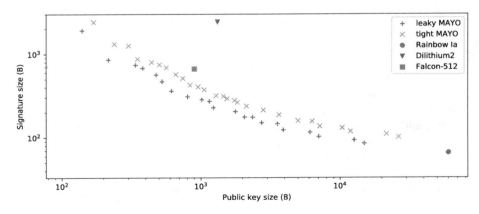

Fig. 3. A comparison of the key and signature sizes of the MAYO signature scheme with various parameter sets, and the key and signature sizes of the NISTPQC signature finalists.

Implementation. We made a C implementation with some preliminary AVX2 optimizations of MAYO for the parameter set ($n = 62, m = 60, o = 6, k = 10, q = 31$), which aims for NISTPQC security level I. We instantiate the H and Expand random oracles with the SHAKE128 extendable output function. With these choices, the public key and signatures have a size of 803 Bytes and 420 Bytes respectively. On an Intel i5-8400H CPU at 2.5 GHz, a signing operation takes 2.50 million cycles, and a verification operation takes 1.3 million cycles (i.e., 1 ms or 0.5 ms respectively). A large fraction of the time is spent expanding the public seed with Expand, therefore, if one can spare 137 KB to store the expanded seed the signing and verification time can be reduced by 30% and 40%, to 1.7 million cycles and 820 thousand cycles respectively (i.e., 0.7 ms or 0.3 ms). We leave a more optimized constant-time implementation of MAYO for future work.

A   Proof of Lemma 3

Before we prove the lemma, we recall the following result, which is useful to prove that certain random matrices are of full rank with high probability. In particular the result applies to uniformly random matrices, and uniformly random symmetric matrices.

Lemma 10. *Let $\mathcal{M}$ be a distribution of matrices in $\mathbb{F}_q^{n \times m}$ with $n \geq m$, such that for all $\mathbf{x} \in \mathbb{F}_q^m \setminus \{0\}$, we have*

$$\Pr_{\mathbf{M} \leftarrow \mathcal{M}}[\mathbf{Mx} = 0] = q^{-n},$$

then the probability that $\mathbf{M} \leftarrow \mathcal{M}$ does not have full rank is bounded by $\frac{q^{m-n}}{q-1}$.

Proof. From the assumption, it follows that the average number of non-zero kernel vectors is $(q^m - 1)q^{-n}$. Since every matrix which does not have full rank has at least $q - 1$ non-zero kernel vectors, it follows that

$$\Pr_{\mathbf{M} \leftarrow \mathcal{M}}[\text{rank}(\mathbf{M}) < m](q - 1) \leq (q^m - 1)q^{-n} < q^{m-n}. \qquad \square$$

A.1   Proof of Lemma 3

Proof. First of all, we show that if $\mathbf{v}_1, \cdots, \mathbf{v}_k \in \mathbb{F}_q^{n-o} \times \{0\}^o$ are linearly independent, then the linear maps $\mathcal{P}'(\mathbf{v}_1, \cdot), \ldots, \mathcal{P}'(\mathbf{v}_k, \cdot)$ from O to $\mathbb{F}_q^m$ are all independent and uniformly distributed. To see this, it suffices to show that for a basis $\mathbf{y}_1, \cdots \mathbf{y}_o$ of O, the matrices $\{p_i'(\mathbf{v}_a, \mathbf{y}_b)\}_{a \in [k], b \in [o]}$ are independent and uniformly random for all $i \in [m]$. If we choose the basis where $\mathbf{y}_b$ is the b-th row of $(\mathbf{O} \ \mathbf{I}_o)$, then a calculation shows that these matrices are

$$\mathbf{V}\left((\mathbf{P}_i^{(1)} + \mathbf{P}_i^{(1)\top})\mathbf{O}^\top + \mathbf{P}_i^{(2)}\right),$$

where the rows of $\mathbf{V} \in \mathbb{F}_q^{k \times (n-o)}$ consists of the first $n - o$ entries of the $\mathbf{v}_i$. Therefore, if the $\mathbf{v}_i$ are linearly independent, then $\mathbf{V}$ has full rank, and if

$k < (n - o)$, then it follows that these matrices are uniformly random and independent because the $\mathbf{P}_i^{(2)}$ matrices are chosen uniformly at random during the key generation algorithm.

In particular, if $\mathbf{M}_1, \dots, \mathbf{M}_k \in \mathbb{F}_q^{n \times o}$ are the matrix representations of $\mathcal{P}'(\mathbf{v}_i, \cdot)$ (i.e. the matrices such that for all $i \in [k]$, we have $\mathcal{P}'(\mathbf{v}_i, \sum_i u_i \mathbf{y}_i) = \mathbf{M}_i \mathbf{u}$). Then we have shown that if the $\mathbf{v}_i$ are linearly independent, then the $\mathbf{M}_i$ are independent and uniformly random matrices.

As a warm-up, let us now look at the case $k = 1$ first. In this case the linear part of $\mathcal{P}^\star(\mathbf{v} + \mathbf{o})$ is $\mathcal{P}^{\star\prime}(\mathbf{v}, \mathbf{o}) = 4\mathbf{E}_{11}\mathcal{P}'(\mathbf{v}, \mathbf{o})$. This has the matrix representation $\mathbf{E}_{11}\mathbf{M}_1$, where if $\mathbf{v} \neq 0$, the matrix $\mathbf{M}_1$ is uniformly random. Therefore, we see that the signing algorithm has to restart with probability bounded by

$$q^{-m} + q^{o-n} + \frac{q^{m-o}}{q - 1}$$

because either $\mathbf{E}_{11} = 0$ or $\mathbf{v} = 0$, which happens with probability bounded by $q^{-m} + q^{o-n}$, and in which case $\mathbf{E}_{11}\mathcal{P}(\mathbf{v} + \mathbf{o})$ is exactly zero, so it definitely is not full rank, or otherwise the linear part of $\mathbf{E}_{11}\mathcal{P}(\mathbf{v} + \mathbf{o})$ is a uniformly random linear map from O to $\mathbb{F}_q^m$, so it fails to have full rank with probability bounded by $\frac{q^{m-o}}{q-1}$ (Lemma 10).

In general, the linear part of $\mathcal{P}^\star(\mathbf{v} + \mathbf{o})$ is equal to

$$\mathcal{P}'^\star(\mathbf{v}, \mathbf{o}) = \sum_{ij} \mathbf{E}_{ij}\mathcal{P}'(\mathbf{v}_i + \mathbf{v}_j, \mathbf{o}_i + \mathbf{o}_j) \tag{2}$$

$$= \sum_{ij} \mathbf{E}_{ij}\left(\mathcal{P}'(\mathbf{v}_i, \mathbf{o}_i) + \mathcal{P}'(\mathbf{v}_i, \mathbf{o}_j) + \mathcal{P}'(\mathbf{v}_j, \mathbf{o}_i) + \mathcal{P}'(\mathbf{v}_j, \mathbf{o}_j)\right) \tag{3}$$

Let $\mathbf{M}_1, \dots, \mathbf{M}_k$ be the matrix representations of $\mathcal{P}'(\mathbf{v}_i, \cdot)$, then the matrix representation of $\mathcal{P}^{\star\prime}(\mathbf{v}, \cdot)$ is $\left(\mathbf{M}'_1 \dots \mathbf{M}'_k\right) \in \mathbb{F}_q^{m \times ko}$, where

$$\begin{pmatrix} \mathbf{M}'_1 \\ \vdots \\ \mathbf{M}'_k \end{pmatrix} = \mathbf{E} \begin{pmatrix} \mathbf{M}'_1 \\ \vdots \\ \mathbf{M}'_k \end{pmatrix} = \begin{pmatrix} \mathbf{D}_1 & \mathbf{E}_{12} & \dots & \mathbf{E}_{1k} \\ \mathbf{E}_{12} & \mathbf{D}_2 & \dots & \vdots \\ \vdots & \vdots & \ddots & \vdots \\ \mathbf{E}_{1k} & \dots & \dots & \mathbf{D}_k \end{pmatrix} \begin{pmatrix} \mathbf{M}'_1 \\ \vdots \\ \mathbf{M}'_k \end{pmatrix} \tag{4}$$

where $\mathbf{D}_i = \sum_{j<i} \mathbf{E}_{ji} + 4\mathbf{E}_{ii} + \sum_{j>i} \mathbf{E}_{ij}$. Since the $\mathbf{E}_{ij}$ are chosen uniformly at random, we see that the matrix $\mathbf{E}$ is just a uniformly random symmetric matrix in $\mathbb{F}_{q^m}^{k \times k}$, so the probability that $\mathbf{E}$ is singular is bounded by $\frac{1}{q^m-1}$ (Lemma 10). Since the $\mathbf{v}_i$ are chosen uniformly at random in $\mathbb{F}_q^{n-o} \times \{0\}^o$, they are linearly dependent with probability bounded by $\frac{q^{k-(n-o)}}{q-1}$ (Lemma 10 again), and otherwise the $\mathbf{M}_i$ are independent and uniformly random matrices. Equation (4) shows that if the $\mathbf{v}_i$ are linearly independent and $\mathbf{E}$ is nonsingular, then the $\mathbf{M}'_i$ are also uniformly random. Therefore, by Lemma 10, $\mathcal{P}'^\star(\mathbf{v}, \cdot)$ has full rank except with probability bounded by

$$\frac{1}{q^m - 1} + \frac{q^{k-(n-o)}}{q - 1} + \frac{q^{m-ko}}{q - 1}. \qquad \qquad \square$$

B   Proof of Lemma 8

Proof. The EUF-KOA adversary $\mathcal{B}$ works as follows. When $\mathcal{B}$ is given a public key $\mathcal{P}$, it starts simulating $\mathcal{A}$ on input $\mathcal{P}$. To simulate random oracle queries $\mathcal{B}$ maintains a list of queries L, that is initially empty. When $\mathcal{A}$ queries a random oracle at input m, $\mathcal{B}$ responds with $(\mathbf{E}, \mathbf{t})$ if there is an entry $(m, \mathbf{E}, \mathbf{t}) \in L$ and otherwise $\mathcal{B}$ samples $\mathbf{E} = \{\mathbf{E}_{ij}\}_{1 \leq i \leq j \leq k} \in \mathbb{F}_{q^m}$ and $\mathbf{t} \in \mathbb{F}_q^m$ uniformly at random, adds $(m, \mathbf{E}, \mathbf{t})$ to L and responds with $(\mathbf{E}, \mathbf{t})$.

When $\mathcal{A}$ makes a query to sign a message M, $\mathcal{B}$ chooses a random salt and aborts if there is an entry $(m\|\mathsf{salt}, \star, \star)$ in L. Otherwise, $\mathcal{B}$ samples $\mathbf{E} = \{\mathbf{E}_{ij}\}_{1 \leq i \leq j \leq k} \in \mathbb{F}_{q^m}$ and $\mathbf{s}_1, \ldots, \mathbf{s}_k \in \mathbb{F}_q^n$, and sets $\mathbf{t} = \sum_{ij} \mathbf{E}_{ij} \mathcal{P}(\mathbf{s}_i + \mathbf{s}_j)$. Then $\mathcal{B}$ adds $(m\|\mathsf{salt}, \mathbf{E}, \mathbf{t})$ to L and outputs the signature $(\mathsf{salt}, \mathbf{s}_1, \cdots, \mathbf{s}_k)$.

Finally, when $\mathcal{A}$ outputs a message-signature pair (m, σ), $\mathcal{B}$ just outputs the same pair.

It is clear that $\mathcal{B}$ runs in time $T + O((Q_h + Q_s + 1)\mathrm{poly}(n, m, k, q))$, so to finish the proof we need to show that $\mathcal{B}$ succeeds in the EUF-KOA game with a sufficiently large probability. We prove this with a sequence of games.

- Let Game_0 be $\mathcal{A}$'s EUF-CMA game against the MAYO signature scheme. By definition we have $\Pr[\mathsf{Game}_0() = 1] = Adv_{n,m,o,k,q}^{\mathsf{EUF-CMA}}(\mathcal{A})$.
- Let Game_1 be identical to Game_0, except that the game aborts and outputs 0 if to answer a signing query m, the challenger picks a salt, such that the random oracle was already queried at input $m\|\mathsf{salt}$. Since there are in total $Q_h + Q_s$ queries to the random oracle, the probability of an abort is at most $(Q_s + Q_h)2^{-2\lambda}$ for each signing query, which makes for a total probability of an abort of $(Q_s + Q_h)Q_s 2^{-2\lambda}$. Therefore, we have $\Pr[\mathsf{Game}_1() = 1] \geq \Pr[\mathsf{Game}_0() = 1] - (Q_s + Q_h)Q_s 2^{-2\lambda}$.
- Let Game_2 be the same as Game_1 except that the game aborts and outputs 0 if during one of the calls to the signing oracle, the challenger has to restart the signing algorithm because he arrives at a linear system $\mathcal{P}^\star(\mathbf{v}_1 + \mathbf{o}_1, \ldots, \mathbf{v}_k + \mathbf{o}_k) = \mathbf{t}$ which does not have full rank. Note that the view of the adversary in Game_1 is independent of the number of signing attempts: if the signing algorithm encounters a system that does not have full rank, it just restarts from the beginning. Therefore, the output of the signing algorithm is independent of the number of signing attempts. It follows from Lemma 3 that

$$\Pr[\mathsf{Game}_2() = 1] = \Pr[\mathsf{Game}_1() = 1 \wedge \text{no restart}] = \Pr[\mathsf{Game}_1() = 1]\Pr[\text{no restart}]$$

$$\geq \Pr[\mathsf{Game}_1() = 1]\left(1 - Q_s\left(\frac{1}{q^m - 1} + \frac{q^{k-(n-o)}}{q - 1} + \frac{q^{m-ko}}{q - 1}\right)\right).$$

- The final game Game_3 is just the EUF-KOA game played by $\mathcal{B}^{\mathcal{A}}$. If Game_2 does not abort, then the view of $\mathcal{A}$ is identical in Game_2 and Game_3, because if no salt is chosen more than once for the same message, then $\mathcal{B}$ simulates the random oracle perfectly. Moreover, since all of the linear systems have full rank, the signatures are computed as $\mathbf{s} = \mathbf{v} + \mathbf{o}$, where $\mathbf{v}$ is chosen uniformly at random in $(\mathbb{F}_q^{n-o} \times \{0\}^o)^k$, and $\mathbf{o}$ is uniformly random in O^k. By construction we have $(\mathbb{F}_q^{n-o} \times \{0\}^o) + O = \mathbb{F}_q^n$, so the signatures in Game$_2$ are uniformly distributed, which means that $\mathcal{B}$ simulates the signing oracle perfectly by just choosing random $\mathbf{s} \in \mathbb{F}_q^{kn}$. Therefore, the probability that $\mathcal{A}$ outputs a forgery in Game$_2$ is at least as big as the probability that it outputs a forgery in Game$_3$ (it could be larger, since Game$_3$ aborts less often, but this is not important for our analysis), so we have $\Pr[\mathsf{Game}_3() = 1] > \Pr[\mathsf{Game}_2() = 1]$.

By combining the 3 inequalities we get that

$$\mathsf{Adv}_{n,m,o,k,q}^{\mathsf{EUF-CMA}}(\mathcal{A}) \leq \mathsf{Adv}_{n,m,o,q}^{\mathsf{EUF-KOA}}(\mathcal{B}) \left(1 - Q_s \left(\frac{1}{q^m - 1} + \frac{q^{k-(n-o)}}{q-1} + \frac{q^{m-ko}}{q-1}\right)\right)^{-1}$$
$$+ (Q_h + Q_s)Q_s 2^{-2\lambda}. \qquad \square$$

C   Proof of Lemma 9

Proof. We do the proof with a short sequence of games. The first game Game$_0$ is the EUF-KOA game played by $\mathcal{A}$. By definition we have $\Pr[\mathsf{Game}_0() = 1] = \mathsf{Adv}_{n,m,o,k,q}^{\mathsf{EUF-KOA}}(\mathcal{A})$.

The next game is the same as Game$_0$, except that during the key generation step the challenger chooses a uniformly random $\mathcal{P} \in \mathsf{MQ}_{n,m,q}$, instead of a $\mathcal{P}$ that vanishes on some oil space O. We construct the adversary $\mathcal{B}$ against the UOV assumption as follows. When $\mathcal{B}$ is given a multivariate quadratic map $\mathcal{P}$, it computes the matrix representation $\{\mathbf{P}_i^{(1)}, \mathbf{P}_i^{(2)}, \mathbf{P}_i^{(3)}\}_{i \in [m]}$ of $\mathcal{P}$. Then, $\mathcal{B}$ pick a random seed, and runs $\mathcal{A}$ on input $\mathsf{pk} = (\mathsf{seed}, \{\mathbf{P}_i^{(3)}\}_{i \in [m]})$, while faithfully simulating a random oracle, and an Expand oracle that outputs $\mathbf{P}_i^{(1)}$ on input $\mathsf{seed}||\mathsf{P1}||i$, that outputs $\mathbf{P}_i^{(2)}$ on input $\mathsf{seed}||\mathsf{P1}||i$, and that outputs random matrices of the appropriate shape otherwise. We designed $\mathcal{B}$ in such a way, that if $\mathcal{B}$ is given a $\mathcal{P}$ that is a (n, m, o, q) UOV map, then $\mathcal{B}$ is exactly Game$_0$, and if $\mathcal{B}$ is given a random map $\mathcal{P}$, then $\mathcal{B}$ is Game$_1$. Therefore we have

$$\mathsf{Adv}_{n,m,o,q}^{\mathsf{UOV}}(\mathcal{B}) = |\Pr[\mathsf{Game}_0() = 1] - \Pr[\mathsf{Game}_1() = 1]|.$$

For the next game we define the adversary $\mathcal{B}'$ against the whipped MQ problem. When $\mathcal{B}'$ is given a WMQ instance $\mathcal{P}, \{\mathbf{E}_{ij}\}_{ij}, \mathbf{t}$, it does the same thing as Game$_1$, except that instead of simulating a random oracle honestly, $\mathcal{B}'$ chooses an integer $I \in [Q_h]$ uniformly at random, and outputs $(\{\mathbf{E}_{ij}\}_{ij}, \mathbf{t})$ for the I-th distinct random oracle query (and all the subsequent queries for the same message). If $\mathcal{A}$ outputs a valid message-signature pair $(m, (\mathsf{salt}, \mathbf{s}))$, then the $\mathcal{B}'$ adversary checks if $m||\mathsf{salt}$ was the I-th random oracle query. If this is the case, then $\mathcal{B}'$ outputs $\mathbf{s}$, which is a correct solution to the WMQ instance, and otherwise $\mathcal{B}'$ aborts. The view of $\mathcal{A}$ in this game is the same as the view of a in Game$_1$, so $\mathcal{A}$ outputs a valid message-signature pair with probability $\Pr[\mathsf{Game}_1() = 1]$. The probability that $\mathcal{A}$ outputs a valid pair $(m, (\mathsf{salt}, \mathbf{s}))$ such that it has not queried the random oracle on input $m||\mathsf{salt}$ is at most q^{-m}. Note that the guess I is information-theoretically hidden from $\mathcal{A}$, so if $\mathcal{A}$ outputs a valid forgery for the J-th random oracle query, then the probability that $I = J$ is $1/Q_h$. Therefore we have $\mathsf{Adv}^{\mathsf{WMQ}}_{n,m,k,q}(\mathcal{B}') \geq (\Pr[\mathsf{Game}_1() = 1] - q^{-m})/Q_h$.

We can now finish the proof by combining $\Pr[\mathsf{Game}_0() = 1] = \mathsf{Adv}^{\mathsf{EUF\text{-}KOA}}_{n,m,o,k,q}(\mathcal{A})$ with inequalities from the two game transitions to get

$$\mathsf{Adv}^{\mathsf{EUF\text{-}KOA}}_{n,m,o,k,q}(\mathcal{A}) \leq \mathsf{Adv}^{\mathsf{UOV}}_{n,m,o,q}(\mathcal{B}) + Q_h\mathsf{Adv}^{\mathsf{WMQ}}_{n,m,k,q}(\mathcal{B}') + q^{-m}.$$

$\square$

References

1. Beullens, W.: Improved cryptanalysis of UOV and rainbow. Cryptology ePrint Archive, Report 2020/1343 (2020). https://eprint.iacr.org/2020/1343
2. Beullens, W.: Sigma protocols for MQ, PKP and SIS, and fishy signature schemes. In: Canteaut, A., Ishai, Y. (eds.) EUROCRYPT 2020. LNCS, vol. 12107, pp. 183–211. Springer, Cham (2020). https://doi.org/10.1007/978-3-030-45727-3_7
3. Chen, M.-S., Hülsing, A., Rijneveld, J., Samardjiska, S., Schwabe, P.: From 5-pass $\mathcal{MQ}$-based identification to $\mathcal{MQ}$-based signatures. In: Cheon, J.H., Takagi, T. (eds.) ASIACRYPT 2016. LNCS, vol. 10032, pp. 135–165. Springer, Heidelberg (2016). https://doi.org/10.1007/978-3-662-53890-6_5
4. Courtois, N., Klimov, A., Patarin, J., Shamir, A.: Efficient algorithms for solving overdefined systems of multivariate polynomial equations. In: Preneel, B. (ed.) EUROCRYPT 2000. LNCS, vol. 1807, pp. 392–407. Springer, Heidelberg (2000). https://doi.org/10.1007/3-540-45539-6_27
5. Ding, J., Yang, B.-Y., Chen, C.-H.O., Chen, M.-S., Cheng, C.-M.: New differential-algebraic attacks and reparametrization of rainbow. In: Bellovin, S.M., Gennaro, R., Keromytis, A., Yung, M. (eds.) ACNS 2008. LNCS, vol. 5037, pp. 242–257. Springer, Heidelberg (2008). https://doi.org/10.1007/978-3-540-68914-0_15
6. Faugère, J.C.: A new efficient algorithm for computing Gröbner bases without reduction to zero (F_5). In: Proceedings of the 2002 International Symposium on Symbolic and Algebraic Computation, pp. 75–83 (2002)
7. Kipnis, A., Patarin, J., Goubin, L.: Unbalanced oil and vinegar signature schemes. In: Stern, J. (ed.) EUROCRYPT 1999. LNCS, vol. 1592, pp. 206–222. Springer, Heidelberg (1999). https://doi.org/10.1007/3-540-48910-X_15
8. Kipnis, A., Shamir, A.: Cryptanalysis of the oil and vinegar signature scheme. In: Krawczyk, H. (ed.) CRYPTO 1998. LNCS, vol. 1462, pp. 257–266. Springer, Heidelberg (1998). https://doi.org/10.1007/BFb0055733
9. Lyubashevsky, V., et al.: Crystals-Dilithium. Technical report, National Institute of Standards and Technology (2020). https://csrc.nist.gov/projects/post-quantum-cryptography/round-3-submissions
10. Petzoldt, A., Thomae, E., Bulygin, S., Wolf, C.: Small public keys and fast verification for $\mathcal{M}$ultivariate $\mathcal{Q}$uadratic public key systems. In: Preneel, B., Takagi, T. (eds.) CHES 2011. LNCS, vol. 6917, pp. 475–490. Springer, Heidelberg (2011). https://doi.org/10.1007/978-3-642-23951-9_31
11. Prest, T., et al. FALCON. Technical report, National Institute of Standards and Technology (2020). https://csrc.nist.gov/projects/post-quantum-cryptography/round-3-submissions

12. Samardjiska, S., Chen, M.-S., Hulsing, A., Rijneveld, J., Schwabe, P.: MQDSS. Technical report, National Institute of Standards and Technology (2019). https:// csrc.nist.gov/projects/post-quantum-cryptography/round-2-submissions
13. Thomae, E., Wolf, C.: Solving underdetermined systems of multivariate quadratic equations revisited. In: Fischlin, M., Buchmann, J., Manulis, M. (eds.) PKC 2012. LNCS, vol. 7293, pp. 156–171. Springer, Heidelberg (2012). https://doi.org/10. 1007/978-3-642-30057-8_10
14. Wagner, D.: A generalized birthday problem. In: Yung, M. (ed.) CRYPTO 2002. LNCS, vol. 2442, pp. 288–304. Springer, Heidelberg (2002). https://doi.org/10. 1007/3-540-45708-9_19

Simple and Memory-Efficient Signature Generation of XMSS^{MT}

Haruhisa Kosuge[1]($\boxtimes$) and Hidema Tanaka[2]

[1] Japan Maritime Self-Defense Force, Tokyo, Japan
harucrypto@gmail.com
[2] National Defense Academy of Japan, Yokosuka, Japan
hidema@nda.ac.jp

Abstract. Stateful hash-based signature schemes are one of the most promising post-quantum signature schemes. Among them, XMSS and XMSS^{MT} have already been specified in RFC 8391 and NIST SP 800-208. The signing time is exponential if the schemes are naively implemented. To reduce the signing time, Merkle tree traversal algorithms are used and the most time/memory efficient one is the BDS algorithm. We focus on XMSS^{MT} (layered XMSS) with the BDS algorithm. Since XMSS^{MT} is vulnerable to incorrect state management, the algorithm and state structure must be simple. Also, the state size for the BDS algorithm must be reduced in order to implement the scheme in resource-constrained devices. To achieve these objectives, we propose a simple and memory-efficient signature-generation algorithm for XMSS^{MT}.

Keywords: Post quantum cryptography · Hash-based signature · XMSS · XMSS^{MT} · Merkle tree traversal

1 Introduction

1.1 Background

Hash-based signature schemes are one of the promising candidates for post-quantum signature schemes. The advantages of the hash-based signature schemes are small key size and fast signature verification; however, the disadvantages are large signatures and relatively slow key/signature generation. The security of the schemes is based on standard properties of internal hash functions and pseudorandom functions. There is a certain belief that the security of these functions will not be broken by large-scale quantum computers

The *eXtended Merkle Signature Scheme* (XMSS) is a stateful hash-based signature scheme proposed by Buchmann, Dahmen, and Hülsing [3]. XMSS has already been specified in RFC 8391 [8] and NIST SP 800-208 [5]. A stateless scheme SPHINCS$^+$ [1] which uses a variant of XMSS as a subroutine is submitted to the NIST post-quantum project. Compared to SPHINCS$^+$, the signature size is smaller and verification is faster in XMSS (signing is also faster with Merkle tree traversal algorithm shown later); however, XMSS must manage its state properly, otherwise no security guarantees are given [2].

© The Author(s), under exclusive license to Springer Nature Switzerland AG 2022
R. AlTawy and A. Hülsing (Eds.): SAC 2021, LNCS 13203, pp. 377–397, 2022.
https://doi.org/10.1007/978-3-030-99277-4_18

XMSS signs a message using Winternitz one-time signature plus (WOTS$^+$) [6] and consists of a hash tree, called *XMSS tree*, whose leaves are WOTS$^+$ public keys. XMSS uses a leaf index to determine which WOTS$^+$ key pair has been used. The number of signatures that can be generated for each XMSS key pair equals to the number of leaves since a leaf is used for a one-time signature. Once all leaves have been exhausted, the XMSS tree cannot be used again. If it is feasible to generate a higher XMSS tree in the key generation, this tree can generate more signatures. To generate a high XMSS tree, e.g., higher than 30, in a realistic time, a multi-tree variant of XMSS called XMSS^{MT} was proposed [9]. In XMSS^{MT}, XMSS trees are layered. The XMSS tree on the bottom layer signs a message and another XMSS tree signs a root of one lower XMSS tree.

A signature of XMSS includes nodes of the XMSS tree called *authentication path*, which are used to compute a root of an XMSS tree. If XMSS naively generates the authentication path, the signature generation requires exponential time complexity $\mathcal{O}(2^h)$ where h is a height of the XMSS tree and the height is specified as $h \in \{5, 10, 16, 20\}$ in RFC 8391 (including heights of individual XMSS trees layered in XMSS^{MT}). The naive signature generation for $h = 5$ is feasible even in client side; however, the application of $h = 16, 20$ typically is limited to high-performance computing servers or servers which do not need to generate signatures immediately such as CA servers ($h = 10$ is in between two groups). XMSS may use Merkle tree traversal algorithms to generate the authentication path efficiently, and the most time/memory efficient one is the Buchmann-Dahmen-Schneider (BDS) algorithm [4]. By time-memory tradeoff, it is feasible to generate signatures in linear time/memory complexity $\mathcal{O}(h)$. While the algorithm of [9] applies the BDS algorithm to XMSS^{MT}, RFC 8391 only shows the naive signature generation not using the BDS and the other Merkle tree traversal algorithms. Hereinafter, the variant of XMSS^{MT} specified in RFC 8391 and the one of [9] are called *naive algorithm* and *Hülsing-Rausch-Buchmann (HRB) algorithm*, respectively.

In this paper, we study the algorithm of XMSS^{MT} with the BDS algorithm. The HRB algorithm has the following disadvantages.

1. A state of the BDS algorithm is called *BDS state*. In the HRB algorithm, a BDS state for the next XMSS tree is generated while generating signatures using the current XMSS tree [9]. As XMSS^{MT} retains two BDS states for every layer (except for the top one), the total state size is large.
2. The state structure is complex in the HRB algorithm since two types of BDS states are retained in each layer. Also, the procedure to update states is complex in the BDS algorithm.

The state size is of concern when implementing XMSS^{MT} in resource-constrained devices. For example, states are stored and updated on a (rewritable) nonvolatile memory if we implement XMSS^{MT} on smart cards [7]. However, the nonvolatile memory has a restriction on the number of times of rewriting memory cells because of its physical feature. Therefore, the memory wears out sooner with higher memory usage.

Also, the state structure and the procedure to update states must be simple in order to prevent mistakes on the state management. Even a minor mistake can lead to loss of security. For example, if a key pair of WOTS$^+$ signs two different messages, no security guarantees are given [2]. Such a critical situation may occur in WOTS$^+$ on higher layers where the key pair of WOTS$^+$ signs a root of one lower XMSS tree. If there is an implementation bug and the root value changes while generating signatures, the key pair of WOTS$^+$ signs two different values. The naive method to compute the root from the secret key (invariant data) as specified in RFC 8391 is relatively simple and hence not very error prone. However, if the root value is computed from a state, the algorithms are more complex and an implementation error might cause a change of the root value for different signatures. One of the most time/memory efficient methods is to compute the root value from an authentication path in the same manner as the signature verification of XMSS (see Sect. 2.2). In the BDS algorithm, the authentication path is stored and updated as a state and it can be incorrect. If the incorrect authentication path is used, the root value changes.

1.2 Contribution

We propose a simple and memory-efficient signature-generation algorithm for XMSS^{MT} which overcomes the disadvantages of the HRB algorithm as follows.

1. Signatures of XMSS trees on the same layer are generated by a single BDS state. Therefore, the state size becomes smaller and the structure is simpler than the HRB algorithm.
2. We simplify two parts of the BDS algorithm and show that the simplified algorithm works without failure.
3. On the bottom layer, the BDS algorithm is recommended because the signature always changes in each signature generation. Since signatures of XMSS trees on higher layers change after multiple signature generations, it is not necessary to generate signatures of the XMSS trees immediately. Therefore, we propose an alternative algorithm called *memory-efficient Merkle tree traversal* (MMT) to be used in the XMSS trees on higher layers. The algorithm retains only $2h$ nodes and the state structure is simple.

Note that we do not investigate side-channel/implementation attacks against the algorithms to generate signatures of XMSS^{MT}. The security evaluation against such attacks is left as an open problem. Disregarding the attacks, we can assume that an adversary cannot access any other information than a public key and signatures. Then, the adversary cannot distinguish which signing algorithm is used since the public key and the signatures have the same format in any algorithm (for interoperability). Therefore, the choice of the algorithms does not impact on the security of XMSS^{MT} (and XMSS) on a formal level.

2 Preliminaries

2.1 Notation

We denote $\{0, 1, ..., l-1\} \subset \mathbb{Z}$ as $[l]$ and $\{m, m+1, ..., l-1\}$ as $[l] \setminus [m]$. Let $(x_i)_{i \in [l]}$ be an abbreviation of a vector $(x_0, x_1, ..., x_{l-1})$. We use sans serif fonts for denoting nodes including leaves of XMSS trees, e.g., $\mathsf{n}_{j.i}^k$ is i-th node on height j in an XMSS tree on k-th layer.

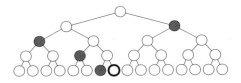

Fig. 1. Example of an authentication path of an XMSS tree of height 4. Red nodes are in the authentication path for a current leaf with thick line. (Color figure online)

2.2 XMSS

We outline key generation, signature generation and signature verification of XMSS. Let n be the security parameter in bytes and let h be the height of an XMSS tree. We use a textbook-like notation in which any kind of one-way function (hash function) is denoted as $H : \{0,1\}^* \rightarrow \{0,1\}^{8n}$ and we omit additional arguments and random bit masking defined in RFC 8391. First, the key generation outputs WOTS$^+$ secret keys, i.e., $(\mathsf{wsk}_0^i, \mathsf{wsk}_1^i, ..., \mathsf{wsk}_{l-1}^i) \in \{0,1\}^{8ln}$ for $i \in [2^h]$, as an XMSS secret key and the root of the XMSS tree as an XMSS public key $\mathsf{xpk} \in \{0,1\}^{8n}$. A (compressed) WOTS$^+$ public key for i-th leaf in the XMSS tree is computed as

$$\mathsf{wpk}^i = L(H^{w-1}(\mathsf{wsk}_0^i), H^{w-1}(\mathsf{wsk}_1^i), ..., H^{w-1}(\mathsf{wsk}_{l-1}^i)) \in \{0,1\}^{8n},$$

where $L : (\{0,1\}^{8n})^l \rightarrow \{0,1\}^{8n}$ is an unbalanced binary hash tree computation called L-tree, w is a constant called Winternitz parameter, and H^j is recursively defined by $H^j(\mathsf{x}) = H(H^{j-1}(\mathsf{x}))$ and $H^0(\mathsf{x}) = \mathsf{x}$. Leaves of the XMSS tree are $(\mathsf{wpk}^0, \mathsf{wpk}^1, ..., \mathsf{wpk}^{2^h-1}) \in \{0,1\}^{2^{h+3}n}$. From the leaves, a node of the tree on height $j \in [h+1]$ is obtained as follows ($\mathsf{n}_{j,i} \in \{0,1\}^{8n}$).

$$\mathsf{n}_{j,i} = \begin{cases} \mathsf{wpk}^i & \text{if } j = 0 \\ H(\mathsf{n}_{j-1,2i} \| \mathsf{n}_{j-1,2i+1}) & \text{otherwise} \end{cases}$$

Then, the root $\mathsf{n}_{h,0}$ becomes the XMSS public key xpk.

Second, the signature generation outputs a signature which consists of a leaf index, a WOTS$^+$ signature, and an authentication path, which are nodes needed to compute the root of XMSS tree (see an example of Fig. 1). Note that we call components of an authentication path as *authentication nodes*. Let φ be the leaf index to sign a message. A message (digest) $m \in \{0,1\}^{8n}$ is encoded as $(m_0, m_1, ..., m_{l_1-1}) \in [w]^{l_1}$. For the encoded message, a checksum $c = \sum_{i=0}^{l_1-1}(w - 1 - m_i)$ is calculated and encoded as $(c_0, c_1, ..., c_{l_2-1}) \in [w]^{l_2}$. Then, the encoded message and checksum are concatenated as $e = (e_0, e_1, ..., e_{l-1}) \in [w]^l$ ($l = l_1 + l_2$). A WOTS$^+$ signature σ_w^φ is computed by e_j times recursive H applications to wsk_j^φ ($j \in [l]$) and an XMSS signature σ_x is obtained as follows.

$$\sigma_w^\varphi = (H^{e_0}(\mathsf{wsk}_0^\varphi), H^{e_1}(\mathsf{wsk}_1^\varphi), ..., H^{e_{l-1}}(\mathsf{wsk}_{l-1}^\varphi)) \in \{0,1\}^{8ln}$$

$$\sigma_x = (\varphi, \sigma_w^\varphi, \mathsf{a}_0, \mathsf{a}_1, ..., \mathsf{a}_{h-1}) \in \{0,1\}^{h+8(l+h)n}$$

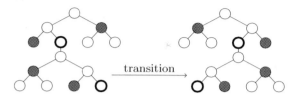

Fig. 2. Example of an authentication path and transition of XMSS^{MT} of two layers.

Note that $(a_j)_{j \in [h]}$ is the authentication path where a_j is a sibling node of either the WOTS$^+$ public key or its parent node on height j. XMSS increases the leaf index by one after the signature generation in order not to sign with the same WOTS$^+$ secret key more than once.

Last, the signature verification computes the root of XMSS tree from the signature and checks if it equals to the one of the public key. The WOTS$^+$ public key is obtained from corresponding WOTS$^+$ signature. Let $(s_0, s_1, ..., s_{l-1})$ be a divided WOTS$^+$ signature σ_w^φ. A node of the XMSS tree is obtained from the XMSS signature as follows ($p_j \in \{0,1\}^{8n}$).

$$p_j = \begin{cases} L(H^{w-1-e_0}(s_0), H^{w-1-e_1}(s_1), ..., H^{w-1-e_{l-1}}(s_{l-1})) & \text{if } j = 0 \\ H(p_{j-1} \| a_{j-1}) & \text{else if } \left\lfloor \frac{\varphi}{2^{j-1}} \right\rfloor \equiv 0 \bmod 2 \\ H(a_{j-1} \| p_{j-1}) & \text{otherwise} \end{cases}$$

Then, the signature is verified if $xpk = p_h$ holds.

2.3   XMSS^{MT}

In the multi-tree variant XMSS^{MT}, XMSS trees are layered. We show an example of layered XMSS trees in Fig. 2. We outline the algorithms of XMSS^{MT}. In XMSS^{MT}, d is the number of layers ($d|h$ as in RFC 8391) and h/d is the height of each XMSS tree (the total height is h). We add another superscript to denote the layer of variables, e.g., pk^k or $sk^{k,i}$ on k-th layer ($k \in [d]$).

In the key generation, a key pair of the top-level XMSS tree, i.e., WOTS$^+$ secret keys $(wsk_0^{d-1,i}, wsk_1^{d-1,i}, ..., wsk_{l-1}^{d-1,i}) \in \{0,1\}^{8ln}$ for $i \in [2^{h/d}]$ and an XMSS public key $xpk^{d-1} \in \{0,1\}^{8n}$ as an XMSS^{MT} public key mpk, is generated.

In the signature generation, the XMSS tree on the bottom layer signs a message and another XMSS tree signs a root of one lower XMSS tree. A signature of XMSS^{MT} is obtained as

$$\sigma_x^k = (\sigma_w^{k,\varphi_k}, a_0^k, a_1^k, ..., a_{\frac{h}{d}-1}^k) \in \{0,1\}^{8(l+\frac{h}{d})n} \ (k \in [d]),$$

$$\sigma_m = (\varphi, \sigma_x^0, \sigma_x^1, ..., \sigma_x^{d-1}) \in \{0,1\}^{h+8(dl+h)n},$$

where $\varphi_k \equiv \lfloor \varphi/2^{k(h/d)} \rfloor \bmod 2^{h/d}$. Note that σ_w^{0,φ_0} and σ_w^{k,φ_k} ($k \neq 0$) are signatures for a message (digest) m and an XMSS public key xpk^{k-1}. In XMSS^{MT}, there is a process called *transition*. Once all leaves have been exhausted, i.e., $\varphi_k = 2^{h/d} - 1$, signatures are generated using the next XMSS tree from the next time. When the transition occurs, a signature on one higher XMSS tree is updated to be the next one since a signed root changes in the transition (see Fig. 2).

In the signature verification, XMSS signatures of all the layers are verified from the bottom layer to the top one. Verification of σ_x^0 for the message outputs a candidate of XMSS public key of the bottom layer xpk^0. This pubic key is signed by σ_x^1 and verification of σ_x^1 for xpk^0 outputs a candidate of xpk^1, and so on. Finally, verification of the signature σ_x^{d-1} for xpk^{d-2} outputs a candidate of xpk^{d-1}, and the XMSS^{MT} signature is verified if this candidate equals to the XMSS^{MT} public key mpk.

2.4 Merkle Tree Traversal Algorithm

A Merkle tree traversal algorithm is used for generating an authentication path of a current leaf on the assumption that the current leaf moves to the next one in each step. Instead of generating the authentication path from scratch, a Merkle tree traversal algorithm efficiently generates using a time-memory tradeoff and various Merkle tree traversal algorithms were proposed [11–13].

The efficiency of the algorithms is affected by a method to obtain WOTS$^+$ secret keys in XMSS. RFC 8391 does not specify any method to generate WOTS$^+$ secret keys [8] but recommends a method to obtain them by inputting a private seed to a pseudorandom function (hereinafter called *PRF method*). There is also a method to generate secret keys from pseudorandom (number) generator [3]; however, we only consider the PRF method since it is recommended in RFC 8391 and NIST SP 800-208. There are algorithms which run in linear time/memory complexity with the tree height, and the BDS algorithm requires the least time and memory in the PRF method [4,12,13]. Therefore, we adopt the BDS algorithm. Note that the choice of the Merkle tree traversal algorithms does not affect the security and the interoperability.

2.5 BDS Algorithm

Intuitive Explanation. The BDS algorithm can speed up the signature generation by generating an authentication path in advance. A state called *BDS state* enables the algorithm to efficiently generate authentication nodes. We denote a BDS state as $((\mathsf{a}_j)_{j\in[h]}, \mathsf{r}, \mathsf{S}, (\mathsf{T}_j)_{j\in[h-2]}, (\mathsf{k}_j)_{j\in[h-1]})$, where we define each variable in the following explanation. The BDS state is initialized (i.e. the key generation in XMSS) and updated in each step while generating an authentication path for the next leaf index (i.e. the signature generation in XMSS). When the leaf index increases by one, the authentication path for this leaf has already been in the BDS state.

The procedures to generate left and right nodes are different as follows.

(*Procedure to generate left nodes*). Left nodes are generated from authentication nodes used in the past. Some of the authentication nodes are kept in $(\mathsf{k}_j)_{j\in[h-1]}$. A new authentication node on height $\tau > 0$ is generated as $\mathsf{a}_\tau \leftarrow H(\mathsf{a}_{\tau-1}\|\mathsf{k}_{\tau-1})$, where H is a one-way function and $\mathsf{a}_{\tau-1}$ is a current authentication node on height $\tau - 1$. We show an example in Fig. 3.

step 0   step 1   step 2

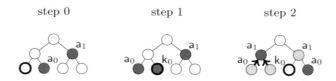

Fig. 3. Example of a procedure to generate a left authentication node. A node with thick line is a current leaf. Red, magenta, and pink nodes are authentication nodes, kept authentication nodes, and (kept) authentication nodes of the last step. (Color figure online)

Fig. 4. Example of the treehash algorithm (four treehash updates) to generate a target node (yellow node). A node with thick line is a current leaf. Blue and light-blue nodes denote pushed and popped nodes on a stack. (Color figure online)

(*Procedure to generate right nodes*). Unlike left nodes, right nodes are generated from scratch. In order to update a_j in the future, the BDS algorithm takes a strategy to generate the target node and keep it in T_j.node before it will be required, where T_j is called *treehash instance* which is a data structure to generate a right authentication node. The BDS algorithm uses *treehash algorithm* [4,8], which is widely used in hash-based signature schemes. The treehash algorithm uses a stack S with ordinal push and pop operations. We show an example of the treehash algorithm in Fig. 4. When a new leaf n is generated, the treehash algorithm pops a node s on the stack and computes $n \leftarrow H(s\|n)$. The algorithm repeats this procedure while a newly generated n has the same height as the top node of the stack. We call the procedure, i.e., a leaf computation and repeated H computations using the stack, as *treehash update*. The treehash algorithm is exponential, i.e., 2^j treehash updates for height j. To reduce the computational time in each step, the BDS algorithm only executes u treehash updates in each step and finish all 2^j treehash updates in $2^j/u$ steps.

The BDS algorithm needs to generate T_j.node for all heights $j \in [h-2]$ but only u treehash updates are executed in each step. In such a restriction, the algorithm prioritizes nodes which are immediately required for the authentication path. An objective of a treehash instance is to generate a target node and store it in T_j.node until it is required as a_j. Since the treehash instance has a leaf index to be generated next time, the algorithm can generate a correct leaf after executing treehash updates for other treehash instances. Also, the algorithm can select a treehash instance to execute treehash updates with priority using some auxiliary data of the instance.

There is an additional parameter k ($k \geq 2$) which controls time-memory trade-off of the BDS algorithm [4]. The BDS algorithm generates $2^k - k - 1$ right nodes on heights from $h-k$ to $h-2$ in the initialization and stores them in r of the BDS state in order not to generate the nodes after the initialization. However, we do not consider the parameter k as a variable and set $k = 2$ in this paper since one of our objectives is to achieve memory efficiency.

Specification. We show the BDS algorithm in Algorithm 1. Let T_j be a tree-hash instance which has four member variables including an area for the target node T_j.node. Also, T_j.idx indicates a leaf which is generated in the next treehash update, T_j.height indicates a height of the lowest node generated by T_j, and T_j.stackusage indicates the number of nodes on the stack pushed by T_j. Let S be a stack having ordinal push and pop operations, S.push and S.pop. A BDS state is initialized as $(a_j)_{j \in [h]} \leftarrow (n_{j,1})_{j \in [h]}$, $r \leftarrow n_{h-2,3}$ and $(T_j.\text{node}, T_j.\text{idx}, T_j.\text{height}, T_j.\text{stackusage})_{j \in [h-2]} \leftarrow (n_{j,3}, 0, h, 0)_{j \in [h-2]}$. The BDS algorithm updates authentication nodes on heights $[\tau + 1]$, where τ is a height of the first left parent node of φ-th leaf (Line 1).

The ways to generate left and right nodes are different. For the left node on height τ, it is generated by a leaf computation if $\tau = 0$ (Line 3) and H computation if $\tau > 0$ (Line 4(a)). For the right nodes on heights $[\tau]$, they are substituted from T_j.node or r in Line 4(b). Also in Line 4(b), a treehash instance is initialized when it substitutes its node to an authentication node of the same height. Before the substitution, the target node must be generated in Line 5, which is the most complex part of the BDS algorithm. To prevent a treehash instance from popping nodes generated by the other instances, the BDS algorithm chooses a treehash instance on height ψ, s.t., T_ψ.height is the minimum in Line 5(a). If T_ψ.height $= T_{\psi'}$.height ($\psi < \psi'$) holds, the algorithm chooses ψ-th one. A chosen treehash instance executes a treehash update in Line 5(b).

To reduce the maximum number of nodes pushed on the stack, the BDS algorithm uses the stack S in a complex manner. If the treehash instance does not store any node (i.e. T_ψ.height $= \psi$), a generated node is stored in T_ψ.node in Line 5(c). Instead of popping a node on S, the treehash instance takes a node of T_ψ.node if the instance does not store any node on S (i.e. T_ψ.stackusage $= 0$) in Line 5(b). In this way, the maximum number of nodes pushed on the stack decreases by one. Note that any detailed procedure for the usage of S is not specified in [4]; therefore, a member variable T_j.stackusage is used to count the number of nodes on the stack as in the reference implementation [10]. In Line 5(d) and 5(e), T_ψ.height is set as defined. If T_ψ.height $= h$ holds, it indicates that T_ψ has already generated its target node. Finally, the BDS algorithm outputs an authentication path for $(\psi + 1)$-th leaf in Line 6.

2.6   Application of the BDS Algorithm to XMSS^{MT}

In XMSS^{MT}, transitions of XMSS trees occur (see Sect. 2.3). When a transition occurs, a BDS state of the next XMSS tree should be ready for signing the next message. Otherwise, XMSS^{MT} must generate the BDS state from scratch in the transition and it requires exponential time (generating $(a_j)_{i \in [h/d]}$ requires $2^{h/d} - 1$ leaf computations). To prevent such an exponential computation, the

HRB algorithm of XMSS^{MT} [9] retains a BDS state for the next XMSS tree (hereinafter called *next BDS state*).

Algorithm 1: BDS algorithm [4]

Input: Leaf index φ and BDS state

Output: Authentication path for $(\varphi + 1)$-th leaf

1. Let τ be the height of the first left parent node of φ-th leaf and authentication nodes on heights $[\tau + 1]$ are updated in this step:
   $\tau \leftarrow \max\{j : 2^j | (\varphi + 1), j \leq h - 1\}$.

2. If the parent of φ-the leaf on height $\tau + 1$ is a left node, keep the authentication node:
   if $\lfloor \varphi / 2^{\tau+1} \rfloor$ mod $2 = 0$ **and** $\tau < h - 1$ **then** $\mathsf{k}_\tau \leftarrow \mathsf{a}_\tau$.

3. If φ-th leaf is a left node, generate φ-th leaf:
   if $\tau = 0$ **then** $\mathsf{a}_0 \leftarrow \mathsf{n}_{0,\varphi}$.

4. Otherwise, the authentication nodes on heights $[\tau + 1]$ are updated:
   else then
   (a) The authentication node on height τ is generated by the current authentication node on height $\tau - 1$ and a node in buffer: $\mathsf{a}_\tau \leftarrow H(\mathsf{a}_{\tau-1} \| \mathsf{b})$.
   (b) For authentication nodes on heights $[\tau]$, substitute nodes of treehash instances and initialize treehash instances which have substituted their target nodes to the authentication nodes if the next indexes are smaller than 2^h (out of the tree):
   for $j \in [\tau]$ **do**
       if $j = h - 2$ **then** $\mathsf{a}_j \leftarrow \mathsf{r}$.
       if $j < h - 2$ **then**
           $\mathsf{a}_j \leftarrow \mathsf{T}_j$.node.
           if $\varphi + 1 + 3 \cdot 2^j < 2^h$ **then** T_j.idx $\leftarrow \varphi + 1 + 3 \cdot 2^j$, T_j.height $\leftarrow j$.

5. Execute treehash update for $h/2 - 1$ times:
   for $i \in [h/2 - 1]$ **do**
   (a) Let ψ be an index of treehash instance, s.t., the lowest node generated by this instance (i.e. T_j.height) is the lowest. If there are more than one such instances, set ψ to the lowest index among them:
   $\psi \leftarrow \min\{j : \mathsf{T}_j$.height $= \min\{\mathsf{T}_{j'}$.height $: j' \in [h - 2]\}\}$.
   (b) Execute one treehash update in the treehash instance on height ψ. If the instance does not store nodes on S, compute H with the node stored in the instance; otherwise, compute H with the popped node from S:
   $\mathsf{b} \leftarrow \mathsf{n}_{0,i}$ $(i = \mathsf{T}_\psi$.idx$)$, T_ψ.idx $\leftarrow \mathsf{T}_\psi$.idx $+ 1$.
   while the heights of either T_ψ.node (if T_ψ.stackusage $= 0$) or the top node on S (if T_ψ.stackusage > 0) and b are the same **do**
       if T_ψ.stackusage $= 0$ **then** $\mathsf{b} \leftarrow H(\mathsf{T}_\psi$.node$\|\mathsf{b})$, T_ψ.height $\leftarrow \psi$.
       else then $\mathsf{b} \leftarrow H(S$.pop$\|\mathsf{b})$, T_ψ.stackusage $\leftarrow \mathsf{T}_\psi$.stackusage $- 1$.
   (c) If the treehash instance does not store any node, substitute the generated node to the treehash instance; otherwise, push the node to the stack:
   if T_ψ.height $= \psi$ **then** T_ψ.node $\leftarrow \mathsf{b}$.
   else then S.push(b), T_ψ.stackusage $\leftarrow \mathsf{T}_\psi$.stackusage $+ 1$.
   (d) If the generated node reaches the target height, finish this instance (substitute h to the height):
   if $j = \psi$ $(j$: height of $\mathsf{b})$ **then** T_ψ.height $\leftarrow h$.
   (e) Else if the generated node has a height lower than the current lowest height, update the height:
   else if $j < \mathsf{T}_\psi$.height $(j$: height of $\mathsf{b})$ **then** T_ψ.height $\leftarrow j$.

6. **return** $(\mathsf{a}_j)_{j \in [h]}$.

We denote nodes and their variables of the next XMSS tree in hat-notation. The next BDS state is generated while the signature generations by the current XMSS tree. In each signature generation in the current XMSS tree, one treehash update is executed. In the next XMSS tree, the HRB algorithm only uses a stack $\hat{\mathsf{S}}$ of the next BDS state and generates $\hat{\mathsf{n}}_{0,i}$ while generating i-th signature ($i \in [2^{h/d}]$). In the end, the root of the next XMSS tree is obtained, and all the nodes required as an initial BDS state are generated in the process. The state structure of the next BDS state in the HRB algorithm is denoted as $\left((\hat{\mathsf{a}}_j)_{j \in [\frac{h}{d}]}, \hat{\mathsf{r}}, \hat{\mathsf{S}}, (\hat{\mathsf{T}}_j)_{j \in [\frac{h}{d}-2]} \right)$. Since the top XMSS tree has no next tree, the HRB algorithm retains d current BDS states and $d-1$ next BDS states.

2.7 Disadvantages of Existing Algorithms

There are two disadvantages in the HRB algorithm. First, the state size is large since two BDS states (current and next states) are retained in each layer except for the top one. The total number of stored nodes is $13h/2 - 3h/d - 10d + 5$, where d is the number of layers and h is the sum of heights of d XMSS trees. For parameters of long-term use, e.g., $h \geq 30$, the state size becomes an obstacle for implementing XMSS^{MT} on resource-constrained devices.

Second, the state structure of the HRB algorithm is complex since two BDS states with different structures are retained. Also, the BDS algorithm itself is a very complex algorithm as shown in Algorithm 1. In the BDS algorithm, the multiple treehash instances take turns to execute treehash updates and they share a single stack. An implementer has to carefully design the schedule of treehash updates, in order to let treehash instances generate nodes in time and prevent them from popping nodes generated by the other treehash instances.

3   Simple and Memory-Efficient Signature-Generation Algorithm for XMSS^{MT}

We design an algorithm of XMSS^{MT} with the BDS algorithm which overcomes disadvantages of the HRB algorithm (see Sect. 2.7) as follows.

1. We modify the BDS algorithm as it can generate authentication paths of XMSS trees on the same layer by a single BDS state.
2. We simplify two parts of the BDS algorithm.
3. In XMSS trees on higher layers, we adopt the MMT algorithm.

First, we show the modified BDS algorithm in Sect. 3.1. Next, we specify the MMT algorithm in Sect. 3.2. Last, we show how to apply the modified BDS and the MMT algorithms to XMSS^{MT} in Sect. 3.3.

Algorithm 2: Modified BDS algorithm

Input: Leaf index $\varphi = \nu \cdot 2^{h/d} + \mu$ and BDS state

Output: Authentication path for $(\varphi + 1)$-th leaf

1. Let τ be the height of the first left parent node of φ-th leaf and authentication nodes on heights $[\min\{\tau + 1, h/d\}]$ are updated in this step: $\tau \leftarrow \max\{j : 2^j | (\varphi + 1), j \le h/d\}$.

2. If the parent of φ-the leaf on height $\tau + 1$ is a left node, keep the authentication node: **if** $\lfloor \varphi/2^{\tau+1} \rfloor \bmod 2 = 0$ **and** $\tau < h/d - 1$ **then** $\mathsf{k}_\tau \leftarrow \mathsf{a}_\tau$.

3. If φ-th leaf is a left node, generate φ-th leaf:
   if $\tau = 0$ **then** $\mathsf{a}_0 \leftarrow \mathsf{n}_{0,\varphi}$.

4. Otherwise, the authentication nodes on heights $[\min\{\tau + 1, h/d\}]$ are updated:
   else then

   (a) If an authentication node on height τ exists, it is generated by the current authentication node on height $\tau - 1$ and a node in buffer:
       if $\tau < h/d$ **then** $\mathsf{a}_\tau \leftarrow H(\mathsf{a}_{\tau-1}\|\mathsf{b})$.

   (b) For authentication nodes on heights $[\tau]$, substitute nodes of treehash instances and initialize treehash instances which have substituted their target nodes to the authentication nodes if the next indexes are smaller than 2^h (out of the tree):
       for $j \in [\tau]$ **do**
       $\mathsf{a}_j \leftarrow \mathsf{T}_j.\text{node}$.
       if $\varphi + 1 + 3 \cdot 2^j < 2^h$ **then** $\mathsf{T}_j.\text{idx} \leftarrow \varphi + 1 + 3 \cdot 2^j$, $\mathsf{T}_j.\text{fin} \leftarrow 0$.

5. Execute treehash update for $h/(2d)$ times:
   for $i \in [\lceil h/(2d) \rceil]$ **do**

   (a) Let ψ be the index of the lowest unfinished treehash instance:
       $\psi \leftarrow \min\{j : \mathsf{T}_j.\text{fin} = 0\}$.

   (b) Execute one treehash update on ψ-th treehash instance:
       $\mathsf{b} \leftarrow \mathsf{n}_{\psi,i}$ $(i = \mathsf{T}_\psi.\text{idx})$, $\mathsf{T}_\psi.\text{idx} \leftarrow \mathsf{T}_\psi.\text{idx} + 1$.
       while the heights of the top node on S and b are the same **do**
       $\mathsf{b} \leftarrow H(\mathsf{S}.\text{pop}\|\mathsf{b})$.

   (c) If the generated node reaches the target height, substitute the node to the treehash instance; otherwise push the node on the stack:
       if $j = \psi$ $(j$: height of $\mathsf{b})$ **then** $\mathsf{T}_\psi.\text{node} \leftarrow \mathsf{b}$, $\mathsf{T}_\psi.\text{fin} \leftarrow 1$.
       else then $\mathsf{S}.\text{push}(\mathsf{b})$.

6. **return** $(\mathsf{a}_j)_{j \in [h/d]}$.

3.1   Modification of BDS Algorithm

We show the modified BDS algorithm in Algorithm 2. Note that we change the height of the tree from h to h/d in accordance with the notation of XMSS^{MT}.

Single BDS State for Multiple XMSS Trees. We modify the BDS algorithm as it can continuously update an authentication path in multiple XMSS trees by a single BDS state. Algorithm 2 generates an initial authentication path of the next XMSS tree while updating an authentication path of the current XMSS tree. Leaf indexes of XMSS trees are integrated as $\varphi = \nu \cdot 2^{h/d} + \mu \in [2^h]$, i.e., μ-th leaf of ν-th XMSS tree. Then, the algorithm initializes a treehash instance even if the index becomes more than $2^{h/d}$ in Line 4(b). A treehash instance, s.t., $(2^{h/d+1} - 1) \geq T_j.\mathrm{idx} \geq 2^{h/d}$, generates a node of the second XMSS tree. While updating the authentication path of the first XMSS tree, the instance generates the node which will be one of the initial authentication nodes of the second XMSS tree. In this way, Algorithm 2 can continuously generate the authentication path of the next XMSS tree while updating the current one.

Right authentication nodes on heights $(h/d - 1)$ and $(h/d - 2)$ are not generated in Algorithm 1 since the algorithm only concerns a single XMSS tree. To generate these two right authentication nodes, the number of treehash instances becomes h/d ($h/d - 2$ in Algorithm 1) and the number of treehash updates per step becomes $h/(2d)$ ($h/(2d) - 1$ in Algorithm 1). We show that the number $h/(2d)$ is adequate in Proposition 1 of Sect. 4.

Simplification of BDS Algorithm. (*Simplification on treehash update*) We change the way to choose a treehash instance to execute treehash updates. The criteria is very simple: choose the lowest treehash instance which has not yet generated its target node. Even if we change the criteria, the BDS algorithm works (see Proposition 2 of Sect. 4). A treehash instance retains a flag $T_j.\mathrm{fin}$ which indicates that this instance has generated its target node or not. Algorithm 2 simply chooses the lowest instance with $T_j.\mathrm{fin} = 0$ in Line 5(a). If T_j finishes generating its target node, sets $T_j.\mathrm{fin} = 1$ in Line 5(c).

(*Simplification on stack usage*) Unlike Algorithms 1, 2 pushes nodes only on the stack S in Line 5(b). In Algorithm 1, the way to store nodes in $T_j.\mathrm{node}$ and S is complicated and we cannot get much benefit from it since the state size decreases by only one node.

As the number of treehash instances increases, the stack S should have at most $h/d - 1$ nodes to generate a node on height $h/d - 1$. Also, the maximum number of nodes on the stack does not decrease because of the second simplification. For these reasons, the maximum number of nodes on the stack increases from $h/d - 4$ to $h/d - 1$. In Algorithm 2, there is a constant increase in the state size. However, we can make the state size smaller than the HRB algorithm, since the proposed algorithm does not retain the next BDS state.

3.2   Memory-Efficient Merkle Tree Traversal (MMT) Algorithm

For XMSS trees on higher layers, the algorithm uses the MMT algorithm shown in Algorithm 3. The MMT algorithm only stores an authentication path and a stack as a state called *MMT state* in the form of $((a_j)_{j \in [h/d]}, S)$. The stack S is used to generate and store nodes which will replace authentication nodes $(a_j)_{j \in [h/d]}$. The maximum number of nodes on S is upper-bounded by h/d (see Proposition 3 of Sect. 4). To update authentication nodes on heights $[\min\{\tau +$

$1, h/d\}]$, Algorithm 3 generates the nodes from $\min\{\tau, h/d - 1\}$ to 0 (descending order of height) by executing 2^j treehash updates (a treehash algorithm) for height j in Line 2. Then, Algorithm 3 pushes the generated nodes on S. To update the authentication path, the algorithm pops nodes on S and substitutes them to the authentication nodes from 0 to $\min\{\tau, h/d - 1\}$ in Line 3.

Algorithm 3: MMT algorithm

Input: Leaf index $\varphi = \nu \cdot 2^{h/d} + \mu$ and MMT state
Output: Authentication path for $(\varphi + 1)$-th leaf
1. Let τ be the height of the first left parent node of φ-th leaf and authentication nodes on heights $[\min\{\tau + 1, h/d\}]$ are updated in this step:
   $\tau \leftarrow \max\{j : 2^j | (\varphi + 1), j \leq h/d\}$.
2. Generate authentication nodes on heights $[\min\{\tau + 1, h/d\}]$ from the highest:
   for $j = \min\{\tau, h/d - 1\}$ **to** 0 **do**
       if $j = \tau$ **then** $\rho \leftarrow \varphi + 1 - 2^j$.
       else then $\rho \leftarrow \varphi + 1 + 2^j$.
       for $i \in [2^j]$ **do**
           b $\leftarrow$ n$_{j,\rho}$, $\rho \leftarrow \rho + 1$.
           while the heights of the top node of S and b are the same **do**
               b $\leftarrow H(\text{S.pop}\|\text{b})$.
           S.push(b).
3. Pop nodes from the stack and substitute them to the authentication path:
   for $j = 0$ **to** $\min\{\tau, h/d - 1\}$ **do**
       a$_j \leftarrow$ S.pop.
4. **return** $(a_j)_{j\in[h/d]}$.

The MMT algorithm stores $2h/d$ nodes and computes at most $2^{h/d} - 1$ treehash updates per step. Though the MMT algorithm is inappropriate on the bottom layer, it is applicable on higher layers.

3.3 Application of Modified BDS and MMT Algorithms to XMSS^MT

The proposed signature-generation algorithm for XMSS^MT uses the modified BDS algorithm on the bottom layer and uses the MMT algorithm on higher layers. The state structure of the whole algorithm is denoted as follows (the left state is BDS sate and the right ones are MMT states).

$$\left(\left((a_j^0)_{j\in[\frac{h}{d}]}, S^0, (T_j^0)_{j\in[\frac{h}{d}]}, (k_j^0)_{j\in[\frac{h}{d}-1]}\right), \left((a_j^k)_{j\in[\frac{h}{d}]}, (T_j^k)_{j\in[\frac{h}{d}]}, S^k\right)_{k\in[d]\setminus[1]}\right)$$

Note that T_j^k is a treehash instance defined in the same manner as Algorithm 2 except that it does not retain node since the target node is kept in the stack S^k. On the bottom layer, the key-generation algorithm generates $(a_j^0)_{j\in[\frac{h}{d}]}$ and

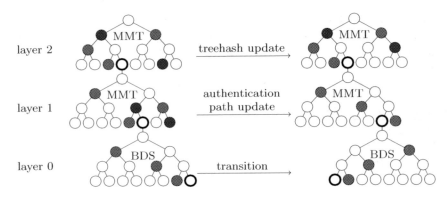

Fig. 5. Example of a treehash update of the MMT algorithm on higher layers. A node with thick line is a current leaf. Red nodes are authentication nodes and blue ones are nodes on the stack. (Color figure online)

the target nodes of $(\mathsf{T}_j^0)_{j \in [h/d-1]}$ and executes $h/(2d) + 1$ treehash updates for $\mathsf{T}_{h/d-1}^0$ to prevent the other instances from popping the nodes pushed by this instance (see Proposition 2 of Sect. 4). For all layers $k \in [d] \setminus [1]$, the algorithm generates $(\mathsf{a}_j^k)_{j \in [\frac{h}{d}]}$ and initializes T_0^k as $\mathsf{T}_0^k.\mathsf{fin} = 0$ and $\mathsf{T}_0^k.\mathsf{idx} = 0$ where $\mathsf{n}_{0,0}^k$ is in the next authentication path.

The MMT algorithm updates the authentication path when a transition occurs in the XMSS tree of one lower layer. Hence, it is sufficient to generate the next authentication path by the time the next transition occurs. The MMT algorithm requires at most $2^{h/d} - 1$ treehash updates. In order to limit the number of treehash updates while generating a signature, we set a condition to update an authentication path and execute a treehash update on k-th layer as follows (the current leaf index is φ).

1. If a transition occurs on $(k-1)$-th layer in the next signature generation, i.e., $2^{k(h/d)} | (\varphi + 1)$, the proposed algorithm updates an authentication path of the MMT state on k-th layer.
2. Else if a transition occurs on $(k-2)$-th layer in the next signature generation, i.e., $2^{(k-1)(h/d)} | (\varphi + 1)$, the proposed algorithm executes one treehash update in the MMT state on k-th layer.

Using the above condition, a treehash update is executed only on k-th layer, s.t., $\max\{k : 2^{(k-1)(h/d)} | (\varphi + 1)\}$. In Fig. 5, we show an example of the MMT algorithm used in XMSS^{MT} . The current index plus one is $\varphi + 1 = 240$ which is divided by 8 ($= 2^{h/d}$). Therefore, the authentication path on the first layer is updated and a treehash update is executed on the second layer.

In order to execute the MMT algorithm of Algorithm 3 following the above condition, we show a divided MMT algorithm in Algorithm 4. In the same manner as Algorithm 2, the proposed algorithm executes Algorithm 4 in every signature generation.

4   Correctness of Proposed Algorithm

Single BDS State for Multiple XMSS Trees. Unlike the HRB algorithm preparing two BDS states, the proposed algorithm generates authentication paths for the current and the next XMSS trees on the same layer by a single BDS state. This is achieved by integrating leaf indexes and increasing the number of treehash instances from $h/d - 2$ to h/d. We can assume all the XMSS trees on the bottom layer as a big XMSS tree of height h. Disregarding authentication nodes higher than $h/d - 1$, the authentication path is updated by $(\mathsf{T}_j)_{j \in [h/d]}$. In addition, authentication nodes are generated in time by increasing the number of treehash updates per step as follows.

Proposition 1. *If the BDS algorithm executes $h/(2d)$ treehash updates per step, T_j can generate T_j.node in time for substituting to a_j for $j \in [h/d]$.*

Proof. Suppose that τ treehash instances $(\mathsf{T}_j)_{j \in [\tau]}$ are initialized. The treehash instance on height j is initialized once in 2^{j+1} steps [4]. In 2^τ steps, the target nodes $(\mathsf{T}_j.\text{node})_{j \in [\tau]}$ are generated multiple times. The number of treehash

---

Algorithm 4: Divided MMT algorithm

Input: Input Leaf index φ of bottom layer and MMT state on k-th layer
Output: Updated MMT state on k-th layer
1. If a transition occurs on $(k-1)$-th layer, update an authentication path:
   if $k2^{h/d}|(\varphi + 1)$ **then**
   (a) Compute a leaf index of k-th layer from φ: $\varphi^k \leftarrow \lfloor \varphi/2^{k(h/d)} \rfloor$.
   (b) Let τ (resp. τ') be the height of the first left parent node of φ^k-th leaf (resp. $(\varphi^k + 1)$-th leaf) and authentication nodes on heights $[\min\{\tau + 1, h/d\}]$ (resp. $[\min\{\tau' + 1, h/d\}]$) are updated in this step (resp. next step): $\tau \leftarrow \max\{j : 2^j|(\varphi^k + 1), j \le h/d\}, \tau' \leftarrow \max\{j : 2^j|(\varphi^k + 2), j \le h/d\}$.
   (c) Pop nodes from the stack and substitute them to the authentication path:
      for $j = 0$ **to** $\min\{\tau, h/d - 1\}$ **do**
         $\mathsf{a}_j^k \leftarrow \mathsf{S}^k.\text{pop}$.
   (d) Initialize treehash instances on heights $[\min\{\tau' + 1, h/d\}]$:
      for $j \in [\min\{\tau' + 1, h/d\}]$ **do**
         if $j = \tau'$ **then** $\mathsf{T}_j^k.\text{idx} \leftarrow \varphi^k + 2 - 2^j$
         else if $\varphi^k + 2 + 2^j < 2^{h-k(h/d)}$ **then** $\mathsf{T}_j^k.\text{idx} \leftarrow \varphi^k + 2 + 2^j$.
         $\mathsf{T}_j^k.\text{fin} \leftarrow 0$.
2. Else if a transition occurs on $(k-2)$-th layer, execute one treehash update:
   else if $(k-1)2^{h/d}|(\varphi + 1)$ **then**
   (a) Choose the highest unfinished treehash instance: $\psi \leftarrow \max\{j : \mathsf{T}_j^k.\text{fin} = 0\}$.
   (b) Execute one treehash update on ψ-th treehash instance:
      $\mathsf{b} \leftarrow \mathsf{n}_{0,i}$ ($i = \mathsf{T}_\psi^k.\text{idx}$), $\mathsf{T}_\psi^k.\text{idx} \leftarrow \mathsf{T}_\psi^k.\text{idx} + 1$.
      while the heights of the top node of S^k and b are the same **do**
         $\mathsf{b} \leftarrow H(\mathsf{S}^k.\text{pop}\|\mathsf{b})$.
      if $j = \psi$ (j: height of b) **then** $\mathsf{T}_\psi^k.\text{fin} \leftarrow 1$.
3. **return** $\left((\mathsf{a}_j^k)_{j \in [h/d]}, (\mathsf{T}_j^k)_{j \in [h/d]}, \mathsf{S}^k\right)$.

---

updates required to generate these target nodes in time is $\sum_{j=0}^{\tau-1}(2^\tau/2^{j+1})2^j = \tau 2^{\tau-1}$. There are $(h/(2d))2^\tau$ treehash updates if $h/(2d)$ treehash updates are executed per step. Therefore, $(h/(2d))2^\tau \geq \tau 2^{\tau-1}$ holds $(h/d \geq \tau)$. Since $\tau 2^{\tau-1}$ is less than or equals to the one executed in 2^τ steps and the fact is true for any τ, the BDS algorithm can generate all the target nodes in time. $\square$

Simplification of BDS Algorithm. The BDS algorithm fails if a treehash instance pops a node pushed by the other instances. We show that the modified BDS algorithm of Algorithm 2 does not fail as follows.

Proposition 2. *If the BDS algorithm updates the lowest treehash instance which has not yet generated its target nodes, i.e., T_ψ for $\psi = \min\{j : \mathsf{T}_j.\mathrm{fin} = 0\}$, with priority, treehash instances do not pop nodes pushed by the other instances.*

Proof. We only show that heights of nodes on the stack S are at least $\tau - 1$ ($\tau \in [h/d+1]\setminus[1]$) when τ treehash instances $(\mathsf{T}_j)_{j\in[\tau]}$ are initialized (hereinafter called *main claim*). Heights of nodes used for generating the target nodes of $(\mathsf{T}_j)_{j\in[\tau]}$ are at most $\tau - 2$ and these nodes never reach the height $\tau - 1$. From the main claim, we can prove that heights of nodes pushed by $(\mathsf{T}_j)_{j\in[\tau]}$ are lower than the nodes pushed by $(\mathsf{T}_j)_{j\in[h/d]\setminus[\tau]}$ and the instances $(\mathsf{T}_j)_{j\in[\tau]}$ never pop nodes generated by the higher instances $(\mathsf{T}_j)_{j\in[h/d]\setminus[\tau]}$.

Let $\varphi_l^\tau = (l+1)2^\tau - 1$ be l-th leaf index such that $(\mathsf{T}_j)_{j\in[\tau]}$ are initialized ($l \in [2^{h/d-\tau}]$). Let t_{stack} be the number of treehash updates spent for generating nodes on S. Since the stack S stores nodes on distinct heights, $2^j | t_{stack}$ implies that the heights of nodes are at least j on S.

We should consider treehash updates which are not executed. Since such treehash updates occur after $(\mathsf{T}_j)_{j\in[h/d]}$ generates their target nodes, we can assume that a virtual treehash instance T_∞ executes treehash updates and pushes generated nodes on S (hereinafter called *virtual-instance assumption*). If the main claim is true on the virtual-instance assumption, the heights of nodes pushed by T_∞ are higher than the nodes pushed by the actual instances $(\mathsf{T}_j)_{j\in[h/d]}$. Because the nodes of T_∞ and the ones of the actual instances are clearly separated upward and downward in S, removing the nodes of T_∞ does not affect the other instances. Hence, we can prove the main claim not on the virtual-instance assumption by removing the nodes of T_∞.

We prove the main claim on the virtual-instance assumption by induction on l for φ_l^τ as follows.

(*Basic step*). We show that the main claim is true for φ_0^τ. In the proposed algorithm, $\mathsf{T}_{h/d-1}$ does not generate its target node and executes $h/(2d) + 1$ treehash updates in the key generation (see Sect. 3.3). Since t_{stack} is computed by subtracting the number of treehash updates spent for the generated target nodes from the total number of treehash updates, we have

$$t_{stack} = \frac{h}{2d} + 1 + (2^\tau - 1)\frac{h}{2d} - \sum_{j=0}^{\tau-1}\left(\frac{2^\tau}{2^{j+1}} - 1\right)2^j = \left(\frac{h}{d} - \tau + 2\right)2^{\tau-1}.$$

Table 1. Comparison of algorithms (the number of leaf computations is counted).

Algorithm	Naive	HRB [9]	Proposed
keygen	$2^{h/d}$	$d2^{h/d} - d - 1$	$d2^{h/d} + h/(2d) - d$
sign (average)	$h/d - 1$	$h/(2d) + 1/2$	$h/(2d) + 1/2$
sign (worst)	$d2^{h/d}$	$h/(2d) + 1$	$h/(2d) + 2$
state (#nodes)	0	$13h/2 - 3h/d - 10d + 5$	$2h + 3h/(2d) - 1$

Therefore, $2^{\tau-1}|t_{stack}$ holds and the main claim is true for φ_0^τ.

(*Induction step*). We show that the main claim is true when the leaf index is φ_{l+1}^τ if it is true for φ_l^τ. Let Δt_{stack} be the number of treehash updates spent for generating nodes on S in 2^τ steps after φ_l^τ. Let t_{higher} be the number of treehash updates spent for completing the target nodes of $(T_j)_{j\in[h/d]\setminus[\tau]}$.

Because the higher instances can execute treehash updates after $\sum_{j=0}^{\tau-1} \frac{2^\tau}{2^{j+1}} 2^j$ treehash updates, we have

$$\Delta t_{stack} + t_{higher} = \frac{h}{2d} 2^\tau - \sum_{j=0}^{\tau-1} \frac{2^\tau}{2^{j+1}} 2^j = \left(\frac{h}{d} - \tau\right) 2^{\tau-1}.$$

Hence, $2^{\tau-1}|(\Delta t_{stack} + t_{higher})$ holds.

As for t_{higher}, we consider two cases. First, T_j generates its target node from scratch by 2^j treehash updates. Second, T_j uses the nodes already pushed on S by generating nodes higher than or equal to $\tau - 1$. In either case, only nodes on heights at least $\tau - 1$ are generated and used for completing the target nodes. By counting treehash updates for generating these nodes, $2^{\tau-1}|t_{higher}$ holds. Therefore, $2^{\tau-1}|\Delta t_{stack}$ holds and heights of nodes pushed on S in 2^τ steps is at least $\tau - 1$. By the induction hypothesis, heights of nodes on S are at least $\tau - 1$ when the leaf index is φ_{l+1}^τ. □

State Size of MMT Algorithm. We show that the maximum number of nodes stored on the stack in the MMT algorithm as follows.

Proposition 3. *The MMT algorithm stores at most h/d nodes on the stack* S.

Proof. When a treehash instance T_j is generating its target node, the higher treehash instances $(T_{j'})_{j'\in[h/d]\setminus[j+1]}$ have already generated their target nodes and these nodes are pushed on S. Then, there are at most $h/d - 1 - j$ nodes stored on the stack S. Also, T_j ($j > 0$) pushes at most j nodes and T_0 ($j = 0$) pushes one node on S at the same time. Therefore, there are at most h/d nodes on S (when T_0 pushes the last node). □

Therefore, the state size of the MMT algorithm is at most $2h/d$ by adding the number of nodes for the current authentication path.

5   Comparison with Existing Algorithms

In Table 1, we compare performances of the naive, the HRB and the proposed algorithms. We show the number of leaf computations corresponding to the WOTS$^+$ key generations. In the comparison, we do not consider *inner node* computation corresponding to a hash function because the computation is negligible compared to the leaf computation. Indeed, a WOTS$^+$ key generation computes hash functions more than 1,000 times assuming parameters of RFC 8391 [8].

Since the signature generation in the worst case of the naive algorithm requires exponential time, the algorithm is impractical for large h/d. For the HRB and the proposed algorithms, the signature generation requires linear time in the average and the worst cases. For the signature generation in the worst case, the proposed algorithm requires one more leaf computation. However, the proposed algorithm has the same signing time on average and the state size is almost half of the HRB algorithm. We show the number of leaf computations as follows.

Proposition 4. *The number of leaf computations in the signature generation of the proposed algorithm is $h/(2d) + 1/2$ on average and at most $h/(2d) + 2$.*

Proof. (*Average case*) First, we only consider the XMSS tree on the bottom layer. As we change the number of treehash instances in a proof of Theorem 1 in [4], we obtain $h/(2d) + 1/2$ as the average number of leaf computations on the bottom layer. Next, we consider the XMSS trees on higher layers. The average of leaf computations on k-th layer is computed by

$$\frac{\sum_{j=0}^{\frac{h}{d}-1} \frac{2^{\frac{h}{d}}}{2^j} 2^j \cdot 2^{h-(k+1)\frac{h}{d}}}{2^h} = \frac{\frac{h}{d} 2^{\frac{h}{d}} \cdot 2^{h-(k+1)\frac{h}{d}}}{2^h} = \frac{h}{d2^{k\frac{h}{d}}},$$

where $\sum_{j=0}^{h/d-1} \frac{2^{h/d}}{2^j} 2^j$ is the total number of leaf computations in an XMSS tree and there are $2^{h-(k+1)(h/d)}$ XMSS trees on k-th layer. Since $d2^{h/d}$ is much larger than h, the average is approximately 0 for any k. Hence, we can estimate the average only by the XMSS tree on the bottom layer.

(*Worst case*). First, we only consider the XMSS tree on the bottom layer. Since there are $h/(2d)$ treehash updates and one leaf computation for generating a left leaf (if $\tau = 0$), the proposed algorithm executes at most $h/(2d) + 1$ leaf computations on the bottom layer. Next, we consider the XMSS trees on higher layers in the proposed algorithm. As shown in Sect. 3.3, treehash updates are executed only on k-th layer, s.t., $\max\{k : 2^{(k-1)(h/d)}|(\varphi+1)\}$. Hence, the number of leaf computations is at most $h/(2d) + 2$ in the proposed algorithm.   □

In Table 2, we show the comparison of the state sizes for parameters of RFC 8391. Note that we count bytes for required auxiliary data such as T_j.idx for the implementation. For large d and h/d, the state size of the proposed algorithm becomes almost half of the one of the HRB algorithm. Also, we show the signature sizes in Table 2. Since the signature sizes are larger than the state sizes of

Table 2. Comparison of the state sizes in bytes.

$(n,\ h,\ d)$	HRB	Proposed	Signature	$(n,\ h,\ d)$	HRB	Proposed	Signature
$(32, 20, 2)$	$2,805$	$1,899$	$4,963$	$(64, 20, 2)$	$5,525$	$3,627$	$18,115$
$(32, 20, 4)$	$2,610$	$1,626$	$9,251$	$(64, 20, 4)$	$5,170$	$3,114$	$34,883$
$(32, 40, 2)$	$6,151$	$3,869$	$5,605$	$(64, 40, 2)$	$12,071$	$7,357$	$19,397$
$(32, 40, 4)$	$6,417$	$3,341$	9.893	$(64, 40, 4)$	$12,657$	$6,349$	$36,165$
$(32, 40, 8)$	$5,542$	$3,080$	$18,469$	$(64, 40, 8)$	$10,982$	$5,848$	$69,701$
$(32, 60, 3)$	$10,115$	$5,410$	$8,392$	$(64, 60, 3)$	$19,875$	$10,178$	$29,064$
$(32, 60, 6)$	$10,029$	$4,913$	14.824	$(64, 60, 6)$	$19,789$	$9,201$	$54,216$
$(32, 60,12)$	$8,474$	$4,669$	$27,688$	$(64, 60,12)$	$16,794$	$8,717$	$104,520$

both algorithms, the signature may dominate consumption of a volatile memory (such as RAM) for the signature generation; however, the state is stored in a (rewritable) nonvolatile memory. Our state size reduction has a big impact if the nonvolatile memory is scarce such as in smart cards.

6   Implementation

We implement the proposed algorithm by modifying part of the codes in the reference implementation of XMSS and XMSS^{MT} [10]. Specifically, we modify xmss_core_fast.c and make xmss_core_simple.c. Our code is available at <https://github.com/HaruCrypto54/xmss_simple>. We confirm that our code is compatible with the reference implementation since signatures generated by our code is successfully verified using reference implementation.

By the implementation, we compare the performances of the HRB and the proposed algorithms. Note that the reference implementation is based on the HRB algorithm. We compile the code using gcc (Ubuntu 9.3.0-17ubuntsu1 20) 9.3.0, with the compiler optimization flag -O3 and execute on a 2.5 GHz Intel Core i5-7200U (Kaby Lake) processor. We show the experimental result for their CPU cycles in Table 3. We use all the parameters of XMSS^{MT} using SHA2-256 specified in RFC 8391 and take an average after generating $2^{h/d}$ signatures since generating all 2^h signatures is unrealistic. Note that parameters are in the format of XMSSMT-[hash family]_[h]/[d]_[8n]. The performance measurements show that the proposed algorithm reduces the memory requirements without having a big impact on the execution time, which means that we improve memory efficiency without losing time efficiency.

Table 3. Comparison of the performance in 10^3 cycles.

Parameters of RFC 8391		xmss_core_fast.c (HRB)	xmss_core_simple.c (Proposed)
XMSSMT-SHA2_20/2_256	keygen	8, 784, 189	8, 818, 217
	sign(average)	25, 145	25, 512
XMSSMT-SHA2_20/4_256	keygen	602, 060	609, 088
	sign(average)	13, 982	14, 030
XMSSMT-SHA2_40/2_256	keygen	8, 955, 852, 682	8, 883, 549, 307
	sign(average)	45, 448	44, 552
XMSSMT-SHA2_40/4_256	keygen	17, 586, 407	17, 522, 011
	sign(average)	24, 355	25, 624
XMSSMT-SHA2_40/8_256	keygen	1, 227, 345	1, 205, 656
	sign(average)	13, 941	13, 893
XMSSMT-SHA2_60/3_256	keygen	13, 410, 972, 836	13, 547, 155, 998
	sign(average)	47, 659	45, 450
XMSSMT-SHA2_60/6_256	keygen	27, 138, 861	27, 394, 427
	sign(average)	25, 831	24, 688
XMSSMT-SHA2_60/12_256	keygen	1, 752, 319	1, 723, 708
	sign(average)	13, 981	14, 187

7   Conclusion

We propose a simple and memory-efficient algorithm of XMSS^{MT} with the BDS algorithm. We make three improvements in the proposed algorithm. First, the proposed algorithm can generate an authentication path of all the XMSS trees on the same layer by a single BDS state. The way of generating the authentication path improves simplicity of the state structure and reduces the state size. Second, we revise the BDS algorithm for simplifying the algorithm. Last, we propose the MMT algorithm to reduce the total state size. In comparison with the HRB algorithm of [9], the proposed algorithm reduces the state size almost by half without increasing the execution time.

References

1. Aumasson, J., et al.: SPHINCS+-submission to the 3rd round of the NIST post-quantum project (2020)
2. Groot Bruinderink, L., Hülsing, A.: "Oops, I did it again" – security of one-time signatures under two-message attacks. In: Adams, C., Camenisch, J. (eds.) SAC 2017. LNCS, vol. 10719, pp. 299–322. Springer, Cham (2018). https://doi.org/10.1007/978-3-319-72565-9_15
3. Buchmann, J., Dahmen, E., Hülsing, A.: XMSS - a practical forward secure signature scheme based on minimal security assumptions. In: Yang, B.-Y. (ed.) PQCrypto 2011. LNCS, vol. 7071, pp. 117–129. Springer, Heidelberg (2011). https://doi.org/10.1007/978-3-642-25405-5_8

4. Buchmann, J., Dahmen, E., Schneider, M.: Merkle tree traversal revisited. In: Buchmann, J., Ding, J. (eds.) PQCrypto 2008. LNCS, vol. 5299, pp. 63–78. Springer, Heidelberg (2008). https://doi.org/10.1007/978-3-540-88403-3_5

5. Cooper, D.A., Apon, D.C., Dang, Q.H., Davidson, M.S., Dworkin, M.J., Miller, C.A.: Recommendation for stateful hash-based signature schemes. NIST Spec. Publ. **800**, 208 (2020)

6. Hülsing, A.: W-OTS+ – shorter signatures for hash-based signature schemes. In: Youssef, A., Nitaj, A., Hassanien, A.E. (eds.) AFRICACRYPT 2013. LNCS, vol. 7918, pp. 173–188. Springer, Heidelberg (2013). https://doi.org/10.1007/978-3-642-38553-7_10

7. Hülsing, A., Busold, C., Buchmann, J.: Forward secure signatures on smart cards. In: Knudsen, L.R., Wu, H. (eds.) SAC 2012. LNCS, vol. 7707, pp. 66–80. Springer, Heidelberg (2013). https://doi.org/10.1007/978-3-642-35999-6_5

8. Hülsing, A., Butin, D., Gazdag, S.L., Rijneveld, J., Mohaisen, A.: XMSS: extended Merkle signature scheme. In: RFC 8391. IRTF (2018)

9. Hülsing, A., Rausch, L., Buchmann, J.: Optimal parameters for XMSS^{MT}. In: Cuzzocrea, A., Kittl, C., Simos, D.E., Weippl, E., Xu, L. (eds.) CD-ARES 2013. LNCS, vol. 8128, pp. 194–208. Springer, Heidelberg (2013). https://doi.org/10.1007/978-3-642-40588-4_14

10. Hülsing, A., Rijneveld, J.: XMSS reference code (2020). https://github.com/XMSS/xmss-reference

11. Jakobsson, M., Leighton, T., Micali, S., Szydlo, M.: Fractal Merkle tree representation and traversal. In: Joye, M. (ed.) CT-RSA 2003. LNCS, vol. 2612, pp. 314–326. Springer, Heidelberg (2003). https://doi.org/10.1007/3-540-36563-X_21

12. Knecht, M., Meier, W., Nicola, C.U.: A space- and time-efficient implementation of the Merkle tree traversal algorithm (2014)

13. Szydlo, M.: Merkle tree traversal in log space and time. In: Cachin, C., Camenisch, J.L. (eds.) EUROCRYPT 2004. LNCS, vol. 3027, pp. 541–554. Springer, Heidelberg (2004). https://doi.org/10.1007/978-3-540-24676-3_32

Zaytun: Lattice Based PKE and KEM with Shorter Ciphertext Size

Parhat Abla[1,2(✉)] and Mingsheng Wang[1]

[1] State Key Laboratory of Information Security, Institute of Information
Engineering, CAS, Beijing, China
parhat@iie.ac.cn
[2] School of Cyber Security, University of Chinese Academy of Sciences,
Beijing, China

Abstract. In this paper, we propose a lattice-based encryption scheme
with a short ciphertext size. Our scheme is somewhat hybrid of the
NTRU type encryptions and RLWE based encryptions. In particular,
the ciphertext of the scheme is a ring element as NTRU type encryptions, yet it can be compressible as RLWE based encryption schemes.
Furthermore, we present a key-encapsulation mechanism that is more
efficient than a direct construction from our encryption scheme.

The IND-CPA security of the schemes is based on the RLWE assumption and the NTRU assumption. Our parameterizations show that the
schemes enjoy almost the same public key size as the NIST PQC finalist lattice-based candidates, yet the ciphertext size is only about 37% of
them.

Keywords: PKE · Lattice · Post-quantum · Encryption · NTRU

1 Introduction

The importance of the design of post-quantum cryptographic schemes has risen
since the work of Shor [24] showed that classic cryptographic schemes based
on the number-theoretic assumptions can be broken by the polynomial-time
quantum algorithms. Although the lattice problems have a long history and
are widely believed to be quantum-resistant, yet the cryptographic designs are
boosted after the groundbreaking works of Ajtai [2] and Regev [23]. Recently the
interest in constructing post-quantum cryptographic primitives was elevated by
the announcement of the National Institute of Standards and Technology (NIST)
that looking towards the standardization of post-quantum cryptography [1]. As a
basic primitive, encryption schemes based on lattice problems are widely studied.
The mainstream constructions are based on two hard problems: Learning With
Errors (LWE) problems and NTRU problems.

Although the plain LWE problems enjoy more plausible reductions [8,19,23],
yet the encryption schemes [6,11,19,23] are suffering from large public keys and
ciphertexts. Therefore, to improve the efficiency, the LWE over rings (RLWE)

© The Author(s), under exclusive license to Springer Nature Switzerland AG 2022
R. AlTawy and A. Hülsing (Eds.): SAC 2021, LNCS 13203, pp. 398–418, 2022.
https://doi.org/10.1007/978-3-030-99277-4_19

problem was introduced [18,21]. The constructions based on RLWE problems [3,5,7,14,16,20,27] still maintains the encryption style from the plain LWE, yet benefit from the compactness of the ring structures and efficient operations. However, there are some drawbacks inherit from the encryption style, and we will describe later.

On the other hand, the NTRU encryption scheme, first introduced by Hoffstein, Pipher and Silverman [12] at the rump session of Crypto96, is constructed over the truncated rings. Even though the security reduction is a concern [25], NTRU type encryption schemes have survived more than two decades of cryptoanalysis. Researchers now have enough confidence in the schemes and recommended it as a post-quantum encryption replacement candidate [1]. However, due to its structure, it suffers from larger ciphertext sizes than that of RLWE based schemes, and we will elaborate on it next.

In this paper, we focus on constructing efficient lattice based public key encryption schemes (PKE) and key encapsulation mechanisms (KEM). Below, we expound challenges in the current constructions and our design idea.

1.1 Motivations and Contributions

Motivations. As we described above, there are two mainstream designs on lattice based PKE. The most efficient design idea is from the works [4,17] (we call it LP type encryption), and is widely used in the follow up works [3,7,20,27], and NIST submissions [1]. The public keys of LP type encryption is an RLWR sample and thus consists of two ring elements, and the ciphertext consists of two ring elements as well. On the other hand, in an NTRU type encryption scheme, the public key is simply a ring element, as well as the ciphertext. However, current encryption schemes suffer from the following shortcomings:

- RLWE based encryption schemes have more ring elements. Although the decryption procedure is very simple as NTRU type encryptions, yet from the inherent reduction idea of the LWE based encryption schemes [4,17], the latest elegant constructions [5,14,22][1] are still need two multiplications of ring elements in the encryption procedure, and the public keys are consist of two ring elements, as well as the ciphertexts.
- NTRU type encryption schemes are incompatible with compression. Comparing with the LWE based encryption schemes, the NTRU type encryption scheme's public key or the ciphertexts is only a ring element. However, the latest construction [28] shows that the public key size and ciphertext size of NTRU type encryption schemes are larger than that of LWE based constructions [5,14]. This is because the LWE based constructions applied compression techniques to the public keys and ciphertexts, yet this seems incompatible with NTRU type encryptions until this work.

---

[1] Since the encryption style is the same, we treat the module LWE in [5,14] as the same dimensional RLWE for simplicity.

Contributions. Motivated by the above challenges, we introduce Zaytun, a suite of cryptographic primitives based on inhomogeneous NTRU problem and RLWE problem. In particular, we introduce the lattice based encryption scheme—Zaytun.PKE which is as compact as NTRU type encryptions and equipped with ciphertext compressibility. The security can be based on the NTRU assumption if one only considers the one-way security[2]. Additionally, instead of the direct design of a KEM via Zaytun.PKE, we introduce a subtle efficient key encapsulation mechanism—Zaytun.KEM, which also enjoys the compressibility. We elaborate technical details of our constructions in the following section, the advantages of our proposals are as follow.

- Our proposals enjoy the best of both the NTRU type encryption schemes and the LWE based schemes that the ciphertexts and public keys are compact as the NTRU type encryption schemes [28] while the decryption procedure is as simple as LP type encryption schemes [5,14,17]. In particular, Zaytun.PKE can be seen as a somewhat carefully designed hybrid of the NTRU encryption [12] and LP type encryption [17].
- Ciphertext compressibility is a particular advantage of our proposals over NTRU encryptions. Although the public key compression is achievable in the NTRU type encryption schemes[3]. However, the ciphertext compression is seemingly incompatible with NTRU encryptions. Our proposals not only enjoy the compactness and efficiency of NTRU type schemes, it further compatible with ciphertext compression, and thus further improve the ciphertext size of NTRU style constructions. Our instantiations show that the ciphertext size of our schemes is only 37% of the NIST 3-rd round lattice based candidates.

Best of our knowledge of lattice based encryptions, our proposals are the first to hybrid the NTRU style schemes and LP style schemes naturally. We also remark that the security of our schemes can be based on the NTRU assumptions if we consider the one-way security of the basic schemes. In this case, our proposals improve the ciphertext size of the NTRU encryptions significantly.

1.2 The Design Idea

We first start with a quick recap of current lattice based encryptions, and then we show the design idea behind our constructions.

Recaps. For a ring R_q, a RLWE sample is the pair $(a, b) \in R_q \times R_q$, where a is uniformly sampled from R_q and $b = a \cdot s + e$ for $s, e \in R_q$ from some distribution

---

[2] Informally, we say an encryption scheme is one-way secure if it is infeasible to decrypt ciphertexts of random plaintexts.

[3] Public key compression in the NTRU type encryption schemes will increases the decryption failure probability, yet it is theoretically feasible.

χ over R_q.[4] In the most efficient designs [4,17] (LP style encryptions) the public key is a RLWE sample, i.e., $\mathsf{pk} = (a, b)$. To encrypt a message μ, the encryption algorithm computes the ciphertexts as: $c_0 = a \cdot r + e_1$, $c_1 = b \cdot r + e_2 + \lceil \frac{q}{2} \rceil \cdot \mu$, where the r, e_1 and e_2 are sampled from the distribution χ, and μ is the message. Intuitively, the ciphertexts are double RLWE samples, and the message is simply added to the RLWE sample. Thus the indistinguishability against the chosen plaintext attacks (IND-CPA) security follows by the uniformity assumption of RLWE samples. Since the decryptor doesn't know how to obtain the value r merely from c_1, thus it needs another RLWE sample c_0, computed by r, for decryption.

When compressing the public key $b = a \cdot s + e$, we simply drop the least significant bits, and thus introduce a new linear error. In other words, compressing the public keys increase the error term e, and thus incurs subtle increment on the decryption failure. Yet the public key compression is feasible via slightly increasing the ring modulus q. Since the message is encoded to the high significant bits of c_1, the error introduced by the ciphertext compression procedure is simply added to the error term e_2. Thus the decryption *success* can be maintained via slightly increasing the modulus. As the 3-rd round submissions [5,14] to the NIST post-quantum standardization showed, the deeply compressed public keys and ciphertexts in the RLWR based encryptions have smaller sizes than that of NTRU encryption [28].

On the other hand, the public key of an NTRU encryption scheme is a ring element $h = s^{-1} \cdot e$, where the s and e are ring elements with small coefficients[5]. The ciphertext corresponding to the message μ is computed as $c = h \cdot r + \mu$, where r is small coefficient ring element in R_q. It is not hard to see that the error introduced by compressing the public key h can be upper bounded, and thus the decryption procedure works correctly via slightly increasing the modulus q. Yet this is not the case when compressing the ciphertext. Note that compressing the ciphertext c (dropping the least significant bits) incurs a small error, and is directly added to the message μ. Since the coefficients of the message μ are very small (actually are in $[-1, 1]$), thus compressing the ciphertext results in a decryption error. Different from the RLWE based encryption schemes, we can't avoid the decryption failure via increasing the modulus q or other parameters.

Our Design. Intuitively, NTRU type encryption schemes enjoy fewer public keys and ciphertexts in the number of ring elements. Yet the RLWE based schemes are nicely compatible with the compression. Aim to combine the best of both schemes, there are two naive ways to combine them: (1) generate the public keys as NTRU style and generate the ciphertexts as in the LP type encryption, (2) generate the public keys as in the LP type encryption and encryption works

---

[4] We use the normal form definition of RLWE here, and χ should close to discrete gaussian over R_q.

[5] For the sake of simplicity, we just use the notation s here, yet letting $s = pf + 1$ for some integer p and small coefficient ring element $f \in R_q$ results in more efficient decryption.

as NTRU style. However, both of the above tries will not work as we elaborate next.

In the case of (1), the public key is a ring element, i.e., $h = s^{-1} \cdot e$, and if the ciphertexts is computed via double RLWE sample style as in the LP encryption, it totally leaks the message; if the ciphertexts is computed via one RLWE sample as $c = h \cdot r + e_1 + \lceil \frac{q}{2} \rceil \mu$, yet the r is unknown to the decryptor. Thus the decryptor is unable to eliminate the term $h \cdot r$ from the ciphertext c, and thus fails to decrypt.

In the case of (2), the public key is $\mathsf{pk} = (a, b) \in R_q \times R_q$, the ciphertext c is computed as NTRU style, that is $c = b \cdot r + \mu$ for some small coefficient ring element r. Since the decryptor is incapable of removing the term $b \cdot r$ from the ciphertext c, and thus fails to decrypt.

As the above natural tries didn't work, we first change the public key of the NTRU type encryptions to $h = s^{-1}(\lceil \frac{q}{2} \rceil + e)$. Then to encrypt the message $\mu \in R_2$, we use RLWE style that

$$c = h \cdot (2r + \mu) + e_1,$$

where r and e_1 are small coefficient ring elements. A routine computation shows that $\lceil s \cdot c \rfloor_2$[6] correctly decrypts the ciphertext if the modulus q is properly set. This is the case, since we have

$$s \cdot c = (\lceil \frac{q}{2} \rceil + e)(2r + \mu) + s \cdot e_1 \mod q$$
$$= \lceil \frac{q}{2} \rceil \cdot \mu + \left(\lceil \frac{q}{2} \rceil \cdot 2r + e \cdot (2r + \mu) + s \cdot e_1 \right) \mod q.$$

Since s, r, μ, e and e_1 are with small coefficients, the terms $e \cdot (2r + \mu) + s \cdot e_1$ and $\lceil \frac{q}{2} \rceil \cdot 2r \mod q$ have small coefficient[7], and thus decryption works correctly. The indistinguishability based security of the scheme is based on the RLWE and NTRU assumptions, we show the security in Sect. 3 with more details. We also remark that the security can be based on NTRU assumptions if we consider one-way security. Since the errors in the NTRU type encryptions are with small coefficients than the LWE based schemes, thus the decryption failure probability, in this case, is smaller than our above construction.

Note that the resulted scheme enjoys the compact public keys and ciphertexts as in the NTRU type encryptions, and the compressibility of the public keys is similar to the NTRU type encryption. Additionally, the above encryption scheme is compatible with the ciphertexts compression. This is the case since the error from the ciphertext compression is added to the error term e_1, and the secret s is with small coefficients, thus the above correctness analysis shows that the term $\lceil \frac{q}{2} \rceil \cdot \mu$ is not affected by the errors if the modulus q been set properly. We show the formal analysis in the main body of the paper.

---

[6] For an integer $x \in \mathbb{Z}_q$, the notion $\lceil x \rfloor_t := \lceil \frac{t}{q} x \rfloor$, and it applies to the ring elements coefficient-wise.

[7] This is the case since the element r is with small coefficients and we have $\lceil \frac{q}{2} \rceil \cdot 2r = r \mod q$ for the odd modulus q, and $\lceil \frac{q}{2} \rceil \cdot 2r = 0 \mod q$ when q is even number.

1.3 Organizations

In Sect. 2, we present some preliminaries; we present our basic public key encryption scheme in Sect. 3, and provide the correctness and the security analysis of the scheme. In Sect. 4, we present a key encapsulation scheme as well as its correctness and security analysis. We present the reference parameterizations of our proposals and a comparison with known schemes in Sect. 5.

2 Preliminaries

Notations. Let $\mathbb{R}$ be the set of real numbers, $\mathbb{Z}$ be the set of integers. For a real number $x \in \mathbb{R}$, use $\lfloor x \rfloor$ to denote the largest integer that $\leq x$, use $\lceil x \rceil$ to denote the integer $\lfloor x + 1/2 \rfloor$, and use $\lceil x \rceil$ to denote the smallest integer that $\geq x$. We use lower-case bold letters to denote the row vectors (e.g., $\boldsymbol{a}$). For a probability distribution χ, we use $x \leftarrow \chi$ to denote that x is sampled from the distribution χ. For a set S, $x \xleftarrow{\$} S$ denotes x is uniformly sampled from the set S. The norm of a vector $\boldsymbol{a}$ is denoted by $\|\boldsymbol{a}\|$. For a ring R, we use $\|a\|_p$ to denote the p-norm of corresponding coefficient vector of $a \in R$, we omit the subscript p if $p = 2$. The function $\mathsf{negl}(\cdot)$ denotes the negligible function, that is $\mathsf{negl}(\lambda) < \frac{1}{\lambda^c}$ for the parameter λ and any constant c. We say two probability distributions $\mathcal{P}$ and $\mathcal{Q}$ are indistinguishable if the distinguishing advantage of any probabilistic polynomial time algorithm $\mathcal{A}$ over the two distributions is negligible, and simply denote as $\mathcal{P} \overset{c}{\approx} \mathcal{Q}$.

2.1 Cryptographic Definitions

Here we present definitions of cryptographic schemes and their security notions that we will use in the following sections.

Public Key Encryption. Our definition of a public key encryption scheme is as follows, and the correctness and security are following.

Definition 2.1. *A public key encryption scheme Π_{PKE} consists of algorithms tuples $(\mathsf{KeyGen}, \mathsf{Enc}, \mathsf{Dec})$ as follows:*

$\mathsf{KeyGen}(1^\lambda) \rightarrow (\mathsf{pk}, \mathsf{sk})$: *On input the security parameter, it outputs the public key pk and secret key sk.*

$\mathsf{Enc}(m, pk) \rightarrow \mathsf{ct}$: *On input the public key pk and the message m, it outputs the ciphertext ct corresponding to the message m.*

$\mathsf{Dec}(\mathsf{sk}, \mathsf{ct}) \rightarrow m$: *On input the secret key sk and ciphertext ct, it outputs the decrypting message m corresponding to the ciphertext ct.*

Correctness. We say a PKE scheme Π_{PKE} is δ-correct if for the security parameter λ and any message m, the following holds.

$$\Pr \left[m' = m \,\middle|\, \begin{array}{l} (\mathsf{pk}, \mathsf{sk}) \leftarrow \mathsf{KeyGen}(1^\lambda); \\ \mathsf{ct} \leftarrow \mathsf{Enc}(\mathsf{pk}, m); \\ m' \leftarrow \mathsf{Dec}(\mathsf{sk}, \mathsf{ct}) \end{array} \right] > \delta.$$

Security. For any PPT adversary $\mathcal{A}$, the advantage of $\mathcal{A}$ against the indistinguishability under chosen-plaintext attacks (IND-CPA) security of a PKE scheme, denoted $\mathsf{Adv}_{\mathsf{PKE}}^{\mathsf{IND-CPA}}(\mathcal{A})$, is negligible.

$$
\mathsf{Adv}_{\mathsf{PKE}}^{\mathsf{IND-CPA}}(\mathcal{A}) = \Pr \left[b' = b \left| \begin{array}{l} (\mathsf{pk}, \mathsf{sk}) \leftarrow \mathsf{KeyGen}(1^\lambda); \\ (m_0, m_1) \leftarrow \mathcal{A}(pk); \\ b \leftarrow \{0,1\}; c^* = \mathsf{Enc}(\mathsf{pk}, m_b); \\ b' \leftarrow \mathcal{A}(c^*, pk) \end{array} \right. \right].
$$

A stronger notion is indistinguishability under chosen-ciphertext attacks (IND-CCA) security, in which the adversary is allowed to query the decryption algorithm except on the challenge ciphertext c^*. Note that there are many works on transforming a IND-CPA secure PKE to IND-CCA secure one via the heuristic way, i.e., classic random oracles [10] or quantum accessible oracles [13,15]. Therefore, constructing IND-CPA secure PKE is the mainstream in the literature and the main focus of this work.

KEM. In a key encapsulation mechanism, instead of requiring the scheme to encrypt a message, we need the scheme to output a random key K and its ciphertext. On input this ciphertext, the decapsulation algorithm outputs the corresponding key K. The correctness of a KEM is defined as the PKE. The IND-CPA security describes that any probabilistic polynomial-time algorithm $\mathcal{A}$ is not able to distinguish the key K from a random string $\hat{K} \leftarrow \mathcal{U}(\{0,1\}^{|K|})$.

2.2   Lattices, Rings and Hardness Assumptions

Lattices and Rings. An n-dimensional lattice is a discrete subgroup in the space $\mathbb{R}^n$. In this paper, we set the ring $R := \mathbb{Z}[x]/\Phi(x)$ where $\Phi(x) := (x^n + 1)$ for some n of a power of 2. We use $\|a\|_\infty$ to denote the ∞-norm of the vector corresponding to the ring element $a \in R$. We defer the concepts and results of Gaussian distributions over lattices and rings to the full version of this paper.

RLWE. The ring Learning With Errors (RLWE) problem, introduced in [18], is the ring version of the LWE problem [23]. Let R_q be the ring defined above, χ be a distribution over R_w, and $s \xleftarrow{\$} R_q$, then the $R\text{-LWE}_{n,q,\chi}$ distribution is the distribution of the pair $(a, b) \in R_q \times R_p$, where a is a uniform sample from R_q and $b = a \cdot s + e$ for some $e \leftarrow \chi$. In this paper, we use the normal form RLWE in which the secret s and the error e are from the same distribution χ. Then the decision version of the $R\text{-LWE}_{n,q,\chi}$ problem is described as follows.

Definition 2.2. *Given a pair $(a, b) \in R_q \times R_q$ for a random $a \in R_q$, the $R\text{-LWE}_{n,q,\chi}$ problem asks to decide if the pair is from the $R\text{-LWE}_{n,q,\chi}$ distribution or from the uniform distribution over $R_q \times R_q$.*

There are quantum reductions [18,21] that showed that the RLWE problems are as hard as the shortest vector problems over the ideal lattices. In the real world crypto, no algorithm that works over the RLWE problem performs better than the corresponding plain LWE problem. Thus, assuming the hardness of the RLWE problems is folklore in lattice based cryptography.

Inhomogeneous NTRU. For the ring R_q and distribution χ over R_q, the inhomogeneous NTRU distribution $\mathsf{iNTRU}_{n,q,\chi,t}$ is the distribution of $h = s^{-1}(\lceil \frac{q}{2^t} \rceil + e)$, where $e, s \in R_q$ are sampled from the distribution χ and $t \in \mathbb{Z}^+$. If t is known from the context, a fixed number, we omit it and simply write as $\mathsf{iNTRU}_{n,q,\chi}$. The decision version of inhomogeneous NTRU problem is defined as follows.

Definition 2.3. *Given a ring element $h \in R_q$, the $\mathsf{iNTRU}_{n,q,\chi}$ problem asks to decide if h is from the $\mathsf{iNTRU}_{n,q,\chi}$ distribution or from the uniform distribution over R_q.*

Note that our definition is similar to the original NTRU assumption, yet with a subtle difference. The work [25] shows uniformity of the $\mathsf{iNTRU}_{n,q,\chi}$ distribution in a carefully designed parameters. Another fact is that this type of problem stays unbroken from more than two decades of cryptanalysis, and thus the researchers have confidence in the assumption [28].

3   The Encryption Scheme

Note that in an NTRU type encryption scheme, the compression of a ciphertext would result in information lost on the encrypted message, and incurs a decryption failure. However, the LWE based encryption schemes are well compatible with the ciphertext compressions, and the decryption correctness is not much affected by the compressions. As for our design, Zaytun.PKE, the message is encoded to the most significant bits, thus our scheme enjoys the ciphertext compressibility as the LWE based schemes while almost maintaining the efficiency of the NTRU type encryptions. The concrete descriptions of Zaytun.PKE and its security analysis are presented in the following sections.

3.1   Scheme Description

Compression Function. For any positive integer q, we define $r' = r \mod^+ q$ to be the unique element r' in the range $0 \leq r' < q$ such that $r' = r \mod q$. For an even (resp. odd) positive integer q, we define $r' = r \mod^\pm q$ to be the unique element r' in the range $\frac{-q}{2} < r' \leq \frac{q}{2}$ (resp. $-\frac{q-1}{2} < r' \leq \frac{q-1}{2}$) such that $r' = r \mod q$. On input $x \in \mathbb{Z}_q$ and an integer $d < \lceil \log(q) \rceil$, the compression and decompression functions Compress and DeCompress are defined as follows:

$$\mathsf{Compress}(x, d) := \left\lceil \frac{2^d}{q} x \right\rceil \mod^+ 2^d, \mathsf{DeCompress}(x, d) := \left\lceil \frac{q}{2^d} x \right\rceil.$$

It is not hard to see that, DeCompress is not the inverse of Compress, yet they have the following property:

$$|x - \mathsf{DeCompress}(\mathsf{Compress}(x, d), d) \mod {}^\pm q| \leq E_d := \left\lceil \frac{q}{2^{d+1}} \right\rceil.$$

The above functions apply on a ring element coefficient-wise.

Construction. Our design of Zaytun.PKE is described in Algorithm 1 to Algorithm 3 as follows, where χ and Bin_η denote two distributions over R_q, t is some positive integer that is prime to the modulus q. On input an integer $x \in \mathbb{Z}_q$, the rounding function $\lceil * \rfloor_{2^t}$ defined as $\lceil x \rfloor_{2^t} := \lceil \frac{2^t}{q} x \rfloor$, and it applies to the ring elements coefficient-wise. All the computations, except the $\lceil * \rfloor_{2^t}$, are over R_q.

Algorithm 1: Zaytun.PKE.KeyGen(param)

1: $(seede, seeds) \overset{\$}{\leftarrow} \{0,1\}^\lambda$
2: $s \leftarrow \chi(seeds)$
3: **if** s invertible **then**
4:   $e \leftarrow \chi(seede)$
5:   $\hat{h} := s^{-1}(\lceil \frac{q}{2^t} \rceil + e)$
6: **else** go to step 1.
7: $h := \text{Compress}(\hat{h}, d_h)$
8: **Return:** pk $:= h, $ sk $:= s$

Algorithm 2: Zaytun.PKE.Enc(pk $= h, \mu \in R_{2^t}$) , $(q, 2^t) = 1$

1: $\hat{h}' = \text{DeCompress}(h, d_h)$
2: $(seedr, seede') \overset{\$}{\leftarrow} \{0,1\}^\lambda$
3: $e' \leftarrow \text{Bin}_\eta(seede')$
4: $r \leftarrow \text{Bin}_\eta(seedr)$
5: $r' = 2^t \cdot r + \mu$
6: $\hat{c} := \hat{h}' \cdot r' + e'$
7: $c = \text{Compress}(\hat{c}, d_c)$
8: **Return:** ct $:= c$

Algorithm 3: Zaytun.PKE.Dec(ct $= c, $ sk $= s$)

1: $\hat{c}' = \text{DeCompress}(c, d_c)$
2: $\mu' := \hat{c}' \cdot s$
3: $\mu'' := \lceil \mu' \rfloor_{2^t}$
4: **Return:** μ''

The compression and decompression parameters d_h and d_c are included in the scheme parameter param.

For simplicity, the public parameter param didn't explicitly input to the encryption and the decryption algorithms, yet they implicitly contain it. Note that the message space of the scheme is R_{2^t}, and the encryption algorithm needs modulus q to be co-prime with 2^t, and thus q should be an odd number. It's not hard to see that the message space can be R_p for any small number p as long as $(q, p) = 1$. In what follows, we show the correctness and the security of the scheme.

3.2   Correctness and Security

Correctness. The correctness result of Zaytun.PKE is given by the following theorem. In Sect. 5, we will show the decryption failure probability of the scheme in the concrete parameter settings.

Theorem 3.1. *For the integer $t \geq 1$ and the modulus $q \geq 2^{3t+3}$, Let e, e', r, s be the random variables as in Algorithm 1 and Algorithm 2, d_h and d_c denote the compression parameters, and δ be the probability that*

$$\delta := \Pr\left[\left(2^t\|r\|_\infty + \left\|e + \left\lceil \frac{q}{2^{d_h+1}} \right\rceil s\right\|_\infty \cdot (\|r\|_\infty + 1)2^t + \left\|\left(e' + \left\lceil \frac{q}{2^{d_c+1}} \right\rceil\right)s\right\|_\infty\right) \geq \frac{q}{2^{t+1} + 1}\right],$$

then Zaytun.PKE described in Algorithm 1 to Algorithm 3 is $(1 - \delta)$-correct.

Due to the space limit, we defer the proof in full version of our paper.

Security. As we stated in the introduction, Zaytun.PKE is a hybrid of NTRU type encryptions and the RLWE based encryptions. Note that the compression and decompression procedures are deterministic and can be publicly executable, and thus they leak no more information than a plain scheme in which the algorithm Compress compresses no information. Therefore, the security of Zaytun.PKE is guaranteed by the security of the corresponding plain scheme. The following theorem shows that we can base the security of Zaytun.PKE on hard problems on lattices.

Theorem 3.2. *The encryption scheme Zaytun.PKE given in Algorithms 1–3 is IND-CPA secure if the underlying problems $R\text{-LWE}_{n,q,\mathsf{Bin}_\beta}$ and $\mathsf{iNTRU}_{n,q,\chi}$ are hard.*

Proof. To show the theorem, we prove a subtle different case where we simply consider the plain scheme in which we compress no information. Additionally instead of proving the standard IND-CPA security game, we show the ciphertext uniformity that the challenge ciphertext c is computationally indistinguishable from the uniform element in R_q if the underlying problems (both R-LWE and iNTRU) are hard. In what follows, we show that ciphertext uniformity of the plain scheme, and thus the IND-CPA security of Zaytun.PKE easily follows. To show this, we introduce the following hybrid games.

Game$_0$	Game$_1$	Game$_2$
1:$seede, seeds \xleftarrow{\$} \{0,1\}^\lambda$	1:$seede, seeds \xleftarrow{\$} \{0,1\}^\lambda$	1:$seede, seeds \xleftarrow{\$} \{0,1\}^\lambda$
2: $e \leftarrow \text{Bin}_\eta(seede)$	2: $e \leftarrow \text{Bin}_\eta(seede)$	2: $e \leftarrow \text{Bin}_\eta(seede)$
3: $s \leftarrow \text{Bin}_\eta(seeds)$	3: $s \leftarrow \text{Bin}_\eta(seeds)$	3: $s \leftarrow \text{Bin}_\eta(seeds)$
4: $h = s^{-1} \cdot (\lceil \frac{q}{2} \rceil + e)$	4: $\boxed{h \leftarrow R_q}$	4: $h \leftarrow R_q$
5:$seedr, seede' \xleftarrow{\$} \{0,1\}^\lambda$	5:$seedr, seede' \xleftarrow{\$} \{0,1\}^\lambda$	5:$seedr, seede' \xleftarrow{\$} \{0,1\}^\lambda$
6: $r \leftarrow \text{Bin}_\eta(seedr)$	6: $r \leftarrow \text{Bin}_\eta(seedr)$	6: $r \leftarrow \text{Bin}_\eta(seedr)$
7: $e' \leftarrow \text{Bin}_\eta(seede')$	7: $e' \leftarrow \text{Bin}_\eta(seede')$	7: $e' \leftarrow \text{Bin}_\eta(seede')$
8: $c = h \cdot (2^t \cdot r + \mu) + e'$	8: $c = h \cdot (2^t \cdot r + \mu) + e'$	8: $\boxed{c \leftarrow R_q}$
9: $\beta \leftarrow \{0,1\}$	9: $\beta \leftarrow \{0,1\}$	9: $\beta \leftarrow \{0,1\}$
10: if $\beta = 1$ then	10: if $\beta = 1$ then	10: if $\beta = 1$ then
11: return (h,c)	11: return (h,c)	11: return (h,c)
12: else $\beta = 0$	12: else $\beta = 0$	12: else $\beta = 0$
13: return $(h, \mathcal{U}(R_q))$	13: return $(h, \mathcal{U}(R_q))$	13: return $(h, \mathcal{U}(R_q))$

Note that the Game$_0$ is subtly different from the original IND-CPA game in which the adversary $\mathcal{A}$ is given the public key h and the challenge ciphertext c, which is generated properly by the challenger or simply sampled from the uniform distribution over R_q depends on the random bit β, and $\mathcal{A}$'s goal is to guess the random bit β. We say $\mathcal{A}$ wins in Game$_i$ if it correctly guesses the random bit β. We use $\text{Adv}_{\mathcal{A}}^{\text{Game}_i}$ to denote the advantage of $\mathcal{A}$ in the Game$_i$ for $i \in \{0,1,2\}$, namely $\text{Adv}_{\mathcal{A}}^{\text{Game}_i} = \Pr[\mathcal{A} \text{ win Game}_i] - \frac{1}{2}$, and the ciphertext uniformity of the plain scheme is obvious if $\mathcal{A}$'s advantage in Game$_0$ is negligible. We show this through the following lemmas.

Lemma 3.3. *If the* iNTRU$_{n,q,\chi}$ *problem is hard, then* Game$_1 \overset{c}{\approx}$ Game$_0$.

Proof. We show the lemma by contradiction. Namely, if there is an algorithm $\mathcal{A}$ that can distinguish Game$_1$ from Game$_0$ with noticeable probability, then we show that there is a simulator Sim which solves the iNTRU$_{n,q,\chi}$ challenge with the same advantage. Our construction of Sim is as follows:

Sim$(h) \to \{0,1\}$ On input an element $h \in R_q$ of iNTRU$_{n,q,\chi}$ challenge, it gives h to the adversary $\mathcal{A}$ as the public key of the scheme. It further simulates every step (including the generation of the challenge ciphertext) of the IND-CPA security game using the element h. Then, it outputs whatever $\mathcal{A}$ outputs: if $\mathcal{A}$ outputs 0 mean that it plays within the Game$_0$, Sim outputs 0 mean that the input h is from iNTRU$_{n,q,\text{Bin}_\beta}$ distribution; if $\mathcal{A}$ outputs 1 mean that it plays within the Game$_1$, Sim outputs 1 mean that the input h is from uniform distribution over R_q.

It is easy to see that if the input h is from iNTRU$_{n,q,\text{Bin}_\beta}$ distribution, then from $\mathcal{A}$'s view it played within the Game$_0$; if the input h is from a uniform distribution over R_q, then from $\mathcal{A}$'s view it played within the Game$_1$. Thus, the Sim perfectly simulated the two games, and thus the advantage of Sim equals the advantage of the adversary $\mathcal{A}$. This completes the proof. □

Lemma 3.4. *If the R-LWE$_{n,q,\text{Bin}_\beta}$ problem is hard, then* Game$_2 \stackrel{c}{\approx}$ Game$_1$.

Proof. To show the lemma, we show that if there is an algorithm $\mathcal{A}$ that can distinguish Game$_1$ from Game$_2$ with noticeable probability, then there is a simulator Sim which solves the R-LWE$_{n,q,\text{Bin}_\beta}$ challenge with the same advantage. Our construction of Sim is as follows:

Sim$(a,b) \to \{0,1\}$ On input the R-LWE$_{n,q,\text{Bin}_\beta}$ challenge $(a,b) \in R_q \times R_q$, it first computes $2^{-t} \bmod q$ (since q and 2^t are co-prime, 2^{-t} efficiently computable). Then it let $h = 2^{-t} \cdot a$ and sends h to the adversary $\mathcal{A}$ as the public key of the scheme. It further simulates every step of the game using h except the challenge ciphertext phase. Instead of generating the challenge ciphertext with h, it let $c = b + 2^{-t} \cdot a \cdot \mu$ as the challenge ciphertext. Finally, it outputs whatever $\mathcal{A}$ outputs: if $\mathcal{A}$ outputs 0 mean that it played within the Game$_1$, Sim outputs 0 mean that the input pair (a,b) is from R-LWE$_{n,q,\text{Bin}_\beta}$ distribution; if $\mathcal{A}$ outputs 1 mean that it played within the Game$_2$, Sim outputs 1 mean that the input pair (a,b) is from uniform distribution over $R_q \times R_q$.

If the input pair (a,b) is from R-LWE$_{n,q,\text{Bin}_\beta}$ distribution, then there is a secret $s \in R_q$ and error $e \in R_q$ such that $b = a \cdot s + e$. Since $a \in R_q$ is uniform and 2^{-t} is invertible in R_q, $h = 2^{-t} \cdot a$ is uniform from $\mathcal{A}$'s view. Furthermore, from the description of the challenge ciphertext we know that

$$c = b + 2^{-t}a \cdot \mu = 2^{-t}a(2^t \cdot s + \mu) + e = h \cdot (2^t s + \mu) + e,$$

and thus from $\mathcal{A}$'s view the pair (h,c) is computed exactly as in the Game$_1$; if the input pair (a,b) is from the uniform distribution over $R_q \times R_q$, then it is not hard to see that the pair (h,c) is also uniformly distributed, and $\mathcal{A}$'s view it is playing within the Game$_2$. Thus Sim perfectly simulates the two games, and thus the advantage of Sim equals the advantage of the adversary $\mathcal{A}$. This completes the proof. □

Complete the Proof. From above lemmas, we have

$$\text{Adv}_{\mathcal{A}}^{\text{Game}_0} \leq \text{Adv}_{\mathcal{A}}^{\text{Game}_1} + \text{negl}(n) \leq \text{Adv}_{\mathcal{A}}^{\text{Game}_2} + \text{negl}(n) \leq \text{negl}(n),$$

where the first inequality is from Lemma 3.3; the second inequality is from Lemma 3.4; the last inequality is from the fact that $\text{Adv}_{\mathcal{A}}^{\text{Game}_2} = 0$. This is the case, since the ciphertext c is uniform over R_q, and thus independent of the random bit β. Since the *compression* procedure is deterministic and publicly known and thus doesn't increase the adversary's advantage. This completes the proof. □

Extentions. A standard security that we require from a PKE is indistinguishability against chosen ciphertext attacks (IND-CCA), in which the adversary has the ability to decrypt the ciphertexts of its choice (other than the challenge ciphertext), and the goal is to guess which one of the adversarially outputted messages the challenge ciphertext is from. As shown in Theorem 3.2, Zaytun.PKE is only able to provide the IND-CPA securiity. However, one can obtain a IND-CCA secure scheme by applying the F-O transformation [10,13]. The security of the resulted scheme now is in the random oracle model. However, the random oracles are publicly available, and may be queried by the adversaries, who owned the quantum computers, with quantum states. In the post-quantum era, we want the post-quantum encryption schemes provide security in this scenario. Fortunately, by applying the variants of F-O transformation [10,13,15] on Zaytun.PKE, we have IND-CCA secure encryption scheme in the quantum (accessible) random oracle model—QROM.

Note that Zaytun.PKE directly implies a key exchange protocol and a key encapsulation mechanism via encrypting a random bit string. However, the KE protocol by itself only provides security against the passive adversary, yet using the general framework, one can construct a protocol with stronger security - authenticated KE [9]. The key encapsulation mechanism only provides IND-CPA security, and we have a CCA secure KEM via applying the variants of F-O transformation [13]. Below, we present a subtle different KEM that is simpler than this direct approach.

4 The Key Encapsulation Mechanism

In this section, we first describe our KEM that is as efficient as the NTRU encryptions, yet with smaller ciphertexts. Our design of KEM is more efficient than that of a direct construction via the encryption scheme presented in the previous section. Then we show the correctness and security of the KEM.

4.1 KEM Description

Our design Zaytun.KEM is presented in Algorithm 4 to Algorithm 6, where χ and Bin_η denotes the probability distributions over the ring R_q; t is a positive integer that is prime to the modulus q. $\lceil * \rfloor_{2^t}$ denotes the rounding function as in the encryption scheme. The function KDF denotes the key derivation function that outputs random strings fed by a string with enough entropy, it is instantiated by the hash function in the concrete applications. On input two integers x and t, the function $\mathsf{LowerBits}(x,t)$ is defined as $\mathsf{LowerBits}(x,t) := x - 2^t \cdot \lfloor \frac{x}{2^t} \rfloor$, and it applies to the ring elements coefficient-wise. Here d_h and d_c are the compression parameters, and the compression functions $\mathsf{Compress}$ and $\mathsf{DeCompress}$ are defined in the previous section. The ring dimension n and the distribution parameter η should guarantee that the lower t-bits of the ring element $r \in R_q$ provides enough entropy to the KDF such that any brute force attack on KDF to fail.

Algorithm 4: Zaytun.KEM.KeyGen(param)

1: $(seede, seeds) \xleftarrow{\$} \{0,1\}^{\lambda}$
2: $s \leftarrow \chi(seeds)$
3: **if** s invertible **then**
4: $\quad e \leftarrow \chi(seede)$
5: $\quad \hat{h} := s^{-1}(\lceil \frac{q}{2^t} \rceil + e)$
6: **else** go to step 1.
7: $h := \mathsf{Compress}(\hat{h}, d_h)$
8: **Return:** pk $:= h, \mathsf{sk} := s$

Algorithm 5: Zaytun.KEM.Encaps(pk $= h, \mu \in R_{2^t})$, $(q, 2^t) = 1$

1: $\hat{h}' = \mathsf{DeCompress}(h, d_h)$
2: $(seedr, seede') \xleftarrow{\$} \{0,1\}^{\lambda}$
3: $e' \leftarrow \mathsf{Bin}_{\eta}(seede')$
4: $r \leftarrow \mathsf{Bin}_{\eta}(seedr)$
5: $\hat{c} := \hat{h}' \cdot r + e'$
6: $c = \mathsf{Compress}(\hat{c}, d_c)$
7: $\mu = \mathsf{LowerBits}(r, t)$
8: $K = \mathsf{KDF}(\mu)$
9: **Return:** $(K, \mathsf{ct} := c)$

Algorithm 6: Zaytun.KEM.Decaps(ct $= c, \mathsf{sk} = s)$

1: $\hat{c}' = \mathsf{DeCompress}(c, d_c)$
2: $\mu' := \lceil \hat{c}' \cdot s \rfloor_{2^t}$
3: $K' = \mathsf{KDF}(\mu')$
4: **Return:** K'

Note that the key generation algorithm above is identical to the key genera-tion algorithm of Zaytun.PKE. However, in Algorithm 5, instead of encapsulating a random message, we encapsulate the lower bits of the randomness r. In fact, the least significant bits of r provide enough entropy if it is sampled from LWE error distributions. For instance, let Bin_η be the binomial distribution for $\eta \geq 1$ and $t = 1$, then μ corresponds to the least significant bits of r' and it contains more than λ-bit of entropy if $n \geq 1.5\lambda$. In the concrete instantiations [5, 14, 22], n can be set at least 4λ, and thus μ provides sufficient entropy to the key derivation function.

4.2   Correctness and Security

Correctness. The correctness of Zaytun.KEM is given by the following theorem. In Sect. 5, we will show the decryption failure probability of the scheme in the concrete parameter settings.

Corollary 4.1. *For the integer $t \geq 1$ and the modulus $q \geq 2^{3t+3}$, Let e, e', r, s be the random variables as in the Algorithm 3, let d_h and d_c be the compression parameters, and δ be the probability defined as*

$$\delta := \mathsf{Pr}\left[\left(\|r\|_\infty + \left\|\left((e + \lceil\tfrac{q}{2^{d_h+1}}\rceil \cdot s) \cdot r + (e' + \lceil\tfrac{q}{2^{d_c+1}}\rceil) \cdot s\right)\right\|_\infty\right) \geq \frac{q}{2^{t+1}+1}\right],$$

then Zaytun.KEM *is* $(1 - \delta)$-*correct.*

For the space limit, we defer the proof to the full version of the paper.

Security. Note that Zaytun.KEM is subtly different from the key encapsulation directly obtained via the Zaytun.PKE, yet the security can be proven in the same way as Zaytun.PKE. Namely, the security of Zaytun.KE is based on both the R-LWE and iNTRU problems as the following theorem shows.

Theorem 4.2. Zaytun.KEM *given in Algorithms 4–6 provides IND-CPA secu-rity if the underlying problems* R-$\mathsf{LWE}_{n,q,\mathsf{Bin}_\beta}$ *and* $\mathsf{iNTRU}_{n,q,\mathsf{Bin}_\beta}$ *are hard.*

Proof. To show the theorem, we show the ciphertext uniformity that the chal-lenge ciphertext c (of a message μ) is indistinguishable from a uniform element of R_q if the underlying problems($\mathsf{iNTRU}_{n,q,\mathsf{Bin}_\beta}$ and R-$\mathsf{LWE}_{n,q,\mathsf{Bin}_\beta}$) are hard, and thus the IND-CPA security follows. Since the compression procedure only decreases the adversaries advantage, we omit it for the simplicity of the proof. To illustrate the proof, we introduce the following hybrid games.

Game_0	Game_1	Game_2
1:$seede, seeds \xleftarrow{\$} \{0,1\}^\lambda$	1:$seede, seeds \xleftarrow{\$} \{0,1\}^\lambda$	1:$seede, seeds \xleftarrow{\$} \{0,1\}^\lambda$
2: $e \leftarrow \mathsf{Bin}_\eta(seede)$	2: $e \leftarrow \mathsf{Bin}_\eta(seede)$	2: $e \leftarrow \mathsf{Bin}_\eta(seede)$
3: $s \leftarrow \mathsf{Bin}_\eta(seeds)$	3: $s \leftarrow \mathsf{Bin}_\eta(seeds)$	3: $s \leftarrow \mathsf{Bin}_\eta(seeds)$
4: $h = s^{-1} \cdot (\lceil \frac{q}{2} \rceil + e)$	4: $\boxed{h \leftarrow R_q}$	4: $h \leftarrow R_q$
5:$seedr, seede' \xleftarrow{\$} \{0,1\}^\lambda$	5:$seedr, seede' \xleftarrow{\$} \{0,1\}^\lambda$	5:$seedr, seede' \xleftarrow{\$} \{0,1\}^\lambda$
6: $r \leftarrow \mathsf{Bin}_\eta(seedr)$	6: $r \leftarrow \mathsf{Bin}_\eta(seedr)$	6: $r \leftarrow \mathsf{Bin}_\eta(seedr)$
7: $e' \leftarrow \mathsf{Bin}_\eta(seede')$	7: $e' \leftarrow \mathsf{Bin}_\eta(seede')$	7: $e' \leftarrow \mathsf{Bin}_\eta(seede')$
8: $c = h \cdot r + e'$	8: $c = h \cdot r + e'$	8: $\boxed{c \leftarrow R_q}$
9: $\mu' = \mathsf{LowerBits}(r, t)$	9: $\mu' = \mathsf{LowerBits}(r, t)$	9: $\mu' = \mathsf{LowerBits}(r, t)$
10: $seedr'' \xleftarrow{\$} \{0,1\}^\lambda$	10: $seedr'' \xleftarrow{\$} \{0,1\}^\lambda$	10: $seedr'' \xleftarrow{\$} \{0,1\}^\lambda$
11: $r'' \xleftarrow{\$} \mathsf{Bin}_\eta(seedr'')$	11: $r'' \xleftarrow{\$} \mathsf{Bin}_\eta(seedr'')$	11: $r'' \xleftarrow{\$} \mathsf{Bin}_\eta(seedr'')$
12: $\mu = \mathsf{LowerBits}(r'', t)$	12: $\mu = \mathsf{LowerBits}(r'', t)$	12: $\mu = \mathsf{LowerBits}(r'', t)$
13: $\beta \leftarrow \{0,1\}$	13: $\beta \leftarrow \{0,1\}$	13: $\beta \leftarrow \{0,1\}$
14: **if** $\beta = 1$ **then**	14: **if** $\beta = 1$ **then**	14: **if** $\beta = 1$ **then**
15: $\mu^* := \mu'$	15: $\mu^* := \mu'$	15: $\mu^* := \mu'$
16: **else** $\beta = 0$	16: **else** $\beta = 0$	16: **else** $\beta = 0$
17: $\mu^* := \mu$	17: $\mu^* := \mu$	17: $\mu^* := \mu$
18: return (h, c, μ^*)	18: return (h, c, μ^*)	18: return (h, c, μ^*)

Note that the Game_0 is subtly different from the standard IND-CPA game that the adversary $\mathcal{A}$ is given h, c and μ^*, which is properly generated as in the encapsulation algorithm that $\mu^* = \mathsf{LowerBits}(r, t)$ or it simply a lower t-bits of a sample form Bin_η, which depends on the random bit β. Then $\mathcal{A}$'s goal is to guess the random bit β. We say $\mathcal{A}$ wins in Game_i if it correctly guesses the random bit β. We use $\mathsf{Adv}_{\mathcal{A}}^{\mathsf{Game}_i}$ to denote the advantage of $\mathcal{A}$ in the Game_i for $i \in \{0,1,2\}$, namely $\mathsf{Adv}_{\mathcal{A}}^{\mathsf{Game}_i} = \Pr[\mathcal{A} \text{ win } \mathsf{Game}_i] - \frac{1}{2}$, and the IND-CPA security of the protocol is obvious if $\mathcal{A}$'s advantage in Game_0 is negligible. We show this through the following lemmas. We omit the proof of Lemma 4.3 since it's identical to the proof of Lemma 3.3.

Lemma 4.3 *If the* $\mathsf{iNTRU}_{n,q,\mathsf{Bin}_\beta}$ *problem is hard, then* $\mathsf{Game}_0 \overset{c}{\approx} \mathsf{Game}_1$.

Lemma 4.4 *If the* $R\text{-}\mathsf{LWE}_{n,q,\mathsf{Bin}_\beta}$ *problem is hard, then* $\mathsf{Game}_1 \overset{c}{\approx} \mathsf{Game}_2$.

For the space limit, we defer the proof of Lemma 4.4 to the full version of the paper.

From above lemmas, we know that:

$$\mathsf{Adv}_{\mathcal{A}}^{\mathsf{Game}_0} \leq \mathsf{Adv}_{\mathcal{A}}^{\mathsf{Game}_1} + \mathsf{negl}(n) \leq \mathsf{Adv}_{\mathcal{A}}^{\mathsf{Game}_2} + \mathsf{negl}(n) \leq \mathsf{negl}(n),$$

where the first inequality is from Lemma 4.3; the second inequality is from Lemma 4.4; the last inequality is from the fact that $\mathsf{Adv}_{\mathcal{A}}^{\mathsf{Game}_2} = 0$. This is the case, since h and c are uniform over R_q, and independent of μ^*. Furthermore, μ and μ' are from same distribution, and thus (h, c, μ^*) is independent of the random bit β, and thus $\mathsf{Adv}_{\mathcal{A}}^{\mathsf{Game}_2} = 0$. This completes the proof. □

In our design of Zaytun.KEM, instead of directly encrypting a random message, we exquisitely used the lowest bits of r. This subtle difference decreases the error bound as reflected in the Theorem 4.1, and thus enables us to compress more bits of ciphertexts. Concrete efficiency comparisons are presented in the following sections.

5   Parameter Settings

In this section, we provide concrete parameterization of the primitives presented in the previous sections.

5.1   Parameter Settings

To instantiate the encryption scheme, we select the concrete parameters such that the resulted scheme has low decryption failure and provides desired bit security. However, setting the parameters according to the theoretical results definitely affects the performance of the scheme. Thus, in practice, we pay more attention to the concrete security of the scheme.

Decryption Failure. The asymptotic correctness results for the Zaytun.PKE and Zaytun.KEM are presented in the previous sections. However, we need a more precise estimation of the failure probability when the primitives are instantiated with concrete parameters. To estimate the concrete failure probability of the schemes, we first compute the distribution function of each coefficient of the error terms involved in the Theorem 3.1. Note that the coefficients of the error polynomials are discrete and upper bounded by small positives, thus we can compute the probability distribution of each coefficient. Then we further compute the failure probability δ in Theorems 3.1 and 4.1. Here we use a python script, provided by [5,14], to estimate the failure probability of Zaytun.PKE and Zaytun.KEM, the results are shown in Tables 1 and 2.

Concrete Security. As we showed in the previous sections, our scheme is based on both the inhomogeneous NTRU problem and the RLWE problem. For concrete security, we estimate the time complexity of the BKZ algorithm to break the scheme. To estimate the time complexity of the BKZ algorithm, we use the folklore estimation model of [22]. For the SVP oracle (called by the BKZ algorithm) complexity, we use $2^{0.292k(1+o(1))}$ for the classic complexity, and $2^{0.265k(1+o(1))}$ for the quantum complexity [5,14]. We remark that this is not a state-of-the-art concrete security estimate, yet it's sufficient to show the advantage of our proposals. We also note that the recent work [26] proposed a quantum key search algorithm for ternary LWE, yet their estimates are currently inferior to the best quantum lattice-based estimates, thus their analysis does not invalidate the security of our schemes. The concrete bit security of Zaytun.PKE and Zaytun.KEM in several parameter settings are presented in Tables 1 and 2.

Parameterization. As we showed in the security proof of our scheme, we need the ring modulus q and the message space parameter 2^t to be co-prime, thus we set the ring modulus q to be a prime such the $q^2 = 1 \mod (2n)$. In this case, we are not able to use the NTT straightly on the polynomial multiplication, yet we use a similar way as [5] to accelerate the multiplications. The concrete parameterization of our scheme is shown in the following Table 1, where η denotes the binomial parameter. For simplicity, we sample the two parameters s and e in the key generation procedure from uniform distribution over $\{-1, 0, 1\}$. Note that this is folklore in the NTRU type schemes, yet other parameterizations are possible. The parameters d_h and d_c are related to the public key compression and ciphertext compression functions, note that the compressibility is a major advantage of our scheme over the NTRU type schemes. In the following Table 1, we present our parameter selections of Zaytun.PKE that provide different levels of security.

Table 1. Parameter settings for Zaytun.PKE.

	n	q	η	d_h	d_c	Failure	Security	
							Classical	Quantum
Zaytun.PKE128	512	3329	3	8	4	2^{-121}	127	116
Zaytun.PKE192	1024	7681	3	6	3	2^{-138}	251	229
Zaytun.PKE256	1024	7681	4	9	3	2^{-188}	260	237

From the column d_c, we know that each coefficient of the ciphertext is compressed more than 60% of the ciphertext bits than an uncompressed one. For the space limit, we defer the parameter selection of Zaytun.KEM to the full version of the paper.

5.2   Comparison with Other Schemes

Although the ciphertext of the NTRU encryption schemes is a ring element, yet the overall bit size of the ciphertext is larger than that of RLWE schemes whose ciphertext is two ring elements [5,14,28]. This is due to the ciphertext compressibility of the RLWE schemes, and this ciphertext compressing procedure compressed almost half of the ciphertexts. As we illustrated in the introduction, Zaytun.PKE enjoys ciphertext compressibility as RLWE schemes, and thus our proposal should have smaller ciphertexts in theory. This is the case in the concrete settings, the following Table 1 shows that the ciphertext size of Zaytun.PKE is only about 37% of the NIST 3-rd round lattice based candidates. Table 2 shows the space complexity of Zaytun.PKE and LWE based NIST 3-rd round candidate schemes [1,5,14,28].

Table 2. Comparison with NIST 3-rd round submissions.

	pk	sk	ct	Failure
128-bit security				
LightSaber	672	832	736	2^{-120}
Kyber512	800	1632	768	2^{-139}
ntruhps2048509	699	903	699	$2^{-214.3}$
Zaytun.PKE128	**512**	**564**	**256**	2^{-121}
192-bit security				
Saber	992	1248	1088	2^{-136}
Kyber768	1184	2400	1088	2^{-164}
ntruhps2048677	930	1202	930	$2^{-213.9}$
ntruhrss701	1138	1418	1138	$2^{-213.9}$
Zaytun.PKE192	**768**	**820**	**384**	2^{-138}
256-bit security				
FireSaber	1312	1664	1472	2^{-165}
Kyber1024	1568	3168	1568	2^{-174}
ntruhps4096821	1230	1558	1230	2^{-769}
Zaytun.PKE256	**1152**	**1204**	**384**	2^{-188}

We also remark that the public key size of our proposals is smaller than that of NIST 3-rd round submissions. Zaytun.KEM provides even smaller ciphertexts.

Acknowledgement. We would like to thank the anonymous reviewers of SAC 2021 for their insightful advices. Parhat Abla would like to thank Abduxukur Turgun for his support and fruitfull discussion.

References

1. NIST:PQC post-quantum cryptography standardization (2020). https://csrc.nist.gov/Projects/post-quantum-cryptography/round-3-submissions
2. Ajtai, M.: Generating hard instances of lattice problems (extended abstract). In: 28th ACM STOC, pp. 99–108. ACM Press, May 1996
3. Alkim, E., Ducas, L., Pöppelmann, T., Schwabe, P.: Post-quantum key exchange - a new hope. In: Holz, T., Savage, S. (eds.) USENIX Security 2016, pp. 327–343. USENIX Association, August 2016
4. Applebaum, B., Cash, D., Peikert, C., Sahai, A.: Fast cryptographic primitives and circular-secure encryption based on hard learning problems. In: Halevi, S. (ed.) CRYPTO 2009. LNCS, vol. 5677, pp. 595–618. Springer, Heidelberg (2009). https://doi.org/10.1007/978-3-642-03356-8_35
5. Avanzi, R., et al.: CRYSTALS-kyber. Submission to the NIST post-quantum cryptography standardization project. NIST National Institute of Standards and Technology (2020)

6. Bos, J.W., et al.: Frodo: take off the ring! Practical, quantum-secure key exchange from LWE. In: Weippl, E.R., Katzenbeisser, S., Kruegel, C., Myers, A.C., Halevi, S. (eds.) ACM CCS 2016, pp. 1006–1018. ACM Press, October 2016

7. Bos, J.W., et al.: Frodo: take off the ring! practical, quantum-secure key exchange from LWE. In: Weippl, E.R., Katzenbeisser, S., Kruegel, C., Myers, A.C., Halevi, S. (eds.) Proceedings of the 2016 ACM SIGSAC Conference on Computer and Communications Security, Vienna, Austria, 24–28 October 2016, pp. 1006–1018. ACM (2016)

8. Brakerski, Z., Langlois, A., Peikert, C., Regev, O., Stehlé, D.: Classical hardness of learning with errors. In: Boneh, D., Roughgarden, T., Feigenbaum, J. (eds.) 45th ACM STOC, pp. 575–584. ACM Press, June 2013

9. Canetti, R., Krawczyk, H.: Analysis of key-exchange protocols and their use for building secure channels. In: Pfitzmann, B. (ed.) EUROCRYPT 2001. LNCS, vol. 2045, pp. 453–474. Springer, Heidelberg (2001). https://doi.org/10.1007/3-540-44987-6_28

10. Fujisaki, E., Okamoto, T.: Secure integration of asymmetric and symmetric encryption schemes. In: Wiener, M. (ed.) CRYPTO 1999. LNCS, vol. 1666, pp. 537–554. Springer, Heidelberg (1999). https://doi.org/10.1007/3-540-48405-1_34

11. Gentry, C., Peikert, C., Vaikuntanathan, V.: Trapdoors for hard lattices and new cryptographic constructions. In: Ladner, R.E., Dwork, C. (eds.) 40th ACM STOC, pp. 197–206. ACM Press, May 2008

12. Hoffstein, J., Pipher, J., Silverman, J.H.: NTRU: a ring-based public key cryptosystem. In: Buhler, J.P. (ed.) ANTS 1998. LNCS, vol. 1423, pp. 267–288. Springer, Heidelberg (1998). https://doi.org/10.1007/BFb0054868

13. Hofheinz, D., Hövelmanns, K., Kiltz, E.: A modular analysis of the Fujisaki-Okamoto transformation. In: Kalai, Y., Reyzin, L. (eds.) TCC 2017. LNCS, vol. 10677, pp. 341–371. Springer, Cham (2017). https://doi.org/10.1007/978-3-319-70500-2_12

14. Jan-Pieter D'Anvers, S.S.R. Karmakar, A., Vercauteren, F.: SABER: submission to the NIST post-quantum cryptography standardization project. NIST National Institute of Standards and Technology (2020)

15. Jiang, H., Zhang, Z., Chen, L., Wang, H., Ma, Z.: IND-CCA-secure key encapsulation mechanism in the quantum random oracle model, revisited. In: Shacham, H., Boldyreva, A. (eds.) CRYPTO 2018. LNCS, vol. 10993, pp. 96–125. Springer, Cham (2018). https://doi.org/10.1007/978-3-319-96878-0_4

16. Jin, Z., Zhao, Y.: Optimal key consensus in presence of noise. Cryptology ePrint Archive, Report 2017/1058 (2017). http://eprint.iacr.org/2017/1058

17. Lindner, R., Peikert, C.: Better key sizes (and attacks) for LWE-based encryption. In: Kiayias, A. (ed.) CT-RSA 2011. LNCS, vol. 6558, pp. 319–339. Springer, Heidelberg (2011). https://doi.org/10.1007/978-3-642-19074-2_21

18. Lyubashevsky, V., Peikert, C., Regev, O.: On ideal lattices and learning with errors over rings. In: Gilbert, H. (ed.) EUROCRYPT 2010. LNCS, vol. 6110, pp. 1–23. Springer, Heidelberg (2010). https://doi.org/10.1007/978-3-642-13190-5_1

19. Peikert, C.: Public-key cryptosystems from the worst-case shortest vector problem: extended abstract. In: Mitzenmacher, M. (ed.) 41st ACM STOC, pp. 333–342. ACM Press, May–June 2009

20. Peikert, C.: Lattice cryptography for the internet. In: Mosca, M. (ed.) PQCrypto 2014. LNCS, vol. 8772, pp. 197–219. Springer, Cham (2014). https://doi.org/10.1007/978-3-319-11659-4_12

21. Peikert, C., Regev, O., Stephens-Davidowitz, N.: Pseudorandomness of ring-LWE for any ring and modulus. In: Hatami, H., McKenzie, P., King, V. (eds.) 49th ACM STOC, pp. 461–473. ACM Press, June 2017
22. Poppelmann, T., et al.: Newhope. Submission to the NIST post-quantum cryptography standardization project. NIST National Institute of Standards and Technology (2019)
23. Regev, O.: On lattices, learning with errors, random linear codes, and cryptography. In: Gabow, H.N., Fagin, R. (eds.) 37th ACM STOC, pp. 84–93. ACM Press, May 2005
24. Shor, P.W.: Algorithms for quantum computation: discrete logarithms and factoring. In: 35th FOCS, pp. 124–134. IEEE Computer Society Press, November 1994
25. Stehlé, D., Steinfeld, R.: Making NTRU as secure as worst-case problems over ideal lattices. In: Paterson, K.G. (ed.) EUROCRYPT 2011. LNCS, vol. 6632, pp. 27–47. Springer, Heidelberg (2011). https://doi.org/10.1007/978-3-642-20465-4_4
26. van Hoof, I., Kirshanova, E., May, A.: Quantum key search for ternary LWE. IACR Cryptol. ePrint Arch. 2021:865 (2021)
27. Zhang, J., Zhang, Z., Ding, J., Snook, M., Dagdelen, Ö.: Authenticated key exchange from ideal lattices. In: Oswald, E., Fischlin, M. (eds.) EUROCRYPT 2015. LNCS, vol. 9057, pp. 719–751. Springer, Heidelberg (2015). https://doi.org/10.1007/978-3-662-46803-6_24
28. Zhang, Z., et al.: NTRU. Technical report, NIST National Institute of Standards and Technology (2020)

A Polynomial Time Key-Recovery Attack on the Sidon Cryptosystem

Pierre Briaud[1,2(✉)], Jean-Pierre Tillich[2], and Javier Verbel[3]

[1] Sorbonne Universités, UPMC Univ Paris 06, Paris, France
`pierre.briaud@inria.fr`
[2] Inria, Team COSMIQ, Paris, France
[3] Cryptography Research Centre, Technology Innovation Institute, Abu Dhabi, UAE

Abstract. The Sidon cryptosystem [21] is a new multivariate encryption scheme based on the theory of Sidon spaces which was presented at PKC 2021. As is usual for this kind of schemes, its security relies on the hardness of solving particular instances of the MQ problem and of the MinRank problem. A nice feature of the scheme is that it enjoys a homomorphic property due the bilinearity of its public polynomials. Unfortunately, we will show that the Sidon cryptosystem can be broken by a polynomial time key-recovery attack. This attack relies on the existence of solutions to the underlying MinRank instance which lie in a subfield and which are inherent to the structure of the secret Sidon space. We prove that such solutions can be found in polynomial time. Our attack consists in recovering an equivalent key for the cryptosystem by exploiting these particular solutions, and this task can be performed very efficiently.

Keywords: Multivariate cryptography · Encryption scheme · Algebraic attack · MinRank problem

1 Introduction

In recent years, many Public Key Cryptographic (PKC) primitives have been proposed to fulfill the need of having quantum-secure Key Encapsulation Mechanisms (KEMs) and Digital Signatures Schemes (DSS).

In the field of DSS, Multivariate Public Key Cryptography (MPKC) has proven to be one of the most promising alternatives. In the ongoing NIST-PQC standardization process, the MPKC schemes Rainbow [11] and GeMSS [8] are in the final round, even though the last as an alternative candidate. But when it comes to KEMs, the situation is less promising. Throughout the last 25 years, many MPKC encryption schemes have been proposed such as HFE, ZHFE, Extension Field Cancellation (EFC), SRP, HFERP, EFLASH and the Simple Matrix Encryption Scheme, see [7,16,19,20,24,25], and all of them are either extremely inefficient or have been successfully cryptanalyzed [1,4,6,17,18,23]. A relative common structure among the MPKC schemes is that the public key

© The Author(s), under exclusive license to Springer Nature Switzerland AG 2022
R. AlTawy and A. Hülsing (Eds.): SAC 2021, LNCS 13203, pp. 419–438, 2022.
https://doi.org/10.1007/978-3-030-99277-4_20

is a system of multivariate polynomials which is hard to solve directly. On the contrary, the private key is a sequence of polynomials which is easy to solve and which is masked in certain way to produce the public key. The two main hard problems considered to build MPKC are the problem of solving a system of multivariate quadratic equations over a finite field (the MQ problem) and the following MinRank problem, which was originally defined and proven NP-complete in [5]. The version of the MinRank problem which is relevant in our case is given by

Problem 1. (MinRank problem).
  Input: an integer $r \in \mathbb{N}$, n matrices $\boldsymbol{M}^{(1)}, \ldots, \boldsymbol{M}^{(n)} \in \mathbb{F}_q^{k \times k}$, $\mathbb{L}$ a finite extension of $\mathbb{F}_q$.
  Output: field elements $x_1, x_2, \ldots, x_n \in \mathbb{L}$, not all zero, such that

$$\text{Rank} \left(\sum_{i=1}^{n} x_i \boldsymbol{M}^{(i)} \right) \leq r.$$

Note that the standard formulation in the literature considers $\mathbb{L} = \mathbb{F}_q$ and possibly non-square matrices. In all cases, solving a particular instance of one of these two problems leads to either a key-recovery attack or a message-recovery attack on a given scheme. Thus, the security of the scheme is usually estimated via the hardness of solving particular instances of MQ or MinRank.

At PKC 2021, Raviv, Langton and Tamo proposed, for the first time, a MPKC encryption scheme based on the theory of Sidon spaces [21]. The concept of Sidon space was originally defined in [2]. A Sidon space is an $\mathbb{F}_q$-subspace of an extension field $\mathbb{F}_{q^n}$ in which the product of any two elements factors uniquely up to multiplicative constants in $\mathbb{F}_q$. The basic idea of the scheme is as follows: the plaintext is the equivalence class of pairs of two elements in a Sidon space $\mathcal{V}$ of dimension k, two pairs with the same product being equivalent, while the ciphertext is the product of these two elements. The private key is some information related to the structure of $\mathcal{V}$ that allows to factor efficiently any ciphertext, while the public key is a bilinear sequence $(p_1, \ldots, p_{2k})$ of $2k$ homogeneous equations in two blocks of variables $\boldsymbol{a}$ and $\boldsymbol{b}$ over $\mathbb{F}_q$ of equal size k. This makes the Sidon cryptosystem to have an additive homomorphic property since the sum of the encryptions of two messages like $\{\boldsymbol{a}_1, \boldsymbol{b}\}$, $\{\boldsymbol{a}_2, \boldsymbol{b}\}$ results in the encryption of $\{\boldsymbol{a}_1 + \boldsymbol{a}_2, \boldsymbol{b}\}$. To the best of our knowledge, this is first MQ- or MinRank- based scheme doted with any kind of homomorphic property.

The private key can be obtained from a solution to the MinRank problem given by the matrices $\boldsymbol{M}^{(i)} \in \mathbb{F}_q^{k \times k}$ defined by $p_i(\boldsymbol{a}, \boldsymbol{b}) = \boldsymbol{a} \boldsymbol{M}^{(i)} \boldsymbol{b}^{\mathsf{T}}$ for $1 \leq i \leq n = 2k$, with $r = 1$ and $\mathbb{L} = \mathbb{F}_{q^{2k}}$. It turns out that this MinRank instance has many solutions, and the structure of the Sidon space can be fully extracted from at least one of these solutions. However, to perform a key-recovery attack, the authors argue that

(i) it is not clear how to solve this particular MinRank instance, since standard techniques are strongly based either on the fact that the base field is small

(Linear Algebra Search [15]) or the number of solutions is small (Minors modeling [12] + XL, and Support-Minors modeling [3]).

(ii) Even if one is able to find a solution to the MinRank problem, it is not clear how this solution can be used to develop a key recovery.

Therefore, the message-recovery attack is arguably the most threatening attack which may be used to design parameters, and this attack can be performed by inverting the public bilinear system. When q is large enough, the Gröbner basis approach outperforms the exhaustive search on $\boldsymbol{a}$ or $\boldsymbol{b}$ in $\mathcal{O}(k^3 q^{k-1})$, and the authors claim a complexity of

$$\mathcal{O}\left(\binom{3k+1}{k+1}^\omega\right) \tag{1}$$

operations in $\mathbb{F}_q$ for this attack, where $2 \leq \omega \leq 3$ is the linear algebra constant. This cost is clearly exponential in k.

Contributions. The purpose of this paper is to give a polynomial-time attack breaking the Sidon cryptosystem. Our attack relies on a rigorous analysis of the solution set of the underlying MinRank problem. In particular, we show here that in addition to generic solutions over $\mathbb{F}_{q^{2k}}$, there exist solutions over the subfield $\mathbb{F}_{q^k}$. Moreover, all these solutions over $\mathbb{F}_{q^k}$ are inherent to the Sidon space used in the scheme. Our attack can be summarized as follows

- The first step of our attack consists in recovering these solutions over $\mathbb{F}_{q^k}$. To this end, we propose a dedicated modeling of the MinRank problem and prove that for this modeling the Gröbner basis computation on this algebraic system terminates at degree 3 independently from the value of k. This shows that this first step can be achieved in polynomial time.
- Second, it is possible to exploit these solutions in order to find an equivalent key which is another Sidon space. This second step can be performed by simple linear algebra operations followed by a sub-algorithm of the original key generation process. Therefore, its cost is also expected to be polynomial.

Along with this paper, we provide a sage implementation of our attack in [26]. This tool can also be used to verify experimentally all the theoretical claims made in the paper and to reproduce the experiments we performed.

Roadmap. The Sidon cryptosystem from [21] is presented in Sect. 2. In Sect. 3, we provide a detailed analysis of the underlying MinRank instance, and this material allows us to introduce our key-recovery attack in Sect. 4 and in Sect. 5.

Notation. Row vectors are denoted by bold lowercase letters $(\boldsymbol{u}, \boldsymbol{v}, \dots)$ and matrices are denoted by bold uppercase letters $(\boldsymbol{M}, \boldsymbol{N}, \dots)$. For a vector $\boldsymbol{v}$ we use the notation v_i for the i-th component of $\boldsymbol{v}$, and for a matrix $\boldsymbol{M}$ we use the notation $\boldsymbol{M}_{i,j}$ for the entry in row i and column j.

For $\boldsymbol{v}$ a vector of length k, we denote by $\boldsymbol{M}(\boldsymbol{v})$ the rank 1 symmetric matrix of size $k \times k$ which is equal to $\boldsymbol{v}^\mathsf{T}\boldsymbol{v}$. In the following, $q \geq 3$ is a prime power and we will consider $\mathbb{F}_{q^k}$ (resp. $\mathbb{F}_{q^{2k}}$) an extension of degree k (resp. $2k$) of $\mathbb{F}_q$. For $j \in \mathbb{Z}_{\geq 0}$ and $\boldsymbol{v} = (v_1, \ldots, v_k)$ a vector whose entries are elements or polynomials over a finite extension of $\mathbb{F}_q$, we define

$$\boldsymbol{v}^{[j]} := (v_1^{q^j}, \ldots, v_k^{q^j}).$$

This corresponds to applying the Frobenius automorphism $x \mapsto x^q$ j times on each coordinate of $\boldsymbol{v}$. Note that this field automorphism is the identity on $\mathbb{F}_q$. We will adopt the same notation for matrices, namely the matrix $\boldsymbol{M}^{[j]}$ is the matrix obtained from $\boldsymbol{M}$ by raising all its entries to the power q^j.

We will also adopt in several places a coding theoretic point of view and view a subspace $\mathcal{C}$ of $\mathbb{F}_q^N$ as a linear code and use the term *parity-check* for it to denote a matrix $\boldsymbol{H}$ whose null-space is $\mathcal{C}$, that is:

$$\mathcal{C} = \{\boldsymbol{x} \in \mathbb{F}_q^N : \boldsymbol{H}\boldsymbol{x}^\mathsf{T} = 0\}.$$

Finally, it is convenient to consider for a vector space V, ordered bases for it, and we will use a vector notation for the basis.

Polynomial Systems. In the following, the expression $\mathbb{K}[\boldsymbol{x}]$ denotes the polynomial ring over the field $\mathbb{K}$ in the coordinates of $\boldsymbol{x} = (x_1, \ldots, x_k)$. We will use Gröbner basis techniques to solve polynomial systems, and we refer the reader to [9] for basic definitions and properties of monomial orderings and Gröbner bases. The most basic algorithm to derive a Gröbner basis with respect to a given monomial ordering for the ideal generated by a sequence $\mathcal{F} := \{f_1, \ldots, f_m\}$ is the so-called Buchberger's algorithm. It starts from $\mathcal{G} := \mathcal{F}$ and computes S-polynomials

$$S(f_i, f_j) := \frac{a_{i,j}}{l_i} f_i - \frac{a_{i,j}}{l_j} f_j,$$

where l_i (resp. l_j) is the leading term of f_i (resp. f_j) and $a_{i,j}$ is the lcm of l_i and l_j. These polynomials are then reduced modulo $\mathcal{G}$ and added to the former sequence, and these steps are repeated until all S-polynomials reduce to zero. At this stage, Buchberger's criterion [9, §2, Thm. 6] ensures that the final $\mathcal{G}$ is a Gröbner basis.

2 The Sidon Cryptosystem

Several explicit constructions of Sidon spaces with relevant parameters and factoring properties were proposed in [22], and the one used in [21] to instantiate the Sidon cryptosystem is of this kind. In Sect. 2.1, we give some background on Sidon spaces in general and on this specific construction. The Sidon cryptosystem is presented in Sect. 2.2, and in Sect. 2.3 we discuss the important notion of equivalent keys for this scheme.

2.1   Sidon Spaces

For integers k and n and q a prime power, let $\mathbb{F}_q$ be the finite field with q elements, let $\mathcal{G}_q(n, k)$ be the set of all $\mathbb{F}_q$-subspaces of $\mathbb{F}_{q^n}$ of dimension k. The formal definition of a Sidon space is the following.

Definition 1. *A subspace $V \in \mathcal{G}_q(n, k)$ is called a Sidon space if for all non-zero $a, b, c, d \in V$, if $ab = cd$, then $\{a\mathbb{F}_q, b\mathbb{F}_q\} = \{c\mathbb{F}_q, d\mathbb{F}_q\}$.*

Then, a first natural question is whether there exist Sidon spaces of arbitrary dimension. A constraint on k was given by [2, Thm. 18][22, Prop. 3], where it is proven that if $V \in \mathcal{G}_q(n, k)$ is a Sidon space, then one has

$$\dim_{\mathbb{F}_q} (V^2) \geq 2k$$

with $V^2 = \mathrm{span}_{\mathbb{F}_q}\{uv \mid u, v \in V\}$. Since $V^2 \subset \mathbb{F}_{q^n}$, this implies that $k \leq n/2$, and Sidon spaces for which this bound is an equality are referred to as *min-span*. Note that regardless of the existence of any factoring algorithm for V, it is crucial for the security of the cryptosystem that the dimension of V satisfies $k = \Theta(n)$, as pointed out in [21, Rem. 2]. In particular, the construction considered to devise the scheme is a *min-span* Sidon space, *i.e.* $n = 2k$. To describe this construction, let $W_{q-1} = \{u^{q-1} | u \in \mathbb{F}_{q^k}\}$ and $\overline{W_{q-1}} = \mathbb{F}_{q^k} \setminus W_{q-1}$.

Construction 1 *[22, Const. 15]. For $q \geq 3$ a prime poewer and k a positive integer, let $n = 2k$ and let $\gamma \in \mathbb{F}_{q^n}^*$ be a root of an irreducible polynomial $x^2 + bx + c$ over $\mathbb{F}_{q^k}$ such that $c \in \overline{W_{q-1}}^1$. Then, the subspace $V = \{u + u^q \gamma | u \in \mathbb{F}_{q^k}\} \subset \mathbb{F}_{q^n}$ is a Sidon space of dimension k.*

A Sidon space V given by Construction 1 admits the following efficient factoring algorithm. This algorithm fully uses the knowledge of the element γ such that $\mathcal{B} := \{1, \gamma\}$ is a basis of $\mathbb{F}_{q^{2k}}$ over $\mathbb{F}_{q^k}$, and for $x \in \mathbb{F}_{q^{2k}}$ we will denote by $[1](x)$ and $[\gamma](x)$ the components of x in this basis. Given a product $\pi = \pi_1 \pi_2$ where π_1 and π_2 lie in V, Algorithm 1 recovers π_1 and π_2 up to constant factors in $\mathbb{F}_q$.

Input: A product $\pi = \pi_1 \pi_2$, where $\pi_1 = u + u^q \gamma$ and $\pi_2 = v + v^q \gamma \in V$, the element $\gamma \in \mathbb{F}_{q^n}^*$ such that $\gamma^2 + b\gamma + c = 0$ from Construction 1.

Output: $\{\pi_1 \mathbb{F}_q, \pi_2 \mathbb{F}_q\}$.
Decompose π in the basis $\{1, \gamma\}$:

$q_0 \leftarrow [1](\pi)$ `// ` $q_0 = uv - c(uv)^q$
$q_1 \leftarrow [\gamma](\pi)$ `// ` $q_1 = uv^q + u^q v - b(uv)^q$
$A \leftarrow T^{-1}(q_0)$ `// where ` T `is map ` $x \mapsto x - cx^q$, $A = uv$
$B \leftarrow q_1 + bA^q$ `// ` $B = uv^q + u^q v$
Compute the roots α, β of $A + Bx + A^q x^2$
`// ` $\alpha = -1/u^{q-1}$, $\beta = -1/v^{q-1}$
From α and β, recover $\{u\mathbb{F}_q, v\mathbb{F}_q\}$ uniquely and therefore $\{\pi_1 \mathbb{F}_q, \pi_2 \mathbb{F}_q\}$.

Algorithm 1: Factoring algorithm for Sidon space from Construction 1.

---

[1] Such a polynomial is known to exist by [22, Corollary 14].

2.2   Description of the Cryptosystem

The Sidon cryptosystem relies on Construction 1, but it might be possible to consider another type of Sidon space such that $k = \Theta(n)$ for which an efficient factoring algorithm exists. In this section, we briefly describe the building blocks of the scheme, and we refer the reader to [21, §3] for further details.

Keygen:

- Select a random element $\gamma \in \mathbb{F}_{q^n}$ satisfying the constraints given in Construction 1 in order to build the Sidon space $\mathcal{V} := \{u + u^q \gamma | u \in \mathbb{F}_{q^k}\}$.
- Select $\boldsymbol{\nu} = (\nu_1, \ldots, \nu_k)$ a random basis of $\mathcal{V}$ and $\boldsymbol{\beta} = (\beta_1, \ldots, \beta_n)$ a random basis of $\mathbb{F}_{q^n}$ over $\mathbb{F}_q$.
- Represent the matrix $\boldsymbol{M}(\boldsymbol{\nu}) = \boldsymbol{\nu}^\mathsf{T} \boldsymbol{\nu} \in \mathbb{F}_{q^n}^{k \times k}$ over the basis $\boldsymbol{\beta}$:

$$\boldsymbol{M}(\boldsymbol{\nu}) = \boldsymbol{\nu}^\mathsf{T} \boldsymbol{\nu} = \sum_{i=1}^{n} \beta_i \boldsymbol{M}^{(i)},$$

  where $\boldsymbol{M}^{(i)} \in \mathbb{F}_q^{k \times k}$ for $1 \leq i \leq n$.
- Output $\mathsf{sk} = (\boldsymbol{\beta}, \boldsymbol{\nu}, \gamma)$ as secret key and $\mathsf{pk} = (\boldsymbol{M}^{(1)}, \ldots, \boldsymbol{M}^{(n)})$ as public key.

As explained in the introduction, the message space correspond to the equivalence class of pairs of elements $\{a, b\}$ in the Sidon space $\mathcal{V}$, two pairs $\{a, b\}$ and $\{c, d\}$ being equivalent if their product is the same: $ab = cd$. If one views an element a of $\mathcal{V}$ as a vector $\boldsymbol{a} \in \mathbb{F}_q^k$, i.e. $a = \sum_{i=1}^{k} a_i \nu_i$, then the equivalence class associated to $\{a, b\}$ corresponds to all pairs $\{c, d\}$ such that either $\boldsymbol{a}^\mathsf{T} \boldsymbol{b} = \boldsymbol{c}^\mathsf{T} \boldsymbol{d}$ or $\boldsymbol{a}^\mathsf{T} \boldsymbol{b} = \boldsymbol{d}^\mathsf{T} \boldsymbol{c}$. This space is of size $\dfrac{(q^k - 1)(q^k - q)}{2(q - 1)} + q^k - 1$ as shown in [21, App A].

Encrypt($\{a, b\}, \mathsf{pk} = (\boldsymbol{M}^{(i)})_{i=1}^n$):

- The ciphertext associated to (the equivalence class of) $\{a, b\}$ is

$$\boldsymbol{c} = (c_i)_{i=1}^n = (\boldsymbol{a} \boldsymbol{M}^{(i)} \boldsymbol{b}^\mathsf{T})_{i=1}^n \in \mathbb{F}_q^n. \tag{2}$$

Note that this definition is compatible with the way the plaintext is defined: the ciphertext does not depend on the particular pair $\{a, b\}$ chosen in the equivalence class of the message. An interesting property of the Sidon cryptosystem is that it is homomorphic under the addition on half of the plaintext. That is, for two given plaintexts $\{a_1, b\}$ and $\{a_2, b\}$ we have

Encrypt($\{a_1, b\}, \mathsf{pk}$) + Encrypt($\{a_2, b\}, \mathsf{pk}$) = Encrypt($\{a_1 + a_2, b\}, \mathsf{pk}$).

To decrypt with the secret key, Bob views the ciphertext $\boldsymbol{c}$ as a product of elements in $\mathcal{V}$. Then, he is able to recover the factors using Algorithm 1 since he completely knows the structure of $\mathcal{V}$.

Decrypt(c, sk $= (\beta, \nu, \gamma)$):

– Compute

$$\sum_{i=1}^{n} \beta_i c_i = \sum_{i=1}^{n} \beta_i \left(\boldsymbol{a} \boldsymbol{M}^{(i)} \boldsymbol{b}^{\mathsf{T}} \right) = \boldsymbol{a} \boldsymbol{M}(\boldsymbol{\nu}) \boldsymbol{b}^{\mathsf{T}}$$

$$= \boldsymbol{a} \boldsymbol{\nu}^{\mathsf{T}} \boldsymbol{\nu} \boldsymbol{b}^{\mathsf{T}} = \left(\sum_{i=1}^{k} a_i \nu_i \right) \left(\sum_{i=1}^{k} b_i \nu_i \right) = ab, \qquad (3)$$

and ab is a product of elements in $\mathcal{V}$.
– From the knowledge of γ, use Algorithm 1 to recover $\{a, b\}$ up to a multiplicative factor in $\mathbb{F}_q$.
– Finally, retrieve $\{\boldsymbol{a}, \boldsymbol{b}\}$ (up to a multiplicative factor) by representing $\{\boldsymbol{a}, \boldsymbol{b}\}$ over the basis $\boldsymbol{\nu}$. Such an $\{\boldsymbol{a}, \boldsymbol{b}\}$ defines the message in a unique way.

2.3   Equivalent Keys for the Sidon Cryptosystem

An important notion for multivariate schemes in general is that of equivalent keys. Two secret keys are equivalent if they lead to the same public key. In the case of the Sidon cryptosystem, one can easily obtain the following result by using the definition of the decryption process given in Eq. (3):

Fact 1. *Any Sidon space $\mathcal{V}'$ generated using Construction 1 with basis $\boldsymbol{\nu}'$ and such that the matrix $\boldsymbol{M}(\boldsymbol{\nu}')$ lies in the linear span of the $\boldsymbol{M}^{(i)}$'s can be used as an equivalent key.*

Proof. Assume that $\boldsymbol{\nu}'$ is a basis of a Sidon space $\mathcal{V}'$ such that the matrix $\boldsymbol{M}(\boldsymbol{\nu}')$ is a linear combination of the $\boldsymbol{M}^{(i)}$'s. From the knowledge of $\boldsymbol{\nu}'$, one can construct $\boldsymbol{M}(\boldsymbol{\nu}')$ and then solve the linear system in the β_i''s given by $\boldsymbol{M}(\boldsymbol{\nu}') = \sum_{i=1}^{n} \beta_i' \boldsymbol{M}^{(i)}$. Finally, the quantity $\sum_{i=1}^{n} \beta_i' c_i$ is a product of elements in $\mathcal{V}'$ which can be factored using Algorithm 1.   □

Equivalent keys are an important feature for our attack, since it will consist in recovering a Sidon space $\mathcal{V}' \neq \mathcal{V}$ which allows to decrypt any ciphertext.

3   Analysis of the Underlying MinRank Problem

Given the public key $(\boldsymbol{M}^{(1)}, \ldots, \boldsymbol{M}^{(n)})$ such that $\boldsymbol{M}^{(i)} \in \mathbb{F}_q^{k \times k}$ for $1 \leq i \leq n$, one has

$$\boldsymbol{M}(\boldsymbol{\nu}) = \boldsymbol{\nu}^{\mathsf{T}} \boldsymbol{\nu} = \sum_{i=1}^{n} \beta_i \boldsymbol{M}^{(i)},$$

where $(\beta_1, \ldots, \beta_n)$ is the basis of $\mathbb{F}_{q^n}$ over $\mathbb{F}_q$ and $\boldsymbol{\nu}$ is the basis of the Sidon space which are part of the private key. In other words, the matrix $\boldsymbol{M}(\boldsymbol{\nu})$ is a linear combination of the $\boldsymbol{M}^{(i)}$'s over $\mathbb{F}_{q^n}$ which has rank 1, and an equivalent key-recovery attack on the scheme requires to find specific solutions over $\mathbb{F}_{q^n}$

of the MinRank instance described by the $\boldsymbol{M}^{(i)}$'s. This MinRank problem is not standard in at least two ways. First, solutions are searched in the extension field $\mathbb{F}_{q^n}$, whereas the $\boldsymbol{M}^{(i)}$'s have their entries in $\mathbb{F}_q$. Second, this system has surprisingly many solutions and it is not clear at all whether the Sidon structure can be recovered from an arbitrary solution to it. Note that the authors of [21] only studied the hardness of finding any solution to this MinRank problem, and the task of determining the whole solution set was not addressed explicitly.

In this section, we examine in greater depth the properties of this solution set. A first remark is that the solutions correspond to rank 1 matrices in the space generated by the $\boldsymbol{M}^{(i)}$'s over $\mathbb{F}_{q^n}$:

$$\mathcal{C}_{mat} := \left\langle \boldsymbol{M}^{(1)}, \ldots, \boldsymbol{M}^{(n)} \right\rangle_{\mathbb{F}_{q^n}}. \tag{4}$$

Our main result will be the existence of solutions over the subfield $\mathbb{F}_{q^k}$, *i.e.* rank 1 matrices in

$$\mathcal{D}_{mat} := \mathcal{C}_{mat}|_{\mathbb{F}_{q^k}} := \mathcal{C}_{mat} \cap \mathbb{F}_{q^k}^{k \times k}.$$

Fact 2. *The subspace* $\mathcal{D}_{mat} = \mathcal{C}_{mat}|_{\mathbb{F}_{q^k}}$ *contains elements of rank 1.*

Such elements are described in Sect. 3.3, and our experiments suggest that these are the only ones in $\mathcal{D}_{mat}$.

3.1 Restricting the Number of the Solutions

We start by reviewing some elementary properties of the solution set. Since the generators $\boldsymbol{M}^{(i)}$ are symmetric, all the elements in $\mathcal{C}_{mat}$ are symmetric as well. Therefore, rank 1 elements in $\mathcal{C}_{mat}$ will be of the form $\boldsymbol{x}^{\mathsf{T}}\boldsymbol{y} \in \mathbb{F}_{q^n}^{k \times k}$ for $\boldsymbol{x}$ collinear with $\boldsymbol{y}$. In particular, we will be interested in the following subset of solutions defined by

$$\mathcal{Z}_{\mathbb{F}_{q^n}} := \left\{ \boldsymbol{x} \in \mathbb{F}_{q^n}^k, \ \boldsymbol{x}^{\mathsf{T}}\boldsymbol{x} \in \mathcal{C}_{mat} \right\}. \tag{5}$$

This set is non-trivial since it contains $\boldsymbol{\nu}$ from the private key. Also, there is still one degree of freedom coming from the $\mathbb{F}_{q^n}$-linearity of $\mathcal{C}_{mat}$. For instance, since $\nu_1 \neq 0$ in $\boldsymbol{\nu}$, the set

$$\mathcal{Z}_{\mathbb{F}_{q^n},s} := \left\{ \boldsymbol{x} \in \mathcal{Z}_{\mathbb{F}_{q^n}}, x_1 = s \right\}$$

is also non-trivial for $s \in \mathbb{F}_{q^n}^*$.

3.2 Generic Solutions Over $\mathbb{F}_{q^n}$

In this section, we describe a generic way to generate many solutions to the MinRank problem. Consider any $\boldsymbol{\omega} \in \mathbb{F}_{q^n}^k$ such that $\boldsymbol{\omega} \in \mathcal{Z}_{\mathbb{F}_{q^n}}$. By definition, there exists $\boldsymbol{\eta} = (\eta_1, \ldots, \eta_n) \in \mathbb{F}_{q^n}^n$ such that

$$M(\boldsymbol{\omega}) = \sum_{\ell=1}^{n} \eta_\ell \boldsymbol{M}^{(\ell)}. \tag{6}$$

In particular, one has for $1 \leq i, j \leq k$:

$$\omega_i \omega_j = \sum_{\ell=1}^{n} \eta_\ell M_{i,j}^{(\ell)}. \tag{7}$$

Then, by iterating the Frobenius map p times on this equation for $0 \leq p \leq n-1$, one obtains

$$\omega_i^{[p]} \omega_j^{[p]} = \sum_{\ell=1}^{n} \eta_\ell^{[p]} M_{i,j}^{(\ell)} \tag{8}$$

since the matrices $M^{(\ell)}$ have entries in $\mathbb{F}_q$. This implies that the matrix

$$M(\omega^{[p]}) = \sum_{\ell=1}^{n} \eta_\ell^{[p]} M^{(\ell)} \tag{9}$$

belongs to $\mathcal{C}_{mat}$ for $0 \leq p \leq n-1$. Overall, this observation can be summarized in the following Lemma 1.

Lemma 1 ("Stability by Frobenius"). *Let $\mathcal{C}_{mat}$ as defined in Eq. (4) and let $\mathcal{Z}_{\mathbb{F}_{q^n}}$ as defined in Eq. (4). If $\omega \in \mathcal{Z}_{\mathbb{F}_{q^n}}$, then $\omega^{[j]} \in \mathcal{Z}_{\mathbb{F}_{q^n}}$ for any $j \geq 0$, and more generally if $M \in \mathcal{C}_{mat}$, then $M^{[j]} \in \mathcal{C}_{mat}$ for any $j \geq 0$.*

The fact that $\mathcal{V}$ is a Sidon space is not used at all in this reasoning. In particular, the very same argument can be applied to a random subspace $\mathcal{W} \subset \mathbb{F}_{q^n}$ of dimension k along with a random secret basis ω for $\mathcal{W}$. In this case, the $M^{(i)}$'s are obtained from the decomposition of the matrix $M(\omega)$ in an arbitrary basis of $\mathbb{F}_{q^n}$ over $\mathbb{F}_q$, and $\mathcal{C}_{mat}$ and $\mathcal{Z}_{\mathbb{F}_{q^n}}$ are defined in the same way as before. For such a random subspace $\mathcal{W}$, the only solutions to the MinRank instance that we observe in practice are given by Lemma 1:

Observation 1 (From experiments). *Let $\mathcal{W} \subset \mathbb{F}_{q^n}$ be a random $\mathbb{F}_q$-subspace of dimension k, let ω be a random basis of $\mathcal{W}$ and let $s \in \mathbb{F}_{q^n}^*$. One has*

$$\left| \mathcal{Z}_{\mathbb{F}_{q^n}, s} \right| = n.$$

Moreover, if $s \in \mathbb{F}_q^*$, then there exists $u \in \mathbb{F}_{q^n}^k$ with $u_1 = s$ such that

$$\mathcal{Z}_{\mathbb{F}_{q^n}, s} = \left\{ u, u^{[1]}, \ldots, u^{[n-1]} \right\}.$$

However, when $\mathcal{V}$ is a Sidon space generated using Construction 1, we observed that there were many more solutions to the MinRank instance than those just described. This behavior can be explained by the fact that there also exist rank 1 linear combinations of the $M^{(i)}$'s over the subfield $\mathbb{F}_{q^k}$, *i.e.* the set $\mathcal{Z}_{\mathbb{F}_{q^k}}$ is non-trivial. More precisely, we obtained the following experimental result.

Observation 2 (From experiments). *Let $\mathcal{V}$ be a Sidon space generated using Construction 1. For $s \in \mathbb{F}_{q^k}^*$, we observed that*

$$\left| \mathcal{Z}_{\mathbb{F}_{q^k},s} \right| = k(q^k - 1).$$

Moreover, if $t \in \mathbb{F}_{q^k}^*$, $t \notin \langle s \rangle_{\mathbb{F}_q}$, we observed that

$$\left| \left\{ \boldsymbol{x} \in \mathcal{Z}_{\mathbb{F}_{q^k},s},\ x_2 = t \right\} \right| = k.$$

3.3 Rank 1 Codewords in $\mathcal{D}_{mat}$ from the Sidon Structure

This section is dedicated to the study of the set $\mathcal{Z}_{\mathbb{F}_{q^k}}$ when $\mathcal{V}$ is a Sidon space generated using Construction 1 with secret basis $\boldsymbol{\nu}$. For $1 \leq i \leq k$, there exists $u_i \in \mathbb{F}_{q^k}$ such that

$$\nu_i = u_i + u_i^q \gamma. \tag{10}$$

Note that $\boldsymbol{u} := (u_1, \ldots, u_k)$ is necessarily a basis of $\mathbb{F}_{q^k}$ over $\mathbb{F}_q$. In the following Proposition 1, we are interested in the rank 1 matrix

$$\boldsymbol{M}(\boldsymbol{u}) = (u_1, \ldots, u_k)^\mathsf{T} (u_1, \ldots, u_k) \in \mathbb{F}_{q^k}^{k \times k}.$$

Proposition 1. *Let $\boldsymbol{M}^{(1)}, \ldots, \boldsymbol{M}^{(n)}$ be the public matrices associated to the secret Sidon space $\mathcal{V}$ and let $\boldsymbol{u}$ be the basis of $\mathbb{F}_{q^k}$ over $\mathbb{F}_q$ associated to $\boldsymbol{\nu}$ by Equation (10). Then, $\boldsymbol{M}(\boldsymbol{u})$ is a rank 1 matrix in $\mathcal{D}_{mat}$, and the same is true for $\boldsymbol{M}(\boldsymbol{u}^{[j]})$ for $1 \leq j \leq k - 1$.*

Proof. We do the proof for $\boldsymbol{M}(\boldsymbol{u}) = \boldsymbol{M}(\boldsymbol{u}^{[0]})$ and the rest easily follows by using Lemma 1. First, one can write $\boldsymbol{M}(\boldsymbol{\nu})$ as a sum

$$\boldsymbol{M}(\boldsymbol{\nu}) = \boldsymbol{A} + \gamma \boldsymbol{B} \tag{11}$$

where the matrices $\boldsymbol{A},\ \boldsymbol{B} \in \mathbb{F}_{q^k}^{k \times k}$ are such that

$$\begin{cases} \boldsymbol{A} = \displaystyle\sum_{i=1}^{n} \delta_i \boldsymbol{M}^{(i)} \\ \boldsymbol{B} = \displaystyle\sum_{i=1}^{n} \eta_i \boldsymbol{M}^{(i)} \end{cases} \tag{12}$$

and where $\beta_i := \delta_i + \gamma \eta_i$ is expressed in the basis $\{1, \gamma\}$ for $1 \leq i \leq n$ with $\delta_i, \eta_i \in \mathbb{F}_{q^k}$. Also, recall that the primitive element γ is a root of the irreducible polynomial $x^2 + bx + c$ over $\mathbb{F}_{q^k}$, so that one obtains for $1 \leq i, j \leq k$:

$$\begin{aligned} \nu_i \nu_j &= (u_i + u_i^q \gamma)(u_j + u_j^q \gamma) \\ &= (u_i u_j - c(u_i u_j)^q) + \gamma(u_i u_j^q + u_i^q u_j - b(u_i u_j)^q). \end{aligned} \tag{13}$$

Therefore, Eq. (13) shows that $A = M(u) - cM(u^{[1]})$, and this matrix belongs to $\mathcal{D}_{mat}$ by (12). By Lemma 1, the same is true for the following matrices

$$A^{[1]} = M(u^{[1]}) - c^q M(u^{[2]})$$
$$A^{[2]} = M(u^{[2]}) - c^{q^2} M(u^{[3]})$$
$$\vdots$$
$$A^{[k-1]} = M(u^{[k-1]}) - c^{q^{k-1}} M(u^{[k]}) = M(u^{[k-1]}) - c^{q^{k-1}} M(u).$$

Then, by performing linear combinations over $\mathbb{F}_{q^k}$, one gets

$$A + \sum_{i=1}^{k-1} c^{1+q+\cdots+q^{i-1}} A^{[i]} = (1 - c^{1+q+\cdots+q^{k-1}})M(u) = (1 - c^{\frac{q^k-1}{q-1}})M(u).$$

Finally, one has $c^{\frac{q^k-1}{q-1}} \neq 1$ since $c \in \overline{\mathcal{W}}_{q-1}$, and therefore the matrix $M(u)$ can be expressed as a linear combination of the $A^{[i]}$'s over $\mathbb{F}_{q^k}$. This proves $M(u) \in \mathcal{D}_{mat}$. □

Also, note that it is easy to find other rank 1 matrices in $\mathcal{D}_{mat}$. Indeed, Eq. (13) shows that the matrix $B \in \mathbb{F}_q^{k \times k}$ defined in (11), (12) satisfies $B_{i,j} = u_i u_j^q + u_i^q u_j - b(u_i u_j)^q$ for $1 \leq i, j \leq k$, and this matrix also belongs to $\mathcal{D}_{mat}$ by (12). Notice that this equality implies that

$$B = u^{\mathsf{T}} u^{[1]} + \left(u^{[1]}\right)^{\mathsf{T}} u - b \left(u^{[1]}\right)^{\mathsf{T}} u^{[1]}$$
$$= u^{\mathsf{T}} u^{[1]} + \left(u^{[1]}\right)^{\mathsf{T}} u - bM(u^{[1]}). \tag{14}$$

Now, let $\lambda \in \mathbb{F}_{q^k}$ and consider

$$M(u + \lambda u^{[1]}) = \left(u + \lambda u^{[1]}\right)^{\mathsf{T}} \left(u + \lambda u^{[1]}\right)$$
$$= u^{\mathsf{T}} u + \lambda^2 \left(u^{[1]}\right)^{\mathsf{T}} u^{[1]} + \lambda \left\{ u^{\mathsf{T}} u^{[1]} + \left(u^{[1]}\right)^{\mathsf{T}} u \right\}$$
$$= M(u) + \lambda^2 M(u^{[1]}) + \lambda B + \lambda bM(u^{[1]}) \quad \text{(by (14))}.$$

This implies that $M(u + \lambda u^{[1]})$ belongs to $\mathcal{D}_{mat}$. Since $M(u + \lambda u^{[1]})$ is of rank 1, we have therefore proved the following generalization of Proposition 1.

Proposition 2. *Let $M^{(1)}, \ldots, M^{(n)}$ be the public matrices associated to the secret Sidon space $\mathcal{V}$ and let u be the basis of $\mathbb{F}_{q^k}$ over $\mathbb{F}_q$ associated to ν by Eq. (10). One has*

$$\left\{ \lambda u^{[j]} + \mu u^{[j+1]} : (\lambda, \mu) \in \mathbb{F}_{q^k}^2, \ 0 \leq j \leq k - 1 \right\} \subset \mathcal{Z}_{\mathbb{F}_{q^k}}.$$

Assumption 1. *We assume that the inclusion from Proposition 2 is an equality.*

Note that Assumption 1 is in particular supported by Observation 2, and a more rigorous analysis of this claim is left for future investigation. Based on this assumption, we are going to describe our (equivalent) key-recovery attack which builds upon the following facts:

- As pointed out by [21], it seems infeasible to recover the Sidon space $\mathcal{V}$ directly as a solution to the MinRank problem.
- However, from Fact 1, it is possible to decrypt by using a different Sidon space. Moreover, contrary to the approach described in [21, Sect. 5.1] which introduces an algebraic system with too many variables to be solved in practice, we will find such a space efficiently. We will then show how this can be exploited to find sufficiently many elements of $\mathcal{Z}_{\mathbb{F}_{q^k}}$ that will be used to recover an equivalent key.

4   Solving the MinRank Instance over $\mathbb{F}_{q^k}$

In this section, we show how to determine elements in the set

$$\mathcal{Z}_{\mathbb{F}_{q^k}} := \left\{ \boldsymbol{x} \in \mathbb{F}_{q^k}^k, \ \boldsymbol{x}^\mathsf{T} \boldsymbol{x} \in \mathcal{C}_{mat} \right\} = \left\{ \boldsymbol{x} \in \mathbb{F}_{q^k}^k, \ \boldsymbol{x}^\mathsf{T} \boldsymbol{x} \in \mathcal{D}_{mat} \right\},$$

which corresponds to particular solutions to the MinRank instance described in the previous section. They will be exploited in Sect. 5 in order to derive an equivalent key.

4.1   Parity-check Modeling

Rather than using the generic techniques described in [21, Sect. 4] to target elements in $\mathcal{Z}_{\mathbb{F}_{q^k}}$, we found experimentally that it was more favorable to consider the following algebraic modeling which is largely inspired by [10, Sect. 5.4]. A first remark is that a square matrix of size k over $\mathbb{F}_{q^k}$ can also be viewed as a vector of length k^2 over $\mathbb{F}_{q^k}$. To make this correspondence explicit, we will use the linear isomorphism

$$\mathrm{vec} : \ \mathbb{F}_{q^k}^{k \times k} \rightarrow \mathbb{F}_{q^k}^{k^2}$$

$$\boldsymbol{M} \mapsto \boldsymbol{m}$$

such that $\boldsymbol{m}_{(i-1)k+j} = \boldsymbol{M}_{i,j}$ for $1 \le i, j \le k$, and we consider the following subspace of $\mathbb{F}_{q^k}^{k^2}$

$$\mathrm{vec}(\mathcal{D}_{mat}) := \{\mathrm{vec}(\boldsymbol{M}), \ \boldsymbol{M} \in \mathcal{D}_{mat}\}.$$

It is a subspace of dimension n over $\mathbb{F}_{q^k}$. We can consider it as linear code and let $\boldsymbol{H} \in \mathbb{F}_{q^k}^{(k^2-n) \times k^2}$ be an arbitrary parity-check matrix for it, $i.e.$ a matrix such that

$$\mathrm{vec}(\mathcal{D}_{mat}) = \left\{ \boldsymbol{x} \in \mathbb{F}_{q^k}^{k^2}, \ \boldsymbol{H}\boldsymbol{x}^\mathsf{T} = 0 \right\}.$$

Note that since the $\boldsymbol{M}^{(i)}$'s have entries in $\mathbb{F}_q$, it is possible to choose a parity-check matrix whose entries lie in $\mathbb{F}_q$ as well. Finally, let

$$\boldsymbol{X} := \boldsymbol{x}^\mathsf{T}\boldsymbol{x} = \begin{pmatrix} x_1^2 & x_1x_2 & \cdots & x_1x_k \\ x_2x_1 & x_2^2 & \cdots & x_2x_k \\ \vdots & \vdots & \ddots & \vdots \\ x_kx_1 & x_kx_2 & \cdots & x_k^2 \end{pmatrix} \tag{15}$$

be a matrix in the unknowns x_i corresponding to a solution $\boldsymbol{x} \in \mathcal{Z}_{\mathbb{F}_{q^k}}$. Since the vector $\mathrm{vec}(\boldsymbol{X})$ belongs to $\mathrm{vec}(\mathcal{D}_{mat})$, one obtains the following system of $k^2 - 2k$ quadratic equations given by

$$\boldsymbol{H}\,\mathrm{vec}(\boldsymbol{X})^\mathsf{T} = 0. \tag{16}$$

Lemma 2. *The sequence given by Eq. (16) contains at most $k^2 - 2k - \binom{k}{2}$ linearly independent quadratic polynomials over $\mathbb{F}_{q^k}$.*

Proof. Let $(\boldsymbol{e}_1, \ldots, \boldsymbol{e}_{k^2})$ be the canonical basis of $\mathbb{F}_{q^k}^{k^2}$. Owing to the symmetry of the $\boldsymbol{M}^{(i)}$'s, one obtains that for $1 \leq i < j \leq k$, the vector

$$\sigma_{i,j} = \boldsymbol{e}_{(i-1)k+j} - \boldsymbol{e}_{(j-1)k+i}$$

belongs to the dual code $\mathrm{vec}(\mathcal{D}_{mat})^\perp$. Therefore, there exists a parity-check matrix for $\mathrm{vec}(\mathcal{D}_{mat})$ of the form

$$\boldsymbol{H} = \begin{pmatrix} \boldsymbol{U} \\ \boldsymbol{H}_\sigma \end{pmatrix},$$

where the rows of $\boldsymbol{H}_\sigma \in \mathbb{F}_{q^k}^{\binom{k}{2} \times k^2}$ are the $\sigma_{i,j}$ and $\boldsymbol{U} \in \mathbb{F}_{q^k}^{(k^2 - 2k - \binom{k}{2}) \times k^2}$. The equations coming from $\boldsymbol{H}_\sigma \mathrm{vec}(\boldsymbol{X})^\mathsf{T} = 0$ all give the zero polynomial. Therefore, the useful part of the system is given by

$$\boldsymbol{U}\mathrm{vec}(\boldsymbol{X})^\mathsf{T} = 0,$$

and it contains $k^2 - 2k - \binom{k}{2}$ equations. $\qquad\square$

Modeling 1 (Parity-check modeling over $\mathbb{F}_{q^k}$). *Let $\boldsymbol{X}$ be the matrix of unknowns defined in Eq. (15), let $n = 2k$ and let $\boldsymbol{H} = \begin{pmatrix} \boldsymbol{U} \\ \boldsymbol{H}_\sigma \end{pmatrix} \in \mathbb{F}_{q^k}^{(k^2-n) \times k^2}$ be a parity-check matrix for the code $\mathrm{vec}(\mathcal{D}_{mat})$ as described in the proof of Lemma 2, where $\mathcal{D}_{mat} = \mathcal{C}_{mat} \cap \mathbb{F}_{q^k}^{k \times k}$. We consider the system $\mathcal{F}$ over $\mathbb{F}_{q^k}$ given by*

$$\boldsymbol{U}\,vec(\boldsymbol{X})^\mathsf{T} = 0. \tag{17}$$

This system contains $k^2 - n - \binom{k}{2}$ quadratic equations in the x_i variables.

It is readily verified that the solutions to Modeling 1 are in one-to-one correspondence with the elements of $\mathcal{Z}_{\mathbb{F}_{q^k}}$. Experimentally, these solutions were also all of the form described in Proposition 2. If one wants to find an element in $\mathcal{Z}_{\mathbb{F}_{q^k}}$ in practice, two variables can be fixed in Modeling 1 to reduce the number of solutions. The corresponding variety over $\mathbb{F}_{q^k}$ has size $\geq k$ still by using Proposition 2, and Assumption 1 states that it is an equality.

Modeling 2 (Recovering an element in $\mathcal{Z}_{\mathbb{F}_{q^k}}$). *Let $(s,t) \in \mathbb{F}_{q^k}^2$ such that $t \notin \langle s \rangle_{\mathbb{F}_q}$. We consider the system $\mathcal{F}_{spec}$ obtained by fixing $x_{k-1} = s$ and $x_k = t$ in the equations of the sequence $\mathcal{F}$ from Modeling 1.*

First, note that the number of solutions does not allow to solve Modeling 2 by direct linearization. Moreover, fixing more variables would result in a system with no solutions with high probability. Therefore, we adopt the standard Gröbner basis approach for a zero-dimensional system: we start by computing a Gröbner basis for a suitable ordering and then we perform a change of order step to deduce a basis for the lexicographic ordering to get the solutions. Using Proposition 2 and Assumption 1, we expect k distinct solutions to Modeling 2, and therefore the complexity of this second step is polynomial in k by using the so-called FGLM algorithm [13]. In the following, we will focus on the complexity of the first step.

4.2   Complexity of Solving the System $\mathcal{F}_{spec}$

In this section, we show that, under the following Assumption 2 and Assumption 3, the system $\mathcal{F}_{spec}$ can always be solved at degree 3 independently from the value of k.

First, note that one can permute the coordinates of the row-vector $\text{vec}(\boldsymbol{X})$ and the columns of $\boldsymbol{U}$ accordingly so that the $\binom{k+1}{2}$ leftmost entries of $\text{vec}(\boldsymbol{X})$ correspond to all the distinct monomials $x_i x_j$ for $1 \leq i \leq j \leq k$. This is equivalent to choosing a grevlex ordering on the x_i variables to label the columns of $\boldsymbol{U}$. Also, by adding rows of $\boldsymbol{H}_\sigma$ to rows of $\boldsymbol{U}$ in $\boldsymbol{H}$, it is always possible to assume that the last $\binom{k}{2}$ columns of the matrix $\boldsymbol{U}$ are identically zero.

Assumption 2. *We assume that $\boldsymbol{U}$ is full-rank, and moreover we assume that the submatrix $\boldsymbol{U}_{*,\{1..\binom{k-1}{2}\}}$ is also full-rank.*

The first part of Assumption 2 ensures that one can find $\binom{k-1}{2}$ distinct leading monomials of the form $x_i x_j$ for $1 \leq i \leq j \leq k$ in the $\mathbb{F}_q$-span of the polynomials $\mathcal{F}$, and a fortiori the equations from Modeling 1 are linearly independent. The second part is a bit stronger: it implies that these leading monomials will not involve x_{k-1} or x_k. Therefore, by doing linear combinations between the equations from the specialized system $\mathcal{F}_{spec}$, one can obtain a set $\mathcal{G}_{spec}$ of $m := k^2 - 2k - \binom{k}{2} = \frac{k^2 - 3k}{2}$ equations $g_1 = 0, \cdots, g_m = 0$ with distinct leading monomials $x_i x_j$ for $1 \leq i, j \leq k - 2$. Since the total number of quadratic monomials of this form is equal to

$$\binom{k-1}{2} = \frac{(k-1)(k-2)}{2} = \frac{k^2 - 3k}{2} + 1,$$

this implies that all monomials of degree 2 appear as leading terms of the g_i's but one. With this assumption it can be proved that computing the Gröbner basis of the algebraic system $\mathcal{F}_{spec}$ is extremely efficient: essentially it amounts to compute the aforementioned echelonized set of quadratic polynomials $\mathcal{G}_{spec}$, and then the Gröbner basis is either already computed or close to be computed. This is easily verified by making the further assumption that

Assumption 3. *The algebraic system $\mathcal{F}_{spec}$ has exactly k distinct solutions which do not belong to a common hyperplane of $\mathbb{F}_{q^k}^{k-2}$.*

This assumption was satisfied in all our experiments and is natural when considering Proposition 2 together with Observation 2, which suggests that the inclusion given in this Proposition is an equality. Indeed, the form of the solutions we get from this Proposition then suggests that Assumption 3 should typically hold.

Buchberger's algorithm for computing a Gröbner basis from $\mathcal{G}_{spec} = \{g_1 = 0, \cdots, g_m = 0\}$ would start by computing the S-polynomials $S(g_i, g_j)$ and reduce them. There are two cases to consider.

Case 1. The missing leading monomial in the g_i's is of the form $x_i x_j$. Note that the only case where $S(g_i, g_j)$ were not reduced to 0 would be when the leading monomials of g_i and g_j have a common factor (see [9, Prop. 4, p.106]). In such a case, the polynomial $S(g_i, g_j)$ is of degree at most 3 and since in our situation

(i) all the monomials of degree 3 appear as multiples of leading monomials of the g_i's,

(ii) all monomials of degree 2 appear as leading monomials in the g_i's but $x_i x_j$,

this implies that $S(g_i, g_j)$ is reduced to a polynomial of the form $g_{m+1} := \mu x_i x_j + L(\boldsymbol{x})$ where L is affine in the x_i's. It is impossible that $\mu = 0$ and $L \neq 0$ since this would imply that all the k solutions to $\mathcal{F}_{spec}$ lie in the affine hyperplane $L(\boldsymbol{x}) = 0$, which contradicts Assumption 3. If $\mu \neq 0$, then it is clear by performing the same reasoning that all S-polynomials $S(g_{m+1}, g_i)$ would reduce to 0 (since they would this time reduce to affine forms which are necessarily 0 by the previous reasoning). We are therefore left with a Gröbner basis.

Case 2. The missing leading monomial in the g_i's is of the form x_i^2. The difference with the previous case is that all degree 3 monomials appear as multiples of leading monomials of the g_i's with the exception of x_i^3. In such a case, $S(g_i, g_j)$ reduces to a polynomial of the form $g_{m+1} := \lambda x_i^3 + \mu x_i^2 + L(\boldsymbol{x})$ where L is again an affine form. It is readily seen that we can not have $\lambda = \mu = 0$ without that $L = 0$ itself (this would contradict in the same way as before Assumption 3). From this, it is readily seen that all S-polynomials $S(g_{m+1}, g_j)$ reduce to 0 and that we have a Gröbner basis again.

Remark 1. *Actually the first part of Assumption 3 is already enough to prove this kind of behavior for the Gröbner basis computation by using the fact that the number of solutions for $\mathcal{G}_{spec}$ is equal to the number of monomials that can not be leading monomials of an element of the ideal generated by the g_i's (this is essentially a corollary of [14, Cor. 5, p.83]). We have avoided to use this result to keep the proof as simple as possible. The constant monomial is an example of such a kind (because $\mathcal{G}_{spec}$ has solutions), there are at most $k-2$ monomials of degree 1, at most one monomial of degree 2 and at most one monomial of degree 3 of such kind. From this, it is for instance straightforward to rule out the possibility that $g_{m+1} \neq 0$ in Case 1.*

Overall, one needs to go up to degree 3 in the worst case to compute the Gröbner basis for $\mathcal{F}_{spec}$. The final complexity is then dominated by that of performing Gaussian elimination at degree 3 on a matrix of size $A \times B$ with $A \leq B := \binom{k-2+3}{3}$, say

$$\mathcal{O}\left(\binom{k-2+3}{3}^{\omega}\right) \tag{18}$$

operations in $\mathbb{F}_q$, where $2 \leq \omega \leq 3$ is the linear algebra constant. Therefore, the complexity of solving the system is in $\mathcal{O}\left(k^{3\omega}\right)$, which is clearly polynomial in the dimension k of the Sidon space.

5   Finding an Equivalent Sidon Space $\mathcal{V}$'

Even if recovering elements in $\mathcal{Z}_{\mathbb{F}_{q^k}}$ can be performed in an efficient way, it remains to explain how it allows to recover an equivalent key. We will prove here that we obtain from a set of $k+1$ elements $t_1, \ldots, t_{k+1}$ in $\mathcal{Z}_{\mathbb{F}_{q^k}}$ a Sidon space $\mathcal{V}'$ obtained by Construction 1 that meets the criterion of Fact 1, namely that there is an ordered basis $\boldsymbol{\nu}'$ for it such that $\boldsymbol{M}(\boldsymbol{\nu}')$ lies in the space spanned by the $\boldsymbol{M}^{(i)}$'s. This procedure consists in

1. From $t_1, \ldots, t_{k+1}$ in $\mathcal{Z}_{\mathbb{F}_{q^k}}$ we recover $\boldsymbol{t} = \lambda \boldsymbol{u}^{[j]}$ for some λ in $\mathbb{F}_{q^k}$ and j in $\{0, \cdots, k-1\}$ where $\boldsymbol{u} = (u_1, \cdots, u_k)$ is defined from the secret basis $\boldsymbol{\nu}$ of the Sidon space of the scheme by (10).
2. From such a $\boldsymbol{t}$, we deduce the aforementioned Sidon space $\mathcal{V}'$ as

$$\mathcal{V}' = \langle t_1 + \gamma' t_1^q, \cdots, t_k + \gamma' t_k^q \rangle_{\mathbb{F}_q},$$

where $(t_1, \cdots, t_k) = \boldsymbol{t}$ and γ' is an element generated like γ in **Keygen**, namely as a root of an irreducible polynomial $x^2 + ex + f$ over $\mathbb{F}_{q^k}$ such that $f \in \overline{W_{q-1}}$.

5.1   Targeting an Element of the Form $\lambda u^{[j]}$

Assuming that the inclusion in Proposition 2 is an equality, one obtains that the set $\mathcal{Z}_{\mathbb{F}_{q^k}}$ is equal to the union of vector spaces

$$\mathcal{Z}_{\mathbb{F}_{q^k}} = \bigcup_{i=1}^{k} \mathcal{W}_i, \quad \text{where } \mathcal{W}_i := \left\langle \boldsymbol{u}^{[i-1]}, \boldsymbol{u}^{[i]} \right\rangle_{\mathbb{F}_{q^k}}.$$

Let us notice that these vector spaces $\mathcal{W}_i$ satisfy a peculiar property, namely that

$$\mathcal{W}_i \cap \mathcal{W}_i^{[1]} = \left\langle \boldsymbol{u}^{[i]} \right\rangle \tag{19}$$

where for a set S of vectors, $S^{[1]}$ stands for the set $\{\boldsymbol{x}^{[1]} : \boldsymbol{x} \in S\}$. (19) follows from the fact that $\mathcal{W}_i^{[1]}$ is the $\mathbb{F}_{q^k}$-vector space generated by $\boldsymbol{u}^{[i]}$ and $\boldsymbol{u}^{[i+1]}$. In other words, we are able to recover one of the $\boldsymbol{u}^{[i]}$'s up to multiplication by an element of $\mathbb{F}_{q^k}$ if we are able to produce one of those $\mathcal{W}_i$'s. This can be achieved by using the pigeonhole principle: two among the solutions $\boldsymbol{t}_i$ for $1 \leq i \leq k+1$ will fall into a same vector space $\mathcal{W}_{j_0}$. These considerations lead to the following procedure for recovering one of those $\boldsymbol{u}^{[i]}$'s (up to a multiplicative constant)

Input: A set of $k+1$ non-collinear vectors $\boldsymbol{t}_1, \ldots, \boldsymbol{t}_{k+1}$ in $\mathcal{Z}_{\mathbb{F}_{q^k}}$.
Output: A set $\mathcal{S}$ of elements containing at least one element collinear
           with one of the $\boldsymbol{u}^{[i]}$'s.
for $i = 1$ *to* k **do**
   for $j = i$ *to* $k+1$ **do**
      $V \leftarrow \langle \boldsymbol{t}_i, \boldsymbol{t}_j \rangle_{\mathbb{F}_{q^k}}$
      if $\dim V \cap V^{[1]} = 1$ **then**
         $\mathcal{S} \leftarrow \mathcal{S} \cup \{\boldsymbol{x}\}$ // where $\boldsymbol{x}$ generates $V \cap V^{[1]}$
      end
   end
end

This algorithm is of complexity $\mathcal{O}(k^2)$ and it remains now just to explain how from one of those elements of $\mathcal{S}$ which is collinear with a $\boldsymbol{u}^{[i]}$ we are able to produce an equivalent key for the Sidon cryptosystem. Notice that we do not even need to have $k+1$ non-collinear vectors $\boldsymbol{t}_1, \ldots, \boldsymbol{t}_{k+1}$ in $\mathcal{Z}_{\mathbb{F}_{q^k}}$, $\Theta(\sqrt{k})$ vectors are indeed sufficient by using the birthday paradox to get an $\mathcal{S}$ containing an element $\boldsymbol{t}$ collinear with some $\boldsymbol{u}^{[i]}$ with probability $\Omega(1)$.

5.2   Deducing $\mathcal{V}'$ from $\boldsymbol{t}$

How a Sidon space $\mathcal{V}'$ with the right properties can be deduced from $\boldsymbol{t}$ collinear with some $\boldsymbol{u}^{[i]}$ is explained by the following proposition.

Proposition 3. *Let γ' be a root of an irreducible polynomial $x^2 + ex + f$ over $\mathbb{F}_{q^k}$ such that $f \in \overline{W_{q-1}}$. Then, the $\mathbb{F}_q$-linear space $\mathcal{V}'$ generated by the ordered basis $\boldsymbol{v}' := \boldsymbol{t} + \gamma' \boldsymbol{t}^{[1]}$ is a Sidon space $\mathcal{V}'$ such that $\boldsymbol{M}(\boldsymbol{v}')$ is spanned by the $\boldsymbol{M}_i$'s.*

Proof. We have

$$
\begin{aligned}
M\left(\nu'\right) &= M\left(t + \gamma' t^{[1]}\right) \\
&= t^{\mathsf{T}} t + \gamma'^2 \left(t^{[1]}\right)^{\mathsf{T}} t^{[1]} + \gamma' t^{\mathsf{T}} t^{[1]} + \gamma' \left(t^{[1]}\right)^{\mathsf{T}} t \\
&= \lambda^2 u^{\mathsf{T}} u + \lambda^{2q} \gamma'^2 \left(u^{[1]}\right)^{\mathsf{T}} u^{[1]} + \lambda^{1+q} \gamma' \left\{ u^{\mathsf{T}} u^{[1]} + \left(u^{[1]}\right)^{\mathsf{T}} u \right\} \quad \text{(since } t = \lambda u \text{ for } \lambda \in \mathbb{F}_{q^k}) \\
&= \lambda^2 M\left(u\right) + \lambda^{2q} \gamma'^2 M\left(u^{[1]}\right) + \lambda^{1+q} \gamma' \left\{ (u + u^{[1]})^{\mathsf{T}} (u + u^{[1]}) - u^{\mathsf{T}} u - \left(u^{[1]}\right)^{\mathsf{T}} u^{[1]} \right\} \\
&= \lambda^2 M\left(u\right) + \lambda^{2q} \gamma'^2 M\left(u^{[1]}\right) + \lambda^{1+q} \gamma' \left\{ M\left(u + u^{[1]}\right) - M\left(u\right) - M\left(u^{[1]}\right) \right\} \\
&\in \left\langle M^{(1)}, \cdots, M^{(n)} \right\rangle_{\mathbb{F}_{q^n}} \quad \text{(by Proposition 2).}
\end{aligned}
$$

$\square$

In other words for finding $\mathcal{V}'$, we just have to

1. find an element γ' satisfying the same constraints as γ, i.e. γ' is a root of an irreducible polynomial $x^2 + ex + f$ over $\mathbb{F}_{q^k}$ such that $f \in \overline{W_{q-1}}$;
2. $\mathcal{V}'$ is then generated by the basis

$$
\nu' = \{t_1 + \gamma' t_1^q, \ldots, t_k + \gamma' t_k^q\}
$$

and leads to an equivalent key by Fact 1.

Note that Step 1. for finding $\gamma' \in \mathbb{F}_{q^n}$ can be performed in the same way as in **Keygen**. This was done at random in [21], and the success probability can be estimated using [22, Lemma 13]. Heuristically, this works in constant expected time.

6   Conclusion

The use of Sidon spaces for cryptography is an interesting new idea initially proposed in [21]. However, in this paper we show that this first attempt to build a public-key encryption scheme based on Sidon spaces is insecure. Here, we develop an attack to recover an equivalent key which is polynomial in the dimension of the underlying Sidon space. With a bit more effort, one may also try to eliminate the abovementionned Assumption 1 from our proof by a more precise analysis of the underlying MinRank instance. Besides of that, we consider worth to further study the possibility of using Sidon spaces to devise other cryptographic primitives.

References

1. Apon, D., Moody, D., Perlner, R., Smith-Tone, D., Verbel, J.: Combinatorial rank attacks against the rectangular simple matrix encryption scheme. In: Ding, J., Tillich, J.-P. (eds.) PQCrypto 2020. LNCS, vol. 12100, pp. 307–322. Springer, Cham (2020). https://doi.org/10.1007/978-3-030-44223-1_17

2. Bachoc, C., Serra, O., Zémor, G.: An analogue of Vosper's theorem for extension fields. Math. Proc. Cambridge Phil. Soc. **163**(3), 423–452 (2017)
3. Bardet, M., et al.: Improvements of algebraic attacks for solving the rank decoding and MinRank problems. In: Moriai, S., Wang, H. (eds.) ASIACRYPT 2020. LNCS, vol. 12491, pp. 507–536. Springer, Cham (2020). https://doi.org/10.1007/978-3-030-64837-4_17
4. Bettale, L., Faugère, J.-C., Perret, L.: Cryptanalysis of HFE, multi-HFE and variants for odd and even characteristic. Des. Codes Cryptogr. **69**(1), 1–52 (2013)
5. Buss, J.F., Frandsen, G.S., Shallit, J.O.: The computational complexity of some problems of linear algebra. J. Comput. Syst. Sci. **58**(3), 572–596 (1999)
6. Cabarcas, D., Smith-Tone, D., Verbel, J.A.: Key recovery attack for ZHFE. In: Lange, T., Takagi, T. (eds.) PQCrypto 2017. LNCS, vol. 10346, pp. 289–308. Springer, Cham (2017). https://doi.org/10.1007/978-3-319-59879-6_17
7. Cartor, R., Smith-Tone, D.: EFLASH: a new multivariate encryption scheme. In: Selected Areas in Cryptography - SAC 2018–25th International Conference, Calgary, AB, Canada, 15–17 August 2018, Revised Selected Papers, pp. 281–299 (2018)
8. Casanova, A., Faugère, J.G., Macario-Rat, G., Patarin, J., Perret, L., Ryckeghem, J.: GeMSS: a great multivariate short signature. iN:Research report, UPMC - Paris 6 Sorbonne Universités; INRIA Paris Research Centre, MAMBA Team, F-75012, Paris, France, LIP6 - Laboratoire d'Informatique de Paris 6 December 2017 (2017)
9. Cox, D.A., Little, J., O'Shea, D.: Ideals, Varieties, and Algorithms: An Introduction to Computational Algebraic Geometry and Commutative Algebra, 3/e (Undergraduate Texts in Mathematics). Springer, New York (2007). https://doi.org/10.1007/978-3-319-16721-3
10. Debris-Alazard, T., Tillich, J.-P.: Two attacks on rank metric code-based schemes: RankSign and an IBE scheme. In: Peyrin, T., Galbraith, S. (eds.) ASIACRYPT 2018. LNCS, vol. 11272, pp. 62–92. Springer, Cham (2018). https://doi.org/10.1007/978-3-030-03326-2_3
11. Ding, J.: Rainbow. Second round submission to the NIST post-quantum cryptography call (2019)
12. Faugère, J.C., El Din, M.S., Spaenlehauer, P.J.: Computing loci of rank defects of linear matrices using Gröbner bases and applications to cryptology. In: International Symposium on Symbolic and Algebraic Computation, ISSAC 2010, Munich, Germany, 25–28 July 2010, pp. 257–264 (2010)
13. Faugère, J.C., Gianni, P., Lazard, D., Mora, T.: Efficient computation of zero-dimensional gröbner bases by change of ordering. J. Symb. Comput. **16**(4), 329–344 (1993)
14. Fröberg, R.: An introduction to Gröbner bases. Pure and Applied Mathematics, Wiley, Hoboken (1998)
15. Goubin, L., Courtois, N.T.: Cryptanalysis of the TTM cryptosystem. In: Okamoto, T. (ed.) ASIACRYPT 2000. LNCS, vol. 1976, pp. 44–57. Springer, Heidelberg (2000). https://doi.org/10.1007/3-540-44448-3_4
16. Ikematsu, Y., Perlner, R., Smith-Tone, D., Takagi, T., Vates, J.: HFERP - a new multivariate encryption scheme. In: Lange, T., Steinwandt, R. (eds.) PQCrypto 2018. LNCS, vol. 10786, pp. 396–416. Springer, Cham (2018). https://doi.org/10.1007/978-3-319-79063-3_19
17. Moody, D., Perlner, R., Smith-Tone, D.: Key recovery attack on the cubic ABC simple matrix multivariate encryption scheme. In: Avanzi, R., Heys, H. (eds.) SAC 2016. LNCS, vol. 10532, pp. 543–558. Springer, Cham (2017). https://doi.org/10.1007/978-3-319-69453-5_29

18. Øygarden, M., Felke, P., Raddum, H., Cid, C.: Cryptanalysis of the multivariate encryption scheme EFLASH. In: Jarecki, S. (ed.) CT-RSA 2020. LNCS, vol. 12006, pp. 85–105. Springer, Cham (2020). https://doi.org/10.1007/978-3-030-40186-3_5

19. Patarin, J.: Hidden Fields Equations (HFE) and Isomorphisms of Polynomials (IP): two new families of asymmetric algorithms. In: Maurer, U. (ed.) EUROCRYPT 1996. LNCS, vol. 1070, pp. 33–48. Springer, Heidelberg (1996). https://doi.org/10.1007/3-540-68339-9_4

20. Porras, J., Baena, J., Ding, J.: ZHFE, a new multivariate public key encryption scheme. In: Mosca, M. (ed.) PQCrypto 2014. LNCS, vol. 8772, pp. 229–245. Springer, Cham (2014). https://doi.org/10.1007/978-3-319-11659-4_14

21. Raviv, N., Langton, B., Tamo, I.: Multivariate public key cryptosystem from sidon spaces. In: Garay, J.A. (ed.) PKC 2021. LNCS, vol. 12710, pp. 242–265. Springer, Cham (2021). https://doi.org/10.1007/978-3-030-75245-3_10

22. Roth, R.M., Raviv, N., Tamo, I.: Construction of Sidon spaces with applications to coding. IEEE Trans. Inf. Theory **64**(6), 4412–4422 (2018)

23. Smith-Tone, D., Verbel, J.: A rank attack against extension field cancellation. In: Ding, J., Tillich, J.-P. (eds.) PQCrypto 2020. LNCS, vol. 12100, pp. 381–401. Springer, Cham (2020). https://doi.org/10.1007/978-3-030-44223-1_21

24. Szepieniec, A., Ding, J., Preneel, B.: Extension field cancellation: a new central trapdoor for multivariate quadratic systems. In: Takagi, T. (ed.) PQCrypto 2016. LNCS, vol. 9606, pp. 182–196. Springer, Cham (2016). https://doi.org/10.1007/978-3-319-29360-8_12

25. Tao, C., Diene, A., Tang, S., Ding, J.: Simple matrix scheme for encryption. In: Gaborit, P. (ed.) PQCrypto 2013. LNCS, vol. 7932, pp. 231–242. Springer, Heidelberg (2013). https://doi.org/10.1007/978-3-642-38616-9_16

26. Crypanalysis tool for the sidon cryptosystem (2021). https://github.com/Javierverbel/cryptanalysis-sidon-cryptosystem

Isogenies

Verifiable Isogeny Walks: Towards an Isogeny-Based Postquantum VDF

Jorge Chavez-Saab[1(✉)], Francisco Rodríguez-Henríquez[1,2], and Mehdi Tibouchi[3]

[1] Computer Science Department, Cinvestav IPN, Mexico City, Mexico
jorgechavezsaab@gmail.com
[2] Cryptography Research Centre, Technology Innovation Institute, Abu Dhabi, United Arab Emirates
[3] NTT Corporation, Tokyo, Japan

Abstract. In this paper, we investigate the problem of constructing postquantum-secure verifiable delay functions (VDFs), particularly based on supersingular isogenies. Isogeny-based VDF constructions have been proposed before, but since verification relies on pairings, they are broken by quantum computers. We propose an entirely different approach using succinct non-interactive arguments (SNARGs), but specifically tailored to the arithmetic structure of the isogeny setting to achieve good asymptotic efficiency. We obtain an isogeny-based VDF construction with postquantum security, quasi-logarithmic verification, and requiring no trusted setup. As a building block, we also construct non-interactive arguments for isogeny walks in the supersingular graph over $\mathbb{F}_{p^2}$, which may be of independent interest.

Keywords: Isogeny-based cryptography · Postquantum cryptography · Verifiable delay functions · Supersingular elliptic curves · SNARGs · Verifiable computation

1 Introduction

A *Verifiable Delay Function* (VDF) is a cryptographic primitive first formalized by Boneh, Bonneau, Bünz and Fisch in 2019 [8], which has since gathered increasing interest due to its various applications such as power-efficient blockchains, benchmarking, and randomness beacons (these and other applications are discussed in [8,14]).

The intuitive idea of a VDF is that it acts as a function whose value is uniquely determined at the moment that we pick an input, but no one is able to compute its output faster than a guaranteed prescribed wall-clock time T. To achieve this, it is crucial that the only known approaches for computing a VDF must be inherently sequential, such that no reasonable amount of parallelism could be effective on speeding up the VDF evaluation. At the same time, we also require the peculiar feature that the VDF's output must be efficiently and publicly verifiable, meaning that any other party can confirm its correctness, without relying on secret parameters nor on repeating the lengthy evaluation work that was required to produce it in the first place.

Constructing an ordinary delay function is a simple task, as it suffices to use T iterations of any function that can be composed with itself and whose output is unpredictable (such as a hash function). However, achieving an efficient verification is usually a much bigger challenge. For this, one may rely on general techniques for verifiable computation, specifically on *Succinct Non-interactive Arguments* (SNARGs) which allow for efficient proofs of any computation, where the time complexity of the proof construction is asymptotically close to that of the original computation, and its verification is polylogarithmic. This paper presents a quantum-resistant VDF, whose evaluation involves isogeny walks over supersingular elliptic curves that can be publicly verified by means of a SNARG-based validation process.

In terms of quantum security, none of the current VDF constructions proposed as of today manage to achieve an exponential time gap between evaluation and verification while still being based on commonly studied postquantum assumptions. Our construction benefits from being derived from isogeny-based cryptography, which provides security guarantees that have been carefully scrutinized in the postquantum setting for over a decade. These studies add confidence in our security assumptions as well as in providing accurate estimates of how fast isogeny evaluations can be performed using optimized software and hardware libraries.

Previous Work: The usage of SNARGs for constructing a VDF was first proposed by Boneh et al. [8], and independently by Döttling et al. [15]. The concept of verifiable computation branched out from probabilistic checkable proofs, as proposed by Babai et al. [3], and its development towards proofs that are short, efficient and non-interactive began with Micali's work [25].

In the context of verifiable delay functions, as of today the only isogeny-based construction was proposed by De Feo et al. in 2019 [14]. The main computational task for the evaluation of this VDF is that of finding images of points under a fixed large degree isogeny of a supersingular elliptic curve, whereas its verification essentially consists of performing a bilinear pairing computation. This verification is much more efficient than a SNARG-based verification, but the trade-off is that a quantum attacker can compute the VDF output by solving an associated discrete logarithm problem rather than going through the intended isogeny evaluation. Moreover, the construction has the added drawbacks of requiring a trusted setup and the setup itself being slow (requiring about as much time as an evaluation).

More recently, Leroux [23] proposed an isogeny-based verifiable random function that makes use of a proof of knowledge of a secret isogeny. While it is pointed out that this proof provides an exponential gap between prover and verifier, it cannot be adapted to a VDF since it only convinces the verifier that the prover knows *some* isogeny without any guarantee that the isogeny was somehow derived from an input. The evaluation of the random function actually maps the input to points, and then evaluates the images of those points, but this is not quantum-resistant unless it is treated as a single-use function.

Our Contribution: We present an isogeny-based VDF that is free of the three main drawbacks suffered by the construction of De Feo et al.: the setup is fast, is not required to be trusted, and the construction is postquantum. By using a SNARG verification, we are able to obtain an evaluator with $\tilde{\mathcal{O}}(T)$ time complexity using $\mathcal{O}((\log T)^4)$ parallelism, and a quasi-logarithmic verifier with $\tilde{\mathcal{O}}((\log T)^{4+\log \log T})$ time complexity using no parallelism. This result is of interest not only due to its asymptotic complexity, but also because of the fact that it could directly benefit from future advances in SNARG constructions.

Since our VDF construction performs a random walk in the supersingular isogeny graph over $\mathbb{F}_{p^2}$, it can be seen as an instance of the Charles-Lauter-Goren hash function [10] augmented with a SNARG verification of this random walk. While there exist general-purpose SNARGs that can be applied for any computation in a straightforward fashion (see for example [5,32]), we save as much as possible on overhead by specializing to the isogeny setting and constructing a SNARG over the field $\mathbb{F}_{p^2}$, which verifies the computation at the field-arithmetic level as opposed to the ALU-operation level. This implies that we have to generalize various SNARG results to work efficiently over a prescribed field, which leads us to present a framework that connects the SNARG with the isogeny walk setting in a natural way. Moreover, we describe the process for "ordering" the possible isogenies at each vertex of the isogeny graph so that the walk can be derived from an input string. This was never presented explicitly in [10], and in order to be compatible with our SNARG, our method selects an isogeny using only $\mathbb{F}_{p^2}$ arithmetic (i.e. we refrain from using arbitrary rules that look at the bit-representation of the field elements).

Organization: The remainder of the manuscript is organized as follows. Section 2 contains an overview and background of both isogeny-based cryptography and time-sensitive cryptography. In Sect. 3 we present the evaluation method of our isogeny-based delay function, and in Sect. 4 we present its SNARG-based verification. We then provide our security analysis in Sect. 5, and concluding remarks in Sect. 6.

2   Background

In this section we present some basic definitions and background material used throughout this paper.

2.1   Elliptic Curves

Basic Definitions of Elliptic Curves over Finite Fields. Let $\mathbb{F}_p$ be a finite field with p a large odd prime, and let $\mathbb{F}_q = \mathbb{F}_{p^2}$ be its quadratic extension. We denote the algebraic closure of $\mathbb{F}_q$ as $\overline{\mathbb{F}}_q$.

Let E be a Montgomery elliptic curve over $\mathbb{F}_q$, expressed as,

$$E(\mathbb{F}_q): \quad By^2 = x^3 + Ax^2 + x, \tag{1}$$

such that $A, B \in \mathbb{F}_q$, $A^2 \neq 4$ and $B \neq 0$. The set of solutions of (1) plus the neutral element $\mathcal{O}$, known as the point at infinity, form an abelian additive group, with the inverse of a point (x, y) being $(x, -y)$. For $N \in \mathbb{N}$, the N−torsion subgroup $E[N]$ is defined as the kernel of the multiplication-by-N map.

The cardinality of $E(\mathbb{F}_q)$ is given by $\#E(\mathbb{F}_q) = q + 1 - t$, where t is the trace of E over $\mathbb{F}_q$ and satisfies $|t| \leq 2\sqrt{q}$. An elliptic curve E is said to be supersingular if $p \mid t$, and ordinary otherwise. When $q = p^2$, it follows that $t \in \{0, \pm p, \pm 2p\}$ for any supersingular curve. In the rest of this paper we only consider supersingular curves with $t = -2p$, so that the group order is $(p+1)^2$.

An elliptic curve E is uniquely defined up to isomorphism by its j-invariant, given by

$$j(E(\mathbb{F}_q)) = 256\frac{(A^2 - 3)^3}{A^2 - 4}. \tag{2}$$

Since the parameter B does not appear at all in (2), it follows that Montgomery curves are completely determined by the parameter A up to isomorphism. Let $E'/\mathbb{F}_q$ be another elliptic curve with parameter $A' \in \mathbb{F}_q$. Then, E is isomorphic to E' over $\mathbb{F}_q$, denoted by $E \cong E'$, if and only if $j(E) = j(E')$. Appropriate values for A always result in supersingular curves. In particular, $A = 0$ and $A = 6$ correspond to supersingular elliptic curves whenever $p \equiv 3$ mod 4. Moreover, even when E is defined over $\overline{\mathbb{F}}_q$ we always have $j(E) \in \mathbb{F}_q$ if E is supersingular, so there exists an isomorphic curve defined over $\mathbb{F}_q$. We therefore assume without loss of generality that all supersingular curves are defined over $\mathbb{F}_q$.

Isogenies. An isogeny $\phi\colon E \to E'$ over $\mathbb{F}_q$, is a non-constant rational map between elliptic curves defined over the finite field $\mathbb{F}_q$, which satisfies $\phi(\mathcal{O}) = \mathcal{O}$. It is known that two curves E and E' are isogenous over $\mathbb{F}_q$ if and only if they have the same number of points [30, Theorem 1]. Therefore, E is supersingular if and only if E' is.

Isogenies inherit the notion of degree and separability from rational maps. A separable isogeny has a kernel size equal to its degree, and is uniquely determined by its kernel up to composition with an isomorphism. The fastest known method for computing the co-domain curve of a smooth-degree isogeny is to decompose it into prime-degree components, so a degree-ℓ^T isogeny requires T isogeny evaluations of degree ℓ.

We refer to an isogeny of prime degree ℓ as an ℓ-isogeny. For any ℓ-isogeny $\phi: E \to E'$, there exists a dual $\hat{\phi}: E' \to E$ which is also an ℓ-isogeny, such that the composition $\hat{\phi} \circ \phi$ equals the multiplication-by-ℓ map.

Supersingular Isogeny Graphs. See [19] for a comprehensive study of supersingular isogeny graphs. For any prime ℓ, the supersingular isogeny graph $G_{\mathbb{F}_q}(\ell)$ is the directed graph having $\mathbb{F}_q$-isomorphism classes of ℓ-isogenous supersingular elliptic curves (represented by their j-invariants) as vertices, and ℓ-degree isogenies as edges. The graph $G_{\mathbb{F}_q}(\ell)$ is a Ramanujan graph [28], meaning that random walks in it have an asymptotically optimal mixing rate. Moreover, $G_{\mathbb{F}_q}(\ell)$ is $(\ell + 1)$-regular whenever $\left(\frac{-p}{\ell}\right) = 1$. There are two special vertices, $j = 0$ and $j = 1728$, which represent the only curves with non-constant automorphisms. Outside of these two vertices the graph contains no self-loops, and can be taken to be undirected since edges are symmetric.

Modular Polynomials. For any prime ℓ, there exists a polynomial $\Phi_\ell \in \mathbb{Z}[X, Y]$ of degree $\ell + 1$, called the ℓth modular polynomial, such that two curves E and E' are ℓ-isogenous if and only if $\Phi_\ell(j(E), j(E')) = 0$. Given a starting curve E, we can walk a step in the ℓ-isogeny graph by finding a root of $\Phi_\ell(j(E), X)$ rather than explicitly computing an isogeny.

2.2 Time-Sensitive Cryptography and Verifiable Delay Functions

Time-sensitive cryptography was first proposed in 1996 by Rivest, Shamir and Wagner [29]. The authors of [29], presented time-lock puzzle constructions that must be computed by performing a prescribed number of sequential squarings over an RSA modulus of unknown order. More recently, Lenstra and Wesolowski introduced in [22], a slow-timed hash function dubbed *sloth*. The evaluation of sloth is accomplished by the iterated computation of a fixed number of sequential functions. Also, the notion of Proof of Sequential Work (PoSW) was introduced by Cohen and Pietrzak in Eurocrypt 2018 [13]. Then, Boneh, Bonneau, Bünz and Fisch formalized this branch of cryptography by rigorously defining verifiable delay functions.

A Verifiable Delay Function (VDF) as defined in [8,22] is a function $f : \mathcal{X} \mapsto \mathcal{Y}$ that cannot be computed in less than a prescribed delay, regardless of the amount of parallelization available for its evaluation. At the same time, once a VDF has been computed, it can be easily verified by any third party, typically with the help of a companion proof produced during the evaluation. Moreover, the verification should be achievable with a limited amount of parallel cores, and ideally, by performing a single-core computation. Formally, a VDF is composed of three main algorithms:

- Setup: takes as input a security parameter λ and a delay parameter T and outputs public parameters pp.
- Eval: Takes a certain input x and public parameters pp and calculates an output y and a proof π.
- Verify: Takes as input x, y, π and pp and outputs 1 if and only if π is a valid proof for the input-output pair (x, y).

Moreover, a secure VDF satisfies the following properties:

- *Sequentiality*: The eval procedure can be completed in time $\mathcal{O}(T, \lambda)$ using $polylog(T)$ parallelism, but cannot be completed in time $o(T)$ even when $poly(T)$ parallelism is available.
- *Completeness*: An honest evaluation always causes the verifier to accept.

– *Soundness*: If y is not the output of Eval(x, pp), then no PPT adversary can find a proof π such that the verifier accepts (x, y, π).

VDFs have important applications for Blockchain proof of work, space and stake [12], constructing a trustworthy randomness beacon [16], benchmarking of high-end servers and many more [9,31]. Several examples of VDFs proposed in the literature can be found on [8,14,27,33].

Isogeny-Based VDFs. The only isogeny-based VDF construction proposed as of today is the one presented by De Feo, Masson, Petit, and Sanso in Asiacrypt 2019 [14].

The authors of [14], proposed an isogeny-based VDF where the evaluator must compute the image of a point under a large smooth-degree isogeny ϕ (consisting of the composition of T isogenies each of prime degree ℓ), between two ℓ^T-isogenous supersingular curves E and E'. The order of the elliptic curves E and E' has a large prime divisor N, and their N-torsion subgroups are used for the verification via a pairing comparison using a point P with known image $\phi(P)$ (these points are public parameters and are computed at setup time).

This VDF construction has three important drawbacks. The first one is that it requires a trusted setup. This implies that a dishonest party computing the setup, can easily backdoor the function to make the evaluation much faster (as discussed in [14], knowledge of the random walk that generated E, can be used to compute the endomorphism ring of the curve E, which can be used to reduce the degree-ℓ^T isogeny to a shorter one). A second issue is that the setup computation is slow, taking as long as the delay from the evaluation itself. A third drawback is that the verification crucially depends on the computation of a pairing, which opens the door against any quantum attack targeting discrete logarithm computations.

VDFs From Iterated Sequential Functions. Given an input parameter x, the authors of [8,14] gave as an example of a naive VDF the chained computation of a one-way function as,

$$x_i = H(x_{i-1}), \text{ for } i = 1, \ldots, T,$$

with $x_0 = x$, and where the output $y = x_T$ can only be calculated sequentially independently of the amount of parallelism available for the evaluator. Notice however, that if the evaluator publishes some of the intermediate values x_i for $i = 1, \ldots, T$ (see Fig. 1), then a verifier with access to many independent processors, can verify the work of the evaluator in a wall-clock delay significantly shorter than the time invested by the evaluator for producing y. This simple version of a VDF was discussed in [22, §3.1] as a *trivial design*, and later proposed by Yakovenko as a *Proof of History* consensus protocol with direct applications to blockchains [34]. Although this type of construction cannot achieve a polylogarithmic-time verification without requiring $poly(T)$ parallelism from the verifier, they are still sufficiently efficient for various applications. In particular, Yakovenko's Proof of History consensus protocol is massively used by the cryptocurrency Solana as its main consensus mechanism.

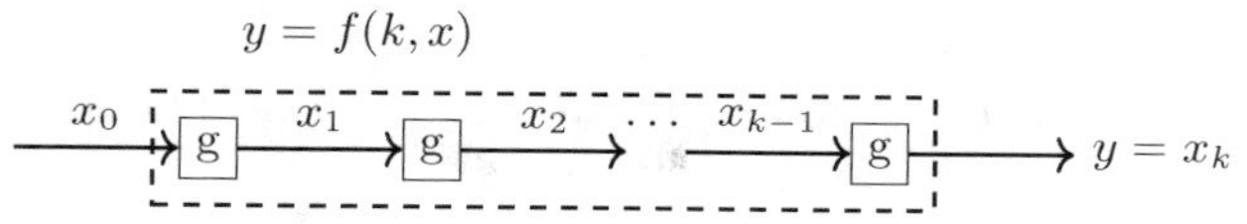

$$y = f(k, x)$$

Fig. 1. Ilustration of an iterated sequential function $f : \mathbb{N} \times \mathcal{X} \mapsto \mathcal{X}$, defined as $f(k, x) = g \circ g \circ \ldots \circ g$. In the figure, $x_0 = x$, and the output of the function $f = (k, x)$ is $y = x_k$.

In order to obtain an asymptotically efficient verification without parallelism, the verification can be improved by means of verifiable computation. Verifiable computation can be used by the evaluator to compute a succinct non-interactive argument (SNARG), which certifies that a given computation was performed honestly. An important characteristic of a SNARG is that its verification can achieve a complexity that is logarithmic in the size of the original computation.

Both Boneh et al. [8] and Döttling et al. [15] proposed that any iterative sequential function can be augmented with a SNARG to produce an asymptotically efficient VDF. This is precisely the steps that we follow for our isogeny-based VDF, with the iterative function being instantiated by a step in the supersingular isogeny graph and the SNARG being constructed at the $\mathbb{F}_{p^2}$ arithmetic level.

3 An Isogeny-Based Delay Function

We now present an overview for the evaluation method of our VDF, leaving the SNARG-based verification for Sect. 4.

Our function involves computing a walk of length T in the 2-isogeny graph of supersingular curves over $\mathbb{F}_{p^2}$, where $p^2 \equiv 9 \mod 16$ (which is required for applying Kong's square-root algorithm [21]) and $p = poly(T)$ (which is required to make field arithmetic efficient for the verifier). The walk itself is determined from a string that is derived from the input to the VDF, starting from a prescribed initial curve, and the $j-$invariant of the final curve is taken as the output of the VDF. Therefore, our output exactly matches the output from an instantiation of the Charles-Goren-Lauter hash function [10], where the isogeny at each step is determined after assigning some ordering to the outgoing isogenies. In order to make the procedure suitable for a SNARG construction, however, we develop a procedure that makes this ordering not only explicit but also verifiable using only field arithmetic.

3.1 Evaluation Overview

Given a delay parameter T, we ask the evaluator to compute a walk of length T on the 2-isogeny graph, where the exact path is determined by a string s and is non-backtracking. We would not be able to specify kernel points of order ℓ^T as in the SIDH setting, since doing so would require either $p = \mathcal{O}(\ell^T)$ or working over an $\mathcal{O}(T)$ field extension, both of which would make all field arithmetic inefficient for the verifier. Therefore, each step in the isogeny walk has to be determined "on the fly", and we chose to derive it from the modular polynomial root-finding problem since it is naturally expressed in $\mathbb{F}_{p^2}$ arithmetic.

Given two curves with j-invariants j_i and j_{i+1}, they are 2-isogenous over $\mathbb{F}_{p^2}$ if and only if the modular polynomial $\Phi_2(j_i, j_{i+1})$ vanishes. Thus, for fixed j_i, the next curve in the path can be computed by finding a root of $\Phi_2(j_i, X)$. This is a cubic polynomial, but we can exploit the fact that we already know one of the roots (namely j_{i-1}, the previous curve in the walk) to factor out a linear term: if $X = j_{i-1}$ is a known root of $\Phi_2(X) = X^3 + aX^2 + bX + c$ then we can rewrite

$$\Phi_2(X) = (X - j_{i-1})(X^2 + (a + j_{i-1})X + b + aj_{i-1} + j_{i-1}^2)$$

and focus on finding the roots of the quadratic factor. This accomplishes three distinct goals:

1. It ensures the walk is non-backtracking by discarding the $X = j_{i-1}$ root
2. It reduces the root-finding problem to a quadratic equation (reducing the size of the computation yields heavy savings on SNARG overhead)
3. It enables the step in the walk to be defined by a canonical square-root along with a bit indicating its sign

Taking into account the explicit form of Φ_2, the other two roots are given by

$$j_{i+1} = \frac{1}{2}\left(j_i^2 - 1488j_i - j_{i-1} + 162000 \pm \sqrt{D_i}\right) \tag{3}$$

where

$$\begin{aligned} D_i =& j_i^4 - 2976j_i^3 + 2j_i^2 j_{i-1} + 2532192j_i^2 - 2976j_i j_{i-1} \\ &- 645205500j_i - 3j_{i-1}^2 + 324000j_{i-1} - 8748000000 \end{aligned} \tag{4}$$

The evaluator computes a canonical square root $S_i = \sqrt{D_i}$ using Kong's algorithm [21]: first fix any quadratic nonresidue d and precompute $t = d^{\frac{p^2-9}{8}}$, then compute

$$R_i = (2D_i)^{\frac{p^2-9}{16}} \tag{5}$$

and set

$$S_i = \begin{cases} R_i D_i (2D_i R_i^2 - 1) & \text{if } (2aR_i^2)^2 = -1 \\ R_i td D_i (2R_i^2 t^2 d^2 D_i - 1) & \text{if } (2aR_i^2)^2 = +1 \end{cases} \tag{6}$$

which can be combined into

$$S_i = \left(\frac{1 - (2aR_i^2)^2}{2}\right) R_i D_i (2D_i R_i^2 - 1) + \left(\frac{1 + (2aR_i^2)^2}{2}\right) R_i td D_i (2R_i^2 t^2 d^2 D_i - 1) \tag{7}$$

After the square root has been calculated, the evaluator uses the input string to choose the sign, yielding a deterministic process for the walk. Note that the input string cannot have length $\mathcal{O}(T)$ (since the verifier must receive it and process it in time $polylog(T)$), so we will construct the signs pseudorandomly from a smaller string, as detailed in Sect. 4.1.

Note also that the evaluator could use any algorithm for computing square roots, but for the SNARG verification process it is convenient to use a procedure that is deterministic and also produces a fixed choice of sign, hence the choice of Kong's algorithm. For the verification process, the evaluator will keep track of j_i, D_i, R_i, S_i at each step and construct a SNARG that shows that Eqs. (3), (4), (5) and (7) are satisfied.

Initial Conditions. Since Eq. (3) requires knowledge of the $j-$invariant two steps into the past, we need to specify the first two curves as initial conditions. The 2-isogeny graph is a 3-regular graph without repeated edges or self-loops except for the two special vertices $j = 1728$ and $j = 0$. At $j = 1728$ there is one self-loop and two edges going to the vertex $j = 287496$, so we use the initial curve $j_0 = 287496$ and take $j_{-1} = 1728$ to avoid going back to the non-regular vertex. Note that the SNARG will only access values at indices 0 through $T - 1$, so we replace $j_{-1} = 1728$ by an equivalent condition on D_0 using Eq. (4).

4   SNARG-Based Verification

In this section we deal with the verification process of the VDF, specifically how to fit the evaluation into a SNARG framework.

The notion of verifiable computation emanated from *Probabilistic Checkable Proofs* (PCP), a term first coined by Arora and Safra [2] to refer to a protocol between a prover who generates a proof of membership in a language (known as the PCP witness) for a given input and a randomized verifier which interacts with it. Both Babai et al. [3] and Feige et al. [17] independently proposed algorithms for transforming any $\mathcal{NP}$ witness into a PCP witness which, at the cost of making the verification probabilistic and the witness polynomially larger, allow for logarithmic-time verification by sampling only a logarithmic number of bits from the witness.

The results from [3] and [17] show that the history of any computation can be put into an alternate form which can be verified with an exponential speedup. In practice, however, these PCP constructions have two major drawbacks. First, they require interaction between the two parties throughout the protocol, and second, the amount of communication is still inefficient since the full PCP witness must be transmitted even if only a few bits of it are sampled. *Succinct Non-interactive Arguments* (SNARGs) are an alternative primitive which overcomes both limitations (they do not require interaction and are succinct in the sense that the witness is of logarithmic size). It was shown by Micali [25] that any PCP construction can be efficiently transform into a SNARG.

General-purpose SNARGs aim to verify a computation by working at the level of a RAM model and translating the correctness of the computation into either a circuit satisfiability or an algebraic constraint problem. For our construction we have focused on the latter approach, and use a checksum-type PCP to verify said constraint problem.

In this section we review how the different construction ingredients are adapted to our particular problem. Section 4.1 describes the process of transforming the correctness of our computation into an algebraic constraint problem (known as *arithmetization*). Section 4.2 then gives a high-level summary for the rest of the SNARG construction and the complexities of the resulting verification scheme. Finally, Sect. 4.3 discusses the parallelization of the SNARG proof construction to obtain a concrete proof construction time close to the evaluation time.

4.1   Arithmetization

The sumcheck protocol that we work with is a PCP that verifies conditions of the form

$$\sum_{\vec{x} \in B^n} P(\vec{x}) = 0, \tag{8}$$

where P is a polynomial in n variables over some ring $R \supset B$.

To turn the verification of our VDF into an instance of this problem we *arithmetize* by storing the intermediate values into polynomials that act as lookup tables. Specifically, for the computation with T steps, we pick a base b and integer n such that $T \approx b^n$, and let $B = \{0, 1, \ldots, b - 1\}$. The time steps $t \in \{0, 1, \ldots, T - 1\}$ can then be expressed as $b-$ary strings of length n, where we refer with $t_{\vec{x}}$ to the integer represented by string $\vec{x} \in B^n$.

For $\vec{y} \in B^n$ we define the polynomial

$$\delta_{\vec{y}}(\vec{x}) = \prod_{j=0}^{n-1} \prod_{z \in B - \{y_j\}} \frac{x_j - z}{y_j - z} \tag{9}$$

which maps $\vec{x} \in B^n$ to 1 if $\vec{x} = \vec{y}$ and 0 if $\vec{x} \neq \vec{y}$. Regarding B as a subset of $\mathbb{F}_{p^2}$, the above formula can be seen as a polynomial over $(\mathbb{F}_{p^2})^n$, and is in fact the unique degree-$(b - 1)$ polynomial that agrees with the δ function on B^n (note that throughout this paper, the "degree" of a multivariate polynomial refers to the maximum degree of any individual variable).

The δ polynomial can be used as an auxiliary tool to select a specific index when summing over all indices. Given the sequence j_i of j-invariants at each step, we can define the polynomial

$$j(\vec{x}) = \sum_{y \in B^n} j_{t_{\vec{y}}} \delta_{\vec{y}}(\vec{x}). \tag{10}$$

This polynomial encodes the history of the computation since it maps $\vec{x} \in B^n$ to $j_{t_{\vec{x}}}$, but can also be evaluated (with less predictable outcome) over all of $(\mathbb{F}_{p^2})^n$.

We can then define similar polynomials $D(\vec{x})$, $R(\vec{x})$, $S(\vec{x})$ for the quantities D_i, R_i, S_i defined in Sect. 3, and also use the constants

$$L_{t_1,t_2} = \begin{cases} 1 & \text{if } t_2 = t_1 + 1 \\ 0 & \text{else} \end{cases}$$

to define the polynomial

$$L(\vec{x}, \vec{y}) = \sum_{\vec{x}', \vec{y}' \in B^n} L_{t_{\vec{x}'}, t_{\vec{y}'}} \delta_{\vec{x}'}(\vec{x}) \delta_{\vec{y}'}(\vec{y}) \tag{11}$$

which vanishes in B^{2n} unless $\vec{x}$ and $\vec{y}$ represent consecutive integers. Similarly to the δ polynomial, this polynomial will be used as a sequential counter that selects only consecutive indices when summing over all pairs of indices.

With this in hand, Eqs. (3), (4), (5) and (7) can be represented as polynomial conditions. For instance, (3) becomes

$$P^j(\vec{x}, \vec{y}, \vec{z}) = 0 \quad \forall \, (\vec{x}, \vec{y}, \vec{z}) \in B^{3n}, \tag{12}$$

where

$$P^j(\vec{x}, \vec{y}, \vec{z}) :=$$
$$[2j(\vec{z}) - j(\vec{y})^2 + 1488j(\vec{y}) + j(\vec{x}) - 162000 - s(\vec{y})S(\vec{y})] \, L(\vec{x}, \vec{y})L(\vec{y}, \vec{z}).$$

Here, $s(\vec{x})$ represents the choice of sign at step $t_{\vec{x}}$, which we have also represented as a polynomial. We have not specified how the sign is derived from the input, but it will be necessary for the verifier to be able to efficiently evaluate $s(\vec{x})$. Therefore, we will take

$$s(\vec{x}) = \prod_{i=0}^{n-1} s_i(x_i), \tag{13}$$

where s_i are single-variable polynomials of degree $b - 1$ mapping B to $\{+1, -1\}$. Since a polynomial of degree $b - 1$ is determined by its values at any b points, we only need b bits to uniquely specify each s_i. This means that we use a total of nb bits to define $s(\vec{x})$, and we now define these bits as the input to the VDF (the input bits can be passed through a hash function first to enforce pseudorandomness of the resulting polynomial).

We then turn equations (4) and (7) into polynomial conditions

$$P^D(\vec{x}, \vec{y}) = 0 \quad \forall \, (\vec{x}, \vec{y}) \in B^{2n}$$

and

$$P^S(\vec{x}) = 0 \quad \forall \, \vec{x} \in B^n$$

in an analogous way.

As for Eq. (5), the polynomial that we would obtain by arithmetizing it directly would be of large degree, which is undesirable for the SNARG construction (the sumcheck protocol verification, described in [24], is linear in the degree of the polynomial). Therefore, we introduce additional state and break the exponentiation down into a right-to-left strategy: let $K = \lceil \log((p^2 - 9)/16) \rceil$ and $e_0, e_1, \ldots, e_{K-1}$ be the bits of $(p^2 - 9)/16$. We define $R_i^{(0)} = 1$, $D_i^{(0)} = D_i$ and for $0 < k < K$,

$$D_i^{(k)} = (D_i^{(k-1)})^2, \tag{14}$$

and

$$R_i^{(k)} = R_i^{(k-1)} (D_i^{(k-1)})^{e_k} \tag{15}$$

so that $R_i^{(k-1)} = R_i$. For each $0 \leq k < K$ we define polynomials $D^{(k)}(\vec{x})$ and $R^{(k)}(\vec{x})$ from the values of $D_i^{(k)}$ and $R_i^{(k)}$, respectively, and use them to write polynomial conditions

$$P^{R,k}(\vec{x}) = 0 \quad \forall \, \vec{x} \in B^n$$

and

$$P^{D,k}(\vec{x}) = 0 \quad \forall \, \vec{x} \in B^n.$$

Note that we now have $K = \log p$ pairs of polynomials to work with, but each being of degree $d = \mathcal{O}(b)$ just as P^j, P^D and P^S (this is inherited from the degree of the δ polynomial).

Finally, to wrap the whole verification into the form of (8), we use the weighted sum

$$\begin{aligned} P(\vec{x}, \vec{y}, \vec{z}) = \, & w^J(\vec{x}, \vec{y}, \vec{z}) P^J(\vec{x}, \vec{y}, \vec{z}) \\ & + w^D(\vec{x}, \vec{y}) P^D(\vec{x}, \vec{y}) + w^S(\vec{x}) P^S(\vec{x}) \\ & + \sum_k \left(w^{D,k}(\vec{x}) P^{D,k} + w^{S,k}(\vec{x}) P^{S,k} \right), \end{aligned} \tag{16}$$

where each w is a weight polynomial. These polynomials are defined in the same way as $s(\vec{x})$ in Eq. (13), but are chosen randomly by the verifier so that proving that

$$\sum_{\vec{x}, \vec{y}, \vec{z} \in B^n} P(\vec{x}, \vec{y}, \vec{z}) = 0$$

is enough to convince the verifier that $P^J, P^D, P^S, P^{k,D}, P^{k,S}$ vanish at all points, and hence that the whole computation is correct.

We stress that general-purpose SNARGs exist that can be applied to any program (see for example [5] and [4]), but they usually perform arithmetization at the ALU level, which increases the overhead cost. For instance, they may have lookup polynomials that encode the values of CPU registers at each time step and obtain polynomial conditions that represent the correctness of ALU operations (which in our case would include even the breakdown of all $\mathbb{F}_{p^2}$ arithmetic into basic ALU operations). The arithmetization that we propose is performed directly at the field arithmetic level, meaning that the values encoded into our polynomials are $\mathbb{F}_{p^2}$ elements and our polynomial conditions represent equality over this field, without actually including the correctness of $\mathbb{F}_{p^2}$ arithmetic procedures in the SNARG proof since it is within the verifier's capabilities to perform them directly.

4.2   Overview of the SNARG Construction

We now present a high-level summary of the steps required to complete the SNARG construction. For a more detailed account, the reader may consult the appendix in the extended version of this work [11].

We have reduced the verification process to the verification of a condition of the form[1]

$$\sum_{\vec{x} \in B^n} P(\vec{x}) = 0,$$

where P is of degree $d = \mathcal{O}(b)$ in n variables, and $T = n^b$. This verification is handled by the sumcheck protocol of Lund, Fortnow, Karloff and Nisan [24], detailed in the appendix of [11]. The sumcheck protocol is a PCP that reduces the problem to the verifier's ability to evaluate P at a random point $\vec{x} \in (\mathbb{F}_{p^2})^n$. To enable this, the prover publishes a PCP witness that contains the table of values for each of the polynomials $j(\vec{x}), D(\vec{x}), S(\vec{x}), R^{(k)}(\vec{x}), S^{(k)}(\vec{x})$ in all of $(\mathbb{F}_{p^2})^n$. The table of values for $L(\vec{x}, \vec{y})$ is assumed to be precomputed and publicly available (since it is independent of the input), while the polynomials for the sign and the random weights are directly evaluated by the verifier.

The next step is to apply Micali's transform [25], which both eliminates interactiveness and shortens the proof to a polylogarithmic size. The core idea is to encode the tables of values into a Merkle tree and publish only the root of the tree as a commitment, answering specific queries with a value along with its verification path in the Merkle tree. We then apply the Fiat-Shamir transform [18] to replace all random choices from the verifier (including the choice of the weight polynomials in (16)).

The resulting verification scheme has a prover time complexity of $\mathcal{O}((n^2 b)^n b \log b)$ with $\mathcal{O}(n^2 \log p)$ parallelism and space complexity of $\mathcal{O}((n^2 b)^n \log p)$ field elements (from computing and storing the tables of values), and a verifier time complexity of $\mathcal{O}(n^3 b \log(nb) \log p)$ with no parallelization nor significant storage requirements (from performing a *degree test* on said table). Both of these complexities are derived in the appendix of the extended version of this work [11]. We argue in Sect. 5 that a choice of $p = poly(T)$ is natural, so the evaluator parallelism is $polylog(T)$.

There is still some freedom regarding the choice of parameters n and b, since they only need to satisfy $n^b \approx T$. Choosing $b \approx (\log T)^{1/\epsilon}$ for some $\epsilon > 0$ means that

$$n \approx \frac{\log T}{\log b} = \frac{\epsilon \log T}{\log \log T},$$

and

$$n^n \approx \left(\frac{\epsilon \log T}{\log \log T} \right)^{\frac{\epsilon \log T}{\log \log T}} < \log T^{\frac{\epsilon \log T}{\log \log T}} = T^\epsilon,$$

---

[1] For ease of notation we collapse $\vec{x}, \vec{y}, \vec{z}$ into a single vector, implicitly substituting $n \mapsto 3n$ throughout.

so the prover complexity becomes $\tilde{\mathcal{O}}(T^{1+2\epsilon})$ time (which can be made arbitrarily close to linear) and $\mathcal{O}(T^{1+2\epsilon} \log p)$ space, while the verification complexity becomes $\tilde{\mathcal{O}}((\log T)^{4+1/\epsilon})$.

Another option is to chose a slowly decreasing function $\epsilon = 1/\log\log T$. This causes the proof construction to be strictly quasi-linear, but at the cost of making the verification only quasi-polylogarithmic.

4.3   Parallelization of the Proof Construction

It is also desirable for the evaluation algorithm of a VDF to take time that is concretely (as opposed to asymptotically) close to T. Both Boneh et al. [8] and Döttling et al. [15] independently proposed similar methods for exploiting parallelism to finish evaluation of an iterative function and its SNARG proof construction at the same time by working with subsegments of geometrically decreasing size. Assuming that computing the proof is slower than the function evaluation by a factor of α, the evaluator stops after completing $T/(1+\alpha)$ iterations of the computation and then starts a proof for this partial computation in parallel with the remaining $\alpha T/(1+\alpha)$ steps. This is repeated recursively, so the evaluator does proof constructions of size $T\left(\frac{\alpha}{1+\alpha}\right)^i$ for $i = 1, 2, 3, \ldots$ until $i \approx \log(T)/\log(1+\frac{1}{\alpha})$ when approximately a single step remains and it can be computed directly by the verifier without proof. Since $\log(1+\frac{1}{\alpha}) = \frac{1}{\alpha} + \mathcal{O}(\frac{1}{\alpha^2})$, this increases the parallelization requirement by a factor of $\alpha \log T$.

Note that in the case when $b = (\log T)^{1/\epsilon}$ for constant ϵ this results in an amount of parallelism polynomial in T, which is coined a *weak VDF* by Boneh et al. [8, Definition 5]. We favor the case when $\epsilon = 1/\log\log T$ instead, which means the parallelism is strictly logarithmic at the cost of making the verification slightly slower (quasi-polylogarithmic).

5   Security Analysis

The soundness of the VDF relies entirely on that of the SNARG proof, which is discussed in [25]. In this section we discuss the other crucial security property of a VDF, namely its sequentiality.

As a side note, we point out that any protocol where the isogeny walk is not prescribed in some way is insecure in terms of sequentiality. For instance, one could have asked the evaluator for a SNARG proof of *any* large-degree isogeny and naively hope that this makes for a good proof of sequential work even if the output is not unique. However, much like the proof of isogeny knowledge proposed by Leroux [23], this does not constitute proof of a sequential computation if the evaluator is free to choose the path. Indeed, even if backtracking is avoided it has been shown by Adj, Ahmadi and Menezes [1] that it is easy to find cycles of any length in the ℓ−isogeny graph, which allows a cheating evaluator to construct a SNARG for a "long" walk by repeating a short cycle as many times as necessary. Of course, the prescribed walks in our construction may still contain cycles, but this is not a problem so long as they cannot be forced nor predicted by the evaluator.

In our context, sequentiality relies on a similar version of the *Isogeny Shortcut Problem* defined by De Feo et al. [14]:

Problem 1 (Isogeny Shortcut Problem). *Let $E/\mathbb{F}_p$ be a random supersingular elliptic curve and $\phi : E \to E'$ an isogeny of degree ℓ^T to a curve $E'/\mathbb{F}_{p^2}$. After a precomputation time $poly(T, \lambda)$, find the image of a given point whose order is coprime to ℓ in time $o(T)$.*

Our setting differs from the one in this problem in three important ways:

1. Our problem is not to find images of points, but codomain curves. Since the codomain curve can be computed from any three point evaluations, the problem in our setting could be considered more general. However, all known point-evaluation methods have complexities asymptotically equal to those of codomain-evaluation, so we do not expect our security assumption to be significantly stronger.

2. The precomputation time that we allow in our setting is granted before learning the isogeny to be evaluated, which reflects the fact that our VDF uses a different isogeny for each input as opposed to fixing the isogeny at setup time. In this regard, our security is stronger since it relies on a much weaker assumption.

3. We do not assume that the starting curve was randomly sampled, which is done in [14] to prevent shortcut attacks (see below) when the endomorphism ring is known. However, we argue that such attacks are unimportant in our setting precisely due to the previous point. Starting from a public curve means we do not need a trusted setup.

Despite these differences, our security analysis is very similar to De Feo's et al., as we still distinguish two types of attacks: either finding a way to perform the isogeny walk faster (possibly exploiting parallelism), or attempting to find an equivalent isogeny walk of smaller degree (which we call *isogeny shortcuts*).

Faster Isogenies. The best known method for computing a degree-ℓ^T isogeny is by sequentially performing the composition of T consecutive ℓ-isogenies, where each ℓ-isogeny is computed using Vélu's formulas. We consider the time of this computation as a lower bound for the delay parameter offered by our VDF, even though our specification of the evaluation algorithm does not use kernel points. While Vélu's formulas parallelize almost perfectly, attempting to directly evaluate an isogeny of degree ℓ^T in time $O(T)$, would require an amount of parallelism exponential in T which exceeds the evaluator's capabilities. This is leaving aside the fact that our isogeny is not readily presented as a kernel that could be plugged directly into these formulas, and even if such a kernel could be obtained it would be defined over a degree-T field extension. Assuming then that the best strategy is to decompose into small-degree isogenies, it is unlikely that any algorithm would be able to compute the composition of all such isogenies without going through each intermediate curve.

While none of the above premises are often studied as security assumptions, they are long-standing conjectures that have endured the test of time, despite considerable incentives to optimize isogeny evaluations. For instance, finding a way to compute an isogeny of degree ℓ^T in linear time without exploiting the smooth decomposition would be equivalent to computing an arbitrary-degree isogeny in time logarithmic in the degree, which would be ground-breaking for all isogeny-based cryptography.

It should be noted that recent improvements to the evaluation of $\ell-$isogenies do exist, most notably the algorithm of Bernstein et al. [6], which achieves a square-root time complexity improvement over the previous state-of-the-art. Although this does not affect the asymptotic complexity of computing T isogenies in series, having the possibility for variations in the concrete cost is still problematic for a VDF. However, the gains in these new formulas are asymptotic in ℓ and we only use $2-$isogenies for which the formulas are so simple that they can be conjectured to be already optimal.

Isogeny Shortcuts. The second possibility is for the evaluator to produce a different isogeny path between the two end curves, and hope that it is shorter than the original. Because construction of the proof requires the evaluator to know each of the j-invariants in the original isogeny path, one might mistakenly assume that such an attack would be useless. However, an attacker that is able to predict the output in a shorter time, even if unable to produce a proof for it, would still violate the security of the VDF.

A shorter path always exists because the isogeny graph is of size $\mathcal{O}(p)$ and the optimal expander property of Ramanujan graphs [28] implies the distance between any two curves is bounded by $\mathcal{O}(\log p)$ (which is necessarily logarithmic in T, otherwise all field arithmetic would be inefficient). However, the sequentiality property only requires that such path cannot be found in time $o(T)$. In the case of arbitrary curves, when the endomorphism ring is not known, the best one can do is to try to solve the isogeny problem between the curves, disregarding the already known isogeny. The best algorithm for this is a birthday attack, which takes $\mathcal{O}(p^{1/4})$ time using a quantum Grover search [7]. This sets a theoretic limit on the admissible delay parameters of $T = \mathcal{O}(p^{1/4})$. However, it should be noted that even this attack would not apply directly since it requires previous knowledge of the codomain curve.

In our construction, we take an additional risk of fixing the starting curve $j = 1728$ where not only is the endomorphism ring known, but also elements of norm ℓ^n can be easily found with the KLPT algorithm [20]. This leads to an attack analogous to the CGL hash collision-finding algorithm that was described in [26] and optimized by [14], which computes a shorter isogeny in time $poly(T, \log p)$. One could always start from a curve of unknown endomorphism ring to avoid this attack at the cost of requiring a trusted setup, but in our case even this attack is admissible because there is a different isogeny used in each input and computing the shortcut is still slower (in the VDF from De Feo et al. [14], this is more of a problem because the same isogeny is always used, so the shortcut breaks the VDF for all inputs after being computed once).

More generally, it is unlikely that any kind of reduction could be computed fast enough since our isogeny is not readily represented as an ideal in the quaternion algebra. Any reduction that works over the endomorphism ring would have to translate the isogeny at each step into the language of quaternion ideals, necessarily resulting in a $\Omega(T)$ complexity, and the concrete time of whatever parsing need to be performed is unlikely to be much faster than a simple degree-2 isogeny.

6   Conclusions and Future Work

We have presented a framework for applying a SNARG at the field-arithmetic level to verify an isogeny walk, and used it to obtain a postquantum isogeny-based VDF that does not require a trusted setup and is less susceptible to isogeny shortcut attacks since it uses a different isogeny walk for each input.

In terms of asymptotic complexity, our VDF is less efficient relative to other constructions: for example, the VDF from De Feo et al. [14] has $\mathcal{O}(T)$ evaluator-space complexity and verification time constant in T. However, no previous VDF construction achieves post-quantum security.

Although SNARG-based VDFs have been deemed mainly of theoretical interest by Boneh et al. [8], alluding to the fact that current SNARG constructions have concrete costs about 100,000 times larger than the original computation, it should be noted that this is the case for general-purpose constructions which verify every step of the computation at the bit-operation level. Since our construction verifies steps of the computation at the field-arithmetic level, it has the potential to save significantly on overhead. Therefore, it could prove an interesting future work to implement and benchmark our construction.

We leave it also as future work to propose concrete parameters for our construction. We stress that definitions such as 128-bit security level are not meaningful for the sequentiality property of a VDF, whereas for soundness our security is completely derived from Micali's work [25] and based on symmetric cryptography. This means that the choice of parameters should be based only on the desired delay time, which is impossible to fine-tune until a working implementation is obtained.

We also point out that there is a factor of $\log p$ in both the evaluator's parallelism complexity and the verifier's total complexity that emanates from the breakdown of an exponentiation to verify a square-root computation, as represented by Eqs. (14) and (15). If the square-root computation was verified via a squaring rather than repeating the computation, this factor could be eliminated. However, the longer computation is required due to the fact that we perform our arithmetization at the field arithmetic level, meaning that we need a deterministic way of picking a sign that uses only field operations. We leave it as an open question whether one can design a method to, given both roots of a quadratic polynomial, choose one of them deterministically using only field arithmetic and without resorting to a large exponentiation.

Finally, it should also be noted that the SNARG mechanism we have described is fairly rudimentary and there are various recent developments that achieve slight optimizations. However, most of these improvements rely on reducing the arithmetic over ad hoc fields (such as [4], which uses a binary field) whereas our SNARG is constrained to work in the field of the elliptic curve. We note that this problem is likely to be ubiquitous when adapting SNARGs to work with existing cryptographic frameworks, since such frameworks usually include arithmetic over a prescribed field. Working directly over this prescribed field is bound to save significantly on overhead when constructing SNARG proofs, so we also encourage further optimizations of SNARG constructions over arbitrary fields.

Acknowledgements. We thank Khashayar Barooti and Abdullah Talayhan for pointing out a typo in the complexities that appeared in a previous version of this work.

References

1. Adj, G., Ahmadi, O., Menezes, A.: On isogeny graphs of supersingular elliptic curves over finite fields. Finite Fields Appl. **55**, 268–283 (2019). https://doi.org/10.1016/j.ffa.2018.10.002
2. Arora, S., Safra, S.: Probabilistic checking of proofs: a new characterization of NP. J. ACM **45**(1), 70–122 (1998). https://doi.org/10.1145/273865.273901
3. Babai, L., Fortnow, L., Levin, L.A., Szegedy, M.: Checking computations in polylogarithmic time. In: Proceedings of the Twenty-Third Annual ACM Symposium on Theory of Computing, STOC 1991, 21–32. Association for Computing Machinery, New York (1991). https://doi.org/10.1145/103418.103428
4. Ben-Sasson, E., Bentov, I., Horesh, Y., Riabzev, M.: Scalable, transparent, and post-quantum secure computational integrity. IACR Cryptol. ePrint Arch. **2018**, 46 (2018). http://eprint.iacr.org/2018/046
5. Ben-Sasson, E., Chiesa, A., Genkin, D., Tromer, E., Virza, M.: SNARKs for C: verifying program executions succinctly and in zero knowledge. In: Canetti, R., Garay, J.A. (eds.) CRYPTO 2013, Part II. LNCS, vol. 8043, pp. 90–108. Springer, Heidelberg (2013). https://doi.org/10.1007/978-3-642-40084-1_6
6. Bernstein, D.J., De Feo, L., Leroux, A., Smith, B.: Faster computation of isogenies of large prime degree. In: Galbraith, S. (ed.) ANTS-XIV - 14th Algorithmic Number Theory Symposium. Proceedings of the Fourteenth Algorithmic Number Theory Symposium (ANTS-XIV), Auckland, New Zealand, vol. 4, pp. 39–55. Mathematical Sciences Publishers, June 2020. https://doi.org/10.2140/obs.2020.4.39. https://hal.inria.fr/hal-02514201
7. Biasse, J.-F., Jao, D., Sankar, A.: A quantum algorithm for computing isogenies between supersingular elliptic curves. In: Meier, W., Mukhopadhyay, D. (eds.) INDOCRYPT 2014. LNCS, vol. 8885, pp. 428–442. Springer, Cham (2014). https://doi.org/10.1007/978-3-319-13039-2_25
8. Boneh, D., Bonneau, J., Bünz, B., Fisch, B.: Verifiable delay functions. In: Shacham, H., Boldyreva, A. (eds.) CRYPTO 2018, Part I. LNCS, vol. 10991, pp. 757–788. Springer, Cham (2018). https://doi.org/10.1007/978-3-319-96884-1_25

9. Cai, J., Lipton, R.J., Sedgewick, R., Yao, A.C.: Towards uncheatable benchmarks. In: Proceedings of the Eigth Annual Structure in Complexity Theory Conference, pp. 2–11. IEEE Computer Society (1993)

10. Charles, D.X., Lauter, K.E., Goren, E.Z.: Cryptographic hash functions from expander graphs. J. Cryptol. **22**(1), 93–113 (2007). https://doi.org/10.1007/s00145-007-9002-x

11. Chávez-Saab, J., Rodríguez-Henríquez, F., Tibouchi, M.: Verifiable isogeny walks: towards an isogeny-based postquantum VDF. IACR Cryptol. ePrint Arch., p. 1289 (2021). https://eprint.iacr.org/2021/1289

12. Chia Network Collaboration: Chia DAQ. Chia network (2021). https://www.chia.net/faq/

13. Cohen, B., Pietrzak, K.: Simple proofs of sequential work. In: Nielsen, J.B., Rijmen, V. (eds.) EUROCRYPT 2018, Part II. LNCS, vol. 10821, pp. 451–467. Springer, Cham (2018). https://doi.org/10.1007/978-3-319-78375-8_15

14. De Feo, L., Masson, S., Petit, C., Sanso, A.: Verifiable delay functions from supersingular isogenies and pairings. In: Galbraith, S.D., Moriai, S. (eds.) ASIACRYPT 2019, Part I. LNCS, vol. 11921, pp. 248–277. Springer, Cham (2019). https://doi.org/10.1007/978-3-030-34578-5_10

15. Döttling, N., Garg, S., Malavolta, G., Vasudevan, P.N.: Tight verifiable delay functions. In: Galdi, C., Kolesnikov, V. (eds.) SCN 2020. LNCS, vol. 12238, pp. 65–84. Springer, Cham (2020). https://doi.org/10.1007/978-3-030-57990-6_4

16. Drake, J.: Minimal VDF randomness beacon. ETH Research (2018). https://ethresear.ch/t/minimal-vdf-randomness-beacon/3566

17. Feige, U., Goldwasser, S., Lovász, L., Safra, S., Szegedy, M.: Interactive proofs and the hardness of approximating cliques. J. ACM **43**(2), 268–292 (1996). https://doi.org/10.1145/226643.226652

18. Fiat, A., Shamir, A.: How to prove yourself: practical solutions to identification and signature problems. In: Odlyzko, A.M. (ed.) CRYPTO 1986. LNCS, vol. 263, pp. 186–194. Springer, Heidelberg (1987). https://doi.org/10.1007/3-540-47721-7_12

19. Kohel, D.: Endomorphism rings of elliptic curves over finite fields. Ph.D. thesis, UC Berkeley, December 1996

20. Kohel, D., Lauter, K., Petit, C., Tignol, J.P.: On the quaternion ℓ-isogeny path problem. LMS J. Comput. Math. **17**(A), 418–432 (2014). https://doi.org/10.1112/S1461157014000151

21. Kong, F., Cai, Z., Yu, J., Li, D.: Improved generalized Atkin algorithm for computing square roots in finite fields. Inf. Process. Lett. **98**(1), 1–5 (2006). https://doi.org/10.1016/j.ipl.2005.11.015

22. Lenstra, A.K., Wesolowski, B.: Trustworthy public randomness with sloth, unicorn, and trx. Int. J. Appl. Cryptogr. **3**(4), 330–343 (2017). https://doi.org/10.1504/IJACT.2017.10010315

23. Leroux, A.: Proofs of isogeny knowledge and application to post-quantum one-time verifiable random function. IACR Cryptol. ePrint Arch. **2021**, 744 (2021). https://eprint.iacr.org/2021/744

24. Lund, C., Fortnow, L., Karloff, H.J., Nisan, N.: Algebraic methods for interactive proof systems. J. ACM **39**(4), 859–868 (1992)

25. Micali, S.: Computationally sound proofs. SIAM J. Comput. **30**(4), 1253–1298 (2000)

26. Petit, C., Lauter, K.E.: Hard and easy problems for supersingular isogeny graphs. IACR Cryptol. ePrint Arch. **2017**, 962 (2017). http://eprint.iacr.org/2017/962

27. Pietrzak, K.: Simple verifiable delay functions. In: Blum, A. (ed.) 10th Innovations in Theoretical Computer Science Conference, ITCS 2019. LIPIcs, vol. 124, pp. 60:1–60:15. Schloss Dagstuhl - Leibniz-Zentrum für Informatik (2019)
28. Pizer, A.K.: Ramanujan graphs and Hecke operators. Bull. Am. Math. Soc. **23**, 127–137 (1990). https://doi.org/10.1090/S0273-0979-1990-15918-X
29. Rivest, R.L., Shamir, A., Wagner, D.A.: Time-lock puzzles and timed-release crypto. Technical report. MIT (1996). https://tinyurl.com/time-lock-puzzles
30. Tate, J.: Endomorphisms of abelian varieties over finite fields. Inventiones Mathematicae **22**, 134–144 (1966)
31. VDF Alliance: VDF research. VDF Alliance (2021). https://vdfresearch.org/
32. Wahby, R.S., Setty, S., Ren, Z., Blumberg, A.J., Walfish, M.: Efficient ram and control flow in verifiable outsourced computation. In: Network & Distributed System Security Symposium (NDSS), February 2015
33. Wesolowski, B.: Efficient verifiable delay functions. J. Cryptol. **33**(4), 2113–2147 (2020)
34. Yakovenko, A.: Solana: a new architecture for a high performance blockchain v0.8.13. Solana cryptocurrency whitepaper (2020). https://tinyurl.com/solana-whitepaper

Towards Post-Quantum Key-Updatable Public-Key Encryption via Supersingular Isogenies

Edward Eaton, David Jao, Chelsea Komlo[✉], and Youcef Mokrani

University of Waterloo, Waterloo, Canada
ckomlo@uwaterloo.ca

Abstract. We present the first post-quantum secure Key-Updatable Public-Key Encryption (UPKE) construction. UPKE has been proposed as a mechanism to improve the forward-secrecy and post-compromise security of secure messaging protocols, but the hardness of all existing constructions rely on discrete logarithm assumptions. We focus our assessment on isogeny-based cryptosystems due to their suitability for performing a potentially unbounded number of update operations, a practical requirement for secure messaging where user conversations can occur over months, if not years.

We begin by formalizing two UPKE variants in the literature as Symmetric and Asymmetric UPKE, which differ in how encryption and decryption keys are updated. We argue that Asymmetric UPKE constructions in the literature cannot be straightforwardly instantiated using SIDH nor CSIDH. We then describe a SIDH construction that partially achieves the required security notions for Symmetric UPKE, but due to existing mathematical limitations, cannot provide fine-grained forward secrecy. Finally, we present a CSIDH Symmetric UPKE construction that requires a parameter set in which the class group structure is fully known. We discuss open problems which are applicable to any cryptosystem with similar requirements for continuous operations over the secret domain.

Keywords: Secure messaging · Post-quantum cryptography · Isogenies · Key-updateable encryption

1 Introduction

Secure communication protocols are quickly evolving [3,28,29], driven by the need to meet simultaneous usability and security requirements, such as asynchronous communication while ensuring forward secrecy and post-compromise security for conversations that can occur over months, if not years. *Key-Updatable Public-Key Encryption* (UPKE) schemes have been proposed as a solution to improve weak forward secrecy properties of existing secure messaging protocols such as the Signal and Message Layer Security (MLS)

© The Author(s), under exclusive license to Springer Nature Switzerland AG 2022
R. AlTawy and A. Hülsing (Eds.): SAC 2021, LNCS 13203, pp. 461–482, 2022.
https://doi.org/10.1007/978-3-030-99277-4_22

protocols [1,2,10,21,25,33,34]. In addition to standard public-key encryption functionality, UPKE schemes allow encryption and decryption keys to be asynchronously *updated* with fresh entropy, thereby *healing* the protocol by restoring security even after exposure of secret values. Unfortunately, the security of all UPKE schemes proposed to date relies on the hardness of the discrete logarithm problem.

In this work, we perform the first assessment of the viability of quantum-secure UPKE schemes. We begin by formalizing two UPKE variants presented in the literature which we call *Symmetric UPKE* and *Asymmetric UPKE*,[1] and assess the extent to which existing isogeny-based cryptosystems can instantiate both variants. We model Asymmetric UPKE after a construction proposed by Jost, Maurer, and Mularczyk [25], in which encryption keys are updated using elements in the public domain, while decryption keys are updated using private values. We model Symmetric UPKE after a construction proposed by Alwen et al. [1] to improve the forward-secrecy and post-compromise security of TreeKEM [5], the group key-exchange primitive used by MLS, where both encryption and decryption keys are updated using the *same* secret update value. Further, we introduce the notion of IND-CPA-U security, a generalization of a security model by Alwen et al. [1] for UPKE constructions.

We argue that Asymmetric UPKE constructions as currently defined in the literature *cannot* be instantiated by either Supersingular Isogeny Diffie Hellman (SIDH) nor Commutative Supersingular Isogeny Diffie-Hellman (CSIDH). We then present a series of steps demonstrating that while SIDH can in theory be used for Symmetric UPKE constructions, a viable construction in practice is hindered by existing mathematical limitations. We then present a CSIDH-based Symmetric UPKE construction which can be used today with the existing CSIDH-512 parameter set, or any CSIDH parameter set where the class group structure is fully known. Knowing the class group structure ensures unique group element representation and uniform sampling of secret key material. Taken together, these properties ensure that knowledge of a secret key prior to an update will not leak information about the key *after* an update operation, thereby fulfilling forward secrecy and post-compromise security. We prove that our CSIDH construction fulfills IND-CPA-U security.

We focus our analysis on isogeny-based cryptosystems, as alternative quantum-secure cryptographic primitives have undesirable usability or efficiency trade-offs for secure messaging protocols, or simply cannot support the algebraic structure required for UPKE. In the setting of secure messaging, user conversations can potentially endure months, if not years, and so supporting ongoing protocol actions without bounds on the number of consecutive update operations is desirable. By contrast, lattice-based cryptosystems accumulate errors for each additional operation, and so require either bounding the number of operations or performing some expensive compression function to limit growth of errors [17,18]. Code-based primitives similarly accumulate errors over repeated

---

[1] Note that symmetric and asymmetric here refers to the requirements of how the update operation is performed, not the style of encryption.

operations, and so have similar restrictions on the number of possible operations that can be performed [30].

Contributions. In this work, we assess the viability of post-quantum secure key-updatable public-key encryption (UPKE) schemes, and define constructions using isogeny-based cryptosystems for a subset of these schemes. Towards this end, we present the following contributions:

- We give formal definitions of Symmetric UPKE and Asymmetric UPKE as two UPKE variants presented in the literature. We also present IND-CPA-U, a generalized security model for proving IND-CPA security specifically for UPKE schemes, a setting in which the adversary is assumed to be able to adaptively choose updates and corrupt secret key material.
- We argue that the most prominent Asymmetric UPKE construction currently in the literature [25] *cannot* be straightforwardly instantiated by either SIDH or CSIDH.
- We then describe a SIDH-based Symmetric UPKE construction that is possible in theory, but requires further mathematical advancements and careful cryptanalytic scrutiny to be instantiated in practice. We present this scheme in order to make clear these gaps and possible future research directions.
- We present a Symmetric UPKE construction that can be used today with CSIDH-512, or any CSIDH parameter set where the class group has been fully computed. We prove this construction to be IND-CPA-U secure, and provide an implementation.

Related Work. The most closely related work to our own is the already mentioned work of Alwen et al. [1] as a mechanism to improve forward secrecy and post-compromise security of TreeKEM [5]. Our Symmetric UPKE primitive is modeled after their construction, and our work is an effort to define a post-quantum UPKE variant suitable for similar use. Further, we prove security in a more robust model that models the adversary's capability to both adaptively choose update values for the victim as well as corrupt their local state. The work by Alwen et al. was in turn based upon work by Jost et al. [25], which is most akin to our Asymmetric UPKE notion.

Both secure messaging protocols and post-quantum protocols are still in active development. Efforts to combine the two into post-quantum secure messaging are so far rare in the literature, although we refer to [7] as a recent example of exactly this. Their work constructs a version of Signal's X3DH protocol out of the (ring)-LWE problem.

Alternative (Unrelated) Notions of UPKE. There exists a separate notion of "updatable encryption" in the literature [6,24]. In these schemes, a *ciphertext* is updated using an update token such that the encrypted message becomes an encryption under a new public key without decrypting the message. These schemes should not be confused with *key-updatable* UPKE schemes.

2   Preliminaries

Let λ denote the security parameter in unary representation. We denote sampling a value a from a non-empty set S uniformly at random as $a \xleftarrow{\$} S$.

As we are constructing a hybrid encryption scheme, we will rely on the standard notions of a key encapsulation mechanism, or KEM, and a data encapsulation mechanism, or DEM. However we do not define our scheme as a KEM in order to match the interface presented in previous work in this area [1]. In order to use our protocol as a hybrid encryption scheme we will use a data encapsulation mechanism, which we keep as an abstract interface for flexibility.

Definition 1. *A Data Encapsulation Mechanism DEM [19] is a tuple of three algorithms: a non-deterministic key generation algorithm $KeyGen(\lambda)$ that accepts a security parameter λ and outputs a randomized key K, a non-deterministic encryption algorithm $Encrypt(K, m)$ that accepts K and a message m and outputs a ciphertext ctxt, and a deterministic decryption algorithm $Decrypt(K, ct)$ that outputs the message m.*

In Appendix A we will show that our CSIDH-based construction satisfies our IND-CPA-U definition so long as CSIDH combined with the DEM scheme is IND-CPA. Thus we do not specify the security requirements of the DEM specifically, only that it is enough to ensure that the hybrid system is IND-CPA.

We now give further background on isogenies and their use in public-key cryptosystems.

2.1   Isogenies and Isogeny-Based Cryptography

Let p be a prime number and $\mathbb{F}_p$ be a finite field of characteristic p, and let E_0 and E_1 be elliptic curves defined over $\mathbb{F}_p$. An isogeny $\phi\colon E_0 \to E_1$ is a rational map from $E_0(\overline{\mathbb{F}_p})$ to $E_1(\overline{\mathbb{F}_p})$ which is also a group homomorphism [36], where $\overline{\mathbb{F}_p}$ is the algebraic closure of $\mathbb{F}_p$. When two curves are isomorphic, they share the same *j-invariant*. which remains a constant value for all isomorphic curves.

An endomorphism of an elliptic curve $\phi\colon E \to E$ is a rational map from E to itself, defined over an extension field $\mathbb{F}_{p^n}$. The set of all endomorphisms for an elliptic curve (over an algebraic closure) forms a ring under the operations of point-wise addition and composition; we denote this ring of endomorphisms as $\mathrm{End}(E)$. When $\mathrm{End}(E)$ is isomorphic to an order in a quaternion algebra, the curve is classified as *supersingular*, otherwise, $\mathrm{End}(E)$ is isomorphic to to an imaginary quadratic field and the curve is classified as *ordinary*[36].

We next describe two existing cryptosystems—SIDH and CSIDH—whose security has been demonstrated to reduce to the hardness of the Supersingular Isogeny Problem (or variants thereof), described in Definition 2.

Definition 2. *Supersingular Isogeny Problem [23]* *Given a finite field K and two supersingular elliptic curves E_1, E_2 defined over K such that $|E_1| = |E_2|$, compute an isogeny $\phi\colon E_1 \to E_2$*

Supersingular Isogeny Diffie-Hellman (SIDH). Introduced by Jao and De Feo in 2011 [23], SIDH is a Diffie-Hellman like scheme defined using secret isogenies between supersingular elliptic curves to perform a key exchange protocol. SIDH can also be constructed as a PKE scheme [23]. SIDH has been adapted as a KEM with additional Fujisaki-Okamoto techniques [20] as an IND-CCA2 secure candidate for the ongoing NIST competition to standardize quantum-resistant key exchange protocols [22].

Performing key exchange via SIDH begins with each party agreeing to a starting public curve $E_0(\mathbb{F}_{p^2})$, where p is a prime of the form $2^{e_1}3^{e_2} - 1$, and two sets of basis points $\{P_A, Q_A\}, \{P_B, Q_B\} \subset E_0$, which are generators of the 2^{e_1} and 3^{e_2}-torsion subgroups respectively. For this work, we assume secret values—which define the kernel of an isogeny—are of the form $\langle [1]P + [n]Q \rangle$, such that participants only need to randomly generate the scalar n to define their secret key. Alice begins by selecting $n_A \xleftarrow{\$} \mathbb{Z}_{2^{e_1}}$ which defines her secret isogeny $\phi_A \colon E_0 \to E_A$, such that $E_A = E_0/\langle [1]P_A + [n_A]Q_A \rangle$. Similarly, Bob selects $n_B \xleftarrow{\$} \mathbb{Z}_{3^{e_2}}$, which defines his secret isogeny $\phi_B \colon E_0 \to E_B$, such that $E_B = E_0/\langle [1]P_B + [n_B]Q_B \rangle$. Alice publishes her public key $(E_A, \phi_A(P_B), \phi_A(Q_B))$, while Bob publishes his public key $(E_B, \phi_B(P_A), \phi_B(Q_A))$.

After obtaining each other's public curves, their shared secret is a common curve E_{AB}, which is the same for Alice and Bob up to isomorphism. Alice arrives at E_{AB} by calculating $E_B/\langle \phi_B(P_A) + [n_A]\phi_B(Q_A) \rangle$ using her secret term n_A, whereas Bob calculates $E_A/\langle \phi_A(P_B) + [n_B]\phi_A(Q_B) \rangle$ using his secret term n_B. Alice and Bob obtain the same shared secret by finding the j-invariant of E_{AB}, as their resulting values $E_B/\langle \phi_B(P_A)+[n_A]\phi_B(Q_A) \rangle \cong E_A/\langle \phi_A(P_B)+[n_B]\phi_A(Q_B) \rangle$ are equal up to isomorphism.

Commutative Supersingular Isogeny Diffie-Hellman (CSIDH). CSIDH [8] builds upon the Couveignes-Rostovtsev-Stolbunov [11,35] scheme, but instead uses the graph of supersingular curves. The security of CSIDH is based on the Supersingular Isogeny problem defined in Definition 2, but CSIDH restricts the supersingular isogeny graph (where nodes are supersingular curves, and edges are isogenies) to curves defined over $\mathbb{F}_p$.

While the full ring of endomorphisms of supersingular curves over $\mathbb{F}_{p^2}$ is non-commutative, restricting consideration to the subring of endomorphisms defined over $\mathbb{F}_p$ yields a (commutative) imaginary quadratic order $\mathcal{O}$. A consequence of this restriction is that the isogeny graph must also be restricted to curves and isogenies defined over $\mathbb{F}_p$. To ensure that isogeny operations can be computed efficiently using Vélu's formulas [37], the prime p in CSIDH is defined to be of the form $p = 4 \cdot \ell_1 \cdot \ell_2, \ldots, \cdot \ell_d - 1$ for some set of small primes ℓ_d generating the class group $cl(\mathcal{O})$.

Similarly to SIDH, participants performing a key-exchange must agree to some starting curve $E_0(\mathbb{F}_p)$. A secret key in CSIDH is a vector $\boldsymbol{e} \in \mathbb{Z}^d$; each element in $\boldsymbol{e}$ is within some bound to ensure the values are "small." The vector $\boldsymbol{e}$ represents a secret ideal $\prod_{i=1}^{d} \ell_i^{e_i}$. By the Deuring correspondence, this ideal corresponds to exactly one isogeny from the starting curve to another curve in the graph.

While CSIDH is normally presented as if it were a group action, there are limitations to interpreting it as such. Sampling uniformly random elements from the group and efficiently computing the group action on those elements requires computing the structure of the class group $cl(\mathcal{O})$, which takes subexponential time in general. The authors of CSI-FiSh [4] solved this problem by explicitly computing the structure of $cl(\mathcal{O})$ for the CSIDH-512 parameter set, which is a specific parameter set using a 511-bit prime p. Such a computation requires subexponential time, and cannot reasonably be extended to much larger parameter sets using present technology. In this case, the group is cyclic, and the group order N is now known. Furthermore, the authors computed a basis of short vectors generating the relation lattice of the set of small prime generators, allowing one to convert elements of $\mathbb{Z}_N$ to vectors $\boldsymbol{e} \in \mathbb{Z}^d$ given a choice of group generator, so that the representation $\prod_{i=1}^{d} \ell_i^{e_i}$ can be used for isogeny computation. Fully computing $cl(\mathcal{O})$ allows for efficient and uniform sampling of elements in $\mathbb{Z}_N$ and canonical representation in $\mathbb{Z}_N$. While the authors of CSI-FiSh used these properties to define a signature scheme, we employ the same structure for the purposes of constructing UPKEs.

Efficient Algorithms for the ℓ-Isogeny Path Problem. The *Deuring correspondence* establishes a mapping between supersingular curves over the quadratic extension field $\mathbb{F}_{p^2}$ and maximal orders in a quaternion algebra.[2] The endomorphism ring $\mathrm{End}(E)$ of a supersingular curve E is isomorphic to a maximal order $\mathcal{O}$ in $\mathbf{Q}_{p,\infty}$ (the quaternion algebra over $\mathbf{Q}$ ramified at p and ∞). For each maximal order $\mathcal{O} \in \mathbf{Q}_{p,\infty}$, there are at most two supersingular curves (up to isomorphism) with endomorphism rings isomorphic to $\mathcal{O}$. The correspondence also provides information about isogenies. If there is an isogeny $\phi \colon E_0 \to E_1$, then looking at the corresponding maximal orders $\mathcal{O}_0$ and $\mathcal{O}_1$, there is a left ideal in $\mathcal{O}_0$ which is also a right ideal in $\mathcal{O}_1$. If the isogeny has degree ℓ^k for a prime ℓ, the ideals will have the same norm.

Kohel et al. demonstrated that finding a path in the ℓ-isogeny graph is easier when working over the maximal orders and ideals [26]. Their algorithm (commonly referred to as the KLPT algorithm), takes as input the endomorphism ring of an elliptic curve $\mathrm{End}(E_1)$ and a prime ℓ and finds an ideal with norm ℓ^k for some k that is a left ideal of $\mathrm{End}(E_0)$ and a right ideal of $\mathrm{End}(E_1)$. This ideal can then be converted back to an isogeny $\phi \colon E_0 \to E_1$.

These algorithms have proven to be quite useful in constructing cryptographic protocols. Finding a second isogeny between two curves is useful for proving knowledge of a secret isogeny $\phi \colon E_0 \to E_1$. By concatenating a commitment isogeny $\psi \colon E_1 \to E_2$, KLPT can be used to generate an isogeny $\eta \colon E_0 \to E_2$ that does not go through E_1. This technique has been used to construct signature schemes, beginning with [16], and most recently to construct the signature scheme SQI-Sign [12], based upon an improved version of the KLPT algorithm,

---

[2] The mapping is not quite bijective. Curves with conjugate j-invariants are mapped to the same maximal order, so the mapping is at most two-to-one for isomorphic curves.

which we call KLPT*. This improved version reduces the degree of the output isogeny from $\frac{9}{2}\log_\ell(p)$ to $\frac{15}{4}\log_\ell(p)$. Note however that KLPT* relies on two assumptions (Assumptions 1 and 2) to prove that the output of KLPT* leaks no information about its input. In summary, KLPT* assumes that an isogeny of fixed degree between two curves can be found with high probability, and that the output is statistically close to a uniform sampling (a random walk).

3 Key-Updatable Public-Key Encryption (UPKE)

We begin by formalizing the notion of a generalized UPKE scheme. We then present two variants of UPKE schemes in the literature [1, 25], which differ in how update operations are performed.

Definition 3. Key-Updatable Public-Key Encryption (UPKE) *A UPKE scheme $\mathcal{U}$ is a tuple of six algorithms: a key generation algorithm KeyGen, an encryption algorithm Encrypt, a decryption algorithm Decrypt, an algorithm to generate update values GenUpdate, and algorithms to update private and public keys UpdatePrivate, UpdatePublic, respectively.*

UPKE schemes must fulfill the following correctness, security, and usability notions.

- *Correctness*: The scheme should correctly perform public-key encryption and decryption both before and after a series of updates.
- *Forward secrecy*: If an attacker learns the secret key for epoch n, the updated secret keys in epochs $1 \ldots, n-1$ should not be recoverable.
- *Post-compromise security*: If an attacker learns the secret key for epoch n, all updated secret keys in epochs $n+1, n+2, \ldots$ should not be recoverable.
- *Asynchronicity*: Anyone with knowledge of a public key should be able to initiate an update, so that the update operation to the public key is immediately available, and only the update operation to the secret key should be performed *eventually*.
- *Key Indistinguishability*: An adversary that has access to both a freshly generated keypair and an updated keypair has a negligible advantage to distinguish between the two. Note that while such a property may be desirable in practice for privacy reasons, our reason for requiring this property is for the reduction to IND-CPA in our proof. However, alternative proof strategies may not require this property.

Symmetric UPKE. We model Symmetric UPKE after a construction described by Alwen et al. [1], which is presented as a mechanism to improve the forward-secrecy and post-compromise security properties of TreeKEM.

In this construction, the sender of a message also generates the update value, which is transmitted privately to the holder of the decryption key along with the ciphertext and message. The sender of a message applies the update value to the other party's encryption key, and then the receiver applies the *same* update value to their decryption key.

Definition 4. Symmetric UPKE *A Symmetric UPKE scheme instantiates $\mathcal{U}$ as follows:*

- $KeyGen(\lambda) \rightarrow (sk, pk)$: Accepts a security parameter λ and outputs a public encryption key pk and secret decryption key sk.
- $Encrypt(pk, m) \rightarrow c$: Encrypts a message m using pk, resulting in a ciphertext c.
- $Decrypt(sk, c) \rightarrow m$: Decrypts c using sk, producing the plaintext message m.
- $GenUpdate(\lambda) \rightarrow \mu$: Accepts λ and outputs a randomly-generated update value μ.
- $UpdatePrivate(sk, \mu) \rightarrow sk'$: Takes as input sk and the update value μ and produces a deterministic output that is the updated sk'.
- $UpdatePublic(pk, \mu) \rightarrow pk'$: Takes as input pk and update value μ, and produces a deterministic output that is the updated pk'.

Correctness. Symmetric UPKE constructions are correct if they correctly perform *Encrypt* and *Decrypt* operations both before and after a series of *UpdatePublic* and *UpdatePrivate* operations.

Asymmetric UPKE. We first define a generic Asymmetric UPKE construction, and then present Asymmetric UPKE[†] that is modeled after an existing construction in the literature. In the Asymmetric UPKE setting, encryption and decryption keys are updated using *distinct* update values.

Definition 5. Asymmetric UPKE *An Asymmetric UPKE scheme instantiates $\mathcal{U}$ as follows, where KeyGen, Encrypt, Decrypt remain identical to the Symmetric setting:*

- $GenUpdate(\lambda) \rightarrow (\mu_{sk}, \mu_{pk})$: Produces the update for the encryption key μ_{pk} and an update for the decryption key μ_{sk}.
- $UpdatePrivate(sk, \mu_{sk}) \rightarrow sk'$: Accepts as input sk and a secret update value μ_{sk}, and produces an updated secret key sk'.
- $UpdatePublic(pk, \mu_{pk}) \rightarrow pk'$: Accepts as input pk and a update value μ_{pk}, and produces as output a updated public key pk'.

Correctness. As in the Symmetric setting, Asymmetric UPKE constructions are correct if *Encrypt* and *Decrypt* operations can be correctly performed. before and after a series of *UpdatePublic* and *UpdatePrivate* operations.

Asymmetric UPKE[†]. Jost, Maurer, and Mularczyk [25] presented an ElGamal-based Asymmetric UPKE construction that we refer to as Asymmetric UPKE[†]. In Asymmetric UPKE[†], the update value for the encryption key is in the *public* domain, while the update value for the decryption key is in the *secret* domain. Updates require a homomorphic one-way function f, such that $pk' = pk \circ \mu_{pk} = f(sk') = f(sk \circ \mu_{sk})$.

IND-CPA-U (Indistinguishability Under Chosen Plaintext Attack with Updatability) Game:

$(pk_0, sk_0) \leftarrow KeyGen(\lambda); \; i = 0$ // *Derive the starting keypair*

$j, m_0, m_1, \mathsf{st} \leftarrow \mathcal{A}_0(pk_0)$ // *Adversary queries oracles, returns index and challenge messages*

$b \xleftarrow{\$} \{0, 1\}, \; c_b \leftarrow Encrypt(pk_j, m_b)$ // *Generate challenge ciphertext*

$b' \xleftarrow{\$} \mathcal{A}_1(c_b, \mathsf{st})$ // *The adversary outputs a guess for* b

Adversary wins if $\mathsf{IsFresh}(j)$ and $b' = b$.

where in addition to the normal IND-CPA oracles, the adversary has access to the oracles:

- $\mathsf{GiveUpdate}(\mu) \to pk_i$, after performing   // *The adversary can update keys with chosen value*

     $i = i + 1; (pk_i, sk_i) \leftarrow UpdatePublic(pk_{i-1}, \mu), UpdatePrivate(sk_{i-1}, \mu);$

     $U = U \cup i$ // *Keep track of updates the adversary has provided*

- $\mathsf{FreshUpdate}() \to pk_i$, after performing   // *Update with value not chosen by adversary*

     $i = i + 1; \mu \xleftarrow{\$} GenUpdate(); (pk_i, sk_i) \leftarrow UpdatePublic(pk_{i-1}, \mu), UpdatePrivate(sk_{i-1}, \mu)$

- $\mathsf{Corrupt}(j)$, returning sk_j after performing the following steps: // *Allow the adversary to learn the* j^{th} *keypair*

     $C = C \cup j$

     $i = j;$ while $i \in U$ do: $C = C \cup i, \; i = i - 1;$ // *Left-adjacent updates chosen by* $\mathcal{A}$ *are now corrupt*

     $k = j;$ while $(k + 1) \in U$ do: $C = C \cup k, \; k = k + 1;$ // *Right-adjacent updates from* $\mathcal{A}$ *are also corrupt*

We define $\mathsf{IsFresh}(j)$ to return true if and only if $j \notin C$

Fig. 1. IND-CPA-U experiment, where the adversary issues a guess in the regular IND-CPA game after performing a series of arbitrary updates and corruptions. To ensure the adversary cannot trivially win, we require the secret key under which the challenge is issued to be fresh, meaning the adversary cannot derive its value from simply having corrupted that key or a prior key from which its value can be derived.

3.1 Security

We now present a generalization of IND-CPA (Indistinguishability under Chosen Message Attack) security for UPKE schemes described by Alwen et al. [1], which we define as "Indistinguishability under Chosen Plaintext Attacks with Updatability", or IND-CPA-U. We present this notion of IND-CPA-U security in Fig. 1. Our notion assumes a Symmetric UPKE construction, but extends to the Asymmetric UPKE setting by simply allowing the adversary to learn public update values.

Let W_b denote the event that Experiment b defined in Fig. 1 outputs b. We define the advantage of an adversary $\mathcal{A}$ against a UPKE scheme $\mathcal{U}$ as $\mathsf{Adv}(\mathcal{A}, \mathcal{U}) = \Pr[W_b] - 1$.

Definition 6. *A UPKE scheme is IND-CPA-U secure if for any polynomial-time adversary $\mathcal{A}$, the value of $\mathsf{Adv}(\mathcal{A}, \mathcal{U})$ is negligible.*

Unlike IND-CPA games for plain PKE schemes, the IND-CPA-U definition presented in Definition 6 captures the notion of forward secrecy and post-compromise security by allowing $\mathcal{A}$ to learn any secret key material and provide whatever update values that it wishes, with conditions preventing the adversary from trivially winning the IND-CPA game.

We provide further detail on our notion of IND-CPA-U and how it relates to prior related notions in the extended version of this work [14].

4   Assessing Isogeny-Based UPKE

As seen in Sect. 3, UPKE constructions require that *UpdatePrivate* output an sk_u whose distributed is *independent* from sk, to ensure forward secrecy and post-compromise security. Further, this operation should be *asynchronous*, so that external parties can update the public key without requiring the keyholder to be online.

With these requirements in mind, isogeny-based cryptography presents an attractive option for UPKE constructions. While lattice-based cryptography can support key-exchange operations, in the setting where an unbounded number of update operations can be performed, the security of existing lattice-based constructions unfortunately degrades with each update operation.[3]

We now discuss the extent to which existing isogeny-based schemes—SIDH and CSIDH—can support Symmetric and Asymmetric UPKE constructions.

Isogeny-Based Symmetric UPKE. As described in Sect. 4, Symmetric UPKE constructions apply the same update value μ to both sk and pk. Unfortunately, several practical limitations impact both SIDH and CSIDH-based UPKE constructions, which we discuss in Sects. 5 and 6.

We compare our constructions against a naive "online" UPKE construction that we call *Double Encrypt*, that does *not* achieve the desired goals of asynchronicity and fine-grained forward secrecy, which we aim to improve upon. As a naive "starting point" construction, *Double Encrypt* simply allows any party to select a keypair at random and perform nested encryption to the recipient using the recipient's long-lived keypair and this ephemeral public key (after sending the recipient the corresponding secret key, encrypted to their long-lived keypair). When the recipient comes online, they simply generate a fresh long-lived keypair. *Double Encrypt* achieves all properties required of a UPKE scheme as defined in Sect. 3 except for asynchronicity and fine-grained forward secrecy. Specifically, *Double Encrypt* maintains a static key for each "window" before and after the keyholder performs an update, and so the forward secrecy of *Double Encrypt* is maintained only for each window.

Isogeny-Based Asymmetric UPKE. Definition 5 describes a generalized notion of Asymmetric UPKE, followed by Asymmetric UPKE[†], a concrete construction in the literature [25]. We now describe why there is no straightforward way to use SIDH or CSIDH to instantiate a Asymmetric UPKE[†] style construction. We narrow our assessment to Asymmetric UPKE[†] in order to effectively determine the assumed mathematical structure.

---

[3] For example, the obvious thing to do with a lattice-based system is to add together two (ring)-LWE samples to update a public key. However the corresponding secret key will then be the sum of two (ring)-LWE secrets. The distribution of the resulting secret will be dependent on the previous secret, making it difficult to argue for the security of such a system.

In Definition 5, *UpdatePublic* applies a public update value μ_{pk} to pk, whereas *UpdatePrivate* applies a *private* update value to sk. As such, Asymmetric UPKE† requires a homomorphic structure between the public and private domains.

More formally, the Asymmetric UPKE† construction assumes the existence of a function f that maps the private domain to a public one. For example, $pk = f(sk)$, and $f(\mu_{sk}) = \mu_{pk}$. For a discrete logarithm-based system like Asymmetric UPKE†, f is the simple mapping $f : x \mapsto g^x$. The public key update operation then works because the domain and codomain of f have group operations $\times$ and $\star$, and $f(\mu_{sk} \times sk) = f(\mu_{sk}) \star f(sk) = \mu_{pk} \star pk$.

The failure of both SIDH and CSIDH in trying to instantiate Asymmetric UPKE† is that the protocol requires f to be a group homomorphism, and current isogeny schemes offer, at best, a group action. SIDH defines only one operation—applying isogenies via Vélu's formula—over elements in the set of supersingular curves over $\mathbb{F}_{p^2}$. While SIDH can "combine" public and private values by some (non-group) operation, SIDH does not define a group operation between group elements. More clearly, it is difficult to imagine how to apply one public value in SIDH—a supersingular curve—to another. As such, SIDH *cannot* be used in a straightforward way as the underlying public-key encryption primitive to construct the Asymmetric UPKE† scheme.

For similar reasons, CSIDH cannot be used for an Asymmetric UPKE† construction. The private values in CSIDH form a commutative group, so one might hope for more algebraic structure to be useful. But for Asymmetric UPKE, we need some sort of structure in the public domain. Public values in CSIDH are still elliptic curves, and without an operation that can be applied between elliptic curves or a new way to separate private and public values, CSIDH as currently defined also cannot support Asymmetric UPKE constructions.

5 Symmetric UPKE via SIDH

A naive SIDH-based Symmetric UPKE construction would simply generate an isogeny μ as a secret update, and perform a plain SIDH key exchange using μ to update the keyholder's public key $(E_A, \phi_A(P_B), \phi_A(Q_B))$ under $\mu(E_A)$, to obtain the updated public key $(E_{A\mu}, \phi_{A\mu}(P_B), \phi_{A\mu}(Q_B))$. After sending μ via an encrypted channel to the keyholder, the keyholder would similarly update their secret key $\phi_A : E_0 \to E_A$ by performing a plain SIDH key exchange obtaining $sk' = \phi_{A\mu} = \langle \phi_\mu(P_A) + [n_A]\phi_\mu(Q_A) \rangle$. Unfortunately, this naive construction is *not* forward secure, as the torsion points remain linearly dependent after each update.

We now describe an "online" SIDH UPKE construction that achieves roughly the same windowed forward secrecy as *Double Encrypt*. Our construction requires the keyholder to publish their updated public key after updating their corresponding private key using KLPT*. However, other participants can perform a "partial update" of other participant's public keys non-interactively to achieve some measure of forward secrecy. Note that we present this construction purely as a proof of concept and to demonstrate where gaps exist in the effort to instantiate SIDH-based Symmetric UPKE.

At a high level, the output of KLPT* will be broken into SIDH-sized chunks. The elliptic curve after each chunk will form part of the public key. This means that we will be performing an SIDH-style key exchange with the secret isogeny of one party being significantly longer than the other. Instances where one party's isogeny is longer than the others are called 'unbalanced' or 'overstretched', and have been considered in a cryptanalytic context previously [27]. We touch on this further in Sect. 7. Due to these potential security problems and because we only introduce this scheme to motivate a potential approach, we do not provide a security proof, nor do we claim the existence of one.

An "Online" Construction. Since KLPT* outputs isogenies of degree greater than 2^{e_1} and the point generating the isogeny's kernel lies outside of $E_0(\mathbb{F}_{p^2})$, our construction represents secrets as a composition of k SIDH-sized isogenies, and public keys as a set of k curves. Let the curves E_{A_1} to E_{A_k} represent part of Alice's secret key, and the curves E_{A_1B} to E_{A_kB} be a shared secret between Alice and Bob obtained by performing one SIDH operation per curve in each party's keys. The issue to avoid is that after performing an update, Bob cannot send both of his auxiliary points to Alice on the shared curve E_{A_iB}, as an attacker could compute the curve using these two points. This is because elliptic curves used in SIDH have two parameters and the knowledge of two point on a curve generates a solvable linear equation system. Hence, an attacker having access the intermediate shared secret curves would then only need to break the final SIDH exchange, making the scheme less secure. We describe a fix that sends only both auxiliary points on the first curve but only a single point for each subsequent curve.

Let (P_{A_i}, Q_{A_i}) be a basis of the 2^{f_1}-torsion of E_{A_i} and let $(P_{A_{i+1}}, Q_{A_{i+1}})$ be a basis of the 2^{f_1}-torsion of $E_{A_{i+1}}$. Alice can write $\phi_{A_{i+1}}(P_{A_i})$ and $\phi_{A_{i+1}}(Q_{A_i})$ as linear combinations of $P_{A_{i+1}}$ and $Q_{A_{i+1}}$. This can be done by using a pairing defined on points of $E_{A_{i+1}}$, for example, the Weil pairing, to reduce the problem of finding a linear combination to finding a discrete logarithm. Since $\phi_{A_{i+1}}$ has a cyclic kernel, we have that $(P_{A_{i+1}}, \phi_{A_{i+1}}(P_{A_i}), \phi_{A_{i+1}}(Q_{A_i}))$ or $(Q_{A_{i+1}}, \phi_{A_{i+1}}(P_{A_i}), \phi_{A_{i+1}}(Q_{A_i}))$ generates the entire 2^{f_1}-torsion of $E_{A_{i+1}}$. Using linear algebra, Alice can then check which of $P_{A_{i+1}}$ or $Q_{A_{i+1}}$ is required to generate the entire torsion, using the corresponding auxiliary point $\phi_{B_{i+1}}(P_{A_{i+1}})$ sent by Bob. From this, Alice can use the commutativity of SIDH key exchange to compute the other auxiliary point. Once all k SIDH schemes have been completed, the shared secret between Alice and Bob is the j-invariant of the final curve E_{A_kB}. We call this variation on the scheme "extended SIDH" as the secret key is a chain of isogenies whose composition is of much higher degree than the usual SIDH isogeny.

This induces the following "online" UPKE scheme. Note that this construction deviates from the definition of Symmetric UPKE presented in Definition 4, in that *UpdatePrivate* outputs the completely updated public key (achieving better forward secrecy), whereas *UpdatePublic* outputs a partially updated public key (achieving partial forward secrecy). Note that *UpdatePrivate* is necessary to obtain forward secrecy since, otherwise, the initial secret chain of isogenies would simply be a subchain of the updated secret key.

- *KeyGen*(λ): Sample $(\alpha_1, \beta_1), \ldots (\alpha_k, \beta_k) \xleftarrow{\$} \mathbb{Z}_{2^{e_1}}^2$. Let $sk = (\phi_{A_1}, \ldots, \phi_{A_k})$ as a chain of 2^{f_i}-isogenies $E = E_{A_0} \xrightarrow{\phi_{A_1}} E_{A_1} \xrightarrow{\phi_{A_2}} E_{A_2} \xrightarrow{\phi_{A_3}} \cdots \xrightarrow{\phi_{A_k}} E_{A_k}$ with $f_i \leq e_1$. Set pk to be the tuple $(E_A, \phi_{A_1}(P_B), \phi_{A_1}(Q_B))$ and a list of tuples $(E_{A_{i+1}}, \phi_{A_{i+1}}(P_{B_i}), \phi_{A_{i+1}}(Q_{B_i}), G_i)$. Both sk and pk are defined recursively by doing the following:
  - P_{A_i} and Q_{A_i} form the canonical basis of the 2^{e_1}-torsion of E_{A_i}. P_{B_i} and Q_{B_i} form the canonical basis of the 3^{e_2}-torsion of E_{A_i}.
  - $\phi_{A_{i+1}}$ is the $2^{f_{i+1}}$-isogeny from E_{A_i} whose kernel is the cyclic group generated by $\alpha_{i+1} P_{A_i} + \beta_{i+1} Q_{A_i}$.
  - $E_{A_{i+1}}$ is the codomain of $\phi_{A_{i+1}}$.
  - G_i is the additional auxiliary point on $E_{A_i B}$ used to complete the SIDH scheme for the $(i + 1)$th isogeny, either $\phi_{B_{i+1}}(P_{A_{i+1}})$ or $\phi_{B_{i+1}}(Q_{A_{i+1}})$. To determine which, we define a *ChooseAuxiliary* algorithm, described in Sect. 5.1.
  - Output (sk, pk).

- *Encrypt*(pk, m): Sample $b \xleftarrow{\$} \mathbb{Z}_{3^{e_2}}$ which defines $\phi_B \colon E_0 \to E_{\mathsf{enc}}$. From E_{enc}, compute $E_{A_k B}$ using the 'Extended SIDH' algorithm in the extended version [14]. Compute $K \xleftarrow{\$} KDF(j(E_{A_k B}))$ and $ctxt \leftarrow DEM.Encrypt(K, m)$. Let $ct = (E_{\mathsf{enc}}, ctxt)$. Output ct.

- *Decrypt*(sk, c): Parse ct as $(E_{\mathsf{enc}}, ctxt)$; set $K \xleftarrow{\$} KDF(j(E_{\mathsf{enc}}))$. Output $DEM.Decrypt(K, ctxt)$.

- *GenUpdate*(λ) $\to \mu$: Sample $(\alpha', \beta') \xleftarrow{\$} \mathbb{Z}_{2^{e_1}}^2$. Produce the isogeny $\mu = \phi_{A'} \colon E_{A_k} \to E_{A'}$, of degree $2^{f'}$ with $f' \leq e_1$ and kernel generated by $\alpha' P_{A_k} + \beta' Q_{A_k}$. Output μ.

- *UpdatePublic*(pk, μ) $\to pk'$: Add the tuple $(E_{A'}, \phi_{A'}(P_{B_k}), \phi_{A'}(Q_{B_k}), G_k)$ to pk, resulting in pk'.

- *UpdatePrivate*(sk, μ) $\to (sk', pk'')$: Append $\mu = \phi_{A'}$ to the isogeny chain sk. Apply KLPT* on the composition of the isogenies in sk to obtain a new chain of isogenies $E \xrightarrow{\phi_{A'_1}} E_{A'_1} \xrightarrow{\phi_{A'_2}} E_{A'_2} \xrightarrow{\phi_{A'_3}} \cdots \xrightarrow{\phi_{A'_\ell}} E_{A'}$. Output $sk' = (\phi_{A'_1}, \ldots, \phi_{A'_\ell})$ and completely updated public key pk''.

So long as Alice and Bob choose the same canonical torsion basis of each elliptic curve, G_i can be encoded using a single bit and does not depend on Bob's ephemeral key. This can be done by having Alice and Bob use the same algorithm to find the basis.

We now elaborate on the extent to which our construction can achieve the required properties of a UPKE scheme.

Correctness: Since both the initial and updated keys are a chain of SIDH protocols, correctness is respected.

Forward secrecy: Because the output of KLPT* will not leak information about its inputs (if the underlying assumptions of KLPT* regarding fixed-length outputs and the randomness of the output hold), an attacker obtaining the updated key gains no information on the keys before the last application of KLPT*. As such, our scheme achieves forward secrecy roughly comparable to *Double Encrypt*, since all participants get some measure of "windowed" forward secrecy between when an external party performs *UpdatePublic*, and the keyholder performs *UpdatePrivate*.

Post-compromise security: Since the output of KLPT* will not leak information about its inputs (again, if its underlying assumptions hold), an attacker looses all information once KLPT* is reapplied during the next update.

Asynchronicity: This scheme cannot support asynchronous updates.

Key Indistinguishability: This scheme does not provide key indistinguishability.

As this construction does not fully instantiate the requirements for Symmetric UPKE (due to the lack of asynchronicity), we purely present this construction as a proof of concept not intended for use in practice. For this reason as well as the potential security problems introduced by overstretching SIDH parameters, we do not make formal claims of security. Hence, while we discuss how to avoid current torsion point attacks in Sect. 7, we omit a formal proof of security.

5.1   Choosing and Getting Auxiliary Points

Recall that in *KeyGen*, the public key includes one additional auxiliary point on E_{A_iB}, which is used to complete the SIDH scheme for the $(i+1)$th isogeny. We now describe the implementation of *ChooseAuxiliary*, an algorithm to determine whether this auxiliary point is on $\phi_{B_{i+1}}(P_{A_{i+1}})$ or $\phi_{B_{i+1}}(Q_{A_{i+1}})$.

Let G_i be the received auxiliary point (either $\phi_{B_{i+1}}(P_{A_{i+1}})$ or $\phi_{B_{i+1}}(Q_{A_{i+1}})$) and let $\psi_{A_{i+1}} : E_{A_iB} \to E_{A_{i+1}B}$ be isogeny induced by the ith SIDH exchange. Let $\mathsf{WeilPairing}(E, P, Q, n)$ be the Weil pairing of two points P and Q of order dividing n in the elliptic curve E, and $\mathsf{DiscreteLog}(a, b, n)$ be the discrete logarithm of a by b, two elements in a group of order dividing n. Let $\mathsf{IsLinearCombination}([U_1, \ldots, U_k], V)$ be a function returning True if V is a linear combination of $U_1, \ldots, U_k$ and False otherwise. Finally, let $\mathsf{LinearCombination}([U_1, \ldots, U_k], V)$ be a function returning $(a_1, \ldots, a_k)$ such that $V = \sum_{i=1}^{k} a_i U_i$.

The *ChooseAuxiliary* algorithm selects the information required to evaluate the auxiliary points for the next exchange, by the following steps.

- Use Weil pairings and discrete logarithms to define $\phi_{A_i}(P_{A_i})$ and $\phi_{A_i}(Q_{A_i})$ as linear combinations of $P_{A_{i+1}}$ and $Q_{A_{i+1}}$.
- Use linear algebra to check if $Q_{A_{i+1}}$ is a linear combination of $P_{A_{i+1}}, \phi_{A_i}(P_{A_i})$ and $\phi_{A_i}(Q_{A_i})$. If that is the case, choose $\phi_{B_{i+1}}(P_{A_{i+1}})$. Otherwise, choose $\phi_{B_{i+1}}(Q_{A_{i+1}})$.

We define how to implement *ChooseAuxiliary* more precisely in the extended version of this work [14].

6   Symmetric UPKE Construction via CSIDH

We described in the prior section the difficulties in constructing a SIDH-based UPKE scheme due to the simultaneous requirements for asynchronicity, forward secrecy, and post-compromise security. We now show how CSIDH, combined with knowledge of the class group structure, can overcome these challenges and construct a scheme that satisfies all notions of a secure and useful UPKE.

CSIDH UPKE, First Attempt. CSIDH admits operations that are much closer to those used in the classical construction from Alwen et al. [1]. Recall that secret keys in CSIDH are represented by a vector of ℓ integers. For efficiency reasons, the integers are usually chosen to be within a bound B, for example, $B = 5$ so that all entries are between -5 and 5. Then the group element $[e_1, e_2, \ldots, e_\ell]$ represents the group element

$$\mathfrak{g}_1^{e_1} \mathfrak{g}_2^{e_2} \cdots \mathfrak{g}_\ell^{e_\ell},$$

for a set of canonical generators $\{\mathfrak{g}_i\}$. Since the group is commutative, we have that if g is represented by $[e_1, \ldots, e_\ell]$ and h is represented by $[f_1, \ldots, f_\ell]$ then $g \cdot h$ can be represented by $[e_1 + f_1, \ldots, e_\ell + f_\ell]$. A basic design for a symmetric UPKE scheme would then be for the update value to be a random group element, to update the public key by applying the group action, and to update the secret key by adding the group elements together.

Unfortunately, this simple design is not secure. If each entry for the update value is drawn uniformly from $-B$ to B, then the distribution of each entry of the new public key is centered at the old public key. This leaks a certain amount of information about the old secret key. For example, if only one update has occurred, if an entry is $2B$ then the adversary immediately knows that the corresponding entry before the update must have been B.

One fix may be to increase the bound B in an attempt to show that leaking the secret key between certain updates still doesn't reveal enough of the secret key to allow a break. Such an analysis must be done carefully, but reveals another fundamental problem. As more updates occur, the size of each entry in the vector is likely to grow. The efficiency of CSIDH is directly dependent on the ℓ_1-norm of this vector, and so allowing it to grow with updates will result in a slower and slower decryption process, eventually becoming unacceptable.

Note that this is almost exactly the same problem that a first attempt at a lattice-based scheme would run into. If one were to define a scheme based on the LWE problem, then updates could be generated by sampling an LWE secret. The secret key would then be updated by adding the update value to the old secret. But as described for CSIDH, this will cause the error term to grow over time, eventually causing the system to fail. Furthermore, because errors are not chosen uniformly, the distribution of a secret will always be dependent on the previous secret, meaning some information about previous keys is leaked in the event of a compromise.

One technique to circumvent this problem that has been to employ rejection sampling, as in the signature scheme SeaSign [15]. However, rejection sampling only works when we can reject the group elements that would leak information on the secret key. Since the party selecting the update value is not the owner of the public key, rejection sampling is not an option in our scenario. Instead, we will need the group elements to be represented in a way that has better properties.

As mentioned in Sect. 2.1, the signature scheme CSI-FiSh uses a different representation for group elements. Let N denote the order of the group. To compute the group action (i.e., apply the isogeny to an elliptic curve) one converts an element of $\mathbb{Z}_N$ (represented simply by an integer) to an ideal in $\mathbb{Z}^\ell$ and then applies the action as in CSIDH. Representing group elements as an integer in $\mathbb{Z}_N$ gives a unique representation. It is also still very easy to apply the group operation in this representation - it is just addition modulo N.

Our Construction. To prevent leakage from secret key updates described above, our construction requires a class group structure that is fully known, so that the secret key and update value can both be represented in $\mathbb{Z}_N$. To update a public key, we apply the group action, and to update the secret key we add modulo N. Because we can sample uniformly over $\mathbb{Z}_N$, we have that the updated secret key leaks no information about the previous secret key, as desired.

We now describe the scheme in full, relying heavily on group action notation. Let N be the order of the class group $cl(\mathcal{O}) \cong \mathbb{Z}_N$. To apply the group action onto a supersingular elliptic curve E (denoted $g \star E$), we first need to convert the element to a representation in $\mathbb{Z}^\ell$ with a low L_1 norm, and then apply the action as in the original CSIDH paper.

- $KeyGen(\lambda)$: Sample $g_{sk} \overset{\$}{\leftarrow} \mathbb{Z}_N$ and set $E_{pk} := g_{sk} \star E_0$. Output $(sk, pk) = (g_{sk}, E_{pk})$.
- $Encrypt(pk, m)$: Sample $g_{\mathsf{enc}} \overset{\$}{\leftarrow} \mathbb{Z}_N$ and compute $K \leftarrow KDF(g_{\mathsf{enc}} \star pk)$, $E_{\mathsf{enc}} \leftarrow g_{\mathsf{enc}} \star E_0$, and $ctxt \leftarrow DEM.Encrypt(K, m)$. Output $ct = (E_{\mathsf{enc}}, ctxt)$.
- $Decrypt(sk, ct)$: Parse ct as $(E_{\mathsf{enc}}, ctxt)$, set $K \leftarrow KDF(sk \star E_{enc})$, output $DEM.Decrypt(K, ctxt)$.
- $GenUpdate()$: Sample $\mu \overset{\$}{\leftarrow} \mathbb{Z}_N$.
- $UpdatePrivate(sk, \mu)$: Output $sk' \leftarrow sk + \mu \pmod{N}$.
- $UpdatePublic(pk, \mu)$: Output $pk' \leftarrow \mu \star pk$.

Theorem 1. *Let $\mathcal{A}$ be an adversary capable of winning the IND-CPA-U game with advantage ϵ that makes q_{gen} queries to the* FreshUpdate *oracle. We will construct an adversary capable of winning an IND-CPA game in time approximately equal to the running time of $\mathcal{A}$ with advantage $\epsilon/(q_{gen} + 1)$.*

We demonstrate that our construction attains IND-CPA-U security, by showing a reduction from an adversary capable of winning the IND-CPA-U game to one that can win a plain IND-CPA game. By a plain IND-CPA game, we mean a game in which no calls to the *GenUpdate*, GiveUpdate, or Corrupt oracles are made. We present our complete proof in Appendix A.

Implementation. Because our scheme requires the structure of the class group to be known, our CSIDH-based scheme can only be instantiated if such a computation has been performed. At the present time, this requirement limits us to the CSIDH-512 parameter set, which claims 64 bits of post-quantum security. Peikert [31] has questioned this security claim, and more recent analysis [9] indicates that CSIDH-4096 is necessary for NIST level 1 security. Computing the structure of the class group is a sub-exponential computation, and so becomes feasible with the availability of a quantum computer to perform the computation. As such, the scheme may not be able to be instantiated until it is most needed.

Other than computing the class group, the main challenge in an implementation is in computing the group action. To compute the group action, the element of $\mathbb{Z}_N$ is converted to a vector in $\mathbb{Z}^\ell$, which represents the group element $\prod_{i=1}^{\ell} \mathfrak{g}_i^{e_i}$ for a vector e and set of generators $\{\mathfrak{g}_i\}_i$. This vector is then applied to the elliptic curve as is done in CSIDH.

Thus the additional complication over any other CSIDH implementation is in converting the element of $\mathbb{Z}_N$ to a vector of integers. This process is described in the CSI-FiSh paper, and the authors have provided code to do this (for the CSIDH-512 parameter set). The authors of CSI-FiSh found that the process of converting to a vector only makes a key negotiation 15% slower. Using their implementation of CSI-FiSh, we have a proof of concept script that illustrates the process of updating the secret and public keys. Our script is available at https://github.com/tedeaton/CSIDH-UPKE.

7 Future Research Directions

Recall that in UPKE constructions, to ensure post-compromise and forward secrecy, the update value must be properly 'mixed in' with the secret key when performing an update. The KLPT* algorithm performs a functionality very close to what is needed; however, the outputs of KLPT* are too long to be computed within SIDH. As we have seen, while 'breaking up' the KLPT* output into SIDH-sized segments allows for computation, it does not result in an asynchronous protocol. Furthermore, since each update increases the length of Alice's total isogeny, a large number of updates would make Alice's isogeny much longer than both Bob's isogeny and the usual isogenies used in SIDH. The security analysis of such a version of SIDH is challenging since prior work has shown that 'unbalanced' [32] and 'overstretched' [13,27] versions of SIDH where the degree of one isogeny is much larger than the other may be less secure. We remark that these attacks require knowledge of the initial curve's endomorphism ring, and thus could potentially be countered by choosing the initial curve E to be a random elliptic curve with unknown End(E), and including this curve in the original public key. It may also be of interest to note that while several published schemes in the literature employ unbalanced SIDH parameters, as far as we know our scheme is the first cryptosystem proposal that actually uses overstretched SIDH parameters in an essential way. Note that while simply re-initializing the protocol can prevent arbitrarily unbalanced parameters, but such an approach creates complexity tradeoffs for implementations, in turn opening to door to alternative security issues.

Overcoming these issues likely means improving both KLPT* or widening the range of isogenies SIDH can compute with. However, there are limitations to how much KLPT* variants can be improved. A simple counting argument shows that paths of length e_1 on the ℓ-isogeny graph will only reach a small fraction of available elliptic curves. The cryptographer's dream is to have the output of KLPT* match the input of SIDH, but this cannot happen only with improvements to KLPT*; new versions of SIDH working with a wider class of isogenies must be designed and shown to be secure.

8   Conclusion

In this work, we have performed the first assessment of the post-quantum readiness for *key-updatable* public-key encryption schemes by determining the extent to which two isogeny-based cryptosystems can be used to instantiate Symmetric and Asymmetric UPKE constructions. We provided formalizations for both Asymmetric and Symmetric UPKE and a generalized security notion, denoted IND-CPA-U. Because neither SIDH nor CSIDH define a group action among elements in the public domain, neither supports Asymmetric UPKE designs that require update operations between public update values and encryption keys. However, both SIDH and CSIDH can be used for Symmetric UPKE constructions. The SIDH-based Symmetric UPKE construction, while possible in theory, requires mathematical improvements for a construction in practice. Our CSIDH-based construction can be instantiated today using CSIDH-512 as the parameter set. We highlighted several open problems that would improve our constructions, including the need for security analysis for unbalanced or overstretched SIDH parameters, as well as stronger CSIDH parameter sets. Such improvements will benefit any protocol that requires ongoing and asynchronous randomization of secret terms.

Acknowledgments. We thank Martin Albrecht, Alex Davidson, and Fernando Virdia for discussion of lattice-based UPKE operations. We thank Douglas Stebila for his review of our proof and suggestions on modeling an adaptive adversary that can both select update values and compromise a victim's local state. We thank Chris Leonardi for understanding limitations on the KLPT algorithm, and Richard Barnes for his help in understanding the details of the MLS protocol. This work is supported in part by NSERC, CryptoWorks21, Canada First Research Excellence Fund, Public Works and Government Services Canada, and the Royal Bank of Canada.

A   Proof of CSIDH-Based UPKE

In Sect. 6, we present a CSIDH-based UPKE construction. We present the proof of its IND-CPA-U security here.

Proof. As we are showing a reduction to a plain IND-CPA game, we will start by being given a public key pk^*. To begin, select a uniformly random index $i \xleftarrow{\$} \{0, \ldots, q_{gen}\}$. The idea of the proof is to set the public key after the ith FreshUpdate query to be pk^*, and hope that the adversary requests the IND-CPA-U challenge to be issued on a public key that occurs before the next FreshUpdate. If we are correct, then the adversary's ability to distinguish which message was encrypted under pk^* (or a related key) will allow us to win the IND-CPA game.

At the start of the game, if $i = 0$ then we set $pk_0 \rightarrow pk^*$. Otherwise, we sample a new uniform pk_0 from *KeyGen*. From here we proceed as normal. If the adversary makes a corruption query, then we provide them with the corresponding private key. When a GiveUpdate(μ) query is made, we update the secret and public key and make note of the μ value.

When the ith query to FreshUpdate is made, we set the resulting public key to pk^*. We carry on, and when the next FreshUpdate query is made we sample a fresh public key from *KeyGen*. If the adversary ever makes a Corrupt query on any of the keys between these FreshUpdate queries, then we abort. We will consider the probability of having to abort occurring momentarily.

Eventually, the adversary requests the IND-CPA-U challenge on a public key with index j. We hope that this index means a key that falls between the ith FreshUpdate and the $i + 1$th call to FreshUpdate. When this happens, the adversary submits m_0, m_1 as part of the challenge.

We then forward m_0, m_1 to receive back an encryption of m_b, consisting of $C = g \star E_0$ for a random g, as well as $DEM.Encrypt(K, m_b)$. Let $\mu_1, \mu_2, \ldots, \mu_k$ be k queries to GiveUpdate after the ith FreshUpdate query. We provide the adversary with $(-\mu_1 - \mu_2 - \cdots - \mu_k) \star C$ and $DEM.Encrypt(K, m_b)$.

Note that $K = KDF(g \star pk^*) = KDF((-\mu_1 - \cdots - \mu_k) \star g \star (\mu_1 + \cdots + \mu_k) \star pk^*)$, which means that the message is encrypted under the correct key. So, when the adversary submits a guess for b, we can guess the same value, and if the adversary is correct, so are we.

When we set the public key to pk^* after the ith call to FreshUpdate, the adversary cannot notice that we have not genuinely updated the public key, unless they issue a Corrupt query. If such a Corrupt query is issued, we must abort. However, note that if our guess is correct, and the IND-CPA query is requested in this segment of public keys, then no Corrupt query will be issued, or else the adversary's advantage is 0.

Because updates are sampled uniformly over $\mathbb{Z}_p$, the resulting public key is uniformly random over the public key space (this follows from the fact that the group action is regular). So after a FreshUpdate has occurred, the adversary has no information on the distribution of the secret key, and we can thus replace the public key with the challenge public key pk^*. The adversary has no advantage in distinguishing that we have done this. As a result, we have a $1/(1 + q_{gen})$ chance of correctly guessing where the challenge will be requested. If we are correct, the adversary does not change their behavior at all, as they have no advantage in distinguishing that we are not managing the game honestly. This means the chance that we abort is exactly $q_{gen}/(1 + q_{gen})$.

Our advantage in winning the IND-CPA game is thus the adversary's advantage in winning the IND-CPA-U game times the probability we do not abort, which is $\epsilon/(1 + q_{gen})$, as desired. $\qquad\blacksquare$

We note that the techniques in this proof can also be applied to the classical construction of Alwen et al. [1]. While they couple together the public key update and encryption functions, the same general strategy can be used to show that the stronger IND-CPA-U notion can be satisfied by their construction.

References

1. Alwen, J., Coretti, S., Dodis, Y., Tselekounis, Y.: Security analysis and improvements for the IETF MLS standard for group messaging. IACR Cryptol. ePrint Arch. **2019**, 1189 (2019)
2. Balli, F., Rösler, P., Vaudenay, S.: Determining the core primitive for optimally secure ratcheting. In: Moriai, S., Wang, H. (eds.) ASIACRYPT 2020, Part III. LNCS, vol. 12493, pp. 621–650. Springer, Cham (2020). https://doi.org/10.1007/978-3-030-64840-4_21
3. Barnes, R., Beurdouche, B., Millican, J., Omara, E., Cohn-Gordon, K., Robert, R.: The Message Layer Security (MLS) Protocol, March 2020. https://tools.ietf.org/pdf/draft-ietf-mls-protocol-09.pdf
4. Beullens, W., Kleinjung, T., Vercauteren, F.: CSI-FiSh: efficient isogeny based signatures through class group computations. In: Galbraith, S.D., Moriai, S. (eds.) ASIACRYPT 2019. LNCS, vol. 11921, pp. 227–247. Springer, Cham (2019). https://doi.org/10.1007/978-3-030-34578-5_9
5. Bhargavan, K., Barnes, R., Rescorla, E.: TreeKEM: asynchronous decentralized key management for large dynamic groups a protocol proposal for Messaging Layer Security (MLS). Research report, Inria Paris (2018)
6. Boneh, D., Eskandarian, S., Kim, S., Shih, M.: Improving speed and security in updatable encryption schemes. In: Moriai, S., Wang, H. (eds.) ASIACRYPT 2020. LNCS, vol. 12493, pp. 559–589. Springer, Cham (2020). https://doi.org/10.1007/978-3-030-64840-4_19
7. Dunkelman, O., Jacobson, Jr., M.J., O'Flynn, C. (eds.): SAC 2020. LNCS, vol. 12804. Springer, Cham (2021). https://doi.org/10.1007/978-3-030-81652-0
8. Castryck, W., Lange, T., Martindale, C., Panny, L., Renes, J.: CSIDH: an efficient post-quantum commutative group action. In: Peyrin, T., Galbraith, S. (eds.) ASIACRYPT 2018, Part III. LNCS, vol. 11274, pp. 395–427. Springer, Cham (2018). https://doi.org/10.1007/978-3-030-03332-3_15
9. Chávez-Saab, J., Chi-Domínguez, J.J., Jaques, S., Rodríguez-Henríquez, F.: The SQALE of CSIDH: square-root vélu quantum-resistant isogeny action with low exponents. Cryptology ePrint Archive, Report 2020/1520 (2020). https://eprint.iacr.org/2020/1520

10. Cohn-Gordon, K., Cremers, C., Dowling, B., Garratt, L., Stebila, D.: A formal security analysis of the signal messaging protocol. In: 2017 IEEE European Symposium on Security and Privacy (EuroS P), pp. 451–466 (2017)

11. Couveignes, J.M.: Hard homogeneous spaces. Cryptology ePrint Archive, Report 2006/291 (2006). https://eprint.iacr.org/2006/291

12. De Feo, L., Kohel, D., Leroux, A., Petit, C., Wesolowski, B.: SQISign: compact post-quantum signatures from quaternions and isogenies. In: Moriai, S., Wang, H. (eds.) ASIACRYPT 2020. LNCS, vol. 12491, pp. 64–93. Springer, Cham (2020). https://doi.org/10.1007/978-3-030-64837-4_3

13. de Quehen, V., et al.: Improved torsion-point attacks on SIDH variants. In: Malkin, T., Peikert, C. (eds.) CRYPTO 2021, Part III. LNCS, vol. 12827, pp. 432–470. Springer, Cham (2021). https://doi.org/10.1007/978-3-030-84252-9_15

14. Eaton, E., Jao, D., Komlo, C., Mokrani, Y.: Towards post-quantum updatable public-key encryption via supersingular isogenies. IACR Cryptol. ePrint Arch., 1593 (2020)

15. De Feo, L., Galbraith, S.D.: SeaSign: compact isogeny signatures from class group actions. In: Ishai, Y., Rijmen, V. (eds.) EUROCRYPT 2019, Part III. LNCS, vol. 11478, pp. 759–789. Springer, Cham (2019). https://doi.org/10.1007/978-3-030-17659-4_26

16. Galbraith, S.D., Petit, C., Silva, J.: Identification protocols and signature schemes based on supersingular isogeny problems. In: Takagi, T., Peyrin, T. (eds.) ASIACRYPT 2017, Part I. LNCS, vol. 10624, pp. 3–33. Springer, Cham (2017). https://doi.org/10.1007/978-3-319-70694-8_1

17. Gentry, C.: Fully homomorphic encryption using ideal lattices. In: Proceedings of the Forty-First Annual ACM Symposium on Theory of Computing, STOC 2009, pp. 169–178. Association for Computing Machinery, New York (2009)

18. Gentry, C., Sahai, A., Waters, B.: Homomorphic encryption from learning with errors: conceptually-simpler, asymptotically-faster, attribute-based. In: Canetti, R., Garay, J.A. (eds.) CRYPTO 2013. LNCS, vol. 8042, pp. 75–92. Springer, Heidelberg (2013). https://doi.org/10.1007/978-3-642-40041-4_5

19. Herranz, J., Hofheinz, D., Kiltz, E.: Some (in)sufficient conditions for secure hybrid encryption. Inf. Comput. 208(11), 1243–1257 (2010)

20. Hofheinz, D., Hövelmanns, K., Kiltz, E.: A modular analysis of the Fujisaki-Okamoto transformation. In: Kalai, Y., Reyzin, L. (eds.) TCC 2017. LNCS, vol. 10677, pp. 341–371. Springer, Cham (2017). https://doi.org/10.1007/978-3-319-70500-2_12

21. Jaeger, J., Stepanovs, I.: Optimal channel security against fine-grained state compromise: the safety of messaging. In: Shacham, H., Boldyreva, A. (eds.) CRYPTO 2018. LNCS, vol. 10991, pp. 33–62. Springer, Cham (2018). https://doi.org/10.1007/978-3-319-96884-1_2

22. Jao, D., et al.: Supersingular Isogeny Key Exchange (2019). https://sike.org/files/SIDH-spec.pdf. Accessed 20 Apr 2020

23. Jao, D., De Feo, L.: Towards quantum-resistant cryptosystems from supersingular elliptic curve isogenies. In: Yang, B.-Y. (ed.) PQCrypto 2011. LNCS, vol. 7071, pp. 19–34. Springer, Heidelberg (2011). https://doi.org/10.1007/978-3-642-25405-5_2

24. Jiang, Y.: The direction of updatable encryption does not matter much. In: Moriai, S., Wang, H. (eds.) ASIACRYPT 2020, Part III. LNCS, vol. 12493, pp. 529–558. Springer, Cham (2020). https://doi.org/10.1007/978-3-030-64840-4_18

25. Jost, D., Maurer, U., Mularczyk, M.: Efficient ratcheting: almost-optimal guarantees for secure messaging. In: Ishai, Y., Rijmen, V. (eds.) EUROCRYPT 2019. LNCS, vol. 11476, pp. 159–188. Springer, Cham (2019). https://doi.org/10.1007/978-3-030-17653-2_6

26. Kohel, D., Lauter, K., Petit, C., Tignol, J.P.: On the quaternion ℓ-isogeny path problem. LMS J. Comput. Math. **17**(A), 418–432 (2014)

27. Kutas, P., Merz, S.-P., Petit, C., Weitkämper, C.: One-way functions and malleability oracles: hidden shift attacks on isogeny-based protocols. In: Canteaut, A., Standaert, F.-X. (eds.) EUROCRYPT 2021, Part I. LNCS, vol. 12696, pp. 242–271. Springer, Cham (2021). https://doi.org/10.1007/978-3-030-77870-5_9

28. Marlinspike, M., Perrin, T.: The Double Ratchet Algorithm (2016). https://signal.org/docs/specifications/doubleratchet/

29. Marlinspike, M., Perrin, T.: The X3DH Key Agreement Protocol (2016). https://signal.org/docs/specifications/x3dh/

30. McEliece, R.J.: A public-key cryptosystem based on algebraic coding theory. Deep Space Netw. Progr. Rep. **44**, 114–116 (1978)

31. Peikert, C.: He gives C-Sieves on the CSIDH. In: Canteaut, A., Ishai, Y. (eds.) EUROCRYPT 2020, Part II. LNCS, vol. 12106, pp. 463–492. Springer, Cham (2020). https://doi.org/10.1007/978-3-030-45724-2_16

32. Petit, C.: Faster algorithms for isogeny problems using torsion point images. In: Takagi, T., Peyrin, T. (eds.) ASIACRYPT 2017, Part II. LNCS, vol. 10625, pp. 330–353. Springer, Cham (2017). https://doi.org/10.1007/978-3-319-70697-9_12

33. Poettering, B., Rösler, P.: Towards bidirectional ratcheted key exchange. In: Shacham, H., Boldyreva, A. (eds.) CRYPTO 2018, Part I. LNCS, vol. 10991, pp. 3–32. Springer, Cham (2018). https://doi.org/10.1007/978-3-319-96884-1_1

34. Poettering, B., Rösler, P.: Asynchronous ratcheted key exchange. Cryptology ePrint Archive, Report 2018/296 (2018). https://eprint.iacr.org/2018/296

35. Rostovtsev, A., Stolbunov, A.: Public-key cryptosystem based on isogenies. Cryptology ePrint Archive, Report 2006/145 (2006). https://eprint.iacr.org/2006/145

36. Silverman, J.H.: The Arithmetic of Elliptic Curves. GTM, vol. 106. Springer, New York (2009). https://doi.org/10.1007/978-0-387-09494-6

37. Vélu, J.: Isogénies entre courbes elliptiques. C. R. Acad. Sci. Paris Sér. A-B, **273**, A238–A241 (1971)

Secret Keys in Genus-2 SIDH

Sabrina Kunzweiler[1], Yan Bo Ti[2], and Charlotte Weitkämper[3(✉)]

[1] Ruhr-Universität Bochum, Bochum, Germany
[2] DSO, Singapore, Singapore
[3] University of Birmingham, Birmingham, UK
C.Weitkaemper@pgr.bham.ac.uk

Abstract. We present a polynomial-time adaptive attack on the genus-2 variant of SIDH (G2SIDH) and describe an improvement to its secret selection procedure. G2SIDH is a generalisation of the Supersingular Isogeny Diffie–Hellman key exchange into the genus-2 setting and achieves the same security as SIDH while using fields a third of the size.

We analyze the keyspace of G2SIDH and achieve an improvement to the secret selection by using symplectic bases for the torsion subgroups. This allows for the near uniform sampling of secrets without needing to solve multiple linear congruences as suggested by Flynn–Ti. More generally, using symplectic bases enables us to classify and enumerate isogeny kernel subgroups and thus simplify the secret sampling step for general genus-2 SIDH-style constructions.

The proposed adaptive attack on G2SIDH is able to recover the secret when furnished with an oracle that returns a single bit of information. We ensure that the maliciously generated information provided by the attacker cannot be detected by implementing simple countermeasures, forcing the use of the Fujisaki–Okamoto transform for CCA2-security. We demonstrate this attack and show that it is able to recover the secret isogeny in all cases of G2SIDH using a symplectic basis before extending the strategy to arbitrary bases.

Keywords: Genus-2 SIDH · Isogenies · Adaptive attack

The Supersingular Isogeny Diffie–Hellman (SIDH) protocol is a key exchange protocol which is the basis of a third round alternative candidate in the NIST post-quantum cryptographic standardisation process [9]. The SIDH protocol was first described in 2011 by Jao and De Feo [7]. The G2SIDH key exchange [4] is a natural generalisation of SIDH to a higher-dimensional setting. In this variant, the supersingular elliptic curves of SIDH are substituted with principally polarised superspecial abelian surfaces (PPSSAS) and ℓ-isogenies are replaced by (ℓ, ℓ)-isogenies. Due to the increased number of neighboring isogenies, the security of G2SIDH can be maintained while using primes a third of the size when compared with SIDH.

In the original description of G2SIDH, the secret keys were encoded by multiple secret scalars that need to fulfil a certain linear congruence property and it

R. AlTawy and A. Hülsing (Eds.): SAC 2021, LNCS 13203, pp. 483–507, 2022.
https://doi.org/10.1007/978-3-030-99277-4_23

required the user to solve these linear congruences during the selection of secrets. This is cumbersome and increases the computational cost of key exchange during run time. Moreover, random sampling of keys was left as an open problem in [4].

We propose a simplification of the methods in [4] which makes the sampling procedure more straightforward. This is achieved by introducing specific conditions on the torsion basis points. In particular, we require the users to choose torsion generators which form a *symplectic* basis. The use of a symplectic torsion basis enables us to classify general genus-2 isogeny kernel subgroups and find canonical expressions for their generators in terms of the suggested basis points. It allows both parties of the G2SIDH key exchange protocol to choose secrets uniformly from a large keyspace simply by choosing 3 to 4 scalars, and furthermore provides a framework in which to present the adaptive attack.

In most aspects, G2SIDH closely resembles SIDH. This leads to natural generalisations of attacks on SIDH to G2SIDH, and also the concept of equivalences of secret keys. In [4], the authors noted that they expected attacks on SIDH to generalise naturally to G2SIDH. One of the contributions of this paper is to demonstrate an adaptive attack on G2SIDH which is similar, but not the same as the Galbraith–Petit–Shani–Ti (GPST) attack on SIDH [6] since a straightforward adaptation thereof fails due to the difference in types of kernel subgroups for SIDH-isogenies and those in G2SIDH.

Adaptive chosen ciphertext attacks work by recovering the secret key from a decryption oracle by sending the oracle adaptively chosen inputs. Such an attack on isogeny-based cryptosystems was first introduced by Galbraith et al. in 2016 [6]. This attack only requires that a decryption oracle returns a single bit of information at a time. In fact, the decryption oracle can be viewed as a decisional Diffie–Hellman oracle, and the adaptive attack can be seen as the reduction of the computational Diffie–Hellman problem to the decisional Diffie–Hellman problem.

More practically, the use of a weaker oracle demonstrates the strength of the attack. The GPST attack meant that non-interactive key exchange implementations of SIDH are no longer secure and can only be safely used with CCA2-protections. As noted in [3], a different cryptosystem will necessitate modifications in the adaptive attack. This continues to hold true in the adaptive attack on G2SIDH.

The authors of [4] claimed that an adaptive attack which can break a static-key implementation of G2SIDH should exist. The implications of the existence of such an attack on G2SIDH would be the same as the GPST attack had on SIDH. Namely the reduction of the computational Diffie–Hellman problem to the decisional Diffie–Hellman problem, and that static keys are insecure without CCA2-protections. However, such an attack is not found in the state-of-the-art.

The main difference between our adaptive attack and the SIDH attack lies in the number of secret scalars and the number of kernel generators associated with each cryptosystem. This requires a thorough analysis of the keyspace.

Contributions. In this paper we present the two results:

- Use of symplectic bases enabling a classification of the isogeny kernel subgroups appearing in the genus-2 SIDH protocol. This allows us to generate secret keys without needing to solve cumbersome linear modular equations. Moreover, we propose a simplified version of secret selection that allows for the uniform selection of keys from a restricted (but large enough) keyspace. This was not addressed in the original paper [4]. Furthermore, the classification provides a framework for the G2SIDH attack to be carried out.
- An adaptive attack on G2SIDH that recovers the secret kernel when provided with an oracle that returns a single bit of information. This attack will be presented with the assumption that the users are using a symplectic basis. However, we will also show how this attack can be extended to users using an arbitrary basis by recovering equivalent keys in a symplectic basis. Finally, this adaptive attack is able to bypass simple countermeasures such as Weil pairing and order checking.

  The only countermeasure that we are aware of is to implement CCA2-protections such as the Fujisaki–Okamoto transformation [5].

Outline. We first give an introduction to principally polarised supersingular and superspecial abelian surfaces and G2SIDH in Sect. 1. In Section 2, we analyze the G2SIDH keyspace and suggest a slight restriction thereof to allow for easier uniform sampling. The adaptive attack is then presented in Sect. 3 where we first sketch an algorithm to determine the type of secret subgroup Alice is using, and then give a detailed description of the strategy for recovering secret keys.

1   Preliminaries

Traditionally, isogeny-based cryptography considers isogenies between (certain types) of elliptic curves. Elliptic curves are abelian varieties of dimension one which are principally polarised, though the polarisation is not usually of concern when cryptography is instantiated with elliptic curves. It is thus natural to consider generalising isogeny-based cryptography by broadening the scope to isogenies between principally polarised abelian varieties of higher dimensions. In particular, G2SIDH is a protocol which adapts SIDH to using principally polarised abelian surfaces.

In this section, we will first give a brief introduction to PPSSAS following [8], and isogeny-based cryptography using principally polarised abelian varieties of dimension two instead of elliptic curves when describing G2SIDH as in [4].

1.1   PPSSAS

Let p and ℓ be distinct primes, let n be a positive integer. Further, let A be an abelian surface defined over some finite field $\mathbb{F}_q$ of characteristic p, i.e. an abelian variety of dimension two. Then an *isogeny* is a homomorphism between two abelian surfaces which is surjective and has a finite kernel.

In order to obtain a higher-dimensional analogue of an elliptic curve, we need to consider *principally polarised abelian surfaces* (PPAS). A *polarisation* of A is an isogeny $\lambda : A \rightarrow A^\vee$, where $A^\vee$ is the dual variety of A, derived from some ample divisor of A. This polarisation is called *principal* if the isogeny is an isomorphism of varieties. If a principally polarised abelian surface $A/\mathbb{F}_q$ is isogenous to a product of supersingular elliptic curves over $\mathbb{F}_q$, we consider A to be *supersingular*. If A is isomorphic to a product of supersingular elliptic curves, we call A a principally polarised *superspecial* abelian surface (PPSSAS).

As shown in [4, Thm. 1], any PPSSAS A defined over $\overline{\mathbb{F}}_p$ is either isomorphic to the Jacobian of a smooth hyperelliptic curve of genus two, or to the product of two elliptic curves. This implies that A can be explicitly represented either by the equation $y^2 = f(x)$ for some polynomial $f \in \overline{\mathbb{F}}_p[x]$ of degree 5 or 6 representing a genus-2 curve, or as the product of two elliptic curves defined by the equations $y^2 = g(x)$ and $y^2 = h(x)$ for some degree-3 polynomials g and h. We represent the $\mathbb{F}_q$-isomorphism class of some PPSSAS A in the genus-2 setting by any valid isomorphism invariant.

As with elliptic curves, there exists a non-degenerate, alternating pairing on any abelian surface $A/\mathbb{F}_q$, the *Weil pairing*

$$e_{\ell^n} : A[\ell^n](\overline{\mathbb{F}}_q) \times A^\vee[\ell^n](\overline{\mathbb{F}}_q) \rightarrow \boldsymbol{\mu}_{\ell^n}$$

where $A[\ell^n](\overline{\mathbb{F}}_q)$ denotes the ℓ^n-torsion group of A and $\boldsymbol{\mu}_{\ell^n}$ denotes the group of ℓ^n-th roots of unity. If A is a PPAS, we can use the isomorphism $A \simeq A^\vee$ to obtain the pairing $e_{\ell^n} : A[\ell^n](\overline{\mathbb{F}}_q)^2 \rightarrow \boldsymbol{\mu}_{\ell^n}$. This pairing allows us to examine the correspondence between subgroups and isogenies of abelian surfaces which preserve the principal polarisation.

Definition 1 (Maximal ℓ^n-isotropic subgroup). *Let A be an abelian variety and K a proper subgroup of $A[\ell^n]$. Then we call G a maximal ℓ^n-isotropic subgroup if*

(i) the ℓ^n-Weil pairing (on $A[\ell^n]$) restricts trivially to G, and
(ii) G is a maximal subgroup with respect to Property (i).

As shown by Flynn and Ti, principal polarisations of PPAS are preserved under isogenies whose kernel is a maximal ℓ^n-isotropic subgroup, hence any maximal ℓ^n-isotropic subgroup of A defines an isogeny between PPAS.

Remark 1. An isogeny $\phi : A \rightarrow A'$ defined by an ℓ^n-isotropic subgroup G can be represented as a sequence $\phi_1, \ldots, \phi_n$ of (ℓ, ℓ)-isogenies between PPAS, each defined by a kernel generated by two order-ℓ elements. In this paper, we are only interested in non-backtracking isogenies, more precisely, we exclude sequences of isogenies that contain both an (ℓ, ℓ)-isogeny ϕ_i and its dual $\phi_j = \hat{\phi}_i$. This is equivalent to the condition $G \not\subset A[m]$ for any $m < \ell^n$.

1.2   G2SIDH

The G2SIDH key exchange scheme is a natural generalisation of SIDH to dimension two. The key exchange scheme requires the selection of a prime of the form $p = 2^{e_A} \cdot 3^{e_B} \cdot f - 1$ where $2^{e_A} \approx 3^{e_B}$ and f is a small cofactor not divisible by 2 or 3. A principally polarised superspecial abelian surface is then chosen to be the base abelian variety. This is achieved by first considering the hyperelliptic curve $H : y^2 = x^6 + 1$.

The curve H is a double cover of the elliptic curve $E : y^2 = x^3 + 1$, given by

$$\phi_1 : E \to H \qquad \text{and} \qquad \phi_2 : E \to H$$
$$(x, y) \mapsto (x^2, y), \qquad\qquad (x, y) \mapsto (x^{-2}, yx^{-3}).$$

These maps induce a $(2,2)$-isogeny from $E \times E$ to $J_H := \mathrm{Jac}(H)$ [2, p. 155].

Also, we have that E is supersingular and $\#E(\mathbb{F}_{p^2}) = (p+1)^2$ since $p \equiv 2 \pmod 3$ by computing the criterion in [10, Thm. V.4.1(a)]. Hence the Jacobian $J_H = \mathrm{Jac}(H)$ is indeed a PPSSAS. As a consequence $\#J_H(\mathbb{F}_{p^2}) = (p+1)^4$ using the theorem of Tate [11, Thm. 1]. Furthermore, we have that $J_H(\mathbb{F}_{p^2}) = J_H[2^{e_A}] \times J_H[3^{e_B}] \times J_H[f]$ as a group.

Then a short random walk is taken from J_H in the $(2,2)$-isogeny graph to obtain a random PPSSAS J. It follows from the above that we can fix torsion-bases $\langle P_1, P_2, P_3, P_4 \rangle = J[2^{e_A}]$ and $\langle R_1, R_2, R_3, R_4 \rangle = J[3^{e_B}]$ with all points P_i and R_i defined over $\mathbb{F}_{p^2}$.

To perform the key exchange, Alice chooses a secret maximal 2^{e_A}-isotropic subgroup G_A of $J[2^{e_A}]$ corresponding to an isogeny ϕ_A with kernel G_A and codomain J_A. This kernel can be determined by three generators (one of which may be $\mathcal{O}$), given as linear combinations of the P_i known only to Alice. In particular, each generator is determined by the four coefficients of the P_i and thus, Alice's secret can be described explicitly by a collection of secret scalars that is dependent on the basis[1]. She sends the tuple

$$\big(J_A, \phi_A(R_1), \phi_A(R_2), \phi_A(R_3), \phi_A(R_4) \big)$$

to Bob. He analogously completes his side of the computation so that Alice receives the tuple $(J_B, \phi_B(P_1), \phi_B(P_2), \phi_B(P_3), \phi_B(P_4))$. She can then use her linear combination of torsion points with the secret scalars as coefficients which generate the kernel of her secret isogeny ϕ_A to compute an isogeny from J_B using $\phi_B(P_i)$ as the basis instead of P_i. Denote the codomain of this isogeny by J_{AB}. Bob will complete his side of the protocol and obtain the abelian surface J_{BA}. By construction, J_{AB} and J_{BA} are isomorphic as principally polarised abelian surfaces. This allows for the use of isomorphism invariants as the shared key.

Flynn and Ti outline a procedure to select Alice's scalars $\alpha_{i,1}, \ldots, \alpha_{i,4} \in \mathbb{Z}/2^{e_A}\mathbb{Z}, 1 \leq i \leq 3$, such that the points

$$A_1 = \sum_{i=1}^{4} [\alpha_{1,i}] P_i, \quad A_2 = \sum_{i=1}^{4} [\alpha_{2,i}] P_i, \text{ and } A_3 = \sum_{i=1}^{4} [\alpha_{3,i}] P_i$$

---

[1] Throughout the remainder of this work, we will use different encodings of Alice's secret subgroup G_A, such as a description in terms of scalars or as an isogeny.

generate a maximal 2^{e_A}-Weil isotropic subgroup of $J[2^{e_A}]$ which can be used as her secret $G_A = \langle A_1, A_2, A_3 \rangle$. For details, specifically which congruences need to be satisfied to obtain a trivial Weil pairing on the A_i, we refer to [4]. We discuss a more efficient method of secret selection in Sect. 2.3 and also address random sampling from the keyspace, which was left as an open problem.

2   Keyspace

A secret key of Alice can be expressed as an isogeny of principally polarised abelian varieties $\phi_A : J \to J_A$. We have seen in Sect. 1.1 that this isogeny corresponds to a maximal 2^{e_A}-isotropic subgroup of J. In the same way, Bob's secret key corresponds to a maximal 3^{e_B}-isotropic subgroup of J. Moreover, we require that the isogeny is non-backtracking (cf. Remark 1). This allows us to identify the keyspace with the set

$$\mathcal{K}_\ell = \{ G \subset J \mid G \text{ maximal } \ell^n\text{-isotropic and } G \not\subset J[m] \text{ for any } m < \ell^n \},$$

for $\ell \in \{2, 3\}$ and $n = e_A$ or e_B, respectively. The groups in $\mathcal{K}_\ell$ can be specified as follows.

Proposition 1 [4, **Prop. 2**]. *Let $G \in \mathcal{K}_\ell$, then G is isomorphic to*

$$\mathcal{C}_{\ell^n} \times \mathcal{C}_{\ell^n} \quad or \quad \mathcal{C}_{\ell^k} \times \mathcal{C}_{\ell^{n-k}} \times \mathcal{C}_{\ell^k}$$

for some $1 \le k \le \lfloor \frac{n}{2} \rfloor$.

Note in particular that, in comparison to kernels usually considered for elliptic curve isogenies, the groups in $\mathcal{K}_\ell$ are not cyclic.

In this section we analyze the set $\mathcal{K}_\ell$ and show how to (almost) uniformly sample from the entire keyspace. Moreover, we introduce the subset $\mathcal{K}_\ell^{\mathrm{res}} \subset \mathcal{K}_\ell$. This subset is of the same order of magnitude as the entire keyspace, and allows for very simple and truly random sampling. An important step in the analysis is the normalisation of secret keys that allows us to classify the groups in $\mathcal{K}_\ell$ and define canonical generators. This is achieved by considering so-called symplectic bases of the ℓ^n-torsion of J.

2.1   Symplectic Basis

Let m be an integer not divisible by p. The m-torsion of J is a finitely generated group of rank 4, more precisely $J[m] \xrightarrow{\sim} (\mathbb{Z}/m\mathbb{Z})^4$.

Definition 2. *We say that a tuple (P_1, P_2, Q_1, Q_2) is a basis for $J[m]$ if it generates $J[m]$ as a group. We say that the basis (P_1, P_2, Q_1, Q_2) for $J[m]$ is symplectic with respect to the Weil pairing if*

$$e_m(P_i, Q_j) = \zeta^{\delta_{ij}}, \quad e_m(P_1, P_2) = e_m(Q_1, Q_2) = \zeta^0 = 1,$$

where ζ is a primitive m-th root of unity, $\delta_{ij} = 1$ if $i = j$ and $\delta_{ij} = 0$ otherwise.

Note that $e_m(Q_j, P_i) = \zeta^{-\delta_{ij}}$ for a symplectic basis (P_1, P_2, Q_1, Q_2) since the Weil-pairing is alternating.

There always exists a symplectic basis for $J[m]$ and indeed, given any basis for $J[m]$ it can be easily transformed into a symplectic one.

Finally, symplectic bases are preserved under isogenies as shown in the lemma to come. This allows us to use symplectic bases in G2SIDH.

Lemma 1. *Let* (P_1, P_2, Q_1, Q_2) *be a symplectic basis of* $J[m]$ *with respect to a primitive root* ζ, *and let* $\phi : J \to J'$ *be an isogeny with degree coprime to* m. *Then* $(\phi(P_1), \phi(P_2), \phi(Q_1), \phi(Q_2))$ *is a symplectic* $J'[m]$-*basis with respect to* $\zeta^{\deg(\phi)}$.

Proof. Observe that for all $i \neq j$ we have

$$e_m(\phi(P_i), \phi(Q_j)) = e_m(P_i, Q_j)^{\deg \phi} = 1 \text{ and } e_m(\phi(Q_i), \phi(P_j)) = e_m(P_j, Q_i)^{-\deg \phi} = 1.$$

Likewise, we have that $e_m(\phi(P_i), \phi(Q_i)) = e_m(P_i, Q_i)^{\deg \phi} = \zeta^{\deg \phi}$ for $i = 1, 2$. Finally, since $\langle \phi(P_1), \phi(P_2), \phi(Q_1), \phi(Q_2) \rangle = J'[m]$ and the torsion subgroup is of rank 4, we can conclude that $(\phi(P_1), \phi(P_2), \phi(Q_1), \phi(Q_2))$ is a symplectic basis of $J'[m]$. $\square$

2.2 Classification of Secret Keys

In this section we suggest a normalisation algorithm that produces canonical generators for each group $G \in \mathcal{K}_\ell$. For this purpose, we let

$$(P_1^*, P_2^*, P_3^*, P_4^*) := (P_1, P_2, Q_1, Q_2)$$

be a symplectic basis for $J[\ell^n]$.[2] Of course, one can adapt the procedure to general bases by performing a basis change to a symplectic basis before applying the algorithm.

Let $(\alpha_{1,1}, \ldots, \alpha_{3,4})$ be the secret scalars defining the group $G = \langle G_1, G_2, G_3 \rangle \in \mathcal{K}_\ell$, where

$$G_1 = \sum_{i=1}^4 [\alpha_{1,i}] P_i^*, \quad G_2 = \sum_{i=1}^4 [\alpha_{2,i}] P_i^*, \text{ and } G_3 = \sum_{i=1}^4 [\alpha_{3,i}] P_i^* .$$

By definition G is maximal ℓ^n-isotropic. This property imposes different conditions on the scalars $(\alpha_{1,1}, \ldots, \alpha_{3,4})$.

The idea for the normalisation is similar to Gaussian elimination. We set

$$A = \begin{pmatrix} \alpha_{1,1} & \alpha_{1,2} & \alpha_{1,3} & \alpha_{1,4} \\ \alpha_{2,1} & \alpha_{2,2} & \alpha_{2,3} & \alpha_{2,4} \\ \alpha_{3,1} & \alpha_{3,2} & \alpha_{3,3} & \alpha_{3,4} \end{pmatrix} \in M_{3,4}(\mathbb{Z}/\ell^n\mathbb{Z}).$$

Using elementary row operations and permuting columns if necessary, we can obtain a matrix of the form

$$A \sim_\sigma \begin{pmatrix} 1 & 0 & * & * \\ 0 & 1 & * & * \\ 0 & 0 & 0 & 0 \end{pmatrix} \quad \text{or} \quad A \sim_\sigma \begin{pmatrix} 1 & * & * & * \\ 0 & \ell^k & * & * \\ 0 & 0 & * & \ell^{n-k} \end{pmatrix} \quad (1)$$

---

[2] The notation $(P_1^*, P_2^*, P_3^*, P_4^*)$ is necessary because we are going to work with permutations of the basis elements. It is only used in this part of the notes.

if $G \simeq \mathcal{C}_{\ell^n} \times \mathcal{C}_{\ell^n}$ or $G \simeq \mathcal{C}_{\ell^n} \times \mathcal{C}_{\ell^{n-k}} \times \mathcal{C}_{\ell^k}$, respectively.

Here σ denotes the permutation $\sigma \in S_4$ corresponding to the permutation of the columns, and $*$ is meant as a placeholder respecting certain divisibility conditions. The first case is obtained from the second by setting $k = 0$, hence this will not appear explicitly in the discussion below.

Note that this normalisation procedure does not affect the corresponding group. More precisely, let

$$A' = \begin{pmatrix} \alpha'_{1,1} & \alpha'_{1,2} & \alpha'_{1,3} & \alpha'_{1,4} \\ \alpha'_{2,1} & \alpha'_{2,2} & \alpha'_{2,3} & \alpha'_{2,4} \\ \alpha'_{3,1} & \alpha'_{3,2} & \alpha'_{3,3} & \alpha'_{3,4} \end{pmatrix}$$

be obtained from A by applying elementary row operations and potentially swapping columns. Let $\sigma \in S_4$ denote the corresponding permutation of the columns. Then $G = \langle G'_1, G'_2, G'_3 \rangle$, where

$$G'_1 = \sum_{i=1}^{4} [\alpha'_{1,i}] P^*_{\sigma(i)}, \quad G'_2 = \sum_{i=1}^{4} [\alpha'_{2,i}] P^*_{\sigma(i)}, \quad G'_3 = \sum_{i=1}^{4} [\alpha'_{3,i}] P^*_{\sigma(i)}.$$

We only used the knowledge of the group structure of G to obtain a presentation as an upper triangular matrix as in (1). Additionally, we also know that the Weil pairing $e_{\ell^n}(G_i, G_j) = 1$ for all $i, j \in \{1, 2, 3\}$. Using this property, we can work out the relations between the non-zero entries of the matrices. The result is captured in the following proposition.

Proposition 2. *Let A be a matrix corresponding to a maximal ℓ^n-isotropic subgroup of the form $\mathcal{C}_{\ell^n} \times \mathcal{C}_{\ell^{n-k}} \times \mathcal{C}_{\ell^k}$ for some integer $0 \le k \le \lfloor \frac{n}{2} \rfloor$. Then there exist a permutation $\sigma \in D_8 = \langle (1234), (13) \rangle$ and scalars $a \in \{0, \ldots, \ell^n - 1\}$, $b \in \{0, \ldots, \ell^{n-k} - 1\}$, $c \in \{0, \ldots, \ell^{n-2k} - 1\}$, $d \in \{0, \ldots, \ell^k - 1\}$ such that*

$$A \sim_\sigma A' = \begin{pmatrix} 1 & d & a & b \\ 0 & \ell^k & s_\sigma \ell^k (b - cd) & \ell^k c \\ 0 & 0 & -s_\sigma \ell^{n-k} d & \ell^{n-k} \end{pmatrix} \in M_{3,4}(\mathbb{Z}/\ell^n\mathbb{Z}),$$

where $s_\sigma = \mathrm{sgn}(\sigma)$ denotes the sign of the permutation σ.

On the other hand, if A' is as above and $G' = \langle G'_1, G'_2, G'_3 \rangle$, where

$$G'_1 = \sum_{i=1}^{4} [\alpha'_{1,i}] P^*_{\sigma(i)}, \quad G'_2 = \sum_{i=1}^{4} [\alpha'_{2,i}] P^*_{\sigma(i)}, \quad G'_3 = \sum_{i=1}^{4} [\alpha'_{3,i}] P^*_{\sigma(i)}$$

for some $\sigma \in D_8$, then G' is maximal ℓ^n-isotropic.

Proof. Following the Gaussian elimination process one obtains a matrix A' of the form given in Eq. (1). Note that the rank-2 case is just the special case obtained by setting $k = 0$. Examining this process more closely , one sees that σ can be chosen to lie in the dihedral group $D_8 = \langle (1234), (13) \rangle$.[3]

Let us write

$$A' = \begin{pmatrix} 1 & d & a & b \\ 0 & \ell^k & \ell^k x & \ell^k c \\ 0 & 0 & \ell^{n-k} y & \ell^{n-k} \end{pmatrix}$$

---

[3] In the rank-2 case, we moreover have $\sigma \in V_4 = \langle (13), (24) \rangle \subset D_8$.

for some $a, b, c, d, x, y \in \{0, \ldots, \ell^n - 1\}$, now including the divisibility by ℓ-powers which was omitted in (1). First, note that after adding a multiple of the second line to the first line of A', we may assume that $d \in \{0, \ldots, \ell^k - 1\}$. Similarly, we can achieve $b \in \{0, \ldots, \ell^{n-k} - 1\}$ and $c \in \{0, \ldots, \ell^{n-2k} - 1\}$. It remains to show that x and y are determined by the scalars a, b, c, d. This is done using the Weil pairing. For the following computation, it is important to note that

$$e_{\ell^n}(P^*_{\sigma(1)}, P^*_{\sigma(3)}) = e_{\ell^n}(P^*_{\sigma(2)}, P^*_{\sigma(4)})^{s_\sigma} \tag{2}$$

for all $\sigma \in D_8$.

Let G'_1, G'_2, G'_3 be the generators corresponding to the matrix A'. Then

$$e_{\ell^n}(G'_1, G'_2) = e_{\ell^n}(P^*_{\sigma(1)} + [d]P^*_{\sigma(2)} + [a]P^*_{\sigma(3)} + [b]P^*_{\sigma(4)}, \ell^k \cdot (P^*_{\sigma(2)} + [x]P^*_{\sigma(3)} + [c]P^*_{\sigma(4)}))$$

$$= e_{\ell^n}(P^*_{\sigma(1)}, P^*_{\sigma(3)})^{\ell^k x} \cdot e_{\ell^n}(P^*_{\sigma(2)}, P^*_{\sigma(4)})^{\ell^k (cd-b)}.$$

Using Property (2), we obtain the condition $\ell^k x = s_\sigma \ell^k (b - cd)$. Computing the Weil pairing on G'_2 and G'_3 shows that $\ell^{n-k} y = -s_\sigma \ell^{n-k} d$.

For the other direction, it remains to show that the group $G' = \langle G'_1, G'_2, G'_3 \rangle$ is maximal ℓ^n-isotropic. This can be done by verifying that G' meets the criteria from Definition 1.   □

The following consequence of the proposition will be helpful for determining the type of a group in the adaptive attack (cf. Sect. 3.3).

Corollary 1. *Let $(P^*_1, P^*_2, P^*_3, P^*_4)$ be a symplectic basis for $J[\ell^n]$ and let $G \subset J$ be an isotropic group isomorphic to $\mathcal{C}_{\ell^n} \times \mathcal{C}_{\ell^{n-k}} \times \mathcal{C}_{\ell^k}$. Assume that $G_1 = P^*_{\sigma(1)} + [d]P^*_{\sigma(2)} + [a]P^*_{\sigma(3)} + [b]P^*_{\sigma(4)} \in G$ for some permutation $\sigma \in D_8$ and scalars a, b, d. Then*

$$\mathcal{C}_{\ell^k} \times \mathcal{C}_{\ell^k} \simeq \ell^{n-k} \left\langle P^*_{\sigma(2)} + [s_\sigma \cdot b]P^*_{\sigma(3)}, \; [-s_\sigma \cdot d]P^*_{\sigma(3)} + P^*_{\sigma(4)} \right\rangle \subset G.$$

Proposition 2 shows that each group $G \in \mathcal{K}_\ell$ may be represented by a tuple of the form (a, b, c, d, k, σ), where $a \in \{0, \ldots, \ell^n - 1\}$, $b \in \{0, \ldots, \ell^{n-k} - 1\}$, $c \in \{0, \ldots, \ell^{n-2k}\}$, $d \in \{0, \ldots, \ell^k - 1\}$, $0 \le k \le \lfloor \frac{n}{2} \rfloor$ and $\sigma \in D_8$.

Clearly, such a representation is not unique in most cases. However, it is possible to make the elimination algorithm deterministic by imposing conditions on the choice of the permutation $\sigma \in D_8$. In that way, it is possible to obtain canonical representatives of the form (a, b, c, d, k, σ), where each $\sigma \neq \mathrm{id}$ comes with some additional constraints on the parameters a, b, c, d.

Definition 3 (Classification). *Let $(P^*_1, P^*_2, P^*_3, P^*_4)$ be a symplectic basis for $J[\ell^n]$ and denote by $\mathbf{P}^*$ the column vector $\begin{pmatrix} P^*_1 & P^*_2 & P^*_3 & P^*_4 \end{pmatrix}^T$. For a group $G = \langle G_1, G_2 \rangle \simeq \mathcal{C}_{\ell^n} \times \mathcal{C}_{\ell^n}$ in $\mathcal{K}_\ell$, we say that G_1, G_2 are the canonical generators if one of the following is true for some $a, b, c \in \mathbb{Z}/\ell^n\mathbb{Z}$.*

2.1 $\begin{pmatrix} G_1 \\ G_2 \end{pmatrix} = \begin{pmatrix} 1 & 0 & a & b \\ 0 & 1 & b & c \end{pmatrix} \mathbf{P}^*.$

2.3 $\begin{pmatrix} G_1 \\ G_2 \end{pmatrix} = \begin{pmatrix} a & 0 & 1 & b \\ -b & 1 & 0 & c \end{pmatrix} \mathbf{P}^*,$
and $\ell \mid a, b.$

2.2 $\begin{pmatrix} G_1 \\ G_2 \end{pmatrix} = \begin{pmatrix} 1 & b & a & 0 \\ 0 & c & -b & 1 \end{pmatrix} \mathbf{P}^*,$
and $\ell \mid c.$

2.4 $\begin{pmatrix} G_1 \\ G_2 \end{pmatrix} = \begin{pmatrix} a & b & 1 & 0 \\ b & c & 0 & 1 \end{pmatrix} \mathbf{P}^*,$
and $\ell \mid a, b, c.$

For a group $G = \langle G_1, G_2, G_3 \rangle \simeq \mathcal{C}_{\ell^n} \times \mathcal{C}_{\ell^{n-k}} \times \mathcal{C}_{\ell^k}$ with $0 < k < \frac{n}{2}$ in $\mathcal{K}_\ell$, we say that G_1, G_2, G_3 are the canonical generators *if one of the following is true for some $a \in \{0, \ldots, \ell^n - 1\}$, $b \in \{0, \ldots, \ell^{n-k} - 1\}$, $c \in \{0, \ldots, \ell^{n-2k} - 1\}$, $d \in \{0, \ldots, \ell^k - 1\}$.*

3.1 $\begin{pmatrix} G_1 \\ G_2 \\ G_3 \end{pmatrix} = \begin{pmatrix} 1 & d & a & b \\ 0 & \ell^k & \ell^k(b - cd) & \ell^k c \\ 0 & 0 & -\ell^{n-k}d & \ell^{n-k} \end{pmatrix} \mathbf{P}^*.$

3.5 $\begin{pmatrix} G_1 \\ G_2 \\ G_3 \end{pmatrix} = \begin{pmatrix} d & 1 & b & a \\ \ell^k & 0 & \ell^k c & \ell^k(b - cd) \\ 0 & 0 & \ell^{n-k} & -\ell^{n-k}d \end{pmatrix} \mathbf{P}^*,$
and $\ell \mid b, d.$

3.2 $\begin{pmatrix} G_1 \\ G_2 \\ G_3 \end{pmatrix} = \begin{pmatrix} 1 & b & a & d \\ 0 & \ell^k c & -\ell^k(b - cd) & \ell^k \\ 0 & \ell^{n-k} & \ell^{n-k}d & 0 \end{pmatrix} \mathbf{P}^*,$
and $\ell \mid c.$

3.6 $\begin{pmatrix} G_1 \\ G_2 \\ G_3 \end{pmatrix} = \begin{pmatrix} b & 1 & d & a \\ \ell^k c & 0 & \ell^k & -\ell^k(b - cd) \\ \ell^{n-k} & 0 & 0 & \ell^{n-k}d \end{pmatrix} \mathbf{P}^*,$
and $\ell \mid b, c, d.$

3.3 $\begin{pmatrix} G_1 \\ G_2 \\ G_3 \end{pmatrix} = \begin{pmatrix} a & d & 1 & b \\ -\ell^k(b - cd) & \ell^k & 0 & \ell^k c \\ \ell^{n-k}d & 0 & 0 & \ell^{n-k} \end{pmatrix} \mathbf{P}^*,$
and $\ell \mid a.$

3.7 $\begin{pmatrix} G_1 \\ G_2 \\ G_3 \end{pmatrix} = \begin{pmatrix} d & a & b & 1 \\ \ell^k & -\ell^k(b - cd) & \ell^k c & 0 \\ 0 & \ell^{n-k}d & \ell^{n-k} & 0 \end{pmatrix} \mathbf{P}^*,$
and $\ell \mid a, b, d.$

3.4 $\begin{pmatrix} G_1 \\ G_2 \\ G_3 \end{pmatrix} = \begin{pmatrix} a & b & 1 & d \\ \ell^k(b - cd) & \ell^k c & 0 & \ell^k \\ -\ell^{n-k}d & \ell^{n-k} & 0 & 0 \end{pmatrix} \mathbf{P}^*,$
and $\ell \mid a, c.$

3.8 $\begin{pmatrix} G_1 \\ G_2 \\ G_3 \end{pmatrix} = \begin{pmatrix} b & a & d & 1 \\ \ell^k c & \ell^k(b - cd) & \ell^k & 0 \\ \ell^{n-k} & -\ell^{n-k}d & 0 & 0 \end{pmatrix} \mathbf{P}^*,$
and $\ell \mid a, b, c, d.$

For a group $G = \langle G_1, G_2, G_3 \rangle \simeq \mathcal{C}_{\ell^n} \times \mathcal{C}_{\ell^k} \times \mathcal{C}_{\ell^k}$ with $k = \frac{n}{2}$ in $\mathcal{K}_\ell$, we say that G_1, G_2, G_3 are the canonical generators *if one of the following is true for some $a \in \{0, \ldots, \ell^n - 1\}$, $b, d \in \{0, \ldots, \ell^k - 1\}$.*

4.1 $\begin{pmatrix} G_1 \\ G_2 \\ G_3 \end{pmatrix} = \begin{pmatrix} 1 & d & a & b \\ 0 & \ell^k & \ell^k b & 0 \\ 0 & 0 & -\ell^k d & \ell^k \end{pmatrix} \mathbf{P}^*.$

4.3 $\begin{pmatrix} G_1 \\ G_2 \\ G_3 \end{pmatrix} = \begin{pmatrix} d & 1 & b & a \\ \ell^k & 0 & 0 & \ell^k b \\ 0 & 0 & \ell^k & -\ell^k d \end{pmatrix} \mathbf{P}^*,$
and $\ell \mid b, d.$

4.2 $\begin{pmatrix} G_1 \\ G_2 \\ G_3 \end{pmatrix} = \begin{pmatrix} a & d & 1 & b \\ -\ell^k b & \ell^k & 0 & 0 \\ \ell^k d & 0 & 0 & \ell^k \end{pmatrix} \mathbf{P}^*,$
and $\ell \mid a.$

4.4 $\begin{pmatrix} G_1 \\ G_2 \\ G_3 \end{pmatrix} = \begin{pmatrix} d & a & b & 1 \\ \ell^k & -\ell^k b & 0 & 0 \\ 0 & \ell^k d & \ell^k & 0 \end{pmatrix} \mathbf{P}^*,$
and $\ell \mid a, b, d.$

Moreover we say that a group $G \in \mathcal{K}_\ell$ is of Type 2.i, 3.i *or* 4.i *for $i \in \{1, \ldots, 8\}$ depending on which of the cases above applies.*

Table 1. Classification of maximal ℓ^n-isotropic subgroups.

	Type	σ	Condition on (a, b, c, d)	Cardinality
$k = 0$	2.1	id	-	ℓ^{3n}
	2.2	(24)	$\ell \mid c$	ℓ^{3n-1}
	2.3	(13)	$\ell \mid a, b$	ℓ^{3n-2}
	2.4	$(13)(24)$	$\ell \mid a, b, c$	ℓ^{3n-3}
$0 < k < \frac{n}{2}$	3.1	id	-	ℓ^{3n-2k}
	3.2	(24)	$\ell \mid c$	$\ell^{3n-2k-1}$
	3.3	(13)	$\ell \mid a$	$\ell^{3n-2k-1}$
	3.4	$(13)(24)$	$\ell \mid a, c$	$\ell^{3n-2k-2}$
	3.5	$(12)(34)$	$\ell \mid b, d$	$\ell^{3n-2k-2}$
	3.6	(1234)	$\ell \mid b, c, d$	$\ell^{3n-2k-3}$
	3.7	(1432)	$\ell \mid a, b, d$	$\ell^{3n-2k-3}$
	3.8	$(14)(23)$	$\ell \mid a, b, c, d$	$\ell^{3n-2k-4}$
$2k = n$	4.1	id	-	ℓ^{2n}
	4.2	(13)	$\ell \mid a$	ℓ^{2n-1}
	4.3	$(12)(34)$	$\ell \mid b, d$	ℓ^{2n-2}
	4.4	(1432)	$\ell \mid a, b, d$	ℓ^{2n-3}

Table 1 summarizes the classification of the groups in $\mathcal{K}_\ell$ defined above. The classification of the groups in $\mathcal{K}_\ell$ also allows us to determine the cardinality of $\mathcal{K}_\ell$. The number of groups of a given type can be directly read off from the description and is provided in the last column of Table 1. Adding up the numbers for Types $2.1, 2.2, 2.3, 2.4$, we obtain $\ell^{3n-3}(\ell^2+1)(\ell+1)$, the number of maximal isotropic subgroups of rank 2. Adding up the numbers for Types 3.1–3.8, we find that there are $\ell^{3n-2k-4}(\ell^2+1)(\ell+1)^2$ groups isomorphic to $\mathcal{C}_{\ell^n} \times \mathcal{C}_{\ell^{n-k}} \times \mathcal{C}_{\ell^k}$, where $0 < k < \frac{n}{2}$. Finally the sum over the numbers for Types 4.1–4.4 is equal to $\ell^{2n-3}(\ell^2+1)(\ell+1)$, the number of groups isomorphic to $\mathcal{C}_{\ell^n} \times \mathcal{C}_{\ell^k} \times \mathcal{C}_{\ell^k}$, where $2k = n$. These cardinalities coincide with the numbers provided in [4, Prop. 3].

2.3 New Uniform Sampling from the Keyspace

In the previous section we described a classification of the groups in $\mathcal{K}_\ell$. This can be used to sample uniformly from the entire keyspace. Here, we introduce a slightly restricted keyspace $\mathcal{K}_\ell^{\text{res}}$ that allows a particularly easy way of sampling from the keyspace which chooses elements uniformly at random. For the convenience of the reader, Fig. 1 provides an explicit description of the G2SIDH protocol in this setting.

For some fixed symplectic basis (P_1, P_2, Q_1, Q_2) of $J[\ell^n]$, we define the restricted keyspace as

$$\mathcal{K}_\ell^{\text{res}} = \{\langle P_1 + [a]Q_1 + [b]Q_2, \ P_2 + [b]Q_1 + [c]Q_2\rangle \mid a, b, c \in \mathbb{Z}/\ell^n\mathbb{Z}\}.$$

Setup

- prime $p = 2^{e_A} \cdot 3^{e_B} \cdot f - 1$
- superspecial hyperelliptic curve $H/\mathbb{F}_{p^2}$ with Jacobian J
- symplectic bases $(P_{A,1}, P_{A,2}, Q_{A,1}, Q_{A,2})$ for $J[2^{e_A}]$ and $(P_{B,1}, P_{B,2}, Q_{B,1}, Q_{B,2})$ for $J[3^{e_B}]$

Key Generation

- $a_1, a_2, a_3 \xleftarrow{\$} \{0, \ldots, 2^{e_A} - 1\}$ $J_A, \phi_A(P_{B,i}), \phi_A(Q_{B,i}), i \in \{1,2\}$ $b_1, b_2, b_3 \xleftarrow{\$} \{0, \ldots, 3^{e_B} - 1\}$
- $A_1 = P_{A,1} + [a_1]Q_{A,1} + [a_2]Q_{A,2}$ $\xrightarrow{\hspace{3cm}}$ $B_1 = P_{B,1} + [b_1]Q_{B,1} + [b_2]Q_{B,2}$

   $A_2 = P_{A,2} + [a_2]Q_{A,1} + [a_3]Q_{A,2}$ $B_2 = P_{B,2} + [b_2]Q_{B,1} + [b_3]Q_{B,2}$

- $\phi_A : J \to J_A = J/\langle A_1, A_2 \rangle$ $J_B, \phi_B(P_{A,i}), \phi_B(Q_{A,i}), i \in \{1,2\}$ $\phi_B : J \to J_B = J/\langle B_1, B_2 \rangle$

                                         $\xleftarrow{\hspace{3cm}}$

Shared Key

$$J_B/\langle \phi_B(A_1), \phi_B(A_2) \rangle = \quad J/\langle A_1, A_2, B_1, B_2 \rangle \quad = J_A/\langle \phi_A(B_1), \phi_A(B_2) \rangle$$

Fig. 1. G2SIDH with restricted keyspace $\mathcal{K}_\ell^{res}$.

In the terminology of the previous section this means that $\mathcal{K}_\ell^{res}$ is the set of all groups of Type 2.1 (cf. Definition 3 and Table 1).

First of all, note that every secret key $sk \in \mathcal{K}_\ell^{res}$ is indeed a maximal ℓ^n-isotropic subgroup as per Proposition 2. A very beneficial feature of the new keyspace is that every secret key $sk \in \mathcal{K}_\ell^{res}$ is uniquely encoded by a tuple $(a, b, c) \in (\mathbb{Z}/\ell^n\mathbb{Z})^3$. This means that a secret key can be sampled by choosing three random integers $a, b, c \in \mathbb{Z}/\ell^n\mathbb{Z}$.

Moreover, the restricted keyspace still has the same order of magnitude as the original keyspace. To see this recall the number of maximal ℓ^n-isotropic subgroups from [4, Thm. 2]:

$$\#\mathcal{K}_\ell = \ell^{2n-3}(\ell^2 + 1)(\ell + 1)\left(\ell^n + \frac{\ell^{n-1} - 1}{\ell - 1}\right) = \ell^{3n} \cdot \underbrace{\frac{(\ell^2 + 1)(\ell + 1)}{\ell^3}\left(1 + \frac{\ell^{n-1} - 1}{\ell^n(\ell - 1)}\right)}_{\alpha_\ell}.$$

Evaluating the expression on the right, one finds $\alpha_2 \approx \frac{45}{16}$ and $\alpha_3 \approx \frac{140}{81}$ for large n.

We would like to point out that a similar restriction of the keyspace is made in the SIDH protocol for elliptic curves. While the space of all ℓ^n-isogenies from a fixed starting curve is of size $(\ell + 1)\ell^{n-1}$, the keyspace used in the optimised implementation is only of size ℓ^n.

Remark 2. We can also obtain uniform sampling on the entire keyspace $\mathcal{K}_\ell$ by taking into consideration the canonical generators and the distribution of the possible subgroup structures in the keyspace.

Suppose $\ell = 2$. The formulae of [4, Thm. 2] and [4, Prop. 3] then show that the proportion of rank-2 subgroups among all admissible subgroups is

$$\frac{2^n}{2^n + 2^{n-1} - 1} \approx \frac{2}{3}$$

if n is large.

Performing the same computation on rank-3 subgroups, for large n we have

$$\frac{3 \cdot 2^{n-2k}}{3 \cdot 2^n - 2} \approx \frac{1}{2^{2k}},$$

where k is the parameter determining the subgroup structure.

Therefore, we obtain a method to almost uniformly sample the keyspace. First, $0 \leq k \leq N$ is determined for some bound $N \leq \lfloor \frac{n}{2} \rfloor$, weighted according to the proportion stated above. Next, one has to make a choice of canonical generators based on the distribution of the different types presented in Table 1. Finally, uniformly selecting the required scalars will ensure the near-uniform sampling from the keyspace.

3   Adaptive Attack on G2SIDH

The attack as presented in this section is able to recover Alice's secret kernel when she uses a static secret kernel which is maximal 2^n-isotropic. In particular, we will describe a method that can recover secret kernels of various group structures. In the exposition to come, the scalars θ_i are used to ensure Weil pairing countermeasures are unable to detect our attack. This method is employed in tandem with the symplectic transformations that are primarily used to isolate the bit under attack. The adaptive attack on G2SIDH is similar to adaptive attacks on SIDH [6], 2-SIDH [3], and Jao–Urbanik's variant [1]. It interacts with an oracle by sending points on some starting variety that correspond to the auxiliary points provided in the protocol. The oracle is "weak" in the sense that only one bit is returned per query. By sending malformed points, the adaptive attack is able to recover scalars that determine the secret kernels.

The first step of the adaptive attack is to recover the kernel structure used by Alice and is presented in Sect. 3.3. The next step then recovers the scalars associated with the kernel structure recovered in the first step and is divided into two parts depending on the rank of the kernel structure (Sect. 3.4 for rank 2 and Sect. 3.5 for rank 3). In each case, we will recover the first bit of the secret scalars before iteratively recovering the remaining bits.

In the following, we will assume that all users of the G2SIDH protocol (or at least Alice, the honest party whose key we want to recover) are using a symplectic basis as described in Sect. 2.1. This attack will still work on users not using a symplectic basis as one can perform a linear transformation from an arbitrary torsion basis into a symplectic basis. For clarity, we present the attack directly on a symplectic torsion basis here and describe the extension to arbitrary bases in Sect. 3.6.

Notations and Setup

Let us fix some notation. Let J be the starting variety, and let J_A be the codomain of the secret isogeny with kernel $\langle A_1, A_2, A_3 \rangle$, where the orders of the points are 2^n, 2^{n-k}, 2^k respectively.

Furthermore, suppose $\langle P_1, P_2, Q_1, Q_2 \rangle = J[2^n]$ is a symplectic basis such that $e_{2^n}(P_i, Q_j) = \zeta^{\delta_{ij}}$, where ζ is a primitive 2^n-th root of unity, and $e_{2^n}(P_1, P_2) = e_{2^n}(Q_1, Q_2) = \zeta^0 = 1$.

We write $\phi_B : J \rightarrow J_B$ for Bob's isogeny. Then $(\phi_B(P_1), \phi_B(P_2), \phi_B(Q_1), \phi_B(Q_2))$ is a symplectic basis for $J_B[2^n]$ as per Proposition 1. To ease notation, we set

$$R_1 = \phi_B(P_1), \ R_2 = \phi_B(P_2), \ S_1 = \phi_B(Q_1), \ S_2 = \phi_B(Q_2).$$

We will assume that Alice is the party under attack, and that she is using secret scalars $\alpha_{1,1}, \ldots, \alpha_{3,4}$ which define a maximal 2^n-isotropic subgroup of $J[2^n]$. We can write any of the secret scalars, say a, as $a = \sum_{i=0}^{n-1} 2^i a_i$ for bits $a_i \in \{0, 1\}$. For $i = 1, \ldots, n-1$, let us then denote the partial key consisting of the first i bits of a as $K_i^a = \sum_{j=0}^{i-1} 2^j a_j$ so that $a = K_i^a + 2^i a_i + 2^{i+1} a'$ for some a'. This convention will help us keep track of the known information at each step of the attack below.

3.1   Attack Model and Oracle

The attack we present in the following assumes that an honest Alice uses a static key which a malicious Bob is trying to learn through repeatedly providing malformed torsion point information during the G2SIDH protocol execution. Bob's overall goal is to recover Alice's full key or a valid tuple of scalars forming an equivalent key. While this means we explicitly work with elements of $J[2^n]$ and focus on recovering a kernel corresponding to a sequence of Richelot isogenies, this strategy can be translated to recover a key for more general small primes ℓ and therefore ℓ^{e_ℓ}-torsions of J due to Proposition 2. The resulting attack on different ℓ may not return a bit of information with every single query, but may require a small number of additional queries to determine a bit of information. The attack can still be carried out successfully.

It is customary in similar attacks to consider two distinct oracles which can model the information obtained by the attacker which differ in their inherent strength. One which, on input of a variety J and four points $R'_1, \ldots, R'_4 \in J[2^n]$, provides the isomorphism invariants of the codomain variety J/G_A of the isogeny corresponding to the kernel subgroup $G_A = \langle \sum_{i=1}^{4}[\alpha_{1,i}]R'_i, \sum_{i=1}^{4}[\alpha_{2,i}]R'_i, \sum_{i=1}^{4}[\alpha_{3,i}]R'_i \rangle$. The second, less powerful oracle is the one we will utilise to model our attack in the following, as is done in [6].

Our oracle, which replaces Alice in an honest execution of the protocol,

$$O\left(J, J', (R'_1, R'_2, R'_3, R'_4)\right)$$

returns 1 whenever the subgroup $G_A = \langle \sum_{i=1}^{4}[\alpha_{1,i}]R'_i, \sum_{i=1}^{4}[\alpha_{2,i}]R'_i, \sum_{i=1}^{4}[\alpha_{3,i}]R'_i \rangle$ is isotropic and the variety J/G_A has the same isomorphism invariants as the second input variety J'. Otherwise, it returns 0. Moreover we assume that the oracle checks whether an input is valid and returns $\perp$ if this is not the case. Here, we say that a tuple $(J, J', (R'_1, R'_2, S'_1, S'_2))$ is a *valid* input if (R'_1, R'_2, S'_1, S'_2) is a symplectic basis for $J[2^n]$ and $e_{2^n}(R'_i, S'_i) = e_{2^n}(P_i, Q_i)^{3^{e_B}}$. Note that an honest run of the protocol generates the valid input $(J_B, J_{AB}, (R_1, R_2, S_1, S_2))$.

For ease of reading, we will represent malformed points to be queried as linear combinations of R_1, R_2, S_1, S_2 and laid out in a 4×4 matrix. That is, for any points R'_1, R'_2, S'_1, S'_2 that the adversary sends to the oracle, we can write

$$\begin{pmatrix} R'_1 \\ R'_2 \\ S'_1 \\ S'_2 \end{pmatrix} = \begin{pmatrix} a_1 & a_2 & a_3 & a_4 \\ b_1 & b_2 & b_3 & b_4 \\ c_1 & c_2 & c_3 & c_4 \\ d_1 & d_2 & d_3 & d_4 \end{pmatrix} \begin{pmatrix} R_1 \\ R_2 \\ S_1 \\ S_2 \end{pmatrix},$$

and we will represent the queries R'_1, R'_2, S'_1, S'_2 by the 4×4 matrix.

3.2   Symplectic Transformations

When constructing malformed torsion points for the oracle queries, we need to make sure that the input is still valid. In our setting, an oracle query

$$O\left(J_B, J_{AB}, (R'_1, R'_2, S'_1, S'_2)\right)$$

is valid if and only if (R'_1, R'_2, S'_1, S'_2) is a symplectic basis and $e_{2^n}(R'_i, S'_j) = e_{2^n}(R_i, S_j)$ for $i, j \in \{1, 2\}$.

A change of basis $t : (R'_1, R'_2, S'_1, S'_2) \leftarrow (R_1, R_2, S_1, S_2)$ with this property is called a *symplectic transformation*. The matrices corresponding to symplectic transformations are called *symplectic matrices*. We are going to write M_t for the matrix corresponding to the transformation t.

Using symplectic transformations has yet another advantage. Let $G = \langle G_1, G_2, G_3 \rangle \subset J$ be maximal 2^n-isotropic and $t : J[2^n] \to J[2^n]$ a symplectic transformation, then $G' = \langle t(G_1), t(G_2), t(G_3) \rangle$ is maximal 2^n-isotropic as well. Note that this is not true for general isomorphisms of $J[2^n]$.

One can easily verify that the following matrices are symplectic. We will use different combinations of these to construct the transformations for the oracle queries.

$$M_{t_0} = \begin{pmatrix} 1 & 0 & 0 & 0 \\ 0 & 1 & 0 & 0 \\ 1 & 0 & 1 & 0 \\ 0 & 0 & 0 & 1 \end{pmatrix}, \quad M_{t_1} = \begin{pmatrix} 1 & 0 & 1 & 0 \\ 0 & 1 & 0 & 0 \\ 0 & 0 & 1 & 0 \\ 0 & 0 & 0 & 1 \end{pmatrix}, \quad M_{t_2} = \begin{pmatrix} 1 & 0 & 0 & 0 \\ 0 & 1 & 0 & 0 \\ 0 & 0 & 1 & 0 \\ 0 & 1 & 0 & 1 \end{pmatrix},$$

$$M_{t_3} = \begin{pmatrix} 1 & 0 & 0 & 0 \\ 0 & 1 & 0 & 1 \\ 0 & 0 & 1 & 0 \\ 0 & 0 & 0 & 1 \end{pmatrix}, \quad M_{t_4} = \begin{pmatrix} 1 & 0 & 0 & 0 \\ 0 & 1 & 0 & 0 \\ 0 & 1 & 1 & 0 \\ 1 & 0 & 0 & 1 \end{pmatrix}, \quad M_{t_5} = \begin{pmatrix} 1 & 0 & 0 & 1 \\ 0 & 1 & 1 & 0 \\ 0 & 0 & 1 & 0 \\ 0 & 0 & 0 & 1 \end{pmatrix}.$$

Proposition 3. *The following matrices are symplectic for any values* x, x_0, x_1, x_2, x_3, x_4, x_5 *and invertible elements* $\theta_1, \theta_2 \in \mathbb{Z}/2^n\mathbb{Z}$.

$$M_1 = \begin{pmatrix} \theta_1 & \theta_2 x & 0 & 0 \\ 0 & \theta_2 & 0 & 0 \\ 0 & 0 & \theta_1^{-1} & 0 \\ 0 & 0 & -\theta_1^{-1}x & \theta_2^{-1} \end{pmatrix} \quad and \quad M_2 = \begin{pmatrix} 1 & 0 & x_1 & x_5 \\ 0 & 1 & x_5 & x_3 \\ 0 & 0 & 1 & 0 \\ 0 & 0 & 0 & 1 \end{pmatrix},$$

$$M_3 = \begin{pmatrix} \theta_1(1+x_0x_1-x_4x_5(1+x_0x_1)) & \theta_2x_2x_5 & \theta_1^{-1}x_1(1+x_4x_5) & \theta_2^{-1}x_5 \\ \theta_1x_0x_5 & \theta_2(1+x_2x_3+x_4x_5(1+x_2x_3)) & \theta_1^{-1}x_5 & \theta_2^{-1}x_3(1+x_4x_5) \\ \theta_1x_0 & \theta_2x_4(1+x_2x_3) & \theta_1^{-1} & \theta_2^{-1}x_3x_4 \\ \theta_1x_4(1+x_0x_1) & \theta_2x_2 & \theta_1^{-1}x_1x_4 & \theta_2^{-1} \end{pmatrix}.$$

Proof. It is easy to check that M_1 is symplectic since the scalars satisfy $\theta_1\theta_1^{-1} = \theta_2\theta_2^{-1} = 1$. The matrix M_2 can be easily written in terms of the transformations t_i, namely $M_2 = M_{t_1}^{x_1} \cdot M_{t_3}^{x_3} \cdot M_{t_5}^{x_5}$. Finally, M_3 can be written as

$$M_3 = M_1 \cdot M_{t_0}^{x_0} \cdot M_{t_1}^{x_1} \cdot M_{t_2}^{x_2} \cdot M_{t_3}^{x_3} \cdot M_{t_4}^{x_4} \cdot M_{t_5}^{x_5}.$$

$\square$

All our queries to the oracle are obtained by combining the transformations in the proposition above. In order to choose a transformation, it is necessary to examine the effect of a transformation on a secret subgroup. To illustrate this, assume that Alice uses a group $\langle A_1, A_2, A_3 \rangle$ of Type 3.1. This means $A_1 = R_1+[d]R_2+[a]S_1+[b]S_2$, $A_2 = 2^k(R_2+[b-cd]S_1+[c]S_2)$ $A_3 = 2^{n-k}([-d]S_1+S_2)$. As in Sect. 2.2, we let A be the associated matrix, i.e. here

$$A = \begin{pmatrix} 1 & d & a & b \\ 0 & 2^k & 2^k(b-cd) & 2^kc \\ 0 & 0 & -2^{n-k}d & 2^{n-k} \end{pmatrix}.$$

Applying a basis transformation t corresponds to computing $A' = A \cdot M_t$. As an example, consider the second basis transformation from the above proposition.

$$A' = A \cdot M_2 = \begin{pmatrix} 1 & d & a+x_1+dx_5 & b+x_5+dx_3 \\ 0 & 2^k & 2^k(b-cd)+2^kx_5 & 2^kc+2^kx_3 \\ 0 & 0 & -2^{n-k}d & 2^{n-k} \end{pmatrix} = A + \begin{pmatrix} 0 & 0 & x_1+dx_5 & x_5+dx_3 \\ 0 & 0 & 2^kx_5 & 2^kx_3 \\ 0 & 0 & 0 & 0 \end{pmatrix}.$$

This means that the matrices A and A' correspond to the same group G_A if and only if $\langle [x_1+dx_5]S_1 + [x_5+dx_3]S_2, [2^k]([x_5]S_1+[x_3]S_2) \rangle \subset G_A$.

3.3   Case Distinction

Recall that in [4], Alice's secret can be described by $(\alpha_{1,1}, \ldots, \alpha_{3,4})$. A priori we do not know, if the group G_A defined by these scalars has rank 2 or 3. Moreover we do not know which canonical form is obtained when normalising the generators (cf. Definition 3, Table 1). In total, when $k = 0$ there are 4 types of maximal 2^n-isotropic groups, 8 different types when $0 < k < \frac{n}{2}$ and 4 different types when $k = \frac{n}{2}$. The type can be recovered by sending at most $4k + 4$ queries that mimic the normalisation process outlined in Sect. 2.2. The approach is illustrated in the decision tree in Fig. 2, where each node is labelled with the condition we want to test for. Note that at most two queries have to be made per "equivalence" node while at most four queries are necessary to test for divisibility by a power of 2.

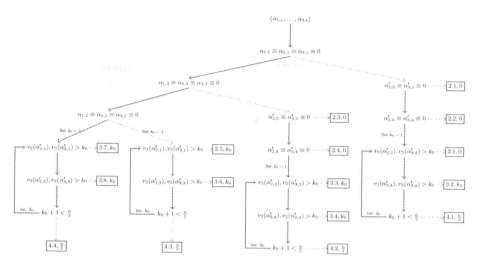

Fig. 2. Strategy for type distinction of normalised kernel generators as in Table 1. We begin with Alice's scalars $(\alpha_{1,1}, \ldots, \alpha_{3,4})$. Each node below represents one or multiple malformed queries which determine whether the displayed condition holds. All equivalence conditions are viewed modulo 2 here. For example, the first query node corresponds to checking whether $\alpha_{1,1} \equiv \alpha_{2,1} \equiv \alpha_{3,1} \equiv 0 \pmod 2$ which can be done with the transformation $t_1^{2^{n-1}}$.

At each node, a true response indicates that the next query can be found along the blue and solid arrow, while the red and dotted path is taken when the condition is not fulfilled. Note that when an odd scalar is found, the subsequent conditions use further normalised scalars denoted by $\alpha'_{i,j}$. Leaves show which type of normalised generators define the secret subgroup Alice uses (as classified in Table 1), followed by k which indicates the order of the generators of the subgroup.

For distinguishing types of rank-3 subgroups, it is necessary to use iterative queries to find the correct type and determine the value of k. At each step, we test whether $k = k_0$ for increasing values of $0 < k_0 < \frac{n}{2} - 1$ by checking if certain scalars are divisible by 2^{k_0+1}. We use that for any integer x, $v_2(x)$ denotes the largest integer such that $2^{v_2(x)}$ divides x. If a scalar is found to not satisfy the divisibility condition, we can again normalise at this position and deduce the type of the subgroup along with k indicating the order of its generators. (Color figure online)

Assuming that the key $(\alpha_{1,1}, \ldots, \alpha_{3,4})$ is drawn uniformly at random from the entire key space $\mathcal{K}_2$, the algorithm illustrated by the decision tree will in many cases terminate at an early stage.

Recall from Sect. 2.3 that roughly one third of the key space consists of groups of Type 2.1. In that case the algorithm terminates after three queries; one to find that one of $\alpha_{1,1}, \alpha_{2,1}, \alpha_{3,1}$ is odd, and another two to determine that one of $\alpha_{2,2}, \alpha_{3,2}$ is odd. In total, the rank-2 subgroups constitute two thirds of the key space, in which case the algorithm terminates after having made at most six queries. Finally, if we encounter a rank-3 group, it will usually not be necessary to perform many iterations to find k because the probability that $k > k_0$ for some fixed k_0 is less than $\frac{1}{3 \cdot 2^{2k_0}}$.

Observe that an attacker obtains some information about the value of certain bits during the course of the type distinction. In particular for rank-3 groups, we recover normalised scalars $b \pmod{2^k}$ and $d \pmod{2^k} = d$ via the iterative queries. At each step of the iteration, we aim to find out whether 2^{k_0+1} divides the coefficients of $P_{\sigma^{-1}(2)}$ and $P_{\sigma^{-1}(4)}$ in the canonical generators of $\langle A_2 \rangle$ and $\langle A_3 \rangle$. In order to achieve this, we need to eliminate the possibility that an oracle query returns 0 because $\langle A_1' \rangle \neq \langle A_1 \rangle$. Hence, we need to query twice for each possible further bit of the coefficients of $P_{\sigma^{-1}(2)}$ and $P_{\sigma^{-1}(4)}$ in $\langle A_1 \rangle$. Therefore we recover the first k bits of b and d fully while we determine the type of G_A. This information can then be used to drastically reduce the number of queries in the main attack algorithm presented in Sect. 3.5, and we thus assume knowledge of $b \pmod{2^k}$ and d for any rank-3 kernel subgroups.

3.4   Kernels of Rank 2

As discussed above, there are multiple canonical forms for rank-2 kernels. In this section, we assume that we have applied the method from Sect. 3.3 to find the correct canonical form of the kernel generators. We illustrate the attack for Type 2.1, where

$$\begin{pmatrix} A_1 \\ A_2 \end{pmatrix} = \begin{pmatrix} 1 & 0 & a & b \\ 0 & 1 & b & c \end{pmatrix} \cdot \begin{pmatrix} R_1 & R_2 & S_1 & S_2 \end{pmatrix}^T.$$

Should the generators be of a different canonical form, slight alterations to the malformed points in the exposition of the attack below will suffice to still recover the correct scalars.

Parity Bits. We want to employ symplectic transformations so that the Weil pairing countermeasure is unable to detect that malformed points have been sent. Table 2 presents transformations that return information about the parity bits, and Fig. 3 illustrates how one can use the transformations to get an optimal adaptive attack.

Table 2. Table of symplectic transformations and how parity bits affect the codomain. The equivalences in the second column are all modulo 2.

Transformation	Same j-invariant iff
$t_0^{2^{n-1}}$	$a \equiv b \equiv 0$
$t_2^{2^{n-1}}$	$b \equiv c \equiv 0$
$t_4^{2^{n-1}}$	$b \equiv ac$
$t_0^{2^{n-1}} t_1^{2^{n-1}}$	$a + 1 \equiv b \equiv 0$
$t_0^{2^{n-1}} t_3^{2^{n-1}}$	$a \equiv b + 1 \equiv 0$
$t_2^{2^{n-1}} t_1^{2^{n-1}}$	$b + 1 \equiv c \equiv 0$
$t_2^{2^{n-1}} t_3^{2^{n-1}}$	$b \equiv c + 1 \equiv 0$

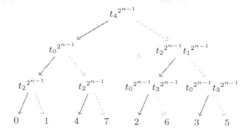

Fig. 3. Optimal strategy for recovering parity bits. The top node represents the first malformed query which will use the t_4 transformation to determine whether $b \equiv ac$ (mod 2), as shown in Table 2. A true response indicates that the next query can be found along the blue and solid arrow, while the red and dotted path is taken when the condition is false. Leaves are decimal representations of the parity bits a_0, b_0, c_0, i.e. 6 corresponds to $[a_0, b_0, c_0] = [1, 1, 0]$. (Color figure online)

As an example, we examine how the first transformation, $t_4{}^{2^{n-1}}$, affects the kernel generators. This step corresponds to sending malformed points obtained via the matrix

$$
M = \begin{pmatrix} 1 & 0 & 0 & 0 \\ 0 & 1 & 0 & 0 \\ 0 & 2^{n-1} & 1 & 0 \\ 2^{n-1} & 0 & 0 & 1 \end{pmatrix}
$$

and leads to Alice using

$$
A' = \begin{pmatrix} 1 & 0 & a & b \\ 0 & 1 & b & c \end{pmatrix} \cdot M = \begin{pmatrix} 1+2^{n-1}b & 2^{n-1}a & a & b \\ 2^{n-1}c & 1+2^{n-1}b & b & c \end{pmatrix} \sim A + \begin{pmatrix} 0 & 0 & 0 & 2^{n-1}(b^2+ac) \\ 0 & 0 & 2^{n-1}(b^2+ac) & 0. \end{pmatrix}
$$

during her internal computations. Note that in the last step, Gaussian elimination is used to normalize A'. We can observe that $O\left(J_B, J_{AB}, (R'_1, R'_2, S'_1, S'_2)\right) = 1$ if and only if $2^{n-1}(b^2 + ac) \equiv 0 \pmod{2^n}$. This occurs whenever $b \equiv ac \pmod 2$, as displayed in Table 2, and from the response we can determine whether $[a_0, b_0, c_0]$ is among $\{[0,0,0], [0,0,1], [1,0,0], [1,1,1]\}$ or $\{[0,1,0], [0,1,1], [1,0,1], [1,1,0]\}$.

Iterative Step. The recovery of subsequent bits will not follow the optimal strategy from the recovery of the parity bits. However, it will still recover a bit of information per query on average.

Suppose now that we have learned the first i bits of each key scalar. Then we know K_i^a, K_i^b and K_i^c, where $a = \sum_{j=0}^{n-1} 2^j a_j = K_i^a + \sum_{j=i}^{n-1} 2^j a_j$ (and similarly for b and c).

Now assume that $i < n - 3$ and set $e_i := n - i - 1$. By the lemma below, the element $T_i = 1 - 2^{e_i}$ is thus a quadratic residue modulo 2^n.

Lemma 2 [6, Lem. 4]. *Let $n \geq 5$ and $i \in \{1, \ldots, n-4\}$. Then $T_i := 1 - 2^{n-i-1}$ is a quadratic residue modulo 2^n.*

In the following, $\theta_i \in \{0, \ldots, 2^n - 1\}$ denotes one of the square roots of T_i, i.e. $\theta_i^2 \equiv T_i \pmod{2^n}$. Note that θ_i is necessarily odd, hence there exists an inverse θ_i^{-1} modulo 2^n. Intuitively, θ_i is a masking scalar that allows us to defeat the Weil pairing countermeasure.

We use three different sets of malformed points to determine a_i and c_i, and then learn b_i with one further query.

First, we send the malformed points obtained from

$$\theta_i^{-1} \begin{pmatrix} T_i & 0 & -2^{e_i} K_i^a & 0 \\ 0 & 1 & 0 & 2^{e_i} K_i^c \\ 0 & 0 & 1 & 0 \\ 0 & 0 & 0 & T_i \end{pmatrix}.$$

Upon which, the subgroup computation[4] will entail

$$A' = \theta^{-1} \begin{pmatrix} T_i & 0 & -2^{e_i} K_i^a + a & T_i b \\ 0 & 1 & b & 2^{e_i} K_i^c + T_i c \end{pmatrix}$$

$$\sim \begin{pmatrix} 1 & 0 & a + T_i^{-1} 2^{e_i} (K_i^a - a) & b \\ 0 & 1 & b & c + 2^{e_i} (K_i^c - c) \end{pmatrix} = A + \begin{pmatrix} 0 & 0 & T_i^{-1} 2^{n-1} a_i & 0 \\ 0 & 0 & 0 & 2^{n-1} c_i \end{pmatrix}.$$

Hence A' defines the same group as A, exactly when both a_i and c_i are zero.

If we have not yet recovered the two bits in question, we proceed with sending malformed points corresponding to the transformation matrix

$$\theta_i^{-1} \begin{pmatrix} T_i & 0 & -2^{e_i}(K_i^a + 2^i) & 0 \\ 0 & 1 & 0 & 2^{e_i} K_i^c \\ 0 & 0 & 1 & 0 \\ 0 & 0 & 0 & T_i \end{pmatrix}.$$

In this case

$$A' \sim A + \begin{pmatrix} 0 & 0 & T_i^{-1} 2^{n-1}(a_i + 1) & 0 \\ 0 & 0 & 0 & 2^{n-1} c_i \end{pmatrix}.$$

The groups associated to A and A' coincide exactly when $a_i = 1$ and $c_i = 0$.

If both queries fail to recover the bits a_i and c_i, i.e. $(a_i, c_i) \notin \{(0,0), (1,0)\}$, then we can conclude that $c_i = 1$. To find the bit a_i, we then send the third set of malformed points obtained from

$$\theta_i^{-1} \begin{pmatrix} T_i & 0 & -2^{e_i} K_i^a & 0 \\ 0 & 1 & 0 & 2^{e_i} K_{i+1}^c \\ 0 & 0 & 1 & 0 \\ 0 & 0 & 0 & T_i \end{pmatrix}.$$

Here, the oracle will return 1 exactly when $a_i = 0$. If this is not the case, then $a_i = 1$.

After these series of queries, we have recovered the bits a_i and c_i, hence we know K_{i+1}^a and K_{i+1}^c. It remains to recover the bit b_i. This is done by querying the oracle on the points corresponding to the matrix

---

[4] To verify the computation below note that $T_i^{-1} \equiv 1 + 2^{e_i} T_i^{-1} \pmod{2^n}$.

$$\theta_i^{-1}\begin{pmatrix} 1 & 0 & 2^{e_i}K_{i+1}^a & 2^{e_i}K_i^b \\ 0 & 1 & 2^{e_i}K_i^b & 2^{e_i}K_{i+1}^c \\ 0 & 0 & T_i & 0 \\ 0 & 0 & 0 & T_i \end{pmatrix}.$$

Here,

$$A' \sim A + \begin{pmatrix} 0 & 0 & 2^{e_i}(K_{i+1}^a - a) & 2^{e_i}(K_i^b - b) \\ 0 & 0 & 2^{e_i}(K_i^b - b) & 2^{e_i}(K_{i+1}^c - c) \end{pmatrix} = A + \begin{pmatrix} 0 & 0 & 0 & 2^{n-1}b_i \\ 0 & 0 & 2^{n-1}b_i & 0 \end{pmatrix}.$$

The oracle returns 1 exactly when $b_i = 0$. Otherwise, we know that $b_i = 1$.

It follows from Proposition 3 that all of the transformations used in these queries are symplectic. Therefore they constitute valid queries in our oracle model. As a consequence the attack is not detectable by the Weil pairing.

Note that we are not able to use these transformation for $i \in \{n-3, n-2, n-1\}$. We suggest to use a brute force method to deduce the last three bits of each scalar. This is consistent with the adaptive attack described in [6].

Complexity. Taking into account that the case distinction strategy outlined in Sect. 3.3 requires at most 6 queries to determine any type of rank-2 kernel subgroup as well as the information we learn about the parity of Alice's scalars throughout the process, we find that this attack requires at most $6 + 4(n-4) = 4n - 10$ queries, each corresponding to one isogeny computation. This leaves 3 bits per secret scalar, hence 9 bits in total, to be recovered through brute force.

3.5   Kernels of Rank 3

Now suppose Alice's secret kernel subgroup has rank 3, i.e. $k > 0$. Let $1 \le k \le \lfloor \frac{n}{2} \rfloor$ be fixed. We assume that the attacker has determined the type of Alice's secret subgroup as outlined in Sect 3.3, and therefore knows k. We present the attack for a kernel of Type 3.1, hence the generators are of the form

$$\begin{pmatrix} A_1 \\ A_2 \\ A_3 \end{pmatrix} = \begin{pmatrix} 1 & d & a & b \\ 0 & 2^k & 2^k(b-cd) & c \\ 0 & 0 & -2^{n-k}d & 2^{n-k} \end{pmatrix} \cdot \begin{pmatrix} R_1 & R_2 & S_1 & S_2 \end{pmatrix}^T$$

for some $(a, b, c, d) \in \{0, \dots, 2^n - 1\} \times \{0, \dots, 2^{n-k} - 1\} \times \{0, \dots, 2^{n-2k} - 1\} \times \{0, \dots, 2^k - 1\}$, where $b \pmod{2^k}$ and d are known from the case distinction algorithm. As usual, we denote the resulting variety $J_B / \langle A_1, A_2, A_3 \rangle$ by J_{AB}.

We again fix $e_i = n - i - 1$, $T_i = 1 - 2^{e_i} \in \mathbb{Z}/\ell^n\mathbb{Z}$, and $\theta_i^2 = T_i \in \mathbb{Z}/\ell^n\mathbb{Z}$ for $1 \le i \le n - 4$, where θ_i is any one of the two square roots. Recall that θ_i exists since $T_i \equiv 1 \pmod 8$.

Recovering a $\pmod{2^{k-1}}$. We first recover the parity of the secret scalar a by sending the malformed points obtained from the transformation matrix

$$\begin{pmatrix} 1 & 0 & 0 & 0 \\ 0 & 1 & 0 & 0 \\ 2^{n-1} & 0 & 1 & 0 \\ 0 & 0 & 0 & 1 \end{pmatrix}.$$

These allow us to recover the bit a_0 since

$$A' = \begin{pmatrix} 1+2^{n-1}a & d & a & b \\ 0 & 2^k & 2^k(b-cd) & 2^k c \\ 0 & 0 & -2^{n-k}d & 2^{n-k} \end{pmatrix} \sim A + \begin{pmatrix} 0 & 0 & 2^{n-1}a^2 & 0 \\ 0 & 0 & 0 & 0 \\ 0 & 0 & 0 & 0 \end{pmatrix}$$

This means that A and A' correspond to the same group if and only if $a_0 = 0$, hence we can deduce a_0 from the oracle response.

Now, we iteratively recover the bit a_i for $i = 1, \ldots, k-2$ using the knowledge of $K_i^a = \sum_{j=0}^{i-1} 2^j a_j$ obtained from the previous steps. Fix $\alpha = -2^{e_i}(dK_k^b + K_i^a)$, and $\delta = -2^{e_i}d$ and send the malformed points obtained from the transformation

$$\theta_i^{-1} \begin{pmatrix} T_i & \delta & \alpha & 0 \\ 0 & 1 & 0 & 0 \\ 0 & 0 & 1 & 0 \\ 0 & 0 & -\delta & T_i \end{pmatrix}.$$

This transformation applied to A yields

$$A' = \theta^{-1} \begin{pmatrix} T_i & \delta+d & \alpha+a-\delta b & T_i b \\ 0 & 2^k & 2^k(b-cd-\delta c) & 2^k T_i c \\ 0 & 0 & 2^{n-k}(-d-\delta) & 2^{n-k}T_i \end{pmatrix} \sim \begin{pmatrix} 1 & d & a+2^{e_i}(a-K_i^a) & b \\ 0 & 2^k & 2^k(b-cd) & 2^k c \\ 0 & 0 & -2^{n-k}d & 2^{n-k} \end{pmatrix} \sim A + \begin{pmatrix} 0 & 0 & 2^{n-1}a_i & 0 \\ 0 & 0 & 0 & 0 \\ 0 & 0 & 0 & 0 \end{pmatrix}.$$

To verify the above simplifications, note that $T_i^{-1} = 1 + 2^{e_i}$ (when $k \geq 1$ and $i \leq k-1$ as is the case here). Hence, we can determine the desired bit from the oracle response since $O(J_B, J_{AB}, (R_1', R_2', S_1', S_2')) = 1$ implies $a_i = 0$, and $a_i = 1$ otherwise.

Recovering mod 2^{n-k-1} and c. We recover the bits a_i and c_{i-k+1} for $i = k-1, \ldots, n-k-2$ simultaneously. Recall that we know the first k bits of b, i.e. K_k^b, as well as d from the type distinction of kernel subgroups. In the following we assume that d is an odd integer. The queries can be easily adapted to the case where d is even by shifting the indices of c accordingly.

In the first query we send the malformed points obtained from the transformation

$$\theta_i^{-1} \begin{pmatrix} T_i & \delta & \alpha & \beta \\ 0 & 1 & \beta & \gamma \\ 0 & 0 & 1 & 0 \\ 0 & 0 & -\delta & T_i \end{pmatrix}$$

where $\alpha = -2^{e_i}K_i^a$, $\beta = -2^{e_i-1}K_{i-k+1}^c d$, $\gamma = 2^{e_i}K_{i-k+1}^c$, $\delta = -2^{e_i-1}d$. Then we obtain

$$A' \sim A + \begin{pmatrix} 0 & 0 & 2^{n-1}a_i - 2^{n-k-1}d^2 c_{i-k+1} & 2^{n-k-1}dc_{i-k+1} \\ 0 & 0 & 2^{n-1}dc_{i-k+1} & 0 \\ 0 & 0 & 0 & 0 \end{pmatrix}$$

This means that A and A' define the same group if both $[2^{n-1}a_i]S_1 + [2^{n-k-1}dc_{i-k+1}]([-d]S_1 + S_2)$ and $[2^{n-1}dc_{i-k+1}]S_1$ are in G_A. Recall that we assume d odd and note that $[2^{n-k}]([-d]S_1 + S_2) \in G_A$. Hence the oracle returns 1 if and only if $a_i = c_{i-k+1} = 0$.

If the oracle returns 0, we proceed with a query to test if $a_i = 1$ and $c_{i-k+1} = 0$. This is achieved by setting $\alpha = -2^{e_i}(K_i^a + 2^i)T_i^{-1}$ in the query above. Similarly, we test for $a_i = 0$ and $c_{i-k+1} = 1$ by setting $\beta = -2^{e_i-1}(K_{i-k+1}^c - 2^{i-k+1})dT_i^{-1}$ and $\gamma = 2^{e_i}(K_{i-k+1}^c + 2^{i-k+1})$.

Recovering b. Recall that K^a_{n-k-1}, K^b_k, c and d are known from previous oracle queries. We now utilise this knowledge to find the remaining bits of b. Again, assuming d to be odd here allows us to perform the queries below for any $k \leq i < n - \max\{k, 3\}$ which can be adapted via some shift in indices to accommodate even d. Let $\alpha = 2^{e_i}(K^a_{n-k-1} + K^b_i d - cd^2)$, $\beta = 2^{e_i}cd$, $\gamma = 2^{e_i}c$, and $\delta = 2^{e_i}d$.

We then send malformed points obtained via

$$\theta_i^{-1}\begin{pmatrix} 1 & \delta & \alpha & \beta \\ 0 & T_i & \beta & -\gamma \\ 0 & 0 & T_i & 0 \\ 0 & 0 & -\delta & 1 \end{pmatrix}$$

to the oracle resulting in

$$A' \sim \begin{pmatrix} 1 & \delta+T_i d & \alpha+\beta d-\delta b+T_i\alpha & \beta-\gamma d+b \\ 0 & 2^k & 2^k(T_i^{-1}\beta+b-dc-T_i^{-1}\delta c) & 2^k T_i^{-1}(c-\gamma) \\ 0 & 0 & 2^{n-k}(-T_i d-\delta) & 2^{n-k} \end{pmatrix} = A + \begin{pmatrix} 0 & 0 & 2^{e_i}d(K^b_i-b) & 0 \\ 0 & 0 & 0 & 0 \\ 0 & 0 & 0 & 0 \end{pmatrix}$$

so that the oracle returns 1 if $b_i = 0$, and 0 if $b_i = 1$.

Recovering a. It remains to recover the last bits of a, given K^a_{n-k-1} as well as b, c and d. Let $i = n - k - 1, \ldots, n - 3$. We again fix $\alpha = 2^{e_i}(K^a_i + bd - cd^2)$, $\beta = 2^{e_i}cd$, $\gamma = 2^{e_i}c$, $\delta = 2^{e_i}d$ and query the oracle with the symplectic transformation

$$\theta_i^{-1}\begin{pmatrix} 1 & \delta & \alpha & \beta \\ 0 & T_i & \beta & -\gamma \\ 0 & 0 & T_i & 0 \\ 0 & 0 & -\delta & 1 \end{pmatrix}.$$

We obtain

$$A' \sim A + \begin{pmatrix} 0 & 0 & 2^{e_i}(K^a_i-a) & 0 \\ 0 & 0 & 0 & 0 \\ 0 & 0 & 0 & 0 \end{pmatrix}.$$

Hence, we can deduce the bit a_i from the response of the oracle whereby $O(J_B, J_{AB}, (R'_1, R'_2, S'_1, S'_2)) = 1$ implies $a_i = 0$, and $a_i = 1$ otherwise.

Since the square root of $T_i = 1 - 2^{e_i}$ is not defined when $i \geq n-3$, we cannot scale the malformed points in order to obtain a valid symplectic transformation. Therefore, the last three bits of a need to be recovered by brute force.

Complexity. If Alice's kernel has rank 3, we can learn the type of the subgroup as well as the scalar d and b (mod 2^k) following Sect. 3.3 with at most $4 + 4k$ queries. We further require $k - 1$ queries, one for each of the first $k - 1$ bits of a, and then 3 queries for each step of the parallel recovery of a_i and c_{i-k+1}, summing to $4 + 4k + k - 1 + 3(n - 2k - 2) = 3n - k - 3$ queries thus far. Each remaining bit of b and a, potentially bar the last $4 - k$ and 3 bits respectively, requires exactly one query to recover, adding $n - 6$ queries. This leads to a total number of at most $4n - k - 9$ queries to recover Alice's secret key while leaving 3 bits of a as well as $4 - k$ bits of b and $3 - k$ bits of c (if $k < 4$ and $k < 3$, respectively) to brute force.

3.6   Adaptive Attack on Arbitrary Basis

In the above, we were able to show that the adaptive attack is able to recover a static key when a symplectic basis is used. In this section, we will present an extension of the attack to recover a static key when an arbitrary basis is used (as originally described in [4]).

We are able to obtain a symplectic basis from an arbitrary basis using a 4×4 change of basis matrix. In particular, such a basis has the following form:

$$\begin{pmatrix} 1 & 0 & 0 & 0 \\ \gamma_1 & -\gamma_2 & 1 & 0 \\ 0 & 1 & 0 & 0 \\ \mu_1\mu_3^{-1} & -\mu_2\mu_3^{-1} & 0 & \mu_3^{-1} \end{pmatrix}$$

up to swapping certain rows. This matrix, together with its inverse, allows us to transform points in one basis to another. Each time we need to query the oracle on a particular set of malformed points, we map these malformed points under the inverse of the matrix to get the malformed corresponding points of the arbitrary basis. We still obtain the same bit of information in return: either the oracle returns the reference variety, or it does not. This ultimately allows us to recover the secret for a symplectic basis which is equivalent to knowing the secret isogeny. Note that the attack is still not detectable by the Weil pairing if the transformations from the previous sections are applied.

Acknowledgements. We would like to thank Christophe Petit and Tanja Lange for the helpful discussions. We would also like to thank Ben Smith and the anonymous reviewers at SAC for their insightful comments and advice to improve the exposition of our results. The first author was supported by the Deutsche Forschungsgemeinschaft (DFG) Cluster of Excellence 2092 CASA.

References

1. Basso, A., Kutas, P., Merz, S.-P., Petit, C., Weitkämper, C.: On adaptive attacks against Jao-Urbanik's isogeny-based protocol. In: Nitaj, A., Youssef, A. (eds.) AFRICACRYPT 2020. LNCS, vol. 12174, pp. 195–213. Springer, Cham (2020). https://doi.org/10.1007/978-3-030-51938-4_10
2. Cassels, J.W.S., Flynn, E.V.: Prolegomena to a Middlebrow Arithmetic of Curves of Genus 2. London Mathematical Society Lecture Note Series. Cambridge University Press, Cambridge (1996). https://doi.org/10.1017/CBO9780511526084
3. Dobson, S., Galbraith, S.D., LeGrow, J.T., Ti, Y.B., Zobernig, L.: An adaptive attack on 2-SIDH. Int. J. Comput. Math. Comput. Syst. Theory **5**(4), 282–299 (2020). https://doi.org/10.1080/23799927.2020.1822446
4. Flynn, E.V., Ti, Y.B.: Genus two isogeny cryptography. In: Ding, J., Steinwandt, R. (eds.) PQCrypto 2019. LNCS, vol. 11505, pp. 286–306. Springer, Cham (2019). https://doi.org/10.1007/978-3-030-25510-7_16
5. Fujisaki, E., Okamoto, T.: Secure integration of asymmetric and symmetric encryption schemes. J. Cryptol. **26**(1), 80–101 (2013). https://doi.org/10.1007/s00145-011-9114-1

6. Galbraith, S.D., Petit, C., Shani, B., Ti, Y.B.: On the security of supersingular isogeny cryptosystems. In: Cheon, J.H., Takagi, T. (eds.) ASIACRYPT 2016. LNCS, vol. 10031, pp. 63–91. Springer, Heidelberg (2016). https://doi.org/10.1007/978-3-662-53887-6_3

7. Jao, D., De Feo, L.: Towards quantum-resistant cryptosystems from supersingular elliptic curve isogenies. In: Yang, B.-Y. (ed.) PQCrypto 2011. LNCS, vol. 7071, pp. 19–34. Springer, Heidelberg (2011). https://doi.org/10.1007/978-3-642-25405-5_2

8. Milne, J.S.: Abelian varieties. In: Cornell, G., Silverman, J.H. (eds.) Arithmetic Geometry. Springer, New York (1986). https://doi.org/10.1007/978-1-4613-8655-1_5

9. NIST (National Institute of Standards and Technology): NIST post-quantum cryptography project (2017). http://csrc.nist.gov/groups/ST/post-quantum-crypto/

10. Silverman, J.H.: The Arithmetic of Elliptic Curves. GTM, vol. 106. Springer, New York (2009). https://doi.org/10.1007/978-0-387-09494-6

11. Tate, J.: Endomorphisms of abelian varieties over finite fields. Invent. Math. **2**, 134–144 (1966)

Author Index

Printed in the United States
by Baker & Taylor Publisher Services